BLUMBERG'S HISTORY OF THE ROYAL MARINES 1755-1914

(PUBLISHED PRIVATELY IN 1934 AS
'A RECORD OF THE ROYAL MARINES
FROM 1755 TO 1914')

COMPILED BY
GENERAL SIR H. E. BLUMBERG, K.C.B.,
ROYAL MARINES

EDITED BY ALASTAIR DONALD, BRIAN CARTER AND
JOHN RAWLINSON

ROYAL MARINES HISTORICAL SOCIETY
SPECIAL PUBLICATION NO 49

BLUMBERG'S HISTORY OF THE ROYAL MARINES
1755-1914

Copyright © Royal Marines Historical Society 2020

All Rights Reserved

No part of this book may be reproduced in any form by photocopying or by any electronic or mechanical means, including information storage or retrieval systems, without permission in writing from the copyright owner.

ISBN

978-1-908123-20-6

First published 2020 by the
ROYAL MARINES HISTORICAL SOCIETY
The National Museum of the Royal Navy
Portsmouth PO1 3NH
United Kingdom

Cover, design and layout
Tim Mitchell
www.tim-mitchell.co.uk

Printed and bound in Great Britain by
CPI Antony Rowe Ltd, Chippenham and Eastbourne

To

My Brother Officers

In the hope that it may
be of some interest to them

Blumberg's History of the Royal Marines 1755-1914

Contents

Editor's Introduction	ix
Preface	xiii

Volume One 1755 – 1792
1.	Formation of the Corps 1755	3
2.	The Seven Years' War 1756 - 1763	11
3.	Peace 1763 - 1774	41
4.	American War of Independence 1774 - 1783	57
5.	Peace 1783 - 1792	95

Volume Two 1793-1836
6.	French Revolutionary Wars 1793 - 1801	117
7.	Peace 1801 - 1803	157
8.	Trafalgar 1803 – 1807	163
9.	After Trafalgar 1808 – 1814	191
10.	American War 1812 – 1815	225
11.	Demobilisation and Reorganisation 1814 – 1816	245
12.	Peace 1816 - 1836	249

Volume Three 1837-1914
13.	Carlist War 1837 – 1839	265
14.	Syria and China 1840 – 1843	271
15.	Around the Globe 1844 - 1852	297
16.	Crimea and the Baltic 1853 – 1856	307
17.	India and China 1857 - 1860	325
18.	Woolwich and Deal; Japan and New Zealand 1861 – 1869	357
19.	Long Service, Army Reform and Africa 1870 - 1880	369
20.	Egypt 1881 - 1882	383
21.	Egypt and Specialisation 1883 - 1886	405
22.	Jubilee, South Africa and China 1887 - 1898	429
23.	South Africa and China 1899 - 1901	445
24.	Reorganisation and the Rising Threat 1902 – 1914	469

Appendix	**I**	The Divisional Colours	485
Appendix	**II**	Commanding Officers	515
Appendix	**III**	The Earl St Vincent	525

Index — 527

BLUMBERG'S HISTORY OF THE ROYAL MARINES 1755-1914

Editor's Introduction.

'In memory of one whose devotion to the Corps was second to none.'

Herbert Blumberg was commissioned in to the Royal Marines Light Infantry in 1888. He is now best remembered for his highly respected 'Britain's Sea Soldiers, A History of the Royal Marines 1914-1919'. This is considered to be the companion volume to Cyril Field's 'Britain's Sea Soldiers' Volumes I and II that record Corps history from 1664-1914. Blumberg's tome was known as Volume III. Both Field and Blumberg had long and distinguished careers in the Corps, both were passionate about the Corps and its traditions and both were frustrated at the lack of a complete history of the Royal Marines.

The first Corps history was published in 1803, when Alexander Gillespie produced 'The History of the Royal Marines'. Later in 1845, Paul Harris Nicholas published in two volumes his 'Historical Records of the Royal Marine Forces'. Neither book formed a complete or reliable history of the subject. They were 'notoriously inaccurate and unreliable and shed hardly any light upon the internal economy and discipline, uniform and equipment of the corps.'

Considered much more satisfactory was Laurence Edye's work published in 1893. He had been honorary secretary of the Arts Section of the Royal Naval Exhibition and took in hand the preparation from original sources of a history of the Marine Corps from its formation in 1664. The first volume, 1664-1701, appeared as planned and the second, 1702-14, was promised for 1895, but never appeared. After many delays the manuscript was believed lost at sea in a torpedoed ship during the First World War. Edye's notes for the second unpublished volume survive in the Royal Marines Museum archive. Whilst in recent years a hand written and uncorrected manuscript supplemented by a detailed and printed contents section of this second volume has come to light in the library of the National Museum of the Royal Navy.

Frustrated with the lack of a modern and complete history of Royal Marines, Field had determined to publish a Corps history from 1664 to the eve of World War One. Originally published in 20 parts the project took several years to come to fruition and it was funded through subscription appeals in the Globe and Laurel. Eventually turning a small surplus, subscribers were asked to allow their surplus subscriptions to transfer to Blumberg's work. It was only in November 1924 when the final part of Field's work was completed that the news of Blumberg's work was announced. It took until January 1927 for the final work to be published.

Field and Blumberg collaborated on a number of projects and indeed Blumberg is credited as a key source for Field's work whilst both were co-authors of the scarce 'Random Records of the Royal Marines' published by the Globe and Laurel in 1930. However, shortly before his death between January and July 1934 Blumberg also privately published 'A Record of the Royal Marines', a three-volume work that recorded the history of the Corps from 1755-1914. Amongst the rarest of Corps histories, the original print had a minuscule circulation and in 1979 the RMHS decided to publish extracts from Blumberg's "Royal Marines Records", covering 'the administrative, social and domestic detail and excluding the 'fighting' which is covered in detail in other places.'

The different styles and interests of Field and Blumberg mean that even when recording the same piece of history both focus on different matters with vastly different emphasis. The RMHS pamphlets have been long out of print and with falling publication costs the RMHS has revisited Blumberg's work and the result is 'Blumberg's History of the Royal Marines 1755-1914' in its entirety for the first time.

Blumberg's career was well recorded in the Globe and Laurel, his obituary tells us much of how well placed he was as a Corps historian but also how respected he was, it was published in autumn 1934, shortly after he distributed the last installment of his history to the Divisions.

We announce, with very great regret, the death, which occurred on 16th August 1934, of General Sir Herbert Edward Blumberg, RMLI (ret.) late Adjutant-General, Royal Marines. The son of Captain F. W. Blumberg, 17th Lancers, he was born on 20th March 1869 and received his first commission in 1888. In the following year he was promoted Lieutenant and also at an early period in his career obtained a first-class certificate as an Instructor of Gunnery.

From 1890 to 1892 he served in H.M.S. "*Hibernia*." On disembarkation he qualified as Instructor of Musketry, obtaining an Extra Certificate. In 1894 he passed for Adjutant, obtaining the envied "Very creditable" certificate of passing. During this period, 1893 to 1896, he held the appointment of Asst. Instructor of Gunnery to the Plymouth Division, RMLI.

He served for a short time in H.M.S. "*Pembroke*" in 1896-97, and in the latter year, on promotion to Captain, he was appointed temporarily as 2nd Assistant to the Professor of Fortifications at the R.N. College, Greenwich. For his good work he received a special report; he had previously received an expression of their Lordships' satisfaction for good work afloat. Thereafter, for two years, he served in H.M.S. "*Australia*" and on disembarkation he was appointed Adjutant to the Portsmouth Division, Royal Marines, an appointment which he held from 1900 to 1905. During this period, he was member of committees on drill and equipment of the Corps, which it was sought to standardise throughout the Divisions.

Introduction

From 1905 to 1907 he served in H.M. Ships *"Duncan"* and *"Good Hope"*. He had been promoted Major on 10th February 1906. On disembarkation he was attached to the War College at Portsmouth and underwent the Course of 1907-08. After embarking in H.M.S. *"Goliath"* in 1909 for manoeuvres, his next tour afloat was in H.M.S. *"Indomitable"* from 1909 to 1911, from which ship he transferred to H.M.S. *"Neptune"*, where he served for a few months only, being relieved in October 1911 to take up the appointment of Deputy Assistant Adjutant General, Royal Marines. He held this appointment until 1st October, 1914, when he was appointed Assistant Adjutant and Quartermaster General, H.Q. Staff, Royal Naval Division. He had been promoted Brevet Lieutenant-Colonel in 1913 and Lieutenant Colonel in 1914.

On 11th November 1914 he was appointed Assistant Adjutant General Royal Marines, but his tour of duty in this office was interrupted by his appointment as Assistant Adjutant General, Salonica Army from November 1915 to April 1916. In the latter year he returned to complete two more years as A.A.G., Royal Marines, but during this period his services were required as commander of the R.M. Special Service Battalion in Ireland during the rebellion of 1916. He had been promoted Brevet-Colonel in June 1917 and Colonel 2nd Commandant in October of the same year. In July 1918 he was given the appointment of Brigadier-General and selected for the command of the Aegean Islands. He received an expression of Their Lordships' appreciation of services rendered while holding the appointments of G.O.C. Troops in the Aegean Islands and Military Governor of Lemnos, Tenedos and Imbros.

In 1919 he returned and assumed command of the Portsmouth Division R.M.L.I.. In 1920 he was selected as Adjutant General, Royal Marines. He was promoted Major-General on 1st January 1921. It was a period of exceptional administrative difficulty, for it was during this period that the amalgamation of the R.M.A. and the R.M.L.I. was ordered. In March 1924 he vacated the appointment and in 1925 he was appointed Honorary Colonel Commandant of the Chatham Division, Royal Marines, an appointment which he held until ill-health compelled him to relinquish it in May 1934.

He had been promoted Lieutenant-General on 1st January 1923 and General the following year when he received an expression of their Lordships appreciation for the zealous and able manner in which his duties were carried out as Adjutant-General, Royal Marines. His Orders comprised the C.B., awarded for services during the War and the K.C.B., awarded on 1st January 1923.

He held the following medals: Coronation Medal 1911, 1914-15 Star, British War Medal, and the Victory Medal. He was an Officer of the Legion of Honour and a Commander of the Order of the Redeemer.

"Blummy" as he was universally, and affectionately, called by all who knew him, was extraordinarily popular with all ranks. He was possessed of a charm of manner which gained in force from the fact that it was exercised quite unconsciously. During the last years of his life his health was bad and the death, in 1931, of Lady Blumberg, was a blow from which he never fully recovered. He lived for the Royal Marines and it is significant that one of the last actions of his life was to present to Divisions and the Depot his "Records of the Royal Marines, 1837-1914," which will stand beside "Britain's Sea Soldiers, Vol.III," in memory of one whose devotion to the Corps was second to none.

The funeral service for the late General Sir Herbert Blumberg, K.C.B., R.M., took place at Stoke Damerel Parish Church at 10.30 a.m. on the 20th August, and the interment at Lelant Parish Church, Cornwall, at 3 p.m.

Some 80 years after his death Blumberg's final work is published in this single volume. We have sought to stay with the original text as closely as possible so that grammar, place names and spelling as much as possible remain the same as in Blumberg's manuscript. However, the author's random and inconsistent use of underlining, bold text and use of sub-headings in the three different parts of his work would have driven the most forgiving of reader to distraction so these have been simplified. Blumberg published this book without maps or illustrations and after much discussion we decided we should do likewise. The Notes are Blumberg's unless otherwise stated. He also produced a separate Preface for Volume 3, but we have combined the two Prefaces into one at the beginning. We, the editors, would like to acknowledge the assistance of John Gilbert in the preliminary lengthy task of scanning the original work and doing the first draft proof read, and Tim Mitchell for preparing the final draft for printing. Blumberg was not good at indexing and so Colonel Michael Reece, Chairman RMHS, who did such a good job indexing the new edition of Blumberg's First World War (Britain's Sea Soldiers, Vol 3) has once again used his talents to index this work as well.

Very special thanks are due to RMHS members Mark Phillips and Hugh Affleck-Graves, who most generously donated the cost of producing this book.

"His work is marked by no heroics, nor has he made any attempt to join in the controversies which have been the distinguishing feature of some war books."

Preface

I have selected the date 1755 for the commencement of these records, as from this time more or less continuous letters and orders exist at the RM Divisions from which it is possible to trace the development of the Corps and its peculiar customs and traditions. In preparing the records, I have consulted every source of information open to me in the shape of Letter Books and Order Books and all the standard naval and military histories, such as James' Naval History, Beatson's Naval and Military Occurrences, Fortescue's 8 volume History of the British Army, Corbett's works, the histories of the Royal Marines by Gillespie, Nicolas and Field, original reports, Battalion War and other diaries, accounts in the Globe and Laurel, etc. Also the Lives of Admirals and Generals bearing on the campaigns. The War Office official accounts, where extant, the London Gazette, and Orders in Council have been taken as the basis of events recounted. The authorities consulted have been quoted for each campaign, in order that those desirous of making a fuller study can do so.

The volumes of the Navy Records Society and some of the Record Office Publications have been most useful.

I have also included as much administrative social and domestic detail as I have been able to glean. I have made no pretence of writing a history or making comments, but have tried to place on record all facts which can show the development of the Corps through the second half of the Eighteenth, the Nineteenth and early part of the Twentieth Centuries.

I hope these notes may be of interest and use to my brother officers and may serve as an introduction to the standard histories for more detail.

H E Blumberg.

Devonport

January 1934

Volume One
1755 – 1792

BLUMBERG'S HISTORY OF THE ROYAL MARINES 1755-1914

1 - Formation of the Corps 1755

In 1755 the war clouds were again gathering over Britain, and the clash of interests between France and Great Britain was becoming more acute; each was seeking to found a Colonial Empire and to expand its trade.

In March 1755 the King - George II - sent a message to Parliament requesting an augmentation of the forces by sea and land. In February some addition had been made to the infantry by raising the strength of the Guards and of seven regiments of the line, but a further increase was necessary.

"The Ministry under Newcastle employed the powers thus given them in raising 5,000 Marines in 50 Independent Companies and placing them under the command of the Lord High Admiral. It is said that Newcastle refused to raise new regiments from jealousy of the Duke of Cumberland's (the Commander-in-Chief) nomination of officers and there is nothing incredible in the suggestion." So writes Fortescue in his great History of the British Army, but the fact remains that Admiral Lord Anson was the First Lord and the strong man of the Ministry, and he took the new Corps under his wing. He had to resist many efforts by politicians to foist unsuitable officers on the Corps.

Thus was born the Corps as it exists today amidst the threatenings of a war in which it was soon to take such a distinguished part. The old regiments of Marines had been disbanded in 1748, and though they had been transferred to Admiralty control the regimental system had been very difficult to work. The provision of drafts had led to a hopeless mixing of the different regiments, and at this period the raising of independent companies was a very common device. The Admiralty divided the companies into three groups, stationed at Chatham, Portsmouth, and Plymouth.

In the London Gazette of 28th April 1755, twenty Companies were allotted to Portsmouth, eighteen to Plymouth and twelve to Chatham; they were numbered in rotation No 1 to Portsmouth, No 2 to Plymouth and No 3 to Chatham and so on; this was changed in 1783 when No 1 was allotted to Chatham, No 2 to Portsmouth, No 3 to Plymouth, etc.

The Officers were gazetted to Companies; a Captain, 1 First Lieutenant and two 2nd Lieutenants to each Company. A Lieutenant Colonel and a Major were appointed to each group and contrary to later practice these latter were not appointed to Companies.

The Field Officers were;
Portsmouth, Lieutenant Colonel J Paterson, 23rd March 1755. Major R Bendyshe.
Plymouth, Lieutenant Colonel T Dury, 24th March 1755. Major F Leighton.
Chatham, Lieutenant Colonel O Gordon, 25th March 1755. Major J Burleigh.

Parliament passed a Marine Mutiny Act and Articles of War for their governance, which was renewed annually, and after being signed by the Lords of the Admiralty was promulgated to the Fleet and Divisions. Their numbers were fixed from time to time, usually annually by Order-in-Council.

A study of the Officers' Lists shows that the majority were officers on half pay from the old Marine Regiments and other regiments. Their commissions were signed by the King and apparently, they were appointed to a definite company, and for any change fresh commissions were issued; also when brought in from half pay, though they took seniority from their first commission. Commissions were never purchased as in the Line and the fact that they were looked on as Grenadiers is shown by the fact that the lowest rank was Second Lieutenant and not Ensign. Also, Colours were not issued.

At first there seems to have been no officer corresponding to Adjutant General and orders were sent direct to Divisions by one of the Secretaries of the Admiralty who corresponded direct with the Divisions, a system that continued even after the appointment of a Commandant Resident in Town. Apparently, however on 19th December 1755, Lieutenant Colonel Paterson was promoted to Colonel, and seems to have performed the duties in London as Lieutenant Colonel Dury was transferred to Portsmouth. On the introduction of Naval Officers as Generals and Colonels in 1780 he was pensioned, but Colonel Dury appears to have performed the duties from February 1781 though borne on the strength of the Portsmouth Division.[1]

A Paymaster of the Marine Forces was appointed in London, and dealt with all their financial arrangements. A Mr W Adair was the first Paymaster and Agent, and he was succeeded by a Mr Tucker. A deputy Paymaster was borne at each Division from the duty officers. An Adjutant and a Quartermaster (who held appointments for a period of years) were appointed in the following year to each Division. A Surgeon was appointed to each Division being commissioned as such; Mr Rickman was appointed to Portsmouth and Mr James Scott to Plymouth.

Non-Commissioned Officers.
There is no doubt many of the old regiments flocked to the Colours. An early Order reads; *The names of men who have been in service are to be reported to the Commanding Officer, so as to make them Corporals.* Sergeants and Corporals were also obtained from the out pensioners of Chelsea Hospital and from invalids doing duty in garrison.[2] Also ten men from each of the Regiments of Foot commanded by Major General Bookland, Colonel Boneywood and Lieutenant General Wolfe were sent to make Sergeants and Corporals for the Marine Companies.[3]

The only Staff Sergeants appointed were a Sergeant Major and a Drum Major at each Division. There must also have been an Orderly Room Clerk, for the Admiralty letters were copied into books and there were also the General Weekly Returns to London and the Sea and Promotion Rosters to be kept. The latter were probably educated men - the one at Portsmouth begins and ends the letter book with a Latin verse.

Each Sergeant was ordered to have an Orderly Book. In the samples of orders extant at Plymouth, each day is written out with the parole of the day and the name of the Commanding Officer in the

---

1   See Appendix.
2   Calendar of State Papers 1780-85, No 937.
3   Plymouth Letter Book 6 May 1755.

margin. Orders were dictated to the Orderly Sergeant of the Company who communicated them to his company officers, a practice which remained in force till the introduction of duplicating machines well on in the 1880's.

Barracks.
No barracks were in existence; officers and men were in quarters, i.e. billeted in the various inns etc. At Chatham in the purlieus of lanes that stood on the ground where the barracks now stand, in Old Brompton, Chatham and even in Rochester, those who can remember The Brook of even twenty years ago can perhaps visualise the conditions. At Portsmouth in the medley of streets and lanes where Curtis' warehouses now stand and round the High Street, and where the present Clarence Barracks are built, closed in by the fortifications and marshes now occupied by the Recreation Grounds and Victoria Barracks. At Plymouth round the Barbican, where it is easier to realise the conditions as there have been fewer changes in the old buildings and stores; the Orderly Room was in the Printing Office in Southside Street and the Parade is still the Parade at the head of Sutton Pool. Houses were taken at each place for Infirmaries, and it is presumed the Officers' Mess was in one of the larger inns. As the men were billeted the allowance to the Innkeeper was fourpence a day which seems to have covered an allowance of beer, but the men were under stoppages of pay towards payment for their bread and meat. If one remembers the smallness of the companies and the large size of the detachments afloat - to say nothing of special battalions - the numbers at Headquarters must have been very small.

Recruiting.
No doubt one of the first duties was to send out recruiting parties, usually consisting of one Officer, one Sergeant, one Corporal, one Drummer and one Private, who were despatched to different parts of the kingdom, provided with "Beating Orders" and a Route or Billeting Order so that they could obtain accommodation. Men were enlisted for life, but from various applications for discharge after the war we gather that many men were enlisted during hostilities for three years or the duration.[4]

The Bounty or Levy Money for Recruits was apparently two guineas, whilst foreign Protestants had been enlisted at Portsmouth for as little as £1.7.0.

Pay. The rates of pay were those which had been established in 1689:

		Servants Allowance
Colonel	20/-	4/-
Lieutenant Colonel	15/-	2/-
Major	13/-	2/-
Captain	8/-	2/-
Lieutenant	4/-	-/8
2nd Lieutenant	3/-	-/8

---

[4] Portsmouth Letters.

Quartermaster	4/-	-/8
Sergeant	1/6	
Corporal	1/-	
Private	-/8	

There were numerous stoppages for rations and clothing and a curious stoppage called the 'Naval Sixpences' which apparently went to Greenwich Hospital. In effect it looks very much as if the men depended principally on their Sea Pay which was paid when they disembarked, and which no doubt was well augmented by Prize Money, because they seem to have generally embarked in debt. From Plymouth Order 1st June 1755 we learn that the stoppage when in hospital was fourpence a day.

Clothing.
The men were clothed as Grenadiers[5]. They all wore 'rollers', which seems to have been a kind of stock. The gaiters were brown linen spatterdashes[6] and were pretty useless things too (they can be seen today on the Drum Majors of the Guards in Review Order). Sergeants carried halberds and wore swords; Corporals were distinguished by 'knots' worn on the shoulder. Officers in addition to the sword carried a 'fuzee', a sort of light musket. Arms and accoutrements were issued by the Board of Ordnance; uniform or 'King's Clothing' (i.e. coat, waistcoat and breeches) were supplied by the Navy Board; necessaries etc were purchased locally by the Company Officers.

Men at first had waist belts for the bayonets and cartouche boxes, but knapsacks were not common if used at all. Nor do greatcoats appear to have been issued generally, but 'watch coats' as we know them were in use for guards and sentries. At first side arms were worn by all ranks when walking out, but in 1780 - in consequence of rows in the streets - an order was issued on 24th May that no one was to wear side arms except on duty, but Sergeants were allowed to wear their swords.

For Necessaries Plymouth Orders 19th February 1758 says: *"2 good shirts, 2 good pairs of stockings, 1 good pair of shoes"*; Chatham Orders 4th March 1757 say: *"3 shirts, 2 pairs shoes, 3 pairs stockings."* McIntyre, as a detachment officer, gives a more comprehensive list which probably was general -

4 Check Shirts	1 pr Spatterdashes.
1 White Shirt	1 Best Leather Stock
4 pr Coloured Stockings.	1 Set Uniform Buckles
1 pr White Stockings.	1 Hair Cockade.
Hair Band, Needles, Thread.	Combs.
1 pr Shoe Soles.	Small Bag Hair Powder

As a proof that many trained officers and men must have re-joined, there are orders for the embarkation of detachments almost at once; the first at Plymouth dated 16th July when Captain Dalton, Lieutenants Cathcart and Cotton with 3 Sergeants, 3 Corporals, 3 Drummers and 100 Privates were embarked in HMS *Ramillies*, and Captain Webb and Lieutenant Maltby with 2 Sergeants, 2 Corporals, 1 Drummer and 70 Privates embarked in HMS *Vanguard*.

---
5   Colonel Field has described all details as to clothing.
6   Plymouth Orders 12 September 1758.

Before describing the operations of the war which commenced in 1768, a perusal of the Letter and Order Books and also of a book by Lieutenant McIntyre, published after the war, throws many interesting sidelights on the life of the Corps, and shows us where many of our peculiar orders and customs originate.

Drummers.
An Order of 4th February 1768[7] states that Drummers were to be paid 3/- a week for subsistence until such time as they *'are perfect in their beating;' the remainder of their subsistence was to pay for necessaries after deducting '£1.1.0 which is to be paid to the Drum Major for all such as he makes perfect in their beating.'* This payment was only abolished by Order-in-Council 5th July 1918.

Adjutants.
At first only one was allowed for each Headquarters, but they had risen to three by the end of the war, a second being added on 22nd April 1758 and a third in September 1782. In 1758 a Quartermaster was appointed to each Headquarters; they were duty officers detailed for a period of years like the Adjutants. They only dealt with Arms and the Uniform Clothing.

Bundles.
An order of 19th February 1758[8] says that no Marine is to carry bundles in the streets.

Garrison Duty.
There seems to have been some friction with the regiments as to the standing of the Marines, because in June 1756 the Secretary at War censured Anstruther's Regiment about some difficulty concerning their taking over guards from the Marines. It was ruled that *"Officers of Marines have rank according to the dates of their Commissions."*

Squads.
By 1758 it had evidently been found that it was impossible for the Company Commander, constantly embarking etc, to keep all the accounts of NCOs and men, purchase and supply necessaries etc, so Parade Companies called Squads were formed by grouping the Divisional Companies. The number of Companies to a Squad varied from 4 to as many as 44 to 6 squads. Officers called Squad Officers were appointed to take charge of the accounts, etc.

An Admiralty Warrant of November 1783 gives an idea of their duties. *"It has been represented to us that from the various accounts of receipts and disbursements which Squad Officers of Marines are obliged to keep, not only a thorough knowledge of accounts, but a regular minute exactness therein, as well as some experience in business is requisite to enable them to execute all the several parts of their duties."* [9] An Order of 1760 shows that *"Officers who pay Squads are to return accoutrements and Kings Clothing to the Quarter Master."* This also shows that as early as this the difference between public and personal clothing was recognised.

---

7   Plymouth.
8   Plymouth.
9   Letter Books. Plymouth.

Sergeant Majors.

A second Sergeant Major was added to each Division on 17th November 1756. At the same time the senior Sergeant Major at Plymouth, John Christian, was given a commission and appointed Adjutant, an appointment which he held for nineteen years; on 18th October 1775 when a Captain Lieutenant he was appointed Adjutant of the Portsmouth Division.

Saluting.

An Order of 17th August 1758[10] lays down the manner of saluting Officers; *"Taking off their hats in speaking or passing an officer."* McIntyre amplifies this *"When a soldier has acquired a good air, he should be taught to take off his hat properly with his left hand and let it hang at his side; in that position to look the officer in the face, taking care at the same time not to stoop or hang down his head."* This custom was certainly observed in the Brigade of Guards when in fatigue dress down to the Boer War.

Fortescue gives the weight of clothing and equipment carried by the Army and presumably the Marines in 1762.

Coat	5 lbs 2 oz.[11]
Firelock and Sling	11 lbs.
Other items and 6 days' provisions	39 lbs. 7 oz.
Total	83 lbs 3 oz.

The knapsack contained 2 shirts, 2 stocks ('rollers' in Marines), 2 prs stockings, 1 pr summer breeches, 1 pr shoes, brushes and blackball. Marines carried a pair of tartan trousers in the valise until about 1904. But from various letters a knapsack was not generally issued to Royal Marines and as late as 1775 when drafts were ordered to America it is said that knapsacks were being sent in the transport, though they are shown in the list of necessaries to be supplied by the contractor and cost 3/7d in 1785. A letter speaks in 1793 of them as more in the nature of haversacks and asks for knapsacks the same as Line Regiments.[12]

Sea Roster.

No general Corps rosters for Officers were kept, but one for each rank at each Division, and there were many difficulties and complaints at the unequal incidence of embarkation. The men also seem to have been detailed by roster, but there was much marching of drafts from one Division to another to meet requirements. The complements for each class of ship were laid down from time to time.

Drill and Training.

We have very little to go on as to the training imparted, but it is pretty clear that during the war the recruits were in many cases embarked with little or no training at all; in fact the battalions sent to

---

10 Plymouth.
11 It is doubtful if the Marines had one.
12 See also McIntyre on this point.

Rochefort in 1757 were composed of more or less untrained recruits.[13]

According to Plymouth Orders the first drill parade took place on the Hoe on 12th May 1755 and on this subject our best authority is Lieutenant McIntyre's book. There used to be an old drill book in the Forton library which gave the instructions for the Manual and Firing Exercises about 1760. Drill at that time was in three ranks, the firings in use were those used by the army adapted as necessary for ship use eg 'Barricade firing' was used for repelling boarders. The officers carried fuzees not only in action but on parade.

The arms seem to have been very bad, and certainly the wooden rammers were most unserviceable. McIntyre says: *"they are unfit for service – he has to have two or three motions to ensure the shot being home; they frequently break, and the brass heads fly off."* He says they *"ought to be replaced by iron rammers."* *"Every Soldier must keep his arms as bright as possible, particularly the brass work and barrel; stocks to be well rubbed and side of lock well oiled; cock and flint screwed fast. The bayonet to fix properly, rammer to fit tight so as not to fall out at exercise,"* whilst by Order lst May 1759 it says, *"the Bayonets must be made to fit the firelock."* Barrels were kept bright till after Waterloo and one of the earliest orders of the peace in 1816 was that the barrels were to be browned.

It was not until 1764 that it was ordered that the firelocks should be marked with the number of the company and the number of the firelock in the company. *"Sergeants and Corporals to keep a list"* So that from the earliest times it was the custom for the Marine to retain his own firearm.

---

13   Beatson.

2 - The Seven Years' War 1756 - 1763

This war, which established the sea power of Great Britain and laid the foundations of her vast Empire, is of peculiar interest to the Royal Marines not only as the first war in which the Corps as at present constituted took part, but for the numerous examples of the work for which the Corps is peculiarly fitted and trained. Those who would learn how 'Striking Forces' should be employed and combined landings under hostile fire carried out, can find invaluable lessons in the standard works on this war.

Although the War originated and was principally fought in efforts to obtain the mastery in North America and the East and West Indies, the various expeditions involved action by the fleets in the home and Mediterranean waters; whilst the King of England at that time was also Elector of Hanover, so that the country was to a certain extent involved in the continental war which was being waged between France, Austria and Russia on the one side and Frederick of Prussia and his Allies - among whom were the British - on the other. The British assistance mostly took the form of subsidies and the employment of the King's Hanoverian and Hessian troops, but the standards of our cavalry and infantry bear witness that the small numbers employed bore a very great share in the success achieved.

The majority of the British troops were however employed in conjunction with the fleet in the combined expeditions in America and the West Indies; also on the coasts of France, which must be considered in relation to the operations on the Continent. France, which was then the most powerful nation in Europe, was also in possession of Canada and was pushing her forces down the great Ohio River, establishing posts with a view to joining forces with her settlements at the mouth of the Mississippi - St Louis, etc - which would have cut off the English Colonies from the great west. Her settlers were therefore coming to blows with the English settlers of the Atlantic coast for the possession of the vast territories drained by the Ohio and its tributaries.

In the East Indies, French adventurers - backed by their Government - were extending their influence with the native princes, which brought them into collision with the English of the East India Company and led to the great campaigns which established British power in India. In those days by a curious convention a "Colonial" war did not apparently involve the home countries in a declaration of war, so that in 1754 the French were reaching southward from Canada and northward from New Orleans. In April and May of that year they established Fort Duquesne where Pittsburgh now stands, whilst the British dispatched a squadron under Admiral Keppel with two regiments under General Braddock to help the Colonial Forces. Unfortunately, the British columns which advanced on Fort Duquesne and Fort William Henry met with disaster.

Meanwhile the home countries were waking up, although the Whig Government under Newcastle, which was in power, was most inefficient and matters in England were in a very bad state. In January 1755 France dispatched six regular regiments to Canada. In England Lord Anson, First Lord of the Admiralty, mobilised the fleet and 13,000 seamen - an increase of 8000 - were voted. In April he instituted the Marines on their present basis as already related.

On the news of the French reinforcements reaching England, Admiral Boscawen, who was lying with the British Fleet at Torbay, probably the last fleet without its complement of Marines, was ordered to Halifax. He sailed on 27th April with orders to take station off Louisburg, the French fortified naval base in Cape Breton Island, and if he met the French transports to seize them. The French sailed on 3rd May. Admiral Holleburne with six more battleships was sent to reinforce Boscawen on 11th May

Boscawen, or rather one of his captains (the celebrated Howe) met the French and captured two small battleships with three companies of La Reine and four companies of the Languedoc Regiments, but the remainder escaped, the fleet going into Louisburg and the troops on to Quebec. As it was said, Boscawen had *"done too much or too little."*

Naturally diplomatic relations were broken off, but still no declaration of war was made. Meanwhile the position in Europe was growing worse, and Hanover was being threatened. It was therefore necessary to isolate France by land and sea.

Admiral Hawke went to sea with the Channel Fleet of sixteen battleships on 28th July to intercept the French Squadron returning from America and also their home coming trade. He went first to Finisterre and then to a rendezvous off Ushant on 23rd August. We may conclude that the first Marine detachments were in the fleet, because we know that the detachment of the *Ramillies* (Flag), 3 officers and 109 men, and of the *Vanguard*, 2 officers and 75 men, embarked on 18th July at Plymouth and must have soon been earning their prize money, because Hawke's Fleet captured many prizes though the French Fleet slipped into Brest when he was driven off by bad weather.

Each Government was now playing for safety and trying to make the other appear to be the aggressor, in order to be able to call on their allies in Europe. The treaty with Frederick of Prussia was signed in August 1755.

Throughout the war it is noticeable how very good was the Intelligence Service of the British Government, which by 14th February 1796 was in possession of the French plans for an invasion of England and a raid on Minorca, our Naval Base in the Mediterranean.

On 27th February, Hawke with sixteen battleships and numerous cruisers was ordered to blockade Brest and the Bay of Biscay and now began for the first members of our Corps that weary watch in all weathers off Ushant and the Bay which lasted for seven long years and which was to be their experience in all the wars of the eighteenth century and repeated in another form in the twentieth amidst the dreary wastes of Scapa Flow. In spite of the vigilance of the fleet, Montcalm - the great defender of Quebec - and his staff slipped out of Brest on 1st April.

We must now turn to the Mediterranean where the British Naval Base, Minorca, was threatened by the French. The Mediterranean Squadron under Commodore Edgcumbe, consisted only of one 90-gun ship, two of 50 guns and four frigates. The Marines of the squadron were landed to help the garrison, and the Commodore sailed for Gibraltar. Admiral Byng with ten battleships was ordered to the Mediterranean and sailed on 6th April 1756; he appears to have landed his Marines and embarked the 7th Royal Fusiliers to reinforce the Minorca garrison. On arrival at Gibraltar on 2nd May he met Edgcumbe's squadron but delayed trying to persuade the Governor to give him another regiment. The latter refused but gave him 250 men to replace Edgcumbe's Marines. Byng left Gibraltar on 8th May.

The garrison of Minorca consisted of the 4th, 23rd, 24th and 34th Regiments with the Marines of Edgcumbe's Squadron, viz: 1 Captain, 2 Lieutenants, 4 Sergeants, 104 Rank and File, the total strength being 2,800. General Blakeney the Governor was eighty years of age but a very gallant old man. The garrison was short of 35 officers; but Major Cunningham of the Engineers, when proceeding on leave, heard of the projected attack and returned to be the soul of the defence; fortunately, the works of Fort Phillip at Port Mahon were very strong. The small detachment of Marines, the first of many similarly placed, shared all the hardships of the siege, which lasted seventy days.

The French with twelve battleships and 16,000 troops anchored off Port Mahon on 8th April but did not land until the 18th at Ciudadella in north east angle of the island; Port Mahon is in the south west corner. In spite of their numerical superiority, it was five days before the French occupied the town and it was the 8th May before their batteries obtained any effect on the fortress into which Blakeney had withdrawn.

On 17th May, Admiral Byng appeared off Majorca, and on 18th May he got into action with the French Fleet; the result was indecisive and after hanging about until the 24th he decided to return to Gibraltar and left Minorca to its fate. For this action he was subsequently tried by Court Martial and shot.

On 8th June the French having received a reinforcement of six more battalions, opened new batteries, and made a breach which the British repaired; on the 9th two new breaches were made, but on the 14th the garrison made a sortie, drove the French from their batteries and spiked the guns; unfortunately, they pursued too far and were all captured. On the 27th June the French attempted to carry the place by storm but were met by a stubborn defence; three companies of French Grenadiers were blown up by a mine. Unfortunately, three principal outworks were taken and more serious still, Major Cunningham was severely wounded. On 28th June with barely enough men to man the guns, Blakeney capitulated with all the honours of war and the garrison embarked for Gibraltar.

Meanwhile the Government had decided to relieve Byng, and Admiral Hawke sailed on 18th June and reached Minorca on 20th July, but by this date Richelieu, having left a garrison in the captured fortress, was safe back at Toulon. The British losses in the siege were 400 killed and wounded; the French lost 2,200. Fortescue sums it up *"Byng (the Admiral) was shot because Newcastle (the politician) deserved to be hanged."*

In January 1756 thirty more companies were added to the Corps and in July twenty additional companies making one hundred. By the end of 1756 the strength was 11,419.

The British Government declared war as soon as the news of the attack on Minorca reached England, but things were going very badly. In India, Calcutta had fallen to Sujah Dowlah who had perpetrated the atrocity of the Black Hole on the British prisoners. In North America, Montcalm had captured Oswego, the British Naval station, on the great Lakes.

Public indignation was at its height and the Newcastle Ministry was driven from office. Pitt, afterward Earl Chatham, became Prime Minister, and at once a new spirit was infused into affairs. At the end of 1756 Lord Loudon had been sent with reinforcements to North America, and whilst arranging for the defence of the frontiers planned an attack on Louisburg, the French Naval Base, which was approved by the Ministry; in addition to the troops from New York, troops were sent from England and a squadron under Admiral Holleburne of seventeen battleships and five frigates was put under orders, but did not sail till 18th April 1757. In the interval French squadrons had slipped out, one from Brest, and one from Toulon and another under De La Mothe of nine battleships and two cruisers got out of Brest on 3rd May. These all concentrated at Louisburg.

The North American Squadron and Loudon's troops had fortunately reached Halifax where they waited until Holleburne arrived on 9th July. Whilst watering etc, news of the French concentration was obtained, and in view of their naval superiority, it was obvious that the attack on Louisburg was impossible and must be abandoned. Admiral Holleburne, however, maintained the blockade off Louisburg, until 24th September when his Fleet was scattered by a gale and had to return to Halifax and England.

Life for our officers and men afloat must have been that of discomfort and danger; in this storm, one battleship went ashore and was lost, ten lost all or some of their masts, whilst several had to throw guns overboard to lighten the ships. After this De La Moths was able to get to sea and evading Hawke's Fleet returned to Brest, but in such a disabled condition and so riddled with disease that the French Fleet was immobilised for many months.

Efforts were being made by the King and others to have troops sent to Hanover to take part in the Continental War and eventually a few British troops under the Duke of Cumberland were sent. On 6th April 1757 Pitt was dismissed from office and all was in confusion in the political world; at last at the end of June a Coalition Ministry was formed with Newcastle as Prime Minister and Pitt as Secretary at War, and also the latter was charged with the direction of operations.

Things went very badly; on 2nd July the French captured Ems and the Duke of Cumberland had to fall back on Stade, his base on the Elbe. There were consequently vehement demands for reinforcements, but Pitt steadfastly refused to allow his troops to be involved in a Continental War. He however agreed to a diversion in which he could use the fleet and Army in combination and therefore decided on an attack on Rochefort - the French Naval Base in the Basque Roads in the Bay of Biscay - using Hawke's

Fleet and 8,000 troops. It was here the Marines got their first baptism of landing under fire.

On 24th July Cumberland was defeated at Hastenbeck and on the 11th August the French entered Hanover; but they were alarmed at the preparations being made in England as they could not tell where the blow would fall and thought it might be coming to Emden or possibly to the Netherlands. Consequently, their reinforcements were delayed, and all coast troops were reinforced.

By 18th August the troops for Rochefort were assembled in the Isle of Wight; there were ten Line Battalions (100 each), and two Battalions of Marines who can only recently have been recruited, and must have been very raw,[14] two Companies of RFA and a troop of Light Horse. Unfortunately, the GOC, Sir John Mordaunt, was a soldier trained in the continental school and quite unfitted for this work.

Rochefort is situated on the River Charente in the Basque Roads and was one of the principal French dockyards. The Roads were covered by the Islands of Rhe and Oleron; at the mouth of the river is the island of Aix where the ships used to take on their armament and stores owing to the want of water in the river. It was therefore strongly fortified; Fort Fouras was at the mouth of the river covering the channel. This island of Aix was to become well known to the Corps in the following years. The object of the expedition was (1) to create a diversion in favour of the troops in Germany, (2) to injure the French credit, and (3) to impair the strength of their fleet.

On 20th September the Fleet sighted the entrance to the Roads; Admiral Knowles with his Division was ordered to go in and bombard Aix and land sufficient men to demolish it with all dispatch; unfortunately the *Magnanime* carrying the only French pilot went in chase of a French man of war which escaped, and gave the alarm to the whole coast The 21st was wasted owing to the pilots not knowing the way; on the 22nd the fleet again tried to enter but the wind fell and they did not get into the Roads until the evening. On the 23rd the leading ships began the bombardment of Aix at 10 pm; the fort surrendered at 1.45, and a regiment was landed to garrison the fort. The French were in confusion and panic stricken, but no attempt to land on the mainland was made and the opportunity was lost. An Admiral and three Captains were sent to find a landing place – but no military officer went with them. They brought off a very unfavourable report of the shoals etc. and the distance at which the transports would have to lie. In the meantime, the GOC sent Colonel Wolfe the Chief Staff Officer to reconnoitre; he reported a suitable place at Chataillon Bay, where however a small force would have been able to stop any landing party. On the 25th a Council of War was held, and, in view of the reports, decided that attempts against Rochefort must be abandoned and orders were given to demolish the fortifications on Aix.

The French were meanwhile hurrying up reinforcements and improving the defences. On the 25th a second Council of War was held and at midnight the grenadiers and first flight of troops were placed in the boats, but as it came on to blow the naval officers represented that it was too long

---

14 In this resembling our battalions sent to Gallipoli in 1915.

a row for the boats, whilst the boats were too few to admit of the second flight following at once; it was therefore decided to abandon the attempt, and on 1st October the fleet, having completed the destruction of Aix, sailed for home. The GOC was afterwards tried by Court Martial, but Colonel Wolfe learnt some valuable lessons which bore fruit the next year.

In Germany, Cumberland had signed the Convention of Kloster-Zeven, but Admiral Parker's squadron in the Elbe and Weser had disturbed the French and caused them to evacuate Bremen. On 5th November the French were defeated by Frederick of Prussia at Rossbach, and Ferdinand who now commanded the allied detachments in Hanover denounced the Convention on 20th November. The French fell back to the Aller River and their allies the Austrians were defeated and fell back out of Saxony.

The year 1758 opened more auspiciously for the British. The French were still nervous about their coast defences and were employing 60,000 men in that way, but both nations were preparing for the struggle in North America. The British plan aimed at seizing Quebec, but before this could be done it was necessary to capture Louisburg, the French Naval Base in Cape Breton Island. The French plan was to throw reinforcements into Canada.

Before dealing with the main operations, it is necessary to glance at the covering operations by which the British expedition was able to cross the sea in safety, and in all of which the Corps took its part. On the side of Germany, the British squadron got into the Ems River and caused the French to evacuate Emden and gradually fall back behind the Rhine. A British battalion was sent to occupy Emden whilst Ferdinand advanced and took Minden on 14th April; these movements enabled the North Sea Squadron to be withdrawn for the main operation.

In the Mediterranean Admiral Osborne was watching De La Clue in Carthagena and guarding the Straits of Gibraltar. French reinforcements, with a squadron under Du Quesne, left Toulon and arrived off Carthagena on 28th February; De La Clue did not come out, and on the 20th a gale blew Du Quesne into the arms of Osborne with the result that the *Oriflamme* and *Orphee* were driven ashore, and Du Quesne having been killed the *Foudroyante* was captured by the *Monmouth*, *Swiftsure* and *Hampton Court* and was added to the Navy.

In the Atlantic Hawke proceeded to sea on 18th March and went to Belle Isle and Basque Roads, where the French convoys were fitting out. He entered the Roads on 3rd April, on which the French ran seven frigates and forty transports aground, but by throwing their guns overboard they escaped up the River Charente. Hawke cut adrift the buoys showing where they had dumped their gear and landed Captain Ewer and 140 Marines who destroyed the fortifications of Aix for the second time. Leaving Keppel to blockade the Roads and Bordeaux, Hawke went back to the Channel on 11th April, and was able to concentrate his whole force and there we must leave him for a time.

The expedition against Louisburg consisted of twenty battleships under Admirals Boscawen and Hardy, whilst troops under General Amherst were to come from England and America to the number of 11,000. Boscawen sailed from Spithead on 19th February but Amherst did not get away until 18th March. The force, having rendezvoused at Halifax, sailed with 157 ships for Louisburg on 28th May. It arrived at Gabbarne Bay on the south side of the island. There were three possible landing places; (1) Freshwater or Kennington Cove, (2) Flat Point, (3) White Point; there was another at Lorambec to the eastward. All points were threatened simultaneously, whilst Wolfe's Brigade made the real attack at Freshwater Cove which turned out to be the most strongly defended. All attempts at landing were prevented by fog and storms, but on the morning of the 7th June troops were placed in the boats and a fierce bombardment was opened by the frigates on all points. The boats pushed off and pulled for the shore. The Cove was a beach ¼ mile long with rocks at each end; the whole beach was covered by the fire of the French entrenchments which were protected by abattis with eight guns sweeping every approach; the boats came under heavy fire as they approached the beach, but three subalterns saw a chance of landing on the rocks at the east end and succeeded. General Wolfe saw their action and at once recognising its importance diverted the boats and followed himself to this spot to reinforce them, followed by Colonel Lawrence's Brigade to the westward. They were quickly followed by the GOC Amherst.[15]

The French retired to the fortress and the siege commenced, but bad weather delayed the landing of the guns. The French Fleet were inside the harbour and the Fleet did not consequently attempt to force the entrance, though the fire from the French ships interfered with the siege operations. On 25th June Wolfe with 1,200 men and some artillery marched round the harbour and seized Lighthouse Point, on the east side, establishing bomb batteries which he armed from the fleet. On 28th June the Marines of the fleet were landed under Captain Tooker Collins on the west side to replace them and on the 30th helped to repulse an enemy attack. On the 28th the French sunk some ships to block the harbour. On 15th July Wolfe's battery at Lighthouse Point silenced the batteries on Goat Island, and on the 19th the bombardment opened. The French Admiral had wished to break out, but the Governor would not allow him and consequently his fleet was doomed.

On 21st July one of the French battleships was set alight by bombs and blew up, which set fire to two more ships. The batteries continued their fire and the next day two more batteries were opened, and the approaches were made to the covered way. On the 25th the Admiral sent in the boats with 800 seamen to take or burn the two remaining ships, the *Bienfast* and *Prudente*, the former was driven ashore and burnt, and the latter brought out. On 26th July the garrison capitulated and 3,000 soldiers and 3,000 seamen with all the ships were taken prisoners.

It was now too late to go on to Quebec, especially as on the 21st news was received of the failure of the overland expedition - although Frontenac on Lake Ontario was taken and all the French inland naval force was destroyed, whilst Fort Duquesne also was captured. The French squadron from Quebec however got back to Brest after a brush with Boscawen on 27th October. The British

---

15   It is interesting to compare this landing with that on West Beach on 25th April, 1915, when the Brigade Commander with two platoons of D Company of the Lancashire Fusiliers (20th Regt) landed from HMS *Implacable* on the rocky point to the north of the Bay and making good their way up the cliff took the defenders in flank and enabled the main body to succeed. (See Official History Gallipoli Vol I pp 228-229. Also compare it with the similar movement at Belle isle which proved so successful in 1761).

forces were then employed laying waste the French Coast settlements until the weather caused the cessation of operations.

Senegal.
Before dealing with events in Europe it is necessary to glance at a small expedition to the West Coast of Africa which illustrates the value of a Marine Striking Force. It had been represented to the Government that an attack on the French settlements in Senegal would be a serious blow to the French, as they drew the supplies of negro labour for their West Indian Colonies from there. Accordingly a squadron of two small battleships and some cruisers with 200 Marines under Major J T Mason of the Plymouth Division were embarked at Plymouth, with a small detachment of Royal Artillery under Captain Walker with ten guns and two mortars. They arrived off the mouth of the Senegal River on 24th April. Fort Louis which was fortified was about twelve miles up the river, across the mouth of which there was a dangerous bar; the French had a few armed vessels behind the bar which interfered with the boats sounding to find the channel. On the 29th when the channel had been discovered the Marines and Artillery were put into several small sloops and escorted by the *Swallow*, *Sloop*, and some armed vessels made an attempt to cross the bar. The *Swallow* and some of the ships got through all right, but some with the troops and stores and the ship with the tents were wrecked; the Marines waded ashore and fortunately no lives were lost. They were quickly joined by the others from the ships, and entrenchments were thrown up at once as it was feared that the natives might give trouble, but they proved to be friendly. The next day 350 seamen were landed, and the force prepared to march on Fort Louis when the French sent down a flag of truce and proposed a capitulation. At first the natives were inclined to prevent the troops entering the fort, but they were soon reassured as to their safety, and on 2nd May the Marines occupied the forts - capturing 240 soldiers, 90 guns and a large amount of treasure estimated at about £200,000.

It was fortunate that the French capitulated because owing to the losses on the bar it was doubtful if the force could have carried out a siege.

Goree.
The Marines were relieved later by 200 men of the 74th Regiment; the squadron went on and tried to bombard Goree but made no impression, so the attempt was abandoned. On 11th November Commodore Keppel and Lieutenant Colonel Worge with troops from Ireland and the Marines of the fleet left Cork and sighted Goree on 28th December. On the 29th the troops and Marines were embarked in the flat boats and the ships opened fire. The French demanded a parley, which came to nothing; hostilities were then resumed and the French surrendered. Commodore Keppel landed all his Marines who took possession of the Fort until arrangements were made to relieve them, as Colonel Worge had been appointed Governor.

Returning to the Channel. Matters had been going none too well in Germany, and Prussia was demanding that England should make a diversion on the French coast to draw off the French troops.[16] Sixteen battalions including one from each of the Guards Regiments were ordered to be in the Isle of Wight by May 23rd. Lord Anson (First Lord) assumed command of the Channel Fleet in place of Hawke to cover the operation, and it was decided to attack St Malo. The covering fleet consisted of twenty-two battleships and eight frigates (34,000 men). Howe was in command of the attacking fleet of three small battleships, ten frigates with 100 transports - all told 150 sail. Troops were 13,000 (13 Battalions, 9 Troops Light Horse, 3 Companies Artillery and a siege train) in addition to the Marines of the fleet.

Anson's idea was that the object was to force the French Fleet to sea and therefore he did not block Brest, but the Government's intention was to make a diversion to attract French troops from Germany. On 4th June Howe anchored in Cancale Bay; the ships silenced the batteries, and the troops were landed at 9 pm; the Grenadiers formed the covering force followed by the Brigade of Guards and Cancale was occupied. During the night two brigades were landed and the next day the cavalry and artillery. It was a complete surprise. The force advanced on the 7th and occupied Parame. The Light Horse, with infantry support, burnt all the shipping in St Servan harbour; St Malo was summoned to surrender but refused. As the place was too strong to attack without the siege train which could not be landed, and French reinforcements were now reported to be advancing, it was decided to re-embark which was done on the 12th. After delays caused by bad weather they made a demonstration off Havre and Honfleur but disappeared to sea on the 28th; on the 30th the fleet reappeared off Cherbourg but being driven off by a gale went to Spithead. Unfortunately, the effort had not created much of a diversion.

A second attempt was made in August, General Bligh having replaced the Duke of Marlborough. This time they seem to have been handicapped by a more than usually incompetent army staff.

On the 7th they appeared off Cherbourg and bombarded the place; the covering troops were landed under the fire of the ships and drove off 3,000 of the enemy and the remainder of the troops were landed; the next day they advanced on the town which fell at once. For a week they destroyed the docks, forts, shipping etc. but the troops got very out of hand; as French troops were assembling the troops were re-embarked on the 15th without loss.

On 31st August they were off again and on 3rd September anchored in the bay of St Lunaire twelve miles west of St Malo; troops were landed during the two following days with the loss of several drowned. They advanced towards the town but the River Rance lay in front of them, and the weather became so bad that Commodore Howe had to leave the anchorage and informed General Bligh that he must go to the Bay of St Cast to the westward. The army started to march there on 7th September and reached St Cast on the 9th but news was received that large French forces were advancing. Meanwhile - according to Gillespie - three ships had landed their Marines on the night of the 9th at the Castle of St Latte who attacked and carried it without loss (it presumably covered the beach). The retreat of the army appears to have been very badly conducted but they

---

16 The Treaty with Prussia had been signed on 11th April 1758.

commenced to re-embark on the 11th. A strong French force attacked the rearguard who made a strenuous resistance in which they lost their general and 750 killed and wounded, but under the fire of the ships the remainder were got off. The diversion however had proved useful in preventing reinforcements being sent to the French troops acting in Hanover.

The troops in Hanover had been reinforced by all the Heavy Cavalry regiments in England and some of the Hussars, and on 25th July three more battalions had been sent to Emden.

1759

Before the ice conditions in the St Lawrence permitted any action for the great expedition of this year - the Conquest of Canada - Pitt had been considering what he could get hold of in order to exchange for Minorca should peace come, for the Government were quite determined that they would not again give up Louisburg.[17] It was therefore decided in the winter of 1758-59 to make an attempt on Martinique in the West Indies.

The expedition commanded by General Hopson with fortunately Colonel Barrington as second-in-command consisted of six battalions and some Artillery. The 38th Regiment from Antigua and the 2nd Royal Highlanders from Scotland were to join Commodore Hughes who with seven battleships formed the escort and were to join Commodore Moore and his squadron already on the station. The Marines of the squadron had been augmented so as to provide a battalion of 800 men under Major Rycaut (Portsmouth) with local rank of Lieutenant Colonel (19th October 1758). They sailed on 12th November 1758, and on arrival at Barbados on 3rd January Commodore Moore assumed command. He would not use the Marines as a battalion but made use of parties as necessary. How often has this happened in our long story? Beatson comments on this: *"Whereby that useful corps was never permitted to land and act with the land forces which was a very great loss to the army"*[18] Gillespie makes this comment: *"Constantly employed in small detachments, it is frequently his lot at short notice to enter the field against well trained legions of his enemies, and to unite his energies with the regular and brigaded forces of his country; he, in this new scene, perhaps knows not his file leader, and is probably a stranger to his officer."* (As it was in the beginning so always it shall be! Ed.)

The expedition left Barbados on 13th January for Martinique arriving on the 18th. The fleet proceeded off Fort Royal on the west side. The fortress lay within the bay; Point Negro, where there was a small fort, was selected for the first landing of the covering force. Captain Gardiner commanding the Marines of the *Rippon* has left an account: With his own detachment and that of the *Bristol* he was landed at 10 am on the morning of the 16th under the fire of the ships, climbed up the rocks and entered the embrasures of the 7-gun battery with fixed bayonets and found it abandoned by the enemy. At 10.30 he hoisted British colours and the Marines were ordered to hold the fort until required to re-embark. In the meantime, he proceeded to spike the guns, knock off the trunnion. and break up the carriages, assisted by a small party of seamen. Meanwhile three

---
17 It was captured in 1745 by the Marines but was given up at the peace in 1748.
18 Naval and Military Memoirs, II, p. 228.

ships attacked the batteries at Cas de Navires about a league below Fort Negro and silenced them.

At 2 pm the fleet anchored and at 4 pm troops were landed to the north of the bay between Cas de Navires and Point Negro under the fire of the guns of HMS *Winchester*, *Woolwich* and *Roebuck* assisted by the *Rippon* and *Bristol* which destroyed a small fort, and the troops advanced inland. The French were afraid of being caught in a trap, as they could see the Marine centries in Fort Negro and after a short engagement withdrew; but they were in great numerical superiority and contested the ground. It was however found that it would be impossible to drag the siege guns over the difficult ground so that the troops could not attempt to reduce the fortress; whilst it was impossible for the ships to bombard it; the troops were therefore re-embarked on the 17th.

On the 18th the squadron and transports went to St Pierre, the capital of Martinique: the *Rippon* went in and silenced one battery, but there were orders and counterorders, and after a severe battering from various batteries the *Rippon* withdrew, and the fleet hauled off without even attempting to destroy the shipping which lay at their mercy.

It was then decided to abandon the attack on Martinique and to go to Guadeloupe, which was the home of the French privateers and the richest of the islands. Basseterre, the principal town, was well fortified and its citadel was declared to be impregnable. Moore however determined to have a try, and after a reconnaissance on the 22nd at 10 am on the 23rd the Commodore sent in three ships to attack the citadel which was situated so high that their guns could have very little effect. After being bombarded all day the forts ceased firing at 5 pm, though the ships had had a very hot time; the *Rippon* in attacking the *Morne Rouge* ran ashore and came under heavy fire, and eight of the Marines out of twenty-eight on the poop were killed or wounded; the remainder of the detachment were employed at the great guns because the ship had ninety men sick on board. She was rescued by the *Bristol* whose Marines kept down the fire of the troops from the entrenchments on shore. The *Rippon* was got off at midnight.[19] At 5 pm the signal was made to land the troops and they got into the boats, but as it was so late they were recalled.

The bomb ketches stood in at 7 pm and bombarding the town in a wanton manner, the place was soon in a general conflagration and valuable property was destroyed to no purpose. The fleet had 30 killed and 60 wounded; the Marines lost Lieutenant Roberts (*Norfolk*) killed, and Lieutenants Curls (*Lyon*) and Chaundy (*Rippon*) wounded.

On the 24th the troops were landed in the afternoon and the artillery and tents on the 25th, but the enemy were given the chance to recover from their demoralisation and took up a strong position covering the road into the rich territory of Capes Terres.

There were a lot of desultory actions but no advance; Commodore Moore sent the *Berwick*, *Roebuck*, *Renown*, *Woolwich* and *Panther* with three bomb vessels and three transports carrying a

---

19 A parallel instance occurred in the attack on Gaba Tefoe, Gallipoli, the ships concerned being the *Albion* and *Canopus*. See Britain's Sea Soldiers, Vol III, p 40.

detachment of Marines under Major John Campbell of Glenlyon of the Marines and 200 of the Black Watch to attack Fort Louis in Grande Terre in the north east corner of the island; early on 13th February they bombarded the fort and the Marines and Highlanders were placed in the boats ready to land. After five or six hours bombardment, the batteries were silenced and a breach made; Campbell was landed with orders to assault but owing to mangrove roots and the boats not going to the proper place the men had to plunge into the water up to their waists and the ammunition was wetted; Campbell however pushed on with fixed bayonets, drove the French out of their works and hoisted the British colours. *"No troops could behave with more courage than the Marines and Highlanders did on this occasion."* [20] There was considerable loss and the troops were very hurt that this valiant piece of work did not receive any recognition from the Commodore.

General Hopson having died on 27th February, General Barrington decided to abandon the attack on Basse Terre and to move to Grande Terre. A small garrison was left at Basse Terre; the forts were blown up and on 8th March the troops left for Fort Louis where they landed on 11th March. On 13th March Moore received information that a French Squadron with reinforcements under M. Bompart had reached Martinique. He therefore decided to go to Dominica where he would be to windward of Guadeloupe; he therefore recalled all his Marines who were doing duty on shore and put them on board their respective ships but owing to their sickness and casualties Barrington sent a detachment of 300 soldiers to help the complements. We cannot follow Barrington in the fine work by which he eventually forced the French to capitulate on 1st May.

Although Moore's concentration of the Fleet was necessary, and he later sent the homeward convoy back in safety, there were very heavy losses of merchant ships in the West Indies for which he was blamed and eventually removed from his command.

The stage was now set for the great adventure of the year - the capture of Canada and Quebec. The Corps was raised to the strength of 14,845 in 130 companies, and in the summer each ship of the line embarked a double complement of Marines to co-operate in descents on the enemy coasts by the army.

Dealing first with the operations in North America, the attack on Canada was to be made in four columns, three coming up by the Lakes; the fourth, with which alone the Corps is concerned, was to be made by the fleet and army against Quebec. Ten battleships and a similar number of frigates had been left to winter at Halifax under Admiral Durell with orders to get into the St Lawrence River as early as ice would allow, to prevent reinforcements and supplies reaching the French. This he neglected to do, and the French reinforcements and stores arrived safely. Durell repaired his error by forcing his way up the river later and thoroughly surveying the 'Traverses', those difficult obstacles to navigation, so that Saunders' squadron was able to pass through in safety; he was also given 300 troops under the AQMG - Colonel Carleton - and occupied the Isle de Coudres; he then pushed on three ships and a frigate with the troops and occupied the Isle of

---

20   Beatson.

Orleans on 5th June. Meanwhile the main forces were concentrating at Louisburg.

The convoy under Admiral Holmes consisted of six battleships and six frigates with three brigades of nine battalions and a Marine battalion under Major Boisrend of 27 officers 577 Rank and File, embarked at Portsmouth, went first. The Commander-in-Chief, Admiral Saunders, with General Wolfe in command of the troops and ten battleships, three fireships, three bomb vessels and a sloop or two sailed just after, but owing to delays they were not concentrated at Louisburg until the end of May; here they embarked two battalions of Grenadiers - the total force was about 10,000 men. On 1st June the expedition left Louisburg; but unfortunately, owing to Durell's neglect, Quebec was now warned because Bougainville, commanding the French reinforcements, had brought full information of the British design.

Saunders decided to take the whole fleet up to help the army, and they went up in three squadrons. On 27th June the army were landed on the Isle of Orleans, after one of the finest feats of navigation ever performed. Quebec is on a promontory called Cape Diamond and consists of the upper and lower town lying between the St Lawrence and Charles Rivers. There is a broad basin lying between Quebec and Isle of Orleans; on the south shore are the Heights of Levis. To the east of Quebec and lying between the Charles and Montmorenci Rivers was the shore known as Beauport, strongly fortified and the main position of the French. The French force was 12,000 and Wolfe had now only 8,000. The French Fleet had retired up the river to Batiscan and the frigates' crews had been brought down to help in the batteries.

The Fleet had anchored on the south shore of the Island, but it was a bad anchorage. The French made an attack by fireships on 28th June but it failed. On the 29th General Monckton and a brigade were sent to hold Point Levis whilst the fleet moved up to between Point D'Orleans and Point Levis, on 1st July. Monckton on landing at Levis seized the Point almost without a blow and made entrenchments there with the aid of the Marines. Townshend occupied Point D'Orleans. GHQ was placed at St Laurent on the island. On 28th June the Commander-in-Chief ordered Admiral Durell, who had been left at the east end of Orleans as a covering squadron, to send up four more battleships and all his Marines. On 2nd July Wolfe under escort of Monckton's force made a reconnaissance of Point des Pères, immediately opposite Quebec and the siege train was landed on that side and pushed on. On the 4th Murray made a reconnaissance further up the river; on the 5th Webb's Regiment seized Point des Pères and the batteries were commandeered and opened fire on the 12th. On the 10th the French had made an attack on Point Levis which was an absolute failure. Wolfe however had determined to make his main attack on the left flank of the Beauport position under cover of the fire of the *Porcupine* and some sloops, which found the north Channel deeper than they thought; on 7th July Townshend's Brigade was passed over to the east of the Montmorenci River, being relieved in Orleans by the Marines.

On 18th July HMS *Sutherland* covered by the batteries ran the gauntlet and anchored above the town with three transports carrying three companies of Grenadiers and one battalion, 60th Rifles. The French then erected batteries at Sillery and Samos and the British ships moved up to Cap Rouge.

On 26th July two Companies of Marines were sent to the camp on the Montmorenci.

On 28th July the French made another attempt with fire ships which failed.

It was then decided to attack a beach one mile west of the Montmorenci Falls which was accessible by a ford at low water. The attack took place on 31st July; HMS *Centurion* with two armed transports carrying troops, bombarded the beach and the two latter were put aground.[21] All batteries opened fire and a feint was made from Levis. At 1.30 pm the bombardment re-doubled and the troops in the boats made a dash for the shore. They carried the lower redoubts, but the grenadiers got out of hand and rushed on the redoubts above; they were repulsed with heavy loss. A storm of rain drowned their ammunition and the troops re-embarked after losing 800 men.

More ships had meanwhile joined the *Sutherland*, whilst General Murray with one battalion, 200 Marines and some companies of Light Infantry and Rangers marched up to the Echermin River and formed a post there. More troops were also sent up to join the ships. Montcalm sent Bougainville to watch the river above Quebec about Sillery and Cap Rouge, but the movements of the British ships and troops kept him constantly on the move. Admirals Holmes and Murray attacked Point aux Trembles but were beaten off with a loss of 80 killed and wounded; they however seized St Antoine on the south shore opposite, where they formed an entrenched camp garrisoned by the Marines which prevented supplies being drawn from the south shore. Murray and the ships went up to the foot of the Richelieu Rapids and destroyed the stores there.

More ships were then passed up to join Admiral Holmes. At this time Wolfe was very ill and a Council of War advised that an attempt should be made on the communications above the town. On Wolfe's recovery however he determined that the real attack should be made on the town from above. By 3rd September Montmorenci Camp was evacuated and all troops concentrated at Levis. On 5th September a Brigade was sent to Echermin River and only a small garrison left in Orleans.

By 6th all available troops were on board the ships and they moved up to Cap Rouge, drifting up and down with the tide so that the French troops were kept marching up and down and were worn out. The Anse du Foulon and des Noires were consequently left with only a guard of 100 Militia. Owing to bad weather the British troops were landed at St Nicholas opposite Cap Rouge on the 9th, and Wolfe went down to reconnoitre the Anse du Foulon. He was reported, but French GHQ paid no attention. At last on the 12th Saunders moved his ships and ranged them opposite Beauport and put every available Marine into the boats, covered by the smaller ships.[22] Montcalm therefore massed all his troops at Beauport. Wolfe's troops were put into the boats off Cap Rouge at dusk, and at 2 am on the 13th the flotilla dropped down the river. The French were expecting a convoy of provisions so that the guards were deceived, because the British answered the challenges in French.

---

21 This method attack of was often used during the following wars. It was also made use of in the landing at V Beach in Gallipoli on 25th April 1915. See Military Operations, Gallipoli Vol. I for the movements of the *Clyde*. See also later at Manila in 1762.
22 Note the importance of Marines being dressed the same as soldiers.

The covering force consisted of 400 men under Colonel Howe, followed by Monckton and Murray with 1,300 forming the first trip. The second trip of 1,900 men were in the ships, whilst Carleton from Levis was to march up every man he could spare, about 1,200, to form the third trip.

As all know, the landing was successfully affected at the Foulon and the fierce battle was fought on the Plains of Abraham where Wolfe fell in the hour of victory. Siege was laid to the town and Admiral Saunders brought up his ships to assist and landed all the men he could in order to spare the troops all fatigues. The British were most anxious not to injure the town which must be their shelter for the winter. After a short siege the fortress capitulated (on the 20th), the soldiers occupying the Upper Town and the sailors the Lower. The Admiral landed all the stores and provisions he could spare to help the garrison of 7,000 men under General Murray who were left to hold the town during the long Canadian winter, and the fleet sailed on 26th October to avoid the ships being caught by the ice. Some of them with the Admiral arrived home in time to endeavour to join Hawke in his great victory in Quiberon Bay.[23]

We must now turn to Europe to see what steps were being taken by France to help her American Colonies. These took the usual form of a threatened invasion of Great Britain, but the dispositions of the several British Fleets prevented any assistance being sent to America or any descent being made on Great Britain.

By the 5th April Anson, First Lord of the Admiralty, had thirty battleships in hand for the Channel and a Cruiser Squadron was sent to Bordeaux. Boscawen with five battleships was sent to reinforce Brodrick off Toulon. By 24th May, Hawke was in position to blockade Brest and when south west gales forced him to run for shelter to Torbay, the same winds prevented the French squadrons from getting to sea.

The intelligence service kept the British Government informed of all the French plans, and flotillas were stationed along the south coast with cruiser supports to watch Dunkirk, Havre, etc. On 2nd July Rodney left with a small squadron and bombarded Havre for hours; he did a great deal of damage and the French gave up the idea of using flat boats to convey the troops across. In Germany where the British troops had been reinforced by all the British heavy cavalry and a few battalions, the Allies gained the great victory of Minden which shook the French badly.

Hawke who had been clinging to his station - watching Brest and the Biscay ports - all through October and November, experienced terrible weather with the result that his ships and personnel were getting into a very bad state; on 10th November he was driven to Torbay, but he left some frigates on the watch. On the 12th he put to sea, only to be driven back again next day; his flagship the *Ramillies* was in such a leaky state that he shifted his flag to the *Royal George*. On the 14th he was out again. On 7th November Bompart had arrived from the West Indies; and on the 14th Conflans put to sea with twenty-one battleships and five cruisers. On the 18th Hawke learnt that

---

23   See later.

the French Fleet was out and at once made for Quiberon Bay. On the 10th Holmes and Durell from Quebec arrived at Spithead. Saunders following on, arriving off the Lizard, heard the news and went off to try and join Hawke.

On the 16th Conflans was seventy miles west of Belleisle, and on the 18th when 129 miles from that place began to reach back but was becalmed on the 19th. Hawke to the northward of the French experienced the same winds; at daybreak on the 20th when forty miles west of Belleisle he sighted the French squadron; at the same time the French sighted the British inshore squadron and their van and centre started to chase when their rear ships sighted Hawke and the French Fleet was recalled. The French had now to decide whether to fight or run for Quiberon Bay; they decided on the latter and bore away for the entrance which lay among a labyrinth of rocks and shoals. The wind was at North West and there was a very rough sea; should Conflans succeed in getting in he would have concentrated his fleet and the transports in one port.

At 9 am Hawke sighted Conflans and made the signal for general chase, though he kept the fleet in hand. The entrance lay between La Feur Shoal and the Cardinals; beyond it was a lee shore with reefs but still Hawke held on. It is not possible here to give a full account of the gallant action of Quiberon Bay fought by our ancestors in the height of a storm with rocks and shoals all round them; this must be read in one of the standard works, but the French Fleet was scattered and lost six ships and 2,500 men to the British two ships and 300 to 400 men; the ships that escaped were shut up with the transports in Quiberon Bay whilst the others that escaped to the Basque Roads were blockaded in the River Charente. All fear of an invasion or help to America ceased. The British also seized the Isle d'Yeu, destroyed its defences - in which we may be sure the Corps took its part - and the cattle were carried off. The whole French coast was threatened and the army of D'Aiguillon was mobilised.

Boscawen had been keeping Toulon and the country round in a state of alarm, but at the end of July he had to fall back on Gibraltar for provisions and water. On 5th August De La Clue with a squadron got out of Toulon and on the 17th appeared off Gibraltar where the British were refitting. In spite of their dismantled state the British ships got to sea at 10 pm that night and pursued De La Clue who was making for St Vincent. Between two and three am Boscawen's leading ships caught up the enemy and the French rear ships sought refuge in Cadiz; Boscawen held on and at daybreak sighted the French thirty miles south of Cape St Vincent. At 8 am a signal was made for a general chase and at 1.20 pm when off Lagos the action opened and at 4 pm Boscawen's flagship engaged the French flag. The chase continued all through the night of the 18/19th and at daylight the French were sighted making for Lagos; some of the French ships made off, but the *Ocean* and *Redoubtable* were driven ashore and burnt; whilst the *Temeraire* and *Modeste* which sought shelter under the neutral batteries were captured and brought out as prizes. The remainder of the squadron got into Cadiz where they were blockaded by Boscawen, who for this action was created a General of Marines. [24]

---

24   See later.

Of all the invading forces only Thuret, a privateersman, escaped from Dunkirk and going by north of Scotland landed some troops at Carrickfergus in North Ireland who eventually surrendered; Thuret himself was soon rounded up and after a sharp action was killed and sunk off the Isle of Man (on 29th March 1760).

1760

This year a very curious method was adopted of rewarding the Corps for its services. Instead of granting any privileges to the Officers and men of the Corps the following order was promulgated:

"His Majesty anxious to reward such officers as had distinguished themselves in the service of their country on this occasion (viz the great victories of 1759) appointed:[25] *Admiral Boscawen to be General of His Marine Forces with a salary of £2,000 a year (for Lagos). Vice Admiral Saunders Lieutenant General of the same with a salary of £1,200 a year (for Quebec) and the following Captains of the Navy to be Colonels of the above Corps: Sir Piercy Brett Knt at Portsmouth. Hon Augustus Keppel at Plymouth. Richard Viscount Howe at Chatham with a salary of £6800 a year each."*

This system remained in force until 1837, when it was abolished. The strength of the Corps voted for this year was 18,355 in 130 companies.

Although this year was full of great events all over the world the Corps did not take any very prominent part except in the East Indies.[26] In the European and American theatres they, in common with the navy, were employed in the hard and dreary work of blockading the French ports; whilst the army with the assistance of a few flotillas consolidated the conquest of Canada by the capture of Montreal.

Efforts were being made to stop the war and the French and British Governments were negotiating in a half-hearted way. King George II died on 28th October and his successor with his new advisers were very averse to continuing hostilities.

During August, Hawke - who had relieved Boscawen - seized the Isle of Deumet off Morbihan where he was able to grow fresh vegetables for his fleet and get fresh water which greatly eased the work of the blockade and no doubt the Marines found the garrison. He also was preparing a plan to attack the mainland and the ships lying in Quiberon by landing his Marines and sailors at the mouth of the estuary, but the Government had other plans now to be developed.

During the autumn and winter an expedition was preparing to help in the East Indies by capturing Mauritius. On 24th October 1760 apparently a Marine battalion was ordered to form part of the expedition, as a Plymouth letter of this date says that the Admiralty have ordered *"an Adjutant from Plymouth to go along with Major Boisrond upon the expedition in case the Marines are*

---

25 V. Beatson Naval and Military Memoirs Vol II.
26 Dealt with later.

landed and that all the Marines should be provided with knapsacks which you will please to order. PS There are to be Colours sent to ye Battalion." [27] Boisrond seems to have been withdrawn in February 1761 to command Portsmouth Division as Lieutenant Colonel Mackenzie of Chatham commanded the Battalion at Belleisle. But in the spring of 1761, with a view to creating a diversion to assist the Allies in Germany, it was decided to divert the force and to attack a point on the French coast; in consequence on March 25th 1761 the King signed the secret orders for an attack on the Island of Belleisle in the Bay of Biscay, which led to the first honour awarded to the Corps.

Admiral Keppel with ten battleships, eight frigates and a flotilla was told off as the attacking squadron whilst Commodore Buckle formed the covering squadron off Brest. General Hodgson was in command of the troops which consisted of twelve battalions - about 7,000 men. The special battalion of 500 Marines under Brevet Lieutenant Colonel J Mackenzie (afterwards Commandant at Chatham and later Commandant in Town of the Corps) was also embarked. Gillespie says that two battalions were employed, and presumably the other was formed from the Marines of the fleet, as about 1,400 Marines altogether were employed on shore.

On 6th April 1761 the force appeared off the south end of the Belleisle and keeping close inshore reconnoitred possible landing places. All the accessible points were fortified but Loc Maria Bay at the south-east end seemed to be the most practicable whilst the beach at St André seemed possible. The Fleet anchored off Palais, the principal town.

On the 8th Captain Stanhope with the *Swiftsure*, the 27th and 61st Regiments and 500 Marines was sent to demonstrate off Sauzen whilst two battleships destroyed the Fort of St André; the 21st and 67th Regiments and some Marines were placed in the boats. The hills formed an amphitheatre and the troops were landed under heavy fire: sixty grenadiers of the 67th Regiment got up the cliffs beyond the entrenchments,[28] but before they could be reinforced they were all killed or wounded. The troops had to re-embark with a loss of 500 men.

A gale blew in the evening and the next day, so that half the flat boats were lost. On the reports of the reverse reaching England, Pitt at once sent off four more battalions and a regiment of Light Dragoons, with new boats.

Meanwhile the commanders had decided to try again and thought that it was just possible to land and mount the rocks just south of Point Loc Maria, where there was a small fort called Fort D'Arsic. The main attack was to be under Major General Craufurd; there were also to be two feints - the first under Brigadier General Lambert near St Foy on the north side of Loc Maria (the Marines were attached to this force) and the second by the Light Dragoons at Sauzon. The *Sandwich, Dragon, Prince of Orange* and two bomb-ketches were to cover the landing at D'Arsic; the *Swiftsure, Hampton Court, Essex* and *Lynn* under Captain Stanhope to cover Lambert's landing. The attack was fixed for the 22nd April.

---

27 See Appendix.
28 Cf the notes on Louisburg 1758 and Gallipoli 1915.

The batteries were silenced by the ships at 3 pm and the troops were sent in; Crauford was met by a very heavy fire and was checked. Lambert without firing a shot landed half way between St Foy and Point Loc Maria, where the cliffs were considered unclimbable. The Grenadier Company of the 19th Regiment under Captain Paterson led the way, quickly followed by a company of Marines under Captain Murray; they were attacked by the Regiment of Bigerre, but took post behind a wall and kept up a steady and withering fire, Paterson and Murray were wounded, also thirty Rank and File were killed and wounded, *"having with their companies withstood the attack of near 300 of the enemy's best troops."*[29] Lambert arrived with the Grenadier Company of the 30th Regiment and the remainder of the Marines under Lieutenant Colonel Mackenzie, who attacked the enemy flank and forced them to retire to the top of the hill. Captain Stanhope immediately ordered all boats to be manned and armed to support Lambert; this attracted the attention of General Crauford who abandoned his attack and hurried his troops to Lambert's landing place.[30] By 5 pm all troops were landed and by nightfall General Hodgson was securely posted with all his forces three miles inland.

The enemy's troops - three regular battalions and one Militia - and all the inhabitants retired into Palais which was fortified and to which six redoubts were added. On the 25th the British marched on Palais. The heavy guns could not be landed for a fortnight and the British sat down to besiege the place. Lieutenant Colonel Mackenzie having been wounded, Major Tooker Collins took over command of the Marines. The remainder of the Marines were landed on the 24th. On 9th May the batteries opened. Four hundred French made a sortie captured General Crauford and pushed on. A company of Marines under Captain Hepburn counter-attacked and the French were forced to retire with considerable loss.

On the 13th an attack was made on one of the enemy redoubts by 200 men under Captain Carruthers (afterwards Commandant at Chatham) and Captain Smith, 30th Regiment. The enemy were surrounded and the officers, determined to take advantage of the panic, pushed on and attacked and carried two more of the redoubts and the French fled to the Citadel: 370 men of the 69th then carried the other three redoubts with very little loss. The Marines followed up and effected a lodgement in the town. The French named the Marines *"Les petits grenadiers"* as they wore Grenadier caps, so that evidently the standard of height was not up to grenadier form. On 16th May the batteries were completed and on 8th June the French capitulated.

From 22nd April to 7th June the losses were 13 officers and 300 killed, 21 officers and 480 wounded, of which the Marines lost two sergeants, one drummer and thirty-four killed, eight officers one drummer and forty-six wounded. Sickness and the fatigues undergone during the siege and the want of proper refreshment caused a great deal of fever and dysentery which carried off a great number. The island was garrisoned and held for the remainder of the war as an advanced base; as Fortescue says, *"Thus Belleisle was secured as a place of refreshment for the fleet*

---

29   Beatson.
30   It is instructive to compare this quick change of plan with Gallipoli in 1915, when the unopposed and successful landings of the Plymouth Battalion RMLI at Y Beach and the Royal Fusiliers at X Beach and the South Wales Borderers were not exploited. (See Official History pp. 202, 224, 237.)

while engaged in the wearing work of blockading the French Coast". But it had also most important results on the Continent. D'Aiguillon on the mainland was largely reinforced and this prevented Soubise's movement against Frederick and Ferdinand in Germany. As soon as the place had been secured, Sir Thomas Stanhope was sent with a squadron to the Basque roads where he again destroyed the works on the Isle of Aix which was only carried out after a sharp action in which no doubt the Marines again bore their share.

In Commodore Keppel's despatch it was said: *"Major General Hodgson by his constant approbation of the battalion of Marines landed from HM Ships and put under his command gives me the pleasing satisfaction of acquainting you with it that His Majesty may be informed of the goodness and spirited behaviour of that Corps."*

For this service the Corps was awarded the distinction of bearing the Laurel Wreath on the Colours and appointments. When news of the success of Belleisle reached England, negotiations for peace were going on; but a serious danger was threatening Britain because France was endeavouring to draw Spain into the struggle and the 'Family Compact' was signed on 15th August though war was not actually declared until 15th December 1761. Pitt was anxious to strike at Spain at once, but the King and his advisers were against this, with the result that Pitt resigned on 5th October; however, the preparations for the attack on Martinique which he had planned went on and all stations were ordered to commence hostilities against Spain on 24th December.

On 5th June Lord Rollo with four battalions from New York and Admiral Douglas' squadron had by a coup de main seized Fort Roseau in Dominica where there was a fine roadstead well placed strategically.

Ten battalions from North America under General Monckton were ordered to be at Guadeloupe by the end of October. Rollo's troops from Antigua and Guadeloupe were to be added: twenty-two battleships were to form the covering squadron. Four regiments under escort of Commodore Swanton were ordered from Belleisle and on 22nd November Rodney who was to be Commander-in-Chief arrived at Barbados. Later five more regiments were drawn from Belleisle.

Douglas was sent to Martinique to destroy the batteries at St Pierre, followed on 9th December by the remainder of the squadron. The *Temeraire* and the *Belleisle* transports arrived on 14th December, and Monckton's troops on the 24th. Rodney now had eighteen battleships, twenty cruisers, four bombs and Monckton had 13,000 troops.

1762

The strength of the Corps was raised to 19,061 of all ranks formed in 135 Companies.

On 8th January 1762, the Fleet anchored in St Pierre Bay, Martinique, Swanton's Squadron and two brigades were sent to Petit Anse d'Arlet in the south-west portion of the island; five frigates were sent to La Trinité on the windward side to threaten a landing. Rodney with the remainder of the fleet anchored in St Anne's Bay on the south of the island. On the 10th the batteries having been silenced, Monckton's troops were landed with the object of marching against Fort Royal overland, but it was found that the deep ravines made it impossible to move the artillery; meanwhile Captain Hervey in the *Dragon* had proceeded to Grand Anse and landed all his Marines and seamen, silenced the battery and occupied it with his Marines until reinforced by General Haviland; marching inland they seized Gros Point opposite Pigeon Island which closed the mouth of Fort Royal Harbour. They were attacked by the French but drove them off; they reported however that the country was impractical for artillery.

The Citadel of Fort Royal lay deep in the bay, the shore bristled with batteries and above it were the batteries of Morne Tortenson, Morne Garnier, and Morne Capuchin. On the 14th the Fleet anchored in the mouth of the bay and a landing place was found at Cas Navires north of Negro Point, the north headland of the bay. On the 16th the fleet stood in and silenced the batteries; at sunset Monckton established himself ashore and after daybreak the next morning the whole army was landed. On this day (17th) the Admiral reinforced the army with a body of Marines 900 strong formed into two battalions of 450 each.[31] They were attached to Rufane's Brigade. It took a week to complete the batteries against Morne Tortenson, 1,000 seamen being employed to pull up the guns.

On the 24th a general assault took place; Brigadiers Haviland and Walsh were sent to turn the enemy's right on Morne Tortenson and were successful; Rufane's Brigade with the Marines stormed the redoubts on the enemy left near the sea, post after post being carried. In this they were much helped by 1,000 seamen who accompanied the advance in flat boats. By 9.0 am the British had gained all the batteries on Morne Tortenson and the French retired to Morne Grenier and Fort Royal.

On the 27th Haviland who had got across the deep ravine started the batteries against Morne Grenier. The Marines had been taken and the 24th from Rufane and posted to cover the road between the two wings which were in two plantations. The French counter attacked but the attack failed; they were followed up and the lower batteries were captured; the light companies on the left under Major Leland creeping up found the redoubts on top deserted. They were quickly supported, and the position made good.

The Citadel was then bombarded and two days later the Morne Capuchin was captured; on 3rd February the citadel surrendered with 170 guns. Pigeon Island surrendered to Rodney who also took possession of 14 fine privateers. Captain Hervey in the *Dragon* had proceeded to La Trinité and landed 500 seamen and Marines and the whole district surrendered. On 15th February the whole island capitulated and the French power in the West Indies was broken. Swanton and a

---

31   Commanders probably Majors Collis and Campbell.

Brigade took Grenada, whilst St Lucia with its magnificent harbour surrendered to Hervey.

Meanwhile the French squadron at Brest had given the blockading ships the slip and had come over but finding Martinique in the hands of the British sailed on to Cape Francis in Cuba to join the Spaniards who had by this time entered into the war.

The British Government had now decided to strike at the two sources of the colonial power of Spain and for this purpose expeditions were launched against Havana and Manila.

For the Havana expedition, the object of which was *"to stab Spain in the heart of her colonial power and wealth"* Admiral Pocock and General Lord Albemarle were dispatched from England. Albemarle brought 4,000 more troops, mostly from Belleisle; he was to be joined by Monckton and his men and further troops were to come from New York making 16,000 to 17,000. Unfortunately, Albemarle was a Continental soldier and out of place for the work in hand. Pocock arrived at Barbados on 20th April and reached Cas Navires Bay on the 25th only to find that Rodney had dispersed the fleet and it was only possible to effect a concentration at Cape St Nicholas in the windward passage. Pocock therefore determined on a most daring move to concentrate his squadron and bring them into position by surprise. He determined to make use of the Old Bahama Channel which was supposed to be impossible for a fleet. The naval combination deserves study but is out of place here. Albemarle had been wasting time reorganising Monckton's troops in the transports.[32]

On 6th June the fleet appeared off Havana and twelve battleships were sent to block the Spanish Fleet in the harbour whilst Commodore Keppel in charge of the disembarkation of the troops went to the north of the city and landed them without opposition between River Bocanao and Coximar, the fort having been silenced by the *Dragon*. Whilst the ships were bombarding all the Marines were placed in the boats as a feint of landing on the west side.

There were two forts at the mouth of the harbour Fort Moro to the east and Fort Punta on west side. On the north side the ground rises to a ridge known as the Cavannos and Fort Moro was at the end of the ridge separated by a deep ravine. Moro was a very strong fort with deep ditch, but the town itself particularly on the west side was in a very poor state of defence. The troops were landed in three divisions of boats and made for the inner edge of the ridge; the troops directed against Fort Moro moved along the shore and reached their objective before dark. General Elliott was sent to seize the village of Guanabocoa at the head of bay where he could get fresh provisions and out of communications of the garrison. Albemarle in the approved continental fashion proceeded to ram his head against the strongest point - the Moro (where the Spanish ships could help in the defence). He laid formal siege to the fort; although the QMG had seized the end of the Cavannos Ridge it was not utilised. Admiral Pocock quickly found an anchorage to westward and anchored off Chorera River and seized the villages as a watering place. On 13th June, Colonel Howe with some troops was sent over to him and the Admiral landed 800 Marines who were formed into two

---

32 To see how history repeats itself read Official History Gallipoli Vol I, Chapter VI, for the time taken by General Hamilton in reorganising the transports.

battalions under Majors Campbell and Collins. It was the 15th July before the batteries could be made effective against the Moro and on the 20th a mine was sprung against the counterscarp; the fort was carried by a storm after a most gallant defence principally by the Spanish sailors.

On 1st July the *Dragon* (Captain Hervey), *Cambridge* and *Marlborough* had been sent in, in a mad attempt to bombard the fort but were driven off with a loss of 42 killed, 140 wounded, and the ships very badly damaged.

On 31st July Batteries were commenced on the Moro and Cavannos Ridge against the town; at last the GOC went over to reconnoitre the west side; the two divisions of troops from America had also been landed on this side.

On 4th August the CRE reported that there was a favourable line of attack on the Polygon next to the Punta Fort owing to the cover of a bank running along the shore; there was a road along the bank covered from fire of the fort but obstructed with abattis. Unfortunately, these lines of advance were in line with the fire of the British batteries being erected on the east side.

On 5th August GHQ was moved to the west side but the construction of batteries on both sides was continued for the next three days. On the 8th the GOC ordered the advanced posts to be moved further forward; on the 9th the entrenching tools were landed on the west side and 200 men ordered to make a redoubt on the road to Punta Fort under cover of another party of 200 whilst all the rest were set to make an abattis for front and flank defence.

On the 10th the batteries on the east being ready to open fire and those on the west on the point of opening ground, a flag of truce was sent in; the enemy after some delay returned it and opened fire. On the 11th all batteries opened fire at dawn. Fort Punta was silenced between 9 and 10 am and the North Bastion about an hour afterwards. Between 1 and 2 pm the enemy were observed to be evacuating Punta, and at 2 pm flags of truce were hung out from the town. On the 12th the truce was continued, and terms were discussed; the capitulation was signed on the 13th, and on the 14th General Keppel and 500 men occupied Fort Punta and about noon the Punta gate and bastion were taken over; Colonel Howe taking possession of the landgate with two battalions of grenadiers.

We had won the Gibraltar of the west which for 150 years had baffled the British even to approach, and the naval effect was incalculable, though at a heavy cost: 580 were killed or died of wounds and 4,500 of disease. The booty was enormous including nine battleships, three more sunk and two building, six frigates and one hundred merchantmen. The prize-money amounted to three quarters of a million; Privates got £9.1.8½ and Bluejackets £3. 14. 9¾. The Admiral and General got £122,000 each. In spite of the fine seamanship of the Admiral "it was the devotion of the subordinate officers and the co-operation of the men which by sheer pluck and endurance forced through the bad plan of the General."[33] The King and Lord Bute had meanwhile very nearly

---

33   Corbet.

brought about peace and almost threw away what had just been so hardly won.[34]

The last effort of the French in America was made by Captain Ternay with a few ships, who landed his troops and captured St John's, Newfoundland. On 24th June Captain Graves fortified Placentia and when Admiral Colville arrived he landed some Marines to reinforce the garrison and arrived off St John's on the 28th. The Marines of the Syren were sent to the Isle of Boys which prevented the place falling into the hands of the enemy. Troops were sent from New York and Halifax and joined the Admiral on 11th September. The troops were landed in Torbay and after some skirmishing De Ternay's ships slipped out in a fog and returned to France and the French troops capitulated on 18th.

East Indies.
It is usual to think because the Corps never serves in India that it has had very little connection with that great dependency, yet as we shall see, in its early days the Corps bore a considerable part during the Seven Years War in laying the foundations of the British Empire in India.

After the dreadful tragedy of the Black Hole in Calcutta Admiral Watson and Colonel (afterwards Lord) Clive arrived in Calcutta on 5th December 1756, but it is probable that there were no Marines in that squadron. Chandernagore surrendered on 23rd March 1757 and Clive won his great victory at Plassey on 23rd June 1757. Admiral Watson died on 10th August 1757 and was relieved by Admiral Pocock. Admiral Stevens brought out a squadron in 1758 to join Pocock which undoubtedly carried complete Marine detachments. Admiral D'Ache and General Lally were sent out by the French in 1757 with four battleships and 1,200 troops.

Admirals Pocock and Stevens concentrated in Madras Roads on 24th March 1758 and on 28th April sighted the French Fleet, which had come from Mauritius, off Fort St David. The French had nine battleships against the British seven and one frigate. The frigate the *Queenborough* was ordered to send all her Marines on board HMS *Cumberland*. There was a confused fight and the French made off to Pondicherry, their main base; the British had 29 killed and 89 wounded, the French 182 killed and 360 wounded. On 3rd May French troops captured Cuddalore and laid siege to Fort St David and on 2nd June the fort surrendered. Meanwhile the fortifications at Madras were being completed in expectation of the coming siege.

On 3rd August the fleets had another fight off Negapatam and the British retired to Carical and the French to Pondicherry the British with 31 killed and 158 wounded, French 251 killed and 602 wounded. On 3rd September the French Fleet sailed for Mauritius. Pocock landed one Captain, one Lieutenant, and 103 Marines to reinforce the garrison at Madras *"who proved of excellent service during the siege."*[35] The siege commenced on 14th December (Colonel Draper's regiment - the 79th - were also part of the garrison). Colonels Lawrence and Draper abandoned the outworks and retired into the town but held on to Chengalaput which proved of great assistance to the defenders. The

---
34   To realise what politicians are capable of it is well to read Vol. II of Corbet's History of the Seven Years War.
35   Beatson

French were very slow in opening their batteries and when they did they were often destroyed by fire from the town; in one sally the 79th captured D'Estaing whom we meet in high command in the next war; and on 16th February 1759 Admiral Kempenfeldt and a small squadron with the rest of the 79th arrived with stores etc. and on 17th February 1759 Lally raised the siege and retired leaving forty guns. The sum of 50,000 rupees was paid to the troops as reward and no doubt the Marines got their share and returned on board their ships when the fleet returned.

After a lot of manoeuvring, on 10th September 1759 Pocock again brought the French Fleet under D'Ache to action off Pondicherry and a hot fight ensued. The French lost 1500 killed and wounded; the British 174 killed or died of wounds, and 285 wounded. Captain Gore and Lieutenant Renshaw of the Marines were killed.

On 27th Pocock sailed past D'Ache trying to get him to come out and fight but the Frenchman was not willing. On 17th October Admiral Cornish arrived to relieve Pocock and bringing Colonel Eyre Coote, soon to be so celebrated, with his regiment. The troops were landed at Madras and the fleet sailed for the Malabar Coast on account of the monsoon.

There were great events in 1760. Colonel Eyre Coote having won his great victory at Wandewash, the French retired to Pondicherry followed by Coote. To assist the operations Major Monson of the 79th was landed on 28th March with 7 gunners, 50 Native Pioneers and 300 Marines from the fleet in the bay about four miles north of Carical, and advanced the following morning against Carical which was defended by Forts Dauphin and Louis. Carical was gained with trifling loss, and the Marines following up the enemy drove him from Fort Dauphin into Fort Louis. On 3rd April reinforcements arrived and invested Fort Louis, which surrendered on 6th April. The possession of Carical was important as it prevented supplies reaching Pondicherry from the rich country of Tanjore. The force then marched on Chilambaum which surrendered, as also Verichilaum, and at the beginning of May joined Coote in front of Pondicherry having in the space of a month deprived the French of many valuable possessions. The Marines were then re-embarked with the thanks of Colonel Coote.

The English forces were not strong enough for a regular siege and could only blockade the town; Admiral Stevens having joined Cornish, seventeen battleships participated in the blockades throughout July and August. On 29th August Admiral Stevens landed all his Marines at Cuddalore who joined the army to assist in the taking of Ariancopang. Major Monson with 800 men was ordered to attack that place whilst Coote attacked Cullagary. On 4th September the French made a gallant sortie in hopes of relief by the French Fleet. The attack on Cullagary was made and succeeded on 9th September. The arduous and active service of the blockade went on. On 1st January 1761 a hurricane sank three battleships, drove three more ashore and wrecked the works of the besiegers, but within a week the squadron had resumed its post off the port and as the French squadron did not appear Pondicherry surrendered on 15th January 1761 and by the 5th April the French flag ceased to fly in India.

There were no great events to chronicle in 1761, but on the entry of Spain into the War as already related it was determined to attack their eastern possessions and the expedition to Manila took place.

In June secret orders were sent to Admiral Cornish, and on 1st August he embarked General Draper with 1,000 Europeans (including the 79th Regiment) and 2,000 Sepoys and left Madras. The Admiral also formed 550 Seamen and 270 Marines into separate battalions to work with the land forces. During the voyage gabions were made for the batteries. On 23rd September they anchored in Manila Bay; the Spaniards were surprised and were found quite unprepared; on the 25th the landing was made two miles south of the town under the cover of three frigates. The covering force was provided by the 79th and some artillery. The main landing including all the Marines was made at Malata; the boats being formed in three divisions commanded by Captains Parker, Brereton, and Kempenfeldt. On the 26th Polverista was seized and the Marines occupied Hermita Church. The Marines were detailed to remain at Malata to secure the retreat of the advanced forces if necessary and to preserve the communications. On the 26th the seaman battalion was landed and encamped between the 79th and the Marines. A detached battery was seized, and the ships sailed up to the forts. One of the ships went aground but it served as a screen to Draper's camp and in spite of a gale it enabled them to land the stores.

There were insufficient troops to invest the place so that the garrison were able to obtain supplies. The garrison consisted of 800 regulars and 10,000 Indians. The British prepared their batteries and on the 27th eight 24 pdrs and two 18pdrs were landed. On 29th the *Elizabeth* and *Falmouth* were ordered to bombard, and at end of the month the ships' carpenters were lent to help with the gabions and fascines. On October 1st and 2nd a battery of 24 pdrs with some 10" and 13" mortars was completed and on 4th October the ships and batteries opened fire and a breach was made. On the night of 4/5th October the Spaniards made a sortie and attacked the seaman battalion but were repulsed and the next day all the Indians but 1,800 deserted. On the morning of the 6th the 79th and the seaman battalion attacked the breach and carried the fortifications. Manila and Luzon then capitulated and £4,000,000 was paid to ransom the town.

Captain Champion with 100 Marines and 100 sepoys was sent over in the *Seahorse* and received the surrender of Fort Cavite which they garrisoned. In the operations 13 seamen and Marines were killed and 29 wounded. Colonel Draper's despatch said: *"the Marines from the good conduct and example of their officers behaved very well and were of great use upon all occasions."*

The peace negotiations were now drawing to a close and the Treaty of Paris was signed on 10th February 1763; the politicians were in such a hurry that they nearly threw away the fruits of the victories at Havana and Manila as the reports had only just reached England in time.

By the treaty France ceded Canada, Nova Scotia and Cape Breton Island and all the territory between the Atlantic and the Mississippi River; also Granada, St Vincent, Dominica and Tobago in the West Indies; they also restored Minorca. Great Britain gave up Guadeloupe, Marie Galante and Martinique in the West Indies; Belleisle; Gorse, West Africa (but kept River Senegal) and Pondicherry in the East Indies. Cuba was restored to Spain, but Britain received Florida in exchange.

1764

Although peace had been signed in 1763, as has happened time and again, it did not mean cessation of active service for the Corps, because we find detachments attached to the army in an unusual field - India. Presumably the two companies were landed from the ships to reinforce the small force of Europeans at Calcutta during the anxious times then prevailing.[36]

There is no space to describe the whole operations that led up to the Battle of Buxar. Suffice it to say that Sujah Dowlah, Nabob of Oude, with three other potentates made up their minds to attack the British and marched on Benares. After skirmishes the British retired to Patna on 14th August and the Chiefs to Buxar. The British Commander was replaced by Major Hector Monro who dealt severely with the insubordinate native troops and re-organised his force for an advance.

The troops consisted of:
    8   Companies of   101st (HEIC troops)
    2   "   103rd "
    2   "   Marines (Captain Wemyss)
200 details of various regiments.
2 Companies of Artillery.
1 Troop Cavalry.
8 Battalions of Sepoys.
1,000 Moghul Cavalry.

Monro decided to attack and ordered the main body to march on Kalverghat on the River Sone.

Major Champion with two companies of Marines and two battalions of Sepoys to cross the Ganges and join the main body at Kalverghat on 10th October. Both parties marched off on 8th October. Sujah Dowlah had control of all the allied troops including some brigades trained on the regular model under a General called Sumroo.

Sujah Dowlah had 40,000 men. His artillerymen were Europeans and his cavalry included besides Sumroo's regulars, Durani and Rohilla Horse. On 10th October Monro reached Kalverghat and found the enemy on the opposite bank of the River Sone. Champion arriving punctually moved up the west bank hidden by fog; the enemy changed front to meet Champion, uncovering the ford and retired on Arrah. Monro took two days to cross the river and another day was spent in reorganising the army into three divisions. On the 13th the advance was resumed in a new formation to meet cavalry. On the 22nd the enemy's entrenched camp at Buxar was sighted; they were drawn

---

36 Note. I am indebted for this account of a little-known piece of Corps history to Sir John Fortescue's monumental work.

up in front of their trenches about three miles away. Both forces after watching each other retired to camp. The force rested on the 23rd and orders were issued for the 24th; but Champion going out with a small party on the 23rd observed enemy moving out of their entrenchments to give battle in the plain. Monro's left flank was covered by a swamp beyond which was a village distant about 1000 yards, whilst about 1000 yards in front of his right wing was a large grove; ground was clear between village and grove. To right of grove and beyond right of Monro's right wing was another village. The grove and villages had been occupied as advanced posts. Enemy's left rested on Ganges.

The British force was formed in two lines.

Front Line. In the centre, two composite battalions, the first - Marines and details of the King's regiments; the second - four Companies of the 101st. On either flank two battalions of Sepoys; twenty guns in pairs in intervals between battalions and on the flanks. Reserve between the lines two Grenadier Companies of the 103rd, some Cavalry.

Second Line. In the centre, four companies of the 101st. Two Sepoy battalions on each flank and eight guns in pairs on each flank of Europeans and on the flanks. Fifty yards between lines.

Baggage Guard.

Four Companies of Sepoys and the Moghul Cavalry.

Total strength, 1,000 Europeans, 5,300 Sepoys, 900 Moghul Horse.

The British Line in advancing had to incline to the right to clear the swamp under heavy fire; the Durani Horse charged and the British formed square; the enemy horse swerved away and attacked the Baggage Guard and drove them on to the main body, the Moghul Horse bolting. They then attacked the rear of the second line and after two gallant charges, in which they were joined by the Rohilla Horse, were driven off.

Meanwhile the First line was hotly engaged with the regular troops - artillery and cavalry - and the right wing came under heavy oblique fire from the guns in the village. The right battalion was ordered to storm, and Lieutenant Nicoll made a wide detour round the enemy flank and carried the village with the bayonet. He then advanced on the grove but was driven back with severe loss.

Monro realised that the grove must be captured and ordered all that was left of the right wing (viz. the Marine Composite Battalion and a Sepoy Battalion) to Nicoll's assistance. Champion recalled the battalion from the first village and advanced in line with artillery support, ordering no firing; the grove was to be carried with the bayonet.

Nicoll's battalion rallied and took its place on the right flank and the whole body dashed into the grove and a volley completed the enemy discomfiture and he fled leaving seventeen guns in

Champion's hands. The retreating troops were driven across Sumroo's front but taking ground to the right he rallied the fugitives. About 8,000 horse and foot then made their way along the swamp and attacked the British left front and flank but were very scattered and ineffective besides masking Sumroo's fire. Sumroo then retired in good order and the British ordered a general advance. The army broke into columns, the left flank following the retreating enemy, the right flank turning towards the entrenchments, and Monro followed with the 2nd line. The right column entered Buxar, the enemy fleeing. In rear of the position was a small stream, mostly mud, and crossed by a bridge of boats. As soon as Sumroo's force with Sujah Dowlah, his escort and treasure had crossed, the Nabob ordered it to be burnt. The fugitives rushed for the bridge under a hot fire from the sepoys. Elephants, camels, men, horse and women fled shrieking to the Nullab and floundered in the mud until it is reported a causeway 300 yards long had been formed of their corpses over which the rearmost escaped.

Europeans lost 2 officers and 37 other ranks killed, 9 officers 55 other ranks wounded.

Sepoys lost 250 killed, 435 wounded, 85 missing.

Enemy had 2,000 dead alone, 187 guns were captured, £12,000 loot taken.

On 8th November Benares surrendered and the campaign finished by the surrender of Sujah Dowlah on 28th May 1765, but the Marines must have returned to their ships soon after the battle because the detachments arrived at Portsmouth in July 1765. One Marine Officer - Captain F T Smith - transferred to the East India Company service.

Volume One 1755 – 1792

3 - Peace 1763 - 1774

The Corps was now to experience its first period of peace conditions. Hitherto it had been customary to disband or transfer to the Army the Marine Regiments on the conclusion of a war. In consequence the letters and orders extant, which are now continuous, deal largely with administration, clothing, etc., and we see the Institution of many rules and customs that are still in force to-day. Further it became possible to properly drill and train officers and men, as from many allusions during the war period we gather that untrained recruits were often sent afloat.

Demobilisation.
No sooner was peace declared,[37] than demobilisation was ordered, though as we have seen many detachments were still on active service. On 1st May the Corps was reduced to 4,510 officers and men with an establishment of 18 Field Officers and Staff, i.e. 1 Lieutenant Colonel, 1 Major, 1 Adjutant, 1 Lieutenant and Quartermaster, 1 Deputy Paymaster at each Headquarters and presumably 1 Commandant resident in Town (Colonel Dury) though not officially borne as such.

There were 70 Companies (Chatham 16, Portsmouth 27, Plymouth 27), each consisting of 1 Captain, 1 First Lieutenant, 1 Second Lieutenant, 2 Sergeants, 2 Corporals, 1 Drummer and 52 Privates; the organisation in Squads or Parade Companies was maintained with a Squad Officer who provided necessaries and kept the company accounts.

The opportunity was taken to renumber the Companies: No 1. being allotted to Chatham, No 2 to Portsmouth, No 3 to Plymouth, and so on, and the officers received fresh commissions.

On 1st July 1763 the Admiralty promulgated Regulations for the Government of Marines on shore. Plymouth Orders of 1st May 1763 give the demobilisation orders: "The following Officers are to be placed on half pay at once - 22 Captains, 54 First Lieutenants and 60 Second Lieutenants the juniors of each rank being placed on the half pay list " The Orders for NCOs and Men were: "(a) *Each NCO and man to be allowed to take clothes, belt, knapsack and twenty-one days pay from day of discharge and to be given a pass;*" (b) They were "*not to travel with arms, nor more than three together on pain of punishment.*"

It is interesting to compare these orders with the demobilisation orders of 1783, 1802, 1814-5, and 1919.

Quarters.
Officers and men were still billeted, or *"in quarters"* as it was termed, but having regard to the numbers afloat and the smallness of the companies there must have been ample accommodation in the numerous inns and alehouses; for instance there were eleven inns in Old Brompton at Chatham alone.

---

37   The Treaty of Paris was signed in February 1763.

Enlistment was for life, but from various letters concerning discharges men seem to have been enlisted during the war for *"3 years or the duration of the War."* Discharge by purchase was allowed, the amount being ten guineas, but there seems to have been considerable difficulty in keeping up the number of recruits; eg on 22nd November 1763 the Commissioned Officer at Portsmouth was told to get as many recruits from Colonel Rufane's Regiment - which was being disbanded - as possible (the Marines had served under his command at Guadeloupe), and although the sum paid as levy money during the war had been two guineas, he was to get them "as cheap as he could."

The Adjutants which had been three at each Division were reduced to one.

Chatham, William Sabine. Portsmouth, Colin Campbell 10.6.1757 till his death in 1773. Plymouth, John Christian 10.6.1757. He had been the first Sergeant Major at Plymouth and was promoted to commissioned rank on this date. He held the Plymouth Adjutancy for many years and on 2nd November 1773 when a Captain Lieutenant became Adjutant at Portsmouth, vice Campbell.

Quartermaster.
There was a Lieutenant and Quartermaster at each Division who dealt with arms, accoutrements, and King's Clothing; he had nothing to do with rations or necessaries. He was a combatant officer appointed for a term of years like the Adjutant.

Sea Roster.
The Officers' Sea Service Roster was established very early. It was kept by Divisions and not generally throughout the Corps, which led to a lot of trouble and inconvenience. It was carefully watched, as service afloat was evidently not popular; a ruling was given on 31st August 1763[38] probably in consequence of officers applying for half pay to avoid sea! *"None such were to be restored to full pay until after every other officer who from want of seniority to entitle him to continue on full pay, when present establishment took place."*

There is no record how officers were entered for the Corps, but during the next few years at all events vacancies were filled by bringing in officers from half pay. Officers were given commissions to certain companies and not generally to the Corps and commissions were signed by the King. This arrangement remained in force until the demobilisation of 1814-5.

Discipline.
The Marine Mutiny Act and Articles of War were passed each year by Parliament, and sent to the Admiralty for signature, who promulgated them by Warrant to Commanding Officers in April of each year.

There were two Courts-Martial - the General and the Divisional. The Admiralty issued

---

38 Portsmouth Books.

the Warrant for the GCM to the Commandant who assembled the Court which was entirely composed of Marine Officers, eg [39] *"A GCM being ordered to be held at Plymouth and not sufficient officers to compose the same"* orders two Majors and two Captains to go forthwith - one Willan being disembarked from HMS *Superb* for the purpose, to be re-embarked on conclusion of the duty - to be sent from Portsmouth. A PS says, *"they will be allowed their travelling expenses."*

The Admiralty confirmed the sentences and varied the punishments as they thought fit. It also seems to have been the practice to send offenders waiting trial at other Divisions before a court when ordered to assemble. The Adjutant usually acted as Judge Advocate.

1764

The strength of the Corps remained at 70 Companies. During this year many rulings and orders were issued which moulded the Corps into its present shape.

The question early arose as to the Marines providing Garrison Guards such as Haslar etc and after much bickering with the local army authorities a ruling was given on 28th September 1764 which has been in force ever since, though there have been many variations of it. It is curious that the question should have arisen with our Chummy regiment, the 31st East Surrey.

Admiralty.
28th September 1764.
Sir
. . . signify Their Lordships directions to you to relieve the 31st Regiment at Haslar Hospital, if you had a sufficient number of Marines at Quarters to enable you to do so; and your having in return represented in your said letter that you not only find it difficult to carry out Their Lordships' directions on that head into execution, but are prevented from complying with the demand for Marines by the Admiral of the Port for the ships fitting out there, by the orders which Colonel Welldon, Commanding Officer of the Garrison has thought fit to issue; in return to which I am to acquaint you that an extract of your said letter and copy of the papers which accompany it are sent to the Secretary at War for his information; and that he is acquainted that as he will see thereby, how much His Majesty's Naval service is likely to suffer by the very extraordinary orders which Colonel Welldon has issued, their Lordships have no doubt of his giving the most effectual orders to the Commanding Officer of the Garrison to prevent his interfering with the Commanding Officer of the Marine Forces in the disposition of the Marines.

I am etc
(Signed) Ph. Stephens
Lieutenant Colonel Boisrond,
Portsmouth.

Difficulties continued to be experienced in raising sufficient recruits and on 12th May 1764 the

---

39 20th December 1763; Portsmouth Books.

Admiralty called attention to the shortage shown in the Weekly Returns and the Commanding Officer is directed to send out more recruiting parties, "Beating Orders and Recruiting Instructions" being sent to them.

Drill and Training Afloat.

In this year we get the first mention of a question which has agitated the minds of Marine Officers and the Admiralty to the present day, i.e. the perennial question of the drill and training of the detachments in the harbour ships and their period of service in those ships. After various suggestions, on 6th July 1764 the Admiralty issued the following orders:[40]

By The Lords Commissioners of the Admiralty.

Whereas our instruction to the Commander in Chief at Portsmouth (Plymouth, Chatham) of the Guardships, there is inserted an article to the following affect viz: "And in order that we may be enabled to judge of the ability of the Marine Officers, and the Progress they have made in the Discipline of the Marines for Service on Shore, as well as their other duties, so far as the same is practicable while they remain embarked, you are to direct upon application from the Commanding Officer of Marines at the Port, that leave may be given for a Field Officer of Marines from the Division to go on board in order to review and exercise the detachments on board them; and to apply for the Marines to be landed for these purposes once a month, and you are to transmit to us the opinion of the Field Officer on the progress that has been made in the discipline of the Marines accordingly. Given under our hands 6th July 1764.

(Signed) George Hay
Carysfort,
Digby

Following on this we get the Field Officer's monthly reports with constant complaints of the badness of the firelocks, but in September the Field Officer's report said that *"in the firings they were not at all steady, and that it will be necessary to have them on shore together to make them in any degree masters of that part of their duty, it being impossible to do it on board;"* the Board directed the Commander in Chief to cause the Marines to be landed once a fortnight in the summer time. And in the December following appeared an order that they were to be disembarked every six months - in July and December.

On 4th May 1764 a ruling was given that one year constituted a tour of sea duty for roster purposes as it does today.

Brevet Rank.

There appears to have been an order in July 1763 about the grant of Brevet rank (the Brevet commissions being signed by the King), but in 1764 a question arose as to the ranking of officers

---

40 Apparently the fact that there was a Marine Mutiny Act and Articles of War got over the modern difficulty of the Naval Discipline Act.

holding Brevet rank, in which a ruling was given (15th July 1765) that holds to the present day *"As these officers (Brevet Majors Marriott and Howarth) are only Majors by Brevet. Major Marriott must by seniority of his commission as Captain command Major Howarth who is a junior Captain on all duties among the Marine Corps, conformable to what is practical among each particular regiment in the Army in pursuance of the Article of War on that head."* This holds to-day as it did between RMA and RMLI as laid down in Orders-in-Council 1883 and 1909.

Squad Officers.
An Admiralty Warrant dated 1st December 1763 gives us information as to the duties of the Squad Officers, that is the Pay Captains of the Parade Companies and the difficulty experienced with that system: *"Whereas it has been represented to us that from the various accounts of Receipts and Disbursements which Squad Officers of Marines are obliged to keep, not only a thorough knowledge of accounts, but a regular minute exactness therein, as well as some experience in business is requisite to enable them to execute well the several parts of their duty; and that the frequent removal of officers from the squad duty to take their turn of sea duty as the 114th Article of the Regulations established in July last directs, must unavoidably be attended with many inconveniences to the service, we have taken the same into consideration and in order to prevent the inconveniences which might attend the frequent changing of Squad Officers, as well as to re-move every obstacle to officers taking their regular tours of sea duty, we have resolved that for the future officers upon half-pay shall be appointed squad officers to the several Divisions of Marines with an allowance of forty pounds a year each for their care and trouble in addition to their half-pay."*

This system remained in force until 1785 when a contractor in London for the supply of necessaries to the whole Corps was appointed, and the Squad Officers were relieved by Squad Sergeants (apparently our Company QMS), who however were not satisfactory and were later replaced by Company Pay Captains.

The proceedings of a Court Martial held in March 1765 gives a very good example of the crimes and punishments and the usual procedure together with the care exercised by the Admiralty in the confirmation of the sentences. The Court was convened by Admiralty Warrant and was composed entirely of Marine Officers.

Gilbert Wright	Theft & Desertion	Guilty	To be shot to death
William Cotton	Desertion	Guilty	(Each to receive
Laughlin Kelly	Striking a Sergeant	Guilty	1,000 lashes on his
Christopher Magee	Desertion	Guilty	bare back with a Cat
John Lees	Desertion	Guilty	of nine tails)
Thomas Hopkins	Desertion	Guilty	To receive 600 lashes
John Parker	Desertion	Guilty	To receive 400 lashes
John Adams	Desertion	Guilty	(Each to receive
Robert Leeson	Desertion	Guilty	300
George Brown	Desertion	Guilty	Lashes)

Admiralty approved and signified the King's pleasure that sentence on Gilbert Wright was to be carried into execution and orders accordingly; a laconic letter of 3rd June 1765 says: *"he was shot to death on Friday last"* Sentences on Kelly and Cotton confirmed; Hopkins reduced to 300 lashes; Adams *"appears to be very simple and of weak understanding"* is to be released and discharged. The others pardoned *"in consideration of their penitence and desire they showed to return to their duty."*[41] The warrant is signed by five Lords of the Admiralty. From other courts martial we learn that the lashes were inflicted by *"the drummers of the Division."*

The other court martial was a Divisional CM convened by the C.O. and confirmed by him.

Dockyard Guards.
On 13th October 1764 the Admiralty issued an order that profoundly affected the Marines for many years.

"My Lords of the Admiralty being of opinion that the guarding of H.M. Dockyards with Marines instead of watchman selected from the Labourers of the Yards, as is now the practice, may contribute greatly to the security of HM Magazines and Stores as well as the safety of H.M Ships . . . the Navy Board having concurred with their Lordships . . . the guard should consist of as many men as will admit of three reliefs. Said Guard with proper number of Officers should march into the yard every day and remain on duty for 24 hours . . . and Captain of Guard is to obtain from the Commissioner of the Yard orders and instructions . . . all duties to be performed in the most punctual garrison duty.[42] *If numbers are insufficient now or at any future time the Commandant is to apply to the Commanding Officer of HM Ships to land such number from the guardships as may be necessary."*[43]

(N.B. It is a curious coincidence that after the War of 1914-18 the Admiralty made a similar proposal to replace the Metropolitan Police. Owing to the shortage of numbers this was impossible, and the upshot was the formation of the Royal Marine Police in 1922).

Evidently NCOs at Headquarters were insufficient because by Order-in-Council 26th October 1764 each company was increased by one Sergeant and one Corporal in lieu of two Privates reduced, making fifty Privates in each company. Guards were visited by the FO of the Day, but as apparently only two Majors were allowed at Headquarters there were some complaints and senior Captains were placed on the roster.

At Plymouth this order led to two of the Parade Companies being placed in barracks at Dock (now Devonport) and the Officers Mess being established in Marlborough Square: the actual order was that *"Marlborough and Granby Squares within the lines of Plymouth Dock were to be allotted for use of HM Marine Forces of 500 men with usual proportion of officers, which detachments are to take care of the Barracks and do all necessary"*. On 25th January 1765 Frederick Square was added.

---

41   Nowadays they would only have been tried for absence without leave.
42   At Portsmouth the guard took 66 Privates.
43   Admiralty Letter of 20th October 1764.

At Chatham, Officers and men were billeted in Old Brompton. There were numerous complaints and difficulties, and the Yards must have been in a very bad state as the Commandants constantly complain of the amount of sickness caused by the mud and wet.[44]

Desertion seems to have been very rife and writing in 1765 the Commandant at Portsmouth reports that the only solution he can suggest is to put the men into barracks. In reply the Admiralty inform him on 16th July 1765 that *"as soon as the old Cooperage at Portsmouth can be spared from the Victualling Service it will be fitted up as a barracks for the Marines"*[45] These became the old Clarence Barracks but they were not occupied until about 1767 or later and the other Divisions waited for many more years.

On 15th July 1765 Lieutenant Colonel Mackenzie at Chatham, who seems to have been a very live wire especially when he became Commandant in Town, pointed out that deserters afloat could not be dealt with by a land court martial, and that when they were brought back they should be handed over to the Senior Naval Officer at the Port, which was approved by the Admiralty.

In reply to a very important letter from the Commandant at Portsmouth the Admiralty say *"that it will be a great advantage to the discipline of the Corps to give the men accoutrements better than they have at present; want of pouches (they only had cartouche boxes) preventing them being put through the firings of a battalion and they approve of an alteration being made."*

Colours.
The Commandant had also represented *"that it would be an advantage that Officers and men should be made acquainted with the use to be made of Colours in a Battalion,"* and desiring that *"those in store at Portsmouth may be delivered to him."*[46] In consequence on 16th July 1765 the Naval Storekeeper is ordered to deliver them to him; and the storekeeper at Deptford is similarly ordered to deliver a pair to the Chatham Division.[47] These were the first Colours borne by the Divisions but we do not know their design. It is possible that they may have been the old Colours of the regiments disbanded in 1748. Plymouth has no record of an issue at this time, but this Division had the Colours used at Belle Isle in 1761, and must have also had a second pair vide the letters when the Botany Bay Detachment went out in 1787.

Sashes.
On 27th March 1766, authority was given for Sergeants of Marines to wear sashes, which have formed part of their uniform ever since.

On 31st July 1765, HRH the Duke of Gloucester reviewed the Portsmouth Division and was pleased to express great satisfaction with their performance, at which their Lordships of the Admiralty express their pleasure; we may be sure that the new Colours were carried on this occasion.

---

44   Chatham Letter Book 11th July 1765.
45   See Order-in-Council 20th May 1765.
46   Portsmouth Letter Book.
47   Chatham Letter Books.

On 22nd May 1765 the eight Senior Lieutenants were made Brevet Captains. Brevet rank seems always to have raised questions in the Corps; on 12th April 1766 the Admiralty issued a Warrant[48] in reply to a memorial from the Captains at Chatham and Portsmouth ordering that in accordance with the Articles of War, all Captains holding Brevet commissions as Major should perform all duties on shore as Captains on the Marine Establishment, except sea duty, which Brevet Majors are to be exempt from until further orders as provided by the order of 30th July 1763. The Captains however returned to the charge on 8th March 1767 about the hardship caused by Brevet Majors being excused from sea duty; the Brevet Majors also memorialised the Admiralty and as a result the Admiralty adhered to their decision.

On 2nd December 1766 the Captains memorialised the Admiralty with a list of the captains of the various Divisions who had done a tour of sea duty since the new establishment and proposing that a general sea roster for the three Divisions should be established for future service. The Admiralty did not approve; yet a study of the letter books shows the great difficulties, expense and hardship that this decision caused and which was not altered until 1815. Portsmouth had a special grievance as the majority of the ships seem to have commissioned there.

A letter of 24th July gives an illuminating account of the difficulty of providing reliefs for the East Indies. These took from twenty months to two years to arrive on the station and the King was therefore pleased to approve of commissions being issued by the Admirals on the station for officers promoted to fill vacancies. This evidently applied to officers who had served in the late war as officers who had served in the Buxar campaign had only just got home.

Elections.
Whenever a Parliamentary Election took place all troops, detachments and recruiting parties had to be marched to a place or places beyond three miles and to be quartered there until three days after the election was over; in consequence the Divisions seem to have been billetted in places like Fareham, Havant, Plympton, Tavistock etc., on many occasions.

Bands.
About this period bands must have been established at the several Headquarters. The Portsmouth Band was inaugurated about 1765 or 1766; the Plymouth Band was apparently formed in 1767, for on 10th March of that year an agreement was signed with a Mr Antonio Rocca to be enrolled as a Private Marine on 2nd April 1767, but to be given his discharge when obligation ceases. He was to be allowed to play at balls and concerts for his own advantage with the Commanding Officer's permission, but the service to come first. In the following year there is an order of 11th June 1768 for the Band to wear white breeches and stockings with black buckled garters at guard mounting.

In 1767 Grenadier Companies were formed, as orders on 10th March 1767[49] direct that Officers of the Grenadier Company are to wear *"two epaulets and fringe and Officers of Battalion Companies*

---
48 Portsmouth Letter Books.
49 Plymouth Orders.

one on right shoulder only." It is possible that about the same time Officers and men ceased to be equipped generally as Grenadiers.

There seems to have been a certain amount of selection for promotion, because on 23rd April a Brevet Captain 'K' protested against being passed over for promotion; he was informed that Lieutenant 'J' had been chosen for a particular service; 'K' at once applied to retire, which was approved. But the practice of bringing in officers from half-pay introduced some queer questions of seniority. The rule was that they took their seniority from their original commission. In 1766 a Lieutenant 'H' had been tried by GCM and dismissed the service; the Admiralty had commuted the sentence and placed him on half-pay; on 22nd May 1767 he was brought back to full pay. The subalterns naturally protested at his being given his original seniority, and the Board ruled that he was to take rank from the date of being brought back.

Ramrods.
On 11th August 1768 a much-needed reform was approved. The Master General of the Ordnance was ordered to issue new firelocks fitted with iron rammers to the Marines instead of the old wooden rammers about which there had been constant complaints since the beginning.

1768 and 1769

These years, as usual in peace, were filled with uniform changes, and on 15th May 1769 new uniform was issued. Was it then that the change was made from the Grenadier caps to the three-cornered hats? In October 1769 the breeches were red, and on 24th October 1769 a new gorget was ordered for Officers.

On 11th December 1770 the first increase in numbers since the war was authorised, each of the seventy companies being increased by one Lieutenant, one Sergeant, one Corporal, one Drummer, and fifty Privates. This must have brought the total to about 8,800; the augmentation was occasioned by the dispute with Spain over the Falkland Islands, when in addition to 18 battleships in commission, 25 battleships and 10 frigates were commissioned, whilst there were 42 ships on foreign stations. The matter was settled between the two Governments in February 1771, when the Spanish Government restored the islands to the British, the small garrison of which had been obliged to capitulate to superior force in July 1770. The islands were handed over to Captain Stot of HMS *Juno*, who landed with a party of Marines on 16th September 1771, and the British Colours were rehoisted at Port Egmont.

1771

This year is an important one in the Corps annals. The First Lord of the Admiralty, the Earl of Sandwich, proved himself a good friend to the Corps: foremost in his reforms was the raising of the Commanding Officers to the rank of Colonel Commandant and Captain dated April 1771. The first holders were.

Chatham,   Colonel J Mackenzie to No 1 Company vice Bendyshe,   16th April 1771.
Portsmouth, Colonel Hecter Boisrond to No 2 Company, promoted   17th April 1771.
Plymouth,   Colonel John Bell to No 3 Company vice Burleigh,   18th April 1771.

They retained the additional rank of Captain and their Companies until 1814, their companies being commanded by Captain Lieutenants in lieu of one of the First Lieutenants. Captain Lieutenants now introduced also commanded the Companies of all Field Officers.

A second Adjutant was appointed to each Division on 18th April 1771, the new holders being:
Chatham,   David Johnstone [50]
Portsmouth, T Archbold
Plymouth,   James Waller [51]

Funds.
To this period is due the foundation of the various funds of the Divisions; chief among which is the Divisional Fund. The earliest mention is in Plymouth Orders of 17th April 1771, when "A Fund called the Eighteen penny Fund" is mentioned. This Fund *"had been established by the late Commanding Officer [52] to supply accidental expenses not authorised by the Admiralty."* The eighteen pence per week was stopped from the pay of men who were allowed to work for civilians; there are many references to this later on and at one time the amount stopped was raised to 3/-. It is believed that some of the levy money for recruits was also paid into the fund.

On 8th November 1766 the Officers' Widows Fund, which is still in existence, continuing its valuable work, was established at Plymouth.

1772

On 3rd February 1772 there was a reduction in numbers, the companies being reduced from 100 Privates to 80 each. It is interesting to compare how this was done with later occasions.

The men selected for discharge were to be those least fit for service. They were to be properly accounted with for Sea Pay and arrears up to date of discharge. Portsmouth were to select a draft of 60 of the best men and send them to Plymouth which was short of establishment. If any men were desirous of entering as 'landsmen' in HM Ships, the Senior Naval Officer was to be informed, and he was to take any he approved of; any who wanted to change to Plymouth being sent there. *"Men who so enter to be given twenty-one days' pay each. Those who want to go home to be given what is usual and given the proper papers."* All surplus arms were to be returned to the Storekeeper.

---

50 See later America and Australia.
51 Adjutant at Bunker's Hill.
52 Colonel Burleigh evidently here refers to Colonel Dury or Colonel Bendyshe.

Volume One 1755–1792

Accoutrements.
On 14th June 1771 it was ordered that accoutrements were to be made of buff. There were evidently only a few issued at first as they were ordered to be retained at Headquarters until more were received. Also, in this year accoutrements were ordered to be whitened, so that it is to this date that we probably owe the introduction of pipeclay. Officers were also ordered to provide themselves with new pattern swords.

About this time the Commissioner of the Dockyard at Portsmouth objected to the drums beating when marching detachments to embark, but he was promptly sat on by the Admiralty.

On 18th April 1772, Lieutenant Colonel H Smith was appointed Colonel Commandant and Captain of No 2 Company at Portsmouth, vice Boisrond to retired half pay.

It has often been said that prior to 1813 commissions from the ranks were not given in the Marines, but this is not borne out by the facts. Lieutenant Christian the Adjutant at Plymouth has already been mentioned and on 9th September 1772 Sergeant Major C Olive was appointed 2nd Lieutenant in 31st Company at Chatham and again on 29th March 1774 there is a letter saying that Sergeant Major Harry Rudd had been promoted to a 2nd Lieutenancy on the recommendation of the Officers of Portsmouth Division, and that as the Officers at Plymouth desired that he should be removed to Portsmouth it was proposed to post him there.[53]

In spite of the reduction at the beginning of the year, on 5th December the number of Privates in a Company was again reduced from 60 to 50; they were allowed what was usual, and on 9th December one Sergeant one Corporal one Drummer per Company was also reduced.

It would seem that in those days Governments were as short-sighted and foolish as those of the present day because the mutterings of the American War were already beginning to be heard. As far as the Corps was concerned it had the usual results, they could not find their drafts for embarkation, as the numbers embarked exceeded the establishments of the Divisions and on 9th January 1773 complements of all Guardships were reduced. The standard of height in this year was 5'4".

1773

There was an enlargement of the Portsmouth Barracks in this year; the Commandant applied for a quarter in barracks but was refused and told that accommodation was to be appropriated for Privates only. The standard of height was raised to 5'5".

There seems to have been a war scare in April of this year, because the companies were ordered to be raised to 70 Privates each, with 4 Sergeants, 4 Corporals and 3 Drummers each, but it did not last long as on 6th May they were ordered to be reduced again to 3 Sergeants, 3 Corporals, 2

---

53 For numerous other instances see 1797.

Drummers, and 50 Privates.

With reference to the Divisional Fund we learn that in July[54] that *"Battalion men may be given leave by Officers Commanding Companies to go to work, as there will be not many Field Days until further orders."*

Review.
On Tuesday 23rd June 1773, HM the King came to Portsmouth to review the fleet and establishments. It seems to have been an even more awe-inspiring function than nowadays; the visit lasted until Saturday the 26th and from the number of dinners eaten and the number of salutes fired the Corps must have had more than its share of 'Guards and Bands', but there is no mention of his having visited the Marine Barracks. The Plymouth Band was also ordered to Portsmouth *"to be disposed of by the CO of Marines there"* as *"there will in all probability be occasion for the said band during the time His Majesty may be at Portsmouth; to arrive at Portsmouth before 20th June."*[55] This was followed by the usual query from the Plymouth Commanding Officer as to how he "was to charge the expense for the Musick", and he was told to charge it to the Contingent Account of the Division.

1774

An interesting light is thrown on the pay arrangements by a letter from the Admiralty dated 8th January 1774.

"My Lords consider it will benefit the service as well as the Marines themselves that they should not receive the whole of the Sea Pay due to them[56] *but a sufficient portion should be retained to furnish them with necessaries while at Quarters, and to provide them with sea necessaries when they embark. Commissioners at Chatham, Portsmouth and Plymouth have been directed to retain £3 of the Sea Pay to be paid into the hands of the Deputy Paymaster who shall account for it to the Marine. If he has not got £3 or if he has not got £3 credit, half of what he has is to be retained."*

The Commissioners of the Yards, who were the officers in charge of the Dockyards, like the modern Admiral Superintendent, evidently dealt with the pay of ships when they were paid off.

In these days of railway trains, motors and aeroplanes, it is rather a shock to remember that when the Corps was first formed all moves were carried out either by march route or by sea, and when one reads of the distances that escorts for deserters had to proceed to fetch back the erring ones - sometimes as far as Newcastle - it is not surprising that it was necessary to issue the following order: April 1774. It has been represented to *"us that owing to the frequent necessity of sending for deserters, the Sergeants, Corporals, and Privates are put to great expense for breeches shoes and stockings"* and *"that it is not*

---

54   Plymouth Order.
55   Plymouth Letter Books, 11th June 1773.
56   As was practised in the late war.

in their power to appear so clean as their characters and station require" the Admiralty therefore ordered the Deputy Paymasters to pay the following allowances and to charge them in the Contingent Account (*"To be equally shared among the party"*):

Distance from Quarters	Parties of 2 men	Parties of 3 men
Between 8 and 20 miles	2/-	3/-
Between 20 and 50 miles	4/-	6/-
Between 50 and 100 miles	8/-	12/-
Between 100 and 150 miles	10/-	15/-
Between 150 and 200 miles	12/-	18/-
Above 200 miles	15/-	£1.1.0

In course of time this allowance seems to have become called "Shoe money".

Clothing.

As this period is one of peace, there is continual changing and modification of uniform etc. As Colonel Field has so fully described all the uniforms in *"Britain's Sea Soldiers"* the following notes only deal with administrative matters.

23rd March 1764. Firelocks were ordered to be numbered with the number of the Company and the number of the firelock in the Company, whilst Sergeants and Corporals were ordered to keep a list.

The men of course were only known by the number of their company; regimental numbers were not introduced until about 1882.

The Division between Public and Personal Clothing and necessaries must have been established early because an order of 11th December 1760 [57] orders Officers who pay squads to return *"Arms, Accoutrements, and King's Cloathing"* to the Quartermaster when men are discharged. The *"King's Cloathing"* apparently consisted only of hats, uniform coats, waistcoats and breeches which was supplied by contract through the Admiralty and Naval Storekeepers, and it seems to have been pretty bad. Necessaries were purchased locally, by the Squad Officers and stopped out of the men's pay. Arms, accoutrements, and swords for Sergeants were supplied by the Board of Ordnance and also seem to have been very bad. Pouches were apparently issued in place of cartouche boxes in 1765.

1. Sergeants carried swords and halberds and on 27th March 1766 in response to a request from the Commandant at Portsmouth the Admiralty authorised their wearing sashes. They also wore special hats. Corporals wore 'knots' on the shoulder. All ranks wore 'rollers' which was a form of stock.[58]

2. Annual Clothing was apparently due on 1st June; it was forwarded to Divisions in time to be altered and fitted to the men before that date. (It was issued for wear on the King's Birthday

---

57 Plymouth Orders.
58 Portsmouth Letter Books.

a custom that survived up till death of Queen Victoria; during her reign new clothing was taken into use on 24th May, her birthday.)

3. The life of a tailor was evidently not an easy one. 59 Their hours were from 4.0 am to 8.0 pm with one hour for dinner. They were to work in the Black Hole in Frederick Square. 60 A Sergeant was to be detailed to supervise them.

4. The use of the Black Hole was prescribed in 1757 as a punishment for Sergeants found drinking with the men; for a second offence they were to be tried by Court Martial.

5. In 1771 accoutrements were ordered to be whitened, and on 14th June 1771 buff accoutrements were introduced, but evidently there were only a few available as they were ordered not to be taken from Headquarters. The bayonet and pouches were slung on waistbelts which on March 24th 1772 were ordered to be made into cross belts, and on 25th December 1771 the Admiralty notified that they had no objection to officers getting buckles for their belts.

6. On 28th July 1771 officers were ordered to provide themselves with new pattern swords, the first of many changes in this his weapon.

7. The kit to be taken by men on embarkation included:

    3 white and 3 check shirts.
    4 pairs of stockings (2 of thread).
    2 pairs of shoes.

    For gaiters the men wore spatterdashes, which seem to have been very useless articles; they were made of white linen and may be seen now on the Drum Majors of the Guards in Review Order 61 and McIntyre says they should be replaced by wool ones as the linen are useless on board and give the men rheumatism from being put on wet with pipeclay. One of the first orders for the drafts for America in the next war was to have proper black spatterdashes, probably of leather.

8. In 1772 the Surgeons belonging to the Divisions were ordered to wear uniform. They seem to have been civilians appointed locally, a custom in force for many years. Eventually when Naval Surgeons were appointed they were given Marine Commissions and wore Marine Uniform until 1887. The uniform laid down in 1772 was red coat with red cape, cuffs and lapels with Marine uniform buttons; white waistcoats and breeches with uniform hat; on duty to wear a small sword and black buckle garters.

---

59 Plymouth Orders 9th July 1766.
60 Where Raglan Barracks now stand.
61 See page 6.

In 1773 army ideas were permeating the Marines; Grenadier and Light Companies were in existence, the uniforms of which seem from the correspondence to have occasionally brought the Divisions into collision with Captains of ships and on 21st January 1773 Plymouth were told it was unnecessary to keep up a light company.

But we are now approaching a new war period and for the next eight years the Corps was engaged in the great struggle with America and France, in which they gained further laurels.

VOLUME ONE 1755 – 1792

4 - American War of Independence 1774 – 1783

1774

No hint appears in the letter books of the coming struggle and no increase of numbers took place this year. Since the close of the Seven Years War, in which the Americans had nobly borne their share side by side with the regular army, the politicians in England had decided that the Americans should bear their share of the expenses of what, after all, had been a war undertaken to protect their interests. The British Parliament, under the guidance of a singularly futile and inefficient Cabinet of politicians, therefore imposed taxes which were bitterly resented by the Colonies, and which led to open defiance and refusal to pay, culminating in the Boston 'Tea Party.'

Matters were therefore rapidly drifting towards war. On 5th September 1774 the Americans held a General Congress; the proposals put forward were rejected by the British Ministry. In dealing with the events that follow, in which Great Britain single-handed was fighting most of the nations of Europe, as well as her rebellious colonists, it has only been possible to try and recount the actions of the Marines ashore and to deal generally with the fleet actions, ignoring the numerous gallant single ship actions which would have made the account unmanageable.

The Headquarters of the British Army in America under General Gage were at Boston, where he had a considerable force. He therefore took steps to protect the town by fortifying the neck leading to the Dorchester Heights of the peninsula on which it stands, and also seized the provincial arsenals at Cambridge and Charlestown on the other side of the Harbour. HMS *Somerset* was placed in the ferry way between Boston and Charlestown.

As regards the Corps, the first intimation of coming hostilities was given when an Admiralty letter was sent to the Divisions dated 10th October 1774. This followed on a division of the Cabinet dated 3rd October. [62]*As it is possible that tents, kettles and camp equipage may be ordered to accompany the party of Marines intended to proceed to North America, I shall be obliged if you will send me an account, by return of post, what articles of each sort there are in store, and whether they are in a proper condition for use.*

(Signed) George Jackson DS

These were for Major Pitcairn's Detachment, consisting of 460 men[63] which arrived at Boston in HMS *Asia*, *Boyne* and *Somerset* on 4th December with Major Pitcairn on board; one of the Captains was Captain Souter who eventually brought the Battalion home in 1778. As late as the 26th December Lieutenant Barker says that the Admiral would not land them, but the reason he

---
62   Sandwich Papers.
63   Diary of Lieutenant Barker, 4th King's Own Regiment.

57

gives is strange, viz "……...*as he wanted to have the advantage of victualling them.*"[64] At any rate they were landed during the next few days, because on 30th December they were detailed with the 43rd Regiment to defend the passage between Barton Point and Charlestown Ferry. On 26th January 1775 Major Pitcairn's Battalion was ordered to do duty with the 1st Brigade under Lord Percy; "*up till then they had done no duty because they had no watch coats or leggings.*"

1775

In spite of the imminence of hostilities no great increases were ordered, but by Order-in-Council 15th February 1775 the number of privates per company was raised to 56 per company - an addition of 420 men - but it was not till Order-in-Council 21st June that 1 Sergeant, 1 Corporal, 1 Drummer and 14 Privates were added to each company - an increase of 1,190. It was easier to give orders than to carry them out, because in July the Portsmouth Division alone was 500 short of establishment.

Early in the New Year, General Gage obtained information that the Americans were collecting a quantity of military stores at Concord and he determined to seize them. On 26th February a small force under Major Pitcairn came into collision with the Colonial Militia but without serious result.

A most interesting letter from Major Pitcairn to the First Lord dated 14th February 1775 says: "*I have great desire to convince everybody of the utility of keeping a large body of Marines who are capable of acting either by sea or land as public service may require.*"

He also complains of the shortness of the men, who are shorter than the regiments and wishes "*the standard were raised; no Marine in my humble opinion ought to be taken who is under five feet six inches and were not at that size if under twenty years of age.*"[65]

Meanwhile drafts were being got ready in England. On 21st January, 1775, the Admiralty notified that a reinforcement of 2 Majors, 10 Captains, 27 Subalterns, 28 Sergeants, 25 Corporals, 29 Drummers and 600 Privates were to be sent to Vice Admiral Graves in North America as soon as transports could be got ready to receive them.

Portsmouth were to send Major Tupper and Adjutant Fielding with 3 companies, consisting of 3 Captains, 6 Subalterns, 6 Sergeants, 6 Corporals, 6 Drummers, and 180 Privates. Plymouth sent Major Short and Adjutant Waller with 6 companies, consisting of 6 Captains, 12 Subalterns, 12 Sergeants, 12 Corporals, 12 Drummers, and 360 Privates. Chatham sent 1 company, of 1 Captain, 2 Subalterns, 2 Sergeants, 2 Corporals, and 2 Drummers and 60 Privates, also 7 Subalterns, 8 Sergeants, and 5 Corporals, were sent by Portsmouth and Plymouth for the companies already in America.

---

64   From a letter of Major Pitcairn to Lord Sandwich, the greater number seem to have come from Chatham, having volunteered to go with him and he complains bitterly that these were the men the Admiral was keeping on board. - Sandwich Papers.

65   Sandwich Papers.

If there were insufficient men at Headquarters the senior Naval Officers at the ports were ordered, on the 25th January, to disembark the numbers necessary from the harbour ships; Portsmouth drew as many as 130 Privates from this source and Plymouth Division probably the same.[66] Chatham was evidently cleared out of men as it drew from the Harbour ships after the draft had sailed.

At the end of January, the Majors and Adjutants were sent to the Admiralty to receive instructions, and on 2nd February, 1776, important orders were issued. Portsmouth and Plymouth were ordered to *"send the Colours of your Division to Boston with the Marines and to acquaint you that they will be replaced with new ones."*

Chatham, Portsmouth and probably Plymouth were ordered to send 60 Grenadier caps with this detachment so that the formation of Grenadier Companies was evidently contemplated.[67]

Provision was made in the transports for women to accompany the draft: Chatham provided 6 and 4 for detachments already there Portsmouth provided 18 and 6 for detachments already there, and Plymouth provided 36 and 10 for detachments already there.

From this it seems that companies were allowed six each. It must be remembered that these women performed the duties of medical orderlies as well as doing the laundry and some of the cooking.

The Captain of one of the Light Companies (the Hon J Maitland) seems to have been a Member of Parliament as he could not sail at the same time as the draft. He signally distinguished himself at Savannah in 1779 in command of a Light Infantry Battalion of the army.

The kit taken was as follows:[68] Officers to have long leather gaiters with Hessian tops (as pattern) except to have buttons instead of springs and also with proper accoutrements.

Men to have following kit:
    4 good white shirts.
    4 pairs good stockings (2 white, 2 worsted) 1 check shirt.
    3 pairs good shoes.
    1 pair long gaiters Hessian tops.
    1 pair short gaiters.
    2 pairs good Prussian drab drawers.
    1 brush, wire, picker, turnkey, etc.
    1 set uniform knee and shoe buckles.
    1 knapsack (which are arriving in the transport).
    2 black Manchester velvet stocks.

---

66 Cf. 11th Battalion in 1921.
67 Samples of these caps and of the Light Infantry caps can be seen in the Officers Mess at Eastney. Editor's Note: Now in the RM Museum see Britain's Sea Soldiers Vol II p164.
68 Plymouth Orders, 8th February 1775.

Buckles for Grenadiers, clasps for Battalion Companies.

Sea Kit:
> 1 old hat.
> 1 jacket, etc.

Plymouth Orders state: [69] *"They will muster at 5.30 pm for muster master parade, and march off parade (the old parade in the Barbican) at 5.30 am tomorrow."*

The first portion arrived at Boston on 16th May and the remainder on the 23rd. [70]

Lexington.
On 18th April General Gage dispatched a force composed of the Grenadier and Light Companies of his force under Lieutenant Colonel Smith of the 10th Regiment and Major Pitcairn of the Marines to destroy the stores at Concord. The force proceeded up the Charles River, disembarked at Phipps Farm and advanced on Concord. The Colonial Militia, who had been roused by Paul Revere, had assembled at Lexington. Six companies of Light Infantry were sent on in advance under Major Pitcairn to seize the bridges beyond Concord, whilst the remainder destroyed the stores. These companies came into collision with the Americans at Lexington about 4 am on the 19th, and rivers of ink have been expended on the subject 'as to who fired first '. Colonel Smith then joined up with the main body and all marched to Concord where they arrived about 9 am. Captain Pearson with 6 companies of Light Infantry was sent to hold the bridges beyond the town where there was another engagement. The Light Companies then fell back on Concord and joined the Grenadiers. They saw some of their killed had been scalped, which embittered the subsequent proceedings. The Grenadiers had meanwhile destroyed the stores. The force then fell back. General Gage's papers have been purchased by an American and are now in the Clements Library of the University of Michigan. Among them are General Gage's instructions to Colonel Smith as to the guns, ammunition and stores to be destroyed at Concord, which shows that his intelligence service must have been very good. Among them also is Major Pitcairn's report given below.

As soon as the retirement commenced, the Militia attacked on all sides, and matters became very serious; casualties were numerous, and the retreat became rather disorderly. On the 19th Brigadier Lord Percy was sent with 10 companies and a body of Marines to help Smith's force and reached Lexington.

He had with him two field pieces, which materially helped in keeping off the Americans. Pitcairn's horse was wounded and his pistols were captured. The Americans had assembled in large numbers on the route to harass the retreat, but Lord Percy retired by a different road to Charlestown and

---
69   24th March 1775.
70   Lieutenant Barker's Diary. In the meantime a letter from Pitcairn to Lord Sandwich dated 4th March tells him that the "Battalion is getting the better of their drunkenness and I hope all will be well soon. As the rum is so cheap, it debauches both Navy and Army and he fears it will destroy more of us than the Yankies will do" (Sandwich Papers).

reached the heights of Bunker's Hill [sic] about 8 pm. As soon as Admiral Graves heard that the force was retiring he landed all the Marines of the fleet under Lieutenant Colonel Johnstone at Charlestown who, assisted by HMS *Somerset*, covered the passage of the troops from Charlestown to Boston.[71] The casualties were 65 killed and 270 wounded.

Major Pitcairn's report was as follows:

Sir,

As you are anxious to know the particulars that happened near and at Lexington on the 19th instant, agreeable to your desire, I will in as concise a manner as possible state the facts, for my time at present is so much employed as to prevent a more particular narrative of the occurrences of that day.

Six companies of Light Infantry were detached by Lieutenant Colonel Smith to take possession of the two bridges on the other side of Concord. Near three in the morning, when we were advanced within about two miles of Lexington, intelligence was received that about 500 men in arms were assembled, determined to oppose the King's troops and retard them in their march. On this intelligence I mounted my horse and galloped up to the six Light Companies. When I arrived at the head of the advanced company, two officers came and informed me that a man of the rebels advanced from those that were there assembled, had presented a musquet [sic] and attempted to shoot them, but the piece flashed in the pan. On this I gave direction to the troops to move forward, but on no account to fire, or even attempt it without orders; when I arrived at the end of the village I observed drawn up on a green near 200 of the rebels: when I came within about one hundred yards of them they began to file off towards some stone walls on our right flank. The Light Infantry observing this ran after them. I instantly called out to the soldiers not to fire, but to surround and disarm them, and after several repetitions of those positive orders, not to fire, etc, some of the rebels, who had jumped over the wall fired four or five shots at the soldiers, which wounded a man in the Tenth and my horse was wounded in two places. From some quarter or other, and at the same time, several shots were fired from a Meeting House on our left. Upon this, without any order or regularity the Light Infantry began a scattered fire and continued in that situation for some little time, contrary to the repeated orders both of me and the officers that were present. It will be needless to mention what happened after, as I suppose Colonel Smith hath given an account of it.

I am, Sir
Your most obedient humble servant
    John Pitcairn.
26th April 1775.
Boston Camp.

After the arrival of the reinforcing draft the following order was published on 20th May 1775:

---

71   Beatson.

The Commanding Officer finds it necessary, *"for the good of the service, to form the whole under his command into two battalions."* The strength of Companies at Headquarters at this time was 1 Captain, 2 Subalterns, 3 Sergeants, 3 Corporals, 2 Drummers and 56 Privates, so presumably these numbers were adopted.

The Battalion Staffs were:

	1st Battalion	2nd Battalion
Commanding Officer	Major Short	Major Tupper
Adjutant	Lieutenant J Waller	Lieutenant J Fielding
Quartermaster	Lieutenant J Pitcairn	Lieutenant T Smith
Grenadier Company	Captain T Averne	Captain George Logan
Light Infantry Company	Captain W Souter	Captain A Campbell

Superintending Adjutant and Deputy Paymaster, Captain D Johnstone - 2/Marines.

The Admiral with the seamen and Marines of the fleet constructed a battery of six 24 pdrs on Cope's Hill in Boston, which was taken over by the Royal Artillery and rendered good service in the coming battle and was afterwards called Cope's Hill Battery.

Noddles Island.
Whilst the Americans were investing the town on 27th May they tried to seize Noddles Island where supplies for the army and timber for the fleet had been placed; HMS *Diana* was sent to prevent boats crossing and the Marines of the fleet were landed with two guns from HMS *Cerberus*; though the *Diana* went aground and was destroyed the rebels who were in strong force were prevented from effecting their object; HMS *Britannia*, sloop, also came to the assistance. The action altogether lasted about eleven hours.[72]

Bunker's Hill.
The Americans now invested Boston and gradually closed on the town. General Gage therefore determined to attack the Dorchester Heights to the south of the town, but on the morning of Saturday 17th June, the Americans were seen building a redoubt and breastwork on the hill known as Bunker's Hill, or rather Breed's Hill, at the end of the ridge above the town of Charlestown on the opposite side of the harbour. At dawn, HMS *Lively* bombarded Charlestown.

General Gage at once issued the following Morning Order:

General Morning Order 17th June 1775.

The 10 eldest companies of Grenadiers and 10 eldest companies of Light Infantry[73] *(exclusive of regiments lately landed), the 5th and 38th Regiments to parade at 11.30 am, with area,*

---
72   Beatson.
73   Note. Fortescue says that the Grenadiers and Light Infantry Companies were drawn from 4th, 10th, 18th, 22nd, 23rd, 35th, 63rd and 65th.

ammunition, blankets and provisions cooked, and march by files to the Long Wharf - the 62nd and 43rd, with remaining Companies of Grenadiers and Light Infantry to parade at the same time with same directions and march to the North Battery - the 47th and 1 Battalion Marines will also march as above directed to the same Battery after the rest are embarked, and be ready to embark when ordered. Rest of troops to be kept in readiness to march at a moment's warning. 1 Subaltern, 1 Sergeant, 1 Corporal, 1 Doctor and 20 Privates to be left by each Corps for the security of respective encampments.

The order of Battle was:

	C-in-C General Howe	
	Major General Burgoyne	
1st Brigade	2nd Brigade	4th Brigade
Brigadier General Lord Percy	Brigadier General Pigot	Brigadier General Jones
23rd	38th	18th & 65th
59th	1/Marines	49th
44th	47th	2/Marines
4th	10th	40th
	Major General Clinton	
3rd Brigade		5th Brigade
Brigadier General Grant		Brigadier General Robertson
43rd		5th
52nd		45th
22nd		63rd
		35th

According to the above order the Grenadier and Light Infantry Companies of 2/Marines must have completed the ten companies, because we know that these companies of the 1st Battalion, were with their own battalion.

For the interesting personal narratives of officers who were present, see *"Britain's Sea Soldiers" Volume I;* the following is a purely tactical account from the History of the British Army (Fortescue) and Gillespie's History of the Marines [sic]. The Americans had actually placed their redoubt on Breed's Hill, which was just above Charlestown, on the end of the Bunker's Hill Ridge. It consisted of a strong redoubt on the summit with a line of trenches from the redoubt to the water on the north side.

In *History MS. Commission XIV Report* Vol. Appendix, Part I, page 2, there is an interesting account of the nature of the ground on Bunker's Hill, over which our troops had to attack:

> "The ground on the peninsula is the strongest I can conceive for the kind of defence the rebels made, which is exactly like that of the Indians, viz, small enclosures, with narrow lanes bounded by stone fences, small heights which command the passes, proper trees to fire from, and very rough and marshy ground for troops to get over. The rebels defended well and inch by inch."

This writer says that floating batteries had been ordered to go close in and prevent rebels moving reinforcements over the neck, but that they did not go close enough and withdrew too early, and that the rebels consequently had been reinforced to a strength of 7,000 men.

The orders for the scows were to prevent the enemy crossing the isthmus, but the ebbing tide prevented their getting near enough.[74] This also prevented the *Glasgow* and *Somerset* covering the disembarkation effectually. This is probably the reason why a frontal attack was made by the troops.

The Grenadier and Light Companies under General Howe, with the 5th and 38th Regiments, under General Pigot, landed on the extreme east point of the Charlestown peninsula, under the fire of the ships which had opened on the entrenchments at daylight. The Generals, after a reconnaissance, asked for two more battalions. The 52nd and 43rd Regiments with six more companies of Grenadiers and Light Infantry were disembarked. The attackers were drawn up in three lines; the left wing, under Howe, in column of battalions formed of the Grenadiers, 5th and 52nd; the Right Wing, under Pigot, formed of the Light Infantry Companies, the 38th and 43rd.

They were covered by the fire of eight guns and howitzers, which was ineffectual as the wrong ammunition had been sent over. The day was very hot, the grass was up to the men's knees and the ground was broken by a succession of fences. The men were carrying their knapsacks and three days' provisions.

The infantry advanced, and during this advance of 600 yards the columns deployed. The Light Infantry Companies were directed against the left of the Americans with a view to outflanking them; during the advance the left wing was galled by fire from the village of Charlestown, but that place was quickly set on fire by Cope's Hill Battery. The smoke of the burning town was driven into the eyes of the attackers. Not a shot was fired by the enemy until the troops nearly reached the entrenchments, when a tremendous and effective fire was opened which staggered the attackers; the American riflemen picked off the British officers. Howe rallied the troops and led them to a similar attack - from left to right - Grenadiers, 52nd 43rd 5th and Light Infantry. They were again swept down and fell back with heavy loss. Howe ordered the packs to be thrown off and the bayonet to be used; he abandoned the attack on the left flank and directed all his force on to the redoubt and breastwork.

---

74   Beatson.

The 1/Marines and 47th had now arrived with General Clinton; as Gillespie says *"Having been formed in two lines they advanced with slow but steady steps to the conflict, Majors Pitcairn, Short and Tupper led the Corps."* The advance was covered by fire from the ships and batteries. The British advanced without firing a shot, and the Americans reserved their fire; the last volley mortally wounded Major Pitcairn who died shortly after in the arms of his son.[75] Major Short, commanding the battalion was also killed, but the Americans shrunk from meeting the bayonets and were driven down and across the neck of Charlestown, where they were harassed by the fire of HMS *Glasgow* and suffered heavily.

Lieutenant and Adjutant Waller, 1/Marines, says that two companies of 1/Marines and part of the 47th were the first to cross the breastworks.

The Americans withdrew to a position on a hill on the road to Cambridge, about two miles away, which they commenced to fortify. The troops on Bunker's Hill were reinforced that night by the 2/Marines and 83rd Regiment; entrenchments were thrown up on the neck. The British casualties were heavy: 1 Lieutenant Colonel, 2 Majors, 7 Captains, and 9 Subalterns were killed including 2 Majors, 2 Captains, 3 Subalterns of Marines; 70 Officers were wounded, of whom 7 were Marines. Other ranks casualties were 207 killed (22 Marines), 758 wounded (87 Marines). Major Tupper was mentioned in despatches. The Officers killed were Major Pitcairn; 1/Marines: Major Short, Captain S Ellis, Lieutenants R Shea and W Finnie; 2/Marines: Captain A Campbell, Lieutenants Gard and F Gardiner. Officers wounded: 1/Marines: Captains T Averne, Stavel, Chudleigh, David Johnstone, Lieutenant Ragg; 2/Marines: Captain G Logan, Lieutenant J Dyer, A Brisbane. Those of the 2nd Battalion belonged to the Grenadier and Light Companies. NCOs and men 1/Marines, 17 killed, 57 wounded; 2/Marines: 5 killed, 30 wounded. Also, a Mr Bowman - probably a volunteer.

On Sunday the 18th there were apparently skirmishes, but the rebels on each occasion were driven off by the artillery and the British troops completed the entrenchment guarding the neck, "extending from the left of the hill quite to the waterside on the right." The tents were sent over and the troops encamped, except the Light Companies who had to guard the works. On 23rd June the 2/Marines returned to Boston town.

On 18th June the Commander-in-Chief published the following order: *"The Commander-in-Chief returns his most grateful thanks to Major-General Howe for the extraordinary exertion of his military abilities on 17th instant. He returns thanks to Major General Clinton and Brigadier Pigot for the share they took in the success of the day as well as…… Major Tupper……… and the rest of the officers and soldiers who by remarkable efforts of courage and gallantry overcame every disadvantage and drove the rebels from the redoubt and strongholds on the heights of Charles-town and gained a complete victory."*

From orders at Headquarters ordering subalterns to embark, the casualties were evidently soon

---

75 This is the usual story, but Major Tupper's official report to the Admiralty says "Major Pitcairn was wounded a few minutes before the attack was made on the redoubt and he died about two or three hours after."

made good; and on 16th July orders were issued for Lieutenant Colonel Gauntlett to proceed to Boston to take over command, but he had already left for Ireland, where he had been detailed for recruiting duty and could not be got hold of. This officer died when 2nd Commandant at Portsmouth and Colonel A T Collins was sent instead from Plymouth.[76]

During the following months they must have drawn on the ships for reinforcements, as, on 15th November, a list was sent to the Divisions of NCOs and men who were serving ashore from 17th June to 9th October 1775.

After Bunker's Hill, the Americans set to work to fortify themselves on the Dorchester Heights to the south of the town and mounted guns there, so that Boston was isolated from the mainland. The garrison remained passively on the defensive, the 1/Marines were certainly left in Charlestown, and Gillespie says that during the winter of 1775-76, the Marines were in tents on Bunker's Hill. The position was most difficult; they were cut off from communication with the Continent and could get no supplies. Store ships arrived slowly, and several were intercepted by the enemy.[77]

The Fleet was so badly provided and weak that when the Admiral sent the *Cerberus* home, the officers and Marines were distributed to the ships which had need of them. And the British troops remained invested in Boston.

In September 1776 Captains of Companies were granted 1/- a day contingent allowance for paying their companies.

During the winter of 1775-76 parties of New England and New York Militia under Generals Montgomery and Arnold, advancing via Lake Champlain, invaded Canada; they reduced the Forts at Chamblee and St John and even took Montreal. Fortunately, Sir Guy Carleton arrived in Quebec; and put the place into a state of defence. All the Marines of the squadron (about 40) and 400 seamen were landed for the defence of the town. On 31st December 1775 the Americans assaulted the Lower Town but were driven off with loss; General Montgomery was killed and they abandoned the siege.[78] Carleton's despatch said *"The Corps of Marines had their proportion of desert in defending the town of Quebec."*

Meanwhile in England the British workman had been showing his quality.

The Navy Board having represented that a number of shipwrights at Portsmouth have absented themselves, and they have reason to apprehend they may obstruct and assault the orderly and well-disposed workmen, and thereby deter them from going to their duty in the Yard; Commissioner Gambier is authorised to apply to you and the Commanding Officer of the Land Forces for a sufficient number of

---

76 Letter dated 27th July 1775.
77 Cf The same work of the Corps in 1914-18.
78 When the ice permitted ships came up the river and landed the 29th Regiment and the Marines of the fleet who, with the garrison, hustled their retreat.

men as well for the security of the Dockyard, as to assist the Civil Magistrates in preserving the peace, until the refractory workmen shall be brought to order. You are to supply as many Marines as you can.

Commanding Officer.
Portsmouth,
16th July 1775.

On 10th August 1775 there is a most interesting letter from the Admiralty which throws a vivid light on the training of young 2nd Lieutenants. It appears that when a gentleman was appointed a 2nd Lieutenant he took the place on the sea roster of the officer in place of whom he was gazetted. On 30th July the Commandant at Chatham (Colonel Mackenzie) pointed out that these officers might be embarked before they *"are qualified in the Requisites personally necessary for their appearance on duty;"* and even sometimes *"embarked in sloops on their own they will be ignorant of the care and command of troops in action or other necessary parts of the Service."* The Board agreed with the Colonel that *"giving time to the new appointed 2nd Lieutenants to perfect themselves in their duty at Quarters before they are sent to sea or on other service is highly necessary and proper."* It was therefore ordered that 2nd Lieutenants (*"who have not been in the service before"*) were to be placed at the bottom of the roster according to dates of appointment, and not to be sent to sea until the whole number of Lieutenants before them on the roster *"shall have been embarked or allowed one tour, in case they shall have served more than one tour before they were last relieved. To be applied to 2nd Lieutenants appointed since 7th June last".*

On 31st October the number of Privates per company was raised from 70 to 80, a total of 700 men; and on 16th February 1776 another 2nd Lieutenant was added to each company and 70 gentlemen were gazetted.

1776

The seriousness of the rebellion was gradually coming home to the Government in England; the vote for the Navy provided for 26,000 seamen and Marines, of which the Marines had 6,665, but the increase took effect slowly.

On 20th February 1776 there were complaints from the Division that as the army were giving levy money of five guineas for each recruit, and the Marines only three guineas that the latter could not get recruits. The Board raised the amount to four guineas but would not give more on account of *"the particular advantages of the Marine Service being considered."* [79]

The Army apparently issued a King's Pardon to deserters, but it was not applied to the Marines until 3rd May 1776.

By Order-in-Council 3rd April 1776 each of the seventy companies were increased from 80 to

---

[79] Cf The action of the Accountant General and Board as regards Naval Separation Allowance 1914-18 and its disastrous consequences in the winter of 1918-19 in the Grand Fleet.

90 Privates, ie 700 men, and by Order-in-Council 10th July from 90 to 100 Privates - a further 700. It was not until the end of the year (8th November 1776) that 15 more companies were added - 3 to Chatham and 6 each to Portsmouth and Plymouth. The establishment of all companies was 1 Captain, 2 First Lieutenants, 2 Second Lieutenants, 5 Sergeants, 5 Corporals, 4 Drummers, and 100 Privates, making a total of 10,145.

All through the year more ships were being brought forward for commission and the Navy was expanding generally.

The expansion and casualties of the Corps were evidently opening the number of vacancies for candidates for officers, who were obviously not all suitable. An Admiralty letter 9th November says. *"Several applications having been made to the Earl of Sandwich for 2nd Lieutenancies for persons of an improper age, I am commanded by My Lords to signify their direction to you to make it publicly known at your Division that no gentlemen under the age of 15 years nor above 21 can, by the rules laid down by Their Lordships, have a commission to be a 2nd Lieutenant in the Marine Corps."* And from various letters gentlemen who were serving as volunteers with the battalions in America were appointed to commissions.

Returning to the battalions, on 1st January 1776 the fleet attacked Norfolk in Hampton Roads and landed the seamen and Marines to collect stores, but the inhabitants set fire to the town themselves. Meanwhile things were going badly in Boston and supplies were short.

A Detachment of Marines under Major Grant was sent to Savannah under escort of an armed ship (HMS *Scarborough*) to collect supplies; and there was a fight and laden ships were burnt but the party returned to Boston with what remained, and which afforded some relief to the garrison.

At the beginning of March, American batteries on Dorchester Heights and at Phipps Farm, commenced a severe bombardment, and an attack on Dorchester Heights ordered for the 5th March was cancelled owing to the weather.

General Howe had succeeded General Gage in command, and, in the middle of March, the combined effects of hunger and the bombardment determined them to evacuate the town; the embarkation was carried out on 17th.

It was a very big business as the loyalist inhabitants had to be evacuated as well as the troops and stores. The embarkation took over a week. Castle William was blown up.

The Marines were embarked in the *Grand Duchess of Russia*, 200 in the *Centurion* and 200 in the *Chatham* and *Renown* and the army sailed for Halifax, Nova Scotia, where they landed early in April; the strength of the force being 9,000 effectives. As early as 8th February 1776 the King suggested to the First Lord that the two Marine Battalions should be sent from Boston to Halifax as the regiment there was very young and sickly.

A letter from Colonel Collins to the First Lord dated 21st March 1776 written from Nantasher Roads says they embarked by daylight on 17th March and although Boston was surrounded by 25,000 rebels, who did not interfere with them; although the town had been bombarded for several nights, whilst works at Phipps Farm and Cobb Hill had played on the west side. He also reports that the two battalions of Marines had been distributed in detachments on board different ships to assist in the navigation and says; *"And I can with pleasure assure your Lordship that the Marines on this service have proved beyond a doubt that every soldier should be a Marine."* [80] The Marines were told off to garrison the place. The battalions were reorganised, the 1st under Colonel Collins and the 2nd under Major Tupper.

After the arrival of the force at Halifax, General Howe formed a plan to seize New York and by an advance up the Hudson River to join hands with a force from Canada and so cut off the New England states. This force left Halifax on 10th June 1776; Beatson says the two Marine battalions - strength 1,172 - were attached but if they did they must have returned very soon as they were in Halifax in July. But the two Grenadier Companies under Captains Averne and Logan were present at all the subsequent fighting.

The Marine Companies appear to have been attached to the 2nd Battalion of Grenadiers and Major the Hon J Maitland of the Marines commanded the 3rd Battalion of Light Infantry, but the Light companies do not seem to have been present. The battalions of Grenadiers and Light Infantry landed on 3rd July on Staten Island and the remainder of the army on the next day; some men of war were sent up the river for about 25 miles.

Admiral Lord Howe arrived with his squadron on 12th July, and on the 24th General Clinton from Charlestown also re-joined. Under cover of the fire of the ships the troops were landed at Gravesend Bay on Long Island on 22nd July in three flights, and by noon 15,000 troops were on shore; the troops advanced up the island, the ships pushing up the river. A night march was made on 26th/27th August and the enemy were encountered near Brooklyn, who after a fierce engagement were heavily defeated, the Grenadiers getting round their rear. On 27th August Captain Logon (2/Marines) was killed, Lieutenant Nugent (1/Marines) was wounded and Lieutenant R Ragg (2/Marines) was missing.

In September the operations were continued on New York Island. On the 14th the Light Companies were landed; on the 15th the 1st Division of the army (the Grenadier and Light Battalions with a Brigade of Hessians) embarked in boats at Newtown Inlet and proceeded in three divisions to Brunswick Point; here under cover of fire of five ships which prevented the advance of great numbers of rebels, from forts near the city and the high banks of the Kipps Bay the troops landed safely, the landing being most creditably performed. The boats then returned for the second flight under Earl Percy. The Grenadier and Light Companies pushed forward to the heights, and the Hessians were attached but the rebels were driven off and left their camp in

---

80 Sandwich Papers.

great confusion and the army secured posts across the island near the village of Haarlem. Three ships made their way up the North River, and a squadron in East River blockaded the south part of the island, the city and its dependencies. At 4 pm the rebels struck their flag at Fort George, and the local loyalists of the town guard secured possession of the forts and batteries evacuated by the rebels and hoisted the British flag.

At 7 am on 16th September the Marines of the *Eagle* were landed and took possession of the forts etc. at New York from the town guard, being relieved during the morning by the 48th Regiment. On the 17th Haarlem was occupied, when the Light companies were engaged by the rebels and were reinforced by Grenadiers who drove the enemy off. They saved New York from being burnt.

Washington's troops retired across King's Bridge.

The fleet co-operated with the army movements in these operations and had several engagements, particularly on 9th October when the *Phoenix*, *Roebuck*, and *Tartar* forced their way past the batteries in the North River when 1 Lieutenant of Marines and 3 other ranks were wounded.

It is impossible to follow the movements of the Marine Companies through the severe fighting and clever handling of ships and troops by which Washington was eventually driven back to Whiteplains, but those who would wish to learn something of combined operations would gain some valuable information. The Americans would not accept the British terms, so Howe returned to New York and made it his Headquarters through all the following campaigns. During the winter the rebels under Washington suffered great hardships.

On 4th July 1776 the Americans had published their 'Declaration of Independence.' Soon afterwards France and Spain opened their ports to the American privateers and supplied them with guns and stores, and also sent French engineers and officers to the American armies. This threw an additional responsibility on the navy and increased the difficulty as regards transport of supplies and reinforcements. Admiralty letters dated 23rd August 1776 order *"Armed guards of 1 Subaltern, 1 Sergeant, 1 Corporal and 18 Privates to be placed on board the 'Success' and 'Increase' (transports) with Naval Stores"* for Halifax - *"to assist in defending them from rebel cruisers should they be detached from the convoy; the party to be sent to the RM [sic] Battalion at Halifax on arrival."* A similar order for the *Elephant* on 5th September and again on 18th November for the *Kent*.[81]

On 12th June 1776 the Admiralty forwarded a return to the Divisions showing the Marines who had been transferred from the *Somerset* and *Glasgow* to the battalion. There is also a report from the Commanding Officer, Colonel Collins, saying that he was keeping some of his invalids for garrison duty and sending the rest to England in the *Glasgow*. Incidentally we learn of a hardship; apparently NCOs invalided had to revert to the ranks when sent on board as others

---

81 Cf Similar precautions 1914-18.

were appointed in their places. Colonel Collins asked that they might be reinstated on reaching Headquarters. The Adjutants, who were Headquarter Adjutants, also had a grievance, because they did not receive their share of the Levy Money for raising recruits. On 12th July Major Tupper was given leave to England and was succeeded by Major Souter. He did not return.

The Captains' Contingent Allowance was raised to 1/6 for repairing arms and burying the dead.

Detachments were trained at the guns in the batteries defending the harbour, and the command given to Lieutenant Tantum, so we find Marines at their duty of defending a naval base.

Charlestown.
On the 1st January 1776 a fleet, under Admiral Sir Peter Parker, with reinforcements of troops under General Lord Cornwallis left Cork for America; they were met off Cape Fear by 3,397 troops under General C Clinton (who was senior to Cornwallis) from New York. They were ordered to make an attack on Charlestown in South Carolina but being ignorant of the topography of the place the enterprise had disastrous results. They arrived off Charlestown on 4th June, and on the 23rd the troops were landed on Long Island, with the idea of attacking Sullivan's Island on which were the Batteries defending the town. The islands were connected by a ford reported to be eighteen inches deep at low water; actually, it was seven feet! The fleet attacked the forts, but the troops failed to pass the ford. The Admiral continued the action for ten hours and lost a ship with a lot of officers and men (84 killed, 141 wounded) and had at last to withdraw, finally abandoning the attack on 29th June. On 12th December this force seized Narragansett Bay and Rhode Island, which proved very useful bases and hampered the movements of the enemy's privateers. Against the advice of Admiral Rodney, they were given up in 1779.

In November 1776 a body of rebel troops and disaffected inhabitants made an irruption into the province of Nova Scotia. They made an attack on Fort Cumberland on 20th November, but men and stores with some ships of war having been sent from Halifax, the troops made a sally and destroyed the American siege works; on which the Americans abandoned the siege and retired from the province. Apparently, the reinforcements included some Marines for on 19th December General Massy commended the Marine Light Companies. From a letter of Major Souter's dated 11th January 1777 the Marines were very happy under General Massy's command.[82]

A letter from Major Souter shows that promotions were made on the same principles as the present day: *"He understands many of the Corporals serving in the Battalions have been appointed Sergeants in their respective Divisions at home and asks that when such promotions take place he may be informed."*

---

82 Sandwich Papers.

1777 - America

A Board Order was issued on the 1st January 1777, ordering the two battalions to be consolidated into one on the 2nd April.

Companies to consist of 1 Captain, 4 Subalterns, 5 Sergeants, 5 Corporals, 4 Doctors, and 100 Private men each, conformable to the present establishment of the Corps, together with the following Field Officers and Staff, 2 Majors, 1 Adjutant, 1 Quartermaster, 1 Chaplain, 1 Surgeon and 1 Surgeon's Mate. The balance to be embarked in HM Ships short of complement; the officers to be sent to England.

By order of their Lordships,

(Signed) Philip Stephens.

The plan of campaign for 1777 included an advance from New York via the lakes to join hands with forces from Canada, and a force was detached under General Burgoyne for this purpose. Leaving General Clinton with 8,000 troops in New York, General Howe for some unexplained reason did not reinforce Burgoyne, who suffered the disastrous defeat at Saratoga,[83] but accompanied by the fleet diverted his main forces to Philadelphia. One result of this disaster was to decide the French to enter the war on the side of the Americans.

General Howe embarked his troops in 200 transports and with them went the Marine Grenadiers. The channel of the Delaware River leading to Philadelphia was blocked with chevaux de frise, the British troops were therefore landed under cover of the fleet at the head of the Elk River (Elk Ferry), in Maryland - 13 miles from Delaware Bay - on 23rd August and marched on Philadelphia. The armies came into collision on 3rd September near Wilmington. On 11th September the Americans were assembled at Brandywine Creek barring the road to Philadelphia; Washington was strongly posted, his left on a cliff, centre at Chad's Ford and the right upstream in thick wooded country. Although the British were inferior in numbers, Howe ordered General Knyphausen to attack the centre and General Cornwallis, whose force included the two battalions of Grenadiers (the RM companies were in the 2nd Battalion) to attack the American right. This was done after a march of 18 miles in two lines - 8 battalions in the first line, 7 battalions in the second line. Washington was driven off and retreated to Chester. There was another action at Germanstown, after which Philadelphia was occupied by Lord Cornwallis and the British Grenadiers. Cornwallis immediately erected three batteries of 12 pdrs and howitzers to act against any enemy shipping that might approach the town. These were attacked by rebel vessels on the 27th, the USS *Delaware* grounded, and the four battalion guns of the Grenadiers did such execution that in a short time she struck her colours and was boarded and taken by the Marine Company of Grenadiers under Captain Averne.[84]

---

83   Lieutenant Haggart RM was among the killed at Saratoga.
84   Beatson.

The greater part of the army encamped at Germanstown, about six miles from the city. In order to secure the communications of the army it was necessary to clear the river, and Admiral Lord Howe tried to enter the river with the fleet. Owing to the enemy batteries, however, he was obliged to anchor between Reedy Island and Newcastle on 8th October. The Americans were holding Mud Fort near the junction with the River Schuykill, and Red Bank opposite on the New Jersey shore, whilst the river itself was blocked.

Till the river was cleared all Army supplies had to come overland from the Chesapeake River. The enemy were first driven from a place called Billinghuret, and then in conjunction with fire on Mud Fort from guns on the Pennsylvania Bank. HMS *Augusta* (64) and the *Merlin*, (sloop) attacked Red Bank; both ran aground and were destroyed by fire. Captain Barclay[85] was in the *Augusta*. The Hessians under Von Donop also attacked Red Bank on 22nd October and were repulsed with heavy loss. Guns were then established on Providence Island and under cover of their fire on 18th November the ships attacked various parts of Mud Fort.

After a long and destructive cannonade, the enemy deserted in the night. The army also occupied Red Bank and the enemy withdrew after partly destroying the works and setting fire to some of their vessels but left their artillery. Navigation was now open for the supply of the army, but the capture of Philadelphia served no useful purpose as it had to be abandoned as soon as the war with France made control of the sea even doubtful. This was almost the first occasion on which the Corps came into collision with its sister Corps, the US Marines, that had been formed in 1776.

To assist both General Burgoyne and General Howe's movements Sir Henry Clinton sent four columns from New York to make an irruption into New Jersey on 12th September. The 4th Column was composed of 400 Loyal Americans and 40 Marines under Lieutenant Colonel Campbell and was sent to Tapan; they had several skirmishes, also secured some valuable supplies of live cattle and sheep with milch cows for the hospital.

During 1777 many quaint methods of raising recruits were adopted. There are also interesting references to the prisoners of war confined at Forton, with complaints by the officers of the guard as to their treatment by the Civil Commissioner. Portsmouth Division was frequently called on to provide additional guards.

On 2nd October 1777 *"In order to preserve to them their rank when doing duty in line with the Land Forces"* the King granted brevet rank to a number of senior Majors and Captains, and the Commandants seem to have been made Major Generals.

The Battalions remained at Halifax as there is a report of the punishment of three Privates for murder in October 1777.

---

85 Afterwards 'Commandant in Town'.

1778

It is clear from the number of ships ordered to be commissioned that the danger of complications with France were being realised all through the autumn of 1777. On 8th February 1778 the French concluded a Treaty with the Americans, and Great Britain immediately recalled her Ambassador and declared war. The centre of interest for the Corps now shifts to the service afloat.

In May the King held a review of the Fleet at Spithead, and he also visited the Marine Barracks.

On 26th December 1777 the 85 companies of the Corps were increased by 1 Sergeant 1 Corporal and 18 Privates each, making the total establishment 11,829 which was the number voted by Parliament. On 18th March 1778 an Order-in-Council ordered 15 more companies to be raised making a total of 100 (28 at Chatham, 36 each at Portsmouth and Plymouth): total establishment 14,000. The standard of height was five feet four inches. Committees of subscribers were formed at various places for raising recruits.

In this year we get the first mention of "Light Clothing" being supplied to detachments under orders for the East Indies.

On 13th April the French sent Admiral D'Estaing with twelve battleships and five frigates to Delaware Bay, and on 10th June the British sent Admiral Byron with thirteen battleships and a large convoy with supplies for the West Indies. Admiral Keppel with thirty battleships was sent to blockade Brest, but the French under the Comte D'Orvillers with thirty battleships and fifteen frigates got out of Brest and from 23rd to 27th July was fought the Battle of Ushant (100 miles west of that island) without any decisive results. The British lost 133 killed and 373 wounded. Lieutenant McDonald Marines (*Prince George*) was wounded.

This action was followed by the usual crop of courts martial; Keppel was tried and honourably acquitted; and his second in command, Palliser, who had brought the charges was also tried and acquitted.

On 18th March 1778 the Cabinet decided that the Marine battalions should be sent home being relieved by troops from Philadelphia. Evidently the manning of Keppel's Fleet was causing great difficulties.[86]

In North America Lord Howe decided on the evacuation of Philadelphia, and the British Fleet was concentrated to the north of the Delaware River and embarked all the army stores whilst the army marched overland to New York on 10th June. General Clinton, after an action at Freshfield where Lieutenant Desborough of the Marine Grenadiers was wounded, arrived on 30th June; and on 5th July crossed over a bridge of boats to Sandy Hook and was conveyed to New York. The fleet

---

86   See Sandwich Papers.

did not clear Chesapeake Bay until 28th June, and on 8th July D'Estaing arrived, just missing the British. The French Fleet anchored four miles south of Sandy Hook on the 11th. They were superior in strength having one 90 gun ship, one 80 gun, and six 74's, whilst the British only had six 64's and the crews had to be completed by volunteers from the merchant ships. On 22nd July the wind and tide were favourable for D'Estaing to attack, but he would not take the risk of crossing the bar, and at 3 pm stood off to the southward and on 29th July attacked Narragansett Bay. Here General Pigot concentrated his troops at Newport on 30th July but continued to hold the batteries at Goat Island and sank four frigates and a sloop to block the channels, using the guns and crews (over 1,000 men) to serve in the fortifications. On 8th August the French ships ran past the batteries and anchored above Goat Island and 10,000 American troops arrived in the northern part of Rhode Island. D'Estaing also landed 4,000 soldiers and seamen. The British garrison was only 8,000.

On 9th August Lord Howe arrived, but as he was in inferior strength, he anchored twelve miles off; on 10th August D'Estaing came out and Howe retired; a hurricane scattered both fleets and at the end of the month D'Estaing withdrew his fleet to Boston to refit; the Americans abandoned Rhode Island and the garrison was saved.

On 25th August 1778 the Marine Battalion was struck off the strength of the garrison at Halifax and embarked on 1st September for England.

On 11th November the Commandant at Portsmouth reported the arrival of the first portion and the remainder landed on 21st November. The accounts were ordered to be closed by 24th November before they re-joined their Divisions. The Chatham draft was sent to Chatham, but only the officers, corporals and men recommended for promotion were sent to Plymouth, the remainder were retained at Portsmouth for embarkation. On 17th January 1779 the Commandant at Portsmouth was ordered to report the number of men of the battalion still at Portsmouth and to embark them in the *Royal George* (flagship of Lord Rodney). It would be interesting to know how many of these were lost in the terrible tragedy of this ship, which was sunk when flagship of Rear Admiral Kempenfeldt at Spithead in September 1782. The ship had been careened out at Spithead for repairs to her bottom; she was crowded with 800 of the crew and about 300 visitors seeing their relations; she was heeled to too great an angle, when a sudden and unexpected squall struck her and she heeled over. The gun ports were open, so she filled with water and sank. The Admiral was lost and it was believed about 900 or 1000 people lost their lives - among them Major Graham and two Lieutenants of Marines and the bulk of the Marine detachment.

On 24th June 10 Companies were added (5 each to Portsmouth and Plymouth) making a total of 110 of a strength 15,300; and by Order-in-Council 14th December 1778 15 more (5 each to Chatham, Portsmouth and Plymouth) making a total strength of 17,300. Yet in spite of these increases, letters show that soldiers were also being embarked as Marines, among other regiments the 50th.[87] The letters from Admiral Keppel of this year show the great difficulties of manning the

---

87   Now Royal West Kent. (Editor's Note. Today a part of the Princess of Wales's Royal Regiment.)

Fleet. On 28th April 1778 it was ordered that the Marines should be relieved from the guards at Haslar and Forton Prison which would give 150 men for the squadron [sic]. And he seems to have filled up some ships with Marines in lieu of seamen.

The question of soldiers as Marines does not seem to have been altogether simple as a letter of 16th July 1778 says *"I would have sent Captain Walsing transports of soldiers ashore and given him a complete number of Marines, indeed they would have been raw and undisciplined men as well as the soldiers but yet as men really belonging to the Fleet they must be more desirable!"*[88]

In America, Admiral Hyde Parker arrived on 11th September with six more battleships and Lord Howe went home. In the West Indies the French seized Dominica, and on 4th November the French squadron under D'Estaing sailed from Boston for Martinique. The British Admiral in the West Indies was Barrington, with a few battleships. On 10th December he was joined at Barbados by Commodore Hotham with two 64-gun and three 50-gun ships conveying 5,000 troops under General Grant from New York. They proceeded at once to St Lucia, anchoring on the 12th in the Cul de Sac. The seamen and Marines were landed to man the batteries at the entrance on each side to cover the fleet, and the ships were anchored so that their broadsides could fire out to sea. Two brigades of troops were landed and forced the heights to the north and opened the way to Castries Bay, where the remainder of the troops disembarked and captured Morns Fortune commanding Castries Bay on the 13th. The troops also gained the peninsula of Vigie between the Cul de Sac and Carenage Bay and all forts and batteries with 59 guns, occupying also all the strong points in the hills on either side of the Cul de Sac.

On 15th December D'Estaing with a large fleet attacked Carenage Bay but hauled off and attacked the British Fleet at the Cul de Sac. He was compelled however to draw off again; he renewed the attack in the afternoon but was again driven off by the ships assisted by the land batteries. On the 16th he anchored off Gros Islet Bay and landed about 9,000 men at the Anse du Choc and attacked the British on the Vigie Peninsula, because he found that General Grant's position on the heights was impregnable. He was driven off with tremendous loss after three attacks and had to re-embark with a loss of 400 killed, 500 severely wounded, and 600 slightly wounded. He then left the island on 29th December, and on the 30th the French garrison capitulated. *"Thus, was a fortified naval base gained ready made at a trifling cost."*[89]

On 29th October 1778 Plymouth Orders contain an interesting regulation dividing the duties of a soldier from works services: *"Entrenchments, roads, making posts, clearing grounds are part of a soldier's duties and are not paid; building forts and fortresses and any other public works are paid at the rate of 9d per hour"*.

Naval Gunnery.
In this year in a letter to the First Lord dated 10th August 1778 Lieutenant Colonel Collins

---
88 Sandwich Papers.
89 Fortescue.

suggests that Marines should be trained in heavy guns to assist in manning the fleet, a suggestion which had already been made in 1773 by Captain Wood (Marines) to have practice batteries on shore.

1779

70,000 men including 17,389 Marines were voted by parliament for the navy this year.

On 20th January orders were issued to commission the following ships: HMS *Vengeance, Worcester, Exeter, Eagle, Actaeon. Nymph,* and *Sybil* to form Sir Edward Hughes' squadron for the East Indies. They carried 4 Captains, 14 Subalterns, 14 Sergeants, 20 Corporals, 7 Drummers and 455 Privates, and we shall presently hear about the hard fighting they experienced. They do not seem to have sailed until March.

Spain now declared war against England and, joining with France, imposed additional duties on the British Navy; the great siege of Gibraltar also commenced.

In European waters the British Channel Fleet had only forty battleships against the strength of sixty-six for the Allies, but the latter did not affect their concentration until 25th July; at Portsmouth alone in the middle of April seven battleships were commissioned taking 25 officers and 850 marines.

The War continued on the continent of America, but the Corps took no further part except in coastal operations. In the West Indies in June Admiral Byron had to leave the North American Station in order to convey home the West Indian convoy which was waiting at St Kitts. On 16th June the French under D'Estaing seized St Vincent and - on 4th July - Grenada.

On 6th July Byron appeared with twenty-one battleships and a convoy of troops; D'Estaing also had twenty-one battleships; the resulting fight was the most disastrous since 1690 and only *"the incompetence of the French Commander-in-Chief saved the British from disaster."*[90] The British loss was 183 killed and 346 wounded among which one Lieutenant of Marines was killed and one wounded, also two lieutenants of the army serving as Marines.

Byron retired to St Kitts and D'Estaing to Grenada. Admiral Hyde Parker took over command of the British until Rodney arrived March 1780.

In European waters the French were making their usual plans for an invasion of England; 50,000 troops were concentrated at Havre and St Malo whilst the Allied Squadron of 68 ships under D'Orvillers was approaching the Channel. Sir Charles Hardy, who had completed the Channel Squadron of 25 battleships at Portsmouth, got to sea on 16th June. The Marine complements had

---

90   Mahan.

been revised at this time and we further learn [91], that *"Hardy's ships were to be completed to the scale except those that are to have soldiers instead of Marines,"* followed by a further letter on 16th June that the squadron was to be completed by Marine Headquarters and if not sufficient they were to be taken from the ships in the harbour - *"unless the draft from Plymouth arrives in time."*

Admiral Hardy rendezvoused SW of the Scilly Islands; the Jamaica convoy and the Leeward Islands Fleet arrived before the French appeared; whilst eight East Indiamen took refuge in the Shannon River. On 16th August the French Commander-in-Chief was instructed that Falmouth was to be the landing place, and on 17th he was off Plymouth, but an easterly gale drove him out of the Channel. On the 29th he sighted Hardy's squadron; the latter with his inferior numbers declined action and reached Spithead on 3rd September. D'Orvillers returned to Brest on 4th September, and the Spanish ships went on to Cadiz. Yet another attempt gone wrong.

Savannah.
In America, in order to help the Loyalists in the southern states, Colonel Prevost and some British troops had been sent to occupy Savannah in Georgia. General Lincoln with a large force of Americans was threatening the place, when D'Estaing with his fleet and troops appeared on 10th September. With him were 22 battleships, 11 frigates and a large number of troops. Captain Harvey RN moved his few ships close up to the town and landed his guns and seamen; he also incorporated his Marines with the Grenadiers of the 60th Regiment. D'Estaing landed 5,000 men; he marched on the town and summoned it to surrender on 16th September. Colonel Prevost delayed his reply in order to allow Colonel Hon J Maitland (late Marines) to join him with 800 men from the outposts inland; this raised the garrison to 3,700 (of whom only 2,200 were fit for duty), consisting of 200 of 2/60th, 720 Fraser's Highlanders, 350 Light Infantry, the Marines and a few of the 16th Regiment, 2 Battalions of Hessians and Provincial troops. The north front of the town was covered by the river, the west front by a morass. D'Estaing broke ground on 23rd September, and on 4th October the besiegers opened fire which continued until 8th October when Prevost made two sorties. D'Estaing had decided to storm on the 8th, the American Militia to make two feigned attacks on the South and East fronts, D'Estaing and Lincoln with two columns of 4,000 regulars to deliver the attack on Springhill Redoubt at the south west angle of the lines. Count Dillon with another column was to move along the morass and gain the rear of the British lines but lost his way: he was exposed to fire while in the morass and was put out of action. D'Estaing approached the redoubt at daybreak on 9th October but was received with a heavy fire by 100 Provincial Dragoons and the 60th. There were repeated attacks and counter-attacks; Colonel Maitland brought up the 60th and the Marines with charged bayonets who soon decided the struggle and drove the enemy back to camp; Lieutenant Colonel Glazier led the Marines and the 60th. The enemy lost 900 killed and wounded; D'Estaing re-embarked his troops and returned to France; the Americans retreated to South Carolina, so that this action freed the coast from the menace of a powerful Fleet.

The growing menace of the European war led to further increase in the Corps, and by Order-in-

---
91 Admiralty Letter 20th May 1779.

Council 20th August 1779, ten more companies were added (5 each to Portsmouth and Plymouth) bringing the total companies to 125 and on 13th September an increase of Field Officers was approved; a Colonel Commandant as Second-in-Command was added to each Division, the Lieutenant Colonels were raised to nine and the Majors to twelve.

Great efforts were being made in recruiting and a Lieutenant Colonel and several officers were sent specially to Ireland; an Act something resembling the National Service arrangements of 1917-18 was passed and curiously enough in both cases the Marines were given the first choice of men.

Drills.
From an order 30th June 1779[92] we learn that the three deep formation was still in existence. *"Ranks to be 6 paces or 12 feet asunder, files 6 inches asunder"*. An order of 12th July gives instructions for making ball cartridges.

Powder	3 Drachms (½oz)
Ball	1 lb of lead to make 14½ bullets
Fine Paper	One sheet to make 16 cartridges
Thread	1 oz will tie 1,000 cartridges.
One whole barrel of powder will make	*"4,266 cartridges for Musquets"*.

Omoa.
The entry of Spain into the war had extended the area of operations in America; in Honduras the Spaniards expelled the log cutters who were British and Irish from the bay and had taken many prisoners; in order to rescue them the Governor of Jamaica dispatched a small expedition. Commodore Luttrell with the *Charon*, *Lowestoft* and *Pomona* embarked a small body of troops under Captain Dalrymple; these, with the seamen and marines of the squadron and a party of the log cutters and bay men from Truxillo, formed the attacking force. They first captured St George's Key and then disembarked at Porto Cavallo on 16th October. A night march was made to the Fort at Omoa; the British encountered morasses and precipices in their march, added to which there was heavy rain. Dawn found them six miles from their objective when they were discovered. After a rest they drove the Spaniards from an ambuscade, established posts round the town and fort, and set the town on fire. The Commodore brought his ships into the harbour and completed the blockade by sea. Guns were landed, and batteries opened but with little effect. Dalrymple then found the siege so slow that he determined to make an assault on the 20th. Covered by the fire of the ships and batteries he advanced at 4 am with 150 seamen and marines formed in four columns - two of seamen, two of marines and some log cutters. By means of scaling ladders the seamen got over the walls 28 feet high and being reinforced by the marines captured the place. The booty was a ship and 3,000,000 dollars in gold, for it was the storehouse for Guatemala. Dalrymple then left. The Admiral sent orders that the fortifications were to be blown up and evacuated, but on 28th December in view of the menace of attack from the interior the place had to be abandoned.

---

92   Plymouth.

1780

On 1st October 1779 Admiral Rodney was appointed to the command in the West Indies with his flag in the *Royal George*. He left England on 29th December with 28 battleships and 14 frigates convoying the store ships for Gibraltar and Minorca. Off Finisterre on 8th January 1780 he captured the home coming Spanish convoy from America, so that all hands had quickly earned prize money. Off Cape St Vincent on 16th January he sighted the Spanish Fleet of 11 battleships with 2 frigates under Admiral de Langara. Rodney attacked at once; one of the enemy ships blew up, six were captured some of which were added to the British Fleet and only four escaped; Lieutenant Straghan Marines (Edgar) was killed. The British loss was 32 killed and 102 wounded.

After relieving Gibraltar and Minorca, Rodney sailed for the West Indies on 13th February; on arriving at St Lucia with 4 battleships he found 16 there.

On 17th April De Guichen, the French Admiral, left Martinique with 3,000 troops to make an attack on the British West Indian islands. Rodney was waiting at St Lucia, and after a severe action when a great opportunity was lost by the bad behaviour of certain Captains in the British Fleet, De Guichen withdrew to Guadeloupe and Rodney returned to St Lucia. The British loss was 120 killed and 355 wounded, Captain Carey (*Montagu*) and Lieutenant Heriot (*Elizabeth*) of the Marines were wounded and an officer of the 88th Regiment was among the wounded so that some of that regiment appear to have been acting as Marines. De Guichen reached Guadeloupe on the 30th, but as Rodney had no troops and insufficient Marines for a striking force he could not follow up his success. The action however cleared the seas for trade.

In May the French attempted a fresh attack on St Lucia, but after the indecisive actions of 15th and 19th May off Martinique, De Guichen withdrew to Martinique and Rodney to Barbados. For fourteen days and nights the fleets had been so close that there had been no rest for Rodney or his officers. In the first action the British loss was 21 killed and 100 wounded, and on the 19th 47 killed and 193 wounded; among the officers wounded were one of the 87th Regiment and one of the 5th, so that portions of these regiments were evidently serving as Marines.

In June the Spanish Fleet of 12 ships joined De Guichen at Martinique and Guadeloupe; the great hurricane of 1780 however immobilised both fleets in the West Indies, and in August De Guichen left for Europe and Rodney for New York.

According to a return of the Volunteer forces at New York on 19th February 1780, there was a unit called 'The New York Marine Artillery' - one company, 98 strong - with a note that it was formed from the Marine Society established by Royal Charter.[93]

---

93 Beatson.

Owing to D'Estaing's repulse at Savannah and his return to Europe, General Clinton was able by aid of the fleet to move his troops to any part of the coast; therefore, in order to support the loyalists in the Carolinas and to obtain a new base, he determined to occupy Charlestown in South Carolina, which had been the scene of Cornwallis' repulse in 1776.

The town was strongly entrenched on the land side and to seaward it was guarded on the south by Fort Johnston on James Island and on the north by Fort Moultrie on Sullivan's Island. There was a dangerous bar below which the American Fleet could lie,

On 10th February 1780 Clinton with 7,600 men were landed on John's Island and pushed forward to James' Island; on 9th April Admiral Arbuthnot with the squadron ran past Fort Moultrie, cutting it off from the town, and anchored within range of the town. The garrison could however communicate overland by the Cooper River to the north east. The British cavalry drove off the Americans; General Webster cut them off in an engagement at Monk's Corner, so that Lord Cornwallis was able to occupy the ground to north of the Cooper River.

The trenches were then opened and pushed on, and on 9th May the third parallel was opened within 200 yards of the abattis. Captain Hudson was landed with 200 seaman and Marines on Sullivan's Island to storm Fort Moultrie, covered by the guns of the fleet; the fort surrendered to the party on 6th May and the town finally capitulated on 12th May.

On 20th June 1780 Captain Allen from Portsmouth was appointed Barrack master at Chatham; some of the rooms in the barracks had apparently been fit for occupation on 2nd September 1779[94] and so it would appear as if the barracks had been completed at this time.

On 1st July by Order-in-Council there were an increase of five companies - one to Chatham, two each to Portsmouth and Plymouth - and again on 27th October six more - three each to Portsmouth and Plymouth. The companies were now thirty-four at Chatham, fifty-nine each at Portsmouth and Plymouth, making a total strength of 20,888.

With reference to recruiting, Gillespie, the Corps historian, makes this comment on the rapid raising of recruits and our history - especially in the Great War 1914-18 - bears out all his statements made in 1803:

"It was at this period and has since been too prevalent a custom to embark recruits, not only unscienced in discipline, but utterly untrained to arms; such deficiencies can only be compensated for by native valour, aided by the care of officers in rendering them good marksmen, and by that punctual system which prevails in our ships of war. A few regular built soldiers should always be intermingled with every detachment, a rule that can only be observed by maintaining a sufficient strength during peace or by a prompt levy at the commencement of hostilities."

---

94   Chatham Orders.

There is an interesting ruling on 30th June 1780 that officers were not liable to pay the tax on men servants for their batmen.

Death of Captain Cook.
We have all read of the gallant conduct of Lieutenant Molesworth Phillips of the Marines on the lamented occasion of the death of Captain Cook RN, the celebrated explorer, and it is pleasant to think that it was recognised by the Admiralty:[95]

> In reply to your letter reporting that Lieutenant Phillips had been constantly returned on board the Drake and has not acquainted you with his being in this kingdom, but that you have no objection to the leave he has requested. My Lords inform you that Lieutenant Phillips proceeded in the Resolution sloop upon her late voyage of discovery, and is but lately returned to England, and their Lordships have in consideration of his being so employed appointed him Captain Lieutenant of the 5th Company of Marines.

But he did not become Captain until 11th January 1792.

The following account of the death of Captain Cook and the action of the Marines is taken from Beatson.[96]

> Captain Cook had gone ashore to interview the natives with reference to the theft of a cutter, being accompanied by Lieutenant Molesworth Phillips and nine Marines. He landed at Kowrowa and marched to the village where he was received with the usual marks of respect. Negotiations were ineffective, and the crowd of natives began to throng round Captain Cook and the Chief. Lieutenant Phillips begged leave to draw his men from the crowd, who pressed upon them, and to permit of their being drawn up regularly close to the water's edge.
>
> This being granted, the natives readily making way for them, they were drawn up in a lane at a distance of thirty yards from the crowd. Captain Cook continued to press the Chief to come on board with him, but the priests would not allow him to move; so, the Captain gave up the task, and was walking towards the boat when news arrived that one of the ship's boats had fired at a canoe across the bay and had killed an important Chief.
>
> Everything was immediately in a ferment; one of the natives came up and threatened Captain Cook with a long iron spike and a stone. As the man would not desist, Captain Cook fired one barrel of small shot which failed to pierce the mat he was wearing. Stones were then thrown at the Marines, and a native tried to stab Lieutenant Phillips with a long iron spike but failed as Lieutenant Phillips hit him a blow with the butt end of his musket.
>
> Captain Cook now fired his second barrel and killed one of the natives. A general attack with stones

---
95   Portsmouth Letter Books - 3rd November 1780.
96   Vol VI.

followed, which was answered by a discharge of musketry from the Marines and the people in the boats. The islanders stood the fire with great firmness, and before the Marines had time to reload broke in on them with dreadful shouts and yells. What followed was a scene of the utmost horror and confusion. Four of the Marines were cut off among the rocks in their retreat; three more were dangerously wounded; Lieutenant Phillips, who had received a stab between the shoulders with an iron spike, having fortunately reserved his fire, shot the man who had wounded him, in time to prevent a second blow. The last time that Captain Cook was seen distinctly, he was standing at the water's edge, calling out to the boats to cease firing and to pull in. As soon as he turned his back he was fallen on and brutally slaughtered by the natives.

Towards the end of 1780 the Admiralty were beginning to get anxious about casualty returns, and also about financial matters, and various returns were called for from the Divisions.

1781

Recruiting difficulties were present in March. Among others, foreigners and prisoners of war were enlisted provided that they were not Frenchmen.

From the letter books it is obvious that the majority of ships were commissioned at Portsmouth, as there are constant orders for drafts of officers and men to be sent from Chatham and Plymouth. The Officers Rosters kept by Divisions instead of a Corps Roster gave constant trouble.

Dogger Bank.
As usual, the prolonged hostilities led to difficulties with neutrals as regards contraband etc, and in consequence war was declared with the Dutch which led to a fierce fight on the Dogger Bank on 5th August 1781 between the British under Hyde Parker with six battleships and ten cruisers, and the Dutch six battleships and nine cruisers which lasted for forty-eight hours. The British lost 104 killed and 339 wounded, among which Captain Campbell and Lieutenant Stewart (*Berwick*) were wounded. The Dutch had 142 killed and 403 wounded.

In the West Indies, Admiral Rodney - with General Vaughan in command of the troops - sailed for St Eustatius Island, from which the Dutch had been carrying on a lucrative trade supplying the Americans and the French. They sighted the island on 3rd February 1781 and occupied it at once, which caused great anger and distress to the Americans. Demerara, Essequibo and the Dutch Settlements on the Spanish Main also fell into British hands.

In April 1781 a large fleet under Admiral Darby (20 battleships, 7 frigates) relieved the garrison at Gibraltar, throwing in supplies and reinforcements.

On 11th May 1781 Fort George in East Florida capitulated to the Spaniards; among the garrison fit for duty were 1 Sergeant and 11 Marines.

As a French Fleet was reported approaching the West Indies in February 1781, Admiral Hood was sent towards Martinique to cruise to windward and intercept them. As a matter of fact, Admiral De Grasse with 26 battleships only sailed from Brest on 22nd March; after detaching Admiral Suffren with 6 ships to the East Indies whom we shall meet later, he went on with 20 battleships to Martinique. The fleets sighted each other on 28th April, the French with 24 battleships to Hood's 17. A long range motion began on the 29th Hood held his own, British loss being 38 killed and 181 wounded among whom was the Lieutenant of Marines of the *Centaur*. De Grasse hauled off and went to St Lucia, where he landed 12,000 troops in May; the Pigeon Island Batteries kept them off and the French abandoned the attempt. They then turned to Tobago; Rodney had sent six ships to help in the defence but meeting De Grasse they withdrew to Barbados. Rodney then sailed himself for Tobago with all his fleet but arrived too late as the island had capitulated on 2nd June. Rodney then withdrew to Barbados and De Grasse to Martinique, whence he sailed on 5th July for the continent of North America.

Meanwhile Lord Cornwallis had decided to abandon his campaign in the Carolinas and to work his way up to General Clinton at New York. It was realised that his troops would require supplies and the only method of supply was by sea to Cape Fear in North Carolina and then up the Cape Fear River. HMS *Blonde* with *Delft* and *Otter* sloops and some gunboats were sent with 300 of the 82nd Regiment from Charlestown on 21st January 1781 and arrived in the river on the 25th, landing on the 26th, Lieutenant Griffiths (*Blonde*) and 81 Marines were landed with the troops. The gallies and gunboats pushed up the river in line with them and in the afternoon the town of Wilmington surrendered and the guns of the batteries defending the river were spiked. They captured some ships and stores and placed the town in the best state of defence that they could. Lord Cornwallis arrived on 5th April and was very pleased to find the arrangements made for him. From there he marched to join Major General Phillips at Petersburgh in Virginia where he arrived on 20th May.

On 18th May Admiral Arbuthnot had fought an indecisive action with the French off the Chesapeake River and had retired.

Lord Cornwallis was now ordered to occupy a defensive position which would cover an anchorage for ships of the line and to strengthen it; in other words, to provide a sort of advanced base. He chose Gloucester and Yorktown on the peninsula between the James and York Rivers. He had 7,000 troops, with 1,000 seamen and Marines landed from the ships; the batteries were largely armed with ships' guns. These waters inside Hampton Roads have become well known to Marines of later dates.

De Grasse arrived off Cape Henry at the entrance to Hampton Roads on 30th August; Graves sailed from New York on 31st for the same place. The French General Lafayette was investing Yorktown; De Grasse sent him 3,300 men and General Washington also came south and reinforced him with 6,000 Americans whilst the French cruisers were stationed in the James River to prevent Cornwallis crossing over into the Carolinas.

On 5th September 1781 Graves and De Grasse met, the British with 19 ships and the French with 24, which were also greatly superior in gun power. The action commenced on 5th September and fighting continued till dark; the next day was spent in repairing damages. On the 7th the French got the wind and approached; the next day the 8th the wind favoured the British, but their line was badly formed and had to surrender the weather gage; manoeuvring went on throughout the 8th and 9th but the British as usual had suffered in sails and rigging and in the night of 9th/10th the English disappeared to the northward. The British losses were 90 killed and 246 wounded. Graves returned to New York and abandoned Cornwallis to his fate. The British lost the command of the sea and the fate of the British campaign was sealed.

Yorktown was strongly entrenched, and the British were holding the outer works successfully, but Cornwallis withdrew into the works round Yorktown on 29th September. The enemy - French and Americans - broke ground on 30th September and the batteries were opened on 9th October; they also fired at the redoubt where the Marines were posted. About 120 men of the Marines and the 23rd Regiment were defending with great gallantry a redoubt on the right of the British lines which had been advanced over a creek. The French attacked the picquets in a wood in front of the redoubt, but they retired into the redoubt and the enemy did not venture to continue the attack. This party under Captain Apthorpe later reinforced by detachments under Lieutenant Colonel Johnstone received the thanks of Lord Cornwallis [97] at the close of the operations.

On 14th October the enemy carried two advanced redoubts on the left and on the 18th the lines were in such a ruined state that Cornwallis ordered a sortie, which was successful and spiked some guns, but it could not affect the general result.

On 19th October Cornwallis capitulated with 7,247 troops and 640 seamen and Marines; this practically concluded the campaign on land. Admiral Graves withdrew to Jamaica, Admiral Hood to Barbados. De Grasse remained in command on the coast of North America until 5th November when he went to the West Indies.

Kempenfeldt's Action.
In Europe a French Fleet of 21 battleships and 8 cruisers under Admiral De Guichen were met off Brest by a British squadron of 13 battleships and 4 cruisers under Rear Admiral Kempenfeldt and forced to return to port; whilst Kempenfeldt secured 19 prizes and sank two or three transports.

Minorca.
Minorca was besieged by the Spaniards and the French from 19th August 1781 to 4th February 1782. The enemy did not make the mistake of landing at Ciudadella but landed near Mahon; the British garrison had withdrawn into the Castle of St Phillip. Among the troops was a 'Marine Brigade' of about 400, but it is not clear if all these were of the Corps; it is probable that they were mostly seamen; for during the great contemporary siege of Gibraltar a Marine Brigade under Brigadier Curtis is often mentioned, but these were seamen under Captain Curtis RN.

---

97 Marines.

When Admiral Darby relieved Gibraltar he also threw supplies into Port Mahon. The garrison made a brave defence against large forces of the enemy but were eventually so reduced by sickness and scurvy that the Governor capitulated on 4th February 1782. Beatson says that of the Marine Corps, Lieutenants Davis and Drew were killed with 37 rank and file, and Captain Harman and Lieutenant Hodges wounded with 134 rank and file.

By Order-in-Council 27th June 1781 the Corps was increased by two men per company, a total of 292 men, and again by Order-in-Council 16th November 1781 five more companies were added (1 to Chatham, 2 each to Portsmouth and Plymouth), giving a total of 21,497. There were also a considerable number of Line Regiments embarked as well as Marines.

On 20th August 1781 HM the King reviewed the troops at Chatham and held a levee at which the sea and Marine Officers were presented to him.

1782

Field Officers.
On 19th January 1782 the Admiralty ordered three Field Officers to proceed to the West Indies to serve in the squadron under Sir George Rodney, in order to take command of such bodies of Marines as it may be necessary to land; these were Lieutenant Colonel Tupper and Major Rotheram from Portsmouth with Major Rycaut from Plymouth; they were to embark in the *Duke* or other ship and report to Admiral Rodney and follow his orders. But the course of operations does not appear to have given them any opportunity of landing operations.

St Kitts.
De Grasse with the French Fleet and troops intended to make an attack on Barbados but hearing of the arrival of Admiral Hood with a squadron from America he attacked St Kitts instead. On his landing troops the British garrison retired to Brimstone Hill where they were invested. Hood hearing of this embarked some troops under General Prescott at Antigua and sailed to relieve St Kitts. De Grasse was covering his attack with his fleet; Hood enticed him out to sea and then slipped into the roadstead and anchored; there was a fierce naval engagement, but the French were driven off on 25th January. The French attacked again on the 28th but were again repulsed.

The garrison considered that they were safe and though the Admiral offered to land General Prescott with the 28th Regiment and two companies of the 13th, and also to land two battalions of Marines of 700 each together with the 69th Regiment serving as Marines (altogether about 2,400 men) General Prescott did not think they could maintain their post. Prescott, who was anxious to be disembarked with the Antigua troops and the 69th - they were landed on 28th January - engaged the troops the French CO had left in the town of Basse Terre and compelled them to retreat. On the 29th the French GOC brought up 400 men against him. By this time, however, Prescott was too strongly posted, and the French returned to the investment of Brimstone Hill. Under these conditions Prescott could not save the island and his troops were re-embarked that evening and returned to Antigua. The garrison eventually capitulated on 13th February, and the French then prepared to mount guns to attack the British Fleet, so on the night of 14th February Hood cut his cables and slipped away by the north end of the island and the French found the roadstead empty the next morning.

Hood joined Rodney on 25th February with twelve battleships; De Grasse retired to Martinique and Rodney to St Lucia; the French convoy reaching Martinique on 20th March.

The stage was now set for one of the greatest sea victories in the annals of England, when Rodney introduced his great tactical move of breaking the Line.

The Battle of the Saintes.
On 8th April De Grasse put to sea from Martinique with 35 battleships with the object of capturing Jamaica. Rodney left St Lucia with 59 battleships. On the 9th there was a partial action, but there was no hope of bringing the French to full action until the 11th. At 7 am on 12th April 1782 the famous battle began, which resulted in a great victory for Rodney and the capture of De Grasse. As a result of the action the *Ville de Paris*, the flagship, (110 guns) was captured as well as the *Glorieux, Caesar, Hector,* and *Ardent*. Four more battleships struggled into Curacoa but were not allowed to stay there by the Dutch and went on to Cape Francois in Hispaniola. These were caught by Hood in the Mona Passage who captured the *Jasen* and *Caton* battleships and two frigates. In the ships captured was the siege train intended for the attack on Jamaica; the *Diademe* was also sunk and the French Fleet ceased to exist as such; several of the prizes were incorporated in the British Fleet and others were sunk in gales on the way home. The French lost 539 killed and 2,500 wounded; the British casualties were 240 killed and 797 wounded; of the Marines, Lieutenant Mournier (*Torbay*) was killed, the Captains of Marines of *Royal Oak, Repulse,* and Lieutenant Bagg (*Magnificent*) and Lieutenant Laban (*Princessa*) were wounded. Lieutenants Bell and Bagg were mentioned in despatches.

For this action the 69th Regiment serving as Marines[98] were awarded the Naval Crown with the date 12th April 1782. This practically ended the fighting in the West Indies and in North America.

"In July 1782 each company was increased from 120 to 140 Privates, and by Order-in-Council 19th July 1782 six more companies - two to each Division - were added to the Corps, making 157 with 181 to each company, totalling 25,290.

In August 1782 as a result of the experiences in America we get the first orders modifying drill and formations. [99]

The Order of the troops in future to be two-deep.

---
98 Now the 2/Welch Regiment. (Editor's Note. Today a part of the Royal Welsh Regiment.)
99 Plymouth Orders 19th August.

Slow March 75 paces per minute.

Quick March 120 steps per minute.

Parade movements to be as short and simple as possible.

After every war we see the order to improve drill and training.

Gibraltar Relief.
On 11th September Lord Howe with a large fleet convoying a large convoy of supplies and with the 25th and 59th Regiments left Spithead to relieve Gibraltar, which was successfully accomplished during the next month, a sharp action taking place off Cape Spartel on 21st October with the French and Spanish Fleets (68 killed 207 wounded). He reached England on 14th November having detached a squadron of eight ships to the West Indies.

On 22nd November 1782 peace with the Americans was signed in Paris and the preliminary Articles of Peace with France and Spain were initialled on 20th January 1783.

1783

111,000 seamen including 25,290 Marines were voted for 1783.

East Indies.
It is now necessary to turn to the East Indies, where the Corps was also bearing its part and we must go back a short time. By the Treaty of Paris - after the Seven Years War - Pondicherry, Chandernagore and Mahe had been restored to the French. Another enemy of the East India Company had arisen in the person of Hyder Ali, Sultan of Mysore. This potentate was more or less in league with the French on the Malabar Coast as he wanted to make Mahe his source of supply and therefore helped the French to defend it. It was however captured by the British.

When the French joined the Americans and the news reached India, war was declared on 7th August 1778. The Governor General, Warren Hastings, was ready with his plans and an attack on Pondicherry was ordered. Commodore Sir Edward Vernon was in command of the station with one battleship and four small cruisers, and as command of the sea was necessary for the attack, the Commodore attacked the French Fleet on 10th August. The result was indecisive, for the fleets were about equal. The French withdrew to Pondicherry, but soon after left for Mauritius. The army under Sir Hector Munro had advanced by land, arriving before Pondicherry on 8th August and they at once laid siege to the town.

The city made a fine defence, but after two months very exhausting work the way was prepared for a general assault on 17th October. There were three points of attack! (a) L'Hopital Bastion on the south (b) the east face of the South West Bastion, and (c) from the sea on the north side. Two hundred seamen and all the Marines of the squadron were landed on 15th October to join in the storm on the 17th. The French Governor however proposed terms of surrender and the place capitulated on 18th October.

As we have seen, Admiral Sir Edward Hughes' squadron had commissioned in January 1779 and left England on 7th March, but during 1779 and 1780 he was unopposed at sea by the French who remained at Mauritius. The British however were waging a desperate war with Hyder Ali and the Mahrattes and *"all depended on the command of the sea."*

In 1780 Hyder Ali with 90,000 troops advanced in the Carnatic on to Madras. The British troops were much scattered, Colonel Baillie was at Gumtee with 2,500, Braithwaite at Pondicherry with 1,500, Crosby with 2,000 at Trichinopoly. Whilst trying to concentrate, Baillie and his force were destroyed and before the menace of Hyder Ali, Munro retreated from Conjeveram and the Carnatic was overrun.

On 17th October 1780 Sir Edward Hughes left Madras to go to the Malabar Coast to Tillicherry, which was being invested by some of Hyder Ali's troops and the Nairs, and then on to Bombay to clean his ships. Arriving at Tillicherry on 27th November he left a Captain of Marines with 4 Officers and 108 Rank and File with 100 barrels of gunpowder to reinforce the defenders; he sailed again on 5th December and on the 8th being off Mangalore he saw some of Ali's ships. Immediately he sent in the boats, manned and armed, and destroyed several.

On the Coromandel Coast, reinforcements marched from Bengal and Colonel Sir Eyre Coote was sent to take charge; owing to defective equipment he had to remain quiescent for two months, but then with 7,400 men he marched south to relieve the beleaguered garrisons by drawing Hyder Ali after him. Hyder abandoned his sieges and made after Coote, though Pondicherry had revolted in his favour. On 27th November 1780 Coote gained a great victory at Porto Novo, three miles north west of Cuddalore.

In January 1781 the French squadron appeared off the Coromandel Coast, but would not co-operate with Hyder Ali.

As related before war had now been declared with the Dutch, and a British Squadron under Commodore Johnstone with a considerable body of troops were sent to capture the Cape of Good Hope. They accompanied Admiral Darby's Fleet which effected the relief of Gibraltar and were then detached for their mission. When at Porto Praya on 16th April 1781 they were surprised and attacked by Admiral Suffren, who had been detached from De Grasse's Fleet on its way to the West Indies. Johnson beat off Suffren but allowed him to escape so that Suffren reached the Cape first, and landed his troops which secured the Colony. Johnstone went to Saldanha Bay, where after capturing five Dutch East Indiamen and sending on the *Hero, Monmouth and Iris* to India to join Hughes he returned home, whilst Suffren continued on to India to prove himself such a doughty opponent.

Negapatam.
Sir Eyre Coote and the Government were determined to attack the Dutch settlement of Negapatam, which Hyder Ali had agreed to protect. Hyder had also agreed to cede Nagore to the Dutch.

Sir Henry Munro's force was composed of Braithwaite's troops from Tanjore and 4,000 seamen and Marines drawn from Hughes Fleet. Hyder had placed a strong garrison in the fort and had occupied many other strong places in the province. The expedition arrived at Nagore on 21st October 1781; the East India Company's troops and 443 Marines landed that day and a battalion of 827 seamen on the 22nd. The lateness of the season and the shift of the monsoon necessitated promptness; guns were conveyed ashore on rafts through the surf by Captain Ball RN, and the force proceeded south to Negapatam at once. The town was defended by five redoubts on the north side flanking strong lines; these were carried by storm on 29th October and the siege was opened. The seamen and marines rendered good service in constructing the batteries. The Dutch attempted two sorties which were repulsed and after nine days of well-directed fire (3rd – 12th November) the Dutch proposed terms which were accepted and the place surrendered.

The Dutch troops were sent to Batavia or Colombo. The numbers of the besieged were 8,000 and of the attackers only 4,000. The breaking of the monsoon prevented the re-embarkation of the Naval Brigade until 25th November and delayed further operations.

Hyder Ali also evacuated Tanjore and all the ports. The Marine casualties were 13 killed and 29 wounded of whom most died, but we read: *"Downfall of Negapatam is ascribed, no doubt with justice to the extraordinary gallantry of the seamen and Marines of the fleet, yet no small credit must belong to Munro."* [100]

The capture of Negapatam not only deprived the French of large supplies of stores etc, but also of the place which had been designed as the principal depôt for the troops expected from France.[101]

1782

Trincomali.
Continuing the attack on the Dutch, Sir E. Hughes proceeded to Trincomali in Ceylon, where a small fort of ten guns commanded the only place where troops could land their stores. As soon as he arrived on 4th January 1782 he landed first the Marines and two field pieces with a detachment of Artillery and two companies of Sepoy Pioneers about three miles from the Port. These were followed by the second flight of seamen, whilst the third flight were Sepoys. The covering force of Marines marched on the Fort and next day Lieutenant Orr with the Marine Grenadier Company rushed through the gateway (and took prisoners 3 officers and 40 men) as it commanded the only place where provisions and supplies could be landed.

---
100 Fortescue.
101 Cf Walfisch Bay 1914.

The enemy now retreated to Fort Ostenberg, which was on top of the hill commanding the harbour; the 7th was occupied in reconnoitring the approaches; on the 8th the troops marched to a high hill where there was an officer's guard, which was captured by a detachment of seamen and Marines that night.[102]

A general assault was planned and executed on the 11th by 450 seamen and Marines in column, the flanks covered by the sepoy pioneers and followed by seamen with scaling ladders. They were supported by a reserve column of three companies of seamen and three companies of Marines supported by field pieces with native parties in rear.

A Sergeant's party of Marines got into the embrasures unperceived and were promptly reinforced. The Dutch were driven from the works and the fort was gained, and with the ships in the harbour, fell into British hands. Throughout the fighting had been very severe and the losses were Lieutenant Long and twenty seamen and Marines killed, Lieutenant Wolseley RN, and Lieutenant Orr, Marines (acting Brigade Major) and forty seamen and Marines wounded. As Fortescue says, on 11th January 1782 *"the finest harbour on the eastern coast of the East Indies"* fell into British hands. Admiral Hughes in his despatch says, *"the whole of the officers who have been landed from the squadron for the attack on Negapatam and Trincomali have on all occasions manifested much honour, courage and good conduct, and the private seamen and Marines have acted with great steadiness and bravery."* And we see the value of a Marine Striking Force at the disposal of the Admiral of a squadron.

But now began the series of naval actions that jeopardised the British power in the East Indies. On 9th February 1782 the French Admiral died and Admiral Suffren assumed command of the French Fleet. On 15th February the French Fleet - four 74s, six 84s, and two 50s, with 3,500 troops on board - sighted Admiral Hughes with his flag in the *Superb* - two 74s, one 68, five 84s, and one 50 - off Madras. Hughes captured six transports, but the action on the 17th was indecisive; the British lost 32 killed, 83 wounded.

Admiral Hughes then went to Madras and leaving there on 12th March was joined by the *Sultan* (74), and *Magnanime* (84). Suffren having landed his troops to assist in the siege of Cuddalore, then held by the British, sailed on 22nd March.

On 9th April the fleets sighted each other and there was another fierce and desperate engagement without any decisive results: the British lost 137 killed and 430 wounded, the French 137 killed and 357 wounded. Among the killed were the Lieutenants of Marines of the *Burford* and *Monmouth*. When the almost impossibility of replacing personnel is considered, the seriousness of these casualties is realised; the ships themselves were quickly repaired.

The fleets remained at anchor within two miles of each other repairing damages, and then

---

102 "The Marines always in front" - Gillespie.

Suffren went south to flank the British convoys and protect his own. On 22nd April Hughes got into Trincomali, where he remained until 23rd June when he sailed for Negapatam. Suffren was at Cuddalore which had surrendered to Hyder Ali on 4th April.

On 5th July Hughes' squadron again sighted the French and stood towards them, and on 6th July began the sea battle of Negapatam - eleven ships on each side and called the 'Third Action'.

The fight began at 11 am and lasted until 6 pm with great fury, when the British, damaged as usual in spars and rigging, anchored near Negapatam and the French ten miles to the north. The British lost 77 killed 223 wounded, the French 178 killed and 601 wounded. Of the Marines Captain Adlam (*Magnanime*), Lieutenant R Williams (*Sultan*), Lieutenant Johnstone (*Worcester*) were wounded. From the casualty lists detachments of the 98th Regiment were serving as Marines on board as they had an officer killed and several NCOs and men killed and wounded.

On 7th July Suffren left Cuddalore going south, and on the 21st he picked up his reinforcements; on the 25th he was off Trincomali and invested that place which capitulated on 30th August 1782.

Hughes did not leave Madras until 20th August and arrived off Trincomali on 2nd September, by which time Suffren had re-embarked his troops and guns. On 3rd September took place the 'Fourth Action' off Trincomali. The fleets were fairly matched and the British lost 51 killed and 283 wounded. Of the Marines, Captain R Clogstone and Lieutenant Barrel, (*Monarca*) Lieutenant Edwards (*Worcester*) were killed, and Lieutenant Orr (*Superb*) wounded, whilst an officer of the 98th in the *Superb* and one of the 78th in the *Monarca* were wounded as well as NCOs and men of both the 78th and 98th Regiments.

The British Fleet was well handled, and the French got into disorder. Fighting continued until dark and because his fleet was damaged, and the change of the monsoon Admiral Hughes sailed for Madras, where he arrived 9th September. Suffren withdrew into Trincomali.

Hughes then sailed for Bombay where he was joined by Sir T Bickerton with five more ships. Suffren went to Achen for the winter and returned to Trincomali on 10th March 1783, receiving a reinforcement of three battleships and 2500 troops; the latter were sent at once to Cuddalore. On 7th December 1782 Hyder Ali had died and was succeeded by Tippoo Sahib.

On 10th April 1783 Hughes passed Trincomali on his way to Madras with 18 ships to Suffren's 15. In June Cuddalore was invested, Hughes fleet covering the besiegers to the south west. On 13th June the French sighted the British off Porto Novo. From 17th to 20th the fleets were manoeuvring, but Suffren threw 1,200 more troops into Cuddalore and it was evident that the result of the siege would depend on the command of the sea.

On 20th June Hughes decided to accept the action that Suffren was offering and the engagement lasted from 4 pm to 7 pm. The British were again crippled by loss of spars. Suffren remained off

Cuddalore and on the 23rd Hughes went to Madras because he was short of water and had large numbers down with scurvy. It was a French victory and decided the fate of Cuddalore, but as it was fought five months after peace had been signed on 20th January 1783 it did not affect the results of the war. The British lost 99 killed and 431 wounded, the French 102 killed, 2,386 wounded. No Marine officers figured in the casualty lists.

By the various treaties signed in Paris on 2nd and 3rd September 1783:

Great Britain recognised the 15 states of America; the boundaries of Nova Scotia and Canada were fixed, and the navigation of the Mississipi was to remain open.

Great Britain gave up to Spain - Minorca, East Florida, and West Florida, but retained the right of cutting logwood for dyeing in what is now British Honduras. Spain restored Providence and the Bahama Islands.

In the Treaty with France, Great Britain retained Newfoundland and islands except St Pierre and Miquelon, and an agreement was come to about fishing rights.

Great Britain restored St Lucia and Tobago; France restored Grenada and the Grenadines, St Vincent, Dominica, St Christopher, Nevis and Montserrat. In West Africa, Great Britain ceded the River Senegal and Forts Louis, Poder and Goree and others, but received Fort James and the Gambia River.

In the East Indies, Great Britain gave up Pondicherry, Carical, Mahe and the factory at Surat and all settlements in Orissa and Bengal. Great Britain also gave up all rights to the claim that Dunkirk should not be fortified.

5 - Peace 1783 - 1792

Peace was no sooner signed than demobilisation became the order of the day. The first intimation came from the Admiralty on 10th February 1783 in the following Order:

To Commanding Officers

"Whereas it is probable a reduction will soon take place in the Marine Forces; you are directed and ordered, as any parties of Marines are landed from ships at the several ports, to discharge such as belong to your division on their arrival at Headquarters, as shall appear to you from their age, size or any other consideration unfit to be continued in the Marine service; taking care that they are (a) accounted with for their sea pay, arrears and other just pretensions (b) furnishing them with passes and (c) paying them the usual bounty of twenty-one days' pay each to carry them to their homes."

This last provision led to trouble with the Commander-in-Chief at Portsmouth, who because the Irishmen had received this money refused to give them free passages to Ireland; he was promptly sat on by the Admiralty.

On 26th February the Senior Naval Officer was ordered to discharge to Headquarters all Marine Officers from ships under orders for foreign service whose commissions bore date subsequent to:

Captains	1st January 1780
First Lieutenants	1st January 1781
Second Lieutenants	1st August 1780

Others of like rank, whose commissions bore date prior to those dates, to be embarked in lieu, so that again the juniors were placed on half pay.

The paying off of ships in large numbers had serious consequences. First, we get a complaint on 25th February 1783 *"as crowding more Marines together in quarters than can properly be provided for must be inconvenient to the publicans and unhealthy for the men."* We must remember that at Portsmouth the Clarence Barracks were small and never held all the men; at Chatham the barracks were open but small, whilst at Plymouth, Stonehouse Barracks were not yet occupied. The Commanding Officer at Portsmouth was directed, whenever numbers were more than could be provided for in barracks, to quarter them at The Common Gosport, Southampton or Chichester as most convenient, and the necessary billeting orders were sent to him.

Apparently riots broke out among the paid-off seamen and at Portsmouth and Plymouth, and many ships - as well as several regiments - mutinied.

On 21st March 1783 their Lordships informed the Commandant at Portsmouth. It gives them *"very great satisfaction to hear of the obedient and soldier like behaviour of the Officers and Marines of the Portsmouth Division which you have represented, and they desire you will cause it to be given out in Public Orders."*

Beatson [103] gives the following account of the Riots in March 1783.

"In all the mutinous and disorderly proceedings at Portsmouth none of the Marines joined in that disgraceful affair; on the contrary they conducted themselves in so becoming a manner (when both navy and army shook off all discipline) that they were employed in keeping the peace and guarding the town; for which their Officers were particularly thanked by Lord George Lenox who commanded. The Commanding Officer, having acquainted the Lords Commissioners of the Admiralty with this, received instructions to assure his men that their Lordships highly approved their conduct."

Matters were composed by Lord Howe, the First Sea Lord, going to Portsmouth and interviewing the men. Gillespie in his History of the Royal Marines written just after the Great Mutinies of 1797 and 1800 says of this period: "To the spirit of compromise then pursued may be traced in part that predilection for revolt which addled the minds of our seamen during the late contest."[104]

"Demonstrations of loyalty and zeal in every Marine Detachment still evinced a readiness to seal with their lives in the support of good order.........Fatal means, which were used to appease the spirit, hushed the murmurs indeed, but invigorated the growth of the untamed monster."[105]

On 22nd March the civil magistrates again called on the Commandant at Portsmouth *"to suppress some outrages threatened to be committed by a disorderly body of seamen who are assembled on Portsmouth Common."* The Commandant, in reporting to the Admiralty, says that *"though the trouble had subsided without his interference yet it might be renewed,"* and *"as the Marines were quartered in houses which rendered them liable to intoxication and other debauchery,"* he had obtained permission from the GOC to quarter the surplus Marines in Hilsea Barracks, especially as the Marines were also finding a lot of garrison guards in the lines. The Admiralty highly approved but put in the usual tag: *"parties will shortly be required for ships fitting out, and that therefore it may be attended with inconvenience to employ them on other services."*

Hilsea Barracks were often used by the Marines, as we shall see.

In April the complements for different classes of ships were laid down:

---

103 Naval and Military Memoirs.
104 i.e. 1792-1802.
105 Cf. proceedings in 1918-19 and again in 1930.

Guardships 17 April, 1783[106]

Guns	Captains	Subs	Sergts	Cpls	Drmrs	Ptes
90 1	2	2	2	1	45	
74 1	1	2	2	1	40	
64 1	1	2	2	1	35	
Frigates	-	-	1	1	-	12 for 'Centinels'

Sea-going Ships, 9th April, 1783

60 or 50	1	1	2	2	1	50
44 1	1	2	2	1	40	
36 1	1	1	1	1	35	
32 -	2	1	1	1	30	
28 -	1	1	1	1	25	
24 or 20	-	1	1	1	1	20
Large Sloop	-	1	1	1	1	16

Dockyard Guard.

In June a Captain's Guard was ordered to be mounted in the Dockyards in the same manner and under the same regulations *"as were practised in the last peace."* This was followed by a Board order on 24th December 1783 for Marine guards *"to do duty in the Dockyards of Portsmouth, Plymouth and Chatham in like manner and under the same regulations as were practised in the former peace. Same may greatly contribute to safety of HM Magazines and Stores as well as to the safety of the Ships in the said Yards. Guards to be of same strength as in former peace. The Guard Houses and Watch Houses now occupied by Officers and Watchmen to be given up to the Marines and such alterations and additions to be made as shall be necessary for their accommodation and convenience."*

On 31st July 1783 the Order-in-Council and Admiralty Orders for the Reorganisation of the Marines on a peace basis were issued and took effect from 1st September, when the Officers received new Commissions dated 31st August 1783.

Order-in-Council 2nd July 1783

The greatest part of Your Majesty's Fleet, which was in commission at the time the Preliminary Articles of Peace were signed, being paid off, a considerable number of your Marine Forces have been discharged, and "it being still necessary that many others should also be discharged to reduce the said Forces to a number proportionable to the numbers of seamen, that will probably be employed in time of peace, which will require an establishment different from that which is now In force." *Following Establishment is proposed:*

1.) That they be divided into 70 companies each of 1 Captain, 2 First Lieutenants,

---

106 Evidently nucleus crews.

1 Second Lieutenant, 3 Sergeants, 3 Corporals, 2 Drummers, 52 Private Men = 64.

69 more companies = 4,416.   Total 4,480[107]

2.) For their proper and regular management 1 General, 1 Lieutenant General, 3 Colonels , 4 Colonels[108] *Commandant - one of whom to reside constantly in London to attend the Board of Admiralty in the nature of Adjutant General.*[109]

> *6 Lieutenant Colonels*
> *6 Majors*
> *6 Adjutants*
> *3 Quartermasters = Total 30.*

3.) The three Colonels Commandant at Headquarters of each Division, the Lieutenant Colonels and Majors to be allowed one of the Companies, with a Captain Lieutenant instead of one of the First Lieutenants as is now the practice, which will make the whole amount to 4,510.

This was not quite correct as under this arrangement, there could only have been 55 Captains, but it is noticed that the three Deputy Paymasters and the Squad Officers are omitted.

The Commandants' Companies were Nos. 1, 2 and 3.

Lieutenant Colonels.' Companies
>   at Chatham, 4 and 7
>   at Portsmouth, 5 and 8
>   at Plymouth, 6 and 9

Majors' Companies
>   at Chatham, 10 and 13
>   at Portsmouth, 11 and 14
>   at Plymouth, 12 and 15

4.) As a considerable number of the present Marine Officers will be reduced, we propose that they may be allowed Half-Pay whilst unemployed, as has been usual with regard to Officers of the Corps under similar circumstances.

5.) The Admiralty ordered the Establishment to take effect from 1st September 1783; the King

---

107 Chatham were allotted 20 Companies, Plymouth and Portsmouth 25 each.
108 These were Naval Officers the General Officers were sinecures, the Colonels seem to have taken some interest in the Divisions.
109 This is the first mention of DAGRM, though we know Colonels Paterson and Dury performed the duties before this.

signed new commissions for those retained on Full Pay; all Officers not named in the lists attached to be informed that they will be allowed Full Pay until 31 August 1783 and afterwards Half-Pay until otherwise provided for; they were also informed that they were at liberty to depart from quarters 'as soon as they think proper.'

Those remaining on the Establishment who had been longest on shore were to be considered first for sea.

30th July 1783.

Signed.   Keppel
Hugh Pigot
J Lindsay

The First Commandant in Town (DAG) was Colonel J Mackenzie from Chatham. He seems to have been a very active and energetic officer and the Letter Books of the next few years bear testimony to his reforming zeal.

Embarkation Muster Roll.
Apparently one of the first subjects taken in hand was the Embarkation Muster Roll, bringing in a new form on 19th December 1783 making it the same for each Division - *"to show debts brought from former ships and prevent mistakes in putting debts in proper columns in Ships' Books."* From later references it must have been much the same as at present.

A new Order came out on 20th February 1784 that Guard (or Harbour) Ships were only to be relieved once a year - on 30th June.

Leave.
In May he stopped the practice of officers applying to the Admiralty for leave; if they wanted it they were to apply to their Commanding Officers.

Stonehouse Barracks.
In December 1783 Plymouth Division took over Stonehouse Barracks. These had apparently been nearly finished in October, because the first guard was mounted on 5th October; the order to take over was given by the Admiralty on 2nd December. Evidently officers' quarters were short, as subalterns had to send in a list of those who wished to live in and those who wanted to lodge out. In 1784 Subaltern Officers were ordered *"to double up in quarters."* Men were forbidden to bring dogs into barracks.[110] Officers' servants were to sleep in the garrets over their masters' apartments.[111] One Barrack-woman was allowed per room. They were to do their washing at the saltwater tank at rear of the barracks and not with fresh water.

---

110   How often has this order been repeated.
111   These can still be seen above the Officer's Mess.

On 6th December the Division was ordered to march at 10 am on Monday morning into Stonehouse Barracks, leaving 6 Sergeants, 6 Corporals and 10 Privates at Plymouth to provide guards for Spur Battery, Infirmary and Millbay Prison. On 7th December, orders read: *"Men to be on parade tomorrow clean, short gaiters. Baggage carts for Officers on Town Parade at 8 am till 10 am Three carts for men's baggage will be on road behind glacis. First troop at 7.30 am, second at 9.30 am"* and on 8th December the barrack guard was to be mounted with 1 Lieutenant, 1 Sergeant, 2 Corporals, 1 Drummer, and 20 Privates.

1784

Reforms went on apace and with far reaching results. On 6th May Plymouth Orders give us the first intimation of the formation of schools: *"School to be opened at Orderly Room tomorrow at 9.0 am for benefit of such children of NCOs and men as may be of proper age to be instructed in reading and writing. Soldiers who desire to qualify for promotion can also attend provided it does not interfere with duties."* Sergeant Jewell is appointed Master; hours 9 am to 12 noon, 2-5 pm. Children who want flogging to be reported to the Adjutant.

Defaulter Sheets.
Defaulter sheets were also introduced on 27th June - a book called "The Black Book" being issued to Captains of Companies.

Adjutants.
On 2nd October the duties of Adjutants were laid down: "The Adjutants to be in two distinct departments, one to superintend the business of the Office, the other the Field." This was amplified on 27th March 1785 as follows;

"The Field Adjutant to attend the Drill and Exercise of NCOs and men; attend all parades and do necessary duties of them. Take Band and Drums and Fifes under his entire care as to dress, interior economy and beating of drummers; executive part of Music of Band to be under Lieutenants Gibson and Gordon, 'who have volunteered and undertaken to make them a Martial Band and capable of softer music.' The Master of the Band is as heretofore to instruct the fifers in Martial Tunes only. The Office Adjutant to keep the books of the Division regularly and make usual reports and returns; attend Commanding Officer on all public service and every contingency in his department. Keep and regulate the roster under directions of the Major of the Division."

This system lasted until 1892.

Dockyard Guards.
But on 28th December 1784 an order of importance was promulgated. That the Admiralty had "decided that the Dockyards were to be guarded in future by Warders, Rounders and Watchmen being Labourers and others belonging to the Yard; with the addition of a Subaltern's Guard of Marines (36 Privates with proportion of NCOs to serve as Patrols within the Dockyard Walls as

directed by the Commissioner."

This of course had the usual result, because it was followed by orders for reduction of numbers. Evidently numbers in excess of Establishment had been retained and we see the first swing of the axe on 28th December 1784.

"It is unnecessary to retain any Marines supernumerary as soon as civilians have taken over, Officers and men now at Headquarters supernumerary are to be discharged, taking care that they are properly accounted for as regards their pay. Those retained to be the stoutest, healthiest and fittest men. None to be discharged who are over five feet six inches in height and under forty years of age."

The vote for numbers in the House in February 1785 showing a reduction, the officers memorialized the Admiralty on 28th February begging that *"No reduction might be made in the Officers, whose length of service with the toils and dangers they have experienced, may be taken into consideration."* The Board replied in the usual terms, meaning nothing. The evil day was staved off until the Order-in-Council of 1st March 1788 when ten companies were reduced together with six Field Officers, viz: three Lieutenant Colonels and three Majors (who are Captains of Companies). Each of the remaining 60 companies was reduced by 1 Sergeant, 1 Corporal, and 2 Privates, leaving 2 Sergeants, 2 Corporals, 2 Drummers and 50 Privates per Company. Five of the companies were reduced from Portsmouth and five from Plymouth. Chatham was reduced to 18 Companies - No 55 being transferred to Portsmouth and No 58 to Plymouth - making them each 21. Chatham were short of men so 1 good Drummer and 90 Privates were to be sent from Portsmouth to Chatham, descriptions and attestations being sent, but the men themselves retained for embarkation.

Men discharged were granted the usual 21 days pay to carry them home. Officers were allowed full pay till 30th April. Besides Field Officers the officers reduced were 4 Captains, 6 Captain Lieutenants, 20 First Lieutenants and 10 Second Lieutenants. There were also a certain amount of moves between Divisions.

On 11th October 1785 Lord Howe and the Board of Admiralty inspected the Plymouth Division, and the Commandant was apparently so pleased with the result that he granted *"1 pint of beer for each man and for the Sergeants some punch."* This good old custom lasted well into the twentieth century.

On 7th May 1785 the Admiralty struck the final blow at the system of the companies providing necessaries and obtaining them locally; it was ordered "that the Marines of the three Divisions shall from and after the 1st July next be supplied with necessaries of the same quality and charged at the same price; the necessaries shall be furnished according to samples that will be lodged at each Division by a contractor in London appointed by the Board. Notice to be given to the person or persons who now supply the Marines of the Divisions with necessaries." The time was extended later to 1st October.

This was the death knell of the Squad Officers, and by Admiralty Order of 1st August 1786, two Sergeants were to be appointed at each Division by the Commandant to be called Squad Sergeants; the Squad Officer *"to close his accounts as soon as possible. The Sergeants to be of proved ability and integrity according to the 15th Article of the Regulations for Marines on Shore established this day. The Sergeants to have an allowance, First Sergeant £30, Second Sergeant £20 per annum in addition to their pay and in lieu of poundage and all other perquisites and emoluments."* It was later ruled that *"Squad Sergeants are to have nothing to do with the disbursement of money further than to check the amount."* And apparently for the first time, the Quartermaster appears to be held officially concerned with the issue of necessaries. The system was evidently not popular at Divisions, who put every obstacle in the way, nor from some letters do the Squad Sergeants appear to have been very satisfactory. From a list of prices to be paid to the contractor we gather some idea of the kit of the Marine of that day.

On 30th June 1785 the bane of many Quartermasters - the 'Quarterly List of Remains' - was established.

About this time a new form for clothing demands was established, and a column was added to show when each Marine's clothing became due, so that evidently the system of annual clothing had been established, the date of the general issue being - as already stated - in June.

On 1st August 1785 the appointment of Hospital Sergeant was established, and on 5th of the same month printed copies of Regulations and Instructions lately established for men serving afloat, and also a copy of Regulations for Marines on Shore, were sent to Divisions. One copy of the Sea Instructions were to be given to each Marine Officer who embarked, the names to be reported.

On 10th April 1786 a copy of Standing Orders for the Divisions was promulgated, which must have been the first issue of the General Standing Orders, RM.

Two Colonels Commandant-en-second had been appointed to the Divisions in 1782, viz - Colonel Collins and Colonel Carruthers.

In February 1786 a Grenadier Company was authorised at each Division and the Board approved of the issue of caps and accoutrements for officers and men. From a Plymouth Order of 7th April 1784, we learn that officers of Grenadier Companies had a button and grenade to turn back the skirts of their coat, and wore a grenade on pouch and belts, the gadgets being fastened with black roses: Battalion Companies had rose and buttons on skirts, Corps pattern pouch ornaments, as did Light Infantry, who had the skirts of the coats curtailed.

From some regulations dated 10th April 1788 as to allowances of fuel and light, we gain some idea of the accommodation in the various barracks. Besides the allowances for Officers, there were offices for the Adjutant, Pay or Squad Office, Quartermaster and Barrack master. In the Infirmary

- kitchen and wash-house, men's wards, sergeant's and matron's room, surgery;[112] mess house, Committee Room when used, music and fifers practice room; schoolroom, armourer's and barbers' shop; wash-house, "taylor's shop;" inhabited rooms, uninhabited rooms, guard rooms (a) officer's, (b) Men's.

Although the reductions in the Corps had been ordered in March, in April orders were issued that the reduction of 1 Sergeant and 1 Corporal per company was to be deferred and this was followed by an Order-in-Council 2nd June 1786 allowing 1 Sergeant and 1 Corporal but reducing 2 Privates per company. This was due to representations from the Commandant at Plymouth on 6th April, which throws an interacting light on the duties of the Division. He forwards a state of the Sergeants:

On board ship	31
Usually on Command after deserters	4
Squad Office	2
Infirmary	1
Quartermaster's Office	1
Adjutants Office	1
Sergeants-Major	1
	42

The new establishment only provides for forty-two, leaving none for guards, recruiting or drilling.

From a correspondence that took place in May 1786 about watch coats, it seems that NCOs and men did not have great coats; but that watch coats, evidently of same shape as today with cape, were issued for use of sentries etc. They seem to have been originally made of blue fearnought, but the Commandant at Portsmouth had had some made of light drab cloth *"such as Artillery use."* He got jumped on for the cost of them, and henceforth they were to be supplied by the contractor at 13/5 each, the sealed pattern being sent to all Divisions *"to be issued to Marines on shore and those who embark and mount guard."* [113]

Although all the Barracks were new, the provision of officers' quarters was very inadequate. At Plymouth subalterns were doubled up and at other Divisions requests to use vacant rooms were refused as they might be wanted for privates.

Botany Bay.
We now come to one of the great episodes in the life of the Corps. In the 18th and early part of the 19th centuries, one of the principal punishments for criminals in England was the sentence of transportation to the Colonies overseas. These men and women had generally been sent to the American Colonies, but after the Peace of 1783, when the USA obtained their independence, this

---
112 Rushlights were allowed for sitting up with patients.
113 3rd May 1786.

was no longer possible, and the Government were at a loss to know where to send them. They first tried the west coast of Africa, but there they all died.

In 1770 Captain Cook had discovered the east coast of Australia, or New Holland as it was called, and had first touched at a place that he named Botany Bay. The Government now turned their attention to this place and decided to send out a first batch of convicts to make a settlement. Practically nothing was known of the place or its suitability. Captain Phillp RN was placed in charge of the expedition which consisted of HMS *Sirius*, a supply ship - the *Supply* - and six transports. It was also decided that the guard should consist of Marines.

The letter from the Admiralty was dated 8th October 1786.

"Lord Sydney having signified to the Lords Commissioners of the Admiralty that a Corps of Marines consisting of 150 Privates with a competent number of Commissioned and Non-Commissioned Officers should be embarked in HM Ships that are to conduct the vessels destined for transporting a considerable number of convicts to Botany Bay in South Wales and to be landed for the protection of the Settlement intended to be made there, as well as for preserving good order and regularity among the convicts.

My Lords intend that they should be formed into four companies. Volunteers to be specially preferred upon this occasion. NCOs and men making voluntary tender will, if they desire it, be allowed their discharge on their return to England, after they have been relieved (which is intended to be done at the expiration of three years) provided their good behaviour in the meantime shall entitle them to such favour,[114] or they will be discharged abroad upon the relief and be permitted to settle in the country if they prefer it. The Marines are to be victualled by a Commissary immediately upon their landing, and provision will be made for supplying them with such tools and utensils and implements as they may have occasion for, while they are employed for the protection of the new Settlement. In the appointment of Commissioned Officers, those on full pay at the different Divisions will have the first option; Commandants will please therefore send a list of names who may tender their services that the requisite appointments may be made; the same offer will be made to officers on Half Pay, if the number of officers on full pay is insufficient."

The Commandant at Plymouth reported on 14th October 1786 that 200 men had volunteered and that he had chosen a fine detachment amongst which were men of all trades.

By 8th November the Admiralty say that they have received so many offers from officers that they do not require any more; and on 24th November an Order-in-Council was issued increasing the Corps by four companies, each consisting of 1 Captain, 2 First Lieutenants, 1 Second Lieutenant, 3 Sergeants, 3 Corporals, 2 Drummers and 48 Privates. Nos 61 and 63 were allotted to Portsmouth and Nos 62 and 64 to Plymouth. Major Ross, the Commanding Officer, came from Plymouth,

---

114 Enlistment was for life – Ed.

as also did Lieutenant Purser, the Adjutant. Captain D. Collins the Judge Advocate came from Chatham and also one company officer - Lieutenant Shairp.

On 23rd November the detachments were ordered to be re-armed with 200 short land musquets with steel rammers (instead of their firelocks) the Sergeants to have 12 Sergeants' Carbines with steel rammers.

The following spare parts were supplied:

Flints in Kegs	(Musquets	10,000
	(Carbines	1,000
Musquet Locknails	(Large	200
	(Small	100
Musquet Nails	(Side	100
	(Breech	100
Thumb pieces		100
Swivel pairs		24
Loops		24

In spite of these elaborate orders no ammunition appears to have been supplied. Major Ross borrowed what he could from the Portsmouth Division whilst at Spithead, but they had to get bullets at Rio de Janeiro on their way out.

On 2nd January 1787 Major Ross requested the Commandant at Plymouth that the Detachment for Botany Bay might be supplied with one of the *"Setts of Colours"* now at Plymouth Headquarters. [115] The Board approved and ordered the CO to supply the same *"if they can be spared"*. [116]

The NCOs and men were also issued with two cotton check shirts and two years "Light Clothing" - at their own expense, be it noted.

The ships were in a disgraceful condition, and Captain Philip had a hard fight with the Admiralty to get even necessaries; but in the end they were badly found, though elaborate precautions were made for railing off the spaces occupied by the convicts.

On 3rd January 1787, ten wives per company were allowed to accompany the draft, for which the King's permission had to be obtained.

In addition to the guards in the transports the following embarked in HMS *Sirius* (flagship) which also carried the RM HQ: 2nd Lieutenant Dawes (afterwards the Engineer Officer of the Colony and whose name is now famous in Dawes Point, Sydney), 1 Sergeant, 1 Corporal, 1

---
115 See Appendix I.
116 It appears as if one of these setts was the pair carried at Belleisle: did they go to Australia?

Drummer and 18 Privates. In the *Supply* (Store ship): 1 Sergeant, 1 Corporal, 10 Privates. [117]

The convicts were evidently being collected during the next two or three months; detachments being sent for escort to Woolwich etc.

On 7th March 1787 Plymouth Orders state:

"*Captain Lieutenant Meredith, 2nd Lieutenants Clark and Kay, 2 Sergeants, 3 Corporals, 1 Drummer and 36 Privates to embark in Friendship. Captain Lieutenant W Tench, 1st Lieutenants Cresswell and Poulden, 3 Sergeants, 3 Corporals, 1 Drummer and 34 Privates in Charlotte.*"

On 8th March *"Detachment for Botany Bay to embark at 10 am tomorrow."* We can imagine these parties being solemnly mustered by the Sergeant Major and after inspection marching off with their powdered hair and stiff clothing into the unknown. There was practically no information as to the place they were going to.

The Portsmouth Letters of 2nd March 1787 say that the ships are at the Motherbank and are to be completed when Captain Philip or Captain Hunter (Sirius) desire it as follows:

Alexander	Lts J Johnstone and A Shairp, 2 Sgts, 2 Cpls, 1 Drummer and 30 Ptes.
Prince of Wales	Lts Davey and Timmins, 2 Sergts., 1 Drummer and 25 Ptes
Lady Penrhyn	Capt Campbell, Lts G Johnstone and W Collins. 2 Sgts, 2 Cpls, 1 Drummer and 3 Ptes.

Those for the *Scarborough* - Capt Shea, Lts Kellow and Morrison, 2 Sgts, 2 Cpls, 1 Drummer, 20 Ptes - had embarked on 24th February to receive their convicts who had marched from Woolwich.

Apparently they were hanging about Spithead for a long time, but eventually sailed on 13th May 1787, arriving at Botany Bay on 19th and 20th January 1788, just in time to forestall the French expedition under La Perouse that arrived five days afterwards.

Botany Bay was found to be impossible. Captain Philip, exploring in a boat, found the Sydney Heads and passing in founded the Settlement in a cove which he named Sydney after the First Lord of the Admiralty, which is now the site of the wonderful city of that name.

It is impossible to follow all the happenings, but the detachments had a very hard time; food ran short and in 1789 they paraded barefoot for guard because the relief ships did not arrive. To ease the pressure a detachment was sent off under Major Ross to Norfolk Island which was more fertile; and a detachment went up the harbour to what is now Paramatta to grow vegetables.

---

117 The CO at Portsmouth reported that he had no more men for embarkation.

Those who wish to read a full account of their doings should study the account written by Captain Tench[118] and the large book by Colonel Collins.[119]

On 22nd May 1789 Divisions were informed by the Admiralty that a new Corps was being raised and sent to New South Wales in the ensuing fall to relieve the Marines. On 18th December 1791 Major Ross and the bulk of the Marines sailed for home; but Captain Johnstone and 83 men transferred to the New South Wales Corps that relieved them. Captain Collins became Chief Justice and remained out there until 1796.

Barracks.
During 1787 the Letter Books contain some interesting details of the barracks. For instance, a letter of 16th November 1786 says that the Marine Barracks at the several Divisions were to be supplied with beds and all bedding of a similar pattern. The tender of a Mr Prater was accepted, and the items were:

Bed, Bolster and Flocks	£1- 2-0
9 x 4 Blankets	13-0
9 x 4 Coverlid	8-3
1 pair Sheets	12-9

but there is an interesting light on the beds; 13th May 1788 the carpenter of the dockyard in making a report says that *"If the Bottoms instead of being boarded close were made with deal battens they would be lighter and much easier cleared of vermin!"*

Retirements.
In March 1787 a memorial was got up by the officers of the three Divisions as to the hardships caused by there being no provision for retired pay; officers unless they went on half pay continued serving till they dropped in their tracks. The memorial began *"From age long service and infirmities acquired in foreign climates, incapable of doing their duty according to their wishes…….."* After signature by the Commandants it was presented by General Mackenzie to the Admiralty, but no relief was afforded until 5th November 1791 when the Earl of Chatham obtained from the King the concession that a certain number of Field Officers, Captains and Subalterns could retire on the full pay of their rank. A considerable number of officers took advantage of this concession, but it was not enough, because in May 1802, even after further concessions we find the Commandant at Plymouth reporting *"that few of the officers here are under sixty years of age."*

In August 1787 a controversy arose between the Admiralty and Portsmouth Division which is very redolent of modern times and incidentally throws light on the administration of Divisions.

The Commandant having reported that he could not provide the detachments for HMS *Bedford*

---
118 Afterwards CO at Plymouth.
119 Also accounts in The Globe and Laurel Vols. 1900 to 1904.

and *Magnificent*, the Board want to know (1) What guards are mounted? (2) Why forty Privates at Portsmouth are *"necessarily employed when Plymouth has only thirty?"* (3) Why twenty-seven Privates are sent on recruiting service with eight parties when Plymouth only have sent twelve with eleven parties? Please consider reduction.

This is followed by a state of the employed dated 31st August 1787.

"Give your reasons for employing so many? ... The Board intend to reduce them unless reasons are very satisfactory to same as at Plymouth. Privates on recruiting service to be reduced to two per party. You also have five men on short leave; none to be granted whilst so short."

	Portsmouth			Plymouth		
	Sgts	Cpls	Ptes	Sgts	Cpls	Ptes
Clerks in Offices	3	1	5	2	-	1
Quartermaster Sergeants	2	-	-	1	-	-
Taylors	-	1	9	-	1	6
Boatmen	1	-	9	-	1	6
Sutlers	-	-	3	-	-	1
Superintendents Hospital & Infirmary	2	1	3	2	-	-
Attendants on Staff & Field Officers	-	-	8	None at Plymouth and Chatham		

This was followed by the usual order:

12th September 1787.

> 1 Sergeant in Q.M.'s office to return to duty.
> 1 Private may remain in Infirmary.
> Reduce 3 Taylors and 3 Boatmen.

Servants to FOs and Staff Officers to be placed in returns in same manner as other Divisions.[120] This is followed by a sly dig *"Sergeant Majors are shown as necessarily employed at other Divisions. Their Lordships presume that there are Sergeant Majors at Portsmouth; therefore, report why you do not return them in same manner as other Divisions."* A comparison with to-day's employed is interesting.

At the same time Dockyard Guards were ordered to be withdrawn and held ready for sea service, but they were started again in March 1788 for patrol duty.

Review.
On 11th January 1788 HRH The Prince of Wales inspected Plymouth Division and was pleased to

---

120 So they were not more virtuous! – Ed.

express his approval of the appearance under arms and the cleanliness of the barracks.

Clothing.
There is also quite a modern touch about a letter dated 14th May 1788 addressed to Portsmouth. The Board picked up a charge in the accounts of £6-16-2 for Lace for Sergeant Major and Drum Major's Clothing and for cutting, making and trimming for the said uniforms £2-17-1, "No charges are found in accounts of other Divisions . . . the Quartermaster is not to make such charges, expense ought to be defrayed at Portsmouth" in same manner as other Divisions!

Divisional Fund.
On 3rd February 1789 we learn from Plymouth orders a little more about the "Eighteen-penny Fund." Men are allowed to work, not more than one mile from quarters, nor for longer than two months at a time, as work debases the ideas of a soldier, except artificers appointed to work for the Division; and on 10th November 1791 it was again ordered that men allowed to work were to be stopped 1/6 a week in the squad offices for the support of the Divisional Fund, and later the stoppage was raised to 3/- a week.

French Revolution.
But we are now approaching the period of the French Revolution and see the first signs of anxiety in the Order-in-Council of 21st May 1790. Each of the 64 companies to be increased by 1 Second Lieutenant, 1 Sergeant, 1 Corporal, 1 Drummer, and 20 Privates, and on 8th July 1790 the 64 Companies were raised to 70, each consisting of 5 Sergeants, 5 Corporals, 4 Drummers and 100 Privates Nos 65 and 68 to Chatham, 66 and 69 to Portsmouth, 67 and 70 to Plymouth, and at the same time HMS *Victory* to be commissioned at Portsmouth with 1 Captain, 2 Subalterns, 4 Sergeants, 5 Corporals, 2 Drummers and 150 Privates. On 1st June 1790 22 Second-Lieutenants were commissioned.

Recruiting.
The Levy Money for recruits was raised on 31st May to five guineas, and recruiting parties ordered to be sent out; this was the beginning of the great difficulties in raising recruits during the following years, as will be seen.

In October 1790 the disastrous step, that led to so much trouble, was taken when 3 Lieutenant Colonels and 15 Officers were sent to recruit in Ireland, being sent to Dublin and Cork, because amongst the recruits so raised were the "United Irish-men" who took such a prominent part in the Great Mutinies of 1797 and 1800.

Numbers must have been very short, because it was directed in July that frigates were not to be supplied with Marine detachments, though this was cancelled later.

Soldiers as Marines.
All through this year ships were mobilising, but owing to the shortage of Marines, soldiers were

being embarked and there are many references to exchanging detachments of soldiers and Marines in certain ships. A curious note on 20th August 1790 orders detachments of Marines to be sent to two ships where men of the New South Wales Corps (the Corps which had been raised to relieve the Marines in Australia) had been embarked evidently in error.

Dockyard Guard.
On 31st May orders were given that the Marines were to be relieved from the Dockyard Guard.

Apparently by September 1791 the fear of the results of the French Revolution was wearing off, because by Order-in-Council 6th September 1791 the strength of each company was reduced to 3 Sergeants, 3 Corporals, 3 Drummers and 59 Privates, and the complements of the guardships were also reduced; a further reduction to 54 Privates per company was made on 22nd December. Men reduced were sent to their homes with a gratuity of twenty-one days pay.

On 24th December 1791, Colonel W Soutar became Commandant at Portsmouth, Colonel Commandant H Smith having been appointed Commandant resident in Town; Colonel Tupper also became Commandant at Chatham vice Carruthers deceased 24th December 1791.

As an evidence of the short-sightedness of Governments, Order-in-Council 14th February 1792 ordered further reductions - the 70 Companies were reduced by 1 Second Lieutenant and the number of Privates by four in each company - and yet war broke out before end of the year.

The usual gratuity of twenty-one days pay to the men was granted and the officers were given full pay to 31st March and then half pay with liberty to depart from quarters as soon as they liked.

On 3rd April 1792 the Dockyard Guards were recommenced.

In the Plymouth Orders of 15th April, we get one of the few indications of the drill of the period:

Orders for Reviews.
Ranks to be at two paces; files just touch at elbow. Reviewing Officer received with "Rested Arms" and "General Salute" - "Shoulder Arms" - "Close Ranks" - Battalion forms open column by wheeling to right by Grand Divisions. Arms to be carried.

March Past.
1. By Grand Divisions in slow time; Officers to salute.
2. By Companies in quick time; ranks closed senior officers in front, Subalterns in rear.
3. File off into Indian File; front rank first on arrival on original ground, firings will begin: Twice from flanks to centre by companies. Twice from flanks to centre by Grand Divisions. Once by Wings standing. Other firings, volley and charge. General Salute.

Uniform.
During this year there are also some uniform changes. On 1st May approval was given for issue of Grenadier Caps for the Grenadier Companies, and there must also have been some shuffling of companies because on 24th May 1792 a draft of 2 Captains, 4 First Lieutenants, 2 Second Lieutenants, 6 Sergeants, 6 Corporals, 6 Drummers, and 100 Privates (i.e. two companies) were sent by the *Avintnu* from Chatham to Portsmouth.

Allotments.
At last by Order-in-Council 22nd June 1792 the long overdue increase in rations and allowances for necessaries was made. It was a long and interesting Order-in-Council and by the Act of Parliament 18th July 1792 power was given to the Marines afloat to allot pay etc. to their relatives.

Botany Bay.
In July Lieutenant Dawes and 36 rank and file returned from Australia and were discharged in accordance with the original promise. Lieutenant Dawes went on half pay; another party returned in November.

Lodging Money.
Apparently a more humane power was at the Admiralty, because after ordering certain accommodation for officers to be allocated in barracks (at Portsmouth 1 Captain, 4 Subalterns and the Surgeon's Mate), the other officers were granted lodging money instead of being billeted in the Inns, etc. From 1st December 1792:

Commanding Officer	20/- a week
Field Officers	12/- a week
Captains	8/- a week
Subalterns	6/- a week

But the mutterings of the storm in France were beginning to be heard, and the war in which the Corps was engaged for the next twenty-two years was fast approaching. Ships were being mobilised. On 5th December 1792 orders were given to complete at Portsmouth alone five battleships taking 5 Captains, 10 subalterns, 20 sergeants, 20 corporals, 15 drummers and 550 privates, the other Divisions to act similarly.

On 9th January 1793 the army took over the Dockyard and Hospital Guards from the Marines, and on the 14th a new scheme of complement for all classes of ships was issued.

By Order-in-Council 20th February 1793 the 70 Companies of Marines were each increased by 1 Second Lieutenant, 2 Sergeants, 2 Corporals, 1 Drummer and 50 Privates.

War.
In March 1793 King Louis XVI of France was guillotined; the British withdrew their ambassador

and war was declared against the French Revolutionary Forces.

As usual an Order-in-Council 17th April 1793 was issued ordering thirty more Companies to be added to the Marines - thus bringing Chatham to thirty, Portsmouth to thirty-five, and Plymouth to thirty-five, a total of one hundred. Each company to consist of 1 Captain, 2 First Lieutenants, 2 Second Lieutenants, 5 Sergeants, 5 Corporals, 4 Drummers, 80 Privates. The standard height of the Corps had been fixed on 28th February at

5 ft 5 in for men 20 to 30 years of age
5 ft 6 in for men 30 to 38 years of age
5 ft 4 in for growing lads
Grenadier Companies 5 ft. 10 in
Light Companies   5 ft. 7 in

but the standard soon fell a long way below this.

Children.
Before leaving peace conditions we may note a curious order issued at Plymouth on 11th June 1793: *"Children of Officers, Non-Commissioned Officers and men over six years of age may be shown on musters of Drummers; they will be struck off as soon as service required it, and those of mature age and fitness can be raised."* In the meantime, no doubt the parents drew the pay.

Volume One 1755 – 1792

Volume Two
1793-1836

6 - French Revolutionary Wars 1793-1801

This war period is of a scattered nature, and it is difficult to describe the part taken by the Corps, which as usual was world-wide. It comprises several naval battles of historic importance and there are numerous examples of purely Marine work, e.g. capture and holding of advanced bases for the Fleet, use of Naval Striking Forces, landing operations, cutting-out operations, etc., but it is essential to grasp that the bulk of the Corps, as always, was afloat in the Fleets and Squadrons which were blockading the French coasts; e.g. the Grand Fleet in the Channel Soundings watching Brest and the Biscay ports, the various squadrons watching and attacking the French northern ports, and the Mediterranean Fleet - in the first place dealing with Toulon etc., and as the French armies penetrated into Italy engaged along the Italian coast and eventually the French expedition to Egypt and Palestine.

At the beginning the Corps was reinforced by the embarkation of considerable numbers of regiments and detachments of the Line. In the East and West Indies, the war followed the usual course that we have already followed in the Seven Years' War and the American Revolution.

Numerous detailed histories on the naval side and Fortescue's monumental work on the British Army have given the full history of the War. I have therefore only indicated the principal events to show when and in what manner the Royal Marines were engaged and have expanded more fully where possible the peculiar features of Marine work and the gradual development of the Corps, but we must never forget as a background to the brilliant events recorded that there was the daily dreary duty of blockade off the enemy's ports, and days and months at sea without ever putting foot on shore. When bad weather, ship-wreck, poor food and water, made life a dreary monotony for our forerunners; nothing to read even if they had the ability to read, no newspapers, no wireless, very little mail and no com¬forts. The only excitement was the occasional capture of an enemy ship with its hopes of prize money to eke out their meagre pay and help to pay off some of the debts incurred for food and necessaries during their last period of shore service.

On 21st January 1793 the French beheaded their King Louis XVI, and on the 24th the French Ambassador Chauvelin was ordered to leave England. On 1st February the French National Convention declared war against Great Britain and the United Netherlands, and on the 7th March against Spain. Holland was soon over-run by French troops and formed into the Batavian Republic which in turn declared war on England.

The British efforts[121] at first were directed to supporting the French Royalists, who were holding out in various parts of the world - particularly in Brittany, La Vendee, and round Toulon where the bulk of the French Fleet was Royalist, and also in the West Indian Islands.

---

121 As under similar conditions against Russia in 1919.

Toulon.

Although the Channel Fleet was constantly at sea up till November they did not come into collision with the French Fleet even when French reinforcements sailed for the West Indies. But in the Mediterranean, Lord Hood with his flag in the *Victory* with twenty-one battleships and some troops arrived at Toulon in the middle of August. There were both Royalist and Republican troops in the town; on 23rd August while the French Commissioners treated for the surrender of the town to the British, the Republican troops and crews manned the batteries defending the town.

Toulon is commanded by heights all round, and there is a semi-circular chain of mountains extending from the Bay of Hyères to the Pass of Ollicules, on the west about five miles from the town. Strong batteries were sited there which also commanded the town and anchorage. Fort La Malgue stood on a hill between the inner or Little Anchorage and the outer or Great Anchorage. Fort Mulgrave occupies the tongue of land continued from this hill to the harbour. At a distance of half a mile were Forts Aiguillette and Beccaques whence to Cape Supet was one continuous chain of forts. The heights were difficult and rugged, the tops guarded by redoubts - St Antonio, Artignes, St Catherine's and others. The breadth of the Outer Anchorage was 2000 yards.

On 27th August 1500 troops were landed, also Captain Elphinstone RN with 200 Seamen and Marines, and occupied Fort La Malgue; this fort commanded Fort St Julien so the French Commander evacuated the latter and retired into the interior with 5,000 men of the crews of the battleships. The Spanish Fleet then arrived and landed 1,000 troops to reinforce the British.

There were skirmishes with the French, particularly an action at Ollicules, which drove the French, though superior in force, from the village.

Early in September the French forces consisted of General Casteau's army on the west, and the army of Italy under Le Poypeau on the east. Brigadier General Lord Mulgrave arrived and assumed command of the allied troops. The Marines of the Squadron were dispersed over different parts of the defences.

On 18th September the French opened masked batteries on the Inner Harbour and were engaged by the British ships and floating batteries. On 25th a reinforcement of 2000 Sardinian and Neapolitan troops was received.

On 20th September the French surprised a Spanish detachment and gained possession of the heights of Pharon (immediately over Toulon). The next day the Allies under Lord Mulgrave concentrated, drove them out and regained the heights. The Marines were mentioned for this attack, Captain Dexter being mentioned in dispatches. Lieutenant Carter RM was wounded. Napoleon Buonaparte as a young Artillery Officer was present at these attacks.

On 8th October the Allies attacked the three batteries on the heights of Des Moulines opposite Hauteur de Grace, which were threatening the Allied Fleet. The force consisted all told of 608 under Lieutenant Colonel Nugent, of whom 408 were British including 50 Marines and a party of seamen. They stormed the difficult ascent and carried the batteries; the Marines destroyed the guns on the Haut de Reinier and then withdrew to quarters.

On 27th October General O'Hara arrived with 750 troops. The circumference of the defences was fifteen miles and the Allied Force was only 16,912, of whom 2,114 were British and there were only 12,000 fit for duty.

During this period the French made several attacks on the posts. On one occasion the post held by Lieutenant T Naylor RM with 120 men - principally Marines - was attacked in a fog by 2,000 men; fire was opened by platoons and the French retired with a loss of 400 killed and wounded.

On 15th November the French attacked Fort Mulgrave with a large force; the Spaniards bolted, but a company of the 1/Royals (Royal Scots), Royal Artillery and Marines made a sortie and drove them back, thus saving an important post. Lieutenant Burdwood of the Marines was made a perpetual member of the Mess of the Royal Scots.[122]

The French then opened batteries against Fort Malbousket and shells reached the town. Admiral Jervis left England with a convoy of troops to help the Royalists. On 30th November a body of 2,300 men - including the Marines - under General Dundas attacked the French batteries and carried them but advancing too far they were counter-attacked and driven back. General O'Hara was wounded and captured.

The Allies were being gradually driven from the forts; Fort Mulgrave was captured and by 10 pm on 18th December the defence was restricted to the town and Fort La Malgue, which were held whilst the French men-of-war were burnt and blown up. About 15,000 Royalists men, women and children were embarked in the Fleet and the place evacuated.[123] The Fleet withdrew to the Sardinian and Neapolitan ports, keeping up the blockade. It is interesting to note that claims for the loss of kit by officers and men employed on shore at Toulon were refused by the Admiralty.[124]

West Indies.
Tobago. Meanwhile the efforts to support the French Royalists in the West Indies were being continued. On 14th April a small squadron with 60 Royal Artillery and 418 of the 9th and 80th Regiments with 32 Marines (Major Bright, 1 Lieutenant, 2 Sergeants, 2 Corporals, 1 Drummer and 27 Privates), the whole under Major-General Cuyler, arrived off Tobago and summoned it to surrender, which the French refused; it was decided to assault Fort Castries, where the British entered the works and the place capitulated.

---

122 Gillespie.
123 Cf. Odessa 1919.
124 Portsmouth Letter Books.

Martinique. Another expedition under Rear-Admiral Gardner and Major-General Bruce with 4 battleships and 1,100 British troops and 800 French Royalists landed in Martinique between 14th and 17th April, but the French Royalist troops bolted and after bringing off what Royalist inhabitants they could, the force re-embarked on the 21st. The remainder of the Royalist inhabitants in the island were massacred.

St. Domingo. At the other end of the Station the French Royalists in St. Domingo communicated with Commodore Ford in the *Europa* at Jamaica; the latter embarked the 13th and some of the 45th Regiments and proceeded off the island. The troops were landed and took possession of Jeremie. On 19th September the Commodore proceeded to Cape St. Nicholas Mole which capitulated on 21st. The 58 Marines of the *Europa* under Brevet-Major Robinson landed and took possession of one of the finest harbours in the West Indies guarded by batteries of 100 guns (the *Europa* was only a 50 gun ship). Marines were the only troops on shore - a true Naval Striking Force. The Royalist inhabitants were expecting 800 to 1000 rebellious blacks to attack the town, so a reserve of 200 seamen was kept ready till the grenadiers of the 13th and five companies of the 49th Regiment arrived.

1794

Corsica.
In the Mediterranean Lord Hood was anxious to seize Bastia, Corsica, as a base for the Fleet watching Toulon. General Dundas declined to act until he received his reinforcements from Gibraltar. Lord Hood then took on board that portion of the Land Forces which had originally been ordered to serve as Marines with some Artillery and Ordnance stores. The troops under Lieutenant Colonel Vilettes - and presumably the Marines of the Fleet - with a detachment of Seamen under Captain Nelson and covered by the Agammenon, landed a little north of the town on 4th April. The small force of 1,248 men was joined by 2,000 Corsicans under Paoli. The Fleet anchored in the form of a crescent out of reach of the fort's guns, whilst a flotilla of boats and launches guarded the mouth of the harbour. By 11th April the British batteries on the heights were ready to open fire and the town was summoned. No answer forthcoming, the batteries opened fire.

On 21st May after a siege of thirty-seven days, negotiations were opened and after four days the town and citadel of Bastia surrendered. The Army losses including presumably the Marines were 7 Privates killed; 2 Captains, and 19 Privates wounded; 6 Privates missing: 1 Lieutenant RN and 6 Seamen killed; a Lieutenant and 12 Seamen wounded. On 19th June the whole island surrendered.

Hood also required an advanced base for the Fleet watching Toulon, as his main base was Gibraltar; and with General Dundas' troops he seized San Fiorenze Bay, Corsica on 16-17th September.

Out in the Atlantic great events had been taking place. Lord Howe with 49 men of war (24 of them battleships) and a convoy of 199 ships sailed on 2nd May. They were off the Lizard on the 4th and the convoys were dispatched to their destinations. The Channel Fleet reduced to 20 battleships and 7 frigates proceeded off Brest; on 16th May they sighted the French Grand Fleet under Villaret-Joyeuse with 25 battleships and 16 frigates etc. Contact was not gained until 28th May and a partial action ensued. There was a second action on the 29th when the British lost 87 killed and 128 wounded.

On 1st June was fought the battle known as the Glorious First of June. The action began at 9.15 am. A few British ships cut through the French line and engaged to leeward, whilst others hauled up to windward. By 11.30 am the heat of the action was over. Of the British 11 and of the French 12 were demasted. About 2.30 pm the French ships *Sanspareil, Juste, America, Impetueux, Northumberland* and *Achille* were secured as prizes and the *Vengeur* sank later. The total British loss was 290 killed, 858 wounded; out of which Captain Saunders and 1 Lieutenant (Army) and 36 Marines or soldiers were killed, Captain W Smith (Marines), 1 Captain, 1 Lieutenant and 2 Ensigns (Army) and 100 Marines or soldiers were wounded. The soldiers mostly belonged to the 2nd Queen's and 29th (now 1st Worcester) Regiments who were both awarded the Naval Crown with date 1st June 1794 as a distinction on their colours.

As to the Marine casualties we find a letter to the Commandant Portsmouth Division (dated 16th July 1794) who had reported that the casualties in the Fleet under the command of Lord Howe required more men than he had at Quarters and asking for a draft from Plymouth, elicited the reply that none were available.

Beer Money.
On 7th June 1794 a grant was made to the Royal Marines that lasted in one way or another until 1904. "An allowance of Small Beer to NCOs and men stationed at barracks of several Headquarters, not exceeding the quantity to which those at Quarters (i.e. Billets) are entitled, to receive gratis from their land lords viz. five pints per diem for each NCO or man. Commandants to obtain contracts, and provision to be made for NCOs and men to be supplied at their option with three pints of Twelve Shilling Table Beer per diem instead of five pints of Small Beer".

Martinique.
In the West Indies an attack was made on Martinique by five battleships and eight frigates under Admiral Sir John Jervis and 7,000 troops under General Sir Charles Grey. The British troops were disembarked at three points on 16th March and seized the heights of Souriere; 300 Seamen with a small party of Marines under Lieutenant Tremenheere under Captain Harvey RN landed with some 24 pdrs and 2 mortars at the Cul de Sac Coheu and joined Sir Charles Grey. All the island was captured except Forts Bourbo and Royal with a loss of 71 killed and 195 wounded. The Naval Brigade stormed the Monte Mathurine.

St Lucia.
On 31st March the force sailed to attack the island of St Lucia. Between 1st and 3rd April troops assaulted and carried the French outposts and on the 4th the French Commander on Morne Fortune capitulated. The British force after securing St Lucia returned to Martinique.

Guadeloupe.

On the 8th April Sir John Jervis in the *Boyne* with three battleships sailed for Guadeloupe. On the 11th he landed his seamen and Marines in the Anse du Gosier under cover of the fire of the *Winchelsea*. Troops were then landed the next morning. The post of the Fleur d'Epee was stormed by the 1st and 2nd Battalions of Light Infantry under General Dundas assisted by the Seamen.

1795

On 19th January the French, having overrun the Netherlands, formed the Batavian Republic, with which war was declared on this date.

In the Mediterranean the squadron under Admiral Hotham, based on Corsica, was watching the French ports, and on 4th March off Genoa he fought an action with 13 battleships and 7 frigates against the French and captured the *Ca Ira* and the *Censeur*, having 74 killed and 284 wounded. Bonaparte was now advancing into Italy and his successes resulted in a treaty with the King of Sardinia on 15th May.

By the 10th November the King of the Sicilies, whose capital was Naples, had also signed a treaty with France. In June the French were approaching Leghorn so the British residents and property were evacuated, San Fiorenzo Bay in Corsica being used as a base.

Porto Ferrajo.

On 10th July Commodore Nelson with his flag in the *Captain* (74) with some frigates and troops seized Porto Ferrajo in Elba as an advanced base; 400 regular troops and 100 guns were captured.

Matters however were becoming serious, because on 12th September 1795 the Treaty between France and Spain was ratified and Spain declared war on England on 5th October.

The French and Spanish Fleets, mustering 38 battleships with 18 to 20 frigates, were concentrated at Toulon about 26th October. Sir John Jervis' Fleet consisted of only 14 battleships. The inhabitants of Corsica were also siding with the Republicans, so it became necessary to evacuate that island and to remove the stores and garrison to Porto Ferrajo in Elba, which was to become the Naval Base. The French crossed to Corsica from Leghorn - which the British had omitted to blockade - and on 21st October they summoned Bastia to surrender. Nelson with the *Captain* and *Egmont* embarked all the stores under threat of battering down the town and thus saved £200,000 worth of stores. The troops at San Fiorenzo were also evacuated under cover of the fire of two 74-gun ships. On 22nd October Bonifacio was evacuated; Ajaccio was captured by the French, but the evacuation was completed by 2nd November.

The evacuation of the Mediterranean having been ordered by the government, Sir John Jervis collected his transports and Fleet and withdrew to Gibraltar, which gave Bonaparte his chance in the following year.

Increase.
By Order-in-Council 21st April 1795, 21 more companies were added to the Corps (7 to each Division) and the strength of all companies was raised to 1 Captain, 2 First Lieutenants, 1 Second Lieutenant, 6 Sergeants, 5 Corporals, 6 Drummers, and 100 Privates (modified on 29th April to 4 Drummers). The numbers voted for the year were 15,000.

Recruiting.
Evidently the Corps was experiencing difficulty in raising recruits. On 6th May the Bounty was raised to eight guineas per man, and on 4th November again raised to 15 for each recruit. On 11th May the country was divided into four Recruiting Districts, each with a Field Officer in charge.

Complements.
The shortage difficulty was also met by a reduction in complements, a new scheme being promulgated on 19th August. On 2nd July Commandants were ordered to supply all battleships with detachments that came into port without Marines or Soldiers; there must have been large numbers of soldiers embarked for on 7th November, by which time the increase was taking effect, the Admiralty ordered eight Captains to be held in readiness to embark in ships of the Home and Mediterranean Fleets to relieve a similar number of line Officers. Officers out recruiting to be relieved by Lieutenants, and again on 6th December, Chatham and Plymouth were each directed to send six Captains and Portsmouth twelve to the Mediterranean to relieve Line Officers; also, as many subalterns from Portsmouth, whether of that Division or any other not exceeding fourteen for a similar purpose. Passage in *Boston* (frigate) or *Dromedary*, (store ship); numbers to be reported so that the remainder could be sent from Chatham and Plymouth.[125] As a matter of fact only nine Captains and two subalterns were then available at Portsmouth.

Transfers from Army.
On 7th November the Army Commander-in-Chief, (HRH the Duke of York), gave orders that the NCOs and men of the 86th, 90th (2nd Battalion), 91st and 97th who had been doing duty as Marines afloat could be enlisted into the Marines with a bounty of five guineas; the Commandants were to arrange with the Commanding Officers. There seems to have been quite a lot of trouble with local GOCs, but eventually a number of NCOs and men were obtained from this source. The Officer Commanding 91st at Liskeard, Cornwall reported that almost every man at Headquarters and in the ships at Plymouth had volunteered for transfer; the Admiral at Plymouth was ordered to discharge them to the Marine Headquarters. The 118th Regiment was added to those who might transfer. Dutchmen prisoners of war were allowed to enlist into the Marines also.

Rations.
As in most wars the prices of provisions were rising; this bore hardly on the men who had to pay for their rations, so that in April the Admiralty ordered that men were to be supplied with bread at the same rate as when in camp; the difference between the usual stoppage of 5d per loaf and the actual

---
125 Portsmouth letters.

price being charged to Marine Contingencies, whilst on 18th June 1795 the billeting money was raised to 6d by Act of Parliament.

Portsmouth seems to have been the principal embarking port as on 14th December 6 Subalterns and 500 Marines were sent from Plymouth to Portsmouth to embark.

La Vendée.
In May an expedition under Commodore Sir John Warren with 3 battleships and 6 Frigates was sent to assist the Royalists in La Vendee. He convoyed 80 transports with 3500 French Royalist troops. On 18th June the French Fleet was sighted, but as Lord Bridport's blockading fleet was within call, after a partial action the convoy got through. They entered Quiberon Bay on 25th June. In order to attack the Quiberon peninsula the Commodore landed the French together with 300 British Marines at two points on 5th July, and three ships were sent to bombard Fort Ponthievre. The French Commander, Count D'Hervilly, with this force advanced to the neck of land at the end of the Peninsula; the Fort surrendered and an equal number of English and French Marines took possession of it. The Republican forces were concentrating and captured Vannes.

The Commodore led an expedition up the River Morbihan to prevent the plundering of the inhabitants and to destroy some French ships, which was successfully accomplished, the Marines being landed to clear the banks.

The Republican forces drove back the Royalists into the Peninsula, who took refuge in the Fort and the Republicans occupied the heights of St Barbe. The Commodore armed the Fort with guns from the Fleet, but the besiegers pressed closer. On 16th July more French Republican reinforcements arrived. On this day Count D'Hervilly with 5,000 men made a sortie to attack the enemy right wing which was strongly posted on the heights - whilst 200 British Marines and 1,200 Chouans made a false attack on the left. The Marines drove back two corps of the enemy, but the Chouans refused to advance and fell back. The sortie on St. Barbe failed and the Royalists fell back in confusion; the Commodore ordered Captain Keates RN to occupy the fort with the British Marines and to place the Chouans in the trenches whilst with the ships' boats armed with 18 and 24 pdrs covered the retirement. The Royalists fell back into the fort where the Marines remained until the French had recovered themselves but were withdrawn the next day at noon when relieved by the newly arrived veteran French troops under General Sombreuil.

On 20th July many of the emigres deserted and brought back the Republican troops into the Fort. Some of the garrison resisted and about 1,600 retreated to the beach. Next morning the frigates worked in and took off 1,100 troops and 2,400 Royalist inhabitants but left behind 10,000 stand of arms with stores and clothing for an army of 40,000. Six transports laden with provisions also fell into the hands of the Republicans. The loss of the British Marines was never published.

Sir John Warren occupied the islands of Hoedic and Homat and also decided to take the Isle D'Yeu as a base when reinforcements arrived, but though when the troops eventually came, in

October, nothing could be done and they returned to England at the end of the year.

West Indies.
Our garrisons in the West Indies were so depleted that it became necessary to evacuate St Lucia. Marines under Captain Lambrecht were present at the evacuation of the Vigie peninsula, St. Lucia, on 17th June 1795 and the letter books show that they put in claims for loss of kit on that occasion, which were refused by the Admiralty. Many of the other islands were in revolt.

However Great Britain commenced attacks on Dutch possessions in other parts of the world.

Cape of Good Hope.
Admiral Elphinstone with 5 battleships and 2 sloops with a detachment of troops (78th Regiment) under Major General Craig anchored in Simon's Bay in July 1795. 450 of the 78th and 350 Marines of the Fleet under Major Hill were landed and took possession of the town and prevented its being burnt. The Dutch, having spiked the guns and destroyed the ammunition, retired and occupied the Pass of Muizenberg leading to Capetown six miles distant. There was a steep mountain on the right, and the sea on the left, but it was difficult to approach the shore owing to shallow water and the surf. 1,000 seamen were also landed and formed into two battalions, making 1,800 all told.

On 7th August the troops advanced, covered by the gunboats and the armed launches and sloops as well as by the fire of two battleships which stood in shore. By 1 pm the enemy was driven from his advanced posts. The ships then moved abreast of the enemy's camp and forced them to retreat after spiking their guns before the troops could arrive. At 4 pm, after a fatiguing march over sandy heavy ground, the troops occupied the camp and, in the evening, the 78th drove the enemy from some rocky heights.

On the 8th the Dutch having been reinforced from Capetown advanced again but were forced to retire by the 1st Battalion of Seamen under Captain Hardy and the Marines under Major Hill who had crossed a lagoon to take them in flank; both Seamen and Marines received the enemy's fire without returning a shot. There was a sharp action on the 9th, the British being reinforced by 400 of the East India Company's troops with 9 field pieces and a 10" howitzer. The British were greatly hampered by want of transports and the guns had to be dragged by the seamen and the stores carried by the troops. They remained at Muizenberg for nearly a month. On 18th August 5 Dutch East Indiamen were captured in Simons Bay.

On 1st and 2nd September the Dutch gained some partial successes; on 3rd September all the Dutch forces with 18 field pieces advanced, but fortunately at this moment the reinforcing British squadron with troops under General Alured Clarke and stores arrived, together with 14 British East Indiamen at Simons Bay. The troops were landed and an immediate attack on Cape-town decided on. The disembarkation was completed by 14th September and the advance was begun, the troops carrying four days provisions and the seamen dragging the guns. HMS *America* and three other ships proceeded to Table Bay to make a diversion. The Dutch were found in great strength at Wynberg but were mishandled and on the big ships opening fire they retired. They sent in a flag of truce and on the 16th the capitulation was finally signed, and the town and Colony fell into British hands.

From the services of the late General Wingrove RM we learn that the Marines were in garrison there until the following September. General Craig was left in command of the garrison when Admiral Elphinstone and General Clarke sailed for India on 15th November.

In General Craig's despatch on Muizenberg he says, *"The remarkable steadiness of the First Battalion of Seamen under Captain Hardy who having crossed the water (i.e. of the lagoon) with the Marines received the enemy's fire without firing a shot"* etc. and also, *". . . the Marines displayed an equal degree of steady resolution on this occasion."*

It is interesting to know that the Seamen received extra allowances, the Marines 'bat and forage' the same as the Army. Also, that the enemy's troops were encouraged to desert and that such deserters might choose the station they would prefer. "Many have made election for the Marines. Therefore, they have been enlisted with a bounty of £2; they will be clothed as soon as possible. They have served faithfully and are excellent German soldiers."[126]

In the East Indies also the Dutch settlements were once more attacked and Trincomali fell into British hands.

On 24th July 1795 Admiral Rainier with *Suffolk*, *Centurion*, and *Diomede* with a body of troops under Colonel Stuart sailed from Madras for Ceylon. On 3rd August the troops landed four miles north of Trincomali without opposition, but it took ten days to land all the stores and provisions. On the 18th the troops opened the trenches and by the 26th they had made a practicable breech; when summoned the governor refused to surrender and firing recommenced, after which the garrison surrendered with 679 officers and men with 100 guns.

On 27th Fort Ostenberg was summoned and surrendered on the 31st. On 18th September Battical was surrendered to the 22nd Regiment, Colonel Stuart re-embarked with some troops and landed on the 27th at Point Pecho and on the 28th occupied Jaffnapatam. On 1st October the 52nd Regiment took possession of Molletive.

Another squadron under Captain Newcombe of the *Orpheus* and Major Brown occupied Malacca on 17th August and before the end of the year Chinsura, Cochin, and all the remaining Dutch settlements in India fell into British hands.

L'Orient.
The Channel Fleet under Lord Bridport had been covering all the expeditions leaving England,

---

126   Keith Papers Navy Records.

and the convoys coming to and fro, and on 23rd June gained a victory over the French Fleet off L'Orient.

In December the British occupied the Islands of St Marcou, off the mouth of the River Issigny (Normandy) to keep watch on the movements of the French flotillas and as a base for the blockading frigates. They were only two small islets, each 200 yards long and 120 yards broad, and as a letter says, "within sound of the drums of the enemy." The first intimation is given in a letter to the Commandant at Portsmouth and for the next six weary years detachments of Portsmouth Marines held these bare rocks, and the letter books are full of letters concerning them.

On 19th December 1795 the Admiralty informed the Commandant that the detachment of HMS *Diamond* had been landed as a garrison of the Isle of St Marcou; the Commandant was ordered to find an equal party of invalid Marines to serve at the place in their stead, and "if a party of about 25 can be found they are to be sent over by the Commander in Chief." On the 24th the Commandant reported that he is holding 1 Sergeant, 1 Corporal, and 25 Privates ready but has no subaltern available and is told to recall one from recruiting.

1796

The year opened with renewed activity; the number of Marines voted in April was 18,000. The Order-in-Council 27th January 1796 ordered nine more companies to be raised, three at each Division; the strength of the companies was raised to 1 Captain, 2 First Lieutenants, 2 Second Lieutenants, 8 Sergeants, 8 Corporals, 6 Drummers, and 113 Privates. Evidently the increased numbers of the Corps enabled them to complete the ships as well as to replace the soldiers afloat.

On 23rd February 1796, 2 Captains, 4 Subalterns, 200 Rank and File were ordered to the West Indies and also 1 Captain, 2 Subalterns, 150 Rank and File to Jamaica. In March another 3 Captains, 7 Subalterns and 42 Privates were sent from Chatham and Portsmouth to join Admiral Cornwallis' squadron in the West Indies. The complements of battleships at Spithead were brought up to the new complements issued in August 1795, and in April several celebrated battleships were ordered to be completed - *Triumph, Juste, Bellerophon, Tremendous, Namur, Brunswick*, and *Formidable* - whilst 200 officers and men were sent to Sir John Jervis' squadron at Gibraltar. These orders caused a lot of drafts between Divisions, and in May 70 to 80 Dutch and German prisoners at Porchester were enlisted which opened the recruiting of prisoners of war and foreigners with somewhat unfortunate results as will be seen later.

An Order-in-Council on 28th November 1796 ordered six more companies to be raised - 3 each to Portsmouth and Plymouth - making 130 for the Corps, and each Company was raised to 120 Privates.

Dutch Guiana.
The first moves came in the West Indies. On 5th April the *Malabar* (54 guns) with some frigates and

1,200 troops under Major General Whyte were sent to take possession of the Dutch settlements at Demerara, Essequibo and Berbice River in Dutch Guiana on the South American coast; the first two places capitulated on 22nd April and the last on 2nd May. On 21st April the Squadron and transports from England which had been delayed by storms, arrived at Barbados, and Admiral Christian's squadron also arrived with reinforcements.

It was decided to recapture St Lucia and its fine harbour; the fleet therefore left for Martinique on the 22nd, and Admiral Christian assumed command on the 24th; on the 28th the Squadron with the troops under Sir Ralph Abercrombie stood across to St. Lucia. Three points of disembarkation were chosen: (1) at the Anse du Cap, (2) the Anse Bequere (Longueville Bay) and Choc Bay, and (3) the Anse La Ray (South of the Cul de Sac).

The Anse du Cap was protected by the batteries on Pigeon Island, the guns of the ships silenced the batteries by 5 pm and the first flight of troops landed; the other attempts were deferred owing to the current carrying the boats to leeward.

On the 28th the landing at Choc Bay was effected without opposition, and on the 29th the landing at La Ray was carried out. The main point to be captured was the Morne Fortune. A battalion of Seamen and a Battalion of 320 Marines under Major Bright were landed to co-operate in the attack.

On the 28th/29th Morne Chabot was captured, but on 3rd May the attempt to dislodge the Republicans from the batteries near the Grand Cul de Sac failed. On 17th May the attack on the Vigie peninsula partially failed. Guns were landed from the Fleet which drove back the French and they retired to the fort of Morne Fortune. On 24th May the garrison capitulated. The British losses were 68 officers and men killed, 378 wounded and 122 missing. Sir Ralph Abercrombie acknowledged the services of the Seamen and Marines: "The conduct of the Marines upon this, as upon all other occasions was perfectly correct."

The Squadron and troops then went on to St Vincent and Grenada. On 8th June the troops with a detachment of Seamen and Marines were disembarked at St Vincent under cover of the guns of the *Arethusa* (38). After an obstinate resistance the island capitulated on 11th June, the British having 38 officers and men killed, and 145 wounded.

Proceeding to Grenada the Republicans soon surrendered. The Republican Civilian Deputy in charge of the island murdered several Europeans in full view of the British. He and his men were pursued by the German troops into the woods and cleaned up thoroughly.

Colombo.
In the East Indies on 5th February a squadron of frigates and armed ships of the East India Company with a body of troops from Good Hope under Colonel Stuart landed about eight miles from Colombo (Ceylon) and under cover of the ships' fire took possession of Fort Negumbo

which they found abandoned. They marched overland to Colombo, covered by the ships, and when everything was prepared for the attack on the 14th the town capitulated. Independent of the shipping the value of the merchandise taken was £300,000.

Admiral Rainier, continuing the captures in Malacca, anchored off Amboyna on 16th February; the troops were landed and took possession in the afternoon without resistance.

On 7th March they arrived off Banda Neira (Nutmeg Islands); on the 8th the troops with a detachment of Marines landed on the north side of the island covered by the *Orpheus*; 2 batteries were silenced, and the same evening Fort Nassau in Banda Neira capitulated. Five Captains of the Royal Navy received £15,000 prize money each; the sixth, Captain Page RN, who had done most of the work, was done out of any share at all.

Cape of Good Hope.
At the Cape of Good Hope, Admiral Elphinstone with 8 battleships and small ships was lying in Simons Bay watching over the newly acquired possession. In September a Dutch squadron of 3 battleships, 4 frigates and a sloop approached to try to recover the Colony. A violent storm forced the Dutch to put into Saldanha Bay and the British had to retire to Simons Bay; they were storm bound until the 15th but on the 17th the Dutch surrendered.[127]

Herqui.
The Channel Fleet and the flotillas in the Channel maintained their watch on the French northern and western coasts, which led to several encounters. The attack on Herqui 17th March and the gallant action between the *Glatton* (Captain Trollope) and four French frigates are fully described in Britain's Sea Soldiers Vol I.

On 23rd September 1796 HMS *Amphion* blew up in Plymouth harbour; 100 women and children and civilians were on board as well as 300 of the crew. The sentry on the cabin door had his watch dashed out of his hand; beyond that he knew nothing and yet received little hurt. The ship was close to the Dockyard Jetty, and the cause was never known; so that it was not only in the War of 1914-18 that these things occurred. From this event came the order that all ships were to land their powder before entering harbour. Some severely wounded men were admitted to Greenwich Hospital, but all compensation for losses was refused.[128]

The Mediterranean Fleet was off Gibraltar watching the movements of the French fleets. The Declaration of War by Spain, in the autumn of 1796 led the Government to withdraw the Fleet from the Mediterranean; troops to the number of 5,000 were sent to Lisbon and aided by the Fleet kept the Tagus open as a base for the Fleet.

---

127 Services of Lieutenant Wingrove RM.
128 Plymouth Letter Books.

1797

The year 1797, one of the most momentous in the history of the Corps, opened fairly quietly. The numbers voted were 20,000 - an increase of 2000.

West Indies.

In the West Indies General Sir Ralph Abercrombie, based on the Fleet, continued his career of conquest. With a squadron of five battleships and four smaller ones under Rear Admiral Harvey he left Martinique on 12th February; on the 16th they arrived off Trinidad, and met the Spanish squadron of 4 battleships and one frigate. On the night of the 16th/17th the Spanish Fleet was destroyed by fire except one captured. On the 17th Gasparade Island being abandoned was occupied by the Queen's Regiment; the remainder of the troops landed three miles from Port d'Espagne and next day the island surrendered. In April they sailed for Porto Rico and on the 17th the squadron anchored off Congrejos Point; on the 16th the troops disembarked after slight opposition. The town was found to be too strongly defended and after several days bombardment, Sir Ralph Abercrombie decided on the 30th to abandon the enterprise and re-embarked with a loss of 8 Officers and 30 other ranks killed, 2 officers and 88 other ranks, wounded, 3 officers and 128 other ranks missing.

San Domingo.

On 6th April the boats of the *Magicienne*, and *Regulus* burnt two and sunk 13 merchantmen and destroyed two batteries at the extreme head of the harbour of Cape Rose, San Domingo; Lieutenants Luscombe, Perry and Frazer of the Marines being engaged. The British at this time were holding posts in San Domingo.

Reverting to the Mediterranean Squadron, which was based on Gibraltar, Admiral Sir John Jervis with eleven battleships had been lying in the Tagus to give support to the Portuguese. On 13th January he left to escort the convoy for Brazil and to meet his reinforcements from England. HMS *St George* was unfortunately wrecked.

On 6th February the convoy having been sent on its way, he was joined by 5 battleships and 1 frigate from the Channel Fleet. He now had the *Victory* and *Britannia* (100 guns), *Barfleur, Prince George, Blenheim* (98), *Namur* (90), *Captain* (Nelson), *Goliath, Excellent, Orion, Colossus. Egmont, Culloden, Irresistible* (74's) *Diadem* (64), 4 frigates and 2 sloops. When working up to Cape St Vincent the *Minerva* reported the Spanish Fleet (one 139, one 120, two 80, eighteen 74 and 12 frigates), evidently making for Brest to join the French fleet (25 battleships and 11 frigates) for the invasion of England. On 13th the Spaniards sighted some British ships.

Cape St Vincent.

On 14th February the Battle of Cape St Vincent took place. Nelson in the *Captain* seized his 'golden moment' and broke the enemy line; the detachment of this ship apparently consisted partly of Marines and partly of the 69th Regiment. He says, "Soldiers of the 69th with an alacrity which will ever do them credit and Lieutenant Pearson of the same regiment were almost the foremost in this service" (i.e. boarding the *San Nicholas*). In this ship the Major of Marines, Norris, was killed and 3 soldiers, while 4 soldiers were wounded.

Four Spanish battleships were captured, and the battle had great political results. The total British loss was 75 killed and 227 wounded, of whom great numbers died; the Marines lost besides Major Norris, Lieutenant Livingston (*Culloden*) and 1 Marines killed; 21 Marines wounded, 5 soldiers killed, and 12 soldiers wounded. On 16th February the British Fleet with its prizes anchored in Lagos Bay, and Sir John Jervis was created Earl St Vincent.

Cadiz.
He then proceeded off Cadiz; on 3rd July and again on the 5th he bombarded the place with bomb ketches with a loss of 3 Seamen and Marines killed and 16 wounded, among the latter Major Oldfield of the Marines.

Earl St. Vincent kept his squadron well in hand throughout the troublous times of these years. He worked them hard and the Corps owe him a great debt of gratitude for the manner in which he supported them.[129] He appointed Lieutenant Colonel Flight to be Inspector of Marines in the Squadron.[130] The *Ville de Paris* had been commissioned at Portsmouth on 25th February 1797.

Uniform.
Whether it was the close contact with the Army due to the large numbers embarked as Marines I cannot tell, but the alterations in uniform issued on 3rd April 1797 seem to give some foundation for the idea:

1. The silver-laced hats to be abolished, and crimson and gold ornaments substituted in their room, such as are used by officers of the Line.

2. The epaulets of Captains and Subalterns to be conformable to the pattern sent to Divisions; the Majors to be distinguished by one gold star on the strap, Lieutenant Colonels by two, Colonels by three.

3. The swords to be the old established silver hilted cut and thrust blades with crimson and gold sword knots as worn by officers of the line.

4. The gorget to be plain and to have the King's Arms and Anchor as at present.

5. The breastplates to be square with Lyon and Crown. And on 14th August another order:

"The sashes to be worn over the left shoulder."

---

129 See Appendix I.
130 St Vincent Letters.

On 27th May 1797 it had been ordered that Grenadier Companies were to wear a "Fuze on each epaulet and Light Companies a bugle but no wings."

The Channel Fleet had been watching the French Fleet gathering at Brest for the invasion of Ireland, but returned to Spithead on 3rd February.

On 3rd March Lord Bridport (in command as Lord Howe was sick ascertained that all was quiet at Brest and returned to Spithead on 30th March, a squadron of observation consisting of 9 battleships being sent off again on 8th April. Lord Howe had now resigned and Lord Bridport had assumed command.

Mutiny at Spithead. [131]
On 15th April the signal was made to prepare for sea, when the seamen of the *Royal George* ran up the shrouds and gave three cheers, which were repeated throughout the Fleet and the men refused to weigh anchor.

As usual the fault lay with the Civilian Admiralty. The February petitions, praying for an advance of pay were not attended to; among the causes the price of provisions had been rising as we have seen and now at last the petitions were submitted to the Board at the end of March.

On 16th April the ships' companies each appointed two men as delegates, and on board the *Queen Charlotte*. (the worst disciplined ship of the lot) officers deemed guilty of oppression were ordered ashore, but this was not peculiar to her; the letter books show that a considerable number of officers and men of the Marines who had evidently tried to do their duty had been put on shore by the mutineers.

The seamen's demands were for:
1. Increased wages.
2. That the seamen's pound should be 16 ounces instead of 14 (the two oz. being kept by he purser for waste.
3. That the rations should be of better quality.
4. That fresh vegetables instead of flour should be issued with the beef when procurable.
5. That the sick should receive better attention.
6. That their necessaries should not be embezzled.
7. That they should be granted short leave on returning home from foreign service.

On the 18th Lord Spencer, Lord Arden, Rear Admiral Young, and Mr. Marsden (Secretary) arrived from the Admiralty and granted an increase of 4/- per month in the pay to ABs 3/6d to Ordinary Seamen, and 2/6d to landsmen. Seamen wounded in action were to continue in payment until their wounds were healed or were discharged as unserviceable, pensioned or

---
131 For the outline of these events the account given in Mr James' History of British Navy has been followed; this has been supplemented as far as the Corps is concerned by the reactions shown in the Divisional Letter and Order Books.

admitted to Greenwich Hospital.

The men had asked for 1/- a day for ABs, Ordinary Seamen in the same proportion, and for Marines as for Ordinary Seamen.

On the 20th the Committee through Lord Bridport agreed, except for the grant of vegetables instead of flour when in harbour (the true civilian mind). On 21st the Admirals went on board, but the men insisted that the pardon should be passed through Parliament. Admiral Gardiner lost his temper and cursed them with the result that the delegates returned to their ships and hoisted the Red Flag, loaded the guns and prevented the officers going ashore.

On 22nd the delegates wrote letters repenting a little, and Lord Bridport went on board on 23rd and hoisted his flag in the *Royal George*. The Fleet then put to sea except the *London*, *Minotaur* and *Marlborough*.

Vice-Admiral Colpoys in the *London* on the second day had refused to allow the boats of the delegates to come on board, telling them to wait for the Admiralty reply; the crew of the *London* were encouraging the delegates to come on board, but the Marines were loyal and the boats could not come, until an officer arrived from Lord Bridport ordering the Vice-Admiral to permit them to do so.

The Fleet refused again to sail on 7th May, the *London* at Spithead again causing trouble. The Admiral asked them to state their grievances; on their replying "None" the seamen were ordered below, and the officers and Marines armed themselves. The seamen down below then cast loose the guns on the main deck and pointed them aft up the hatchways; the officers were ordered by the Admiral to fire on those trying to force their way on deck. Five men were mortally wounded and six others. James says that the Marines then threw down their arms and the seamen rushed on deck and the Admiral ordered the officers to cease firing.

On 14th May Lord Howe arrived from London with plenary powers and affairs were settled by the 18th; the Fleet under Lord Bridport cruised off Brest for the remainder of the summer.

As Portsmouth was the nearest Marine Division the Letter Books contain many interesting letters. On 29th April the Admiralty requested to know the names of two Corporals, sent on shore "from one of the ships at Spithead when in a state of mutiny for refusing to join in the measures then pursuing."

On 1st May the Commandant proposed to the Admiralty that some of the Marines "who behaved ill" as well as the whole detachment of the *Marlborough* should be discharged to Headquarters; but the Admiralty replied that this must be deferred for the present.

On the same date the Admiralty express their approval of the exemplary behaviour of the following Marines in the late mutiny at Spithead: Acting Corporal P McGuire, Sergeants Blackaller, Connor, Bullman, Doan, and Lance Corporal J Entwistle.

On 16th May Lord Bridport was instructed to apply for officers to replace those who have been recently sent ashore from the ships of his squadron. This order brought a letter from Major Douglas and Captain Lieutenant Minto on behalf of themselves and the Officers of the Portsmouth Division, pointing out the hardships that would fall on them if they were required to supply the places of those who were sent ashore in the late Mutiny. The Admiralty replied on 23rd "that they will see that the duty falls equally on all Divisions."

The Commandant at Portsmouth having forwarded a declaration of the NCOs of the Division, Their Lordships replied that they "entertain a proper sense of the loyalty and good conduct of the Marines of your Division.[132]

On 11th July ten Marines of the *Phoenix* were ordered to be discharged to Headquarters on account of their improper conduct in the late riots on board that ship - "new men to be sent and these men separated on their next embarkation."

On 11th July a letter from Captain Lock of HMS *Inspector* says "Richard Peters, Private Marine, deserves to be noted; I know him always to be of the officers' party, and so is James Instone, who is worn out in the service and wishes to retire. Peters belongs to the Portsmouth Division; he has been a soldier seventeen years and I should be glad to have him appointed Corporal and let Instone who is worn out retire."

But at Plymouth very serious happenings were taking place. We all know the story published in the History of Plymouth of the Drummer Boy on the Longroom who overheard the United Irish conspirators planning an outbreak in the Barracks; of how he informed the Sergeant (probably Gilborne) who insisted on seeing Colonel Bowater the Commandant who was at Mess and how the latter dealt with it, but it is interesting from the letter books and the court martial proceedings to learn more from Colonel Bowater's own reports.

His report to the Admiralty is dated 20th May as to "the events which took place last Sunday. Immediately on receipt of the Admiralty letter respecting additional pay I had it read to the men in their rooms, and they expressed themselves perfectly satisfied. Having seen the Warrant for the Troops of the Line sent to Lord George Lennox.[133] I directed the Deputy Paymaster to issue the Allowances therein specified. I hope their Lordships will approve.[134]

Regarding the. three persons who had been confined he reports

---

132 Dated 31st May.
133 Given in Fortescue's Vol V Appendix.
134 They approved of the same indulgences to Marines on shore as for the Line on 29th May. Ed

"On further examination of the person who came forward at first, I find the oath they had taken was not only to redress grievances and get additional pay, but also that they would stand by each other till they had made this country like France and America a Free Country. The business however I am happy to add has been entirely confined to the Irish, and more particularly to the recruits lately landed from that country; in consequence of which and disorders arising more frequently from men being out of barracks I have applied to Sir R King to order the Prensburg, Tender, now on her passage here (evidently with more recruits), to Portsmouth on her arrival, as we have already 100 men billed out.

"It is an additional pleasure to me that I have to bear testimony to the good conduct and zeal of all the NCOs under my command who came forward with the utmost alacrity on this occasion."

On 1st June he reports that he has now sufficient evidence to bring home to the ringleader Robert Lee, Private 51st Co. "who was bred an Irish Attorney" and he says he will no longer send a daily report.

A General Court-Martial under Major-General Campbell (2nd Commandant) was assembled for their trial.

51st Co. Pte. R. Lee: For Mutiny and Sedition and endeavouring to excite Marines in Barracks to mutiny and sedition.

58th Co. Pte. Daniel Coffee: For Mutiny and Sedition and for being active in swearing the Marines to join Mutiny and Sedition.

67th Co. Pte. John McGinnis: For Mutiny and Sedition and for exciting Marines to join the same.

122nd Co. Joseph Brannan: For Mutiny and Sedition and for using Mutinous and Seditious words in the Ranks after the intended Mutiny had been discovered, and the men admonished for behaving so improperly.

The Commandant reported that he had not enough Captains of experience to sit on the Court, and the Board arranged for some Line Officers to be detailed.

On 3rd July the Board confirmed the sentences. A laconic report of 6th July says that "Robert Lee, Daniel Coffee and Joseph Brannan were this day at 2 o'clock shot to death on the Hoe" and John McGinnis received 400 lashes (out of the 800 awarded) of his punishment, not being able to bear any more."

For gruesome details of the execution see the History of Plymouth.,

On 9th July 1797 Colonel Bowater recommended Sergeant A Gilborne for his conduct in discovering the late mutiny and enabling the charges to be brought home. He says, "His services have been various and meritorious and he is a child of the service; his father for many years serving here with credit as Sergeant Major." He was promoted 2nd Lieutenant in 135th Company for his services in the Mutiny on 15th July 1797. On 18th July Sergeant John Sweet was promoted 2nd Lieutenant at Plymouth for his services on board HMS *Pompee* in the Mutiny.

On 22nd November 1797 Vice Admiral Gardner brought to the notice of the Admiralty the good conduct of Captain Lewis and a party of Marines on board HMS *Glory* on 27th October, also recommending T Jacques and J Adams for NCOs which was approved. The men who had been threatened by the ships company were to be disembarked.

Simultaneously with these events the ships at the Nore had mutinied. As a result, Admiral Duncan - who had been blockading the Dutch Coast - only had two ships with him in May; gradually they returned to their allegiance however and rejoined him, but after eighteen weeks at sea he returned to Yarmouth to replenish stores, etc. on 3rd October, leaving Captain Trollope with 2 battleships and 2 frigates to watch the Dutch Fleet in the Texel. His full Fleet consisted of 16 battleships (74s, 64s, and 50s), two frigates and some cutters.

Encounter with Dutch Fleet.
On 9th October Admiral de Winter with 15 battleships and 4 frigates with some small ships was reported to be at sea. At 8.30 am on 11th October the Dutch Fleet was sighted; they had been heading for Lowestoft, but now made for Camperdown. The leading British ship cut through the Dutch line; the *Venerable* (Flag) and *Bedford*, cut through the line also and ranged up to leeward of the *Vryheid* (Flag). The *Vryheid* lost all her masts and Admiral de Winter surrendered. Contrary to actions with the French the rigging of the British ships was hardly touched, but they had been badly hulled which accounted for the heavy casualties. Ten Dutch battleships were captured and two frigates, and when the action closed the fleets were close inshore between Camperdown and Egremont. The total losses were British 203 killed and 622 wounded, of which 21 Marines were killed and 62 wounded.[135] Lieutenant Chambers (*Venerable*), Lieutenants G. Walker (*Powerful*), C. Rea (*Isis*), Sandys (*Lancaster*), Captains Cuthbert (*Ardent*) and James Cassel (*Belliqueux*) were wounded. The Dutch Fleet was out of action for the remainder of the war. Admiral de Winter died soon after in England and his son became an officer in the British Royal Artillery.

The Isles of St Marcou continued to occupy the minds of the authorities at Portsmouth. On 25th July 1797 a reinforcement of 50 Marines was ordered to be sent with a suitable number of subaltern officers and NCOs "to consist of recruits to be trained there, and for that purpose you are to send proper officers and NCOs to bring them to a state of discipline."[136]

On 21st September orders were given to send a Captain of Marines with an additional two parties of Marines of 26 each. Captain Burn was detailed and informed that he would be borne on

---
135 Almost the same percentage as at Jutland.
136 Cf. 1914-18 Relief of R.A. in Home Defences Britain's Sea Soldiers Vol. III.

the books of HMS *Badger* gunboat and follow the orders of Lieutenant Price RN, her commander. This officer was in command throughout and though a very gallant officer seems to have had a very difficult temper, judging by the number of rows with Marines, and the complaints and enquiries by Commanding Officers of frigates that followed. Anyway, Captain Burn did not last long; probably he was senior to Price.

Whether due to increased numbers or because they took on additional duties in the garrison, on 21st June the Board approved of 1 Major General (Lewis, the 2nd Commandant), 2 Captains, 1 Adjutant, 3 Subalterns, 12 Sergeants, 12 Drummers and 312 Privates occupying Hilsea Barracks at Portsmouth, also one of the Headquarter Adjutants was to be sent to Hilsea; of course there were objections, but they were peremptorily ordered to send one and also officers capable of bringing recruits into a state of discipline. Portsmouth was evidently up to establishment as further recruits were ordered to be sent to Chatham.

Pay.
On 26th July 1797 an Order-in-Council raised the pay of Privates to 1/- a day.

Pikes.
We note that on 23rd September a supply of pikes for Sergeants was made; the word Halberd was not used and perhaps the weapon itself was changed.

Courts-Martial.
But at the end of 1797 a hitherto unprecedented event took place. The Commandant at Portsmouth (Major General M Wemyss) was tried by General Court-Martial. As it throws a light on Court Martial procedure at that time it is quoted fairly fully. In the first place the Commandant in Town (i.e. the present AG) came down and assumed command of the Division. General and Field Officers of Marines were scraped together from all Divisions. Then General Wemyss objected to being tried by a Court composed entirely of Marine Officers, but this was over-ruled.

General Souter (the Commandant in Town), in despair of not being able to find enough officers (fifteen), applied to the Admiralty and was told that it was his business. Also My Lords decided that although he was convening officer he was eligible to sit as President. The Warrant to assemble the Court was dated 9th December and the confirmation of the sentence 29th January 1798. Wemyss was tried for repeatedly declaring his intention to entirely abolish the Divisional Fund ('being a charitable institution very beneficial to the Marine Corps and service at large'). Also for most gross, violent and insulting treatment of the Adjutant. Also for ordering the Barrackmaster to charge to Government certain things that were for his own private use.

He was found not guilty of third charge, guilty of the first and the second partly proved. In view of his long service and infirmities (he must have been very old as he was in command as a Captain at the Battle of Buxar in 1764) he was sentenced to be placed on half pay, which was confirmed by the Admiralty. He was succeeded by Major General T Avarne, an officer with a splendid war record.

Naval Striking Forces Santa Cruz.
Before leaving 1797 it is interesting to describe an account of a Naval Striking force, which though unsuccessful, contains many lessons.

On 28th May the boats of the *Lively* under Lieutenant T M Hardy RN and Lieutenant R Bulkeley (Marines), cut out a French brig from the harbour of Santa Cruz, Teneriffe. On 20th July, Nelson (with his flag in the *Theseus*), 3 battleships and 3 frigates arrived at Santa Cruz. 200 Seamen and Marines from each battleship and 150 from each frigate with a small detachment of Royal Artillery were detailed to land, a total of 1000-1050 men. Captain Troubridge of *Culloden* was in command, each Captain commanding his own seamen and Captain T Oldfield commanding the Marines.

On the 20th frigates with the boats stood in to land the men and gain possession of a Fort on the north east side of the bay, but the current and a strong wind prevented the boats reaching the desired point and they withdrew. On 22nd at 3 am the battleships bore up for Santa Cruz and just after daylight were joined by the frigates and boats, but the enemy was now thoroughly alarmed.

It was decided to land and attack the heights immediately above the fort and from there attempt to storm the town. On the 22nd at 9 pm the frigates anchored off the east end of the town and landed their men; the town was found to be strongly guarded and they had to re-embark during the night, which they did without loss.

On the 24th the *Leander* (50) arrived and her large detachment of Marines was added to the Marine Battalion. At 5 pm the Squadron anchored to the north east of the town, the battleships about five miles off, the frigates about two, as if to land in that direction. This was a feint. The rendezvous of the boats was fixed on the Molehead. At 11 pm on the 24th 700 Seamen and Marines embarked in the boats, 180 in the *Fox* cutter, and 75 in a large provision ketch, numbering with the Royal Artillery 1,100. Captain Oldfield was in charge of the Marines, Lieutenant Baynes of the RA, Admiral Nelson in command in person.

Rough weather scattered the boats, but by 1.30 am on the 25th the Rear Admiral's boat and two others reached within half gunshot of the Molehead. The alarm bells then rang out and fire was opened from thirty guns and from a body of troops on shore. Two shots reached the *Fox* and when struck by a third she sank and 97 were drowned. A shot struck Admiral Nelson on the elbow as he was stepping ashore, so disabling him that he had to be carried back and his arm amputated.

The British effected a landing, storming and carrying the Molehead in spite of the enemy force of three to four hundred men with six 24 pdr guns; the guns were spiked, but the attackers were met by a heavy fire from the Citadel. Captain Brace and nearly all this party were killed or wounded. Captain Troubridge's boats pushed ashore under a battery south of the Citadel and a few others landed at the same time, but the others were driven back by the surf and all ammunition was wetted.

Troubridge pushed on and reached the Prado, the main square, but of course could not communicate with the Admiral's party. He summoned the citadel, but naturally got no reply and his scaling ladders had been lost. Captains Hood and Muller RN had meanwhile landed to the south west of the spot where Troubridge had got ashore and the three parties joined up; at daybreak the survivors numbered only 340, viz: 80 Marines, 80 Pikemen, and 180 seamen with small arms. This little party tried to attack the citadel without ladders; the streets were full of Spaniards and guns and the boats were stove in.

Troubridge then sent Captain Hood to tell the Governor he would burn the town, if the Spaniards advanced any further and asked the following terms (!!!):

'The British to be allowed to re-embark with their arms or to be provided with others.' In case of compliance he engaged that the ships would not further molest the town nor attack any of the Canary Islands!

Such is the power of sea command.

The Governor was so astonished that he agreed to the terms; Troubridge marched his party to the Molehead and embarked in boats provided by the Spaniards, who also supplied them with a biscuit and ration of wine for each man and received their wounded into their hospital. The squadron was even allowed to obtain provisions etc.

The British losses were as follows:

Killed: 1 Captain and 4 Lieutenants RN; 3 Lieutenants Marines, Raby and Robinson (Leander), W Barham (Emerald); 25 Seamen and 14 Marines.
Wounded: Rear Admiral and 2 Captains RN; 1 Lieutenant RN; 1 Midshipman; 85 Seamen and 15 Marines.
Drowned: 97 Seamen and Marines.
Missing: 5.

St Paul's Thanksgiving Service.
On 11th December the following order was issued to the Chatham and Portsmouth Divisions:

"Order a Captain's Guard of Marines together with the Band of the Division under your command to march from Chatham or Portsmouth to attend in Town by 18th inst. (which, if possible, is to be commanded by officers who were in the actions of 1st June, 14th February, 11th October last) in order to attend His Majesty to St. Paul's Cathedral on the 19th inst. to offer thanksgiving for the many signal and important victories obtained by His Majesty's Navy in the course of the present War.

PS This being a King's Guard the Colours must of course accompany it; and their Lordships desire it may be selected from the best and most orderly men at Quarters."

On 14th December the Order was modified as follows:

"The Captain's Guard is intended to form part of the procession to St. Paul's with the Colours taken from the enemy and not as a guard to His Majesty in the procession and that therefore they are not to bring the Colours with them if they have not begun the march.

1798

The numbers voted for the year were again 20,000, and from the Letter Books they seem to have been fairly well up to strength.

The French were still threatening the invasion of Ireland and this year occurred the abortive rebellion; consequently, the Channel Fleet and the flotillas defending the Channel were constantly on the watch. In January that fleet was off Brest, during which time HMS *Mars* had an encounter with the French *Hercule* in which the Captain of Marines (J White) and 4 Marines were killed, 2 Sergeants, 1 Drummer and 5 Marines wounded.

St. Marcou.
On 7th May the Isles of St Marcou came prominently into the picture. They were attacked by the French and after a severe fight the French who had made the main attack on the Western Battery were beaten off. Lieutenants Bourne and Lawrence were in the Eastern Battery, and Lieutenants Ensor and Mangham in the Western; on 12th May the Commandant at Portsmouth, who had forwarded a report received from Lieutenant Ensor giving an account of the attack and of the good conduct of the party under his command, received from Their Lordships the following reply (12th May 1798): "That they have received from Captain Price the most satisfactory account of the good conduct of the Marine Detachment and that you will do right to take proper notice of the NCOs and Private men who had distinguished themselves on this occasion".

Discontent in Fleet.
This behaviour was all the more creditable as a letter of 14th June orders several men who were incapacitated from duty from old age and injuries they have received in the service to be replaced by effective men. But the excitement of the attack having died away, trouble began to brew there. On 22nd November we learn of complaints of bad accommodation and treatment, particularly by a Sergeant Ruddle; and the SNO of the vessels off Havre being sent to enquire; also, that there were no sentry boxes and that watch coats were deficient: "Coats to be sent over and charged to the accounts of men to whom issued." On 6th December two Dutchmen deserted, taking a boat and the Commandant was told that foreign recruits should not be sent to such a place, which throws yet another light on the difficulties of recruiting and drafting.

But a real row blazed up in December when Lieutenant E Nicholls ("Fighting Nicholls") was ordered to be sent to Portsmouth to be tried by Court Martial. Captain Price asked for an officer senior to Nicholls "to superintend the discipline of a very fine body of men." Anyway, Nicholls and three sergeants were sent to Portsmouth, but after being kept in arrest for a considerable time no action seems to have been taken and peace was declared soon after. One cannot imagine Nicholls serving quietly in such a place.

Expressions of Loyalty.
There are many notes of the aftermath of the Mutinies. On 3rd February 1798 the Sergeants of the Portsmouth Division offered £50 as a voluntary contribution in favour of HM Government and of the Country. In acknowledging the gift, the Admiralty say it is to be paid into the Bank of England. On 15th March the Commandant at Portsmouth reported that the Officers, NCOs and Privates of that Division had voluntarily subscribed and paid into the Bank of England one week's full pay amounting to the sum of £544.0.9, and the Admiralty replied that "They observe with great satisfaction the disposition which has been manifested by the Officers, NCOs, Drummers and Privates of the Portsmouth Division on this occasion." On the 8th February the Plymouth Division had made a similar offer which was accepted, but the amount is not given; the Commandant says that the idea originated with the NCOs and Privates themselves and also that the Retired Officers in the neighbourhood had joined in. There is probably a similar letter from Chatham, and they also contributed.

Clothing.
In March another alteration was made in the supply of clothing; contracts were in future to be made by the Navy Board, requisitions being made to the Board through the Storekeeper of the Dockyard.

Promotion from Ranks.
Here is yet another example of how matters in the Marines work in circles. On 28th April 1798, Sergeant J Mooney at Portsmouth, one of the Squad Sergeants, was promoted to 2nd Lieutenant for his long service and exemplary conduct and placed on half pay to continue his duty in the squad office, so that affairs were now back in the position when Squad Officers were abolished in 1786.

On 29th August 1798, Sergeant O'Neale of the Plymouth Division was promoted 2nd Lieutenant for his exemplary conduct on board HMS *Caesar* in bringing to light a very dangerous conspiracy of some United Irishmen belonging to that ship and also of his having on a former occasion been very active in bringing forward evidences on the Marines who mutinied and were shot at Plymouth in July 1797. The details of his services were to be promulgated in Public Orders at all Divisions, which was the method in those days of notifying all good work by Officers and Men.

United Irishmen.
The United Irishmen were evidently still a course of anxiety as reports are constantly called for as to numbers of suspected men; in forwarding one list in September 1798 the Commandant at Portsmouth expresses satisfaction at so few in such a large body of men, having been implicated in the Mutiny and Sedition, and expressing his entire confidence in the zeal and loyalty of the NCOs and Men of his Division.

Foreigners.

A report from Plymouth dated 15th September 1798 gives some idea of the number of foreigners serving in the Corps. Serving at Plymouth:

From		Sgts	Cpls	Ptes
Ireland		16	7	85
Ireland	Suspects	-	2	18
Holland		-	-	5
Germany		-	-	3
Sweden		-	-	-
Denmark		-	-	1
France		-	1	-
		16	10	113

Recruiting.

In September recruiting was opened in Scotland, a Colonel Duncan being sent to Edinburgh to superintend.

Ireland.

The French had been fomenting trouble in Ireland, and projected assisting the rebels. For this purpose, they sent a squadron with officers, arms, etc. On the 12-14th October they met the British squadron under Admiral Sir J B Warren who captured the frigate *La Hoche* conveying the notorious rebel Wolfe Tone and 50 French officers of rank. Captain Williams of the Marines was sent to take charge of them and was afterwards a principal witness in the trial of Tone in Dublin.

Battle of the Nile.

The main interest of the year lay in the Mediterranean, where Napoleon, benefiting by the withdrawal of the British Fleet to Gibraltar and the Atlantic, had taken the opportunity of leading his expedition to Egypt with a view to his advance on India. He left Toulon on 19th May, reached Malta on 9th June, and soon overcame the Knights of St. John - then holding the island - who capitulated on the 12th. Leaving a garrison of 4,000 men he left on 18th June for Egypt. Admiral Nelson with his flag in the *Vanguard* (thirteen 74s and one 50) had been sent to watch his movements. Going direct to Egypt, Nelson sighted Alexandria on 28th June, but the French had not yet arrived; he hurried back towards Sicily. The French arrived at Alexandria on 1st and 2nd July, and by 25th July had entered Cairo. Nelson left Syracuse on 19th July and on 1st August sighted the French Fleet at Aboukir, where they were anchored off shore in the form of a bow. Their fleet consisted of one 120, three 80s, nine 74s, and four frigates. The British anchored by the stern and dropped down parallel with them; the *Culloden* went ashore but took part in the action. Fire was opened at sunset in the great Battle of the Nile and continued throughout the night. This is no place to describe all the gallant deeds in both fleets. The French under Admiral de Bruis were protected by flanking batteries ashore: the French Flagship *L'Orient* was set on fire and blew up with terrible loss. Day broke at 4 am and the action continued till noon the next day. Of the French ships one blew up, eight surrendered, two escaped, and one went ashore and was burnt by her crew, and on the morning of the 3rd the last ship - *Tonnant* - surrendered.

The French Fleet destroyed, the French Army and Napoleon were locked up in Egypt and all his grandiose schemes of conquest crumbled. The British loss was 218 killed and 678 wounded, of which the Marines lost Captain Faddy (*Theseus*), 18 NCOs and men killed, Captains Creswell (*Alexander*) and Hopkins, Lieutenant Jewell (*Vanguard*) and 78 NCOs and men wounded.[137]

On 13th October 1798 Captain T Oldfield, the Senior Marine Officer, was given a Brevet Majority for his services in the action. Lord Nelson was created a Peer.

On 14th August seven battleships with six prizes arrived at Gibraltar. Lord Nelson received his orders from Admiral St Vincent to return to the westward for the attack on Minorca, Captain Hood with three ships being left to blockade Egypt. Nelson had to refit his ships and arrived at Naples where he fell into the toils of the Queen of Naples and Lady Hamilton. On 1st September Turkey declared war on France in conjunction with the Russians.

Malta.
The British soon set to work to provide themselves with bases in the Mediterranean Sea. On 12th October the *Alexander* (Captain Ball), *Culloden*, and *Colossus* with five Portuguese battleships were sent to blockade Malta, Major Weir and 300 Marines being landed to help the Maltese. The French retired into the fortress, but two French ships escaped. On 24th Nelson arrived with *Vanguard* and *Minotaur*; on the 28th Gozo surrendered and the Castle was occupied by Captain Creswell and the Marines of the *Alexander*, and the French were confined to Valetta.

Minorca.
At the end of October, Commodore Duckworth with *Leviathan* and *Centaur* (74s) and two 44 gun frigates with smaller ships and a detachment of troops under the Hon C Stuart was sent to capture Minorca, the old British base in the Mediterranean. The squadron approached the north side of the island; the battleships anchored off Fornello, the transports and frigates proceeded a little further east and anchored in Addaya Bay on 7th November. The Spaniards were evidently taken by surprise. Covered by a frigate the covering force of 800 men landed and held their own against 2,000 Spaniards until the remainder landed. At nightfall the enemy retired. On the 8th General Stuart seized the pass of Mercadel in the centre of the island, cutting off Port Mahon from Ciudadella, and the main body joined him on the 9th, the seamen dragging up the Battalion guns. A force of 160 men was sent to take Mahon which was almost deserted and capitulated at once. The British then removed the boom and the harbour was opened to the fleet.

A force advanced on Ciudadella in two columns, the Spaniards retiring into the town. The Southern or right flank column proceeded via Ferrerie to seize the sunken road, the main body, to

---

137 A rather larger proportion than in the other great Battles including Jutland, where the Marine losses are generally one tenth of the whole.

which were attached the 90 Marines of the *Centaur* and *Leviathan* under Captain Minto with 6 light guns from the fleet, advancing by the North Road along the coast. At this time four Spanish men-of-war were sighted and Commodore Duckworth, without re-embarking his seamen and Marines, sailed against them and drove them off. Stuart opened his trenches and batteries against Ciudadella and armed them with the light guns - really RHA guns - and drew up his troops to look as if they occupied a line of four miles and having completely bluffed the enemy they capitulated on the 15th. General Stuart writing to the Commodore said: "I have the honour to return you and the gentlemen employed on shore under your command my sincere thanks for your activity, zeal, and assistance in forwarding the Light Artillery of the army."

The *Leander* (50), bringing back prisoners after the Nile, came across the *Genereux* (74) - one of the escaping French ships and after a severe action it was captured. The Captain reported on "the spirited conduct and well directed fire of the Marines on the poop under Sergeant Dair."[138]

1799

The numbers voted for the Corps were again 20,000. The United Irish recruits seem still to have been giving trouble, as there are orders for their disembarkation from various ships.

In January the Marine garrison for St Marcou was fixed; they were to be borne on the books of HMS *Badger* and *Sandfly*, gunboats, as part complement.

HMS *Badger*: 2 Lieutenants, 8 Sergeants, 8 Corporals, 3 Drummers, 170 Privates.
HMS *Sandfly*: 2 Lieutenants, 4 Sergeants, 4 Corporals, 2 Drummers, 90 Privates.

But the rows with the Commanding Officer went on, and Captain Wilkinson of HMS *Success* was ordered to proceed to investigate the complaints of ill treatment of NCOs and Men and send a report on Captain Price's conduct.

By Order-in-Council 5th June 1799 each of the 136 companies was increased by 15 Privates and 4 more Companies were raised - Nos. 137 and 139 to Portsmouth; 138 and 140 to Plymouth, a total of 2,420.

Discharge by Purchase.
We learn also that thirty guineas was not sufficient to raise two recruits and therefore discharge by purchase was fixed at forty guineas.

Income Tax.
In this year Income Tax is first charged on officers, and any who had £60 a year whether from private income or from pay were liable to the tax from 6th June 1799. Paymasters apparently deducted it.

---

138 Lieutenant Robinson had been killed at Tenerife.

Transfer from Militia.
Men from the Militia were authorised by Act of Parliament to enlist into the Regular Forces, and this was extended to the Marines. Considerable numbers of recruits were obtained in this way.[139]

In this year the main interest of the operations was in the Mediterranean where large numbers of the Corps were employed. Napoleon with his army was shut up in Egypt owing to the destruction of his Fleet; he completed the conquest of that country, and then turned his attention to the invasion of Palestine and Syria.

Captain Sir Sidney Smith RN commanding the British squadron had diplomatic powers as well as Military and signed a treaty of Alliance with Russia and Turkey. The Turks proposed an attack on the French in Egypt from Syria.

Whilst at Constantinople the Marines were presented with a pair of Colours on 7th January 1799 by the Ambassador's wife, which were afterwards carried at Acre.

Egypt.
Napoleon anticipated the danger and marched 12,000 men early' in February towards the frontier. On 10th February he left Cairo and arrived at the forts protecting the wells at El Arish on the 17th. On the 25th El Arish surrendered; Jaffa was carried by storm on 7th March and he reached the heights commanding St Jean D'Acre on 18th March. Sir Sidney Smith left Constantinople on 19th February, arriving at Alexandria on 3rd March. He bombarded it in order to divert the French, but to no purpose. Anticipating Napoleon's moves, he sailed for the Coast of Syria, arriving at Caiffa on the 11th and at St. Jean D'Acre on the 15th. Here he arranged measures of defence with the Turkish commander Diezzar Pasha, with whom the late Viceroy of Egypt, Ibrahim Pasha had taken refuge. He sent Colonel Philipeaux, a French Royalist Engineer Officer, to look after the defences and landed the Marines of the *Tigre*, *Theseus*, and *Alliance* under Major Douglas of the *Tigre*, to whom he gave the Brevet rank of Colonel so that the Turks and Seamen might be under his orders.

On the 18th a convoy of French vessels was seen and captured; it proved to contain the French Siege Train, so that Napoleon was reduced to his field guns and howitzers, whilst the British mounted the French Siege ordnance on the walls. From the 17th to the 23rd the British gunboats flanked from the sea the French approaches and constantly harassed the French posts and cut off his supplies, Lieutenant Burton and his Marines distinguishing themselves. On 20th March the French opened fire from their trenches against the East Salient angle of the town within 900 yards, and on 1st April attempted to storm the breach, which was found to be impracticable. They were repulsed by the seamen and Marines and eventually fled in panic. The *Tigre* and *Theseus* were driven from their anchorage by a gale. The French sapped closer to the ditch, where the assault had failed and were trying to mine the tower itself. Part of the counterscarp was destroyed, and a lodgment made on the north east wall. The garrison determined to make a sortie on 7th April, a party of seamen under

---
139 Army Circular 17th July 1799, and Letter Books.

Lieutenant Wright to destroy the mine. The attack was under Colonel Douglas and consisted of three columns, each headed by the Marines, whilst the Turks attacked the trenches on the right and left. The noise made by the Turks aroused the French, but the Seamen and Marines carried the 1st and 2nd parallels, but all except the centre column under Major Oldfield of the Marines were driven back. The French accounts say that Oldfield had advanced boldly to the entrance of the mine - "they attacked like heroes and were received by heroes." Oldfield was killed at the entrance and the column retired. His sword remained in the hands of the French Grenadiers; his body was found by the French and buried by them with military honours. Lieutenant Beatty of the Marines was also wounded.

On 1st May after a bombardment, the French attempted to storm but were again beaten back. The Marines of the *Tigre* and *Theseus* ran out two ravolins on either side of the breach and manned them whilst the ships kept up a heavy fire. Colonel Philipeaux succumbed to heat and fever and Colonel Douglas took over the engineering duties. The French continued their attack every night and nine different attempts at assault were defeated. The French had now got up heavy guns overland from Jaffa and tried to breach the East Curtain; an attempt to effect a lodgment in the tower at the salient angle was also defeated

On the 51st day of the siege (7th May) a Turkish squadron under Hassan Bey arrived and landed some troops trained in the European manner, and on the morning of the 8th the French made another attempt and planted their flag on the North-East Tower; Sir Sidney Smith landed with all the men he could and as the Turkish reinforcements were also landed and pushed into the Town the stormers were driven out. The bombardment was resumed by the French and masses of the wall fell, till a breach was practicable, Though the stormers entered the place on the 10th they were cut to pieces by the Turks and at last on 20th the new Turkish troops made a sortie, and the French abandoned the siege and retreated in disorder - leaving 23 heavy guns behind them - pursued along the beach by Sir Sidney Smith and harassed in rear by the Arabs.

The British losses were 53 Seamen and Marines killed, and 113 wounded, 13 drowned and 8 2 prisoners.

The French retreated by El Arish where they left a small garrison and then retired to Cairo. 'The successful defence fixed a barrier to Buonaparte's ambition; Egypt was conquered at Acre and India preserved.

Sir Sidney Smith continued his coastal raids with varying success. He first got together 1300 Turks in Cyprus and with his Seamen and Marines landed them under Colonel Douglas at Aboukir, but the Turks fled[140] and the Seamen and Marines were re-embarked. Sir Sidney collected another force at Rhodes and other islands and attacked the French at Damietta. This force under Sir Sidney and Colonel Douglas destroyed the French magazines and redoubts, but the Turks again fled and the expedition proved disastrous.

---

140 A letter of Sir J. Douglas in Globe and Laurel Records. p 111 gives some idea of what these Turkish troops were like.

Finally, the Turkish force in Palestine was induced to advance to El Arish. Colonel Douglas was appointed as adviser and joined them at Gaza on 7th December, having landed at Jaffa on 30th November with some officers and a small force of Seamen and Marines. They advanced on El Arish and summoned it to surrender. The French at first refused; Douglas and two officers reconnoitered the fort and batteries were erected. After some days bombardment the French hoisted the white flag (the French troops having revolted)[141] and Colonel Douglas ascended into the fort by means of a rope let down to him; the place surrendered, the enemy announcing that its fall was principally due to the small British detachment. Colonel Douglas reported that "the cheerful way in which the whole detachment performed their duty, exposed as they were in the desert, without tents, ill-fed, and with only brackish water to drink, gained them the admiration of the whole Ottoman Army."

This paved the way for the Convention of 24th January 1800, signed at El Arish, for the evacuation of Egypt by the whole French Army under Kleber. This of course was not recognised, as Sir Sidney had not the necessary powers and was not ratified, and it was not until 1801 that the French were finally driven from Egypt.

Colonel Douglas was selected to take home the dispatches and was knighted by the King and granted a life pension of £400 a year.[142] He died on 4th March 1814 at Greenwich and is buried in Old Charlton Church.

Taking advantage of the absence of Napoleon in Egypt the Neapolitans revolted and were at once supported by the British Squadron under Lord Nelson, so that the Marines had another opportunity of extending the power of the Fleet over the land.

Castel Uovo and Castel Nuovo are the principal sea defences of Naples; Nuovo is in the heart of the City, whilst Uovo is on a tongue of land which runs out into the bay. Fort St. Elmo commanded the town inland on the west side.

Cardinal Ruffo with a motley crowd of Neapolitans, Russians and Swiss had shut up the French troops in the Forts, and on 22nd they capitulated. Lord Nelson would not recognize the capitulation and on the 27th landed his Seamen and Marines. The Marines, 800 strong, were formed into a Battalion under Major (local Lieutenant-Colonel) Strickland with Bt. Major Creswell as second in command, 7 Captains, 23 Lieutenants, 2 Adjutants (Wemyss and Tydesley), and Quartermaster Vyvian. The French evacuated Uovo and Nuovo and retired into Fort St. Elmo. On 30th June at 5 am Captain Troubridge (*Culloden*) with the British Marines, 400 Portuguese Marines, 450 Russians, and 9 heavy guns advanced against St Elmo; he summoned it to surrender but was refused, so trenches were opened. The French garrison consisted of 800 men under Major Mejan. By the 5th July the batteries containing 8 mortars, 4 howitzers, and six 36-pdrs were ready and opened fire. The Russians also opened a battery under Captain Baillie (Marines). On 11th July a British battery was knocked out, but they opened another with six 36 pdrs about 180 yards from

---
141 James.
142 For interesting letters of Sir John see Globe and Laurel Records pp. 108-112.

the wall, screened by trees. After a few hours' bombardment the forts surrendered, and the Marine grenadiers marched into it on 12th July. The enemy were allowed to march out with the honours of war. All the guns and works were destroyed. The British losses were 5 Officers and 32 rank and file killed, 5 Officers and 79 rank and file wounded.

On 20th July, Captain Troubridge with 1,000 British and Portuguese Seamen and Marines marched from Naples, halted for the night at Caserta, and encamped before Capua on 22nd July.

A pontoon bridge was thrown over the Vetturino river and batteries were constructed. By the 26th one battery of four 24 pdrs and one of two howitzers and a mortar were ready and opened fire, which was replied to by 17 guns. On the 26th trenches were opened, and new batteries begun, on which the besieged proposed terms of capitulation and on the 29th it was signed and 2,800 French marched out under escort of 400 Marines and 2 squadrons of General Acton's cavalry. In all 108 guns were captured.

The Squadron then proceeded to Gaeta, landing there on 31st July. The place surrendered the next day with 1,500 French and 73 guns who were handed over to the King of Naples.

On 11th, Captain Troubridge sent the *Minotaur* with two small ships to Civita Vecchia and followed with the *Culloden*, on 29th and 30th September with the Seamen and Marines of the two ships and Neapolitan Royalists he took over the town; he also occupied Corneto and Tolsa. By the same capitulation Rome was handed over and was occupied by the Neapolitans and a detachment of Seamen from the *Minotaur*: 5,000 French were dispatched to France in accordance with the terms of the treaty.

Holland.
In August an expedition under General Abercrombie and Admiral Mitchell had been sent to Holland. Landing at the Helder between the 27th and 30th August they captured the Dutch Fleet and moving south fought a severe action at Bergen. Continuing the advance on 2nd October the Battle of Egmont-Op-Zee (borne on the Colours of several regiments) was fought. A detachment of 167 Seamen and Marines, the Marine officers being Lieutenants M Wybourn, J Howell, J Higgins and R Gardner, had been sent to garrison Lemmerstown in West Friesland; at 5 am on 11th October a small advanced guard of French and Bavarians tried to storm the North Battery. They were caught between the fire from two sides, surrounded by the Seamen and had to surrender. The main body of 670 soon after assaulted the village, but after a sharp fight of 4½ hours were driven off. The Marines pursued, but the enemy escaped, having broken down a bridge. The fire of the Marines cost them a further 18 killed and 20 wounded.

On 18th October the weather and the nature of the country precluding any further advance, a capitulation was signed, and the British troops were evacuated to England.

Puerto Cabello.
On the Spanish Main at Puerto Cabello there was a gallant cutting-out expedition by the boats of HMS Hermione, which is of interest as the Marines were commanded by an Acting Marine Officer - Monsieur de la Tour du Pin. The account says, "At this critical moment M. de la Tour du Pin boarded with the Marines over the larboard gangway, and gave a favourable turn to the then not very promising affair." The Marines were instantly formed and poured a volley down the after hatchway and "the gallant English rushed down with bayonets fixed on to the main-deck." The ship was brought out, and the shore batteries opened on the frigate as the sails filled but she got away; a few shots from the deck quieting the Spaniards, the English loss was only 12 wounded. Of the Spanish crew of 365, 119 were killed and 97 wounded. There is a picture of this incident in the Painted Hall at Greenwich.

1800

Malta.
Early in the year a Battalion of Marines from the Fleet was landed in Malta to assist the Maltese in blockading the French in Valetta - Captain Weir in command. Four Captains, six lieutenants, Adjutant (Tyldesley) and Quartermaster (Scobell). On 4th September Valetta capitulated and the Marines took possession. Soon after Major Weir seems to have opened a Recruiting Station and raised many recruits; the letter books of the next few years contain many references to it. The station was closed in September 1807.

Brest.
The Fleet under Admiral Sir John B Warren was stationed off the Penmarcks blockading Brest, and the Seamen and Marines were employed in many cutting-out expeditions, two of the most noticeable of which were:

1. At the Quimper River 23/24 June. By daybreak on the 24th the boats were off the entrance; to protect them whilst ascending the river two detachments of Marines were landed, that on the right bank under Lieutenant Burke RN of *Renown*; that on the left bank by Lieutenant M A Gerrard, Marines, of *Fisgard*. The enemy ships were found to be too far up to be reached but the Marines blew up a battery and two small forts before returning.

2. Attack on a convoy inside the Isle of Noirmoutier on 1st July. The convoy with escorting corvettes was bound for Brest and was lying under the protection of six batteries at the south east end of the island with flanking guile on every projecting point. The boats were in three divisions containing 192 Seamen and Marines, Lieutenant Burke RN in command with Lieutenants M J Thompson, O H Ballinghall, and Major Gerrard, William Jarrett, and H Hulton. They boarded the armed ships at midnight and captured them after a stout resistance and much loss; they were unable to bring off the 15 merchantmen laden with flour, corn and provisions and timber for the fleet at Brest but destroyed them. On their return the boats stranded on a sandbank and Lieutenant Burke and his party came under the fire of 400 French

and of the forts on Noirmoutier. They promptly attacked some vessels afloat near them in order to capture one large enough to bring them off; this they did and dragged her nearly two miles over the sand until the men were up to their necks in water but succeeded eventually in getting her afloat: 92 men however were captured, including Lieutenant Burke, and Lieutenants Thompson and Ballinghall wounded. Lieutenant Gerrard was invalided on 15th November 1808 and is then spoken of as Sir Mark Gerrard, so he appears to have been knighted either for this or when he was injured later when boarding a French gun brig La Rochelle.

Ferrol.
In August an expedition under General Pulteney, escorted by the squadron under Admiral Sir John B Warren was sent to attack Ferrol (Spain). Lieutenants J Farmer and G Richardson, Marines were landed on 25th August with their detachments as a covering force and stormed a battery of guns which commanded the landing place selected. By the morning of the 26th the whole force was ashore; the operations however were found to be impracticable. The Fleet was lying in an open roadstead, the land side was the only one accessible to attack and was formidably fortified, whilst it would be necessary to keep a strong force to prevent any attempts at relief. The troops were therefore re-embarked and went on to Vigo but could find no object worthy of attack.

Belleisle.
In August there was a projected attack on Belleisle by the fleet, and a battalion of 800 men was formed from the Fleet under Captain Lukin who were to have landed at Vieux Chateau and marched to Sauzon by the coast road, but the enterprise was abandoned.

Rations.
At Headquarters in consequence of the rising price of bread the Government took over the supply to the forces in England, appointing a firm of contractors. Every man was to have a 'four pound loaf every four days, made of good marketable English or foreign wheat, out of which the bran has been taken by means of a twelve seamed cloth.' A stoppage of sixpence to be made from his pay and paid to the contractor; any excess to be charged to Marine Contingencies.[143]

Colours.
In December 1800 the Divisions were supplied with new Colours with the St. Patrick's Cross added to the Union Jack, owing to the Union with Ireland.

Beer Money.
On 1st May 1800 it was ordered that 1d a day Beer Money was to be paid to all NCOs and men in Barracks in lieu of the Beer Ration granted in 1794. This allowance lasted in the case of NCOs till 1831 and for Privates until 1899.

The Portsmouth Letter Books are full this year of drafts and changes in the garrison at St

---

143 Portsmouth Letter Books.

Marcou, but there was no fighting. In December 1800 a letter about the embarkation of a Captain Miles shows that the Marine Officers were tried by Court Martial as well as the Naval Officers when a ship was lost.

1801

In order to celebrate the commencement of the new (nineteenth) century and also to celebrate the Happy Union with Ireland a man was promoted to Corporal in each Company.[144]

The numbers voted for the year were for the first two months 22,696 and for the remainder 30,000. On 16th January an Order-in-Council directed that five more companies were to be raised (two each to Chatham and Plymouth, and one to Portsmouth), each Company to consist of 1 Captain, 2 First Lieutenants, 2 Second Lieutenants, 8 Sergeants, 8 Corporals, 6 Drummers, and 140 Privates.

Pikes.

The supply of Pikes for Sergeants on the augmentation was approved, and from a letter asking for compensation for clothing we see that Marines were employed for fitting out ships for commissioning. The application was of course refused. Also Marines were embarked in ships for the West Indies to make up for the shortage of seamen.

Lieutenant Gillespie, the Corps Historian, who was recruiting at Birmingham, seems to have got into trouble for not answering letters and was placed on half pay, whilst Lieutenant M Phillips (Captain Cook's Marine Officer) was at last promoted to Captain on 23rd May 1801. We also learn that the cost of raising two recruits was £52. On 4th July Brevet Lieutenant Colonel D Collins, the original Judge Advocate at Botany Bay, was brought back to full pay as Captain of 55th Company.

In July a new scheme of complements for HM Ships was promulgated, ranging from 145 Officers and Men for a first rate to 15 men for a sloop.

Copenhagen.

Afloat and ashore the Corps was actively employed. Napoleon had succeeded in organising the Armed Neutrality of the North against England, and to prevent any ill results Great Britain struck first and dispatched a fleet under Admiral Sir Hyde Parker to seize the Danish Fleet lying off Copenhagen.

Sir Hyde Parker anchored his two 98 gun, four 74s and two 64 gun battleships off the Sound and sent in Lord Nelson with his flag in the *Elephant*, with seven 74s, two 64s, one 54 and one 60 gun battleships, four frigates and some sloops to attack the Danish fleet and batteries. The Danes had 18 ships and two batteries flanking them, one of 30 guns the other of 38 guns.

---

144 Plymouth Orders 31st December 1800.

On 2nd April Lord Nelson ordered his squadron to go in and, anchoring by the stern, to bring up abreast of the enemy. The bomb vessels were outside the British line to throw shells over them. At 11 am the squadron opened fire; the bomb vessels proved of no use, so the frigates engaged the batteries and as matters were not going well, Hyde Parker generously made the signal to allow Lord Nelson to break off the action as his squadron was in a very tight place. This was the celebrated occasion when Nelson turned his blind eye to the signals. After five hours' bombardment the Danish Adjutant General came off to arrange terms and the action closed, the Danish ships being surrendered.

The total casualties were 255 killed and 688 wounded. The casualty lists show that a considerable number of troops must have been embarked as Marines as the Marines had 32 killed and 104 wounded and the soldiers 28 killed and 44 wounded; whether these were Royal Artillery in the bomb vessels one cannot say. The Marines had two Lieutenants wounded and the soldiers two Captains and one Lieutenant killed, and one Lieutenant wounded.

In the Channel the flotillas, which were being assembled for the invasion of England, were constantly attacked by the British flotillas with not very successful results.

Ferrajo.
In the Mediterranean Porto Ferrajo in Elba was being held as an advanced base for the squadrons operating on the coasts of France and Italy. It only had a small garrison of 400 men.

On 2nd May the French landed 1,500 men on the Neapolitan part of the island to attack the Tuscan part in which Ferrajo is situated and also blockaded the harbour. On 1st August Admiral Sir John B Warren raised the blockade and captured the French frigate with stores. Lieutenant C Douglas of the Marines lost his leg in the action. On 12th September Colonel Airey commanding the garrison asked Admiral Warren for a battalion of Seamen and Marines to assist in the attack on some French batteries, then closing the port, and asked for the fleet to co-operate. On 13th September 440 Marines under Captain J Richardson with 240 Seamen, some Tuscans and a battalion of Maltese under Major Weir of the Marines - about 1,000 all told - under Captain White RN of the *Renown* were landed.

The attack was made, but the force was not strong enough to complete the whole business; Lieutenant Campbell of the Marines charged and drove the French into a narrow pass where his further advance was checked by the arrival of French reinforcements and he had to fall back on the garrison. Captain Long RN was killed whilst storming a bridge. The Marines lost heavily - 12 killed and 20 wounded, with 64 missing - 8 seamen were killed, 17 wounded and 12 missing.

Warren sailed on 22nd September, but Lieutenant Lawrence and the Marine detachment of the *Pearl* were left and served throughout the siege.[145] Captain Lieutenant A Campbell died on 6th

---
145 Plymouth Letters.

March 1802 in Port Mahon hospital of wounds received at Porto Ferrajo in January.

Colonel Airey maintained his post intact until peace was made in March 1802.

Egypt.
The British Government now decided on an expedition to Egypt to finally clear the French out of the country. A detachment from India under General Baird was to co-operate.

Aboukir.
The Naval Commander-in-Chief, Admiral Lord Keith, with the troops under General Sir Ralph Abercrombie anchored in Aboukir Bay on 1st March but gales delayed the disembarkation until the morning of the 8th; 7,000 French troops were posted in the sand hills with 15 pieces of heavy artillery to oppose the landing. Covered by the Fleet, but under heavy fire from the French and also from the Castle of Aboukir on their right flank, the .covering troops under General Sir John Moore made good their landing at a point where the sand hills rose abruptly and drove back the French; the second flight of boats quickly followed and by the evening of the 9th all were ashore. A thousand seamen under Sir Sidney Smith were landed to drag the guns and also a Battalion of Marines from the Fleet under Lieutenant Colonel W. Smith. One half were first employed to fill sandbags whilst the other half advanced through deep sand, being rejoined at 7 pm by the other half battalion.

The whole Battalion then advanced to join the Army about 15 miles distant, reaching their destination at 1 am on the 19th. They were attached to the 3rd Brigade under General Lord Cavan consisting of the 50th and 79th Regiments which had reached the heights of Nicopolis. A very interesting letter from Lord Keith to Earl Spencer, First Lord of the Admiralty, shows how dependent the Army is on the Navy in a combined operation.[146] "Aboukir Bay 11th March 1801. The General has again required the Marines to be landed and with reluctance I comply, but I am convinced were I to refuse or withdraw a man, the troops would re-embark and charge the failure to me, and so it will be if the enemy throw troops into Alexandria." He adds that 6,000 men from the Fleet were ashore and very hard worked.

Mandora.
At 5 am on the 13th they advanced with the 90th and 92nd Regiments forming the advanced guard. General Hutchinson with the 3rd, 4th and 5th Brigades formed the main body for the attack on the left, General Moore was to attack on the right; the remainder lying down on the plain.

The advance endured heavy loss owing to the French artillery and the French cavalry fell on the 90th and 92nd who drove them off. The left and centre columns deployed into two lines under heavy fire and advanced; the Marines, owing to the narrowness of the peninsula were somewhat crowded in the ranks and suffered severe loss. After heavy fighting the French abandoned the

---
146 Spencer Papers – Navy Records.

attack; this action is known as Mandora (which is only borne on the Colours of the Cameronians and Gordon Highlanders). The Marines lost 2 officers (Lieutenants P Hussey and J L Spear), 22 rank and file killed; 4 officers (Major Minto, Captain Torkington, Lieutenants R Parry and G Peebles), 2 Sergeants, 2 Drummers, 27 rank and file wounded. In Sir R Abercrombie's order of the day they were thanked "for their gallant conduct in the course of service yesterday."

On the 14th the Marines marched to Aboukir for the siege of the castle which surrendered on the 18th and they were employed as garrison, so that they were not present at the battle of Canopus which took place on the 21st; here the French, who had been reinforced, attacked again but after severe fighting were repulsed with heavy loss. Sir R Abercrombie was mortally wounded and died on board the Fleet.

Alexandria.
The Marines were relieved at Aboukir by the 92nd and joined General Eyre Coote's Brigade before Alexandria. On 3rd April the British, reinforced by the Turks, obtained possession of the Rosetta delta and so opened the Nile to the British gunboats. On 18th June Marabout fell to a combined naval and military attack.

On 2nd September Alexandria was surrendered and the French were evacuated from Egypt; the Marines were re-embarked on 5th September, their Brigadier – Major General Finch - taking leave of them in the following order:

"Major-General Finch in taking leave of Lieutenant Colonel Smith and the Marines under his command requests him to accept his warmest thanks for the order, regularity, zeal, and attention that have uniformly marked their conduct during the period he had the honour of commanding the first brigade; and he shall be happy on all occasions to bear testimony to their merit in the correct performance of their duty, in every respect which has come under his observation."

Regiments that took part in this campaign were awarded the badge of the Sphinx superscribed Egypt which might therefore be included among the badges of the Corps.

On 6th July an action took place off Algeciras with a French and Spanish squadron. Among the mortally wounded was Lieutenant D J Williams of the *Hannibal*.

On 16-17 August Lord Nelson, in command of the Channel Fleet, ordered an attack on the invasion flotilla at Boulogne. In spite of the great gallantry displayed and the heavy loss sustained, it had very little result and it was only undertaken owing to the popular clamour and panic in England.

In the West Indies the Squadron under Admiral Duckworth attacked and captured the islands belonging to the Armed Neutrality Powers; on 20th March St Bartholomew (Swedish) and St Martin surrendered. On the 29th St Thomas and St John's (Danish), on 31st Santa Cruz (Danish) and on 10th April the French evacuated St Eustatius and Saba which were occupied by the Buffs.

Funchal.
The French had also incited the Portuguese to exclude British shipping from their ports, so Funchal with two forts was occupied without resistance on 23rd July. On the 29th the French and Portuguese concluded a treaty by which France obtained all Portuguese Guiana.

On 21st June in the East Indies the Dutch Island of Ternate was occupied by the troops and ships of the East India Company.

But peace was approaching. On 1st October preliminary articles were signed and these were ratified on the 10th. On the same day the Divisions were ordered to recall all their recruiting parties, and from now on we read of discharges of men not fit to serve on the Peace Establishment.

The Treaty of Peace was signed at Amiens on 25th March 1802, by which Great Britain surrendered most of her conquests.

In Europe Great Britain surrendered St Marcou, Porto Ferrajo (Elba), as well as islands and forts in the Mediterranean and Adriatic; Malta and Gozo were given back to the Knights of Malta; Portugal and Egypt were restored to their position before the war, whilst the French evacuated Naples and the Roman territory.

In North America St Pierre and Miquelon were restored to France. Great Britain gave back to Holland all her possessions in the West Indies and also the Cape of Good Hope, but retained Trinidad (Spain). Denmark and Sweden regained their islands and Portugal got back Madeira. All her islands St Lucia, Martinique, and Guadaloupe were given back to France. Great Britain retained Ceylon, but gave back Amboyna to the Dutch; also, Pondicherry, Chandernagore, and Fore Point Madagascar to the French.

7 - Peace 1801 - 1803

All through the last months of 1801 the Records are full of orders as to the discharge of men who will not be required for the Peace Establishment.[147] Ships were being paid off in large numbers and the barracks were becoming overcrowded in the early months of 1802. As we know, Portsmouth only held 500 men, and on 23rd April we find the Commandant applying for the use of Hilsea and Fort Cumberland, but the Board ordered that Forton Prison should be handed over to him. At Plymouth there is an Order of 19th April 1802 that Nos 1 and 5 Parade Companies should go to Plymouth, and on the 23rd Nos 2 and 6 Companies to Devonport Dock, whilst on 4th May they sent one Company to Plympton, two to Tavistock one to Modbury - consisting of men longest at sea who required country air.

On 24th April the Resolution conveying the thanks of the Lords and Commons dated 6th April to the Navy, Army, and Marines, was received, and in forwarding the resolutions the Secretary of the Admiralty says: *"The Commanding Officer is to communicate to the Officers, Non-Commissioned Officers and Men of the Division under his command this high testimonial of their splendid and meritorious services."*

Royal Marines.
But on 29th April 1802 the Corps was singled out for particular honour by His Majesty the King and became "The Royal Marines" which was signified to the Divisions in the following letter:

Admiralty
Office.
29th April, 1802.

Sir,
The Earl St Vincent having signified to My Lords Commissioners of the Admiralty that His Majesty in order to mark His Royal Approbation of the very Meritorious Services of the Corps of Marines during the late War, has been graciously pleased to direct that the Corps shall in future be styled The Royal Marines.

I have great satisfaction in obeying Their Lordships' Commands to communicate this intelligence to you and in offering Their Lordships' congratulations on this testimony of the opinion His Majesty entertains of the very distinguished services of that part of his Forces to which you belong.

I am, Sir
Your most obedient humble servant
(Signed) Evan Nepean,
(Secretary of
Admiralty.)

---

147 Peace was actually signed at Amiens on 25th March 1802.

The Order was promulgated at Plymouth on 1st May.[148] The following shows how the news was received. It was probably the same at the other Divisions.

*Morning Order,
1st May 1802,*

"*The Royal Division of Marines will be under arms this evening at 8 o'clock and fire three volleys. The Barracks and offices to be illuminated in consequence of the intelligence contained in the foregoing letter, and the Commanding Officer trusts this high and flattering mark of distinction which the King has so graciously been pleased to confer on the Corps will excite the pride of every individual to persevere in that discipline and conduct which has thus been honoured and distinguished.*"

Demobilisation.
But alas the deadly axe of demobilisation was again to fall on the Corps. On the same day it was notified in orders that an increase in the number of officers to be allowed to retire on full pay was to be made, and volunteers for retirement were called for; the Commandants were to send in lists of those whom they considered unfit for further active service. The Commandant at Plymouth in forwarding the list says *"few of the officers here are under sixty years of age and some of them subject to the infirmities incidental to advanced years; that though equal to the duties, of Parade and what is now required of them, yet if called upon for Foreign Active Service they would certainly not be equal to it . . ."*

The demobilisation and reorganisation arrangements were promulgated by Order-in-Council of 5th May 1802.

After the preamble stating that a large number of ships had been paid off and considerable numbers of the Marines had been discharged, it states that further reductions were necessary "proportionable to the number of seamen to be employed in time of peace" and therefore lays down a new establishment:

"That the Corps be divided into 100 Companies (Chatham 32, Portsmouth and Plymouth 34), each to consist of 1 Captain, 2 First Lieutenants, 2 Second Lieutenants, 6 Sergeants, 6 Corporals, 4 Drummers and 100 Privates - total 121; 100 Companies equal 12,100.

"That there be established for their proper and regular management:

1 General	)
1 Lieutenant General	) These were Naval Officers holding
1 Major General	) the sinecure appointments
3 Colonels	)
	) To reside constantly in town to

---
[148] The Warrant was received by Major-General Bowater, the Commandant; and announced to the men on Parade. The Officers entertained their colleagues of the Garrison at dinner. On the tap of the drum "volleys were fired and the Barracks burst out into colours with a truly electrical effect." (Plymouth in Times of Peace and War. H F Whitfield)

> 1 Colonel Commandant) attend the Board of Admiralty in
>   ) the nature of Adjutant General
> 3 Colonels Commandant)
> 6 Lieutenant Colonels) Included in the above companies.
> 6 Majors)
> 3 Quartermasters
> 6 Adjutants
> Making a total of 12,116.

Each of the Colonel Commandants, Lieutenant Colonels and Majors to be allowed one Company with a Captain Lieutenant in lieu of one of the First Lieutenants.[149]

> *"And as a considerable number of the present officers will by this means be reduced, we propose that they should be allowed half pay while unemployed as has been the usual custom..."*

On 14th May lists of officers to be retained were circulated to the Divisions and new commissions were issued to them dated 1st June 1802. All others were allowed full pay to the 30th June and were told that they were at liberty to leave Headquarters when they liked.

As regards the men:

> *"They were to be paraded by the Commandant and all men who appear unfit or over forty years of age were to be discharged, preference being given for retention to those who have longest service at sea or are most in debt to the Crown. Drummers to be persuaded if possible to remain and serve in the ranks.*
>
> *"All accounts, sea pay, etc. to be cleared up; arms to be returned to Ordnance Stores. Men discharged to be allowed to take cloathes, belt and knapsack and presumably were also paid the usual gratuity of 21 days pay."*

Uniform.

The Letters are now full of the changes of uniform consequent on the grant of the title of 'Royal'.

6th May 1802.

> *"In pursuance of the King's Pleasure signified by the Earl of St Vincent, the Board of Admiralty directed the Navy Board to cause the clothing hereafter to be provided for the Royal Marines to be faced with blue; Sergeants to have yellow metal buttons and gold laced hats instead of silver*[150] *and to send a sufficient quantity to Chatham Portsmouth and Plymouth for the use of those Divisions in due time to be worn on the approaching anniversary of His Majesty's birthday."*

---

[149] As a matter of fact these numbers are not quite correct, as there were also the three Deputy Paymasters and probably the three Medical Officers and the Secretary to the Commandant in Town.

[150] The Board however cancelled this provision on 15th May.

Officers were to have blue facings with gilt buttons and gold epaulets (according to sealed pattern, sent by AG); Captains and Subalterns to be distinguished by one epaulet only, on the right shoulder.

> *"When the Marines assumed their new uniforms for the first time the Barrack square was thronged, and the windows were radiant with toilettes. Salutes having been fired, the Battalion presented arms and the veteran Colonel Elliot exclaimed in a loud voice "Royal Marines, here's God Save the King and Long Life to Him."*
>
> *"The sentiment ran through the lines like lightning and heartier cheers than then raised within and without the Barracks were rarely heard.*
>
> *"Always regarded as a family and constitutional Corps, the Marines were surrounded on this occasion by the aristocracy of the West, and a most brilliant ball was held in honour of the event at Pridham's Long Room."*[151]

All Divisions were in communication with the Admiralty about the new Colours rendered necessary by the Corps becoming Royal [152] but the Commandant at Portsmouth on 1st November 1802 makes the curious statement "it would be preposterous to take out a Red Colour with Blue Facings." He also made a plea for the grant of the Sphinx as allowed to regiments for the Campaign in Egypt 1801, but it was not approved.

On 19th June 1802 Lieutenant General Innes, Commandant at Chatham, was tried by General Court Martial at Chelsea, but was honourably acquitted. It must have been for some old charge as the Orderly Books of the Portsmouth Division for 1793 were ordered to be produced in evidence.

In August the lists of Officers who were to be allowed to retire on full pay were published.

On 25th August a Committee on Corps Administration was ordered to assemble and visit each Division to inspect books and papers, call and examine witnesses and investigate abuses, etc. It was composed of the Hon. George Villiers (the Paymaster of the Marines), Major Generals Campbell, Barclay, and Jackman (the supernumerary Second Commandants). Its report was never completed[153] but it apparently made some recommendations because in 1803 Pay Captains were substituted for the Squad Sergeants who were abolished from 1st May 1803: the four Senior Captains at each Division were to be the Pay Captains. Evidently, they asked for clerks, which were refused and they were told they could decline the duty if they liked and the next senior would be appointed. They also seem to have had difficulty in getting the new books and forms.

From the letters of Lord St Vicent (Navy Records) we learn that this Committee and the

---

151 Plymouth in Times of Peace and War - H. F. Whitfield. Note. Pridham's Long Room - the present Schoolroom. (Ed.)
152 See Volume 1755-1792, Appendix I. Divisional Colours.
153 Because like a similar Committee of which Admiral Lord Jellicoe was president in 1914 it was dissolved by the outbreak of a great war.

evidence given at the trial of General Innes proved that very grave abuses were in existence at the Divisions particularly as regards the men's necessaries, debts, etc., and the Squad Sergeants were very gravely implicated. We also get a glimpse of this in Lord St Vincent's letter to Major General Elliott when appointing him Commandant at Portsmouth in 1804.

Accommodation.

Barrack accommodation was again becoming a difficult question. Chatham was occupying their new barracks; Plymouth Barracks also were small and as usual Portsmouth Barracks were insufficient. The Commandant had pointed this out on 3rd October 1802 and sent up a scheme for building barracks for 1,500 men on Southsea Common. As the Clarence Barracks were in very bad repair he also suggested that the site might be sold to the inhabitants; and he pointed out that this would save the expense of lodging money and billetting. The GOC offered Gosport Barracks on the same terms as were in force at Plymouth.[154] The Commandant in asking if he may accept these terms says he is afraid the Army will give him the casemates at Fort Cumberland "very distant from the Dockyard and any market" (remember the messing system). He wanted the Four House Barracks which in after years the RMA occupied for many years. Apparently matters settled down as they remained for another forty-six years in the Clarence Barracks.

Dockyard Guards.

In December 1802 the mounting of the Guards in the Dockyards was resumed.

At this time the Marines attended the Garrison Church at Portsmouth, and the Chaplain received no allowance, but in 31st March 1803 there was an application for a gallery to be built for the use of the Marines.

The numbers of the Corps voted by Parliament for 1802 are interesting: for the first five months 30,000; for one month 18,000 and for remaining six months 14,000.

The number of officers borne afloat shows the proportion of the Corps at sea:

8th December 1802,

Officers Afloat	Capts	Lts
Chatham	4	37
Portsmouth	6	63
Plymouth	6	36

Australia.

On 3rd February 1803 Lieutenant Colonel D Collins with three Subalterns (one of whom was C

---

154 Practically the same as those under which Scraesdon and Borstal are held nowadays.

Menzies), three Sergeants, three Corporals, two Drummers, and thirty-eight Privates were ordered to be held in readiness to proceed for passage to New South Wales as escort to the convicts in HMS *Calcutta* who were to found the proposed new settlement at Port Phillip in Bass's Strait.

Colonel Collins found the place selected at the mouth of the Bay unsuitable and mainly because his detachment was too small[155] to permit of his penetrating to the head of the Bay (where the magnificent city of Melbourne now stands), he went on to the Derwent lower in Tasmania and founded the settlement at Hobart, because his commission allowed him to select another place provided it was close enough to guard Bass's Strait. He became the first Governor of Tasmania, with which Colony the Corps was long associated as garrison and died there in 1810. The son of a Royal Marine named Thorne was the first white born in the great colony of Victoria. This detachment sailed in the transport *Ocean*, only the junior subaltern going out in HMS *Calcutta*.

But war was again approaching; Recruiting Instructions were issued, and certain counties allotted to each Division. On 7th March 1803 the General Impress Warrant was issued, and Commandants were ordered to assist the Port Admirals in sending out Press Gang parties; the importance of secrecy was impressed upon them and the most discreet officers were to be chosen to be placed in charge of the parties. On 12th March orders were issued to complete the ships to full complement, orders having been issued to the Army on 11th March to take over the Dockyard Guards. On 28th March reports had to be rendered to the Admiralty of the numbers necessarily employed at Headquarters who were to be reduced as much as possible.

---

155 In the St Vincent papers (Navy Records) are some interesting letters showing that St Vincent would not agree to 100 men being sent, as it was not a proper charge on the Navy estimates, and he would only agree to 50 all told

8 - Trafalgar 1803 – 1807

War was declared on 16th May 1803, and on 17th Admiral Cornwallis sailed for Ushant with ten battleships; three battleships were sent to the North Sea and four into the Irish Channel; twenty more were fitting out hurriedly. Cornwallis hoisted his flag in the *Ville de Paris*. On 18th May Lord Nelson was appointed Commander-in-Chief Mediterranean with his flag in the *Victory*. He went out in the *Amphion*, first to Ushant and then to Naples and from there joined Bickerton's Squadron off Toulon. They seem to have made a base in Agincourt Sound, Sardinia (Aranci Bay?).

As usual one of the first steps taken was to increase the Marines. On 22nd June 1803 an Order-in-Council authorised an increase of 2 Sergeants, 1 Corporal, 1 Drummer, and 30 Privates to each of the 100 companies of the Marines and 43 new Companies to be raised (11 to Chatham, 18 each to Portsmouth and Plymouth), each consisting of 1 Captain, 2 First Lieutenants, 2 Second Lieutenants, 8 Sergeants, 8 Corporals, 5 Drummers, and 130 Privates. Also, three Colonels Second Commandant, 6 Lieutenant Colonels, 6 Majors each with command of a company and 15 Captain Lieutenants in lieu of a similar number of First Lieutenants.

Recruiting was opened in Scotland under Major Campbell from Plymouth but evidently the large and rapid increase led to difficulties about NCOs as on 29th June the Commandant at Portsmouth asked that Captains of ships and officers commanding detachments of the Home Station should select a proportion of their Corporals and Privates who could be recommended for promotion and send them in to Headquarters with statements of their character, zeal and abilities, due regard being paid to their length of service. This was apparently approved.

In July 1803 an address signed by the three Commandants was sent, after some discussion, to Earl St Vincent thanking him for his interest in the Corps and for his share in obtaining the grant of the title "Royal". The Portsmouth and Chatham Divisions also asked him to sit for his portrait by Sir William Beechy.

In Home Waters at this period of the war all efforts were concentrated on preparing defence against Buonaparte's threat of invading England; the squadrons were consequently employed in watching the French ports, in raids, and bombardments.

On 27th June three boats of HMS *Loire* cruising off the Isle of Bas attacked the French brig *Venteux* lying under the batteries of the Island; only two boats were able to board and carried her after a fight of ten minutes; *Venteux* had four long 16 pdr and six 36 pdr carronades. It was a very gallant exploit, the Lieutenant RN in command was promoted and Private E O'Reilly RM was promoted to Sergeant for his conduct. The Plymouth Letter Book says he was also awarded £40 by Lloyd's Patriotic Fund.

Arrangements for repelling an invasion were made everywhere in England, and on 11th

October the Commandant at Portsmouth complained that the Marines had not been called on to take their share with the garrison and suggests that at least the senior officers might be employed. But evidently there were no men available, for in September it is reported that officers' servants mounted guard with their masters and that there were only 11 Privates fit for duty - barely sufficient for Barrack and Infirmary Guards.

But even civilian England was arming, as in September 1803 the artificers in the dockyards volunteered to form battalions which were to be embodied and trained to arms; the Commissioners of the Yards to be Colonels. Sergeants from the Marine Divisions were ordered to be employed in training and exercising them every Sunday till further orders and at such hours as most convenient.

The Army was evidently short of arms because on 14th November the Master-General of the Ordnance asked that all spare arms at the RM Headquarters should be surrendered to the local depots.[156]

On 23rd December, Major General Elliot was appointed Colonel Commandant at Portsmouth and Captain No. 2 Company vice Avarne, and there is a very interesting letter from Earl St Vincent to him on his appointment. At Plymouth Colonel R Bright relieved Bowater on 27th December.

West Indies.
Although no great actions were fought in the Home or Mediterranean waters, there was great activity in the West Indies. On 21st June the *Centaur* and *Courageux* under Commodore Hood with the troops proceeded to St Lucia; the troops were landed at 5 pm, and at 5.30 Fort Castries was taken; and the Morne Fortune was summoned to surrender, but the French Commander refused. At 4 am on the 22nd the Morne was stormed and captured with a loss of 20 officers and men killed and 110 wounded. By desire of the Lieutenant General the Marines of the Squadron were landed and ordered to take post near Ilet to prevent supplies being thrown into Pigeon Island (where the Batteries which guarded the harbour were situated). When Morne Fortune fell the island was given up.[157]

On 25th June the *Centaur* and the. troops sailed for Tobago; the troops landed on 30th covered by the fire of the ships; Fort Scarborough capitulated, and Tobago was once more British. The Royal Marines and a body of Seamen were landed to co-operate with the Army under command of Captain Hallowell RN.[158]

On 30th June the boats of the *Aurora* under Lieutenant Davis RN and Lieutenant Baillie RM took St Peter's Island and during September Demerara, Essequibo, and Berbice River again fell into the hands of the British, the Marines being landed to help the Army.

---

156 Cf 1914-15.
157 Hood's Dispatch.
158 Ibid.

At the other end of the Station HMS *Blanche* (Captain Z Mudge)[159] was trying to cut out a French ship from Marcoonelle Bay, St. Domingo; the first attempt failed and on 3rd November Lieutenant Nicolls RM volunteered with 15 men to cut her out. He went in the cutter and Lieutenant Lake RN with 22 men followed in the barge to try and supersede Nicolls whose plan it was. On approaching the ship Lake refused to believe that it was the one they were seeking and went to the other side of the harbour; Nicolls stuck to his plan and at 2.30 am boarded the ship, the *Albion*, which was found to be prepared and received them with a volley; they got in two volleys before Nicolls boarded, he was wounded but killed the French Captain and drove the crew below. As he was within shot of the battery on shore he kept up firing to deceive the French whilst his seamen got sail on her, cut the cable and hoisted the jib. Lake now arrived and took charge and ordered the firing to cease, on which at once the shore battery opened fire and killed and wounded some of the crew, but with the boats towing they got the *Albion* out. In the dispatch all the credit was given to Lake who received a £50 sword from Lloyds Fund; Nicolls received a £30 sword.

On 16th November there is a very instructive incident in the cutting out of the French ship *Harmonie*, a privateer, from the Marin in the Bay of St. Anne Curacao by the boats of the *Blenheim*, and *Drake*. The harbour was protected by a Battery on each side: 60 seamen under Lieutenants Cole and Furber were detailed to attack the ship; 60 Marines under Lieutenants G Beatty and W S Boyd RM were to storm Fort Dunkirk, a battery of nine guns on the starboard side of the harbour to prevent the island militia coming to the point and interfering with the boats. Captain Ferris RN of the *Drake* took command with 144 more Seamen. The Marines surprised the fort and took 15 prisoners; they dismounted and spiked the six 24 pdr guns and blew up the magazine, but they did not fire the barracks for fear of damaging the sugar stores. The seamen gallantly boarded the privateer, which put up a strong resistance, but she was brought out as a prize.

1804

The numbers voted for the year were 22,000.

The arrangements of the squadrons to repel the threatened invasion of England were maintained, whilst there was continued activity by the squadron in the West Indies. Admiral Hood in the *Centaur* was blockading Fort Royal in the Island of Martinique. Lying off the island is an isolated rock known as the Diamond Rock. French ships were able to avoid the blockading ships by running inside, so the Admiral determined to take and fortify it as a base for his boats. In June 1804 the crew of HMS *Centaur* mounted three long 24 pdrs and 2 in one gun batteries on the shore, and one higher up only approached by a rope ladder; also two 18 pdrs on the summit. Shelter was obtained in caves and grottoes on the west side where there was wood and vegetation, but water was bad and scarce. A small garrison of seamen and Marines was provided, and a pennant hoisted, the rock being christened as a Sloop of War HMS *Diamond Rock*.

---

159 For character of Captain Mudge read James Naval History. Lake got into trouble in HMS Hawke in 1805 for his treatment of his Marines.

Curacao.

In January an attack was made on the Dutch Island of Curacao which, though unsuccessful, is a good example of a Naval Striking Force. Captain Bligh with two 74 gun battleships and the frigates *Blanche*, *Gipsy*, and Pique hove to off St Anne's on 31st January. The town and harbour were commanded by batteries, and whilst some frigates were in the Port. The *Blanche*, and Pique were left to block up the harbour, whilst the *Hercule*, *Theseus* and *Gipsy* bore up for a cove; the boats of the squadron with 406 seamen and 119 Marines under Lieutenants E Nicolls (*Blanche*) E Harwood and D Cahusac (*Theseus*), S Perrot (*Hercule*), W A Craig (Pique) assembled on board the *Hercule* under command of Captain Drummond RN of *Hercule*. Fort Piscadero, which with ten 12 pdrs commanded the landing place opened fire, which was returned by the *Theseus*; at 1 pm the covering Division of seamen and Marines stormed and carried the Fort without loss, and by a rapid movement gained the heights with small loss and drove away the Dutch. The second flight of boats then landed, the *Gipsy* anchoring in the cove, whilst the *Theseus* and *Hercule* stood off.

On 1st February two 18 pdr carronades and some light field pieces were landed from *Theseus* and dragged four miles up to a height 800 yards to the west of the town of St. Anne.

On the 2nd two more long 18 pdrs were landed and the battery known as Willoughby's was armed, also some Dutch 12 pdrs from Piscadero were mounted. Other guns were landed and mounted at different points and at 2 pm fire was opened.

The Dutch had 230 regular troops, besides the local militia and the crews of their vessels. On the 4th there was a skirmish at the advanced posts and on the 5th a more serious affair when 500 French and Dutch attacked the Marines under Nicolls; they were most gallantly repulsed, but the Marines pursued too far and lost 20 killed and wounded, from the guns of Fort Republique. On the 6th the bombardment was renewed; the shipping and a considerable part of the town being set on fire. The British however were losing men fast from sickness and fatigue - 60 men were re-embarked for dysentery; there were no camping conveniences and men were lying on the ground.

On the 23rd the Dutch received reinforcements. As an illustration of the dangers of enlisting foreigners, 30 out of the *Hercule*'s Marines, who were Poles enlisted whilst prisoners of war at San Domingo, threatened to desert on the 25th and had to be sent on board their ship.

On the 25th the attack was abandoned and by 9 pm all were on board except a small party left to destroy the guns and Fort Piscadero.

The Marines had Lieutenants Harwood, Cahusac, and Perrot wounded, 2 Sergeants and 7 Privates killed, 2 Sergeants and 21 Privates wounded. The total loss was 18 killed and 42 wounded.

Surinam.

On 25th April an attack was made on the Dutch settlement of Surinam on the Coast of South

VOLUME TWO 1793 – 1836

America by Commodore Hood and General Sir Charles Green. The expedition left Barbados on 7th April and anchored off Surinam River on the 25th. This river entrance was defended by powerful works. Troops were landed on the 26th, 30 miles east of the entrance and marched on the settlements. The ships engaged the batteries at the entrance and then landed more troops. Marines are not mentioned as landing. The Governor was summoned to surrender on the 29th; the remainder of the force landed on 2nd May and on the 5th Surinam capitulated. The British sustained only trifling casualties.

Royal Marine Artillery.
But the Corps were now to make a bold departure that had momentous results on its history.

Although in many engagements the Marines had assisted in manning the great guns and though Colonel Collins (late Commandant at Plymouth) in a letter to the First Lord dated 20th August 1778 had suggested the formation of artillery companies from the Marines to help in manning the ships' guns, and a proposal to form practice batteries of heavy guns had been made in 1773 to Lord Sandwich by Captain Wood of the Marines, no steps to include this work in their training had been made. But now another question had arisen.

It had hitherto been the practice to embark detachments of the Royal Artillery to man the howitzers and mortars with which the bomb ketches for bombarding purposes were armed. Owing to the difficulties of discipline, pay, etc, at the suggestion of several naval officers of whom Lord Nelson was one, Lord Melville (First Lord of the Admiralty) decided that the duty should be transferred to the Royal Marines. Consequently, an Order-in-Council dated 18th August 1804 authorised the establishment of a company of artillery at each Division, *"The officers and men to be selected from the most intelligent and experienced then belonging to the respective Divisions"* so that from the first it was a Corps d'elite.

From Plymouth Orders dated 9th September 1804 we learn that the establishment was to take effect from 1st September and

> *"........in order to stimulate and encourage them to the most active exertions in the execution of this important duty and also in some measure to reward them for the very considerable change and great confinement they may undergo.*[160] *Their Lordships will give directions that they shall have the same pay and advantages in all respects whether on shore or afloat as have been allowed to detachments of the Royal Artillery employed on similar services."*

Commandants were called upon to forward lists of officers they could recommend for transfer to the Artillery Companies and the following were selected to command the three companies: Captain T Minto at Chatham, R Williams at Portsmouth, and T Abernethie at Plymouth. Officers selected

---
160 ie In the Bomb Ketches which were tiny vessels armed each with a 13 inch and 10 inch mortar; on long passages they were towed by the ships.

167

were disembarked and there are various proposals for selecting the men; so that the companies must have soon come into being. Evidently at first, they were only embarked in the bomb ketches.

Captain-Lieutenant.
By Order-in-Council 13th August the rank of Captain Lieutenant (i.e. the Officers borne in lieu of a First Lieutenant in companies commanded by Field Officers) was abolished.

Foreigners.
Authority seems to have been getting anxious about the number of foreigners enlisted and serving in the Marines and returns were called for. The numbers were large and drawn from every country.

Boys.
On 17th October the enlistment of Boys was approved at special rates of pay and continued throughout the War; they were to receive pay as men on attaining the age of fifteen and there are. also references that they were not to be embarked in certain ships.

Rations.
A letter of 5th August shows that the messing of the men was 9d a day, the Government paying all above 6d a lb. for meat.

Straw Bedding.
An interesting item of interior economy existent to this day, dates from 17th December 1804.[161] "Beds to be filled with straw instead of flock and to be fresh filled every two months."

In this year also on 1st November the practice of keeping the two flank companies as Grenadiers and Light Infantry was abolished.

War was declared by Spain on 12th December 1804 under pressure from Napoleon and Great Britain replied on 11th January 1805.

1805

The numbers voted were 30,000.

This was the great and decisive year in which Napoleon's hopes of effecting an invasion of England were brought to nought and his fleet was destroyed. In this record it is not possible to endeavour to give more than the barest outline of the great strategical combinations by which the British defeated his efforts and forced him to over-run Europe in his vain efforts to combat the sea power of Great Britain.

---

161 Plymouth Orders.

Recruiting.

In January recruiting was re-opened in Ireland; from some mistake in the posters, where men were told that they would receive the same rates of pay ashore and afloat, we learn from the Portsmouth Letters that 4½d. a day was deducted from pay of men afloat presumably for rations.

A Return of Recruits enlisted at Portsmouth from 1st January to 31st July 1805 is instructive.

Men			480
Boys			122
Volunteers from Militia	14 Sgts	5 Cpls	371 Ptes
Foreigners enlisted in Mediterranean			82
Foreigners enlisted in West Indies			15
Total			1070

By Order of 23rd April ten out of every hundred men enlisting into the Army were allowed to volunteer for the Royal Marines. A Recruiting Station was also opened in Malta.

On 31st March 1805 Pitt, with a view to enabling the Army to obtain men for the regular army from the militia, who were raised by ballot, and also as a sop to the Militia Colonels, passed a bill through the House to enable men to be enlisted into the Regular Army equal to the actual strength of the Supplementary Militia. Under this Act about 11,000 men passed into the Regular Forces between 10th April and 26th June – four-fifths into the infantry and the remainder to the Marines, so the Corps got about 2,000 men with the advantage that these men were not raw recruits but trained and disciplined men from the militia. [162]

By Order-in-Council 5th April three Sergeants were added to each RMA Company.

During these years of war it is necessary to realise that the greater part of the Corps was afloat in the numerous and large squadrons occupied in blockading the enemy ports of Brest, Rochefort, Ferrol, Cadiz, Toulon etc; also the Netherlands and the Channel ports where Napoleon's flotillas were gathered were being watched so that the Corps was not engaged in any large land operations on shore, but in numerous ship landing parties and cutting out expeditions too many to enumerate.

West Indies.

The moves opened with the escape of Missersy's fleet from Rochefort with troops, which sailed for the West Indies, where they arrived at Martinique on 20th February. The first island attacked was Dominica, but the garrison withdrew to Prince Rupert's Bay after some hard fighting. Having levied a contribution the French left and repeated the performance at St Kitts and Monserrat, returning to the Isle of Aix at Rochefort on 20th May. Meanwhile Admiral Villeneuve had escaped from Toulon and picking up the Spanish squadron at Cartagena managed to slip out of the Straits of Gibraltar and made for the West Indies. Here he was to have met Admiral

---

162 Fortescue Vol V p240.

Ganteaume from Brest, but the latter had failed to break out.

Villeneuve, having waited the specified time, returned to Europe. As soon as Lord Nelson, Commander-in-Chief Mediterranean, learnt that Villeneuve had broken out, he divined his intention and himself started at once for the West Indies, leaving Craig's force with one battleship in Sicily; this was May 11th. Not finding Villeneuve in the West Indies Nelson returned to Gibraltar which he reached on 19th July. He proceeded to Tetuan for water etc. 21st July and sailed again on the 26th.

Calder's Action.
Meanwhile Cornwallis, blockading Brest, suspecting that Villeneuve was returning detached Sir Robert Calder with the following ships - four of 98 guns, one of 80 guns, eight of 74, two of 64, and three frigates to cruise off Finisterre to intercept the combined enemy fleet. On 22nd July Calder sighted Villeneuve with 20 battleships etc, about fifty leagues west of Ferrol. The weather was foggy but the fleets engaged and by 6 pm all ships were in action with visibility very bad due to fog and smoke. At 6.26 pm Calder ordered the ships to break off the action but fighting did not cease till 9.30 pm. The enemy lost two Spanish ships and had 476 men killed and wounded. The British had 30 killed, 159 wounded.

The result was indecisive, because Calder had to remember the threat of the enemy squadron still in Ferrol as well as the fleet he was fighting, but it had important consequences, as the enemy fleet entered Vigo on the 27th. On the 26th Calder having secured his prizes went back to Cape Finisterre to try and meet Nelson but failing to do so he continued his blockade of Ferrol. Nelson as we know was on this date at Tetuan. On 2nd August Villeneuve anchored at Corunna, with his ships in a very bad state and his crews sickly. One's mind turns to our detachments who had been all these months at sea and for whom there was still no rest.

The Ferrol squadron then joined Villeneuve who now had 29 ships in Corunna. On 9th August Calder having reconnoitered Ferrol-Corunna discovered Villeneuve's strength; in view of the disparity of strength he abandoned the blockade and rejoined Cornwallis off Ushant.

On 13th August Villeneuve put to sea, arriving in Cadiz on the 15th. Nelson having failed to meet him joined the Fleet off Brest on 15th August bringing its strength to 39 ships, but he himself with *Victory* and *Superb*, left for Portsmouth where he arrived on the 18th and struck his flag. On 16th August Allemand's French Squadron from Rochefort and the West Indies reached Vigo, but Villeneuve had already left.

On 22nd August Napoleon, having seen that his combinations had failed, marched the Grand Army into central Europe and gained the resounding victories over the Austrians at Ulm and Austerlitz which drove the Allies into making terms and paved the way for the attack on Naples and Napoleon's attempts to gain control of the Mediterranean.

Volume Two 1793 – 1836

Collingwood watching Cadiz with only four battleships on 21st August resumed his blockade, although the French and Spanish had 35 ships. He was reinforced by four battleships under Admiral Bickerton and on the 10th he was joined by Sir Robert Calder with 18 battleships. He cruised off the port until 28th September when Lord Nelson rejoined taking command of the Mediterranean Squadron, bringing with him the *Victory, Ajax,* and *Thunderer.* Nelson now had 22 battleships with him and Admiral Louis with 5 acted as his inshore squadron; Nelson kept the main fleet out of sight off the port to try and entice the French Fleet out. The French now re-embarked their troops as on 28th September Villeneuve had received peremptory orders from Napoleon to put to sea, and land his troops at Naples and then attack the British commerce in the Mediterranean.

Admiral Louis with 5 battleships had been sent to water at Gibraltar. *The Prince of Wales* had sailed with Calder for England, and the *Donegal* had gone to Gibraltar for repairs, but the *Royal Sovereign, Belleisle, Africa,* and *Agammemnon* had now joined, bringing Nelson's strength to 27 battleships and 4 frigates.

From 10-17th October hard gales from the westward prevailed and prevented the French ships from coming out, and we can imagine the hard times that the British Fleet was undergoing.

On the 19th the French weighed anchor with light airs, but only got 12 ships out of port and the rest did not get to sea until the next day - a total of 33 battleships and 5 frigates.

Trafalgar.
It is not in my power to describe the Battle of Trafalgar and it is only possible to mention a few details about the Corps. In this, one of the decisive battles of the world, one third of the Corps bore its part in its usual inconspicuous manner, but with their usual loyalty managed to be well to the front in all the hard fighting.

At 12.50 pm the *Victory* (Flag) opened fire; very soon after a double-headed shot killed eight Marines on her poop and wounded several others; Lord Nelson ordered Captain C W Adair to disperse his men round the ship to minimise the losses. When Lord Nelson was wounded, Sergeant Secker RM and two Marines helped to carry him to the cockpit. Captain Adair was soon after killed in repulsing an attempt by the Redoutable to board the *Victory*; he was struck by a musket ball at the back of his neck while standing on the gangway encouraging his men.

In the action between the Spanish *Algeciras*, and the British *Tonnant,* the *Algeciras* attempted to board, but the Marines of the *Tonnant,* maintained so steady and well-directed fire that the attempt failed; the *Algeciras* when she struck was taken possession of by Lieutenants Bennett and Ball RM.

When the *Bucentaure* (the French Flagship) surrendered, Captain Atcherly RM with one Corporal and four Privates and a seaman were sent to take possession of her; Admiral Villeneuve and his 2nd Captain presented their swords, but Atcherly having secured the keys of the magazine and put two of his men on sentry took the Admiral and his Captain to the *Mars.*

The strength of the Corps in the Battle was 92 Officers, 3500 men. The casualties were very heavy: Killed - Lieutenant R Green (*Royal Sovereign*), Captain C W Adair (*Victory*), Captain S Busigny and Lieutenant Kingston (*Temeraire*), 113 NCOs and Men. Wounded - Lieutenant J Le Vesconte (*Royal Sovereign*), Lieutenant J Owen (*Belleisle*), Captain T Norman (*Mars*), Captain J Wemyss (*Bellerophon*), Lieutenant J Benson (*Colossus*), Captain P Westroop, Lieutenant W Seddon (*Achille*), Lieutenant L B Reeves and J G Peake (*Victory*), Lieutenant S J Paine (*Temeraire*), Captain Fynmore (*Africa*), Captain P Lely (*Revenge*), and 219 NCOs and Men.

Of the combined enemy squadrons, out of 19 ships comprising the rear squadron 17 were captured and one (the *Achille*), blew up. Out of the 27 British ships 14 were more or less badly damaged.

Medals were awarded to all Captains of ships who took part in the Battle, but only one Brevet Majority was awarded to the senior officer of Royal Marines - Major Timmins.

Admiral Collingwood assumed command on Lord Nelson's death. A gale sprang up during the night and scattered the prizes and drove many on shore; the following days were spent in vain efforts to recover the prizes and in fact in face of the gales endeavouring to prevent themselves from being wrecked on the lee shore.

To sum up the French out of eighteen battleships preserved only nine, and the Spanish out of fifteen saved only six, which were driven for refuge into Cadiz and Lord Collingwood resumed the blockade.

Tasmania.
Before continuing the operations, it is necessary to glance at the doings of the Corps in other spheres. On 19th July we learn that drafts were being sent to Lieutenant Colonel Collins, the founder and governor of Tasmania; his son serving in *Orion* evidently tried to exchange to go but was ordered to rejoin his ship.

Woolwich Division.
But of great importance to the Corps was the addition of the Fourth Division and fourth Artillery Company to be stationed at Woolwich. This was the work of Admiral Lord Barham, the first Lord of the Admiralty. The Order-in-Council is dated 15th August 1805 and was signed at the Court at Weymouth.

> The reasons given for the increase are interesting.
> "The present establishment . . . being considerably short of the number voted by Parliament . . . being also found so insufficient for supplying detachments for HM frigates and sloops now in commission and under orders to be fitted for immediate service, that we have been under the necessity of reducing the number of subalterns serving in battleships; and are still unable to furnish a sufficient number of parties

> *for the Recruiting Service and performing other duties required on shore . . . judge it highly expedient that a new and additional Division . . . should be established at Woolwich not only for supplying promptly detachments for HM Ships and vessels fitting in the River Thames, but also for affording security to HM Dockyards at Woolwich and Deptford and furnishing the usual guard in time of peace; and likewise in assisting in fitting and manning ships upon sudden emergency requiring a naval armament, when it may be of great importance to have ships sent to sea."*

It provided that each of the then 143 Companies (47 Chatham, 48 each Portsmouth and Plymouth) should be increased by ten Privates.

The additional Division to be denominated the Woolwich, or Fourth Division, was to be raised and stationed at that place as their proper and established Headquarters to consist of thirty Companies numbered from 144 to 173 of the same strength as the other Companies viz, 1 Captain, 2 First-Lieutenants, 2 Second Lieutenants, 8 Sergeants, 8 Corporals; 5 Drummers, and 140 Privates.

> *"As the greatest advantage is likely to arise to HM Naval Service from the Establishment of RMA Companies to instruct the other Companies in the use of Artillery, to serve on board HM Bomb Vessels and to perform such other duties as may be required.....one more Company of RMA to be raised and attached to said Division to consist of 1 Captain, 3 First Lieutenants, 5 Second Lieutenants, 8 Sergeants, 5 Corporals, 8 Bombardiers, 3 Drummers, and 62 Gunners.*
> *The following number of Field and Staff Officers:*
> *One Colonel (i.e. the Hon. Colonel, a Captain, RN)*
> *One Colonel Commandant*
> *One Second Commandant*
> *Three Lieutenant Colonels*
> *Three Majors.*
> *Two Adjutants.*
> *One Quartermaster.*
> *One Deputy Paymaster*
> *One Barrackmaster.*
> *One Surgeon.*
> *One Surgeon's Mate."*

Pay and allowances to be the same as at other Divisions. Colonel Fletcher Second Commandant at Portsmouth, was appointed to the Command.

The other Divisions were each ordered to send 10 Sergeants, 10 Corporals and 20 Privates qualified and deserving of promotion; 6 disciplined Drummers and 8 undisciplined. They seem to have proceeded about 11th September.

The Division was at first quartered in a hulk in Woolwich Dockyard. The names of the officers appointed to Woolwich can be seen in the Divisional Letter Books.

The promotions given by the addition of the new Division were very welcome to the Corps and the Divisions evidently sent memorials of thanks to Lord Barham, the First Lord, because in acknowledging the letter from Plymouth in a reply dated 3rd September 1805 he says: "He holds their services in high estimation and that the Corps may always depend on that attention from him to which its merits so well entitle it." And in a letter to the King[163] he takes credit for having established the Division and increased the Corps; unfortunately, he ceased to be First Lord in the following year.

King's Regulations.
A new Edition of the King's Regulations for the RM was issued on 15th November 1805, and on 22nd November we see the first fruits of the new increases in the order that frigates with a complement of 300 men were to have a detachment of 45 Marines.

Strachan's Action.
Before the close of the year the French Fleet was to suffer a still further blow. Lord Collingwood lay off Cadiz watching the shattered ships of Villeneuve sheltering there; but after the battle four French ships under Admiral Dumanoir had escaped to the southward; these tried to make for Rochefort and the Isle of Aix and passed Cape St Vincent on 29th October. The Rochefort Squadron of 5 battleships and 3 frigates under Admiral Allemand was still at sea preying on British commerce. The *Phoenix*, frigate, when off the Scillies got news of the French Squadron and stood into the Bay of Biscay, and when in the latitude of Cape Finisterre on 2nd November sighted some French ships which proved to be Dumanoir's Squadron. The *Phoenix* promptly made for Ferrol, off which place a squadron of 5 battleships and 2 frigates under Captain Sir Richard Strachan was cruising. The *Phoenix* and other frigates were now in touch with the two squadrons, and during the night were able to keep Sir Richard Strachan in the *Caesar* informed. About 1.30 am the moon set and as the weather was hazy and blowing they lost sight of the French. All through the 3rd and 4th the British were searching for the French and the *Bellona* (74) was left behind. Early on the morning of 5th November the frigates opened fire on the rear French ship; at 11 am the French Admiral ordered his fleet to form line ahead - the *Duguay-Trouin, Formidable, Mont Blanc, Scipion*. About 12.15 pm the three British battleships got into action (*Hero, Caesar*, and *Conqueror*, the *Namur* was too far astern but came into action later). After about three hours' hard fighting the French *Formidable* surrendered and almost immediately after the *Scipion*. The *Duguav-Trouin* and *Mont Blanc* tried to get away but being pursued by *Caesar* and *Hero* also hauled down their colours at 3.30 pm The casualties were 24 killed, 111 wounded; the Royal Marines had *Hero*, Lieutenant Morrison killed, 2nd Lieutenant C J Stevenson wounded; *Namur*, Captain A Clements wounded.

---

163 Barham Papers.

The news of this disaster reached the Emperor Napoleon in the midst of his successes in Central Europe; he won the Battle of Austerlitz on 2nd December. The *Duguay-Trouin*, under the name *Implacable*, and the others were added to the British Navy.

1806

The numbers voted for the year were 29,000.

San Domingo
In the Atlantic on 13th December 1805, a strong French squadron of 11 sail of the line with troops had escaped from Brest in bad weather; on the 14th they divided into two squadrons, one of six battleships under Admiral Lessegues with troops proceeded direct to San Domingo in the West Indies, the other under Admiral Willaumez was to proceed to St Helena or the Cape and then across to the East Indies to injure British trade; the latter squadron was sighted and phased to the southward by Admiral Sir John Duckworth on 25th December. Duckworth however abandoned the chase on the 26th and sailed for the West Indies, arriving at Barbados on 12th January, proceeding to other islands to water and refit. On 1st February when at St Kitts he received information that Admiral Lessegues' squadron was off San Domingo. Sir John with seven ships started at once, and on 8th February the British squadron arrived off the harbour and city of Santo Domingo. The French ships, five battleships and some frigates, slipped their cables and the two fleets engaged; in less than two hours three of the French ships had been captured and two driven ashore. The British loss was 74 killed and 264 wounded, of which the Royal Marines had 15 killed and 43 wounded.

Meanwhile Admiral Willeaumez had reached the Cape only to find that it was in British hands.[164] After cruising between Africa and America, he proceeded to Martinique. Leaving there on 1st July and cruising near Montserrat and Nevis, he made great efforts to capture the British convoy; but Sir Alexander Cochrane's squadron of three 74-gun ships sighted and chased him; the French avoided the contest and Sir Alexander anchored on 4th July at Tortola with 26 West Indiamen. Willeaumez then went to the Bahamas to intercept the Jamaica convoy; in this he failed and so sailed north in order to damage the fishing fleets off Newfoundland. On 18th August his fleet was scattered by a gale and all the ships damaged. Another British squadron had been detached under Sir Robert Strachan to search for him and two of these ships drove one of the French battleships - the Impetueur - ashore at Cape Henry, USA; later on, several of the others were captured and damaged, and only a few returned to France.

Cape of Good Hope.
As mentioned the Cape of Good Hope was for a second time in the hands of the British. Commodore Sir Home Popham with *Diadem*, Raisonnable, *Belliqueux* (64s) *Diomede* (50), *Leda*, and *Narcissus* frigates with 6,000 troops under General Sir D Baird left Cork on 31st August 1805, reaching Madeira 26-30th October and Bahia 10th November. They made Table Bay on 4th

---
[164] See later.

January 1806 and anchored close to Robben Island. The surf was too heavy to allow landing, and on the 5th General Beresford with the 38th Regiment and some 20th Light Dragoons was sent to land at Saldanha Bay covered by the frigates. On the 6th the surf admitted of landing the main body sixteen miles North West of Capetown; they were covered by the ships, who kept off the Burgher Militia. One transport was run ashore to act as a breakwater, and the Highland Brigade (71st, 72nd, and 93rd) landed with the loss of only one boat swamped; the surf increased in the evening, but the remainder of the troops landed the next day. The Commodore with *Leda, Encounter* and *Protector* and boats with the battering train proceeded to the head of Blueberg Bay.

The Dutch could only muster 2,000 men, including a regiment of Waldeckers, one of Dutch Regulars, and an irregular force of Colonials; as the harvest was being gathered the burghers could not be collected.

On the 8th the Dutch tried to seize a position on the heights near Het Vlei, but were forestalled by Baird with 4,000 men, whilst a battalion of Marines from the Fleet under Major McKenzie was landed further along the Bay between the army and the town and advanced on the enemy's left flank. The Highland Brigade advanced and attacked the front of the Dutch whilst the other Brigade 24th, 59th, and 83rd turned off to turn his right flank. The Waldeckers and Regulars bolted but the remainder put up a good fight. At Rietvlei the Dutch Commander rallied his troops and marched off to the mountains

On the 9th some provisions having been obtained from the ships, Baird advanced and took up a position at Salt River about one and a half miles North of Capetown, where he was joined by Beresford from Saldanha Bay. Overtures were now being made for the capitulation and on the 10th Capetown was occupied; but by the 18th the Dutch General had agreed to surrender the Colony to the British and the final capitulation was signed.

Buenos Aires.
The Corps was now to be involved in a disastrous enterprise, during which they lost a pair of Colours, which may still be seen in the Convent of San Domingo, Buenos Aires,[165] and underwent the humiliating experience of a battalion having to surrender to the enemy, one of the rarest, if not the only instance, of such an occurrence in Corps history.

Reports of a revolt of the Spanish Colonies in South America were prevalent and attempts had been made to get Great Britain to espouse the cause of the revolutionaries, but the government had resisted all these efforts. Commodore Home Popham however, who was an ambitious man, when he had acquired the Cape of Good Hope and inspired (some say) by the hope of prize money, determined to sail for Rio de la Plata and on his own responsibility undertook the expedition against Buenos Aires. He persuaded Sir D Baird to let him have the 71st Regiment and some artillery under General Beresford and sailed with all his squadron for Buenos Aires. At

---

165 See Vol 1755-92, Appx 1. Divisional Colours.

St Helena he persuaded the Governor to let him have 1 Officer, 101 artillerymen, and 8 Officers and 278 of the St Helena Infantry. On 8th June he sighted the entrance of the Rio de la Plata. He had intended to attack Monte Video, but on the pretence of shortage of provisions he decided to attack Buenos Aires.

To the troops he added what was called the Marine Battalion, viz. 9 Officers and 331 Marines together with 10 Officers and 90 Seamen with 2 light 3 pdr guns under Captain King RN. The Officers of the Marine Battalion were Majors A McKenzie, and Gillespie, Captain Ballinghall, Lieutenants Swale, Pilcher, Pollard, Sandell, Forbes, and Fernyhough. This Battalion carried the Colours described in the Appendix.

They were embarked on board HMS *Narcissus* and *Encounter* (frigates). On 16th June these vessels with the troop transports moved up the river, whilst HMS *Diadem* blocked Monte Video, the *Raisonnable* and the *Diomede* being near Maldonado.

Owing to fog and delays they did not arrive at Point Quelmey, 12 miles from Buenos Aires, until the 25th, and landed during night 25/26th June. On the 26th the Spaniards were driven from their position and the British hastened on to secure the bridge over the Chuelo River, (about 3 miles from Buenos Aires) but arrived too late. Boats and rafts prepared by the seamen got them across on the 27th and Beresford then took charge of the town. The capitulation was signed on 2nd July, a ransom of 1,088,208 dollars being paid. One account says that the Marine Battalion was re-embarked (their services being highly and justly extolled by the Major General); whether this was so or not, a portion must at any rate have been soon disembarked again as they were involved in the events to be narrated.

The whole political situation had been miscalculated, and the Spanish Revolutionaries were by no means ready to accept the British. After about six weeks an insurrection broke out in the country and under a General Liniers began to advance on the city. On 4th August Liniers with 1,000 men succeeded in evading the fleet, crossed the river, and landed at Conchas above Buenos Aires whence he advanced on the city. General Beresford despatched 450 of the 71st and 50 Marines to attack them. This force dispersed Liniers' men after a march of five hours and returned to the city, having marched thirty miles in fourteen hours. But the inhabitants were only waiting to join Liniers, and on 10th August the insurrection broke out in the city and on the 11th attacked one of Beresford's advanced posts. On the night of 11/12th August Beresford re-embarked his sick, women and children, and took up a position in front of the fort, selecting a position in the large square, (a space of 100 yards across, divided in half by a long colonnaded building). Two streets came in from the rear and were protected by the guns of the fort; two more on each flank at opposite ends of the central building, two more at each of the further angles. The 71st Regiment were in the building; the St Helena Infantry were placed to enfilade the further angles; the Marines and Seamen were drawn up in front. Guns were brought up to cover the flank approaches, but the enemy had occupied the houses all round and were sniping the British. At 9.30 am on 12th August the enemy (about 10,000) attacked, but the attacks were easily beaten off by the artillery, though the sniping caused very heavy loss and by noon Beresford had 2 Officers and 46 Men killed, 8 Officers and 99 Men wounded. His ammunition was running short and he hoisted the white flag. General Liniers was unable to check the mob, who had lost heavily, but eventually a capitulation was drawn up; the insurgents prevented it being carried out and Beresford and his men were carried off into captivity to Condor about 100 miles away.

Commodore Popham remained blockading the river, but the British Government, on hearing the news, was furious. Meanwhile General Baird had sent Colonel Backhouse with 2,000 more men from the Cape. On the latter's arrival on 13th October he found Beresford a prisoner and he had no orders or any idea of what was required. However, he and Popham landed at Maldonado on 29th October, drove off the Spaniards, secured his position and the next day secured the Island of Goretti with thirty-two guns which covered the harbour and provided the ships with a refuge. He was undisturbed for three months, though in an open town and absolutely insecure.

The Government recalled Popham and tried him by Court Martial. They also recalled the Governor of St Helena and General Baird, though they dispatched Colonel Auchmuty with two Battalions, some artillery, and the 17th Light Dragoons to clear up the mess. Auchmuty arrived on 5th January 1807 at Maldonado; Admiral Stirling replaced Popham. The new commanders decided to attack a small garrison at Goretti. On 16th January they landed about nine miles below Monte Video; the Spaniards were in force but made little attempt to face the fire of the ships; the covering force established itself a mile inland, and landed their stores but they had no siege artillery. On 10th they advanced against the city. The resistance of a mounted force was quickly brushed away, which carried panic into Monte Video, and the suburbs were occupied in the evening; the advanced posts were pushed up to the Citadel and the main body was only two miles away.

They were attacked next morning by 6,000 men who were driven off with great slaughter, so that Auchmuty was free to invest the city. The town was surrounded by water on three sides with 23 heavy seaward batteries; on the east side the land fortifications formed a salient angle, the south side 1,000 yards long, north side 1,200 yards. A square fort at the angle and other defences were heavily armed. The works were in good repair and well armed with 113 pieces of artillery, while the rock was so close to the surface that the entrenching tools were useless. The Garrison of 6.000 were brave but untrained.

Auchmuty's force was slightly superior, but with the exception of three regiments (36th, 40th Regiments and 17th Dragoons) were not very good material and he very much relied on that battalion of Seamen and Marines (about 800 strong) who were attached to his 2nd Brigade under Colonel Lumley. He had one Cavalry Brigade (3 Regiments) and two Infantry Brigades but the artillery only had six guns. Admiral Stirling lent him all the men he could and had 1,400 ashore. Batteries helped by the guns of the ships operated against the northern front, fire being opened on 25th January without any effect; on the 28th another battery of six guns was opened against the Citadel, which knocked the parapet to pieces, but did not do much damage to the rampart.

Although the powder began to run short, they opened yet another battery of six guns to try and break the wall close to the South Gate and on 2nd February the breach was reported practicable. A relieving force was reported to be approaching, so on 3rd February an assault was ordered, which was most gallantly executed and soon cleared up the town and restored order.

The Spaniards lost 800 killed and 500 wounded with 2,000 prisoners, the remainder escaped unmolested by the ships. The British casualties were 6 Officers and 110 rank and file killed, 21 Officers, 258 rank and file wounded.

The British Ministry meanwhile had developed great ideas of obtaining control of the South American Colonies and had dispatched Colonel Crauford with the 6th Dragoon Guards, 9th Lancers, artillery, and 6 battalions of infantry. The Lancers arrived on 6th February, but Auchmuty was not strong enough to continue the offensive campaign until these reinforcements had arrived. When they did come Lieutenant General Whitelook superseded Crauford and attacked Buenos Aires, but the operations of the miserable campaign which followed, ending in the surrender of Whitelook and all his troops, do not concern the Corps. By the capitulations General Beresford with his troops and Marines was liberated and returned to England.

Before describing the operations in the Mediterranean of the year 1806 we must glance at the happenings of the Corps in England.

Lloyds Patriotic Fund.
In January 1806 the Divisions subscribed to Lloyds Patriotic Fund apparently one day's pay; the Portsmouth contribution was £56. 2. 6. There were evidently very few men ashore, because in February when owing to a Parliamentary election the Division had to leave Portsmouth for three days, billets were only required for 300 men.

Canteens and Taxation.
In April of this year a curious controversy arose with the Civil Magistrates about the RM Canteens. They were apparently assessed for Poor Rate, House and Window Tax, and further as they were licenced houses, the Magistrates threatened to billet soldiers on the Canteen premises. The Commandants countered by threatening to saddle the Parish with all the women and children of the Division; and from this correspondence we learn that the Canteen Sutler also supplied the NCOs and men with bread, cheese and groceries.

The Admiralty referred the matter to the Admiralty Solicitor who settled the matter by telling them not to pay Poor Rate or taxes on assessments on Barracks, and that the billeting of soldiers was illegal. The magistrates replied in consequence that they would not grant a licence for the Canteen but in the end they had to give way. This matter has often been fought out - even as late as 1890 - but both sides have had to give way in the present compromise.

Militia Recruiting.
In July the Irish Militia were allowed to volunteer for the Royal Marines as well as the English Regiments.

Pay.
In August the long overdue increase of pay was granted by an Order-in-Council 6th August 1808 *"that it will be a proper encouragement to the Officers, NCOs and Privates of Your Majesty's Royal Corps of Marines (which have upon all occasions gallantly distinguished themselves) if the late augmentation* [166] *is extended to them."* The annual expense was estimated at £36,949 and was approved. It appears to have taken the form of increases after seven years' service and again after fourteen years.

The Order-in-Council 17th September 1806, gives the RMA rates of pay as:

Captain	11/-	For Brevet Major	2/- in addition
First Lieutenant	6/10d	After 7 years	1/- in addition
Second Lieutenants	5/7d		
Sergeants	2/9½d		
Corporals	2/5½d	After 7 years	2/6½d
		After 14 years	2/7½d
Bombardiers	2/3½d	After 7 years	2/4½d
		After 14 years	2/5½d
Gunners	1/5¾d	After 7 years	1/6¾d
		After 14 years	1/7¾d

Expense of the Four Companies, £1221-4-7.
The increases to the Corps generally were:
When serving afloat:

Sergeant		8d	
Corporal		6d	
	After 7 years	7d	
	After 14 years	8d	
Drummer		3¾d	
Private		3¾d	
	After 7 years	4¾d	
	After 14 years	5¾d	
	Boys	3d	Making their pay 9d a day

---

166 ie to Army.

In this year we see to what a large amount the Levy Money for recruits had grown, viz: £17.1.0 for men, and £10.15.0 for boys. An Admiralty Order of 15th December shows how it was distributed.

Gaeta.

Turning to the Mediterranean all Napoleon's schemes for the invasion of England having been exploded by the defeat and destruction of his fleet, he had turned on his enemies in Europe. After the crushing defeats of the Austrians at Ulm and Austerlitz (December 1805) he had determined on over-running the Neapolitan Kingdom in Italy, and his troops had taken the necessary action. The King of Naples had fled to Sicily; and the British squadrons from their bases - Malta and Sicily - were blockading Toulon and harassing the French troops in their march through Italy. Russian troops had occupied Corfu and a British expeditionary force had been sent to Sicily. The Neapolitans were holding Gaeta under the Prince of Hesse-Philipstadt, which was besieged by the French but held out gallantly. Admiral Sir Sidney Smith in the *Pompee* commanding the British squadron arrived in the Bay of Naples at the end of April. As long as Gaeta was held the French hold on Neapolitan territory was very precarious; Smith threw in some ammunition and left HMS *Juno* and some Seamen and Marines to help in a sortie on 15th May when Lieutenant Mant RM (*Juno*) was wounded; the sortie was successful. He then however went off to attack the island of Capri on 12th May. After fire by HMS *Eagle* and two Neapolitan bomb vessels the French were driven within the walls, and the storming party of seamen and Marines was at once landed. The Marine detachments under Captains Bunce and J Stannus with Lieutenant G P Carroll and the seamen mounted the steps; Captain Stannus killed the French commander and the French beat a parley and capitulated. One Marine was killed, and four seamen and Marines wounded. A garrison of Corsicans from the army at Messina was placed in the island.

Sir Sidney Smith then returned to Palermo where he remained dallying at the Neapolitan Court. On 25th June General Sir John Stuart crossed over with his force to the mainland at St Euphemia and having landed won the Battle of Maida, but unfortunately did not exploit his victory. Nor did Sir Sidney Smith take the opportunity of relieving Gaeta which fell on 18th July, but contented himself with raiding places to the southward, which had already fallen to the Army. In spite of the action of Captain Hoste of the *Amphion* and the 78th Regiment off Reggio and Cotrone, Stuart's force was withdrawn to Sicily, but the difficult political currents and the movements of troops and ships are beyond the scope of this record and do not concern the Corps.

However, a coalition was forming against Napoleon and hopes of deliverance from the Napoleonic domination were in formation all over Europe, whilst Spain was opening negotiations with England. But the whole fabric was dashed to pieces by the resounding victories of Napoleon over the Prussians at Auerstadt and Jena on 14th October and by 31st October the Prussian Army had ceased to exist. The Russians also had picked a quarrel with the Turks, which necessitated help being afforded to the former, whilst the chances in Italy had been wasted by Sir Sidney Smith; further home, Popham's adventure in South America had diverted troops that were badly needed in Europe.

1807

The numbers voted were 31,400.

There were few alterations in administration.

Necessaries.
In February a big innovation was made in the supply of necessaries. On 16th February it was ordered that in future the contracts would be made by the Navy Board and that supplies would be drawn from the Board in future. Time was given up to 30th June to use up the stocks of Mr Prater, who had supplied the Corps for over twenty years, and needless to say there were many complaints about the new clothing and the sins of contractors. Among other complaints they supplied shirts without frills.

Bayonet Exercise.
In February also Lieutenant Paden, the Adjutant at Portsmouth, had developed some form of Bayonet Exercise and approval was given for NCOs and men to be instructed in its use. It was not till some years later that its use became general throughout the Corps.

Chevrons.
On 2nd September Lieutenant General Barclay, the Commandant in Town, obtained the Admiralty approval to abolish the Corporal's Knots or Epaulets and to adopt the Army custom introduced in 1802 of distinguishing Sergeants and Corporals RM by chevrons on the right arm; lace for the purpose was ordered to be sent with the uniform clothing.

King's Regulations.
On 1st September there was a new edition of the Admiralty Regulations for the Royal Marines ashore.

Wounded man.
But there is a very interesting instance of difference between present day methods and those then existing. A Private W Fairbrother of HMS *Brunswick*, who had been wounded in the arm at Trafalgar was suffering from the effects of several splinters coming out, which rendered his arm more weakly than formerly. The Admiralty were pleased to order his discharge in consideration thereof, but on a payment of twenty-five guineas to raise a recruit in his stead.

Returning to the operations of the Fleets in which the greater part of the Corps was engaged in watching the French ports to prevent the escape of the few ships remaining, and where therefore action, except in rare instances, was confined to small ship landing parties.

Curacao.
We have seen how a large part of the Army was locked up in Buenos Aires and also in Sicily; but

in the West Indies a most gallant action on the part of some frigates in the capture of the Island of Curacao must be recorded.

HMS *Arethusa* (Captain Brisbane, 38), *Latona* (36), *Anson* (44), and *Fisgard* (44) left Jamaica on 24th December 1806. On 1st January 1807 they were off St Barbarys, the east end of the island, but the object of their attack was the Bay of St Ann on the south east side. The entrance was only 300 feet wide with regular fortifications; on the right of the harbour was Fort Amsterdam with sixty guns in two tiers, there was also a chain of forts on the Misselburg Heights. Fort Republique on a high hill at the head of the harbour enfiladed the whole place. At daylight the four frigates entered the harbour, the Dutch were surprised and sleepy but opened fire from the forts and ships which however were flying the flag of truce. The fire was ineffective but the *Fisgard* went ashore; the others got up the harbour and anchored to engage the forts and also a frigate and corvette lying there. The summons to surrender was not answered but the enemy hauled down the flags of truce and at 6.15 am the fight commenced; after a few broadsides Captain Brisbane boarded and captured the Dutch frigate of which the *Latona* took possession, and the *Anson* secured the corvette. Captains Brisbane and Lydiard (*Anson*) then landed at 7 am with their Seamen and Marines who stormed and carried Fort Amsterdam in ten minutes, breaking in the gates, though the garrison consisted of 275 men. Immediately after they captured some more of the forts together with the town and citadel, The Captains than returned to their ships and opened fire on Fort Republique, at the same time landing 300 Seamen and Marines (senior RN Officer was Lieutenant G Peebles of *Anson*) who attacked the rear of the fort; the attack was very difficult but by 10 am the fort had surrendered, and by noon the Dutch capitulated and the whole island was in British hands. A most amazing and gallant exploit. On 26th February Lieutenant George Peebles was promoted to Brevet Captain. [167]

The island was evidently garrisoned by Royal Marines because on 11th November 1807[168] Captain Reynolds of HMS *Mediator* reports that his detachment had been landed at Curacao by order of Vice-Admiral Davis and were on duty there.

But in Europe Napoleon, foiled in his efforts to attack the British Fleet, was extending his power over the Continent and was doing his best to organise the Northern and Scandinavian nations against the British. The British Government determined to grasp the nettle before his attempts should damage the valuable Baltic trade, so they dispatched a Fleet under Admiral James Gambier to seize the Danish Fleet and keep open the entrances to the Baltic.

After the Battle of Friedland on 14th June and the Armistice with Russia on 25th June, Napoleon completed treaties on 7th and 9th July with Prussia and Russia; he had therefore obtained control of the nineteen or twenty Russian ships and he wanted the Swedish eleven and the Danish sixteen. With these he might have conveyed an army to Ireland.

---

167 Portsmouth Orders.
168 Plymouth Letters.

On 19th July Great Britain demanded the surrender of the Danish Fleet and Admiral Gambier sailed on 26th July with seventeen battleships and twenty-one frigates, bombs, etc., from Yarmouth. On 1st August Admiral Keats with *Games, Vanguard, Orion, Nassau*, two frigates and ten brigs was sent into the Great Belt to prevent supplies being sent to Zealand. On 3rd August the Fleet anchored off Elsinore and on the 5th the *Superb* was sent to join Keats. On the 7th a large convoy of transports under Rear Admiral Essington with *Inflexible, Leyden, Minotaur, Valiant* (74s) arrived and on the 8th came more transports with the *Kars* and *Defence* (74s). Lord Cathcart was GOC Troops and Gambier's force was now twenty-five battleships, forty frigates, bombs, etc. and 377 transports with 27,000 troops, more than half of whom were Germans in British pay.

The Danish troops were about 12,000 with the sailors of the Fleet. Copenhagen lies partly on an angle of the Isle of Zealand and partly on the Isle of Anager, the passage between forming the harbour and arsenal; it was defended by the Trekonen pile Battery of 58 guns on a shoal to the north of the town; the pile battery of 36 guns in front of the citadel north of the town, and the Arsenal Battery of 50 guns. All these Batteries were also armed with mortars. In addition, there were several floating batteries and three blockships had been sunk and converted into batteries to enfilade the channel. The Danish Fleet consisted of 16 battleships, 21 frigates and sloops, with three more 74s on the stocks building. On the land side the works were in good repair with double ditch and outworks; along the western front ramparts with deep ditch, outworks, glacis and covered way; similar works covered the southern front.

Copenhagen.
On 15th August the bulk of the fleet anchored at a village midway between Elsinore and Copenhagen, whilst Admiral Essington went further up. On the 16th troops were landed at Webeck whilst the fleet weighed and stood further up. On the 17th there was skirmishing between the brigs, gunboats and small fry, and the fleet anchored in Copenhagen Roads four miles north east of the Trekonen Battery, whilst General Ludlow's troops invested the town and repulsed a sortie. From the 10-21st the Danish and British gunboats had slight engagements, whilst Zealand was blockaded. Troops under Lord Rosslyn landed in north part of Kioge Bay and a battery of thirteen 24 pdrs was erected at Svan-Moelle. On the 22nd three sloops, five bomb vessels with RM Artillery crews for their mortars, seven gunbrigs - which we know had recently been fitted out at Chatham with Marine detachments [169] - and ten launches fitted with mortars took station in Trekonen Strait and were attacked on the 23rd by the Danish prames. Fire was exchanged till 2 pm, but the British carronades were not long enough for the range and the British lost 1 Officer and 2 Seamen killed, 1 Officer, 7 Seamen and 5 Marines wounded. On the 24th on shore the British centre advanced on Fredinsberg and the Brigade of Guards occupied the suburbs; the Danish posts fell back to the inundation, whilst the garrison made a feeble sortie which was driven back. A new line was chosen for the batteries 800 yards from the ramparts under cover of the suburbs.

---

169 Orders 27th May 1807.

On 25th and 29th the Danish vessels renewed the attack and also fired on left of the investing force. On 29th the troops at Kioge Bay, now under General Sir A Wellesley, drove back a relieving force. On 28th, 29th and 30th there was fighting but on 31st the Danish vessels attacked again and one British gun vessel was blown up. On 1st September the Island of Stralsund, which was now in French hands, was blockaded by Admiral Keats.

By 31st August the batteries against Copenhagen were finished and the town was summoned to surrender but refused; action however was delayed by the Diplomatic Agent until 7.30 pm on the 2nd when all the British batteries opened fire and set the town alight. The bomb vessels also commenced firing and the bombardment continued until 5 am on the 3rd. It was resumed in the evening and continued throughout the night of 3/4th September, firing slowly. The bombardment opened again at 7 pm on the 4th; timber yards were on fire; the steeple of the church was knocked down and firing continued until the evening of the 5th. When the conflagration was threatening the whole city, the Major General asked for an armistice which was refused, and he was informed that the basis of a capitulation would be the surrender of the Danish Fleet. General Sir Arthur Wellesley, Commodore Home Popham, and the DQMG were appointed Commissioners to arrange the terms, which were signed and ratified on the 7th. As soon as the fleet was surrendered, the citadel was returned to the Danes and the British withdrew. British losses were 56 killed, 179 wounded, 25 missing! By 20th October all troops were re-embarked, and all ships were out of harbour. On the 21st the Fleet sailed.

Many of the Danish ships were incorporated in the British Navy and we find their names in the letter books and elsewhere in the demands for detachments etc.

But Denmark had now declared war on England; Sweden and Portugal were also forced into the Continental system and Napoleon endeavoured to exclude British trade from the Continent.

Heligoland.
There was a small but interesting expedition on 30th August, when a 32 gun frigate summoned Heligoland to surrender; on 4th September HMS *Majestic*, anchored off the town and at 8 pm when making arrangements to storm the place with her Seamen and Marines, a flag of truce came off with proposals for capitulation. On the 6th the treaty was signed, and the island became British, only to be given away in the late nineteenth century by our statesmen.[170]

Dardanelles.
The Corps was now destined to make their first attack on the Dardanelles, an attack to be repeated so tragically a hundred years later. The comparison of the two campaigns is of interest and brings home how little their role has varied.

Napoleon, being now master of Austria and having pushed his forces into Dalmatia and

---
170 To prove a thorn in the British side for 1914-18.

Italy, was again aiming at the sea power of Great Britain in the Mediterranean. His ambassador Sebastiani was doing his best to stir up Turkey against the Allies, England and Russia. On 16th September the French Ambassador demanded that the Straits should be closed to Russian ships under threat of war, as the French troops were already in Dalmatia.

On the news reaching England the Government determined, in accordance with the old policy, to attack the point from which harm could come to their trade and commerce.[171] On 22nd October 1806 Lord Collingwood, who was watching Cadiz where the French and Spanish were very quiet, was ordered to dispatch three battleships to reconnoitre the Dardanelles Forts. These ships *Canopus* (80), *Thunderer* (74), *Standard* (74), with a frigate and a sloop under Rear Admiral Louis went first to Malta and left there on 15th November; on 27th the Squadron stood into the Straits with a fair wind and anchored in In Tepe Bay (Azir). The *Canopus* proceeded alone on the 28th and anchored off Seraglio Point (Constantinople) with the *Endymion* (40),

On 23rd November the Russian Army invaded Moldavia (which then belonged to Turkey) and the Russian Ambassador embarked on board *Canopus* on Christmas Day, she sailed on the 28th, leaving the *Endymion* at Constantinople, and joined the other ships at In Tepe Bay. On 31st January the *Endymion* having embarked the British Ambassador and all the British merchants, cut her cables and sailed after dark rejoining Admiral Louis who had gone to Tenedos. Meanwhile Admiral Sir John Duckworth and a squadron were detailed for the Dardanelles and he proceeded with his flag in the *Royal George* (110). His orders were to bombard Constantinople and demand the surrender of the Turkish Fleet. He was told to give them an ultimatum allowing only half an hour for reply. His squadron consisted of 12 battleships, 9 frigates and store ships.

He left Gibraltar on 18th January, picking up the *Windsor Castle* (98) and *Repulse* (74) at Malta, and was joined at Malta by Sir Sidney Smith with *Ajax* and *Pompee*. He joined Louis at Tenedos on 10th February.

The Turkish Fleet was at Constantinople, but one battleship and some smaller ships were off Nagara Point.[172] On 11th February the British Fleet weighed, but as the wind was not fair they anchored off Kum Kale in Besika Bay, and Duckworth was beginning to be doubtful of the enterprise. On the 14th HMS Ajax caught fire and blew up on the 15th, 250 Officers and men being lost; the cause was unknown but it was suspected to be due to spontaneous combustion of coals. The ambassador was on board the fleet and he seems to have been a great incubus. On 19th February the wind veered to south-south-west and at 8 am the *Canopus*. arrived abreast of Seddul Bahr and Kum Kale which opened fire. This was not returned except by the bomb vessels. By 9.30 the *Canopus* leading, the line was abreast of the Chanak and Kulid Bahr Forts. The casualties were very small and the ships very slightly damaged.

The Turkish ships at Nagara Point opened fire, which was returned by *Canopus, Repulse, Royal*

---

171 Cf. Havana and Manila, 1762.
172 Accounts call it Pesquies.

George and *Windsor Castle*, who stood on to the anchorage three miles above the point, leaving Sir Sidney Smith with three battleships and the frigates to deal with the Turkish ships as well as the redoubt of 31 guns. All the Turkish ships were run ashore and destroyed, and Turkish troops which appeared were dispersed by the fire of the *Pompee*. Lieutenant M Oates RM landed and captured a green standard; the boats were sent in and destroyed the frigates. Lieutenant E Nicolls RM (*Standard*) burned the frigate of the Captain Pasha and brought off his flag. The Turks were panic stricken and Lieutenant Nicolls with Lieutenants Fynemore and Boileau RM, entered the redoubt, where they set fire to the gabions and spiked the guns, which were of brass and fired large marble balls.

The 64 gun ship was destroyed by the boats of the *Pompee* and *Repulse*; Lieutenants D Holt and W Laurie RM landed with them, but as the battleship was expected to explode, Lieutenant Nicolls' party had to return to their ships before quite completing the destruction of the redoubt. The total British casualties were only 4 killed and 26 wounded, of which the RM lost 1 killed and 5 wounded.

At 5 pm the squadron weighed and at 8 pm passed the town of Gallipoli. On the 20th they anchored off Princes' Islands.

The bombardment of Constantinople was expected to begin on the 21st as they had to wait for word from the ambassador, but nothing was done. A summons was sent to the Turks to surrender their Fleet, but the flag of truce was not allowed to land and only the *Endymion* went up to Constantinople. Talk and letters went on and nothing happened, but on the 27th the British discovered that the Turks were erecting a battery on Prota Island near the anchorage. The Marines of the Squadron under Captain Kent RM (*Canopus*) prepared to land covered by *Canopus* and *Lucifer*; the ships opened fire and the Turks cleared out, but left a few men in the battery. In the afternoon the Marines of the *Canopus*, were landed and pursued the Turks to a monastery which was loop-holed and defended; Captain Kent and several men were killed and the party repulsed. The Marines and armed boats crews of *Royal George*, *Windsor Castle*, and *Standard* were then hurried ashore and after a smart skirmish were driving off the Turks when Admiral Duckworth directed their recall. They had to retire and regained their ships with a loss of 2 Officers and 5 men killed, 2 Officers and 17 men wounded. They just missed capturing Sebastiani, the French ambassador, and the Chief Aga of the Janissaries who were on the island.

Admiral Duckworth had been given by the Government those feeble instructions "avoid being drawn into danger" and also had been provided with too weak a force.

On 28th February it blew a gale and the Turks began to realise that Duckworth was not going to do anything drastic, so they began to equip their fleet and erect batteries. By the morning of 1st March, when the Turks had got ready 5 battleships and 4 frigates, the wind went to the north east so the British Fleet weighed and on the 2nd anchored six miles above Nagara Point. On the 3rd they weighed with the wind at north east and sailed through the Narrows. When off Chanak and Kilid Bahr, Admiral Duckworth fired a salute of 13 guns which was returned by shot and shell from Forts Hamidish Medjidieh and Kilid Bahr (as they are now called) and other batteries; the defences had been much improved; one stone shot of 800 lbs hit the mainmast of the *Windsor Castle*, and cut through three quarters of its diameter. The *Standard* was also hit by one of 770 lbs.

Bomb Vessels.

The *Meteor* (bomb) had burst her 13 in mortar on the way up, and she now burst her 10 in. She had her Lieutenant RMA wounded. The magazines in the bomb ships *Lucifer* and *Meteor* were above water, as they had originally been merchant ships (vessels regularly built as bombs had their magazines under water). The British lost 29 killed and 138 wounded of which the RM had 4 killed and 16 wounded.

Egypt.

After this unsuccessful effort the *Tigre* (74) with *Apollo* (32), *Wizard* (16) and 33 transports carrying troops under Major General Fraser left Sicily on 6th March for Egypt. On the 7th the *Apollo* and 19 transports parted company in a gale; the *Tigre* with the remainder anchored at Alexandria on the 15th. Reports from the shore being favourable, the transports were anchored in the evening off the entrance to the old harbour. Possession of the town and forts being demanded and refused, on the 17th 600-700 troops with 5 field pieces and 36 seamen were landed at the mouth of the ravine leading to Lake Mareotis; owing to the surf the remaining 300 could not be landed till the following day. On 18th March the troops carried the advanced works; on the 19th the *Apollo* with her transports arrived and were sent to Aboukir Bay, and having secured the Castle of Aboukir on the 20th the remainder of the troops were landed.

On 21st March the Governor capitulated and the troops occupied Alexandria, securing two Turkish frigates and one corvette. On the 22nd Admiral Duckworth arrived, and General Fraser attacked Rosetta and Rhamanieh to obtain supplies. The troops took the heights of Abourmandora but suffered a complete defeat, losing 400 men killed and wounded including Fraser himself. Duckworth then sailed for England leaving Admiral Louis, who died later in command. After hanging about until the middle of September, the troops - who had lost 1,000 men - had to be evacuated and re-embarked.

Meanwhile on 19th July 1807 Napoleon informed the Portuguese that unless they closed their ports to the British and sequestered British property France would declare war. The River Tagus and Portuguese ports were of great importance to the British as naval bases, because at this time they were excluded from Spanish ports. The Regent of Portugal shilly-shallied whilst the British urged him to sail for Brazil; on 19th October the French armies under Junot crossed the Bidassoa and on 20th Napoleon declared war on Portugal, whilst on the 27th a secret convention was signed at Fontainebleau between the French and Spanish. On 29th November the Royal Family and 16,000 Portuguese left Lisbon under the care of the British squadron and sailed for Brazil, a squadron of 9 battleships under command of Sir Sidney Smith being left to blockade the Tagus.

On 30th November Junot at the head of the French armies entered Lisbon, where was the Russian Fleet from the Levant! Among the results of the Treaty of Tilsit (after the Battle of Friedland), the Russians had declared war on England on 2nd December and the Ionian islands had been ceded to France: therefore, their squadron was now blockaded in Lisbon.

9- After Trafalgar 1808 – 1814

This year that saw the beginnings of the Peninsular War, which was to absorb the energies of England for the next six years, is full of instructive examples of the varied work of the Corps, but for the majority it meant the important but never ending work of the Blockade.

In January HMS *Blenheim* was wrecked, Captain Forbes, Lieutenant Farber and the detachment being lost. During this year a number of small vessels and sloops were built at Bermuda, presumably for work in the West Indies, because there are numerous orders to send Sergeants' parties as detachments.

Recruiting.
Apparently recruiting from the Irish regiments of Militia was opened again and an innovation was made in permitting enlistment for limited service as well as for life, but with smaller bounties.

RM Artillery.
Steps were also being taken to improve the technical efficiency of the RM Artillery, because on 5th April it was ordered that officers who were candidates for the RMA were to pass an examination in mathematics before the Master, Mr. Edwards, in order to ascertain their qualifications.

On 5th May a new scheme of complement for all classes of ships was promulgated.

King's Pardon.
On 4th May the King's Pardon to all Seamen and Marines who had deserted since 10th October 1805 was promulgated, and it is clear that recruiting was one of the principal difficulties of the time.

Increases.
The strength of the Corps was fixed at 31,400; the Order-in-Council of 27th July ordered ten more companies to be raised and attached to the Woolwich Division. They were numbered 174-183. The strength of the Companies at this time was 1 Captain, 2 First Lieutenants, 2 Second Lieutenants, 8 Sergeants, 8 Corporals, 5 Drummers, 140 Privates. This made the Corps 183 Companies with 4 Artillery. An additional Lieutenant Colonel and Major were added to Woolwich.

Second Captains.
Further as Captains were badly wanted for embarkation, 16 Second Captains were made to replace Senior Captains employed as Pay Captains. This caused a little flutter on the sea roster as the new Captains had all been put at the top of the roster; but on 31st August the Admiralty ordered that they were to be placed at the bottom of their respective rosters.

In May the Admiralty at last recognised that the Deputy Paymaster required some clerks and accordingly the Paymaster at each Division was allowed £100 a year in addition to the NCO's pay to be divided among the clerks employed, commencing from 8th May.

Drills and Training.
In this year also, the letter books contain a few details about drills and training. We learn that it was a very hot summer and there were protests from the Field Officer of the Week at Portsmouth, asking to be allowed to carry out subaltern's drills in the early morning instead of after guard mounting; and also, to drill in the field instead of the barrack square, as attempts to drill under the colonnade were not very successful. One can realise that it must have been pretty fearsome in that confined paved barrack square. The Field Officer, Major Moncrieffe, also puts forward a plea for the use of the plummet and stepmeasurer by the Drill Sergeants and that "facings" (i.e. 'turnings') should be carried out precisely according to His Majesty's Order of 26th July 1808. These innovations do not seem to have met the approval of the Commandant, General Elliot, as Major Moncrieffe was transferred to Woolwich on 5th August and General Elliot had also got rid of his Adjutant, Lieutenant Faden, on 31st May, for the latter seems to have had some new ideas about bayonet exercise, etc.

Abolition of Powder and Queues. But a great break with the past was made on 18th September by the following letter: "It having been judged expedient to crop the hair of all soldiers liable to foreign service, the Admiralty order the same to be adopted at the Marine Divisions" and this was the end of powdered hair and queues.

General Court Martial.
On 5th October practically all the Field Officers of the Corps were ordered to Woolwich to sit on the Court-Martial on the Colonel Commandant: he was found guilty and sentenced to be dismissed the service, but as he was recommended to mercy, the Board placed him on half pay on 9th November.

Rewards.
There are two cases of rewards being given to Marine Officers and men for good service: In the first case Captain Sir Mark Anthony Gerard Knight (Portsmouth) was placed on the Retired List with full pay in consideration of his meritorious services and injuries received in the act of boarding *La Rochelle*, a French Gun brig (15th November 1806). And on 26th December Captain Seymour RN of HMS *Amethyst* brought to notice Sergeant Packwood for his extraordinary good conduct in the action with *La Thetis*[173] and recommended him for QMS or Barrackmaster Sergeant. The Board directed that he was to be promoted in the first vacancy. In this action Second Lieutenant Kendall and 8 Rank and File were killed, and Lieutenant Payne with 9 Rank and File wounded.[174]

Drummers.
From a letter at Plymouth of 24th February we learn some of the "Beatings" of the Drum in which a

---
173 See James.
174 See Britain's Sea Soldiers Vol I p242.

Drummer had to qualify. "Reveille", "Troop", "Retreat", "Tattoo", "To Arms", "Grenadiers' March", "Pioneers' March," "Dukes' March", and all beats practiced on the Drum.

Operations in Europe.
Turning to the operations, the main centre of interest is in Spain, though the actual operations of the Peninsular War do not concern the Corps, yet in conjunction with the fleet their movements had quite a bearing on the operations, and they were able to render many useful services both to the Army and the Navy.

At the end of 1807 we saw that the French troops had arrived in Lisbon, and that the French armies had seized many of the fortified places in Spain. Napoleon had also decided to replace the Spanish Dynasty and to bring the country under his own domination. But this policy had stirred the Spanish people to revolt. Risings occurred all over the country, which cut the communications of the French, and when they tried to advance south two of their armies were defeated, whilst by the Convention of Baylen (28th July) 20,000 of their troops were surrendered. The Spanish Armies and peasants, though unable to stand against the French forces in the open, rendered their movements precarious and the troops in each province were isolated. The rupture between France and Spain had important results for the British Fleet because now the ports, not in possession of the French, were open to them and the strain of the blockade was relieved. The Spaniards, though eager for British help, did not at first allow the fleet to use Cadiz as a naval base. It was essential, however, for the protection of commerce and as a base against the French Fleets, that Lisbon and the Tagus should be in British hands, or at least in those of an Ally, so in July the British Government determined to send an expedition to help the Portuguese to turn the French out of Lisbon.

Figueiro.
General Sir Arthur Wellesley with a force of 11,000 men was dispatched from Cork and arrived on 20th July 1808 at Corunna. Meanwhile Admiral Sir Charles Cotton, who had been blockading the coast, had placed in his hands by the Portuguese insurgents the Fort of Figueiro at the mouth of the River Mondego. He garrisoned it with 400 Royal Marines under Major G Lewis. General Wellesley having reconnoitered the coast decided to land there, the Marines acting as the covering force. With much difficulty and danger owing to the surf, the disembarkation began on 1st August, but was not completed for five days; on the 6th a further force of about 5,000 men under General Spencer arrived from Sicily, Gibraltar and Cadiz, and took three more days to land.

When Wellesley advanced the French were encountered and defeated in the skirmish of Rolica on 17th August 1806; this was followed by the more serious Battle of Vimiero on 21st August. Junot with about 13,000 men was severely defeated, losing 14 out of 24 guns and his infantry was badly shaken and demoralised.

This action was followed by the unfortunate Convention of Cintra on 31st August, by which the French were allowed to evacuate Portugal and were taken back to France. The Tagus was opened again to the British Fleet and became once more a naval base.

The Corps is not concerned with the movements of the army, which under the command of Sir John Moore advanced into Spain nearly to Madrid, and by its movements and masterly retreat to Corunna upset all Napoleon's plans and rendered still more precarious his hold on Spain; but when the army reached Corunna and fought the Battle there on 16th January 1809 the detachments of the Fleet were landed to hold the forts during the re-embarkation. From the Portsmouth letter books, we gather that when the remnants of Sir John Moore's army were crowding into Portsmouth permission was given by the Admiralty for as many as possible to be accommodated in the Marine Barracks.

During the last months of 1807 Admiral Ganteaume, evading the British blockading fleet in the Basque Roads, slipped out of Rochefort and succeeded in reaching Toulon. Lord Collingwood, who was in charge of the Mediterranean Fleet cruising between Cadiz and Sicily, had his hands full. Early in February 1808 Ganteaume left Toulon with 10 battleships, 3 frigates, 2 corvettes and 7 armed transports, and though constantly reported by British cruisers safely reached Corfu, where he landed his troops and occupied the Ionian Islands which had been ceded to France by the Treaty of Tilsit. He also sent detachments to occupy Jacente, Taranto and Brindisi on 23rd February. On the 25th of that month he sailed again towards Sicily and though watched by British frigates he evaded the Battle fleet and returned to Corfu on 15th March. Leaving again on the 16th and running along the North Coast of Africa and then via Sicily and Sardinia, he was again missed by the British and regained Toulon on 10th April.

And so, it continued throughout 1808, the British Fleet lending assistance to all people resisting the French and protecting our commerce.

In November 1808 Napoleon took personal command of the troops operating in Spain. The subsequent movements led to one of the most gallant episodes in the Corps history.

Rosas.
In order to keep open their communications with Barcelona, the French were besieging Gerona and their line of communications passed close to the Bay of Rosas where, at the town of Rosas, there was a fort still held by the Spanish. HMS *Excellent* accompanied by the bomb vessel *Meteor*, (Lieutenant Ballchild RMA in command of the detachment) saw an opportunity of helping the Spaniards. The Marines of HMS *Excellent* under Captain J Nicholson and Lieutenants Gillespie and Patten were landed to occupy the citadel of Rosas under Captain West RN, whilst Lieutenant Howe and 25 Royal Marines were sent to hold the detached fort of La Trinidad. On 15th November 200 French attacked Fort Trinidad but were repulsed by Lieutenant Howe and his men who beat off two assaults, using hand grenades as well as musketry.

Howe was then reinforced by Captain Nicholson, Lieutenant Patten and 30 Rank and File from the Citadel, who climbed into the fort by a rope ladder with the loss of one man wounded. On 20th November the French opened a battery commanding the fort and drove off the *Lucifer*, bomb vessel (Lieutenant Lawrence RMA) that had been helping the fort. Another battery forced the *Excellent* to move further out. HMS *Fame* then relieved the *Excellent*, and her Marines under Lieutenant Wall RM relieved the *Excellent*'s Marines: but by special request of the Captain of the *Fame*, Lieutenant Howe and his men were left in Fort Trinidad with the Spanish garrison. On 23rd November a breach was made in the Citadel and the Spanish garrison were in such a bad state that the Captain of the *Fame* decided to withdraw his Marines.

On the 24th the Spaniards in Fort Trinidad were on the point of surrendering, when Captain Lord Cochrane, in HMS *Imperieuse*, appeared in the Bay. In spite of the opinion of the Captain of the *Fame*, Cochrane threw Lieutenant Hore (his Marine Officer) with 30 Seamen and 30 Marines into Fort Trinidad and took command himself. The Spanish garrison consisted of two companies, one of which was composed of Irishmen who had been long in Spain. Lord Cochrane improved the defences of the Fort in many ingenious ways.

On 26th the French assaulted Rosas and captured the town; on 30th November the French again assaulted Fort Trinidad but were repulsed - in connection with which there is a legend about Lord Cochrane. On 5th December the Citadel surrendered and as there was no particular reason to continue to hold Trinidad Lord Cochrane sent for the boats and evacuated it, blowing up the tower by one mine. Unfortunately, a second mine failed to explode.

Advanced Bases.
In the West Indies the Corps were concerned in a matter which is the subject of much study today and one which illustrates some of its dangers.

The Navy were blockading the French in the island of Guadeloupe to protect our West Indian commerce, and for this purpose required to occupy the small islands of Marie Galante and Deseada, opposite the Coast, which sheltered the privateers.

Marie Galante was captured on 2nd March which was useful also for the supply of wood and water. On 30th March Deseada was also secured.

Admiral Sir Alexander Cochrane garrisoned Marie Galante with 300 Marines, but soon after he applied to the Governor of Barbados for an army garrison; the latter knowing the unhealthiness of the place hesitated but agreed to supply 150 men to take the place of the Marines in the Fleet. By the middle of August many of the Marines had died and General Beckwith at Barbados was getting anxious about the survivors, as the French were then on their way to attack. The Admiral begged for reinforcements and the General sent 300 of the West India Regiment "which rescued the unfortunate Marines"[175] and took 170 French prisoners. This occurred between August 29th and September 3rd, 1808,

Admiral Sir Alexander Cochrane then increased the garrison of Marie Galante, but called

---
175 Fortescue.

on the General to furnish 800 soldiers to replace the crews in the ships; the General complied but in reporting the matter to the Secretary of the State made the caustic comment: "There is a thing called prize afloat; searching for it on shore tends to a different signification though both words begin with a P. We cannot keep the seas without 800 soldiers in the Fleet such has been the mortality; if seamen occupy islands, soldiers must be turned into Seamen and Marines, but I cannot do this for long." [176] What had happened was that the Admiral had commissioned the islands as a man-of-war with a Post Captain in command and was using them as a base for carrying on trade with North America (which was forbidden to other islands) and the Naval officers concerned were making a handsome profit.[177]

The Marine casualties were made up in February 1809 when 8 Subalterns, 20 NCOs and 200 Privates embarked in HMS *Dolphin*, for passage to the Leeward Islands.

This incident had important results, for the blockade of Martinique was relaxed, food got in during the summer, and in December more ships with men and provisions arrived from France both in Guadeloupe and Martinique, which led to the expedition against Martinique early in 1809.

1809

Admiral Sir Alexander Cochrane with six battleships and nine frigates and a lot of small craft with 10,000 troops under General Beckwith (4 Battalions had joined him from North America) sailed on 28th January. On the 30th they arrived off Martinique. General Maitland with the 2nd Division disembarked at St Luce without opposition, covered by the Belleisle sending one regiment, the York Rangers, to Anse d'Arlet to take the Battery at Cape Salomon in rear and so command Pigeon Island.

Maitland pushed on and reached Rivière Salée on the 31st. Marching to Lamenteu on 2nd February, he reached Fort Desaix (formerly Bourbon) on the 3rd, and covered the landing place of Cohe du Lamentine. The York Rangers had seized the heights commanding Pigeon Island and heavy guns were landed by the *Pompee* in the adjacent bay which the Bluejackets brought up to the battery. Beckwith with Provost's Division (8,500) landed unopposed, covered by the *Acasta* at Baie Robert on the north east or Windward Coast.

Starting late on 30th he made a night march of seven miles and reached the Legarde River at dawn on the 31st. On the 1st he occupied Morne Brumeau. The French were occupying a good position covered by a river at Desfourneaux; the British attacked and were driven back, but after repulsing one or two attacks the French though reinforced were driven back to their entrenched camp, losing 700 killed and wounded. Beckwith extending to the westward tried to carry the entrenched camp but suffered heavy loss and had to abandon the attack.

---

176 Ibid.
177 Perhaps in this we see one of the reasons why the prize regulations were altered in 1914-18.

During the night the French abandoned their position which the British occupied on the 5th. Meanwhile on the 4th the battery had opened on Pigeon Island and it had surrendered. Admiral Cochrane stood in and anchored in Fort Royal Bay on which the French burnt their ships and abandoned all the Forts and retired to Fort Desaix. On the 8th Maitland, marching by Borne Brumeau and Negro Point, completed the investment of Fort Royal on the west side, and on the 10th the town of Fort Royal was occupied. On the 9th February the Polorus and Cherub were sent with a few of the 63rd Regiment to St Pierre, which surrendered.

From the 10th-19th the British were building their batteries against Fort Royal and fire was opened at noon on the 23rd when the French were summoned to surrender but refused; fire continued until the 24th when the French surrendered and accepted the terms.

Before leaving the West Indies, we must record a very gallant bit of work by which the British and Portuguese captured Cayenne in French Guiana. The *Confiance* (20) and the Portuguese *Voada* and *Infanta* landed 80 Seamen and Marines and captured Forts Diamant and De Gras de Caine on 8th December 1809. Lieutenant Read RM, one Seaman and 5 Marines being wounded, this secured the entrance to the river. The French with 1,000 men came down from Cayenne town; the British and Portuguese blew up Fort Diamant and concentrated at De Gras de Gaines. Two forts up the river covering the creeks were attacked and carried by the British who then fell back on De Gras where they were attacked by the French; after three hours fighting the attack was driven off. On the 14th after further fierce fighting they marched up to Cayenne and took it. Lieutenant Read unfortunately died of his wounds.

The Corps was now very active in various parts of the world, and it is difficult to give any connected account. In the first place there was the continuous and main blockade of the French Atlantic ports, the Brest Roads and the Channel. We are not concerned with the great controversy that arose over Lord Cochrane's attempt with fireships on the Basque Roads, but many of the Corps must have been witnesses of that gallant attempt on 11th April 1809.

Naturally we were involved in the great expedition to the Scheldt under Admiral Sir Richard Strachan and the Earl of Chatham, when disease proved the most fatal enemy and incapacitated many of our finest battalions at a time when they were urgently required in the Peninsula. A very favourable report was received of the Battalion under Captain I Liardet which was landed at Walcheren.[178]

First dealing with what was gradually becoming the main British theatre of war - Spain and Portugal - the operations being mainly inland were beyond our reach, but the Corps was able to lend help to the Spaniards in June at Vigo.

Following on Lord Wellington's successful campaign by which he drove Massena out of the

---

178 Plymouth Orders 30th August 1809.

Northern part of Portugal in May, Marshal Ney had been sent by Napoleon to subdue Galicia, and his hands were full of the Galician insurgents, helped by the remnants of Romana's regulars.

Ney advanced from Corunna on Santiago where the French garrison had been defeated on 22nd May and where Ney did not arrive till 5th June. Hearing of his arrival the Spanish General Novoa fell back forty miles south and took post behind the River Oitlaben, his right flank on the Sierrade Suido the left on the Sea. There were four passages over the river, one a ford on the estuary open for three hours at low tide, next a bridge at San Payo just above the tidal water (four arches were broken), then a bridge at Candeles six miles further up and lastly a ford just above the bridge. Seamen from the British frigates manned some gunboats to patrol the estuary. The Marines of the squadron and 60 of Moore's stragglers were put ashore to garrison Vigo about eight miles down the Bay from the River Oitlaben. The officers in command were Lieutenants J H Debrissay, C Griffith, J Laurie, J M Smith, D Miller, Second Lieutenants H Broom, J Dehan, J Brown; Lieutenant P Nicholas (Adjt).[179] They were landed on 14th April.

On 7th June Ney reached the Oitlaben, where he reconnoitered the fords; on the 8th he attempted the passage at both fords but was repulsed. Learning that Soult was not coming to his aid he retreated on Pontevedra and Santiago; Soult also retired to the eastward to Benavente, and on 22nd June Ney evacuated Corunna and Ferrol and retired to Astorga, so that Galicia was free of the French. The Marines re-embarked on 19th June.

The other centre of interest was the Mediterranean where British garrisons held Sicily and Malta, and the Fleet was continually watching the movements of the French in Italy and those of their squadrons from Toulon. The only Naval action took place on 21st October 1809 when Lord Collingwood destroyed a small French squadron and convoy in the Gulf of Lyons. There was constant fighting between the flotillas of gunboats based on Sicily and the French at Naples in which the RMA officers and men were engaged; on 30th June a small force from Sicily captured Ischia, which after dismantling the forts returned to Sicily on 6th July.

Advanced Naval Bases.
The fact that the French were in possession of the Ionian Islands was of great importance, as Fortescue says.[180] "This is a point much neglected in our Naval and Military plans; a vast deal of scouting and watching is expected from the Navy, but with the exception of holding certain definite bases for the Fleet the duties of the Army are held to be offensive, and no account is taken of the new naval stations which Admirals will inevitably require to be held for them, and of the consequent weakening of the offensive military force." This is where the new Marine Organisations come in and the following operations are instructive.

On 25th September Brigadier General Oswald with some 20th Light Dragoons, RA, RE, 35th, and 44th Regiments and the Corsican Rangers, under the escort of a battleship and some

---

179 Portsmouth and Plymouth Letter Books.
180 VII p304.

small vessels, was sent from Sicily to Zante. On 1st October he landed eight Companies under Colonel Hudson Lowe and took the island. Owing to the good Naval dispositions Cephalonia also surrendered. Captain R Church with 300 Corsican Rangers captured Ithaca whilst Major Clarke with two companies of 35th took Cerigo without opposition. Zante and Cephalonia provided a good naval base for blockading Corfu where there were 4,000 French troops.

Peace was signed between France and Austria on 13th October 1809, with the result that the Sicilian garrisons became more concerned for the next two years in the contest between British and French interests in the Levant and Adriatic than in the great contest proceeding in Spain.

Before leaving the operations of 1809, there is an incident to be recorded in West Africa in which the Corps took a characteristic part. The French privateers at Senegal were disturbing trade; the *Solebay* (32), with 166 troops of the African Corps on board the *Agincourt*, left Goree on 4th July with *Derwent* (18) and *Tigre* (12). Anchoring off the bar on the 7th, 160 troops, 120 Seamen and 50 Marines, in spite of the heavy surf, crossed the bar in boats, and Major Maxwell succeeded in landing and took up a position on the left bank of the river. The French (120 troops and 240 militia) were in position about ten miles above the bar. On the 9th the French advanced to the attack; Maxwell, supported by the boats, advanced to meet them, and the French retired to a formidable line of defence at Babague. Here they had a battery on the south point of an island commanding the passage and a chain across the river; behind the chain was a flotilla of armed vessels and gunboats with 31 guns.

On 11th the *Solebay* and *Derwent* took up a position close to a neck of land between the river and the sea where they could bombard Babague and this they did with effect. On the night of the 11/12th the *Solebay* went ashore and was wrecked; the stores however were saved. On the 12th the troops re-embarked and proceeded up the river to Babague and were on the point of attacking when the French Commandant proposed to capitulate for his troops had deserted and broken the boom and the next day the colony surrendered. Lieutenant Reeves and his detachment were commended for their good service by the Governor.[181]

Certain alterations were made at Headquarters which are noteworthy. By Order-in-Council 18th February 1809 a second Colonel Second Commandant was added to each Division and the pay of the senior officers was increased. The pay of the Colonel Commandant Resident in Town was raised from 40/6d to £3 per diem, Senior Colonels Commandant of Divisions from 40/- to 50/- and Second Commandants from 24/- to 30/-.

The numbers voted for the year were 31,400.

Forage and Divisional Fund.
Forage for the chargers of Lieutenant Colonels, Majors and Adjutants was allowed in March.

---

181 Plymouth Orders 24th May 1810.160,

Contributions to the Divisional Funds were increased on 23rd March, when the stoppage of 1/6 per week from the pay of men allowed to work for outside employers, known as the Eighteenpenny Fund, was raised to 3/- a week as the pay of the men had been raised; the 1/6 had been fixed when it was only 8d a day. The money was to be applied to the Divisional Fund and a report made to the Admiralty of numbers employed and the number of days each had been at Headquarters.

NCOs.
There was evidently trouble about NCOs, for on 28th May an order was given that men reduced were not to be promoted again within one year and also *"Not any Marine is to be promoted to NCO from the situation of servant to an officer of the Royal Marines".*

Badges of Rank.
An alteration in badges of rank was made on 6th April, whereby Brevet Field Officers were to wear two epaulets as for Field Officers, and Adjutants one epaulet on right shoulder with a laced strap on left.

Training.
On 7th April allowances of ammunition for training was laid down, and it is interesting to compare them with modern allowances.

> Spring Allowance due 25th March, 20 Rounds Ball Cartridge, 40 Rounds Blank Cartridge and 2 Flints per musket.
> Autumn Allowance due 29th September, 10 Rounds Ball Cartridge, 20 Rounds Blank Cartridge and 1 Flint per musket.

To be issued on certificate of average numbers at Headquarters.

Sea Pay.
On 23rd of October was introduced a rule which remained in force for many years, and in the days of the sharks who used to hang round barracks and fleece the men was of great importance. No Sea Pay, Hospital Money or other credit was to be paid to the men until they reached their own Divisions, unless they re-embarked from the Division at which they were.

1810

Before describing the operations, administrative arrangements deserve attention.

An Order-in-Council 10th January authorised the increase of one Sergeant and one Corporal to each of the 25 senior companies at each Division, or 100 Sergeants and 100 Corporals in all, the Commandants pointing out the great number of small detachments afloat, making the proportion generally 1 Sergeant and 1 Corporal to 16 Privates instead of the established proportion of 1 Sergeant and 1 Corporal to 13 Privates and also to provide for Drill Sergeants, Pay Clerks, etc.

Badges.
Badges of rank were again dealt with by an order of 28th March:

Field Officers	2 Epaulets, Bullion fringe.
Colonels	Crown and Star.
Lieutenant Colonels	Crown
Majors	Star
Captains	1 Epaulet, Bullion fringe on right shoulder.
Subalterns	1 Epaulet with fringe on right shoulder.
Adjutants, Quartermasters and Paymasters	Same as Subalterns but Adjutants, a laced strap on left shoulder as well.
Surgeons and Assistant Surgeons	Neither Epaulets nor Wings. Waistbelts instead of shoulder belt and no sash.

Correspondence.
On 22nd June Divisions were ordered to number their letters sent to the Admiralty in succession (as is now done) but an observation of the letter books shows that this was more honoured in the breach than the observance.

Portsmouth tried to get their Mess Room enlarged but it was refused on 1st August 1810.

Recruiting.
The enlistment of foreigners also was stopped this year.

The numbers voted were 31,400.

Guadeloupe.
Operations opened with the attack on Guadeloupe, but before the main attack the RN and RM were engaged in a gallant little affair at Baie Mahaut Guadeloupe. On 17th January the *Freya* (36) sent four boats under Lieutenants Hope RN and Shillabeer RM with 50 Seamen and 30 Marines to bring out a brig anchored under a fort. This had just been reinforced by a company of infantry and a troop of cavalry and as the boats came in they were greeted by fire from a battery on the north east point and from another at the head of the bay as well as from ships and musketry from the shore. They boarded the brig and the crew fled; they then turned her guns on to the shore, whilst the boats landed, and the men waded ashore. The French abandoned the first battery but took cover under a wall from which the Seamen and Marines drove them, capturing one 24 pdr and 6 howitzers which were thrown over the cliff and the battery burnt. They then pushed on storming and capturing another battery with three 24 pdrs which were spiked. Returning to the brig they got her afloat, but the other vessels could not be moved and were burnt. Lieutenant Hope gave high praise to "the gallant manner in which Lieutenant Shillabeer led his Marines to the charge as well as the steady discipline of the latter in keeping possession of the heights while

the seamen were destroying the batteries."[182]

With the main expedition, except for their usual service afloat, the Corps was not concerned. Leaving Barbados on 22nd January 1810 they arrived off the Isle of Gosier on the 26th. One division landed at Village de Sante Marie covered by the *Abercrombie* (74), and two brigades at Cupes Three covered by the *Sceptre* (74). On the 30th the troops reached Trois Rivières.

It is not possible to follow the whole campaign, but the fleet were enabled to anchor on the 31st in the Anse de Trois Rivières; on 3rd February the French gave way in their strong position and on the 6th the island was surrendered. This led to the fall of the Islands of St Martin on 14th and 15th February and of St Eustatius without any opposition on the 21st, so that the French flag ceased to fly in the islands, but the British were hampered by having to provide 17 garrisons besides Saint and Marie Galante which were held by the Navy.

Indian Ocean.
Turning to the Indian Ocean where the French privateers based on Mauritius and Reunion were seriously damaging the British trade. It was decided that the army should help the navy to clear out these places.

Mauritius and Reunion.
The first step was to dispatch a small force under Colonel Keating, who with Commodore Rowley seized the uninhabited island of Rodriguez; as the force was so small the next step was to seize Reunion (or as it was then called Bourbon). The troops - about 3,650 all told - in 14 transports escorted by the *Boadicea* and *Nereide* left Rodriguez on 3rd July. They were divided into four brigades commanded by Colonels Fraser, Keating, Campbell, and Drummond; the Royal Marines (300 in number) were attached to Drummond's (2nd) Brigade.

The principal town was St Denis; Fraser's Brigade landed at Grande Chaloupe six miles south and west of the capital at 2 pm on the 7th covered by *Sirius*; the other three Brigades were to land at Riviere de Pluies, three miles to the east of the town, covered by *Boadicea*, *Iphigenia*, *Magicienne*, and *Nereide*. There was a shingly beach, surf and bad weather; Captain Willoughby Nisbet RN ran a transport ashore to act as a breakwater but only succeeded in landing a covering force of seamen and about 150 troops who took possession of Fort Sainte Marie for the night, and the landing had to be suspended. Fraser advanced and bivouacked for the night one and a half miles from St Denis, and on the morning of the 8th he advanced and found the enemy in position with one flank on a redoubt and the other on a river. He carried the redoubt with the bayonet. In the meanwhile the *Boadicea* had gone to La Grande Chaloupe and at 11 am Colonel Keating and the troops in the *Boadicea* landed and in course of the day the remainder were put ashore. Drummond's Brigade, with which were the Royal Marines, reinforced Fraser when the French commander proposed a truce. Keating arriving on the scene, hectored the Governor into surrender, the French regulars

---

182 James.

being made prisoners of war and the Militia sent to their homes. On 10th the town of St Paul was captured, and the island passed into British hands.

The next step was to seize the Isle de la Passe at the mouth of the harbour of Port Bourbon, Mauritius. This was done by the boats of the *Sirius* and *Iphigenia* and a small garrison was placed on the islet, the command being given to Captain Willoughby Nisbet RN of the *Nereide*, one of the dare-devils of the Navy.

On 10th August Nisbet with the boats of the *Sirius*, *Nereide* and *Staunch* with 400 seamen, Marines, and soldiers attacked the Point du Diable, but the weather was bad and the attack had to be abandoned. On the 13th however 71 Officers, seamen and Marines under Lieutenant Norman RN (RM Officers - Lieutenants S J Collett and W Bate) attacked again; the French garrison was composed of 88 men with four 24 pdrs nine 13 pdrs and three 13in mortars (most of them commanding the landing places). The French opened fire on the boats causing casualties in spite of which the British landed and drove the French from the works; Norman was killed but Lieutenant Watling carried on and the place was carried, so sealing up the French ships in the harbour.

Unfortunately, the desire to make prizes of the ships led to Captain Nisbet making an attack on them which led to disaster. At the first attempt on 22nd August by the *Sirius* and *Nereide*, the *Sirius* went ashore and on the 23rd when the *Iphigenia* and *Magicienne* joined the attack was resumed. The *Nereide* succeeded in getting inside the harbour but lost 230 men out of 280 and had to surrender, the *Magicienne* had to be abandoned and was blown up on the 24th, the *Sirius* on the 25th. The *Iphigenia* escaped to the Isle de la Passe, but four French frigates came round from Port Louis and she also had to surrender as well as the garrison of the island who were sent to the Cape of Good Hope. The French, being now superior in force, blockaded Reunion.

The next point of attack was Mauritius itself (or Isle de France as it was then called) but for this an expedition from India was needed.

On 13th September the *Africaine* was taken by two French men of war, but was immediately retaken by Commodore Rowley in the *Boadicea*. On the 17th the *Ceylon*, with General Abercrombie the Force Commander and detachments of the 69th and 86th, knowing nothing of the disaster, sailed past Port Louis and were captured by the French; they were fortunately recaptured next day by the *Boadicea*.

On 10th October Admiral Bartle in the *Nisus* with three frigates arrived from the Cape of Good Hope and, leaving the *Africaine* to maintain the blockade, the Admiral and General went on to Rodriguez to concentrate the force.

On 22nd October the first contingent from Bombay arrived under escort of one battleship and six frigates. On 6th November the Madras contingent and on the 27th the final contingent from Bengal about 10,000 troops in all. Three-fifths were Europeans and the rest Sepoys. There were also available 1,500 - 1,700 seamen and Marines. The French had 1,300 regulars (including 500 Irish) and 10,000 National Guard. The British force was organised in five brigades and a reserve; the Royal Marines - 300 in number - under Captain Liardet were in the 4th Brigade commanded by Colonel McLeod of the 69th which consisted of Royal Marines, the 69th, and the flank companies of the 6th and 12th Madras Native Infantry.

The force landed on the 29th in the Grande Baie on north of the Island, having passed through a channel never before attempted by the British and only used by the French in cases of extreme need - a fine bit of pilotage and surveying.

Although the landing was unopposed the Navy landed the force with all due formality as if it was under fire; the 5th Brigade was left to secure the landing place and the remainder marched on Port Louis about 12 miles away. They at first marched along the beach, then for three or four miles through dense forest, coming out on to a plain where they halted for the night, the men having suffered much from thirst and fatigue.

They advanced at daybreak on the 30th and at 8 am reached a strong position with abundant water where General Abercrombie decided to halt; at noon the French General De Caen reconnoitered but was driven back. Supplies were landed during the day. On 1st December the advance was resumed in an easterly direction. The enemy were in position on the bank of the River Seche and opened a heavy fire; Abercrombie turned their left, captured three guns and pursued them until under the guns of Port Louis; he then occupied a hill - Montague Longue - with his left and halted for the night.

On 2nd December General De Caen sent out a flag of truce and by nightfall the surrender of the island was arranged. The French soldiers and seamen were sent back to France. The British captured 200 guns, 36 ships, and liberated 2,000 British prisoners.

With reference to the Irish there are some interesting letters in the Divisional letter books of 1811 of officers and men required for evidence at the trials of some of the Irishmen found in arms at the surrender of Reunion.[183] Probably they were Marine deserters. The courts Martial were held at Sheerness.

The enemy bases in the Molucca Islands were taken - Amboyna on 9th February 1810, and Banda Neira 9th August 1810.

Mediterranean.
Turning now to the Mediterranean, where the Navy had to maintain continuous watch, not only on the French coasts, but also on Italy and Dalmatia where the French troops were still in occupation. The first operation that claims attention is in the Ionian Islands, and without going into the politics

---
183 And also Mauritius; see dates 6th November 1811, and 19th December 1811.

of the Republic of the islands etc., it is sufficient to say that it was necessary for the operations of the fleet to continue the blockade of the French in Corfu, and to complete the operations described in 1809 it was decided to seize the Island of Santa Maura.

This island is twenty miles long north and south, and seven miles from east to west; the town of Amaxichi lies at the north east angle, whilst two miles west of the town is a headland which runs out northwards for about a mile, then turns abruptly to the east in a low sandy spit to form the port of Santa Maura and then turns away in north east direction. The fort is at the north east angle; on the east side of the quadrilateral is an aqueduct 1,300 yards long, very narrow on top, which supplies town and fort with water. The approach to the fort is by the spit of sand 1,300 yards wide, narrowing to 300 yards at the narrowest part. At this point there were two redoubts and an entrenchment calculated to delay an enemy for a month.

Brigadier General Oswald sailed from Zante on 21st March 1810 with three men of war and 2,500 troops; these included 225 Royal Marines under Major Clarke, Captain Snow, and Lieutenant Morrison from HMS *Magnificent, Montagu* and *Bellepoule*. the 35th Regiment, 548 Greek Light Infantry, and troops of the Calabrian Corps, Corsican Rangers and de Roll's Corps besides Royal Artillery and Royal Engineers and a few cavalry. They arrived off the town the same evening and disembarked the next morning. The enemy were driven from the coast batteries by the fire of the ships and evacuated the town retiring to the fortress. The French garrison consisted of 1,600 Regulars and Irregulars, but half of the local Militia deserted.

General Oswald advanced in two columns, one under Colonel Hudson Lowe to watch the town and secure the aqueduct; Oswald reconnoitered the spit but Captain Church and the Greek Light Infantry carried the first redoubt; the French were strengthening the entrenchment which stretched from sea to sea with a wet ditch and with an abatis in front; they had also four guns well flanked and about 500 men.

HMS *Leonidas* was asked to cover the assault and the provisional battalion under Major Clarke (2 Companies RM, 2 Companies de Roll's, 2 Companies Corsican Rangers) was sent to reinforce the Greeks, who skirmished well making good use of the ground, though they would not advance to the storm. Clarke's battalion, the Marines leading the way, broke through the abatis and charged so fiercely with the bayonet that the enemy fled at all points. Lowe brought up two companies of the 35th and some Corsican Rangers along the aqueduct and came in on the rear of the fugitives. The French were so demoralised that they abandoned the remaining strong positions and took refuge in the fort; a very brilliant affair carried out with a loss of 13 killed, 94 wounded and 17 drowned, including 1 officer killed and 11 wounded.

A reinforcement of 650 men and 12 heavy guns arrived from Sicily and the siege was commenced. The batteries opened fire on 8th April and after a week an outwork within 300 yards of the rampart was assaulted and carried. From this point the riflemen made such havoc among the enemy artillerymen that on the 16th the French surrendered, 800 prisoners being taken. The total losses were troops 16 killed, 86 wounded; RN 2 officers and 6 wounded, 2 men killed; Royal Marines 6 killed, Captain Snow, Lieutenant Morrison and 27 men wounded. From the Plymouth Orders of 25th June 1811, we know that Major Clarke, Captain Snow and the Marines were mentioned for storming three entrenched batteries and also that on 23rd March and again on 17th April 1810 General Oswald published in orders *"Congratulations of Brigadier General Oswald"* (Signed R Oswald, A.A.G.).

Grao.
The frigate squadron under Captain Hoste was very active in the Adriatic, and on 28th June the Corps was given an opportunity of gaining further laurels in an operation which we should nowadays consider as coming under the head of the RM Striking Force. The *Amphion* (Captain Hoste, 32), *Active* (38), *Cerberus* (32) when off Trieste chased a convoy on its way to Venice into Grao. The boats of the *Amphion* and *Cerberus* under Lieutenant Slaughter RN with Lieutenants T Moore RM (*Amphion*) and Brattle (*Cerberus*) on the morning of the 29th landed to the right of the town without opposition. They attacked the town at daybreak but were met by troops and peasantry. The British were obliged to retire when the French charged with the bayonet, but received the enemy with great steadiness and captured 1 Officer, 1 Sergeant and 38 Privates of the French 81st Regiment. The British party then entered the town and captured 25 vessels of the convoy. French reinforcements arrived but were also captured by the boats of the *Active* which had just arrived. By 8 pm they managed to float the vessels over the bar and brought them off. Four Marines were killed, and Lieutenant Brattle and four Marines wounded; the seamen had three wounded. On 31st December it was notified that Lieutenant T Moore was promoted to Brevet Captain dated 21st November for gallantry and good conduct displayed by him when landed from HMS *Amphion* at Grao on 29th June 1810.

Lissa.
These three frigates with the *Volage* (22) on 13th March 1811 fought a very gallant action with five French frigates, and a lot of small craft off Lissa in which they captured three French frigates.

We must not forget that the main Mediterranean Squadron was blockading Toulon and on 22nd July they had a sharp action in which the French were driven back to port.

Palamos.
There was also a squadron cooperating with the Spanish forces on the east coast of Spain which did very useful work, but in one attempt to use a striking force and bring out a convoy there was a failure from which some useful lessons can be learnt.

This was at Palamos on the south east coast of Spain. The *Kent* (74), *Aiax* (74), *Cambrian* (40), *Sparrowhawk* (18), *Minstrel* (18) sent their boats with 350 Seamen, 250 Marines and two field guns under Captain Pane of the *Cambrian* to bring out a convoy intended for Barcelona which was lying in the port.

The Mole was protected by a battery of one 24 pdr and one 13 inch mortar with another 24 pdr on a height close by, and a garrison of 250 troops in the town. The British landed under cover of the *Sparrowhawk* and *Minstrel*, and the French retired; the British occupied the batteries and the vessels and spiked the mortar; the guns were thrown into the sea. Two vessels were brought out and the rest burnt with very small loss. The Marines and seamen, who had occupied the hill to cover the operations, in withdrawing did so in some disorder; this encouraged the French who had just been reinforced. Instead of retiring to the beach where the *Sparrowhawk* and *Minstrel* could have assisted them, they passed through the town to the mole; fire was opened from the houses and walls on to the crowded boats and those left on the mole. Two officers, 19 seamen and 12 Marines were killed; 15 Officers, 42 seamen, and 32 Marines were wounded; and 2 Officers, 41 seamen, and 43 Marines captured.

The Mediterranean Squadron was also assisting in the Siege of Cadiz where the Spaniards and a force of British under General Graham were holding up Marshal Victor. Although we are not concerned with the siege there is an incident in which our Corps took part that added yet another laurel to the wreath.

Matagorda.
Cadiz itself lies at the end of a sandy spit, almost midway along the spit is Fort Puntade; opposite it to the westward a sandy spit runs out forming a sort of inner harbour and on the point of this spit is Fort M*atago*rda. The Spaniards had blown it up as of no use. Marshal Victor made an approach on this side, owing to distance to which the approaches had to be made on the other sides.

The Spaniards and British started to repair and re-arm the fort and stationed a naval force to help. Victor therefore concluded that it must be of some use; the fort was 100 yards square, but only had a small garrison. In March 1810 when General Graham took over command he inspected it and also doubted its value but allowed the work to continue.

On 21st April the French started batteries on Trocadero against M*atago*rda, drove off the ships with red hot shot and then turned their fire on to the fort. The garrison consisted of one officer and 25 Royal Artillery, 25 Royal Marines, 1 Officer and 25 seamen, 3 officers, 67 Rank and File of the 94th Regiment. The garrison replied with their eight guns but were short of ammunition; after eight hours the fort was a heap of ruins. At 10 am on the 22nd it was evacuated by order of General Graham; out of 147 defenders there were 64 casualties and General Graham published an order holding up their conduct to the emulation of their comrades.[184]

But we must not forget that all these operations were being covered by the blockading fleet in the Channel and off Brest, and more particularly in the Bay of Biscay and in the Basque Roads. Here, on 27th September, seamen and Marines of the Squadron carried out a very gallant and instructive attack at Point du Che. The *Caledonia*, (100), *Valiant* (74), *Armide* (38) sent their

---
184 See also Britain's Sea Soldiers.

boats under Lieutenant Hamilton RN with 130 Royal Marines under Captains Sherman and A MacLachlan, Lieutenants J Coulter, J Conche and R J Little to destroy three brigs lying under the protection of a battery at Point du Che; the enemy had also four field guns and a force of cavalry in the village of Angouleme close by.

At 3.30 am on the 28th the RM landed at Point du Che; the alarm was given by the brigs and an ineffectual fire opened. Lieutenant Little pushed on with the bayonet to assault the battery, supported by Captain MacLachlan's company and a detachment under Lieutenants Coulter and Conche of Captain Sherman's company was posted on the main road by the sea supported by a launch with an 18 pdr to face the village. A large body of the enemy advanced from the village but were checked by a hot fire; the enemy then brought up a field gun to flank the line but the British charged and took it with the bayonet. In the meantime the seamen had captured two of the brigs and burnt the third. The Royal Marines then re-embarked with the loss of 1 killed, Lieutenant Little and 1 man wounded. Little lost his hand while struggling to get a musket from a Frenchman.

In the Peninsula, Lord Wellington after his summer campaign had retired to the Lines of Torres Vedras covering Lisbon. These consisted of three very strong fortified lines; the third line was very powerful - two miles long - and had been thrown up round Sao Juliao to cover a re-embarkation. Two Battalions of Marines were told off to man this third line in addition to other troops. They had evidently been provided by the fleet lying in the Tagus as the British occupied the lines on 10th Ootober. This led to the formation of the celebrated First Battalion under Major Williams to relieve them.

Orders had been issued on 25th September 1810 to the Divisions to provide companies composed of 80 Rank and File (including 10 foreigners, 'who must be Germans') with a proper proportion of Sergeants and Drummers to be selected from the steadiest and best disciplined men; 1 Captain, 2 Lieutenants to each company to be perfectly fit for active service on shore. Chatham and Portsmouth to provide one Company each, Plymouth two companies and the Division of RMA.

Major R Williams, the senior RMA Captain, was appointed to command with Major Abernethie as his second and ordered to proceed to Chatham for orders. On 8th October the companies were ordered to assemble at Plymouth and two field pieces and ammunition were to be supplied to the RMA. On 2nd November these were ordered to embark on board the *Abercrombie* and a frigate selected by Admiral Sir Robert Calder for passage to Lisbon, taking with them their appointments for service on shore but not the guns and stores belonging to the RMA. The embarkation state signed by Major Williams shows 2 Majors, 5 Captains, 9 First Lieutenants, 3 Second Lieutenants, 28 Sergeants, 11 Drummers, 462 Rank and File, 1 Adjutant, and 2 Staff Sergeants. They embarked from the Devil's Point at 7.30 am on 28th November.

On arrival at Lisbon, after receiving a pair of Colours from the Ambassador, they were detailed to relieve the Marines of the fleet as garrison in the third line of Torres Vedras; Napier the historian of the Peninsula War says of them *"A superb body of Marines"* and they were evidently picked men. They remained in the neighbourhood of Lisbon for twelve months and we know very little of them except that in August 1811 the Admiralty directed that the Battalion should be raised to 8 Companies of 70 Rank and File each, and a draft was sent out of 5 Officers, 4 Sergeants, 2 Drummers, 101 Rank and File under the command of Major Graham and a state dated 9th August 1811 is in the Plymouth Letter Book showing that on that date the Battalion consisted of:

RMA at Cascaes:
    1 Captain
    2 Lieutenants
    4 Sergeants
    45 Rank & File (1 on command)

RM at Lisbon:
    1 Major (Commanding)
    1 Major
    5 Captains
    11 Lieutenants
    3 Second Lieutenants
    4 Staff
    32 Sergeants (2 sick)
    11 Drummers
    459 Rank & File (46 sick)

A letter of 3rd October 1811 throws an interesting light on how extra pay was managed in those days. Each Division was ordered to contribute 4½d a day from their funds to make up the pay of 1/6d a day to Sergeant Hewitt who was Acting Sergeant Major to the Battalion.

1811

The numbers voted for the year were 31,400.

Boy Recruits.
There seems to have been little trouble about obtaining the necessary recruits, but large numbers of boys were evidently serving, in fact on 22nd August there is a letter to Portsmouth saying that 100 stand of light arms were being sent, for use at Headquarters only, for boy recruits. By Order-in-Council, 8th November, their pay was raised from 9d to 10d a day.

Bayonet Exercise.
In this year the Bayonet Exercise was ordered to be taught generally. On 3rd May an order was promulgated that Lieutenant and Adjutant Faden at Woolwich had invented a new principle of Bayonet Exercise and each Division was ordered to send four or five of their best NCOs to be

instructed *"for the purpose thereafter of instructing men in the same, so that officers can proceed with the exercise as part of their drill as soon as the men are expert in their arms and otherwise for duty."*

Prisoners of War.
An interesting case occurred in February of three Marines who effected their escape from the French Army in Spain; they had been taken prisoners of war and joined the French Army, but as they had taken an early opportunity of rejoining, the Board ordered that they were to be received back into the service.

Surgeons.
Surgeons at Headquarters were forbidden to engage in private practice, and orders were given that in future invalids were to be sent to the Naval Hospital for survey.

Regent's Allowance.
On 25th September 1811 Regent's Allowance was introduced. This was an allowance in aid of the expenses of the Regimental Mess when stationed in Great Britain; it was apportioned according to the establishment of the Corps and varied from £250 for a regiment of 10 companies to £25 for a company; after some argument it was allowed to commence in the Marines from 25th December 1809. This allowance was always regarded as an allowance towards officers' expenditure in wine in drinking the King's health; it was variously dealt with, but in the Royal Marines an allowance of 3d a day used to be credited in the mess bill of each single officer messing in the mess.

By Order-in-Council 8th November, the four companies of RMA were each increased by 3 Corporals, 4 Bombardiers and 58 Gunners. There appears to have been great difficulty in obtaining the men. The Headquarters were combed and then in succession the ships in port, the Channel Squadron, the Downs, and the Baltic Squadrons, whilst special officers were sent round to try and obtain volunteers; the age was also extended to thirty years. No doubt the hardships of the life in the bomb vessels deterred the men in spite of the extra pay.

Anholt.
Coming to the operations one of the outstanding events was the defence of Anholt. This Danish Island which lies in the Kattegat had been taken in May 1809 by Captain E Nicolls and Lieutenants Henry and R G Atkinson with 120 Marines and the boats of the *Standard* and *Glendower*, Captain Nicolls was the first Governor but he was replaced in 1810 by a Naval Officer when the island was placed on the establishment as a 50 gun ship. It was useful as a point of communication between Great Britain, the Baltic and the Continent, and some say in order to keep the Lighthouse going for the convenience of the large British Baltic trade.[185] The garrison was composed of 350 RM and 31 RMA with four field howitzers under Major Torrens RM. The Governor was Captain Maurice

---

185 For the second or third time in his service a GCM was ordered on 5th March 1812 to try Bt Major Nicolls, but no charges are given and nothing seems to have come of it. The former case was at St. Marou when he was sent to Portsmouth and was kept waiting trial several months but no more was heard of it. We have seen his name several times at Curacao and in the Dardanelles. He was in action 107 times. His portrait is now in the Plymouth Mess.

RN, who had come to fame at the Diamond Rock.

In a general history such as this only an outline of the defence can be given; a full account is given by Sir R Steele.[186]

The Danes had begun preparations to attack the island in 1810 but, as always in the case of these isolated islands, as long as the British cruisers could keep their station no attack could be made. In this case when bad weather drove them off it also shut up the Danish transports and gunboats in their harbours.

The main octagon fort (Fort Yorke) was near the lighthouse. There was a one gun battery near the south beach and the garrison had four field howitzers manned by the RMA; the cruisers had gone off on the morning of 27th March, when the Danes (about 1,000 strong), landed unopposed in a fog about four miles to the west of Fort Yorke. Two hundred RM and the field howitzers under Major Torrens and the Governor proceeded to the sandhills by the one gun battery on the south side to meet them. The enemy were found in force and the troops returned to Fort Yorke; the Danes followed and sending their reserves along the north beach their flotilla opened fire in support. The fire from the redoubt soon checked the attack from the south and blew them out of the one gun battery. The attack from the fourth beach was also checked. HMS *Tartar* and *Sheldrake* were signalled and the former ran to the south side to attack the gunboats and flotilla whilst the latter went to the north side to cut off their retreat. The Danes made another general attack in which their Commanders were killed and wounded.

The schooner *Anholt* with some of the Light Company under Lieutenant Turnbull now returned and anchored off the north shore on the flank of the attackers, whilst Captain Holtaway RM (commanding in the town at the West end) having commandeered some Danish fishing vessels came firing into the north shore and landed under the guns of the Lighthouse Battery; the attackers on the north side then raised a flag of truce and surrendered. On the appearance of the *Tartar* on the south side the Danish flotilla got under way and made off to the westward so that the attackers on the south side ware also compelled to surrender.

The Danes lost about 200 killed and wounded and the British 2 killed and 50 wounded, Captain Torrens being among the latter. Captain Torrens was promoted to Brevet Major and the senior subaltern - Lieutenant J N Fischer - to the rank of Captain.

The garrison remained in the island until September 1812, when they returned to Portsmouth, when the RMA returned to Chatham and the infantry were formed into six companies under Captain Sterling and were sent to join the Royal Marine Battalions operating on the north coast of Spain as is described later.

---

186 See Britains Sea Soldiers, Vol I, p. 227.

Java.
The other main point of interest in which the RM were concerned was the conquest of Java in August and September.

As Fortescue says, *"The Navy overburdened with the task of protecting commerce called loudly first for fresh naval bases of its own to enable it to maintain effective blockades and next for the destruction of the naval bases of the enemy so as to obviate the necessity of any blockade at all. A powerful army is no less important for the conservation of trade in war than is a strong navy . . . Every hostile base captured means the allotment of a military force to hold it."*

For the capture of Java an expedition was dispatched from India under General Sir Samuel Auchmuty (the Governor General Lord Minto accompanying it). There were 4 battleships and 40 cruisers. The force concentrated at Molucca on 1st June and was formed into three Divisions commanded respectively by Colonels Gillespie, Wetherall, and Wood, a total of 12,280 men. We need only take note of the composition of Colonel Gillespie's Division in which the Royal Marine Battalion was incorporated:

Governor-General's Bodyguard.
Detachment 22nd Light Dragoons.
A Grenadier Battalion.
A Light Infantry Battalion.
Detachment 89th Regiment.
250 Royal Marines under Major Liardet.
Bengal Native Light Infantry.

Batavia was the principal town of Java; Napoleon had sent General Daendels to fortify Java in 1809; Daendels had built roads and, finding Batavia unhealthy, had selected a healthy site called Cornelis seven miles south of Batavia, fortified it elaborately and removed the Government offices there.

He had also built Fort Ludowyk to command the passage between Java and Madura Island.

On 20th July the expedition reached Cape Samber at south west corner of Borneo. General Janssens had relieved Daendels in command of the Franco-Dutch. Lieutenant R White RM of the *Minden* with a detachment of 14th Regiment and some of the 69th was landed by one of the cruisers at a place called Bantam where they completely defeated a force of the enemy sent from Batavia and ascertained that the enemy had concentrated at Batavia.

Reconnaissances were made of the coast and it was decided to land at Chillingching twelve miles from Batavia. Before dark on 4th August all the infantry (8,000) were ashore covered by the frigates, without opposition; the Dutch were surprised, and their patrols were not met with till after dark. Chillingching was on an island, so Gillespie's Division which was the first landed, seized the bridges, and then pushed up the roads leading to Batavia and Cornelis. Wetherall took position on his right, Wood covered the landing place. On 5th August, the advance was continued but slowly owing to the heat and the length of time the troops had been on board ship, there were many deaths, but the discipline of troops was splendid and there was no looting of vegetables or supplies.

On the 6th Gillespie advanced on Batavia and the fleet moved up to Tonjong Priock. On the evening of the 7th the troops passed the Anjole River by a bridge of boats; there was no resistance and by dawn on the 8th they were in the suburbs of the town. Wetherall's Division moved up to the Anjole River. On the 8th the Mayor surrendered the town, but it was half deserted, and the stores of sugar and coffee had been burned so depriving the British of their prize money.

On the night of August 8th, the enemy attempted a counter-attack which was beaten off and on this day the fleet moved up to the town and the next day Rear Admiral Stopford arrived to take command.

On the 10th Gillespie's Division advanced to Welte Vreeden on the road to Cornelis where the Dutch were occupying the strong position; Gillespie turned them out and General Auchmuty arrived just in time to prevent him throwing his troops wildly at the big entrenched camp. Wetherall's Division arrived in time to check the French reinforcements and the British occupied Welte Vreeden, a salubrious cantonment with good barracks and stores where they obtained 300 guns, horses and labourers.

The entrenched camp at Cornelis was shaped like a parallelogram one and a half miles north to south, half a mile east to west; on the west side was the Batavia River, on the east side the Slohan rivulet; there was a deep ditch on north and south sides with redoubts etc. To capture it needed a regular siege.

On the 14th the army opened trenches and on the 20th constructed batteries 600 yards from the entrenchments. By the 22nd the batteries were completed, but on that day the enemy made a sortie which was momentarily successful, especially as at one point they caught the RA and seamen mounting the guns; they were however driven out by the 59th and 69th Regiments, but 6 Officers were killed and 3 wounded.

When the sortie failed the enemy opened fire with 40 guns which was not replied to. On the 23rd both sides were silent. On the 25th fire was opened, and the enemy guns were silenced before dark, 500 seamen having been lent to help to man the guns. There was a lot of sickness; among others Major Liardet died of dysentery and was succeeded by Captain Bunce.

General Auchmuty then decided on an assault. On the 26th two deserters came in who told of a path past the entrenchment along the bank of the Batavia river from north west angle by Redoubt No 1, and that there was another path through the jungle leading to Redoubt No 3 on the east face, situated on east side of the Slohan River and connected to the camp by a bridge.

Colonel McCleod with 69th and a Native Battalion was told off to go by the north west path; Wood with the 78th and a Native Battalion to attack No. 2 Redoubt at north east angle and follow the bank of the Slohan; the Mounted troops and Horse Artillery were sent to watch the Bridge over the Batavia River at Campong Malayo. The main attack was entrusted to Gillespie who was to attack No. 3 Redoubt; he had a queer mixed force - the RM, companies of the 14th, 59th and 78th Regiments, and 5 companies of the 89th; followed by the Grenadier Companies of the 14th, 59th and 69th. He also had in reserve the 59th Regiment and a Battalion of Native infantry under Colonel Gibbs from Wetherall's Division.

His task was difficult for he had to march through the jungle over ravines, enclosures and plantations. Just before dawn on the 27th August Gibb's force was missing. Gillespie would not wait but formed up and though challenged outside No 3 Redoubt by a sentry and then by an officer's picquet charged on, swept them aside and in unbroken order forced his way into Redoubt No 3. There was a fierce bayonet fight but keeping his men together he pressed on to the bridge which was defended by four guns and flanked by Redoubts Nos 2 and 4. In spite of grape shot he carried it after a sharp struggle and then led his men on to Redoubt No 4. The enemy resistance increased but No 4 was carried with heavy loss. Three companies of Gibb's force now came up and fell on the rear face of No 2 Redoubt and cleared it out capturing the French General in command, but the magazine blew up causing heavy loss to both attacked and attackers. The 59th however secured the redoubt.

Wood failed to secure the north east angle but came round by Redoubt No 2 and McCleod with the 89th carried Redoubt No 1. Gillespie then led the 59th against Fort Cornelis, the keep, but the attack was badly made, and no success was obtained until the various columns converged on it, when the enemy abandoned the place and retreated on Buitzenburg. That remarkable man Gillespie then got hold of the mounted troops and hunted the enemy for many miles to Tanjong capturing many guns etc. The British captured nine of the Headquarter staff, 200 Officers 5,000 prisoners and about 1,000 of enemy were killed. The British strength was 5,000 to the Dutch 12,000. On the 28th Gibbs captured Buitzenburg.

General Auchmuty addressing the Royal Marines after the battle said. "I have halted you to express my high opinion of the zeal and gallantry displayed by the Royal Marines, who were attached to the advance under Colonel Gillespie in the action on the 27th. I cannot possibly express my gratitude for their exemplary good conduct. I beg you to accept my warmest thanks and to communicate the same to the officers and men under your command."

The losses from 4th to 27th August were:

	Killed	Wounded	Missing
Army	141	733	13
Navy	1	2 Offrs 29 ORs	3
RM	4	20	

General Janssens had retired to the eastward and on 31st August the *Nisus, President, Phoebe*, and *Hesper* with a Battalion of Native Infantry were sent to Cheribon. The fort there capitulated at once, and after the Marines had taken possession the seamen were put in garrison. The Marines of those ships with those of the *Lion* (64) - 180 all told - and seamen under Captain Welchman RM were sent to Carang Sambang some 35 miles inland, which they captured on 6th September together with more stragglers and large stores of coffee etc, so that the country round was subdued. The RM re-embarked in the *Nisus* and *Phaeton* and went on to the east, capturing Taggel on the 12th. On 5th September General Auchmuty with 1,600 men of the 14th, 78th, Sepoys, and 22nd Light Dragoons embarked and sailed to Zedayo, expecting General Janssens to go to Sourabaya. Admiral Stopford wanted to get possession of the harbour at Sourabaya to shelter the fleet during the monsoon. Janssens had however gone to Samarang and taken up a strong position at Jattoo six miles inland. On 12th September Auchmuty occupied Semarang and on the 16th advanced to attack another strong well protected position garrisoned by 8,000 men, mostly however spearmen. He attacked promptly and by the evening Janssens was hopelessly beaten and capitulated. So, the last of the Dutch East Indian positions passed into British hands.

Meanwhile the seamen and Marines of the *Drake* and *Phaeton* had captured the Island of Madura. Landing in the darkness on night of 30-31st August, they advanced and carried the Fort of Samanap by storm in two columns; Lieutenant Roch RM destroyed a battery of twelve 9 pdrs at the mouth of the river leading to Samanap, but in the attack on the fort was wounded in wresting the Colours from a French Officer whom he slew. The island was then secured. The prize money for the taking of Java amounted to one million sterling.

But we have only followed the adventures of about 1,000 of the Corps. What of the other 30,000? They were scattered over the Seven Seas engaged in the prosaic work of blockade and commerce protection which is the lot of the Navy in all Naval Wars.

1812

The numbers voted were 31,400.

Though there seems to have been no dearth of recruits they were evidently not of a good standard, and there were many boys, in fact in January and March one Division was ordered to relieve nearly half the detachments of two ships because they were not equal in physical strength to the duty in 74-gun ships.

Enlistments must have been made for limited service, also for periods of seven and five years as regulations were made in March for men to extend their time for life with a bounty of five guineas. On 10th March boys on completing the age of 15 years were placed on the same rates of pay and allowances as men.

Attestation Forms.

On 9th March a new Attestation Form was introduced extending the oath of allegiance for service not only to His Majesty but also to His Heirs and Successors as it is to-day.

By Order-in-Council 21st April, another 4 Sergeants were added to each of the Artillery Companies so that they had a very high proportion of NCOs.

From the numerous drafts ordered to the Mediterranean etc. it is clear that the wastage in the squadrons must have been very considerable. From a letter of 14th April 1812 making a request for replacement of clothing, we gather that the Marine detachments must have been often used for fitting out ships for commission as the seamen, who had to be impressed, avoided that duty in newly commissioned ships.

Officers Embarkation.

On 8th May a rule was laid down that remained in force until the harbour ships were abolished in 1904. Subalterns in stationary ships were only to serve therein for a period of twelve months and there is also an order of 1st September that will appeal to many in the Corps. *"Captain W........ is to take his turn for sea as the Board cannot admit seasickness to afford an excuse for any Marine Officer not embarking."*

Barracks.

There are some interesting side lights on the Barrack life in the letters of this year. On 24th March an order was published that *"RM Field Officers, below the rank of Colonel-en-Second who have attained the rank of Major General to become supernumerary on establishment of respective Divisions and be excused from Field Officers duties."* [187]

Also, on 26th October we learn that the allowance for "Bedstead and accommodation of the Barrack Woman should not exceed eight square feet" (one was allowed to each Barrack room). [188]

Duel.

On 11th October the Commandant at Portsmouth reported that Lieutenant Bagnell, who had been wounded in a duel, had died of his wounds and that the officers concerned had absconded. The Board ordered their apprehension and respited (ie stopped) their pay.

Before coming to the main operations of the year in which the Corps was concerned, it is necessary to notice some landing parties carried out on the coast of Italy that are instructive and characteristic.

The French Fleet had been driven from the seas and all the enemy bases in the distant seas had been captured, so that it was only necessary to seal up the Channel and Atlantic ports of France and

---

187 I have been unable to find out how or why these officers were promoted. There must be some orders. - Ed
188 Plymouth Orders 1795.

the Baltic, which was done by the blockading squadrons and to keep a careful watch on Toulon and the Adriatic whence attempts might be made by the French.

The other operations to which we shall come later were in support of Lord Wellington's operations in Spain and Portugal.

Languelia.
On the 9th May a convoy of French vessels took shelter under the batteries of Languelia near Alassio, when pursued by the *America* and *Leviathan* (74s) under Captain Rowley RN. The Marines of those ships (about 250) were landed under Captains Rea (*America*) - afterwards Commandant at Chatham - and John Owen (later Sir John, DAG from 1838 to 1854), Lieutenants J Neame, W B Cock, P H Carden, and J G Hill. In landing the yawl was sunk by fire and ten Marines were drowned. The party under Captain Owen carried a battery of five 24 pdrs and 18 pdrs to the eastward; the main body under a severe fire of grape shot carried a battery adjoining the town of Languelia, armed with four 24 pdrs and 18 pdrs and one mortar; there was a strong escort posted in a wood and buildings close by, but the Marines having carried the batteries turned the guns on to them. The fire from HMS *Eclair* drove the French from the houses lining the beach so that the boats were able to bring off sixteen of the vessels, burning one and sinking one. The Marines were re-embarked in perfect order under cover of the fire of the *Eclair*, although the French reinforcements were coming up from Alassio. The losses were 1 Sergeant, 3 Privates killed, 18 wounded.

Again, on 27th June another convoy was assembled at Languelia and Alassio. The *Leviathan*, *Imperieuse*, *Curacao* (36), and *Eclair* again sent their Marines under Captain Owen, covered by the fire of the *Eclair*. The Marines had just formed up, when they were attacked by treble their number, as the garrisons had recently been reinforced from Genoa, but dashing at the French with the bayonet they drove them from the batteries and spiked the guns (nine and one mortar) and destroyed their carriages. But in spite of all efforts the ships were unable to drive the enemy from the buildings and get the ships of the convoy out. They therefore destroyed them by firing at them, the Marines being brought off with a loss of 3 killed and 9 wounded. Captain Campbell (*Leviathan*) in charge of the operation reported his admiration of the good conduct and gallantry of Captain Owen and the officers and men engaged.

Peninsula War.
Before detailing the part taken by the Royal Marine Battalions in the Peninsula War, we must first recall that in the Spring of 1812 Ciudad, Rodrigo and Badajos had been taken; Lord Wellington had embarked on the campaign which led to the great victory of Salamanca on July 22nd; we cannot go into all his operations but in the winter, after abandoning the siege of Burgos he had to fall back again to the Douro (November). It was most important that the French Army which was in Galicia and the Northern Provinces should not be available to reinforce Marmont who was opposing Wellington.

For this purpose, Admiral Sir Home Popham, assisted by General Sir Howard Douglas, based on Corunna, was doing all he could to encourage the Spanish armies and guerillas, and by threatening descents on the coast was keeping the French in such a state of tension that General Caffarelli refused to part with any of his troops.

On 26th February 1812 Major Williams reported the arrival of part of his battalion from Lisbon at Portsmouth[189] and the Commandant was ordered to inspect the battalion on 6th March and report its state, but an outbreak of an infectious fever on the 14th caused some trouble. On 3rd March the guns and stores of the RMA, which had been left at Plymouth were ordered round to Portsmouth.

From now on the Letter Books are full of orders to complete the clothing and equipment of the Battalion. It is interesting to note that first one and then a second musket sling were issued to each man to improve the carriage of the knapsack. There were many changes in the officers. Major Graham relieved Major Abernethie as second in command and Captain T Mould became Paymaster vice Hornby.

On 18th May the Commandant was ordered to complete the battalion to a strength of 500 effective rank and file (on Fortescue's principle of adding 1/8th for Officers and NCOs that would make 562), and on 20th May Major Williams reported that the battalion was complete except for 50 sick which Portsmouth Division was ordered to make up. Lieutenant Kempster was the Adjutant but seems to have been sent home very soon.

On 6th June the Battalion embarked in HMS *Diadem*[190] to join Sir Home Popham's squadron off the North Coast of Spain.

On 23rd June they arrived off Bermeo and caused the French garrison to evacuate that place and the defences were destroyed, so that their arrival must have had some effect in holding back the French Northern Army and so helped to lighten Wellington's task at Salamanca.

On the 28th the battalion was landed on both shores of the river leading to Bilbao, where they destroyed the batteries. After a reconnaissance of Guetaria, they sailed for Fort Castro, which surrendered after a short bombardment, and Marines were placed in garrison where they shortly after beat off a French attack with heavy loss.

Meanwhile on 9th July orders were sent to the Divisions to form a new battalion known as the 2nd Battalion; two companies were formed at Plymouth, one at Portsmouth, and later 100 men were sent from Woolwich to form two more companies and as on 23rd July the Commandant at Portsmouth was informed that five more companies were being sent to him, it is presumed that two more were coming from Chatham and one from Woolwich as well as the two from Plymouth.

---

189 Portsmouth letter books.
190 Colonel Field says 694 strong.

Major Malcolm was appointed to command, Captain Weaver (Portsmouth) Paymaster, Lieutenant W M Burton, Adjutant. The companies were composed of 1 Captain, 2 Subalterns, 4 Sergeants, 5 Corporals, 2 Drummers and 55 Privates. Dr Lind was appointed Surgeon. In the letter books are interesting details as to the equipping a battalion in those days. On 5th August the Commandant was authorised to issue a pair of Colours to the Battalion should he see fit and it is believed that they took the Portsmouth Division Colours.

On 31st July orders were issued for them to embark in the *Fox* and *Latona*, as soon as the Commander-in-Chief reported that the ships were ready. They sailed about the middle of August and arrived at Santander.

No sooner had they gone than the garrison of Anholt returned to Portsmouth; the RMA were sent back to Chatham, but the remainder were formed into six companies equipped as the 1st and 2nd Battalions but were given no Battalion organisation and were embarked in the *Nemesis* in October 1812 (order is dated 13th October) and sent to join the 1st and 2nd Battalions on the north coast of Spain.

There were numerous actions on the north coast of Spain. Among which some of the principal were as follows:

On 30th July and 1st August there was a combined attack on Santander and the Castle of Ano by the Marines of the *Magnificent*, *Surveillante* and *Medusa*. The British were commanded by Captain Lake RN of *Magnificent* and were to cooperate with the Spanish guerillas under General Portier. The Royal Marines stormed and captured the Castle, but as the garrison of the town had been reinforced Portier was unable to advance; the Marines who had pushed on to join in his attack were obliged to fall back to the Castle with some loss. Captain Lake was wounded as also Captain C Noble RM who was also taken prisoner. On 3rd August the French evacuated Santander which was occupied by a detachment from the frigates in harbour.

In September an abortive attack was made on Guitaria. On 18th September with the Artillery Companies they landed at Sumaga and formed a battery opposite the rock of Guitaria and armed it with two long 24 pdrs and a 5½ inch howitzer, and opened fire. The two battalions landed and joined the Spaniards, but on the 20th the attack was abandoned owing to reports of French reinforcements and they re-embarked.

On 28th September both Battalions disembarked at Santander and were quartered in the Castle.

At the end of October, the 1st Battalion marched from Castello to Santona which was garrisoned by 1,500 French.

The reinforcements (Anholt garrison) having arrived at Santona, two companies were added to the 2nd Battalion.

The principal object of attack was Santona, which was the best winter harbour on the north coast, in fact the Gibraltar of the North. It was situated on a mountain promontory and a sandy neck. It was very strong and had been well fortified by the French engineers. Its possession would have cut off the French from France and made a good base for British attacks on the French Coast and also would form a point of connection with the Spanish guerillas. Napier says that Malcolm's Battalion was formed to garrison it when taken. By 29th October the place was fully invested by the two battalions and attached companies and was kept in a state of strict blockade until 14th December when Sir Home Popham having been ordered to return home and reports of strong French forces advancing to its relief being received whilst Lord Wellington had retired to Ciudad Rodrigo, the Battalions were withdrawn to England. Major Williams and part of the 1st Battalion arrived at Portsmouth, Malcolm's Battalion and the left wing of the 1st Battalion arrived in Plymouth Sound on 4th January 1813. Major Williams and his battalion were concentrated at Portsmouth, and Major Malcolm's at Berry Head Barracks near Brixham, where they were prepared for service in the American War which is dealt with separately.[191]

America had declared war on 12th June 1812 and our frigates matched against their larger and heavier armed vessels of the same nominal class were having a disastrous time in American waters and presumably we were unable to spare any battleships from the European blockades.

1813

The numbers voted were 31,400.

Evidently one effect of the war in America was that the detachments of frigates of 40 and 38 guns were increased.

An interesting General Court Martial was held on a Lieutenant D............ for:

1. Fraudulently obtaining money and property (under particularly disgraceful circumstances).
2. Behaving with contempt and disrespect to Lieutenant General Elliot (Commandant at Portsmouth) in three alternative charges prejudicial to Good Order and Military Discipline.
3. Behaving in a mutinous and disrespectful manner and lifting a weapon and offering violence to Lieutenant General Elliot, etc.
4. Absenting himself from Headquarters and deserting HM Service.

He was sentenced on 28th June to be cashiered. "But in order to mark the abhorrence of the Court at so foul an act as lifting a weapon etc. "......... he was to be cashiered in the most public manner at the head of the Royal Marines doing duty at Headquarters and his sash and epaulet to be cut from his person by the Drum Major."

---

191 For American War see p88.

Levees. It is interesting to note that when the Admiralty Board visited the Dockyards they held Levees at the Port Admiral's House at which all Field Officers of Marines were ordered to attend.

Uniform.
On 30th October the ornament which had been worn in the front of Officers Hats was ordered to be abolished.

RMA.
Four additional Second Lieutenants were added to the establishment of the RMA.

Landing Parties.
Throughout the year there were numerous landing parties by the Mediterranean Fleet particularly on the coast of what we now call the Riviera and also in the Adriatic.

The Hague.
During this year Lord Wellington was making his victorious advance through Spain, including the Battle of Vittoria, and Napoleon after the debacle of his Grande Armee in the retreat from Moscow found his star waning and enemies arising on every side. In fact, so much was his authority weakened that there was a rising of the Dutch in Holland and on 28th November four English men-of-war appeared off Scheveningen; Captain Baker of the *Cumberland* proceeded to the Hague and landed 200 Marines from the *Cumberland* and *Princess Caroline* on the 29th to help keep order and they were welcomed by the inhabitants.

From the records we find that orders were sent to the Divisions on 20th November 1813 to send to the Downs to HM Ships all the Marines at Headquarters fit for duty with a due proportion of Officers and NCOs and whose services were not absolutely required for commissioned ships. Apparently, a Lieutenant Colonel Campbell was in command as there is an Order of 18th December saying that the accounts of the men who proceeded with him to Holland are to be closed on the ledgers and the men struck off the effective list, but to continue to be borne "On Command" so they were evidently not on the books of any ship.

This force with a Battalion of the Guards advanced on Helvoetsluys, Williamstadt and other places; the French falling back on Antwerp. On 17th December another detachment of RM was landed in South Beveland, whilst the detachment of the *Cornwall* (74) landed under Major Bartleman and occupied Crabben-Dyke to keep a check on Fort Batz.

On the 19th a reinforcement of two companies arrived and Major G Lewis assumed command.

The weather was bitterly cold and the men very poorly clad and equipped; they were sleeping in barns and had to repel constant night attacks by the enemy.

On the 22nd the French advanced in force, but after a sharp struggle were driven back from

Crabben-Dyke. On the 25th the British had mounted two guns and advanced towards Fort Batz to reconnoitre but were exposed to heavy fire and lost 3 killed and 3 wounded. This situation continued till 4th January when they were attacked by a very superior force, which turned the Dutch picquets. A small detachment RMA with a 6 pdr gun under Lieutenant Wolrige kept up a fire of grape, which enabled the advanced posts to retire. Lieutenant Wolrige was wounded but continued to direct the fire from the limber. Captain Owen was also mentioned for gallantry. Eventually the RM were relieved by Russians and sailed for England on 18th January in the *Diomede* arriving at Portsmouth on the 21st.[192] We shall find their further history under the records of the Third Battalion in America.

North America.
On the 1st June 1813 off Boston, North America, took place the celebrated action between HMS *Shannon* and the *Chesapeake*. The RM detachment of the former took part in the boarding, and lost four killed and many wounded, and the United States Marine officer was killed. The RM officers were Lieutenants Johns and Law.

1814

The numbers were 31,400.

But the end was approaching. On 20th April orders were issued for all recruiting parties to return to Headquarters. (It is interesting that these are the first printed orders in the books.) On 27th April the first orders for demobilisation were issued.

Colour Sergeants.
On 17th March the Commandant at Portsmouth brought to notice the meritorious conduct of Sergeant Burns in the recapture of the *Mary* (transport) and suggested that he might be promoted to Colour Sergeant according to the late War Office Regulation, but the Admiralty replied that these regulations were not applicable to Royal Marines. (The War Office had approved of one Sergeant per company being granted the rank and pay of Colour Sergeant).[193] But it was not long before they had to take action, because on 22nd August 1814 orders were issued that the rank of Colour Sergeant was introduced into the Marines with 6d a day extra pay; Chatham to promote 18, Portsmouth 14, Plymouth 15, and Woolwich 12, to date 1st July 1814.

Though the orders for demobilisation went on all through the year we cannot forget that the battalions were still fighting in America, whilst Napoleon in his prison island of Elba was seeking an opportunity of regaining his Empire. On 6th July Parliament passed the Resolutions conveying the thanks of both the Houses of Lords and Commons to the Army, Navy, and Royal Marines for their services.

---

192 Nicolas.
193 See Fortescue.

Suddenly towards the end of the year in November orders were sent to the Commandants to put specially selected picquets on the main roads in the vicinity of the ports to arrest deserters and to impress seafaring men. The picquets were to be disguised as much as possible and were to report to the Commander-in-Chief once a week.

1815

In the letter books and routine orders, we find no record of the events that were stirring all Europe and it is not till 16th June 1815 that we find an order to keep the nucleus crew ships ready to be fully manned at a moment's notice. But two days later the Battle of Waterloo settled the matter for all time and the long drawn out war of more than twenty years was finished.

Although the battalions were returning from America in May and June, we were unable to provide a battalion to take a share in that crowning victory.

10 - American War 1812 – 1815

This war arose over the perennial cause of quarrel with America called euphemistically 'the freedom of the seas' - really the claim by America to trade and make profits from both sides in any war, and on the British side a claim that was often wrongly used, that of impressing British seamen from neutral ships.

Owing to the locking up of practically all available British troops in the Peninsula War it was at first a naval war, in which partly owing to the different classification and armament of the frigates, the British were not at all successful; the one bright spot being the duel between the *Shannon* and *Chesapeake*, when the superior gunnery training of the British gave them the victory. Also, the main fleets were fully occupied in blockading the French Coasts and the Continent generally, besides supporting Wellington's Army.

In America the British efforts on land were confined to protecting the long Canadian frontier with very inadequate troops and resources, and in endeavouring to establish naval squadrons on the Lakes Champlain, Ontario, Erie, etc. where their means, in comparison with the American, were very poor, the latter being able to draw on their dockyards in New England, besides having available the crews of their merchant vessels which were laid up owing to the blockade.

War was declared by America on 6th June 1812, and by the end of the year and the spring of 1813 the British had established an effective blockade of the Atlantic coast from the mouth of the Mississippi to Rhode Island, especially in the Chesapeake and Delaware Rivers. The ports of New England, where the war was unpopular were left comparatively open.

On Lake Ontario the British had four ships and two building, the Americans had eight, two of which were larger than any British; on Lake Erie the British had three and three building, the Americans had only one but were busy building with all the resources at their disposal.

We left the 1st and 2nd Battalions arriving in England from Spain on 4th January 1813, the 1st Battalion going to Plymouth, and the 2nd to Berry Head Barracks, Torbay.

On 2nd January 1813 the Admiralty issued orders that the battalions and the attached Anholt companies were to be sent as above in order to be *'inspected, disciplined and refreshed,'* and each battalion completed to the enclosed schedule:

Major Commanding	1	Artillery	
Major	1	Captain	1
Captains	8	Subalterns	4
Subalterns	16	Sergeants	4
Staff Sergeants	2	Corporals	4

Sergeants	32	Bombardiers	6
Corporals	16	Drummers	2
Drummers	16	Gunners	60
Privates	640		
TOTAL	753	TOTAL	81
Adjutant		1	
Paymaster		1	
Surgeon		1	
Assistant Surgeon		1	

The Commandant at Portsmouth was told to complete one battalion with men already arrived and any he could spare and forward them to Berry Head, but this was evidently unnecessary, owing to the arrival of the 2nd Battalion at Plymouth on the 4th.

On 6th January, the Artillery Company of the 1st Battalion was ordered to Plymouth, and Commandants were told to make the number of Sergeants per company up to five; and a draft of 150 men was sent from Woolwich to Portsmouth to complete the numbers.

On 29th January Major Mortimer was appointed Second-in-Command of the 1st Battalion, and Brevet Major Barry of the 2nd Battalion.

On 20th February, Major R Williams received the reward of a Brevet Lieutenant Colonelcy dated 21st January 1813.

They were apparently not left long in peace, because on 17th March Lieutenant Colonel Williams was ordered to report *"the number of invalids it will be necessary to leave behind on the embarkation of the two battalions which will take place forthwith."*

In addition to the battalions, on 8th February the Commandant at Portsmouth was directed to hold in readiness as a garrison for Bermuda (presumably because the 102nd Regiment was being taken) 1 Captain, 3 Subalterns and 100 Privates with a due proportion of NCOs to embark in HMS *Sceptre* and to supply them with the equipment necessary for the purpose.[194]

In a letter in reply to the Admiralty the Commandant at Plymouth reported that the battalions had embarked in the *Diomede, Fox,* and *Diadem.*"

Before the arrival of the battalions Admiral Sir John Warren in the *San Domingo* with Rear Admiral Cockburn and several ships made attacks in the Chesapeake River. On 28th April the latter moved up 2 brigs and some tenders with 150 Royal Marines under Captains Wybourn and Carter and five RMA under Lieutenant Robertson to destroy depots of stores, food, etc., at French Town on Elk River; the boats mistook the way and did not arrive till the following forenoon.

---

194 It is possible that Major Nicholl's detachment in Florida came from these men.

The Marines quickly took a 6-gun battery and the stores were destroyed.

On 2nd May the Rear Admiral attacked Havre de Grace at the entrance to the Susquehanna River with the same force, the while under Captain Lawrence of the *Fantome*; at daylight the boats opened a hot fire on the battery which was returned for some time. The Marines were landed on the left, on which the Americans withdrew to the town, the boats' crews having occupied the battery and turned the guns on the retreating Americans they retired to the furthest part of the town, pursued by the Marines. The Americans after some firing from the houses took to the woods. The six guns of the battery were embarked, and the Admiral proceeding with some boats about three miles up the river discovered a foundry where he disabled about 45 guns of different calibres. Lieutenant Robertson RMA and Captains Wybourn and Carter were mentioned in dispatches.

On 6th May the same light squadron proceeded against the towns of Georgetown and Frederickstown on the Sassafras River, under Captain Byng of the *Mohawk*. Heavy fire was opened on the boats, but the Americans fled when the Marines landed and fixed bayonets under cover of the fire of the boats. Certain houses and four vessels with merchandise were destroyed, and this decided the inhabitants of other places to offer no further resistance and supply the needs of the fleet by purchase.

A small body of troops under General Sir Sydney Beckwith was sent to join Sir John Warren's squadron and assist the blockade by harrying the American Coasts. We know that the two Marine Battalions formed part of this force. Fortescue says it consisted of 2434 Marines, 300 of 103rd Regiment and two Independent Companies, mostly French Deserters. On arrival at Bermuda, Beckwith discharged his 103rd Regiment and embarked in lieu the 102nd Regiment under Colonel Sir C Napier and formed them into two Brigades.

	Officers	NCOs & Men
Charles Napier's Brigade		
RMA		76
2nd Bn Royal Marines	30	720
102nd Regiment	13	310
1st Independent Company		
Lt Col Williams's Brigade	5	149
RMA	5	72
Rocket Bn RA	2	49
1st Bn Royal Marines	31	730
2nd Independent Company	5	148

The operations that followed were not very successful, but did act as a diversion and helped to draw off some of the pressure on the hard pressed British troops on the Canadian frontier. As Fortescue puts it "There were three Commanders. Admiral Warren, Admiral Cockburn, and General Beckwith ...... Admiral Cockburn, an excellent Admiral, tried to be a General; Beckwith, an admirable soldier, tried to be an Admiral."

The expedition left Bermuda on 8th June and arrived in the Chesapeake River on the 16th. There were 13 ships, including three 74 gun, one 64 gun and four frigates. A landing was attempted on 22nd August at Craney Island, where the American batteries were situated. The main body landed in the wrong place, the whole attack was repulsed, and some 50 of the Independent Companies deserted: the casualties were 3 killed, 8 wounded and 52 missing, of which 1/RM and Rocket Artillery had 1 wounded; 2/RM, 2 killed, 1 Captain and 4 wounded, 7 missing.

The troops were then reorganised, the two Marine battalions forming one brigade under Colonel Williams, the 102nd and Independent Companies forming a Light Brigade under Napier; a portion of the artillery was attached to each.

The next point attacked was Hampton in the Hampton Roads, where there was a battery of four to six guns to the right of the town guarding the creeks, with a camp of troops close by.

On 25th June the Light Brigade under Colonel Napier with three companies of RM from the ships and two 6 pdrs RMA landed two miles to the west of Hampton half an hour before daylight; the two RM battalions did not arrive until 5 am, when the force advanced along the shore flanked by the ships' boats with the RMA howitzer and rocket tubes.

The advance was directed towards the great road leading from the country into the rear of the town; after advancing through the woods about one mile, a body of the enemy with two field artillery 6 pdrs were seen on the right flank of the 1st Battalion; the enemy guns opened fire but the British advanced and deployed into line; the enemy retired to the woods at once followed by the 1/RM in column of sections. Arriving in rear of the town the British deployed under cover of a hedge, over which the enemy's guns opened a severe fire, replied to by a RMA 6 pdr under Captain Parke of 1/RM. The enemy had moved from their camp to the rear of the town where they were vigorously attacked by Colonel Napier's Light Brigade. After a short skirmish the town was entered, and the 2/RM occupied the Hampton Churchyard.

While the Light Brigade was securing the town and batteries, Lieutenant Colonel Williams noticed a movement in the camp close by and crossing a rivulet by means of planks he attacked the enemy so suddenly that the whole camp equipment, their last gun and three stands of colours belonging to the 65th and 85th Regiments were captured. The boats' crews and the Independent Companies behaved very badly, pillaging the houses etc.; the good conduct of the Marines stood out in bold contrast. After destroying all munitions and carrying off four 12 pdr and three 6 pdr guns with limbers etc., the force re-embarked.

The Casualties were:

	Killed	Wounded	Missing
RMA	1	4	
Ship Marines		1	1

1/RM	1	1 Lt, 1 Marine	
2/RM		1 Lt, 1 Sgt, 6 Marines	3

Lieutenant Colonel Williams and Major Malcolm were mentioned in General Beckwith's dispatch.

On 4th June 1813 Major Malcolm was promoted Brevet Lieutenant Colonel.

On 6th August further up the River Chesapeake, the RM of HMS *Marlborough* and the frigates with an RMA 6 pdr under Captain Parke occupied a post covering a ferry from the left bank of the river to Kent's Island, at the south point of which the squadron was lying.

The two RM battalions and the 102nd landed on the 7th, and on the 8th with a temperature of 90 degrees in the shade marched fourteen miles from the south to the north of the island. On the 12th an attempt was made to take Queen's Town on the left bank of the river. The Marines of the Squadron relieved all the detached posts in the island so that the battalions were up to strength. At 11 pm General Beckwith with 2/RM, 102nd and two RMA 6 pdrs crossed by the ferry at the narrows. Before daylight they met the enemy picquets but owing to the mistake of a guide the Marines found they were separated from the town by a creek. The operation had no results and the force fell back to Kent's Island which was evacuated on the 22nd.

A landing in Talbot County was also profitless. As fever was prevalent the Admiral abandoned the operations and sailed for Halifax where he arrived on 13th September. The troops were landed and placed under canvas.

These attempts, though void of great results, had detained American troops and so helped General Prevost on the line of the St Lawrence River.

Reinforcements in Canada were urgently required, so the two battalions left for Quebec, and on 26th October the 2/RM was sent on to Montreal followed by the 1/RM, from whence they were sent on towards Prescott on the St. Lawrence River.

We must now glance at the operations on the rivers and lakes. On 7th August a small British Naval Squadron under Captain Yeo, armed only with short carronades, had fought an indecisive action with the Americans armed with long guns. Yeo captured two small schooners and two more were sunk in a squall; they met again on 13th September and after four days manoeuvring with no result, both sides retired to their bases. On 28th September there was another indecisive action, when Yeo retired to Burlington Heights where General Vincent had his troops, the Americans to Fort Niagara.

On Lake Erie the British had been more unfortunate, for Captain Barclay's squadron, after a severe action lasting three hours on the 10th September, had been captured. The British crews were mostly made up of Canadian Militia and a few troops from the various regiments as there were hardly any seamen available.

The Americans were holding Fort George on Lake Ontario, which they had captured, and were also holding Fort Niagara on the other side of the river. Their plan of attack on Montreal was - for one force under General Wilkinson to move down the St Lawrence, the other under General Hampton to come up from Lake Champlain. Wilkinson's force on 9th November reached the head of the Long Sault Rapids; General de Rottenburg had sent 600 of the 49th and 89th Regiments under Lieutenant Colonel Morrison of the latter regiment with a small flotilla under Captain Mulcaster RN from Kingston to hang on their rear; they picked up two more companies of the 49th and some Canadians on the 8th, and on the 9th continued their march and gained contact on 10th November with the American rear guard at the head of the rapids.

Meanwhile the 2/RM and Lieutenant Stevens RMA with two 6 pdrs had been sent on to Coteau du Lac where a British force - consisting of some 19th Light Dragoons, 3 Militia Battalions and a Volunteer Corps - was assembling to oppose the advance whilst the 1/RM with the rocket company had reached La Chine west of Montreal at the rapids below those of Long Sault. On 11th November the Americans commenced the descent of the Long Sault Rapids, but Morrison was attacking their rear, and when their rear guard turned about he took up a position at Chrystler's Farm, whilst Mulcaster opened fire on their flotilla. The American rear guard attacked the British but was driven back after severe fighting and Morrison continued to hang on to their rear.

The Americans passed the rapids on the 12th but hearing that the force which was to co-operate from Lake Champlain in the attack on Montreal had retired to Plattsburg, General Wilkinson transferred his force to the American shore and established himself for the winter at French Mills about eight miles from St Regis. This terminated the invasion of Canada, Chauncey's squadron re-turning to its base on 11th November.

The 2/RM was then sent to Prescott and later to Kingston; the 1/RM went up the Richelieu River to the Isle aux Noix to reinforce the troops on that line. Lieutenant Colonel Williams took over command of the garrison which also comprised two flank companies of the 13th Regiment and the 10th Veteran Battalion - about 550 all told.

The island was the centre of a system of booms and chevaux de frise which barred the river; there was also a fort and two strong redoubts which commanded the passages on either side, and the opposite banks had been cleared of trees. Cole Mill on the Lacolle River had also been fortified; it was of stone, two stories high with a wooden roof on the south bank of the river. On the north bank communicating by a wooden bridge was a small house, converted into a blockhouse with a breastwork of logs, also a large unprotected barn. The woods came up to within 200-100 yards of the buildings.

Major Handcock of the 13th Regiment was in command with a company of his own regiment, 70 RM and 4 RMA with a small detachment of Frontier Light infantry, about 180 all told.

The Battalions remained in garrison throughout the winter of 1813-14.

On 10th December 1813 the Americans, most of whose Militia had deserted after behaving disgracefully, evacuated Fort George and retired to Niagara, after burning the village of Newark, which embittered the rest of the war and for which as well as the destruction of York (now Toronto) terrible retribution was exacted the next year.

Lieutenant General Gordon Drummond had assumed command and General Vincent was not a man to let opportunities slip; after occupying Fort George on 12th December it was determined to capture Fort Niagara and on 10th December this fort was also taken; large quantities of guns, clothing and stores fell into British hands. Following up the success Lewiston and Fort Schlosser were taken and destroyed; the British advanced on Black Rock and Buffalo; on 29th December the batteries were carried and Buffalo itself was burned with its stores as well as three vessels of the Lake Squadron, in fact the American frontier was laid in ashes as a reprisal for the burning of Newark.

In March 1814 the Americans opened their new campaign, General Wilkinson advancing along the Richelieu River from Plattsburg, whilst another force was to advance from Sackett's Harbour, Lake Ontario, on Kingston.

Wilkinson in his advance with 3,000 men to the Lacolle River sent a brigade to capture Cole Mill; they were met by an advanced picquet and delayed: 600 men were then sent across the river to the rear of the Mill and the Americans brought up two guns and one 56in howitzer; the guns opened fire which was returned by musketry. Major Handcock and his little garrison held on until reinforced by the two flank companies of the 13th. He then took the offensive and charged the guns; he was repulsed, and the companies retired across the river to the blockhouse; another company of Canadians arrived and a second attempt was made to take the guns. The artillerymen had to abandon them, but the American infantry kept back the attackers. Owing to the ice the gunboats in the Richelieu River could not render assistance; two Privates were sent for ammunition to the Isle aux Noix but were captured, but Pte J Brown of the Marines succeeded in swimming across.[195] The garrison maintained their position till the evening, when the Americans retreated to Plattsburg.

General Wilkinson was removed from his command. Handcock's party lost 11 killed; 2 Officers and 44 Other Ranks wounded; in his dispatch Lieutenant Colonel Williams mentioned Lieutenants Caldwell and Barton of the Royal Marines.

By April Captain Yeo's squadron on Lake Ontario was superior in number to the Americans, but there were no seamen to man them, so one may imagine the envious eyes cast by the Naval Officers on the two Battalions of trained Marines, with the usual result.

Of the 1/RM on 8th May 3 Officers, 5 Sergeants, 5 Corporals, 89 Privates and 1 Drummer were embarked on board the gunboat *Linnet* on the Richelieu River and the following day 2 Officers, 4 Sergeants, and 112 Rank and File were distributed in the gun-boats the crews of which were

---

195   See Britain's Sea Soldiers Vol I, p. 294.

completed by Canadian Militia, only two seamen were available for each boat and one RMA gunner. On 11th May these gunboats attacked an American 7 gun battery at the head of Lake Champlain, but after a two hours bombardment by a bomb vessel, when it had only dismounted one gun of the battery, the flotilla withdrew to the Isle aux Noix.

Similarly, orders were issued on 5th May for the break-up of the 2/RM and their distribution in the vessels on Lakes Ontario and Erie. Lieutenant Colonel Malcolm and his staff were ordered to Bermuda to take command of the 3rd Battalion on its way from England.[196]

Before the orders could be carried out General Drummond and Commodore Yeo wished to attack the American Naval Base at Sackett's Harbour, but for this the force at their disposal was insufficient and they therefore decided to attack Oswego, at the mouth of the Oswego River, which was the route by which all the American stores etc. came up to the Lakes, and where large stores of munitions were collected. The American Commander however had left the guns and equipment for his new ships about twelve miles up the Oswego River.

On 3rd May General Drummond and Captain Yeo embarked 1,000 men at Kingston (6 Companies, De Watteville's Regiment, 1 Company Glengarry Light Infantry, 2/RM and a detachment of Artillery).

A covering force of a few Marines, the flank companies of Watteville's and the Glengarry Light Infantry were put into the boats on the 5th and were to have landed under a heavy fire from the squadron about 4 pm, but a north west gale drove them off and they anchored for the night about ten miles off. On the morning of the 6th the Flotilla returned; the two flank Companies of Watteville's, the Light Company of the Glengarries, the 2/RM under Colonel Malcolm and 200 seamen with pikes under Captain Mulcaster - about 770 all told under Colonel Fischer of Watteville's - were put into the boats, leaving four companies of Wattevilles, the Artillery and Sappers as a reserve.

The two largest ships could not approach owing to shoal water, but the *Montreal, Niagara, Star*, and *Charwell* covered the disembarkation. The wind was ahead which delayed the boats under heavy fire, but landing and forming on the beach, in spite of heavy fire they ascended a long steep hill to the fort, but as soon as they gained the summit the Americans retreated to the woods Lieutenant J Lawrie RM was the first man to enter the fort and Lieutenant Hewett RM cut down the colours. The garrison as they retired sank three heavy guns and some naval stores in to river; seven heavy and four light guns were taken with their ammunition and also two small schooners, 2,000 barrels of provisions, and great quantities of cordage were captured.

After the capture and destruction of the stores the troops returned on board at 4 am on the 7th and the force withdrew. In his despatch General Drummond mentions the cool and gallant conduct of Lieutenant Colonel Malcolm 2/RM, Lieutenant Stephens of the Rocket Company, and also Lieutenants Lawrie and Hewett. Captain Yeo in his despatch to the Admiralty says, "The Second

---

196 Portsmouth Letters see later.

Battalion of Royal Marines excited the admiration of all; they were led by their gallant Colonel Malcolm and suffered severely."

The casualties were 82 killed and wounded, of which the RM lost Captain Holtaway, 2 Sergeants and 4 Privates killed; Lieutenant Hewett, 1 Sergeant and 32 Privates wounded.

The Battalion was broken up and Colonel Malcolm with his staff proceeded to join his new battalion in the Chesapeake River, but before leaving the RM in the flotillas on the lakes we may give some of their doings.

As we saw, the guns for the new American Squadron on Ontario had been left up the Oswego River and could only be moved to Sackett's Harbour by water: Commodore Yeo therefore established a blockade of the coast. The Americans placed the guns in bateaux up the river and on 28th May dropped down the stream and tried to creep along the shore with a force moving on the land to cover them; he began the voyage northwards on the lake at night, and at noon on the 29th reached Big Sandy Creek, about eight miles from his destination Stony Creek. They entered the creek and anchored two miles from the mouth, but the British small craft had captured two of them and Commander Popham in command realised what was going on. He collected three gun vessels and four smaller boats and manned them with 200 seamen and Marines.

At daylight on the 30th he entered Sandy Creek and landed parties on either bank to protect his flanks. The Americans however were warned and had posted superior forces on the flanks and so cut off every man ashore. After a loss of 40 killed and wounded the remainder of the British had to surrender and the Americans saved their guns. The loss of 200 men of the blockading squadron was so serious that the British had to abandon the blockade of the shore.

Before leaving the 2/RM there is another operation in which they showed their gallantry. In July 1814 the Americans were making a fresh advance from Buffalo and crossed the river to Fort Erie which surrendered on 3rd July. The Americans advanced up that bank to Fort George, but General Drummond who had been reinforced beat them at Lundys Lane and following up attacked Fort Erie which was very strong and well garrisoned. General Drummond divided his force into three columns;

No 1 - Colonel Fischer
        8th Regiment, De Watteville's, Light Companies of the 89th and 100th
        with Cavalry and Artillery to attack Snake Hill.
No 2 - Lieutenant Colonel Drummond (250)
        Flank Companies of the 41st and 104th Regiments;
        Detachment of Seamen and Marines to storm the Old Fort.
No 3 - Lieutenant Colonel Scott (650)
        2 Companies Royal Scots and the 103rd Regiment to attack
        the Douglas Battery which was a stone fort on the water's edge
        because the old fort stood rather back from shore.

Fischer's Column failed and got into some confusion; Scott was driven back with heavy loss but joined Drummond's Column. Drummond's party after three repulses established themselves in one of the batteries and turned its guns on to the Douglas Battery. Unfortunately their magazine exploded, blew the bastion and all its occupants into the air and the survivors ran back in panic. The Royal Scots covered the retreat and the enterprise was abandoned with a loss of 900 killed, wounded and missing, but which the small numbers of Marines lost 1 RMA killed and 10 RM wounded, 3 Sergeants and 17 Rank and File missing.

Troops were now arriving from the Peninsula Army to reinforce the British, and the lines of invasion were securely blocked; whilst forces were also being detached to attack the American Coasts. Therefore on 13th July Lieutenant Colonel Williams 1/RM received orders that the 1st Battalion was to be disposed of for naval service and in consequence 11 Officers, 27 NCOs, 5 Drummers, and 470 Privates were embarked in the flotillas on the lakes, whilst Lieutenant Colonel Williams with 11 Officers, 46 NCOs, 11 Drummers and 48 Privates proceeded to Halifax where he was directed to join Rear Admiral Cockburn in the Chesapeake River and proceeded in the *Ceylon*.

Those left on the lakes had another action, which unfortunately ended disastrously. In September General Prevost decided to advance on Plattsburg, but the Naval squadron under Captain Downie was not quite ready, particularly the new big ship the *Confiance*. On 6th September the troops advanced in two columns and found the enemy in a strongly fortified position on the east side of the River Saranac. Although the troops were now composed of the Peninsula battalions the General did not attack at once but waited for the naval flotilla and set to work to erect batteries. The American squadron were anchored under the protection of their batteries.

The naval flotilla under Captain Downie was not ready to move until the 11th when with *Confiance* (36), *Linnet* (18), *Broke* (10), *Shannon* (10) and 12 gunboats he came up with a fair wind. When Downie opened fire General Prevost's batteries also opened and silenced the American battery bearing on the water and the Brigade advanced to the attack but did not press it home, owing to waiting for the ships. Here disaster had supervened. Captain Downie was killed and after 2½ hours fighting the *Confiance* and *Linnet* surrendered, and the *Broke* and *Shannon* also fell into the enemy's hands. The gunboats, principally manned by Canadian Militia, fled.

General Prevost recalled his troops and as no more was to be gained the army retired to their base. A disastrous example of want of co-operation, for the troops could easily have captured the batteries and turned their guns on the American squadron.

It is interesting to note that the men who were employed in the ships on the lakes were given extra pay for this service.[197]

---

197   Portsmouth Letter Books.

But we must now turn to the formation of the 3rd Battalion in England. On 13th February 1814, the Commandant at Portsmouth reported the arrival of part of the battalion lately serving in Holland together with the Blenheim's Marines. [198] On 15th February orders were received that as they arrived they were to be formed into companies of 100 each including NCOs and Drummers, with 2 Lieutenants to each Company. This was followed on 17th February with detailed orders:

> *"Select 1,000 Marines including Sergeants, Corporals and Drummers from those coming from Holland or at Headquarters for particular service and one company of Artillery consisting of 80 men also including NCOs with guns and equipment.*
> *"The 1,000 to be divided into 10 companies of 100 each; Major Lewis and four of the Captains returning from Holland for the present to take charge of two companies each. The companies to consist of 2 Subalterns, 6 Sergeants, 6 Corporals, 2 Drummers, 66 Privates.*
> *"Lieutenant and Quartermaster Holland if available to be QM. Appoint an Adjutant to act till further orders. Both will receive the usual allowances.*
> *"Communicate with Admiral Sir R Bickerton and send them as soon as possible to Torbay – Berry Head Barracks; if weather does not permit proceed to Plymouth and march thence."*

Then follow details as to equipment, pay, victualling, etc., but there is a very important postscript.

> *"P.S. You will understand that the Staff and a certain number of Captains of the late 2nd Battalion are ordered to meet the Corps at Bermuda and that the appointments etc. now made are only temporary."*

On 24th February the Admiralty gave orders that the excess Captains were to rejoin their Divisions, and ordered ten Sergeants from Woolwich, five from Chatham and fifteen from Plymouth to complete the numbers. They however refused to give Brevet Major Lewis the pay of a Major, but eventually gave him command money of 3/- a day.

Evidently there was great congestion at Portsmouth as it was ordered that men were to be sent off to Berry Head as soon as possible. On 15th March the Commandant was informed that Officers would be paid Regent's Allowance.

On 18th March the Board issued orders that the Artillery Company was to be the same strength as that of the other battalions, i.e. 5 Officers, 76 NCOs and men, the surplus to be returned to Chatham. They were to embark in the *Tonnant* with their guns and equipment. The battalion was to embark in the *Regulus*, *Melpomene* and *Bruno*. On 22nd March orders were issued for the battalion to be embarked forthwith and they sailed on 7th April.

The British Squadron blockading the American coast had occupied and fortified an advanced base at Tangier Island opposite the mouth of the Potomac River, and so hindered the movements of

---

198 Major Torrens of the *Blenheim* tried very hard to get command of the Battalion but was peremptorily ordered to return with his detachment to his ship.

the American flotilla under Commodore Barney between the five great rivers Patuxent, Potomac, Rappahannock, York, and James. They must have garrisoned it with the Marines of the fleet. Also, numerous refugee slaves had fled to join the British ships and these appear to have been formed into companies of what were known as Colonial Marines, though there must have been irregularities as to their attesting. We read[199] of a Marine Battalion formed at Tangier Island, and some of these blacks arrived in England. On 26th April 1815 the Admiralty said they could not remain as Marines but could be entered as seamen or discharged; but on 28th April orders were given that they were all to be sent back to the West Indies.

On 15th June Captain Barrie RN taking 12 boats with 180 Marines and 30 of the Colonial Corps proceeded up the Patuxent to Benedict, and disembarking his Marines drove the enemy into the woods and destroyed their gun and camp equipment together with a lot of tobacco.

After a period of drills at Bermuda the 3rd Battalion was sent across to join Rear Admiral Cockburn on 19th July where[200]. they were employed in various raids with the squadron in conjunction with the Colonial Marines. They first went to Leonards Town and on 21st July to the Nominy River; on the 22nd to the Yecomico River where they advanced ten miles up country and destroyed the stores at Kinsale. "Thus 500 British Marines penetrated ten miles into the enemy's country, and skirmished on their way back, surrounded by woods in the face of the whole collected Militia of Virginia under Generals Eylon and Hungerford and yet after this long march they carried the heights of Kinsale in the most gallant manner".[201] On 7th August there was another move up the Coan River. On 7th August Lieutenant Colonel Malcolm and his staff arrived and relieved Major Lewis in command of the battalion.

The Government had prepared an attack on Washington U.S.A. as a reprisal for the damage done to the towns and villages on the Canadian frontier. General Ross with the 4th, 44th, and 85th Regiments from Wellington's Peninsula Army sailed from Bordeaux, arriving at Bermuda 24th July. Here he picked up the 21st Regiment and sailed from Bermuda on 3rd August with Admiral Sir Arthur Cochrane in HMS *Tonnant* and entered the Capes of the Chesapeake on the 15th. The naval squadron consisted of four ships of the line as well as numerous frigates.

The first objective was the American flotilla under Commodore Barney, which was defending the rivers with great skill and then according to their instructions - Washington. Barney's Flotilla had retreated up the Patuxent River from which it was only a short march overland to Washington. The frigates were sent up the Potomac River to make a feint and secured Fort Washington. On 18th August the main body entered the River Patuxent, the banks being lined with huge trees.

On the 19th and the 20th the troops landed at Benedict and were formed into three brigades:

---

199 Portsmouth letter books. 22nd March 1815.
200 According to the diary of an officer preserved in the mess at Portsmouth.
201 James' Military Occurrences.

> 1st Brigade - Lieutenant Colonel Thornton:
> > 86th Regiment, Light Companies of the 4th, 44th, 21st and 2/RM. Also 1 Company Colonial Marines (negroes) under Captain Reed 6/WIR.
>
> 2nd Brigade - Lieutenant Colonel Brooke:
> > 4th and 44th Regiments less Light Companies.
>
> 3rd Brigade - Lieutenant Colonel Paterson:
> > 21st Regiment and 2/RM less Light Companies and RMA with one 6 pdr and two 3 pdrs.

The Admiral also landed a provisional Battalion of ship Marines under Captain Robyns who were brigaded with the 3rd Brigade.

On the 21st the force advanced north keeping touch with the squadron to Nottingham, to attack Barney's Flotilla, which the enemy blew up on the 22nd, the officers and men having proceeded overland to Washington and then out to join the force defending Washington under General Winder.[202]

On the 22nd the British marched to Upper Marlborough where the Ship Marine Battalion under Captain Robyns was left in garrison. From here there were two roads to Washington; one over the bridge on the Eastern Branch right into the city, the other NW to the bridge at Bladensburg about five miles further up. On the first road, about halfway to the city, was a crossroads called Oldfields, where one road went North West to Bladensburg the other south west to Fort Washington which was the main defence of the capital on the Potomac River.

The Americans had 5,000-6,000 Militia but few regulars beyond Barney's men. Ross, including the ship battalion, had about 4,000. General Winder had taken up a position at Oldfields; on the 23rd Ross advanced on the Western Road and camped three miles from Oldfields; Winder retired on Washington, burning the bridge over the Eastern Branch. On the 24th Ross turned North West and at noon marched into Bladensburg. The Militia had retired behind the river but without destroying the bridge and were formed on the heights astride the road commanding the bridge; the stream however was fordable. Winder came up to take command and extended their left. The 1st Brigade proposed to attack immediately though the 2nd and 3rd Brigades, exhausted by the heat and the time on shipboard, were some way behind. The 1st Brigade launched the attack on the bridge at 1 pm and carried it with some loss. Barney's men and guns with the Marines were holding the main road. The British rockets of the RMA under Lieutenant Lawrence sent the American left off in panic. The 1st Brigade after passing the bridge reformed and then, without skirmishers, advanced up the road to a frontal attack. They were three times repulsed with loss by grapeshot from Barney's guns, and a fourth attack directed at the enemy's right was also driven off. They were ordered to hold on until the 2nd Brigade much exhausted appeared half an hour later.[203]

---

202 The Marines of the Flotilla were under Captain Miller USMC, History of U.S. Marine Corpsl, (Collum).
203 History of U.S.M.C. (Collum) p. 57 says "First (sic, really 2nd - Ed.) RM, were in the attack, they probably mistook the Light Company.

Ross assumed command of the 1st Brigade and the 44th were told off to attack Barney's left flank while the 4th attacked the infantry on his right; the latter bolted and Barney was left alone, but his men stood and were bayoneted at the guns; ten guns were captured as well as the Commodore and Captain Miller both wounded.

The British casualties were 249 killed and wounded of which the RMA had 1 killed and 1 Sergeant wounded; 2/RM, 5 killed; Colonial Marines, 1 killed and 2 wounded.

Ross entered Washington the same evening. All private property was respected and there was no plundering, but in accordance with the Government's instructions and as a reprisal for the American destruction in Canada all public buildings including the Presidents house, Parliament House, Navy Yard, Barracks, and Arsenal were burnt and the troops withdrew on the 20th to Marlborough after a night march. On the 30th they re-embarked in their ships.

Captain Robyns RM and Captain Harrison RMA were mentioned in Admiral Cockburn's dispatch, and the RMA Rocket Company in General Ross's.

Lieutenant Colonel Williams and the staff of the 1st Battalion must have joined the Fleet about this time and there was probably a reorganisation of the battalions.[204]

In Major Lewis' services in RMO[205] it is said that 3rd Battalion was formed on 4th September of three Companies RM from 2nd Battalion and three Companies of Negroes.

Inspired no doubt by the hope of prize money, the Admirals now advised an attack on Baltimore, but General Ross hesitated and for a time the idea was abandoned. An attempt on Rhode Island which would have threatened New York was considered, but the Baltimore plan was revived and the troops re-embarked in the squadron, sailed up the Chesapeake and anchored at the mouth of the Patapsco River on which Baltimore stands; the light vessels went on up to the North Shore, a little above North Point. It would seem as if there were certainly present the 2/RM, 3/RM under Major Lewis and possibly part of the 1/RM under Lieutenant Colonel Williams.[206]

The troops disembarked at North Point on 12th September on the peninsula formed by the Back River on the north and Patapsco River on south, 13 miles from Baltimore. The History of US Marine Corps says that the British were reinforced by the Marines and 600 seamen from the fleet and this is very probable in view of their previous losses and that Admiral Cockburn was present in person.

---

204 See Diary of Officer, 3rd Battalion: Britain's See Soldiers.
205 Editor's Note – Officers' service records now in The National Archives, Kew.
206 James' Military Occurrences says 1st and 2nd (Colonial) Battalions as well as detachments of Marines and Seamen from the Fleet.

Advancing north, they reached the head of an inlet, where the enemy militia were entrenching a neck of land only ½ mile wide from water to water; the Americans abandoned it on the approach of the skirmishers, the British advancing two miles further came into collision with some American skirmishers when General Ross was killed, and Colonel Brooke took command.

The force pressed on to five miles from Baltimore when they were stopped by 5,000 men with six guns posted across a narrow neck of land 1,000 yards wide. The 1st Brigade deployed in skirmishing order, the 2nd Brigade deployed along the whole line (to this brigade the ship Marines under Captain Robyns were attached), and the 3rd Brigade (21st Regiment, 2/RM under Malcolm and a detachment of Marines under Major Lewis of the 3/RM)[207] was formed in columns on the road with orders to deploy to the left, and press the American right as soon as the ground opened sufficiently. The water on the right was fordable where an American battalion had been placed in echelon; the 4th Regiment got into position unseen within twenty yards on the American left and opened fire on which the Americans fled, followed by all the left wing; the right wing stood a bit longer and offered some resistance and then fled leaving two guns.

Brooke halted for the night; advancing the next morning (13th) to a distance of 1½ miles from Baltimore. He found that the town was defended by a ring of hills with palisaded redoubts connected by a breastwork, which was defended by about 15,000 Militia, some US Marine Corps and some seamen with many guns. Lieutenant Colonel Brooke then decided on a night attack, but on the 13th the squadron had made an attack on the batteries at the entrance to the Patapsco River without success, and during the night 13th/14th an attack was made by boats which also failed, whilst the ships found themselves unable to remove the barrier of sunken ships leading up to the harbour. Therefore, Brooke retired slowly on the 14th unpursued and re-embarked at North Point (on 15th) with a loss of 290 men killed and wounded. Fortescue says this was a wicked waste of life for no object, except probably the desire of the Navy for Prize Money.

The squadron withdrew on the 15th and returned to Tangier Island; on 19th September Sir Arthur Cochrane with the *Tonnant* and *Surprise* sailed for Halifax from whence he went to Jamaica arriving on 1st November. Rear Admiral Cockburn in the *Albion* went to Bermuda, Rear Admiral Malcolm with *Royal Oak* and some frigates and the troops remained in the Patuxent and made a petty raid on the Virginian shore on 5th and 6th October, but on 14th October with *Royal Oak*, *Asia*, *Ramillies* and the frigates, bombs, and troopships he sailed for Jamaica. Captain Barrie with *Dragon* (74) was left as SNO in Chesapeake and according to the diary of the officer of 3/RM on 26th September that battalion was landed at Tangier Island; three companies RM and three companies Colonial Marines (Negroes); Major Lewis was invalided to England and Captain Clements took command. The 1st and 2nd Battalions seem to have remained afloat with Rear Admiral Cockburn.

The 3/RM remained in garrison at Tangier Island where they built barracks, a battery, hospital, etc. and even a mess room, evidently a complete advanced base until 11th December when Admiral

---

207 Colonel Brooke's dispatch.

Cockburn came from Bermuda, embarked them in the *Regulus*, finally leaving the Chesapeake on 10th December and went to Amelia Island, East Florida.

Preliminaries of peace had been signed in Europe on 14th December but of course this was not known until the end of January and all the useless waste of life in Georgia and at the mouths of the Mississippi might have been saved.

Dealing first with the doings of the Marine battalions with Admiral Cockburn: on 10th January 1815 all three battalions under Lieutenant Colonel Williams were disembarked on *Cumberland* Island, having lost 60 men from disease on the way round.

On 12th January the brigade crossed the sound to seize the town of St Mary's on the mainland, which was defended by Fort Point Pitre with six or seven guns commanding the entrance to St Mary's River. Landing from the boats of the squadron without opposition they advanced through a wood to attack the American riflemen who were driven from three positions, and at length from the fort itself, which with the barracks, artillery, etc. fell into the hands of the Marines.

Leaving three companies to secure the position, they crossed another branch of the river and entered the town of St. Mary's and found it full of merchandise. Here evidently Sir Richard found it necessary to provide himself with some mounted patrols, for he mounted a Sergeant and seven Corporals as a Cavalry Patrol.[208]

On 24th January, having destroyed all the enemy's works and embarked everything valuable from the town and vessels, they returned to Cumberland Island, which they placed in a state of defense, fortifying the west end of it and a large house called Dungeness. Here they remained no doubt as an advanced base for the squadron blockading the coast till 10th March when news was received of peace having been ratified; they re-embarked on board their respective ships and sailed for Bermuda. Arriving at Bermuda on 21st March under orders for England.

The ships must have returned independently, because we know from the letter books that there is an Admiralty Order dated 6th May that officers and men who arrived at the forts were to be sent to their respective Headquarters forthwith, whilst the Board of Ordnance was to take over the Field Train and stores from the *Asia*.

Evidently Sir Richard Williams arrived before the 8th May as at his request the above order was modified that the RM Battalions were not to be disbanded until the men were paid; but a similar application from Lieutenant Colonel Sir James Malcolm that the staff of the 2nd Battalion might be kept together was refused on 18th May. The RMA in the *Tonnant* must have arrived about the 15th or 16th, as on the 17th it was ordered that they were to be sent to Chatham to be re-equipped. Apparently matters were settled up by July as certain officers were then granted leave and

---

208 On 13 May 1815 he applied for the difference of pay between cavalry and infantry for these men, but it was refused by the Admiralty Portsmouth letter books.

the accounts of the Quartermasters are squared up,[209] though the writer of the diary quoted says that he did not arrive till 3rd August, whilst letters in the books indicate that accounts of the men were still being closed at the end of that month and even later.

It is hard to realise in reading these old letters that England was at the moment being convulsed by Napoleon's last throw and the Battle of Waterloo.

On 1st July Sir Richard Williams brought to notice the exemplary conduct of Sergeant Major William Webb of 1/RM and the Board directed that he was to be borne as a supernumerary Sergeant-Major until a vacancy occurred. On 7th December 1814 a Brevet Majority had been conferred on Captain John Robyns, the Fleet Marine Officer, dated 27th October 1814. Lieutenant Colonels Williams and Malcolm were created Knights of the Bath.

On 11th May 1815 the Commandant Resident in Town sent the following letter to the Divisions.

> "I am directed by My Lords Commissioners of the Admiralty to communicate to the Officers and Men of the Royal Marine Battalions the high sense which Their Lordships entertain of their meritorious conduct during their services in America; I have to desire you will cause the same to be inserted in Public Orders."
>
> (Signed) H. Bell
>
> The Commandants RM

Before leaving this war there is the record of the doings of yet another body of Royal Marines in a different theatre.

Gulf of Mexico.

In May 1814 the Naval Commander in Chief Sir Arthur Cochrane had sent a frigate under Captain Pigot to the mouth of the Apalachicola River in the Gulf of Mexico, whose Captain had reported that the Creek and Choctaw Indians with the aid of a few British Officers and Sergeants could gain possession of Baton Rouge from which place the conquest of New Orleans and the Lower Mississippi was possible.

The project was approved by the Cabinet and Admiral Cochrane sent Major Edward Nicholls RM with some NCOs and men with arms and ammunition to Mobile Bay in August; the Indians had just been defeated by the American General Jackson, who was holding the country. Nicholls went to Pensacola and threatened the forts on the Alabama River and drove off the Americans. He then armed the Indians and raised forts on the Apalachicola, so that the Americans sent 2,000 men who had been intended for Canada to watch him, whilst General Jackson with 500 men took post in Mobile opposite Pensacola.

---

[209] It is to be noted that the accounts only of 1st and 2nd Battalions are dealt with, the 3rd having evidently been merged in theirs.

With 60 Royal Marines, 12 RMA with a 52 inch howitzer and 108 Indians covered by the 20-gun ships *Hermes* and *Charon* with two sloops, Nicholls attacked Fort Bowyer on Mobile Point which mounted two 24 pdrs six 12 pdrs, eight 9 pdrs, four 4 pdrs, with a garrison of about 375 men in order to cut off communication between New Orleans and Mobile. The attack was repulsed, and the *Hermes* ran aground and was burnt; Major Nicholls was wounded in the right eye and leg; owing to dysentery he was directing operations from the *Hermes*. He then returned to Pensacola.

Nicholl's officers were 2nd Lieutenants R Henry Wallen RMA, J McWilliams RM and Sergeant J Chapman, temporary Lieutenant and Adjutant.

On 19th October the Admiralty ordered 3 Captains and 4 Lieutenants from Portsmouth and 3 Captains from Plymouth to be sent out in *Leonidas* and *Iphigenia* to join the North American Squadron; they were not to be taken from the roster, but specially selected as active and intelligent and fit for active service on shore, so they would seem to have been intended for Nicholl's force.

Admiral Cochrane arrived at Jamaica on 1st November, where he was met by fresh troops from France, and with those already with the squadron he proceeded to attack New Orleans. To second these operations and to detain the Americans at Pensacola, Nicholls evacuated the place and fell back to the Apalachicola River where he built a fort in a strong position and by raids etc. caused great loss and inconvenience to the Americans and maintained his position to the end of the war. His force seems to have reached England sometime in June 1815, because there are letters with reference to their pay whilst in East Florida.

The Fleet and troops went on to the attack of New Orleans but we cannot follow this disastrous operation except to say that on 8th January 190 Marines of the fleet under Major T B Adair in conjunction with the 85th Regiment under Lieutenant Colonel Thornton accomplished the one successful action of the campaign when they crossed the river and carried the American lines on the right bank (among the ordnance captured here was a howitzer inscribed "Taken at the surrender of Yorktown 1781"): the main attack on the left bank failed with heavy loss, including the Commander-in-Chief (General Pakenham) and the British naval and military force withdrew on 11th January and re-embarked by the end of the month.

The Royal Marines had 2 killed and 1 Captain (G Elliott), 2 Lieutenants (H Elliot and Morgan), 1 Sergeant, and 12 Rank and File wounded.

From the 8th to 14th February the British besieged and captured Fort Bowyer with slight loss, but the conclusion of peace put an end to hostilities.

The final comment of Fortescue in his History of the British Army[210] is worth remembrance by members of the Corps. "Never employ the Fleet alone for operations which require the combined

---

210 Book XV Chapter XX.

forces of the Army and Navy . . . Never use those combined forces on the sole advice of a Naval or a Military Officer".[211]

---

[211] A lesson driven home by the Dardanelles in 1915, just 100 years later. - Ed.

11 - Demobilisation and Reorganisation 1814 – 1816

The problem now before the Admiralty was to reduce the Corps of 31,400 Officers and Men to a Peace Establishment, and to lay down the lines of future policy for a force that had practically never existed in peace time. To complicate matters when demobilisation of the fleet commenced in 1814, the three battalions and Major Nicoll's force were still on service in America and the escape of Napoleon from Elba with the exciting events that followed in 1815 during the "Hundred Days" and Waterloo were all factors to disturb the arrangements. But we can follow the successive steps taken fairly easily.

On 27th April 1814 it was ordered that all returning prisoners of war were to be paid up to date and discharged; and on 28th April that all recruits in the Recruit Depots, not up to peace standards, were also to be discharged. Efforts were also made to trace men borne on the books, who had not been heard of for any length of time; and one can imagine that under the conditions there must have been many such men.

On 28th April Lieutenant General Barclay retired from the position of Commandant in Town and was succeeded by Major General H Bell from Chatham; Colonel R Winter becoming Commandant at Chatham. On 28th April 1814 the Commandants at Portsmouth (Lieutenant General Elliott) and at Plymouth (Major General R Bright) were also informed that in view of their long and meritorious services they would be placed on Retired Full Pay. Major General Strickland became Commandant at Plymouth, but though Major General R Williams (not the battalion commander) was appointed to Portsmouth on 30th May he does not appear to have taken over command until 1st January 1815, the 2nd in Command Major General Farmer doing the duty.

On 26th May a report on each class of officer was called for who from age, length of service, or debility were no longer able to discharge their duty - with a view to considering their claims to retirement on full pay. As a consequence, a considerable number of officers of all ranks were retired on full pay later in the year.

On 25th June orders were issued to commence reduction by discharging:

1. All foreigners.
2. All sick, infirm, and those likely to become so.
3. All men over forty years of age.
4. All men under 5 ft. 1 in. in height.
5. All undisciplined drummers.

We learn how difficult it was for natives of Ireland, Scotland and the distant parts of England to return to their homes, and the Commanders-in-Chief at the Home Ports were instructed to grant passages when possible. On 6th July peace was proclaimed and thanksgiving services held throughout the country.

On 2nd August the Admiralty promulgated the Order-in-Council of 23rd July 1814:

> The New Establishment for the Royal Marines was to consist of 120 Companies with 23 Field Officers and 14 Staff Officers; to commence on 1st September 1814. Lists of Officers to be retained on full pay were sent to each Division; all those not included in the lists were allowed Full Pay until 31st August and afterwards Half Pay until otherwise provided for, and to be at liberty to depart from Headquarters as soon as they think proper. Of the Field Officers 1 Commandant, 1 2nd-Commandant, 2 Lieutenant Colonels and 2 Majors were allowed to each Division and 1 as Commandant in Town. The Staff Officers appear to have been 8 Adjutants, 4 Deputy Paymasters, the Secretary to the Commandant in Town, and perhaps the Acting Adjutant of the RMA. The 4 Quartermasters and the 4 Senior Captains allowed at each Headquarters as Pay Captains who were mustered in Nos 1, 2, 3 and 4 Companies i.e. the Commandants Companies were presumably counted in the Company lists.

A case occurred on 27th September 1814 that is of interest as showing the relation to the Civil Law of the land. A couple of Marines were sentenced by GCM to transportation as felons to New South Wales for life; but the sentence could not be carried out without a certificate from the Court of King's Bench transmitted by a Secretary of State.

On 7th November a Proclamation was issued allowing the discharge of Royal Marines who had completed the periods of limited service for which they had enlisted.

At the beginning of the next year (1815) it is interesting to learn that the Master and principal performers of the Band of the Oxfordshire Militia (presumably being disbanded) volunteered for and were accepted by the Portsmouth Band.

Early in the year we learn of the arrival of the 1st, 2nd, and 3rd Battalions from America.

The Quartermasters of the two battalions on their return were apparently Lieutenants Griffith of the 1st and Puddicombe of the 2nd as there are orders and amounts which were to be paid to them for surplus necessaries taken over by Headquarters.

But Napoleon was once more stirring Europe and we see orders dated 21st June 1815 allowing men enlisted for limited service to extend their service, but no one would ever imagine from the Divisional letter books that such great events were stirring Europe and the Corps seems to have gone serenely on its way though unfortunately unable to take any share in the great drama in Belgium.

The danger from Napoleon soon passed. An order dated 1st August 1815 is of interest to the Corps as it says that Captain Beatty RM was to relieve Captain Hull RM in HMS *Northumberland*;

this was the ship detailed to take the ex-Emperor to St Helena and Captain Beatty remained in charge of the Marine Guard for many years.[212]

On 17th August the special impressment picquets were withdrawn. The new peace schemes of complement for all ships - amounting to about half war strength - were promulgated.

On 4th September 1815 the fiat went forth that the Peace Establishment of the Corps was only to be 6,000 men and that discharges were to go on i.e. that over 24,000 Officers and men were to be discharged.

A quaint order in view of the fact that the war was over was promulgated on 26th December viz: that in future the barrels of all musquets were to be browned (in this following the army). Hitherto they had always been polished bright. They were to be treated by the Ordnance Board.

On 23rd December 1815 was promulgated the Order-in-Council of 27th November 1815 which regulated the fate of the Corps for many years. The reductions were to take effect from 1st January 1816 and the order made many drastic alterations in the system.

The Corps was to consist of 80 companies only. Instead of commissioning officers to the different companies, a list of officers to be attached to each Division was sent to the several Divisions and the Commandant was told to post Captains and Subalterns to different Companies according to the scale.

The six Colonels Second-Commandant at present on the list were to be allowed to retire on full pay "subject to recall if their Lordships think fit to fill vacancies." As a matter of fact they were nearly all recalled and one, Campbell, became the first DAG in 1825 without apparently being Commandant.

The RMA Companies were all transferred to Chatham and the Commandant of that Division was ordered to make returns of the whole establishment, the Divisions discontinuing to do so. Major and Brevet Lieutenant Colonel Sir Richard Williams was ordered to go to Chatham for the purpose of taking on himself the duty of Major Commandant of that Establishment. They were quartered in Fort Pitt where to this day the names of terraces and walks bear the names of the early Captains and Subalterns of the RMA.

Officers not included in the new establishment were placed on half pay from 1st January 1816 and were at liberty to depart from Headquarters immediately but "sufficient of those who stand first for appointments were to be retained to replace those who were being surveyed for retirement." Those placed on half pay were given full pay for two months from 1st January 1816.

---

212 Beatty had had most distinguished service; he was Major Oldfield's subaltern at Teneriffe, at the Nile and at Acre and since then had been at Trafalgar and many other battles.

And now the Corps entered on the longest nominal period of peace it had ever enjoyed, but a perusal of the following pages will show that very few years of the next hundred passed without some portion of the Corps being actively engaged in the defence of its country's interests.

12 - Peace 1816 – 1836

It is very difficult to deal with the next twenty years, because they are nominally years of peace, during which as usual changes in uniform and administration were rife, but there was very little progress in training. Although large operations were few, portions of the Corps were continually occupied in small operations and police duties.

The numbers varied very little as shown in following table:

1817-1818	-	6,235
1819-1822	-	7,835
1823	-	8,700
1824-1831	-	8,000
1832-1837	-	9,000 in 2 Artillery, 90 Divisional Companies

Sir Henry Bell from Chatham assumed the duties of Commandant in Town and his assistant, known as a 'Secretary' was Captain F J Kempster. General Bell continued in office till 19th July 1825 when by an Order-in-Council of that date the Admiralty represented that owing to age and infirmities he was no longer fit for duty and an extra full pay retirement was created to admit of his retirement. In his place it was ordered that there should be a Colonel Commandant and Deputy Adjutant General at an allowance of £2-10-0 a day, £300 for house rent and forage for a horse together with an Assistant Adjutant General at the full pay of his rank and 10/- per diem, £150 for house rent and forage for a horse. Major General Campbell on half pay from 2nd Commandant Plymouth was the first holder of the post till the reformers had an opportunity of making an appointment constantly advocated up to modern times and invariably found impracticable.

Inspector General.
By. Order-in-Council 31st January 1831 an Inspector General with a Brigade Major were appointed in place of a DAG and AAG. A Major General Sir James Cockburn (apparently an Army Officer) was appointed, but by Order-in-Council 11th May 1836 the Inspector General was abolished and the DAG and AAG reappointed.[213] The DAG evidently made all administrative inspections and conducted the London work, but the local Garrison Commanders carried out the drill and training inspections. Sir John Owen, fresh from the battalion in Spain, was appointed DAG in November 1838 and remained in office till the Crimean war in 1855.

Paymaster.
By Order-in-Council 1st June 1832 the post of Paymaster of the Marines was abolished. This had been in existence since 1755 and was apparently a Parliamentary post of some importance. It was abolished by Act of Parliament 10 Geo iv c.1. and in 1830 by 2 William iv. c. xq lst June 1832: "Whereas by reason of the abolition of the Paymaster of the Marines and transfer of part of the duties to the Treasurer of the Navy Probate of Marines Wills was transferred to the Inspector of

---

213 See 1862.

the Wills of the Navy." This was probably one of the steps by which the Corps became subject in financial matters to the Accountant General of the Navy. The first Paymaster of the Marines had been a Mr W Adair; he was succeeded by a Mr Tucker and among other names that of the Hon George Villiers is mentioned.

Blue Colonels

The system of appointing Naval Officers to be Generals and Colonels of Marines which had originated in 1760 continued until 11th February 1837, when it was abolished. HM King William IV, whilst he was Duke of Clarence and Lord High Admiral, held the appointment of General of Marines till his accession to the throne in 1830.

Pay.

One of the first acts of the government on the approach of peace in 1814 had been to increase the amount of half pay to officers,[214] but judged by present day standards the amounts were very small.

	Present rates	New Rates
Colonel	12. 0	14.8
Lieutenant Colonel	8. 6	11.0
Major	7. 6	9.6
Captain	5. 0	7.0
First Lieutenant	2. 4	4.0
" " after 7 years	2. 4	4.6
Second Lieutenant	1.10	3.0

Promotion.

But the great and increasing problem through all these years was the stagnation of promotion for the officers. First there was the huge list of half pay officers to be absorbed and next the establishments of retired full pay officers were so small that numerous committees were assembled from time to time and reported, followed by numerous Orders in Council, but the difficulty still continued. It may be of interest to note the different ways taken to deal with it.

We get a picture of the situation in the Order-in-Council of 3rd April 1832 reintroducing the rank and appointment of Colonel Second Commandant: *"We have had under consideration the slowness with which the promotion of the Corps has taken place and the consequent gloomy prospects of the officers, more particularly the senior First and Second Lieutenants of whom the former has 28 years service and the latter 18 standing in their present rank."* The Board therefore proposed to add to the Corps 4 Lieutenant Colonels to be Second Commandants, one to each Division at the rate of pay of £1 per diem which will create vacancies for 4 Majors to be Lieutenant Colonels, 4 Captains to be Majors, 4 First Lieutenants to Captains, and 4 Second Lieutenants to be First Lieutenants and *"we venture to submit the said augmentation the more readily as by the late disbanding of the Marine*

---

214 Order-in-Council 15th August 1814.

Artillery a very considerable saving accrued to the Public."

But this did not afford any very great relief and a fresh scheme of retirement was promulgated by Order-in-Council 30th April 1834, the preamble of which throws a light on the conditions *"The rank and numbers of the Officers RM, as now established, are disproportionate to the rank and file. To improve the efficiency of the Corps a certain number of Captains ought to be retired to give promotion to the same number of First Lieutenants who have served during the late war and whose seniority as subalterns is from 26 to 29 years standing."* It was an elaborate scheme, which typically of the Admiralty i.e. worked out in detail, and shows a saving of £375. 5. 5¾ a year to the Government but it did not mend matters very much and in 1837 matters had become so bad that a Royal Commission was held, and the question of pay, promotion, and retirement was more fully gone into, which resulted in the Order-in-Council of 21st June 1837 and this made a decided improvement.

During this period there were many changes of organisation and in training, but it is only possible to follow the more important of these, as at this period Army Regulations were adhered to very closely. The alterations in uniform have not been dealt with here because they are so fully described and illustrated in Colonel Fields *"Britain's Sea Soldiers".*

Algiers.
The principal event in 1816 was the bombardment of Algiers, when the Powers, having settled their differences, turned on the nest of Barbary pirates and destroyed it.

Nineteen men-of-war left Plymouth on 28th July 1816 under the command of Admiral Sir Fleetwood Pellew, arriving at Gibraltar on 9th August, where they were joined by the Dutch Squadron of five frigates and a corvette. Leaving Gibraltar on 14th August they met HMS *Prometheus* with news from Algiers on the 16th.

The Dey of Algiers had called up 40,000 men from the interior and the batteries were very strong. On the north side the batteries were armed with 80 guns and 6 large mortars; in front of them was shoal water. Between the North Wall and the pier connecting with the lighthouse twenty guns were mounted. On the North Mole of the harbour was a 44 gun battery, semi-circular in shape in two tiers. To the south and in line with the pier, circular in shape the Lighthouse Battery with 48 guns in two tiers. Then a long battery in three tiers - called the Eastern Battery - with 60 guns flanked by four other batteries of two tiers with 60 guns. On the south head of the Mole two large 68 pdrs. There were altogether about 220 guns round the molehead, principally 32 and 24 pdrs. South west of the small pier that projects to form the entrance to the harbour was the Fish Market Battery with 15 guns in three tiers, and between that and the southern extremity were two batteries of four and fifteen guns respectively, as well as the castle, and two or three other forts with 70 guns. The city was also fortified on the land side.

On 17th August the Fleet sighted the City and a flag of truce was sent in demanding:

1. The abolition of Christian Slavery.
2. Delivery of all Christian Slaves.
3. Restoration of the ransoms recently paid for Neapolitan and Sardinian prisoners.
4. Release of the British Consul and the boats crew of the *Prometheus*.

No answer was received so at 2 pm the fleet stood into the bay and when about one mile off the town the *Queen Charlotte* hoisted the preparative and anchored with springs on her cable when about fifty yards from the Molehead and opened with her starboard broadside on to the embrasures, each ship coming into action as her guns would bear.

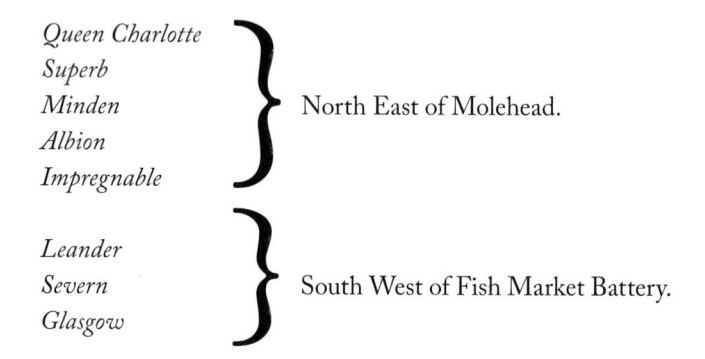

Queen Charlotte
Superb
Minden   } North East of Molehead.
Albion
Impregnable

Leander
Severn   } South West of Fish Market Battery.
Glasgow

The five Dutch frigates engaged the batteries to the southward. The *Granicus* and *Hebrus* with four bomb vessels engaged at about 2,000 yards from the enemy and the battering flotilla of gun and mortar boats with various kinds of ship's boats - about 50 in all - opened on the enemy fleet.

Three broadsides from the *Queen Charlotte* smashed up the south end of the mole and she then turned her batteries on to the town gate leading to the mole. At 3 pm Lieutenant J B Stevens RMA in a boat mounting a 68 pdr carronade, having secured himself to the stern warp of the *Leander*, fired carcasses into the shipping and vessels alongside the mole. At 4 pm the barge of the *Queen Charlotte* was sent to set fire to the Algerine frigate moored across the harbour; this was suggested and carried out by Lieutenant A R Wolrige RM, but he received no recognition though the Lieutenant RN who accompanied him was promoted.

By 4.30 pm the *Impregnable* (2nd Flag) had suffered 150 casualties and the *Glasgow* was sent in to help her. By 7 pm all ships and vessels in the harbour were in flames; the British ships had suffered but contrary to the usual experience of ships versus forts they had been very successful. At 8.30pm an explosion vessel with 143 barrels of powder was run ashore under the semi-circular battery and exploded at 9 pm, which created a diversion in favour of the *Impregnable*. The cannonade continued until 10 pm when the upper tiers of the Mole Batteries were silenced and the lower tiers partly silenced, though the ammunition of the British ships was nearly expended. The *Queen Charlotte* cut her cables and stood off with the land breeze and by 2 am all ships were out of range.

The enemy ships in the harbour and the storehouses were all alight, when a thunderstorm which lasted for three hours came on and added to the horrors of the burning city.

At daylight on the 20th a flag of truce, repeating the demands, was sent in, and the bomb vessels took up their positions to resume the bombardment, but in the afternoon, terms were agreed to.

On the 29th after conferences 1,200 Christian slaves were released and 382,500 dollars restored. Peace with the King of the Netherlands was signed, and 30,000 dollars compensation and a public apology was made to the British Consul.

Major Joseph Vallack (*Superb*) was promoted to Brevet Lieutenant Colonel, Captains J Wright and C F Burton (wounded) were promoted to Brevet Major, and the senior Sergeant Major J K Wilson was promoted to 2nd Lieutenant.

The casualties were:

> Killed: Captain J Wilson and Lieutenant G Baxter (*Leander*), Lieutenant W Morgan, 2nd Lieutenant Henfry (*Granicus*), Lieutenant J P B Bissett RMA (*Infernal*) with 20 NCOs and men.

> Wounded: 1 Captain, 3 Lieutenants, 111 NCOs and men.

> The total loss was 128 killed, 690 wounded.

Royal Marine Artillery.
The first administrative change affected the RMA Companies which were by Order-in-Council 25th November 1816 raised from four to eight; but the Admiralty took the opportunity to take away from them certain allowances which they had drawn when embarked in bomb vessels, following on the original order that they were to receive the same pay and allowances as the Royal Artillery whom they replaced. The wording of the Order-in-Council throws a light on the duties of the RMA which is useful:

> "*It is certainly unnecessary to give them to the RM Artillery whose natural course of service is to embark and which in fact were formed for the special purpose………
> We hope this error will be corrected at this favourable opportunity, when it can be done without injury to individuals because at present none of the Marine Artillery are embarked, nor according to the original regulations would they have been embarked in peace. While we propose to continue the increased shore pay (ie at artillery rates) and to encourage the Artillery in the Corps in general by doubling the numbers who will receive this increased pay, we propose to abolish the extra sea pay*" (which was done).

But the accommodation at Fort Pitt, Chatham, was insufficient and on 7th June 1817 four companies under Brevet Lieutenant Colonel Sir Richard Williams KCB marched to Fort

Cumberland and soon after took over quarters at Fort Monckton, Gosport, and the other four companies were sent one to each Division. An Admiralty Circular of 6th December 1817 defines their position: it was to be assimilated in all respects to that of a detachment of Royal Artillery doing duty with a regiment of the line. It also says that the duty of the Acting Adjutant of the RMA was not to be confined to the instruction of Royal Marines in the use of the sea service gun, but that he is to perform the duties of an adjutant to the detachment, for which he received extra pay of 2/- a day.

Evidently questions had arisen because an RMO letter of 25th July 1818 defines the position of the RMA company on parade. It was to be formed up inspected and dismissed on its own private parade. Its position is to be six paces distant on the right of the band. The position of officer commanding whether in line or column i.e. in front of the centre; "all words of command to be repeated by the officer in charge of the detachment." The officer commanding company kept a roster and detailed his men for duty and was responsible for interior economy and had charge of the Ordnance stores.

1819

Colonels Commandant.
On 4th September an order was issued that Colonels Commandant on attaining the rank of Lieutenant General were to vacate their commands, and all the Commandants were changed. I have not been able to ascertain how they regulated the promotion of these senior officers, because there were often Major Generals as Second Commandants.

1820

Precedence.
On 30th March 1820 an order was issued settling the precedence of the Royal Marines when in Line as next to the 49th (Royal Berkshire Regiment)[215] and before the 50th (Royal West Kent Regiment). On 24th April the Plymouth Division paraded with the troops in garrison for the first time in their recognised place.

Queen Caroline.
In 1820 a detachment of 350 Officers and men were sent from Plymouth to Chatham to strengthen the Division during the trial of Queen Caroline at Westminster from 7th July to 25th November, and a battalion of 700 men from Chatham was attached to a brigade of artillery and held in readiness to set against a mass meeting of a mob at the White Conduit House, Pentonville, whilst the Royal Marines of HMS *Glasgow* under Captain T Aslett furnished a guard of honour over the remains of that unfortunate Queen when she died in 1821.

---

215   See Corps Records Vol I.

Schools.
In 1820 Plymouth, which seems to have led the way in this matter, started schools for the female children of NCOs and men. Schools for boys had been started in 1784. The wording of the order is interesting and in the following years one can follow by the successive Orders in Council the gradual taking over by the Government and the increased pay to Schoolmasters and Schoolmistresses.

On 25th July 1841 schooling was made free of expense to parents.

The final abolition of the RM Schools by the Minister of Education and the Treasury came in 1921, another of the short-sighted acts of HM Civil Service.

Half Pay Officers.
There often seems to have been trouble over the restoration of officers from half to full pay and one such case led to the Commandant at Plymouth in 1821 Major General Watkin Tench - a very distinguished officer, who had been one of the founders of New South Wales and had done a great deal of exploration about which he has written a book - being removed from his command. The trouble appears to have occurred over another very distinguished officer, who after having been tried by Court Martial and dismissed the service was reinstated and eventually became Deputy Adjutant General.

During these years the RM Office was located at 39 Cadogan Place, London.

Royal Marine Artillery.
In 1822 owing to fever at Fort Monckton the RMA Companies were moved back to the Upper Barracks at Chatham, where they remained until 1824 when they returned to the High Street and Gunwharf at Portsmouth

Mess Funds.
In August 1825 the Admiralty for the first time laid down the compulsory contributions to be paid by officers to the mess funds on joining; they were also to pay the difference between the rates on promotion, the amounts being collected by the Adjutant and handed over to the Mess Committee. This was discontinued in 1919 but modifications had been made in 1912.

Bermuda.
From mention in Plymouth orders of the thanks of the Governor there appeared to have been a battalion in Bermuda about 1824.

Burmah.
In 1824 the First Burmah War broke out and a small portion of the Corps was engaged in HMS *Liffey*. On 11th May she silenced the batteries at Rangoon and troops from India were landed and took possession of the town and later the Royal Navy with the 89th Regiment and 7th Madras Native Infantry subdued Tennasserim.

Lisbon.

In consequence of the struggle in Portugal between the Constitutionalists and Absolutionists on the accession of Pedro I of Brazil as Pedro IV of Portugal civil war appeared imminent. The British Government sent 5,000 British troops under Sir William Clinton to restore order and to disband the troops under Chaves, the leader of the Abolitionists. A battalion of Marines under the command of Colonel T B Adair formed part of this force and were quartered in Fort St Julian at Lisbon on the River Tagus. Colonel Adair was in command from 17th August 1825 to 3rd January 1827.

East Surrey Regiment.

In 1825 the *Kent* (transport) when conveying the 31st East Surrey Regiment to India was burnt and destroyed; the bulk of the troops were rescued and brought to Chatham where they were received and entertained by the Chatham Royal Marine Division till they could be refitted and re-embarked. In memory of this episode the Officers of the Chatham Division and the East Surrey Regiment made each other honorary members of their respective messes in perpetuity; this privilege has since been extended to include all the Divisions of Royal Marines and all the regular battalions and depot of the East Surrey Regiment, the 31st being now linked with the 70th Regiment.

Adjutant.

In 1826 the examination to qualify for the appointment of Adjutant was instituted and the first one held at Woolwich on 31st July 1826. The peculiar reward was held out that those who qualified need not attend Adjutant's drill in the early morning at 6 am, a privilege which extended well into the 20th century.

Pay Captains.

On 6th March 1826 a great departure was made in the pay arrangements. From the beginning there had always been Squad Officers who were on half pay or else special officers told off as Pay Captains; from now on Pay Captains were the ordinary Company Captains who did the Pay Duties in addition to their other duties; they however were not to be embarked or sent on recruiting duties[216] and they were paid 1/- a .day contingent allowance, which was abolished in 1919.

Adjutants and Quartermasters.

A curious point arose in 1826 which was settled by an Order-in-Council 1st September 1826: this, was the disproportionate pay of Adjutants and Quartermasters. As the Order says *"Adjutants are selected as the most efficient officers of the Corps and have the most important duties, but they are generally anxious to exchange to Quartermaster as 'more lucrative'"*. Adjutants were now given 2/6 a day in addition to the 4/- a day now received independent of the pay of their regimental rank. Quartermasters from the ranks had not yet been instituted, officers being detailed for the duty.

---

216 This was not adhered to in later times.

1827

Colours.
During 1827 new sets of Colours were presented to each of the four Divisions by HRH the Duke of Clarence, General of Marines. The well known and famous badge of the Globe and Laurel was now awarded to the Corps by HM King George IV in lieu of placing the names of battles on the Colours and he also gave the privilege of bearing his Cypher GIVR as well as that of the reigning sovereign.

Pikes.
In 1827 the carrying of Pikes by Sergeants was abolished finally. There had been several changes in this matter, but on 8th November 1827 it was ordered that Sergeants were to wear arms and accoutrements when men were under arms, at other times to wear their swords.

Navarino.
The Greeks had been struggling for freedom from the savage rule of the Turks. Great Britain, France, and Russia after exhausting the resources of diplomacy, each sent a squadron to intervene in the struggle. Admiral Sir Edward Codrington, with his flag in the *Asia*, was in command. The British squadron consisted of three battleships, four frigates and five brigs; the French of four battleships, one frigate and two schooners; the Russians of four battleships and four frigates.

The Turkish Fleet took refuge in the harbour of Navarino, one of the finest in the Mediterranean, on 4th October 1827. The Allied Fleet assembled before Navarino on 15th October; they proposed at first to blockade the harbour, but if the fleet should be dispersed. by the weather, Ibrahim Pasha, the Turkish Commander, would have been free to move his troops as he wanted. It was therefore decided to attack.

Navarino Bay is six miles across and at the entrance lies the island of Sphacteria; the navigable passage is at the south end about 600 yards wide; on the right hand side of the passage is the town of Navarino where the troops were encamped.

At 1.30 pm on 20th October the fleet stood in; the Turkish ships were formed in the shape of a crescent, reaching from Fort Navarino to the southern point of the island; at the bottom of the harbour were the transports. There were also five fireships at the extremities of the crescent. The Turks had three battleships, six double-banked frigates, fifteen frigates, twenty-six corvettes, eleven brigs and forty transports. The battleships had ten inch guns which fired marble shot.

When fire was opened the forts joined in and casualties on both sides were heavy. All the Turkish ships except two battleships, two frigates and some smaller craft were burnt or sunk, and the forts put out of action. In HMS *Genoa* the Marines on the poop lost so heavily that they were removed to the quarterdeck. In this battle the Marines were largely employed at the great guns. They remained in the harbour till 25th October when the Allied Fleets left.

The Royal Marine casualties were:

Killed: Captains Bell (*Asia*), Stevens (*Albion*), Lieutenant Sturgeon (*Cambrian*), and 16 Privates.

Mortally Wounded: Captain T Moore, who was awarded a Brevet Majority.

Wounded: 39 Privates.

The Total British losses were 75 killed and 197 wounded.

1828

In 1828 the Four House Barracks - next to the Clarence Barracks at Portsmouth - were occupied by the RMA, and the old battery that stood for so many years on Southsea Common was used by them. The Clarence Barracks also were enlarged.

Naval Gunnery.
But a change was coming over the Divisional Companies of the Corps, and Naval Gunnery though not unknown to them was now to become part of their training. On 12th March 1829[217] *"All Captains and Subalterns to attend 'the great gun exercise' under instruction of the Artillery officer who will report the names of such officers as they become perfect in that exercise, who will no longer be required to attend that drill."*

In 1820 the Admiralty had started HMS *Excellent* for the instruction of Naval Officers and men in gunnery, instructors being provided by the RMA, which was the only body that had made any scientific study of gunnery and systematized its teaching. Apparently NCOs of the Royal Marines were soon after sent to the *Excellent* for instruction, because we find in Plymouth Orders 30th October 1833 the Commandant congratulating three NCOs, the first men to qualify in HMS *Excellent* in 'great gun exercise.' On 6th October 1833 the DAG had directed that as these NCOs had qualified as instructors the NCOs of the Division were to be put through a course of gunnery. A report of the number of each rank who qualified was to accompany the monthly returns.

The instruction of the Corps in Naval Gunnery made rapid progress, as we find another Order (8th January 1843), where the Admiralty refused extra pay to Gunnery Instructors as the appointments were only to be for a few years, but they ordered all Captains on being promoted to be embarked in HMS *Excellent* four at a time to receive instruction, these officers to be employed in turn at the Divisions. We shall see later - in 1854 - what progress had been made in instructing the men.

---

217 Plymouth Orders.

In 1830 King William IV ascended the Throne and resigned his appointment as General of Marines, but he was always a good friend to the Corps.

A very noticeable article of uniform, the Officer's Gorget, was abolished on 26th August 1830, the stars indicating rank on the officer's epaulets were changed from the Order of the Garter to those of the Bath as at present.

Sidearms.
Up to this time sidearms must have been generally worn, as an Order of 30th January 1830 shows that deprivation of wearing sidearms, except on duty was a punishment. It was not till 9th November 1837 that the General Order was issued ordering the Army and Navy to discontinue wearing sidearms except on duty; but this did not affect Sergeants' swords in the RM, and for some reason unknown Corporals of the Portsmouth Division were allowed to wear their bayonets when walking out.

Naval Sixpence.
A curious old stoppage ceased in 1830 under 10 Geo. iv c.1 viz "The Naval sixpence" - a payment of 6d a month to Greenwich Hospital out of pay and wages of all people borne on the books of ships in commission only. It apparently continued in other ships. Greenwich Hospital used also to receive one quarter of the freightage of treasure carried in the Queen's ships.

Good Conduct Medals.
By Order-in-Council 24th August 1831 gratuities for Good Conduct were granted and men were entitled after certain periods of service to wear *"a silver medal, the size of half-a-crown, at the 3rd button of their jackets; having on one side 'For Long Service and Good Conduct' and on the other an 'Anchor and Crown'."*

In 1831 was a scare of cholera and the two flannel cholera belts, such an important article of the RM's kit, was introduced on 19th November.

Royal Marine Artillery.
But the institution and success of the *Excellent* brought a heavy blow on the Corps. By the end of 1831 the Navy considered themselves competent to dispense with the services of the RMA who up to that date had been the only people to study gunnery scientifically. The Admiralty letter is quoted in Plymouth Orders of 28th December 1831.

> *"The Lords Commissioners of the Admiralty have been pleased to direct that the corps shall be broken up on and from the 31st inst - to prevent the total extinction of the Artillery science and skill and as a nucleus whereon to form any greater body, which hereafter may be judged desirable Their Lordships further direct that two companies .... be annexed to the Portsmouth Division to be considered and act as artillery companies.*

"The Artillery officers and men being however removed from the Divisional embarkation rosters are to be separately and officially embarked by directions of Their Lordships as occasions may require."

The two Companies were quartered at Fort Cumberland and were again under their old Commandant Sir Richard Williams, now Commandant of the Portsmouth Division. The actual Order-in-Council was published on 6th February 1832 and says: "*It appears to the Board that the RMA are no longer necessary as a separate and distinct body......... but in order to preserve the skill and science attained in that branch of the Military profession and as a nucleus in case it may be necessary to form a greater body*" etc. It allowed an "*extra Captain Laboratory Instructor and Sergeant Major specially attached but to form an integral part of the Division............ to continue on Artillery pay and allowances.*" The Adjutant, Quartermaster and Barrackmaster were abolished from 31st December 1831. By Order-in-Council 21st June 1837 the extra Captain was also abolished, and we learn that each company then consisted of 1 Captain, 2 First Lieutenants, 2 Second Lieutenants, 6 Sergeants, 6 Corporals, 3 Bombardiers, 3 Drummers and 95 Gunners, a total of 238.

Ireland.

Owing to the troubles on 28th July 1832 a Battalion with a company of Artillery was sent to South Ireland under the command of Major T A Parke CB. The Headquarters appear to have been in Spike Island in Queenstown Harbour. They remained in Ireland until 18th February 1834. On their departure a letter of thanks was sent to Colonel Parke by the GOC in Cork for their services.

Portugal.

And again, the Corps had service in Lisbon owing to the renewed troubles over the succession, when a small expeditionary force and fleet calling themselves the Liberators, which had been raised in England, proceeded to the Tagus.

The British Squadron under Admiral Sir William Parker intervened to protect British interests. Lieutenant Colonel T B Adair was sent out specially to command the Marines of the Squadron and assist the Admiral, whilst a reinforcement of 200 RM from Portsmouth - 5 Officers and 90 RMA, and 7 Officers and 200 RM from Plymouth - were sent out in June 1832 in HMS *Caledonia* and the *Romney* (transport). The Battalion was stationed in the River Tagus from 8th June 1832 to 20th June 1834 during which Lisbon was captured by the Pedroists, on 24th July 1833 and Queen Maria II arrived in September. As Don Miguel surrendered on 24th May the Battalion was withdrawn.[218]

Fifers.

On 7th June 1832 orders were given that all drummers were to be instructed in the fife and none embarked until competent. The charge was to be made to the Contingent Fund, but this must have been changed later, as it was included in the £1.1.0 paid to the Drum Major under the old order of

---

218 Life of Sir W Parker.

1760. In 1835 it was ordered that Drummers were to be designated Fifers when embarked, but this did not last long.

Volume 3
1837 - 1914

13 - Carlist War 1837 – 1839

On 20 June 1837, Her Majesty Queen Victoria ascended the Throne and commenced the long reign which was to bring such glory and honour to England, but the year found the fortunes of the Corps at a very low ebb.

The numbers voted were 9007, and the RM Artillery had officially ceased to exist - a School of Laboratory and nominally two companies quartered at Fort Cumberland as part of the Portsmouth Division only being maintained. The Portsmouth Division were still in the old inadequate Clarence Barracks in the High Street; Plymouth and Chatham were in their present barracks, which had not then been enlarged to their present size, and Woolwich were in the western part of the Royal Artillery Barracks.

Owing to the long peace and the neglect of the Services, promotion was stagnant and a Commission was held this year which makes very sad reading: as a result an Order-in-Council was published on 21st June 1837 increasing the Establishment of Retired Officers, which afforded some relief, but gives a sorry picture of the position of affairs: "The Inefficiency of the Officers holding the rank of Colonel Commandant in the Royal Marines who, from slowness of promotion in the Corps, must almost necessarily have reached an age incapacitating them from active exertion before they attain command of a Division, has occupied the serious attention of successive Boards of Admiralty. Further steps are necessary. At a survey held by our orders by a member of the Board, the Physician General of the Navy, and the DAG Royal Marines, three out of the four Commandants were found unfit to discharge their duties. The Board therefore propose to create six additional retirements on Full Pay for Colonels Commandant, the full and retired pay to be £1.18.6 per diem. Also, three retirements on full pay for Colonels 2nd Commandant, one additional full pay retirement for Lieutenant Colonels and five for Captains

This made the full pay retired establishment up to 8 Colonels Commandant, 3 for Colonels 2nd Commandant, 4 for Lieutenant Colonels (there was an increase to 6 on 10 August 1840), 25 for Captains and 10 for First Lieutenants

The Order went on to say that experience of late years had shown that owing to the number of men embarked in small ships without officers etc, the number of officers on shore, in proportion to men, was larger than required; the number of companies was therefore reduced to 90 with 2 Artillery Companies, allowing one Captain and two Subalterns to each, thereby reducing 12 Captains and 4 Subalterns, also abolishing the supernumerary Artillery Captain, though he was restored on 15 May, 1838.

Further, to place the Marine Corps on the same footing as the Artillery and Engineers, and to accelerate promotion the 2nd Commandants were granted the rank of Colonel, and the rank of Major was abolished. Of the Subalterns, two-thirds were to be First-Lieutenants and the remainder Second-Lieutenants.

On 1st January 1838, Lieutenant Colonel Sir John Owen (afterwards KCB KH) became DAG, an appointment that he held until 12 December 1854; under his fostering care conditions in the Corps much improved.

Sidearms.

On 5 November 1837 an order was issued that Army and Marines were to discontinue wearing of sidearms except on duty. This of course did not affect the Sergeants' swords and at the same time the exception must have been made which allowed Corporals of the Portsmouth Division to wear them when walking out. Prior to this they must have been generally worn, because an order of 30 January 1830 (Plymouth) shows that a punishment for misconduct was deprivation of wearing sidearms in streets or at Church Parade except on duty.

In 1838 the numbers voted were 9,000. In 1839 the numbers voted were 9000.

Officers.
On 19th December it was laid down that in future all candidates for Commissions would be required to possess competent knowledge of arithmetic, algebra, euclid and trigonometry, and be able to write English from dictation: the examinations were held at the RN College, Portsmouth.

War in Spain 1836-1839.
We must now turn to the operations that occurred during this period, in which portions of the Corps were gaining further laurels. First, there were the operations in Spain in support of the Christinos against the Carlists, who were trying to usurp the throne and oust the line that later was represented by King Alfonso, well known to the Corps of the present generation.

When King Ferdinand died in 1833 there were two claimants to the throne: his daughter Isabella, with the Queen Mother, whose supporters were known as Christinos; and his brother Don Carlos, who according to the old Salto Law was the male heir. For some reason France and England supported the Christinos, and Great Britain allowed a British Legion to be raised consisting of 2 Cavalry Regiments and 10 Infantry Battalions under Lieutenant General Sir de Lacy Evans. They also lent the assistance of the British Squadron under Lord John Hay, and sent a Battalion of Marines under Major John Owen, and a Field Battery of RMA under Captain R Steele RMA with some RA and RE detachments to assist them. The Squadron secured the possession of the north Coast of Spain, so that they could land where they pleased, but they could not go inland beyond the guns of the Fleet. The Battalion (the Detachment from Plymouth under Major Owen, KH, embarked on 27 April) was formed at Santander in May 1836, and on the 15th of that month 100 men from the Battalion and a part of the detachment of HMS *Castor* under 2nd Lieutenant Halliday were sent to garrison Portugalette at the mouth of the Bilbao river. They were here joined by another detachment under Lieutenant G C Langley. They fortified - and incidentally 'cleaned' - an old Spanish monastery and made a battery armed with two long 32 pdrs and two 9 pdrs.

On 5th May at San Sebastian the Legion, aided by the fire of HMS *Phoenix* and other ships, drove off the Carlists and captured some guns, but had later to fall back to San Sebastian. The RM Battalion was brought round to Portugalette and proceeded to Bilbao, but after a week was withdrawn and returned to San Sebastian.

On 27th May 1836, the Third Brigade of the Legion, supported by the Royal Marines, advanced across the river Urumea to the east of San Sebastian, covered by the fire of the steamers and gunboats, and the guns on the Fortifications together with the RMA Field Battery. They forded the river in three places and bivouacked on a hill near Ametza, whilst a feint was made to the westward by a detachment of Royal Marines in the *Salamander* and *Reyna* to draw off the Carlists.

At 3 am on 6th June the Carlists drove in the pickets of the Legion and attacked in force at 8 am. The Royal Marines were called up to support the Spanish, and the three leading companies deployed and opened fire. The Carlists fell back and the Marines returned to their bivouac, Captain Garmston and two Privates being wounded.

On 28th May, 70 men of the *Castor* under Lieutenants Halliday and Langley were taken to the eastward and landed at Passages, where they marched to the top of the hill, which commanded the harbour and the hills round. On the next day they were reinforced by Lieutenant Clapperton and 12 RMA; here they built a redoubt, under the direction of Lord John Hay, which was shaped like a ship and was given the name of the 'Ship'. It was armed with two 6 pdrs and two 3pdrs, also a 4 pdr and 20 pdr Rocket Tube. Seamen from the Fleet came up to help make and man the redoubt; also a company under a Captain from the Battalion. It was only about six miles across country to San Sebastian, so they could watch the fighting going on there.

About 2 am on the 9th June the little garrison of 300 was attacked by 400 Carlists. At daylight, when visibility was better, the Carlists were driven off: Lieutenant Langley was wounded in the leg and gained the Order of San Fernando.

The garrison of the 'Ship' was than augmented by two companies from the Marine Battalion, also the Marines of the *Pearl*, *Tweed*, and *Royalist*, besides 300 Spaniards and 4 Companies from the Legion.

On 10th July, 1836, the Battalion was concentrated at Passages, and on 11th July, General Evans with about 5000 men moved towards Fuentarabia; Lieutenants Halliday and Clapperton with 52 men being left to hold the 'Ship' redoubt. Brevet General Evans apparently wished to prevent reinforcements being thrown into Irun and Fuentarabia, so he seized the bridge near the Monastery of Guadaloupe. The bridge was secured, but the Carlists counter-attacked and two companies of Royal Marines were brought up to an embankment close by, and later two more were thrown into a convent near the bridge and held the Carlists in check till late in the afternoon: the Christinos then retired to the Isquibel hills and two other companies of Royal Marines checked an attempted sortie from Fuentarabia.

On the 12th the force fell back to Passages, the Royal Marines having lost two killed and 10 wounded. With the exception of a small Carlist attack on the outposts at Passages on 1st October, which was quickly driven off, the Royal Marines were undisturbed during the remainder of the year.

On 10th March 1837 the Legion and a body of Spanish troops, supported by the Royal Marines, made an attack on the Ametzegana position (a redoubt constructed by the Royal Marines at Passages). The Christinos, covered by the guns of San Antonio, made a feint on the villages of Lezo and Rentirea; part of the Legion stormed the Ametzegana position, and a Spanish regiment supported by the Marines captured Gabara. So, the whole position fell into the hands of the Christinos. The guns of the RMA drove out the enemy at San Marco, who put up an obstinate defence.

It was then decided to attack the Carlists who were in position near the village of Hernani, 7 or 8 miles from San Sebastian. On 15th March 1837, the RM Battalion advanced on the Hernani Road as far as the Windmill Battery in the Ayette Lines. The Carlists were strongly posted at the Venta of Oriamendi, and when at 2 pm the Marines advanced they came under artillery fire at about 800 yards, to which the guns of the RMA replied with considerable effect. The Christinos were making a flank attack round the Carlist right, and at 5 pm the Legion drove the Carlists from a line of heights which enabled the guns to be brought to close range of the Venta. At 7 pm the Venta was stormed and its defenders took refuge in the town of Hernani. By 8 am on 16th March the RM Battalion was in position on the Oriamendi plateau, about 1.5 miles from Hernani, covering the movement of the heavy artillery on the right of the Venta Hill; close here the RMA 24 pdr howitzers were posted under Lieutenant Savage RMA.

The RM Battalion was with the 5th Division of the Legion; in their front were the 2nd Spanish LI and the 6th Regiment of the Legion in extended order. When the advance began fire was opened by three Carlist guns on the left of the town, to which the Heavy Artillery Battery replied. At 11 am the Carlist Lancers made a charge which was met by the Lancers of the Legion and overthrown. Four Carlist Battalions then suddenly appeared on the left from a gorge and drove back the skirmishers. Lieutenant Colonel Owen at once deployed 5 Companies of the Royal Marines under cover of a natural breastwork, and opened a heavy independent fire which checked and drove off the Carlists, whilst a flank attack on the right was defeated by the RM as also an attempt to get on to the San Sebastian road in their rear which was met by a company placed en echelon by Colonel Owen. The Carlists in front of the Marines fell back towards Hernani, but on the British left they continued to gain ground, so that the RM Battalion was ordered back to cover the San Sebastian road and eventually halted in column, where they had first come under fire on the day before - ie about 800 yards in rear of the Oriamendi Plateau. By 3.20 pm the Christinos and the Legion were falling back in such disorder that the Carlists were only checked by the Royal Marines deploying into line and showing such a threatening front that the Carlists ceased their pursuit, and the Christinos were able to gain the shelter of the fortifications at San Sebastian: the Battalion marched in that night and was quartered in the Church of St. Francis. The Spaniards and

Legionaries had behaved so badly that it was only the steadiness of the Royal Marines that saved the day from disaster.

On 21st March, General Evans published the following order:

"The unshaken firmness of the British Royal Marines under Lieutenant Colonel Owen, in repulsing, as they did, four times their number, afforded you a noble example of the irresistible force of military organisation and discipline, which the Lieutenant General feels confident on future occasions you will be proud to emulate."

For the remainder of the year (1837) they were constantly moving about over the ground between Passages, Hernani, and San Sebastian. On 18th May, Irun was captured by assault and Fuenarabia surrendered the same day. The Battalion then proceeded to Passages.

On 8th July the Battalion paraded in honour of the funeral of King William IV, who had been a General of Marines and a good friend of the Corps. On the 9th they fired a feu-de-joie to celebrate the accession of Her Majesty Queen Victoria.

On 1st August Lieutenant White was captured by the Carlists by whom he was well treated, and shortly after exchanged.

In September 1837, the Battalion joined the Spanish Army and was present when Hernani was surrendered on 9th September.

On 24th November 1837, Lieutenant Colonel Parke took over command from Lieutenant Colonel Owen, who had been appointed DAG Royal Marines, and it remained in quarters at Passages, assisting the Christino troops when possible till the close of the war in 1840. Lieutenant Colonel Thompson Aslett relieved Colonel Parke in command on 5th February 1840 and brought the Battalion home on 2nd September 1840. Several Officers received Spanish decorations for their services in this campaign.

Lord John Hay, the Admiral, sent the following letter to the Commanding Officer:

"The Lords Commissioners of the Admiralty . . . have directed me to convey to yourself, the Officers, NCOs, and Privates of the Royal Marine Battalion under your command, Their Lordships' marked approbation of the zeal, gallantry, and good conduct which has been displayed by the Battalion on all occasions during the long course of service in which it has been employed on this coast." He also conveyed his own thanks for their steadiness, zeal, ability, etc.

HMS North Star. 16
August 1840.

Karachi.

On 17th January 1839, HMS *Wellesley*, flagship of the East Indian Squadron, embarked the 40th Regiment and sailed for Karachi. On 2nd February under cover of the guns of *Algerine* and *Constance* the boats landed the regiment on the beach to westward of the batteries, which however only fired one shot. As so many seamen were away in the boats, the Marines under Captain E B Ellis, were manning the ships' guns and opened fire until the fort was occupied. On the 4th the boats crews went to the encampment of the regiment on Marharo Hill and the regiment occupied the town. So, fell into British hands one of the most important harbours in India.

Persian Gulf and Aden.

The *Wellesley* then went up the Persian Gulf to Bushire, where the Persians were holding up the Residency. Captain Ellis and 50 Marines were sent in the boats on 25th March to a landing place 8 miles from the *Wellesley*, where the boats opened fire which was not returned, and the detachment landing quickly the Persians fled; 1 Sergeant and 2 Privates were wounded.

They then occupied the Residency and brought off the Admiral and Residency staff. Captain Ellis and 30 Royal Marines were left there until 30th March, when they brought off the Resident. Another small party of the Corps from HMS *Volage* and *Cruiser* were present with the force that captured Aden on 19th January 1839.

14 - Syria and China 1840 – 1843

These years are notable for two campaigns in which the Royal Marines took a prominent part.

In 1840 the numbers were 9000.

On 12th January the franking of letters was abolished, and in future all letters were to be prepaid, and accounts to be kept by the Office Adjutant: this coincided with the introduction of the Penny Post.

Libraries.
We see also the advance in the amenities of the barracks, as on 2nd June the Barrackmasters were called on to furnish estimates for fitting up Libraries for NCOs and Men of the Divisions.

By Order-in-Council 10 August 1840, Marine Cadets were admitted to the Royal Naval College at Portsmouth to train for Commissions. It was laid down that after a short course on board one of HM ships and at the RN College they were to receive Commissions as 2nd Lieutenants It was estimated that 12 cadets would be sufficient to fill vacancies. Their pay was to be the same as Mates RN, viz £65 per annum, and they messed with the Mates and Midshipmen.

The Royal Naval College had been established on 30 January 1816 and the staff allowed is interesting as showing subjects taught: Governor, 1st Lord of Admiralty; a Post-Captain and 2 Lieutenants; a Professor - Master of Classical History and Geography, with 3 Assistant Masters; a French master, a Fencing and Dancing master (abolished in 1827), Drawing master; 2 Sergeants Marine Artillery (with £30 extra pay); Matron and Housekeeper.

In 1841 the numbers voted were 10,500.

Arms.
On 8th February the Corps was rearmed with the new Percussion Muskets, an advance that was to prove its worth in China the following year.

On 8th May presumably in consequence of the War in China, one Lieutenant Colonel RM and a Lieutenant Colonel for the Artillery Companies were added to the Establishment; also, one Company to each Division besides an additional Company to the Artillery of the Marines. The number of Privates in each Company was raised to 107 from 97, and the three Artillery Companies had an addition of 1 Sergeant, 1 Corporal and 15 Gunners each, making the total Staff 41, Royal Marines 10,058, Artillery 405.

Syria 1840.[219]
Another portion of the Corps were occupied in operations at the Eastern end of the Mediterranean.

Mehemet Ali, the Pasha - or as we should say the Khedive of Egypt - had so improved the efficiency of his army and navy that in 1839 he thought himself strong enough to rebel against the Sultan of Turkey. Having invaded Syria, he defeated the Turkish Army at Nizib on the Euphrates. England, Austria and Prussia however took the part of the Sultan; France stood aloof. The bulk of the work fell on the British Mediterranean Squadron, commanded by Admiral Sir R Stopford, assisted by a small Austrian Squadron and a few Turkish ships. Russia and Prussia took no part. The British Squadron consisted of the *Princess Charlotte* (104), *Rodney* (92), three 84-gun ships, eight 74- and 80-gun ships, eight frigates and corvettes, three brigs and six steamers.

An ultimatum was sent to Mehemet Ali to withdraw his troops from Syria, to which he returned a defiant answer.

Colonel Sir C Smith RE was in command of the Allied troops but owing to ill-health the shore operations were taken charge of by the Commodore, Sir C Napier, RN.

At nightfall on 8th September 1840 the Royal Marines of the Fleet, under Lieutenant Colonel Walker, were embarked in the *Gorgon* (steamer), and 5000 Turkish troops in other steamers. At dawn on the 9th September the Fleet weighed and stood towards Beyrout Point, towards which the Egyptian troops concentrated and came under the fire of the Fleet. At noon the steamers with the troops were dispatched to D'Jounie Bay, at the other extremity of the Bay, followed as the wind changed by the *Castor, Pique, Dido, Wasp,* and *Powerful*. The steamers landed their troops, who were safely ashore unopposed by 4 pm

The heights covering the landing place were occupied by the Turks; one Company of Royal Marines was sent along the beach to the Southward and crossed the Dog River (only passable at its mouth) and reinforced a Turkish company that had landed there: a second Company RM with 300 Turks occupied a convent three or four miles from the main position on a hill covering the road to Baalbec via Antura. These formed the outposts behind which the Allies established an entrenched camp with 9 British field pieces, three 5.5 inch howitzers and 8 small Turkish guns. The force consisted of about 1500 Royal Marines, 200 Austrians, 5000 Turks, with a Company of Royal Artillery and some Royal Engineers. The Royal Marines on landing were formed into two Battalions of 8 Companies each, commanded respectively by Lieutenant Colonel Walker and Captain C Fegan. Reinforcements arrived from England shortly afterwards with orders that Lieutenant Colonel Walker was to command the Brigade, and Captains Whylock and Leonard the Battalions. The troops were occupied for some days in strengthening the position at D'Jounie, which was in communication with the Mountaineers of the Lebanon; there were also two roads from Baalbec to Antura which were held by two Turkish Battalions and 5 Companies of Royal Marines.

---

219 Authorities: "Life of Sir C. Napier"; "Britain's Sea Soldiers" (Field); "History of RM Forces" (Nicolas); MSS Letters, etc. (RMO).

HMS *Dido* and *Carysfort* were sent to Gebail to open communication with the Mountaineers of Mount Lebanon, but as the Albanian garrison was still holding the old Castle they did not meet with a very friendly reception.

The Commodore therefore reinforced them with HMS *Cyclops* on the 12th September, which brought four Companies of Marines (220) under Captain Robinson and 150 Mountaineers. Captain Robinson selected a beach to the South of the Castle as a landing place; under cover of the fire of the ships on the Castle and town, the troops were landed, but the fortifications could have defied the whole of the Mediterranean Fleet. They however advanced up the slope, which was intersected by stone walls and dotted with trees, covered by the fire of the boats carronades. The Royal Marines in extended order took every advantage of cover and there was no serious opposition until they arrived within 30 yards of the Castle. On crossing the last wall, a fierce musketry fire broke out, particularly from some loopholes on the ground level; the Marines returned the fire, though Captain Robinson saw there was nothing to be done, but to retire to the cover of the walls, as there were no openings, gates or embrasures by which they could get in. He therefore retired to the beach and by sunset they were on board their ships. The RM lost 5 men killed, Lieutenant C W Adair and 16 men wounded. Lieutenant Gifford RN, who had accompanied them, was also wounded. The Admiral approved of Captain Robinson's action, especially as during the night the Egyptian troops evacuated the Castle, which was occupied and became a very important post as it commanded the main road by which the enemy might advance from the north and was a convenient depot to convey arms to the Mountaineers.

On 22nd September, Commodore Sir C Napier with one Battalion RM and 2 Battalions of Turks reconnoitred the Egyptian camp near Marouba. They advanced by the road of Antura and Argentoum through very difficult country under a blazing sun. The RM Battalion was much knocked up and reached Argentoum with difficulty.

Sir C Napier with two Companies of Turks pressed on; about two hours before sunset they arrived in sight of the enemy entrenched camp, which occupied a very strong position. The Royal Marines were now ordered to move on and show themselves. That evening they returned to Argentoum and the next day returned to D'Jounie.

In order to attack the left of the Egyptian Army near the heights of Ormacaguan, on the evening of 23rd Sir C Napier sent General J Jockmus and three Battalions of Turks into the ravine of the Dog River, between the camp and Beyrout; another Turkish Battalion supported by the 2nd RM under Captain Fegan and the Austrian Rocket Battery were sent across the bridge at the river's mouth to occupy the heights on the Beyrout side and watch the road leading to Beyrout. The Turkish Battalion reached its position unobserved and debouched on the left of the Albanians who were afraid of being cut off from the road leading to Beharsof; they abandoned their entrenchments and gained the heights of Ormacaguan, occupying a strong position on the road on which General Jockmus was approaching. The latter attacked at once and drove the Albanians out with considerable loss so that the Royal Marines were not engaged.

Meanwhile the Fleet had not been idle. On 14th September it bombarded the town of Beyrout and on 20th made an attack on the town of Tortosa where large quantities of stores had been reported.

The Royal Marines of the *Benbow*, *Carysfort*, and *Zebra* were re-embarked for the operation. The *Carysfort* and *Zebra* anchored within 500 yards of the shore, opened fire and 50 RM under Lieutenant R Harrison embarked in the boats and a pioneer party of seamen in the cutter who made for the beach.

A wall ran the whole length of the beach in which only a bricked up archway had been breached. The cutter's party landed though fire was opened all along the wall when she grounded; the boats with the RM however grounded about 30 yards out on the rocks and came under a heavy fire, which they returned though most of their ammunition was ruined by the water. Fourteen men were transferred to the cutter and got ashore to help the seamen who, after breaking open some stores, were compelled to retreat to the cutter. The boats were then recalled with a loss of 1 seaman and 3 Marines killed, 11 seamen and 8 Marines wounded. The losses would have been heavier but for the covering fire of the *Carysfort* and *Zebra*.

Caiffa.
HMS *Castor*, *Pique*, and a Turkish frigate bombarded Caiffa, and a landing party destroyed the guns and ramparts; a castle with 5 guns commanding the rear of the town, was also destroyed by the fire of the ships, and a landing party of Royal Marines and seamen soon dismantled it, although a large Egyptian force was close by.

Tyre.
Tyre, occupied by 5000 Egyptian troops, was next attacked by HMS *Castor* and *Pique*, on 24th September. Fire was opened by the ships and at daylight seamen and Marines were landed and took possession of the town; here they levelled large sandbanks which had been thrown up by the Egyptians to cover the town; they also carried off the stores of grain. The guard boats were kept manned, because they were in full sight of 15,000 Egyptian troops only two miles away.

Sidon.
Sidon was the next place to be attacked. It stands on an eminence rising somewhat abruptly from the sea; high walls enclosed the three landward sides; the houses and barracks along the beach formed practically a line of fortifications toward the sea; from the Barracks a bridge ran out to a castle standing in the sea. Another large castle stood in the centre of the town, and there was another small fort on the south side, crowning a small but steep ascent from the level ground outside. The principal gate, which was well defended, was on the north side near the beach.

The ships told off were the *Thunderer* (84), *Guerriera* (Austrian), *Wasp* (18), and *Gulsefulde* (Turkish); also the *Gorgon* and *Cyclops* steamers. The *Cyclops* carried a Battalion of Turks 500 strong, the *Gorgon* six Companies of the 1st RM and six Companies of Turks under Captain Morrison RM.

The *Hydra* arrived with Walker Bey, the Turkish Admiral, and the *Stromboli* with 284 Royal Marines under Captain Whylock RM. A summons to surrender was peremptorily refused; the plan was for Captain Morrison's Battalion to land on the beach to the north of the town; Captain Whylock's detachment, with 100 Austrian Marines under Prince Frederick, to land to the South-East, whilst the Turks were to capture the outlying castle and bridge. The heavy guns of the *Gorgon* opened on the barracks and shore end of the bridge, whilst the guns of the larger ships were directed at the houses and walls of the town. After half an hour's bombardment, the sea castle was breached, and the Turks effected a lodgement, but the enemy still held the barracks though the walls had been swept away. Captain Whylock's detachment and the Austrians on landing advanced on the small fort on the South side, and with great skill and gallantry forced their way into the fort and houses round with the loss of Lieutenant C F Hoskin RM killed and several men wounded. (Hoskin held the Order of San Fernando for operations in Spain.) Having secured the fort, they were ordered to fight their way to the main citadel in the centre of the town. The Turks, headed by Walker Bey and two British Naval Officers, forced their way over the bridge into the Barracks, whilst the RM Battalion under Captain Morrison which had landed on the north side broke into the North Gate. The Allies, advancing into the centre of the town from all directions, encountered a large house near the Barracks, which made a strong resistance; at last headed by Hassan Bey, the Egyptian Commander, the garrison made a sortie, which was met by the Royal Marines, and Hassan Bey refusing to surrender, was killed. The whole garrison of 3000 men were killed, wounded or captured, although the landing force was only half their numbers. The Governor, Suleiman Pasha, resisted to the last; he was killed and his house destroyed by the Royal Marines.

Lieutenant A Anderson (afterwards Commandant at Plymouth) planted the British flag on the walls of Sidon and one of the enemy standards was captured by Corporal John Symons RM. The Royal Marines remained here until 8th October, when they returned to their ships.

Acre.
The whole coast except Acre had now fallen. The Allied Commanders were doubtful of attacking Acre, as the season was so far advanced, but the British Government decided that the attack should be made. On receipt of the instructions, Admiral Sir R Stopford decided to take the risk. On 31st October, 13 British, 2 Austrian, 1 Turkish, and 1 Arabian men-of-war left Beyrout for Acre, anchoring about two miles from the town on 2nd November. Surveys were made to enable the ships to take up their bombarding positions, and in spite of some misunderstandings the bombardment commenced at 2 pm the following day (3 November) and continued till past 4 pm, when the principal magazine was blown up with disastrous results for the enemy, as two regiments were annihilated. After a pause the bombardment was resumed and continued until sunset, by which time only about 20 of the enemy guns were still in action, when the Admiral made the signal to cease fire. During the night the Egyptian troops evacuated the place, after plundering the inhabitants.

On the 4th November, all the troops and Marines under Colonel Sir C Smith, who had now resumed command, were landed and occupied the place; 2000 of the enemy were made prisoners. Two days later there was a second explosion, which caused some casualties to the Royal Marines.

This terminated the operations of the Allies: 250 RM under Lieutenant Colonel Walker were left in garrison and suffered severely from fever. Colonel Walker died on 8th December, and was succeeded by Lieutenant Colonel John McCallum, who had been with the operations since 10th October and remained in command until the garrison was withdrawn on 10th June 1841.

A return in the Records, dated 'Marmarice Bay, March 1841', shows the effectives of the Royal Marines who were lately on the Coast of Syria, but were now supernumeraries in the Fleet (ie in garrison at Acre) as 1 Lieutenant Colonel, 6 Captains, 3 Subalterns, 1 Acting-Adjutant, 2 Staff Sergeants, 14 Sergeants, 11 Corporals, 4 Drummers, 160 Privates Royal Marines. 1 Captain, 1 Lieutenant, 3 Sergeants, 3 Corporals, 2 Drummers and 47 Gunners, RMA.

The officers were: RMA. - Captain Shute, Lieutenant Parke. Royal Marines – Lieutenant Colonel McCallum, Captains Baker, Brown, Edwards, Brevet Major Whylock, Leonard, Childs. Lieutenants Travers, Suther, Rich, Anderson, and the following were in hospital - Captains Cater and Downman, Lieutenants Land, Miller and Aslett.

China War 1840-43.[220]

This war is of peculiar interest to the Royal Marines, as they appear to have filled most of the roles for which the Corps exists: sometimes landing to secure and hold forts etc., battered down by the Fleet; sometimes to storm places under cover of the ships' fire; at others to assist and reinforce the Army in its operations. The harmonious working of the Corps and its officers throughout these varied operations is very noticeable.

War with China had been pending since 1839. Continued commercial disputes, the question of the opium traffic, the Chinese custom of insisting on all foreigners kow-towing to their officials - an indignity that could not be borne; these were all causes of friction, but the first overt act of war was the attack on 3rd November, 1839, by a fleet of junks on British merchant shipping in Macao Roads; HMS *Volage* (26) and *Hyacinth* (sloop) sank three of the junks and drove the remainder ashore. No serious action was taken until the summer of 1840, when an expedition under Commodore J G Bremer with 15 men-of-war (*Wellesley* (74), the frigates *Amoy* and *Alligator*, with small craft and 4 steamers) went to Chusan, leaving some ships at the mouth of the Canton River to protect the British at Canton.

Chusan.

The Commodore summoned the Chinese to surrender the town of Tinghae, where the Chinese had mounted every gun possible on the Temple Hill. At 2 pm on 4th July 1840, as no reply had been received to their overtures, HMS *Wellesley* opened fire which was returned by the Chinese, but they very soon bolted. The right wing of the 18th Royal Irish, reinforced by 121 Royal Marines (2 Captains, 5 Lieutenants, 114 NCOs and Men) under Captain Ellis (with Captain McArthur, Lieutenants E Ussher, F J White, J Urquhart, Priest, and Hayes Marriott) followed by detachments

---

220 Authorities: Log of HMS *Nemesis*; Life of Sir Hugh Gough; Life of Sir S. B. Ellis, RM; original letters, Reports, etc.

of the 26th and 49th Regiments with Madras Artillery and Sappers landed, and by 3 pm the British ensign was hoisted on the Temple Hill. By daylight of the 6th, eight 9 pdrs, two mortars and two howitzers were in position against the city. However, the Chinese had evacuated it during the night. Chusan Island was occupied, but unfortunately very little impression was made on the Chinese, particularly on the Imperial Government at Peking. The British Superintendent of Trade, or as we should say the Political Officer, seems to have been a pretty hopeless sort of person and hampered the operations very much. Admiral Elliot went up to the Pei-Ho and the remainder of the Fleet blockaded Canton, Amoy, and Ningpo.

Macao.
The British residents at Macao, near Canton, having appealed to the British Admiral for assistance, the Royal Marines of HMS *Druid*, *Larne*, and *Hyacinth* (about 100, under Lieutenants Maxwell and Pickard) landed on 19th August 1840, with some seamen manning a field piece, covered by the *Larne* and *Hyacinth*. The ships opened fire on one of the principal batteries and Chinese encampment with 10 guns, and silenced them in twenty minutes; the Royal Marines advanced to the top of the hill where they came under heavy fire and were counterattacked by a strong body of infantry, who were checked by a volley and retreated leaving a number of killed and wounded; Lieutenant Maxwell then ordered the RM to return to the beach to await the arrival of Captain Mee and the Bengal Native Volunteers, who landed about an hour later. This officer, with the Royal Marines in the centre, the Bengalis on the right, and seamen on either flank, advanced on the fort which was entered without opposition, the Chinese retiring to the war junks and to the old Portuguese battery. After a short bombardment the Chinese abandoned their guns and fled; the guns were spiked, and the magazines destroyed.

The Chinese now took refuge in negotiations. The sickness was very great in Chusan in October 1840, so that no troops were available for any serious attempt to be made on the Canton Forts. An old Return of the number of sick at Chusan has a note against the regiment with the largest number of sick, "a temperance regiment".

On 30th November the Government, realising that they were committed to a serious campaign, offered the command of the troops to General Sir Hugh Gough in India, but he did not arrive on the scene until 2nd March 1841.

Bogue Forts.
At the beginning of the year (1841) the Naval C-in-C determined to attack the Forts on the islands defending the Bocca Tigris, i.e. the Channel connecting the outer and main defences of the Canton River, now known as the Bogue Forts.

On the 7th January 1841, the outer forts were captured. For this purpose a force consisting of a detachment of Royal Artillery, with one 24 pdr howitzer and two 6 pdr field guns with seamen crews; detachments of the 28th and 49th Regiments, 37th Madras Native Infantry (NI), detachment of Bengal Volunteers, and a Royal Marine Battalion from the Fleet under Captain Ellis RM (3 Captains, 9 Subalterns, 17 Sergeants., 11 Corporals, 458 Privates and 8 Privates of the 18th Royal Irish) in all about 1400 men under Major Pratt, 26th Regiment, landed at 8 am, 7th January, in a small sandy bay, two miles below Chuenpee Point.

Chuenpee Point is a projecting headland on the left bank of the river (on north side of the Bocca Tigris). It is a high peak about one and a quarter miles wide; on either side is a sandy beach off which there are good anchorages. On top of the hill are a Watch Tower and the Upper Fort; at the bottom a strong battery and other works recently strengthened; round the rear was a line of entrenchments with mud batteries. Behind the hill was an opening northwards to Ansons Bay, with another small battery and a square barrack. The river at this point is three miles wide.

Captain Ellis led the advanced guard with two companies Royal Marines, supported by the 26th and 49th, and followed by a column composed of the RM Battalion, 37th Madras NI, and the Bengalis. After marching about one and a half miles they came to the edge of a hill crowned with an upper fort and a strong entrenchment with a deep ditch and breastwork connecting with the Upper Fort. The position was flanked by field batteries and deep trenches garrisoned by a strong force of Chinese.

The British guns came into action, as did HMS *Queen* and *Nemesis*, who opened fire on the Upper Fort at 10 am and soon silenced it. The Advanced Guard crossed the shoulder of the hill on the right, driving the Chinese before them, and descended into the valley, where the guns of the *Queen* and *Nemesis* again assisted them: they then captured a field battery and moved against a large force occupying the crest of a wooded hill in front. Two companies of the 37th Madras NI had gone round on their right and drove off the Chinese with much loss. The Advanced Guard, having cleared the wooded hill, Nos 3 and 4 Companies under Captain J Whitcomb passed the valley by the left, and forced an entry into the breastwork and up to the Upper Fort. The British ensign was hoisted by Private Knight. No. 8 Company, Captain Gillespie, crossing on the left, caught the garrison retreating from the Upper Fort. Lieutenant F S White, 2 Sergeants and 7 Marines were wounded out of a total loss of 30.

This success led to a truce, and negotiations took place between the Imperial Commissioner Keshen and the British Envoy, Captain Elliot. The British demands were (i) the cession of Hong-Kong; (ii) Indemnity of 6,000,000 dollars; (iii) Direct official intercourse; and (iv) Re-opening of Trade at Canton.

On 21st January the Forts were handed back to the Chinese and on 26th HMS *Nemesis* and *Madagascar* went up to the Pagoda at the Second Bar where the conference was held. A Guard of Honour under Captain Ellis (*Wellesley*), Lieutenants Maxwell (*Druid*) and Stransham (*Calliope*) with 100 picked Royal Marines from *Wellesley*, *Druid*, and *Calliope* was provided and excited great admiration and wonder among the Chinese.

The British demands were presented on 27th, and on the 28th the Chinese envoy came to pay his respects and the *Nemesis* and *Madagascar* returned down the river.

By 2nd February no ratification of the agreement had been received, and on 11th February HMS *Nemesis* went up the river again to see about the compliance with the terms, on which day the Chinese envoys received an order from Peking to resist the demands. Hong-Kong was however taken possession of on 26th February 1841, and the British had decided to renew hostilities and attack the Bogue Forts on 25th February.

Anunghoy.
These forts were still very powerful. On the East side of the river about 45 miles from Chuenpee is Anunghoy; it is a high hill on an island, the fortifications are the most important at the Bogue; between Chuenpee and Anunghoy is Anson's Bay. The works on Anunghoy were two very strong heavy batteries built of granite connected by a temporary work with a semicircular wall round each fort. There were several strong entrenchments to the South of this, and the ridges of the hills which were armed with guns, led up to a camp calculated to hold 1200 men. On the north side there was a modern work mounting 60 heavy guns, and there were 150 yards of rocky beach between the end of this battery and the Northern circular battery which was armed with 40 guns. These works were protected by a high wall with steps for musketry and in the entrenchments were barracks and magazines.

The breadth of the river at Anunghoy is two miles; in the middle of the river are two rocky islands known as North and South Wang-Tong and a smaller rock; the Channel towards Anunghoy is generally known as the Bocca Tigris or Hogue; the passage to the Westward was barely known but was used by some ships in the attack on North Wang-Tong. The true Bogue is only ¾ of a mile wide and ships have to hug the Anunghoy shore. On the East side of the North Wang-Tong Island was a battery with a double tier of guns to defend the passage of the river on that side, and to cover the rafts of floating timber moored across the river supporting a chain to form an obstruction - one end on South Wang-Tong, the other on Anunghoy. On the West side of the island was a battery of 40 guns, flanked by another with 17. On the western side of the Channel on Ty-Cock-Tow Island was a battery of 22 guns and another field work with 17 guns protecting another encampment for 15,000 to 20,000 men. South Wang-Tong was not occupied; on the night of 24/25th February the British seized it and threw up a work for two 8" iron and one 24 pdr Brass Howitzers, and by daylight on 26th Captain Knowles RA, opened fire on North Wang-Tong.

The *Wellesley* (74) and *Druid* (42) attacked the South-West batteries of Wang-Tong; Admiral Sir F Senhouse, with *Blenheim* (74), *Melville* (74), *Queen* and a Rocket Boat, attacked the Batteries on Anunghoy; the frigates *Calliope*, *Semarang*, *Herald*, *Alligator*, *Sulphur* and *Modeste* fired on the Batteries on the North and North-West of Wang-Tong and those facing Anunghoy. The *Nemesis* and *Madagascar* were told off to land the troops.

The troops under Major Fratt, 26th Regiment, were landed and gained North Wang-Tong without loss, 1300 Chinese being captured.

As soon as the batteries on Anunghoy were silenced by the *Blenheim* and *Melville*, their Marines under Captains Whitcomb and Gillespie with a party of seamen all under the Naval C-in-C landed at the Southern battery, and by 1 pm the Chinese were driven off and the British flag was flying along the whole chain of works. The battery commanding the passage on the Western side of the Wang-Tong Islands was occupied by a party of Royal Marines from HMS *Wellesley*. Admiral Kwan, the Chinese commander, was killed by the Royal Marines at the gate of Anunghoy.

The next day it was found that the Wampoa reach was blocked by forts, camps, and an old British ship called the *Cambridge* mounting 34 guns. The light ships having been sent up to clear the way (*Sulphur, Calliope, Modeste, Hound, Madagascar* and *Nemesis*) the *Madagascar* and *Nemesis* came into action first and at 3 pm the remainder of the squadron arrived. At 3 pm Lieutenant Stransham[221] (*Calliope*) and the Royal Marines landed to storm the works with the seamen under Captain Herbert RN. The Royal Marines carried the gate nearest the landing place and by 4 pm the fort was in their possession. A small party of seamen got off in a boat and captured the *Cambridge*, which was set on fire and blown up. The ships pushed on to reconnoitre, and on 28th all the Royal Marines, to the number of 593, were embarked in the steamers to go up to the attack of the last of the nine Hogue Forts - Howqua's Fort, which was a square battery mounting 30 guns, on the right bank of the river and was at the mouth of a creek running into the main river. In front of it was a long low island dividing the river into two branches and on the Eastern point of the island was a fort with 35 guns; there were well secured rafts forming a bridge extending to both sides of the river, and junks filled with stones had been sunk in the channels.

Little or no attempt was made to hold Howqua's Fort. On 5th March the Royal Marines of *Wellesley, Druid, Blenheim* and *Melville* landed at the Joss House opposite it on the other side of Junk River and strengthened the latter against attack; as the ships stood in to cover them, the Chinese, having fired all their guns, fled.

Macao.
The Chinese reopened negotiations and the troops having re-embarked, the ships dropped down to Wang-Tong. On 13th March the Macao Passage Fort mounting 22 guns, on an islet in the river, having refused to surrender, was bombarded by the *Modeste* and *Madagascar*, and then stormed by the Royal Marines under Lieutenant Stransham. Captain Herbert RN, being in charge of the operations Lieutenant Stransham was left in charge of the Fort which was a valuable point d'appui for further operations.

Above it is the Bird's Nest Fort on Honan Island, where the river was obstructed by rafts well moored; there were also a number of war junks at the point of junction with the Canton River opposite Shameen. On 17th March a flag of truce having been fired on by the Chinese, the ships opened fire and a rocket from the *Nemesis* set Bird's Nest Fort on fire. Captain Herbert brought up a flotilla of 4 Divisions of boats, embarked 6 Officers and 227 Men from the garrison of Macao Fort and on 18th March attacked the whole of the works which defended the river front of

---

221 Inspector General of the Corps from 1862 to 1867, and created GCB in 1887.

Canton. Some hours operations ashore and afloat resulted in great destruction of Chinese junks and shipping. At 11.30 am the *Nemesis* attacked the end forts, the Chinese returned the fire; the *Modeste* and *Madagascar* joined in and soon silenced the Chinese guns. The boats crews mastered the forts and another field work mounting 20 guns. The *Stanley* and *Algerine* got through the rafts and carried another battery and also every junk as the boats arrived. The captures were 113 guns, 6 gunboats and 6 mandarin boats. The *Nemesis* bombarded, and the boats captured Shameen Fort with 10 guns. The *Madagascar* captured Dutch Folly, a circular fort in centre of the river, opposite the city mounting 25 guns; whilst the boats captured another battery close to the Naval Arsenal and recaptured the English Factory.

On 9th April, Captain Ellis and 80 Royal Marines landed to garrison Tay-Wong-Koo (? Dutch Folly Fort) a circular fort with 20 embrasures on a small island in centre of river commanding the branch of the river leading to Macao Fort and within three miles of Canton. Nothing material occurred, but the Chinese were restless, and batteries were erected on the opposite bank of the river and their forces increased from day to day to about 50,000.[222]

Canton.
The capture of the Bogue Forts was now complete, and the way was open to Canton. The Political Officer was however very vacillating and difficult to deal with; by this time General Sir Hugh Gough had taken over the command of the troops and Admiral Sir F Senhouse had replaced Commodore Bremer in command of the Fleet. Operations were therefore suspended until May.

A plot was then discovered to murder the British merchants in Canton, and a proclamation was issued on 20th May. On 21st May the foreigners were warned to leave Canton by the British Envoy and left for Macao; the factories were deserted, and the Marines withdrawn, and that night by means of fire junks the Chinese attempted to burn the *Modeste*, *Pylades*, *Algerine*, *Nemesis*, etc. "Fortunately, that day I had been directed by Captain Herbert of HMS *Calliope* commanding the Advanced Squadron, to detach from the garrison 1 NCO and 12 men to the latter for her protection and accordingly sent them with a large supply of ammunition and they arrived in time to be of the utmost use."[223] No attempt was made on the Fort.

Sir H Gough and the available troops were now making their way up the river. On 21st the Royal Marines evacuated the Fort and proceeded up the river where they were formed into a battalion and joined Sir H Gough's forces.[224]

A second attempt by fire ships was defeated on 23rd and a battery above the town opened on the ships, but was silenced by the *Calliope*, and a party landed and destroyed the fortifications. HMS *Nemesis* also discovered 43 war junks and 32 fire rafts and destroyed them; whilst the mob pillaged the factories.

---
222 Captain Ellis' Report.
223 Captain Ellis' Report.
224 See Captain Ellis' Report later.

A reconnaissance was made by the Naval and Military C-in-C's on 23rd, and Tsing-poo - 4 miles to West of Canton - was selected as the place for landing; here a creek runs up to the base of the hills commanding Canton on the North-West. The foreign factories were in the Western suburbs and there were also suburbs on the East and South sides of the town.

A wall running from East to West divides the old Northern part from the new Southern part of the city. Outside at the South-East corner was a fort called French Folly. Westward almost in centre was the Dutch Folly; both forts commanded the Arsenal. On Northern hills on the high ground were 4 strong forts with 42 guns which were directly above the city, from which they were separated by a ravine.

The Naval Forces consisted of *Blenheim*, *Wellesley* (Flag), *Blonde*, *Calliope*, *Sulphur*, *Hyacinth*, *Nimrod*, *Modeste*, *Pylades*, *Cruiser*, *Algerine*, *Conway*, *Herald*, *Alligator* and the steamers *Nemesis* and *Atalanta*. The Naval personnel amounted to about 3200, of which about 1000 were available for landing.

At 2 pm On 24th May 1841, the troops began to land, with two days cooked provisions. Troops were in light marching order; men's canteens were filled with water and they carried a spare pair of shoes and socks per man. The sappers carried scaling ladders. They were formed as follows:

Right Column - Major Pratt
                26th Regiment - 317
                Madras Artillery - 21 with one 6 pdr and one 5.5" Howitzer, RE
Their duty was to attack and hold the Foreign Factories.

Left Column -   Under Sir Hugh Gough
1st Brigade -   Major General Burrell
                18th R Irish - 535 - Colonel Adams.
                Royal Marines[225] - 377 - Captain Ellis

---

226   The Field State of the Royal Marines was:
     Wellesley   Capt Ellis
                      Lts. White and Ussher. 127 NCOs and Men.
     Blenheim   Capt Whitcomb
                      Lts Whiting and Farmar 116 NCOs and Men
     Blonde   2Lt Polkinghorne 33 NCOs and Men
     Druid   Lt Maxwell 3 NCOs and Men
     Calliope   Lt Stransham (Adjt) 3 NCOs and Men
     Modeste   12 NCOs and Men
     Columbine 15 NCOs and Men
     Pyles   28 NCOs and Men
     Hyacinth   18 NCOs and Men
     Cruiser   16 NCOs and Men
     Nimrod   17 NCOs and Men
                      370
Sergeant-Major - Sgt. Mackay. QMS - Sgt. Chance.

2nd Brigade -   Captain Bouchier RN
                1st RN Battalion - Captain Maitland (*Wellesley*)
                2nd RN Battalion - Commander Barlow (*Nimrod*) about 471
                3rd Brigade
                Royal Artillery - 38
                Madras Artillery - 241
                Madras Sappers – 150

4th Brigade -   Lieutenant Colonel Morris
                49th Regiment - 321
                37th Madras NI - 240

Bengal Native Volunteers – 80

Guns: 4x12-pdrs; 4x9-pdrs; 4x6-pdrs; 3x5.5" mortars; 152x32-pdr rockets

The duty of the left column was to assault the heights above the city.

The Right Column landed about 5 pm on 24th, and easily occupied the factories.

The Left Column, embarked in 80 boats, was towed by the *Nemesis* for about 5 miles; HMS *Sulphur* was covering the landing place, but it was dark on their arrival and no opposition was offered.

General Gough landed first with the 49th. Picquets were posted and during the night the disembarkation continued and by early morning of 25th all was ready for the attack.[226]

The heights were about 3.5 miles off; the ground was undulating and covered with rice fields. The advance was unopposed till near the forts; four forts were near the North-West corner of the City Wall; others were on higher ground and near the centre of the North Wall. The progress of the Artillery was slow, but by 8 o'clock two heavy guns and the rockets had arrived and bombarded the forts for an hour. The troops were in echelon of columns; the 4th Brigade were to carry a hill on left of the nearest of the two most Eastern Forts; the 1st Brigade co-operating by attacking a hill, which flanked the approach to the fort on which the 49th were moving to cut off communication between the two forts. The Naval Brigade advanced on the two Western forts. As the attack was commencing, and the RM Battalion and the Royal Irish were ascending the heights in Reserve, the C-in-C was informed that the enemy were in his rear and had already attacked the shipping and boats. The RM Battalion was ordered to halt and to send a strong picquet to protect the rear and disperse the enemy. Captain Whitcomb with Nos 7 and 8 Companies was sent with No 6 in support, and he fell in with and dispersed several large bodies of the enemy, but "to pursue was useless".

---

226 For the conditions of the Marines' landing see Captain Ellis' Report later.

At 9.30 am the general advance began under cover of the artillery fire, but under heavy fire from the forts and City Wall and by a very difficult road. The 49th captured the two Eastern Forts, and the Naval Brigade under heavy fire, the two Western. Within half an hour all the forts were in British hands.

Heavy fire from the City Wall and 400 men entrenched on rising ground North-East of the Wall harassed the British left. In the afternoon the 49th were sent to dislodge them, and cleared them off, but later the Chinese came on again. The only approach to their cantonment was along a narrow causeway exposed to fire in rear from the walls of the city; the 49th and 18th and one Company of Royal Marines under General Burrell were detailed to clear it. The severest loss of the day occurred in crossing the causeway, but the enemy were driven out, their camps and magazines being destroyed. The rest of the day was spent in reconnaissance because the Artillery had to be brought up before assaulting the city. Meanwhile the Dutch Folly Fort was occupied, and the French Folly carried and occupied on the morning of 26th.

That night the RM Battalion bivouacked in and around a large building at the foot of the heights with strong picquets out, and next day preparations were made to assault the walls. An attack on the landing place was driven off by the baggage guards on 26th. On the morning of the 26th the Chinese hoisted the white flag, but nothing came of it. Ammunition was got up, and on 27th the Royal Marines marched at daylight to form a junction with the Seaman Brigade to co-operate with them in storming the walls near the large Pagoda, but the Political Envoy had agreed to a suspension of hostilities on payment of the 6,000,000 dollars; but as usual the Politicals had made a mess of it and given away all the advantages gained. On May 29th only 2,000,000 dollars were paid.

The Battalion of Marines returned to their former position with four companies on picquet duty; but 150 of the 26th Regiment having arrived, the GOC ordered the Marines to occupy a large Joss House near the North Gate, which with two large houses formed very comfortable quarters.

By the terms the Tartar troops were to evacuate the City, but on 30th a large body of Chinese irregulars were gathering four miles in rear of the British and with increasing numbers threatening to attack the camp. The British were divided into two forces - one to hold the Camp under General Burrell, one to attack under General Gough consisting of a wing of 26th, five Companies of 49th and 37th Madras NI. A Reserve, ready to return and meet any advance from the town, consisted of the Royal Marines and the Bengal Native Volunteers.

There were about 4000 Chinese behind an embankment which was carried by 26th and the Madras NI, who destroyed the post and magazines. They advanced about 5 miles, when the GOC considering that the force was too large for the purpose, sent back the 49th and Royal Marines to camp. General Gough watched the enemy for two hours and as their numbers increased to 6000 or 7000 he opened fire with rockets and two charges were made by the 26th and the Native Infantry, which drove them back.

The heat was very great and the British suffered heavily from it, the RM had 8 men down with sunstroke, and then a rainstorm came on, which made the firelocks useless; the enemy retreated and Sir Hugh's force returned to camp. Captain Duff, commanding the 37th Madras NI had detached a Company under Lieutenant Hadfield to open communication with the 26th on his left, when the retirement took place. This Company was accidentally left behind, and their absence was not discovered till after the return to camp. Captain Duff was sent with two Companies of the 49th and one of the Royal Marines, mostly from the *Blenheim* and the *Blonde*, under Lieutenant Whiting, who had been re-armed with percussion muskets which were unaffected by the wet. They found the native Company, which had formed square and was defending itself as well as it could because its firelocks were useless; two or three volleys from the Royal Marines dispersed the enemy and the Company was brought safely to camp.

Captain Ellis' report to the Admiral is appended and gives a graphic description of the formation of the Battalion - not an example to be followed - and a description of the above incident.

HMS Wellesley.
Anunghoy.
6th June, 1841.

Sir,
I have the honour to report to you that the Battalion of Royal Marines under my command amounting to 370 men, and formed from part of the Squadron under your Command employed in China, viz; Wellesley's detachment, Blenheim's, part of Blonde's, Modeste's, Pylades', Hyacinth's, Nimrod's, Cruiser's and Columbine's landed in cooperation with other Forces of Her Majesty and HEICs Service in the successful and gallant advance, and the capture of the Heights and Forts in front of Canton on the 25th ultimo, and that altho' under the very great disadvantage of having to be formed as they landed into eight companies of 22 files each, and to be proved and officered, many of the men meeting for the first time, unaccustomed to act together, the zeal of all got everything into fair order, and they advanced with steadiness and regularity to the attack. First-Lieutenant Maxwell of the Druid commanded the first company, and cooperated with HM 18th Regiment Royal Irish, in storming the enemy's entrenched camp the evening after the attack: Lieutenant White the 2nd, Lieutenant Polkinghorne the 3rd, Lieutenant Ussher the 4th (for one day only, as he fell sick and returned the next), Colour Sergeant Nicholls commanded the 5th, Colour Sergeant F Fairweather the 6th, Lieutenant Farmer the 7th, Lieutenant Whiting the 8th. Captain Whitcomb assisted as Field Officer and from whom, throughout the whole of the arduous duties the Battalion had to perform, I received at all times and occasions the most cheerful, able, and ready aid; Lieutenant Stransham of the Calliope executed the laborious duties of Adjutant with alacrity, zeal, and ability, and to the officers in command of companies generally I was much indebted for the prompt execution of, and attention to, the orders they from time to time received; to Lieutenant Whiting of the Blenheim, an active and vigilant young officer, my thanks are especially due, in an affair of the 30th ultimo between a large body of armed peasantry, and HM 26th Regiment and the 37th NI, a company of the latter, on the return to quarters was missing, and in consequence, at about sunset, I was directed by the Major General to detach a

Company in search of it - the 49th had two out for the same object. I selected the 8th (Blenheim's) - being armed with percussion muskets - for this important duty, and Lieutenant Whiting to command them. He was accompanied by Captain Duff of the 37th NI. After a long and tedious march of 8 miles through paddy fields filled with water, they succeeded in reaching this company drawn up in square on a rising ground, surrounded by the enemy, then actively engaged in getting up a field gun for their destruction. Lieutenant Whiting announced his proximity to the 37th NI by firing a musket and directing his company to cheer loudly; the effect was instantaneous and beneficial; the Chinese, from the darkness, not knowing the amount of force, so unexpectedly near, separated a little and the 37th retreated; and Lieutenant Whiting, watching his opportunity, judiciously fired a volley amongst them, whereby the two companies were enabled to return to their respective Corps unmolested: the previous very heavy rain to which the 37th Company was exposed had wetted their firelocks and rendered them useless for the time.

The following morning in a letter I had the honour to receive from Sir Hugh Gough on the subject he thus expressed himself: "Many thanks to the officer and party who were out last night.

I shall give out an order on the subject." I am most happy to add that every praise is due to the Non-Commissioned Officers, Drummers, Rank and File of the Royal Marine Battalion engaged in this short and brilliant campaign for the steadiness, zeal, order, and sobriety invariably displayed by them through all the operations, which it is most gratifying to me, their Commanding Officer, to have the honour to make known to you. The casualties are happily but few: one corporal and one private dangerously wounded, four privates slightly. The 1st and 2nd Instant all the men composing the Battalion had returned to their respective ships.

I have the honour to remain,
Sir,
Your obedient servant,
(Signed) S. B. Ellis
Captain, Royal Marines.
Commanding Officer

On 27th May 1841, the GOC published the following General Order.

Fort Yang-gang-Tai.

"Major General Sir H. Gough, from his heart, congratulates the troops of every arm upon their steadiness under fire and their brilliant conduct in the attack of the heights and the capture of the several forts above Canton and of the entrenched camp under cover of the City Wall on 25th instant. The expression of the General's best thanks were as fully merited and as sincerely accorded to the Naval Battalions and the Royal Marines who have nobly upheld the high character of their profession."

On the 1st June the heights above Canton were evacuated and the troops re-embarked. The following extract from Orders refers to the Royal Marines.

"No. 2. The Royal Marines and Brigade of Seamen will not move until a preconcerted signal be given, when the whole of the remaining force will evacuate the forts at the same moment and move down into the plain and form in rear of the Artillery in the following order:

Royal Marines, Brigade of Seamen, 49th Regiment 18th Royal Irish."

The detachments returned to their ships. The RM casualties had been two severely wounded and four slightly wounded.

On 6th June the General expressed his thanks again to the 18th Royal Irish and to Captain Ellis RM.

On 1st June whilst the force was withdrawing the detachments of the *Calliope*, *Conway*, *Alligator*, *Herald*, and *Algerine*, about 45 men under Lieutenants Urquhart, Hewett and Hayes Marriott were employed in the boats of the Advanced Squadron in the destruction of the enemy works including French Folly Fort and along the banks of the river.

Captains Ellis[227] and Whitcomb were given Brevet Majorities. For the next months there was inaction, whilst the politicals tried to negotiate with very little result. There was a great deal of sickness, ague and dysentery, from which the Navy suffered more than the Army, and the C-in-C, Sir F Senhouse, died.

In spite of the Treaty, the Chinese authorities failed to carry out the provisions, and obstacles to trade were thrown in the way; so that at last, in August, orders were issued for a renewal of hostilities. There was a new Naval C-in-C - Sir William Parker - and of almost equal importance, a new and stronger Political Officer - Sir H Pottinger.

Amoy.
It was decided to attack Amoy, and on 25th August the squadron anchored off the Port. The Island of Ku-Lang-Su in the middle of the harbour commands the town; it is separated from Amoy by a passage which practically forms another harbour; every island and headland was fortified. In front of the outer town were a line of batteries with a solid rampart facing the sea about a mile in length, on which 96 guns were mounted in tiers. A castellated wall led to a range of rocky heights running parallel to the beach and rampart. It was therefore protected from flanking attack: the entrance between Ku-Lang-Su and Amoy, thus protected, was only 600 yards wide. On Ku-Lang-Su were several strong batteries mounting 76 guns, some facing the above rampart. There were to be two attacks, one on Ku-Lang-Su, the other on Amoy.

Taking first that on Ku-Lang-Su, there was a frontal attack by the ships, whilst the landing party took the batteries in reverse. Captain Ellis with 40 men from the *Wellesley* transferred to the *Blonde*, Captain Whitcomb with 40 from the *Blenheim* to the *Druid*, and with *Blonde*'s and

---

227 Captain Ellis was afterwards Commandant at Woolwich and the Honorary Colonel of the Portsmouth Division from 28th March 1863 till his death in 1865.

Modeste's detachments making altogether 8 Officers, 7 Sergeants and 172 Rank and File. At 1.30 pm on August 26th, the *Blonde* (44), *Druid* (44) and *Modeste* (18) under Captain Bourchier RN; bombarded the Easternmost battery. The troops - 3 Companies of the 26th - were landed in a small bay to left of Easternmost battery. A Company of Artillery was embarked in the *Blonde* to assist in the bombardment.

Captain Ellis in his Report says: "I landed without accident to the right of fort on a low sandy beach, climbing the rocks with some difficulty, we gained the cliffs; the enemy courageously resisting us. We drove them before us and cleared the fort, Lieutenant Polkinghorne hoisting the boat's Union (flag). Part of the 26th arriving, I sent them to South and right flank to dislodge the enemy from an 8-gun battery in that direction, which they gallantly accomplished. Leaving a guard in the fort under Lieutenant Polkinghorne, I pursued the fugitives. By 3.30 pm Ku-Lang-Su was captured."

The Royal Marines remained in bivouac on the island till 1st September; the officers were Captain Ellis, Lieutenants Hewett, Pickard, Whiting, Ussher, Farmar, Polkinghorne, Maxwell (Adjutant).

In the attack on Amoy the *Wellesley* and *Blenheim* bombarded the extreme end of the rampart nearest the town; the *Pylades* (18), *Cruiser* (16), *Columbine* (16) and *Algerine* (10) continued the attack up to the entrance of the harbour. The selected landing place was at the extreme end of the castellated wall described above; two ships were stationed at this point to guard against flanking fire from the batteries.

The Naval bombardment was not so successful as usual; separate batteries were silenced, but little impression was made on the great rampart, and up to 2 pm very little damage at all was done. At 3 pm the 18th and 49th Regiments were disembarked at the foot of the castellated wall (the 55th Regiment not until the next morning). The 18th were to escalade the wall, the 49th to make along the beach and then mount the rampart. Captain Hall of the *Nemesis* with a few seamen rushed the wall and were followed by two Companies of the 18th, who ran down and opened the gate; the 49th got over the rampart and cleared out the Chinese near the outskirts of the city, being joined by some Royal Marines; i.e. the remainder of the Royal Marines who had not landed at Ku-Lang-Su and who had been required on board to work the ships' guns and were landed under Captain Whitcomb, aided by a few seamen by order of Admiral Sir William Parker.[228]

The outworks at both ends of the rampart were taken by the Naval forces. The 18th, 49th, and Royal Marines formed up on the heights above the rampart, which commanded the outer town of Amoy, but a chain of rocky heights occupied by the enemy guarded the inner city. Guns were brought up and an attack was made in two columns; there was only slight opposition and by evening the British had gained possession of the hills and next morning secured the town. The

---

228 Captain Ellis' Report.

Royal Marines returned to their ships in the evening.

It was then decided to hold only Ku-Lang-Su; accordingly, the defences of the town were destroyed and 500 guns taken possession of; there was a certain amount of plundering by Chinese bandits. On 5th September the troops having re-embarked, sailed north for Chusan.

Chusan.
Storms delayed their arrival until 25th September. The Chinese were busy strengthening the defences of Ting-Hai on the South-West side of the island. This was a walled town two miles in circumference and one mile from the shore. There was a raised bank to guard against inundations, on which was a battery with 80 guns, but very badly constructed.

The Pagoda Hill batteries were close to the landing place; opposite to it were two small islands, one called Trumbull, which proved very useful on which to mount guns for the attack on Pagoda Hill. On the Western side were steep hills called the Forty-Nine Hills, commanding the flank of the battery wall; here were fortified camps and two strong forts not yet manned. This point was selected for the landing place.

On 29th fire was opened on the camp and destroyed the temporary buildings; on 30th a small battery was completed by the RA on Trumbull or Melville Island.

The General Orders issued on 29th September 1841, said:

"It may be necessary to recapture Chusan. Be prepared to land in light Marching Order.
Left Column - Lieutenant Colonel Craigie
   Madras Artillery. 4 Howitzers, 2 Mortars
   Madras Sappers and Miners
   55th Regiment
   18th Royal Irish
   With two days' cooked provisions.
Right Column - Lieutenant Colonel Morris Madras Artillery. 2 guns
   Madras Sappers
   49th Regiment
   Royal Marines[229]
   RN Seaman Battalion

---

229 Field State of Royal Marines landing at Chusan, 1 October 1841.
   Wellesley -   Captain Ellis, 2 Subalterns, 4 Sergeants, 2 Fifers, 89 Rank and File.
   Blenheim -   Captain Whitcomb, 2 Subalterns, 3 Sergeants, 2 Fifers, 78 Rank and File.
   Columbine -   1 Sergeant, 1 Fifer, 12 Rank and File.
   Cruiser -   1 Sergeant, 1 Fifer, 13 Rank and File.
   Lieutenant Farmar, Adjutant. Sergeant Fairweather - Sergeant-Major. The Subalterns were White and Farmar (*Wellesley*), Whiting and Ussher (*Blenheim*).

With one day's cooked provisions.
On Trumbull Island
    Royal Artillery
    Madras Sappers
Scaling Ladders, Powder Bags, and Planks for crossing canals to be provided".

On 1st October, *Wellesley*, *Cruiser*, and *Columbine* covered the landing; the Madras Artillery with 8 guns, the Sappers, 18th, 55th, and Madras Volunteers landed at the West end of the wall; the 55th advanced up the heights which were steep and rugged. The Chinese made a stronger defence, but the heights, encampment and a stand of Colours were captured. The troops also dealt with a long line of batteries along the coast. The 18th, the Marines, and the Artillery were resisted with courage. The Royal Marines had landed and formed up at noon and moved off in support of the Royal Irish advancing to attack the strong position of the Joss House in the suburbs of the city; they joined the Royal Irish at the Joss House Fort, the enemy retreating from it. At sunset by orders of Admiral Sir William Parker the battalion re-embarked in the *Sesostris*, lying off the hills to await further orders, but as none arrived the men were conveyed to their own ships.[230]

Two Companies of the 55th were placed to prevent the Chinese gaining the South gate of the town; they were joined by the 49th and the outer defences were abandoned by the Chinese. The guns and rocket battery were brought up to the hills on the North-West which commanded the town. The Chinese escaped by the North and East gates, the 55th having gained the walls of Ting-Hai and the 18th being on Pagoda Hill.

The importance of the island was due to its situation at the mouth of the Yang-Tse-Kiang.

Ningpo and Chinghai.
The next place for attack was Chinghai, the sea port at the mouth of the Ningpo River, and 12 miles from the city of Ningpo which stood on the left bank of the river. On this side at the South-West corner, separated by a rocky gorge, a precipitous rock known as the Joss House Hill stood out, with a fort on its top. The river was blocked from this point by piles and sunken junks; the rock and the City Wall were strongly garrisoned. The main body of the enemy troops were on the right bank on a range of hills commanding the town, which were fortified; it was a position of great strength, with an entrenched camp, field redoubts, etc.

The Army under Sir Hugh Gough were to attack the right bank, covered by the *Cruiser*, *Nemesis*, *Queen*, *Phlegethon*, and *Columbine*. On 10th October the Army were quite successful and the enemy fled, but they could only help the force on the left bank by bringing the captured guns to bear on the City and by the fire of the Rocket Battery.

At 11 am on 10th October the *Blenheim*, *Wellesley*, *Blonde*, and *Modeste* bombarded Chinghai. Captain Herbert (*Blenheim*) with 400 Seamen and 276 Marines under Captain Ellis, a detachment

---
[230] Captain Ellis' Report.

RA, and 50 Sappers landed with Sir William Parker, and made their way up the Joss House Hill. The magazine exploded as they approached and the Chinese in their panic did not close the gate; there was a second explosion and the British immediately scaled at the South-East angle of the City Wall, and the Chinese escaped by the West Gate. A great arsenal and cannon factory with quantities of warlike stores were captured with practically no loss, owing to the skilful use of the British Artillery

On 12th October, Ningpo surrendered. The force however was not strong enough to make an attack on Hang-Choy or proceed to the Yang-Tse.

Captain Ellis' Report of this action is as follows:

Marine Quarters,
Gate of Confucius, Ningpo
21st October 1841

............*The Royal Marines had to climb a range of precipitous heights (which was quite unexpected by the enemy) .... The walls of the city of Chinhae were 25 feet high, and at part of these which were flanked by some rocks, some Marines of HMS Wellesley by extraordinary perseverance and courage succeeded in ascending and lowering a rope; others soon followed from below, when fire was opened on the enemy who soon fled, having a few killed. Scaling ladders coming up, the remainder of the Marines and armed seamen under Captain Herbert RN, were quickly on the rampart and in possession of Chinhae. Marine sentinels were posted on the gates and on the walls, and the seamen returned to their ships. The troops under General Gough operated on the opposite side of the river, carrying by assault a strongly fortified entrenchment, which the Chinese defended with great obstinacy, and numbers were killed. In the evening the General crossed over to Chinhae and took up his quarters in the Joss House.*

Having decided on a forward movement by water, the 55th Regiment and half the Royal Marine Battalion under Captain Whitcomb were left at Chinhae. The remainder under Captain Ellis accompanied the C-in-C in the Modeste to Ningpo. The RM were ordered to attack the gate I am now holding. Other troops proceeded to other points; the GOC remarked 'His orders were executed without any resistance.' The Chinese Governor and his troops had fled."

The garrison at Ningpo consisted of Captains Ellis, Lieutenants Hewett, Ussher, Farmar (Adjutant), Sergeant Fairbank (Sergeant Major), Sergeant Waldron (QMS), 6 Sergeants, 12 Corporals, 3 Drummers and 84 Privates, belonging to *Wellesley*, *Blonde*, *Columbine*, and *Blenheim*.

A small expedition was undertaken in December 1841 to Yu-You and Tsekee, to cow the province of Fu-Kien, after which operations were suspended for the winter.

On 11th November the Marines under Major Ellis quitted Ningpo and calling at Chinghai embarked the 113 Royal Marines under Captain Whitcomb who were in garrison there.

In February 1842 Major Ellis and a portion of the *Wellesley*'s detachment left for England. The *Blenheim*'s detachment under Captain Whitcomb returned to their ship and went to Macao, and they were replaced by the detachment of HMS *Cornwallis* under Brevet Major Uniacke. Major Ellis was promoted to Brevet Lieutenant Colonel on 26th May 1841, and at the close of the war was given a CB in 1842.

Sir Hugh Gough wrote, "*I cannot allow you to leave the expedition without some assurances on my part of my regret at losing you, and of my best wishes for your future welfare. As you have been repeatedly placed, by the Naval C-in-C, at my disposal for active operations in the field, I have had occasion to notice the gallantry and steadiness of your little Battalion, as well as the zeal, spirit, and judgment with which you exercised the command. The subsequent period of your service in the garrisons of Ningpo and Tinghae, has only tended to increase the satisfaction which I shall always feel at having had you and a portion of the Royal Marines under my orders, and I will beg you to convey the expression of my sentiments to the Officers, Non-commissioned officers and men under your command.*"

Tsekee.
In March 1842 the Chinese made surprise attacks on Ningpo and Chinghai, which were repulsed after some severe fighting, and the Chinese fell back to Tsekee, North-west of Ningpo, where they were reinforced from the North. On 15th March it was decided to attack Tsekee, for which 850 troops of 49th and 18th Regiments with 410 Seamen and Marines were detailed. They were taken up the river and landed as near Tsekee as possible, where they were joined by the guns of the Madras Artillery. After a cannonade by the field guns, the Seamen and Marines escaladed the walls at 4 pm and the force concentrated at the North Gate; the 18th Regiment moved up a steep ravine on the right which commanded the Chinese left. The Naval Brigade were then to attack the Chinese right and the 49th the centre. The 18th were slow in getting into position, so at 8 pm the General sounded the 'Advance'; the Royal Marines covered by the Seamen poured in a heavy fire, when the 49th and two Companies Royal Marines under Lieutenants G Elliot and A J Hambly dashed forward and charged up the steep and rugged hill in front of them; the Chinese put up a strong resistance but were routed and 1000 killed, the troops turning their flanks. The RN Brigade lost 3 killed and 15 wounded, of which the Marines had 1 Private killed, Lieutenants Elliot and Hambly and 10 Privates wounded.

Yang-tse-Kiang.
It was then decided to transfer operations to the Yang-tse-Kiang and to commence by attacking Chapoo, which was the centre of trade with Japan. Ningpo was therefore evacuated on 7th May and the garrisons of Chinghai, Chusan, and Amoy reduced to the smallest dimensions.

Chapoo.
Chapoo was the port of Hang-Chow on the Huan Estuary, and on 17th May the Fleet anchored near Chapoo, which was a walled city with hills extending Eastward for 3 miles. It was defended by batteries near the shore. The plan was to land on 18th at the Eastern end of the promontory and storm the heights. The troops were in three columns:

Right: 18th, 49th, and RE	970.
Centre: RA, RE, and Company Madras NI	388.
Left: 28th, 55th, RM	883.

The Right Column landed first and covered the disembarkation, the Left Column was sent round the base of the heights to get in rear of the enemy and cut the communications with Chapoo, which they successfully accomplished. The Right Column advanced on the defences, covered by the fire of the ships, *Cornwallis, Modeste, Blonde, Sesostris, Algerine, Columbine, Starling*; and *Bentick*. The Tartars in a Joss House put up a stiff resistance and caused casualties. By noon General Gough was on the walls, where he was joined by the Seamen and Marines who had been landed near the suburbs not far from the Joss House, and the gates were secured. The place was held only for a few days, whilst the arsenals and ordnance were destroyed, and on 27th May it was evacuated, and the squadron proceeded round the headland into the mouth of the great river.

The first operation that had to be undertaken before they could advance up the Yang-Tse-Kiang, was the capture of the Woosung Forts, which was carried out by the Navy. On 12th June, 1842, the Fleet reached the anchorage off Woosung; the Admiral and General made a reconnaissance and found that there was no landing place practicable except for a frontal attack.

Woosung.
The Woosung River empties itself into the right bank of the Yang-Tse-Kiang, and the town of Woosung - about 500 houses - stood at its mouth. At its entrance the breadth of the river is about one mile, but the channel for vessels is only about 300 yards wide. Its course is North and South, and the banks widen as it joins the Yangtse. The principal line of defence was along the Western bank; from the approaches of the village of Woosung for 3 miles along the river mouth, and then curving gradually round the bank of the Yangtse River.

The town of Paoushan was nearly two miles in rear of the batteries at that end; there were 134 guns, but the embrasures were too wide, and the batteries were made of earth; there were also stakes along the front. Just above the village of Woosung, skirting it on the Southern side, was a large creek, or canal, communicating with the river, protected by strong semi-circular stone batteries armed with ten brass guns (24 pdrs). They defended the river itself and commanded the whole reach as well as the mouth of the creek.

On the East side of the river - opposite Woosung - was a strong fort, built of brick, circular in shape and flanked by a line of embankments armed with 21 guns. There were 175 guns available for defence at Woosung with the pick of the Tartar troops, who worked their guns with great spirit and kept up a good fire and who, when the principal line of defence was out-flanked by the Seamen and Marines, defended themselves with great courage.

The water shoaled to under three feet within 200 yards of the banks and it was very difficult to find a landing place.

On the 16th June the tide and the state of the weather was favourable: the bombarding ships were towed in by the steamers, which were lashed alongside; only five steamers however were available. The *Cornwallis* and *Blonde*, the heaviest ships, were placed in front of the batteries just below the village of Woosung.

The light squadron – *Modeste*, *Columbine*, *Clio*, towed by *Nemesis*, and *Phlegethon*, and *Pluto* – passed above the village, and engaged the battery at the mouth of the creek and the circular battery on the East Bank; fire was not returned by the ships until they had anchored in position, so that they suffered some-what.

The *North Star* arriving, the *Tennasserim*, after placing the *Blonde* in position, went off and placed her ahead of the *Blonde*. The *Nemesis* engaged the war junks, but they bolted; however, the *Nemesis* went ashore, so sending away her boats with all those of the *Phlegethon*, together they destroyed all the junks.

The Chinese fire having been reduced, Captain Watson RN, with the Seamen and Marines of *Modeste*, *Columbine*, and *Clio*, landed in the creeks to cut off the enemy retreat and to turn their flank near the village. He was received with heavy fire, but the Chinese soon retreated. As the Chinese soon came on again, Watson withdrew to the embankment. Captain Bourchier landed some men from the *Blonde* to assist Watson's men, who renewed the attack, the Chinese putting up a good fight. The Seamen and Marines of the *Blonde* and *Cornwallis* (Captain Uniacke RM) then landed nearly opposite their vessels, and as soon as they were formed up they drove the enemy out of the line of batteries. The *Sesostris* engaged the fort on the East side of the entrance but went ashore; she however brought her guns to bear, and a party landing from her and the *Tennasserim* took possession of the fort. The troops were not landed till the afternoon, as most of the transports had gone ashore. General Schoedder was sent to get in rear of Paoushan. Sir Hugh Gough with the Naval parties moved along the line of batteries, and the Chinese fled to Soo-Chow-Foo.

Lieutenant C C Hewett RM (*Blonde*) and 1 seaman were killed; 3 officers, 15 seamen, 1 corporal and 5 RM were wounded; 250 guns were captured, of which 42 were brass.

The way to Shanghai was now open, and the attack was arranged for the 19th June. One Column of 1000 men under Lieutenant Colonel Montgomerie of the Madras Artillery was to march by land; the Royal Marines of the squadron went up in HMS *Medusa*. One long battery of 49 guns below the town opened fire but was quickly silenced by broadsides from the *North Star* and *Modeste*. Captain Bourchier with the Seamen and Marines landed and took possession of it. The land column reached the city first and the town was captured unopposed. All military stores were destroyed, and a large number of guns captured, but the city was almost immediately evacuated owing to the lateness of the season. The expedition returned to Woosung and having received reinforcements it was decided to attack Nanking, 170 miles up the river at the junction of the Imperial Canal with the Yang-Tse-Kiang. It was fortified, and Chin-Kiang-Foo commanded the Northern entrance to the Canal. The expedition started on 6th July 1842. They had to go 200 miles up an unknown river, but only 10 days were taken in the passage and there was practically no opposition. On 19th July, HMS *Cornwallis* anchored off Kinshan, about 1000 yards from the entrance of the Imperial Canal, which was occupied by a small party of Marines, and on the 20th the Fleet was concentrated.

The Canal formed the moat for Ching-Kiang-Poo, joining the main river near the Western angle; on the North and East sides was a range of heights. Both heights commanded the North angle of the city and on each was a Joss House.

On 21st July the assault was delivered by the Army, which carried the hills and the encampments on them. Whilst the guns were being landed by the *Blonde* near the West Gate, the Chinese attacked the Seamen and Artillery; the *Cornwallis* at once landed 200 Royal Marines at the entrance to the Canal, and being joined by 300 Madras NI, they pushed through the suburbs, supported by the boats which advanced into the Canal. Near the West Gate the Marines and Native Infantry, with the Naval Officers, escaladed the Wall and advanced against the Chinese, who put up the strongest resistance, but were at last driven back by rockets; the outer Gate was blown in by the 3rd Army Brigade, who rushed into the city. The Seamen and Marines then advanced along the Western Wall. The heat was intense, and many men died from sunstroke: among them Captain and Brevet Major J Uniacke RM, of the *Cornwallis*. He had joined the Corps on 28th August 1804 and had 38 years' service.

In addition to Major Uniacke, Lieutenants L Atcherly of the *Cornwallis* and W Herald had died. About 780 Royal Marines had been engaged in this War. This proved to be the last engagement of the War. By August 9th the whole Fleet had arrived, and on 17th the Chinese proposed preliminaries of peace and a preliminary treaty was signed on 29th, by which the island of Hong Kong was ceded to the British, the Chinese paid an indemnity of 21,000,000 Dollars, and the following ports were opened to foreign trade: Canton, Amoy, Foo-Chow, Ningpo, Shanghai; and the British envoys, etc were to be treated on a perfect equality with the Chinese.

The regiments that were engaged in this war were granted the badge of the "Dragon superscribed China", so that this is yet another of the badges to which the Corps is entitled, but which is merged in the 'Great Globe Itself'.

15 - Around the Globe 1844 - 1852

The numbers seem to have remained unaltered until 1845, when there is a very interesting Order-in-Council dated 13th January 1845, which, whilst giving the numbers for that year, affords information as to the employment of the RM Artillery:

"Consideration of the steam vessels and weight of armaments and consequent insufficiency of present numbers of the Companies of Marine Artillery, a portion of whom are embarked in each vessel. Previous to 1831 the Marine Artillery consisted of eight companies; in that year four companies were reduced and in 1832 two more; at which period the horse-power of the Navy amounted to 2660 horses; in 1841 one company was added, making the strength 405. The Steam Navy now amounts to upwards of 26,000 H.P., and this amount will be doubled in a few years; the Board therefore propose to establish two companies of RMA without adding to the total force of RM, viz 10,500"………."The total strength was divided into Staff 62, RM 9,682, Artillery Companies 725. The cost of the change was estimated to be £2741."

On 18th March 1846, two more Artillery Companies were added, making 7 all told; the numbers were taken from the Divisional Companies without altering the total. The RMA Headquarters about this time were moved back to the Gunwharf Barracks, still forming part of the Portsmouth Division; and when there were too many men for these and Fort Cumberland, men were sent to the other Divisions.

Bands.
A subscription of one day's pay from all officers was ordered for the support of the bands from 19th March 1842 and has continued ever since.

Quartermasters.
On 19th May 1846 a big departure was made. For the first time a second Quartermaster was added to each Division and instead of a combatant officer being appointed for a term of years, they were selected from the Staff Sergeants of the Corps; but it was not until Order-in-Council 18th January 1850 that any scales of pay were laid down for them and not until Order-in-Council 26th June 1857 that there was any scheme of Retired or Half Pay.

It would seem that this addition must have been due to the increased duties in connection with rations and quartering, for we learn[231] that it was not till then that the GOC Western District ordered that an evening meal of tea or coffee and a proportion of bread should be provided in addition to breakfast and dinner; and the hour of pm after evening roll-call is suggested.

Duelling.
A very important change in the social customs was made by the Army Order forbidding Duelling

---
231 Plymouth Orders, 8th August 1845.

on 15 March 1844; as we have seen it was more or less officially recognised, though when the Commandant at Portsmouth reported in 1812 that an officer had died of his wounds, the other officers concerned absconded and the Commandant was ordered to 'respite' their pay.

The year 1847 was noteworthy for legislation affecting service which still governs the Corps.

On 24th April 1847 the strength was raised from 10,500 to 12,000, which included three more companies at a strength of 145 each added to the RMA making 10. The Acting Adjutant RMA was put on the same footing as the other Adjutants of the Corps. The Divisional Companies were 100 with a strength of 104 each, and on 22nd July another Lieutenant Colonel was added.

Medals.
On 1st June 1847 the issue of the Naval War Service Medal for the Great War 1793-1815 was authorised with clasps for the numerous and various actions. The same medal was also issued for the Syrian Campaign of 1840 and for Navarino, 1827. There were 230 different bars issued. The distribution took place on 1st January 1849, when naturally there was not a very large number of recipients surviving. An Army Medal was also issued with clasp for their battles, and a certain number of these were issued to the Royal Marines.

Marine Mutiny Act.
Since the Great War the problem of the age of officers had been very pressing, but it would now seem as if some difficulty was arising as regards the men. As we have seen, except for certain exceptions during the war periods when men were enlisted for 3 years or the duration of the war, or from the militia for 'Limited Service', enlistment had always been for life, and no doubt the peace period was producing men too old for the duties required.

Doubtless also the influence of the Army Service Act 1847 was felt and at all events the Mutiny Act of this year passed on 1st August 1847 contained the first provision for limiting service in the Marines, and was known as the Marine Mutiny Act 1847 (d 12 Victoria c 53), the provisions of which are still in force, by which it was ordered that men were to be discharged after 12 years' service, and allowed to re-engage for another 12 years (afterwards modified to 9, in 1853). This was a revolutionary step and had a great effect on the Corps. The Pension Regulations were altered at the same time. Apparently, on 26 June 1837, pensions had been granted after 21 years at sea or on foreign service, two years on shore in England to count as one year afloat and no Marine was entitled unless he had 10 years afloat or on foreign service. Further, since 1st January 1832 service had only counted from the age of twenty; now by an Order-in-Council 17th June 1847 this rule was declared to be unfair, and a reversion to the old Marine system was ordered, by which Marines were entitled to benefit from the whole of their service ashore and afloat and were allowed to reckon service from the age of 15. On 1st August a new scale of pensions was fixed, which remained in force up to 1919, viz 8d a day, with additions of 21 pence for Sergeant-Majors, 2 pence for QMS, 1 penny for Sergeants, a ha'penny for Corporals, with limits of 2/6, 2/3, 2/-, and 1/6 for respective classes. Acting time did not count.

1848

The strength was 12,000 but a fresh distribution was ordered, by which 12 new companies were created, but with reduced strength; which allowed 700 men to be transferred to the Artillery companies and the creation of 3 additional Artillery companies. An additional Lieutenant Colonel was allowed for the Artillery Companies, and one for the Corps generally.

Portsmouth Barracks.
In this year came also the move from the old Clarence Barracks at Portsmouth to the new Barracks, which had been erected on the land where the old hospital for prisoners of war used to stand at Forton. These were exchanged with the War Office for the Clarence Barracks, and at first consisted only of the four large blocks. The transfer took place on 29th March 1848.

At the same time the Barracks for the Woolwich Division on Woolwich Common were completed. These were the latest things of their day and appear to have been a very fine set of buildings. They were called the Cambridge Barracks: since 1846 the Division had been quartered in the old 74-gun hulk *Benbow* alongside the quay in the Dockyard. The Infirmary was established in what is now known as the Red Barracks.

In 1849 the strength voted was:
Staff	70
112 Divisional Companies	10416
10 Artillery Companies	1500
	11986

An Order-in-Council of l6th January 1849 contains many valued concessions to the Marines which exist to the present day. It is laid down that a Marine's service commenced from date of attestation as service towards pension, reckoned from the age of 18 only.

Meritorious Service Medal.
It instituted the Meritorious Service Medal, granting annuities for distinguished service to Sergeants - for which a sum of £250 was allowed, to be divided in sums not exceeding £20 per annum, to be enjoyed whilst serving or after discharge. The medal to be of silver "For Meritorious Service" and not to be liable to forfeiture except by sentence of Court Martial or on conviction of felony. Order-in-Council 11th January 1853 modified the annuities.

Long Service and Good Conduct Medal.
It also instituted gratuities for the Long Service and Good Conduct Medal - Sergeants £15, Corporals £10, Privates £5 - provided they had served 2l years with irreproachable character and never been convicted by court martial. It also laid down the conditions for the grant of Good Conduct Badges and introduced the proviso of the grant of the 4th Good Conduct Badge at 16 years (now obsolete). It also brought in the regulation that deprivation of Good Conduct Badges could only be by Warrant, as for corporal punishment, and that no man wearing a GCB was liable to corporal punishment except for mutinous conduct.

Gunnery.
An Order-in-Council of 1st July 1849 directed that Marines generally should be trained in Naval Gunnery, also in knotting and splicing, hammock-slinging, boat pulling, etc. Hitherto such instruction on shore had been confined to the Artillery training of the RMA., but it was not till the year 1877 that a definite standard of Trained Man as for seamen was laid down for the Infantry of the Corps.

A curious old custom was abolished on 6th October 1849. Apparently, Captains of Marines afloat were liable to a deduction of 1/1 a day to meet cost of provisions. No naval or military officers were so liable, and it was abolished on 1st July. In 1851 another old privilege of RMA Captains went: they had apparently drawn £20 a year Non-Effective Allowance - it is not stated for what it was granted. It was abolished on 24th September 1851, and 1/1 added to their personal pay in lieu.

In 1850 the numbers were 12,000,

In 1851 the numbers were 10,500.

Lodging Money.
(In this year was held the Great Exhibition in London.) On 14th April a great boon was granted to married NCOs and men. They were put on the same footing as the Army for lodging money, viz 2 pence a day; the proportion allowed was 3 men for every 100. Later the allowance was increased to 6 pence a day.

The difficulties caused by stagnation of promotion, however, were still extant. In November 1852 it was reported that four Lieutenant Colonels and four Captains were unfit for further active service (Order-in-Council 10th November 1852) and again in August 1853 Inspection Reports say that four Lieutenant Colonels are unfit for active service owing to advanced age and ill health (Order-in-Council 8th August 1853); they were all specially retired on full pay.

In 1852 the numbers were 10,500.

South America.
It is customary to speak of the period 1815 to the Crimean War (1854) as a period of 40 years' peace, but as we have already seen this did not apply to the Corps, and the accounts of the following operations will show that the Corps was never really free from active service. No sooner were affairs settled in China before attention was turned to another hemisphere and the Royal Marines were engaged in South America, where the Spanish Colonies were all in a state of revolt.

From 1835 there had been two factions in Uruguay, one under Rosas desiring incorporation with the Argentine Confederation, and the opposition led by a M. Rivera. The Acting President was a M. Suarez. Rosas, the dictator of Buenos Ayres, favoured the Argentine party and one of his lieutenants - Oribe - in 1843 began the nine years' siege of Montevideo.

But in 1845 the British and French Governments ordered their squadrons to interfere against Rosas at the moment when his victory seemed assured, and in consequence an attack was ordered.

Admiral Inglefield with 6 British and 3 French ships first proceeded to turn Rosas' men out of Colonia, a town on North bank of the River Plate: these retired after a few shots. The ships then ascended the River Parana to where powerful batteries had been erected at Puente Obligado, about 100 miles from the mouth.

On 18th November they anchored about three miles below Obligado. The batteries on the right bank were armed with 22 guns and a number of field guns. Twenty-four vessels had been secured with a chain as a boom across the river, protected by a schooner and two gunboats. On 20th the Allies attacked, and the leading vessels suffered rather severely, but the chain was cut, and the steamers passed through and enfiladed the forts. At 5 pm Captain T Hurdle with Lieutenant Morrison as Adjutant landed with 145 Marines and 180 Seamen (who had been trained as Light Infantry by Lieutenant Lawrence RMA) and attacked the Uruguayans covering the batteries and drove them out with the bayonet. They destroyed the guns and re-embarked; next day the destruction was completed. The British loss was 30 killed and wounded. The squadron then went up the river to Corrientes, opening up the river to trade.

In the early part of 1846 when the Allied squadron was bringing down a convoy of vessels, Rosas had prepared a warm reception for them at San Lorenzo, where the high banks afforded a good site for his batteries. To facilitate the passage of the convoy, Lieutenant C L Barnard RMA and 12 gunners with Lieutenant Mackinnon and 11 seamen with 4 rocket tubes, were concealed on a small island close to the batteries for three days. As the convoy approached, the rocket tubes opened fire and, assisted by the fire of the ships, the convoy was successfully passed down. That evening Captain Hurdle with the Marines of the squadron landed, and with the seamen small arms men stormed the batteries where they spiked the guns.

The Royal Marines of the Fleet, under Brevet Major Leonard, were landed till 1847 to protect British interests.

Lisbon.
In 1848 the Royal Marines were again in Lisbon. Admiral Sir William Parker, owing to the critical state of affairs in Portugal on 21st October 1846, offered an asylum to Queen Maria II. Some Marines, who had been sent out in the *Terrible*, were available and he was authorised to retain them on 1st November, and the Admiralty hoped that he would be able to occupy Belem Castle with them. They were retained until matters calmed down.

New Zealand.
In quite another quarter of the Globe, in New Zealand, trouble arose over the occupation

of tribal land between the settlers and the Maoris. In March 1845 at Kororareka, the Chief Heke so harried the settlement that it was abandoned, and the inhabitants went to Auckland. Reinforcements were demanded from Australia and on their arrival the 58th and 96th Regiments with the Seamen and Marines of HMS *North Star* and *Hazard* and a body of natives, proceeded against a stockade called Okaihau. As they had no artillery it was found to be impregnable, and they were forced to retire with a loss of 14 killed and 58 wounded. On 23rd June 1845 they attacked another stronghold - Oheawi; the guns were useless till a 32 pdr was brought up from HMS *Hazard*. On 1st July the assault was delivered and again repulsed with heavy loss; on 10th it was found that the Maoris had evacuated the Pah.

In November 1845 Sir G Grey, the governor, sent a force of 1170 soldiers, volunteers, Seamen and Marines against the Chiefs Heke and Kawiti. Heke was at Ikoragi, but the force proceeded against Kawiti in the Pah at Ruapekapeka and. besieged it from 31st December to 10th January 1846, when the Maoris abandoned it. The British loss was 13 killed and 30 wounded.

The Chiefs surrendered and were pardoned, and the War in the North Island ended. A medal was granted for this campaign in 1869.

Ireland 1848.
During the revolutionary troubles in Ireland a small Battalion of 300 men was sent to Dublin in July and proceeded to Waterford. It was present at the attack on Portland Barracks and the attempted destruction of the Granagh Bridge over the River Suir on 12th September 1848. On the 1st March the complements of ships on the Irish station had been increased by 300 men. The Battalion was withdrawn in February 1849.

West Coast of Africa 1851.
On 26th and 27th December 1851, HMS *Bloodhound* and *Tartar* took Lagos on the West Coast of Africa, Lieutenants J C W Williams[232] and E McArthur RMA with 27 RMA and 47 RM taking part. Lieutenant Williams was wounded.

1852

On 26th February the *Birkenhead*, conveying troops to South Africa, was lost, 9 officers and 349 men being drowned, the troops remaining fallen in and keeping their ranks as the ship went down, after the women and children had been saved, providing yet another deathless story for the Annals of the Services.

Burmah.
The (Second) Burmese War, 1852, in which a small portion of the Corps was engaged, commenced this year.[233] Rear-Admiral Austen was in command of the Naval Forces and Major General H

---
232 Afterwards DAG.
233 Authorities: History of Indian Navy; Fortescue's British Army; Officers' Services.

Godwin of the troops who came from India.

On 5th April 1852, after a brief bombardment, the town of Martaban was captured. On 8th April the squadron was joined by the Royal Indian Marine squadron of six ships, bringing 4 transports with troops from Bombay and Madras, and 7 transports from Bengal.

Rangoon.
The Burmese had persisted in their insults to British officers and refused to pay the indemnity of 10 lakhs or rupees, so an expedition was ordered to attack Rangoon. The following forces were available:

    HMS *Rattler, Fox, Hermes, Salamander, Serpent*   818 men, 80 guns.

    Indian Navy - 8 ships 952 men, 31 guns (mostly Bengal Marine 7 ships 500 men, 33 guns 8")

The troops were the 18th Royal Irish (850), 51st (900), 80th (460), Artillery (517), 3 Regiments Native Infantry (2800), Sappers and Miners (170) with two 8" howitzers, six 24 pdr, eight 9 pdr field guns.

On 10th April the Fleet anchored below Hastings Sand. On 11th each ship having two transports in tow crossed the Sand and anchored below the stockades protecting Rangoon: as soon as clear of the Sand the transports were cast off. At 9.30 am the Burmese opened fire, which was returned by the Indian ships *Ferooz*, *Sesostris*, and *Mozaffur* as soon as they were anchored. A stockade mounting nine 18 pdr guns was blown up early in the proceedings. Fire was kept up on Dallah on the left of the British as well as on the Rangoon defences on the right. At first the Burmese replied with accuracy, but soon after the *Fox* and *Serpent* came up at 11 am and the firing on the British right nearly ceased. The ships kept up their fire on both sides till the large stockade of Shoe Dagon blew up. The fire cleared the coast for nearly a mile and made a clear landing place for the troops, who were to land the following morning.

At 4 am on the 12th the 51st with the 9th and 35th NI were landed.

The *Sesostris*, *Zenobia*, and *Mozaffur* went up the river and anchored abreast of the Upper Stockades and burnt them without opposition. Proceeding on till abreast of the Great Pagoda the ships continued fire until ordered to cease by the Admiral. HMS *Serpent* and *Phlegethon* went on to Kemmerdine, where they found the stockade too strong for them, and were reinforced by the *Fero*. On 13th April Kemmerdine was found to be evacuated and was burnt.

The squadron anchored abreast of the Great Pagoda and shelled it during the night of 12/13th. At 2 am they ceased firing to allow the troops to advance, and Rangoon was captured during the afternoon, together with 98 guns and 70 gingalls. The troops also captured the White House Stockade and the Great Dragon Pagoda with a loss of 17 killed and 132 wounded. The troops had three days' hard fighting, the walls being 20 feet high, with spikes.

On 7th May, 450 troops under Colonel Apthorp including the RM of the squadron under Lieutenants J Elliot and Nightingale RM, in the *Medusa*, *Tennasserim*, and *Pluto*, under Commander Tarleton RN left in pursuit of the Governor of Rangoon. After going about 45 miles up the river, the force landed and marched to Mawbee; the Governor had fled, so after burning the village they returned, having suffered a great deal of sickness.

Bassein.
On 17th May, General Godwin and Commodore Lambert proceeded with 800 men in the *Mozaffur, Sesostris, Pluto,* and *Tennasserim* to capture Bassein, which was strongly held. The force comprised 400 of the 51st, 300 Madras NI, 67 Madras RA under Major Errington of the 51st, and included 44 RM under Lieutenants Elliot and Nightingale, and 16 Seamen with a field piece under Lieutenant Rice RN.

Bassein was 60 miles above the Island of Negrais at the entrance to the Bassein River, which they reached on the afternoon of the 19th; on the 20th they sighted the fortifications of Bassein on the left bank; there was an extensive fort and stockade with a strong work round the Pagoda, having a brick parapet facing the river. The ships anchored unmolested and the troops were easily and quickly landed, when fire was immediately opened on them from the stockades. One party under General Godwin stormed and carried the Pagoda, and the ships fired whilst the boats' crews of the *Sesostris* and *Mozaffur* stormed the stockades opposite the town; 54 guns and 32 gingalls were captured. Two days were allowed for the occupation of Bassein, the *Sesostris* was then left in charge and the remainder of the squadron returned to Rangoon on the 23rd May.

Pegu.
On 3rd June an expedition started for Pegu, 75 miles from Rangoon, Major Cotton of the 63rd Regiment in command. With them went HMS *Phlegethon* with 5 boats from the *Fox* in which were the Royal Marines under Lieutenant Elliot, and the boats from the Mozaffur all under Commander Tarleton RN, of the *Irrawaddy* Flotilla. On the 4th Pegu was captured with small loss, the fortifications were destroyed, and they returned to Rangoon.

Prome.
In July an expedition was sent against Prome. Officers and men of the *Medusa* were sent to Yeanjue on the 7th July, followed by the *Prosperine, Mahannuddy, Phlegethon,* and three boats from the *Fox*. The enemy were encountered on the bank opposite Komroughie and a sharp action took place, lasting about an hour. Lieutenant Elliot RM and three other officers were severely wounded. As it was inadvisable to land, they anchored at sunset off Meaony. On the 8th the flotilla weighed and proceeded up river till they sighted an extensive fortification on the end of a ridge of hills above the town of Akouktoung. The Chief Bundoola with 1000 men was reported to be here, so the flotilla proceeded on and the *Medusa* reached Prome on the 9th at daylight. She landed her troops and being joined at 7 am by the *Prosperine* with the *Fox*'s boats, 13 guns were captured and brought

off. The ships then withdrew and later, large reinforcements of troops having been received, they occupied Prome in September and the war was concluded. The Province of Pegu was annexed on 20th December 1852. The India Medal with clasp for Pegu was awarded for this campaign. Lieutenants Elliot and Nightingale were mentioned in despatches (LG 10 August 1852).

VOLUME THREE 1837 – 1914

16 - Crimea and the Baltic 1853 – 1856

This period comprises some of the biggest campaigns of the Nineteenth Century and large numbers of the Corps were engaged both ashore and afloat.

In 1853 the numbers were 10,500.

Employment of Marines.
On 1st April 1853, Continuous Service was introduced into the Navy for the first time, and in the following year it had its repercussions on the Royal Marines.

The first was the Order-in-Council 11 August 1854, when stoppages for rations afloat were abolished for NCOs and Men. The wording of the Order-in-Council is so frank and gives such a picture of the duties of the Royal Marines afloat, that it deserves to be quoted *in extenso:*

"NCOs and Men, Royal Marines, are still liable for deductions from pay originally intended to meet most of sea provisions when afloat; this position has become more anomalous, compared with soldiers of the line, and their own officers, and in consequence of the increased pay to continuous service seamen of the Navy, no corresponding advantage having been granted to the Royal Marines.

"The grounds upon which additional pay to seamen entering for continuous service was granted, had reference to the value which unquestionably attaches to the services of skilful and trained seamen, and to the great demand for such men in the Mercantile Marine; but the bearing of this increase, as affecting the relative conditions of the Marines when embarked, was not taken into account, and it cannot be denied that the reasons which have led unavoidably to the increase of the wages of seamen in the Royal Navy, when entered for long periods, apply in many respects with equal force to the services of Royal Marines when afloat. Of late years and more especially since Order-in-Council 1 July 1849 great care and pains have been bestowed in training Royal Marines ashore, not only in the exercise of the ships' gun batteries, but also to some of the duties of seamen, and the proficiency, which these men have acquired before embarkation, renders them so fully equal to those duties that in the recent equipment of the Fleet[234] *they have been found capable of rendering very efficient and valuable services".*

"Another consideration which should not be overlooked in weighing the claims of the Royal Marines, is the fact that at all times and under all circumstances, but more especially during the repair and equipment of ships in port, they are liable to the performance of many harassing and laborious duties, which have been known to deter seamen, when not entered for continuous service, from volunteering during the period of equipment. The Royal Marines are exposed to much wear and tear of clothing witho ut any additional remuneration, and that as regards the general discipline of HM Fleet too much importance cannot be attached to the contentment and efficiency of the Marine Corps and therefore Their Lordships consider that the NCOs and Men should be placed on a more equitable footing as regards ration deductions."

---

234 ie for the Baltic and Crimean Wars.

Therefore, all differences between pay of Royal Marines ashore and afloat, and deductions for rations afloat, ceased from 1st October 1854; but it was 50 years exactly before the deductions for rations on shore ceased.

1854

The strength for 1854 was 15,500 (Order-in-Council 30 January 1854)

Staff	72
12 Artillery Companies	2112
110 Divisional Companies	13310

Two Orders-in-Council published 9th March and 13th September made another effort to deal with the stagnation of promotion.

1. Lieutenant Colonels to be promoted to Colonels after 3 years.

2. An establishment of 10 General Officers was fixed.

3. Any Lieutenant, Captain, or Lieutenant Colonel may be rewarded for brilliant service in the Field or afloat; such promotion to be by brevet and to be converted into rank on the strength at the earliest period that consideration for the claims of other officers senior will admit of.

4. The retired full pay establishment fixed at £35,000 - i.e. an increase of £6,000.

5. Two Officers were to hold the appointment of A.D.C. to the King and to be promoted to full Colonel.

6. Rates of pay for Captains and Subalterns were laid down that remained in force for 50 years.

The Staff consisted of 1 DAG, 1 AAG, 4 Colonels Commandant, 4 Colonels 2nd Commandant, 18 Lieutenant Colonels, 1 Instructor of Laboratory, 4 Paymasters, 4 Barrackmasters, 4 Quartermasters, 9 Sergeants-Major (1 for Artillery), 4 QMS, 6 Barrack-master's Sergeants (1 for Artillery), 4 Surgeons and 4 Assistant Surgeons.

Arms.

The Corps was at this time,[235] armed with the Minie Rifle, which had replaced the percussion muskets; it was superseded in 1857 by the Enfield Rifle. This rifle remained in use for about 10 years, when the Corps was ordered to be armed with its first breechloading rifle - viz, the Enfield converted on the Snider principle. The date of the order was the 19th January 1867. The Snider rifle carried a very heavy bullet (.577) and was fairly simple in action. It was superseded in 1875 (22nd April) by the Martini-Henry (.45), the rifle with the falling block for insertion of the cartridge, and a needle acting on a detonating cap in the base of the cartridge. It retained the old long triangular bayonet with locking ring. The cartridges were very bad, as they were made of rolled strips of brass and there were constant jams till the solid drawn brass case was introduced.

1855

In 1855 the numbers were 15,500.

Light Infantry.

On the 30th January 1855 the title of the Corps was changed to Royal Marines, Light Infantry. An Admiralty letter of that date says: *"That the Corps of Royal Marines may be designated a Light Corps and equipped and designated as such agreeably to Your Majesty's Regulation for Light Infantry Regiments of the Line; this training being considered best adapted to the nature of the service which the Corps is generally required to perform when employed ashore."*

During the Crimean War was also instituted the Conspicuous Gallantry Medal. This was meant as the Naval counterpart of the Army Distinguished Conduct Medal[236] instituted by Royal Warrant of the 4th December 1854. The Admiralty were authorised to confer rewards of the medal with gratuity to any Petty Officer, Seaman, or Royal Marine who "shall, while serving in action, distinguish themselves in action with the enemy"; the same to be granted in the proportion of 8 Petty Officers or Sergeants and Corporals and 10 Seamen or Privates for every 1000 men, and the gratuities to be granted were also laid down.

By Order-in-Council 8th February 1855 NCOs, Royal Marines, serving on shore from the Fleet in the Crimea, were made eligible for the Army Distinguished Conduct Medal and corresponding annuity and pecuniary awards.

In 1856 numbers were 16,000 (Order-in-Council 28 February 1855) by the addition of 1 Artillery and 2 more Divisional Companies.

By 1st November as the operations in the Baltic had shown the need of more RMA for service in the bomb vessels, Infantry Companies were reduced and the Artillery Companies were raised to 14, whose strengths were also increased.

---

235 1854.
236 By Order-in-Council 13 August 1855.

The Russian War, 1854-1856

In 1855 differences between the Latin and Greek Churches concerning the Holy Places in Palestine had led Turkey to appoint a Commission of enquiry. Russia, always a champion of the Greek Church, thought this to be a favourable opportunity to interfere with a view to breaking up the Turkish Empire. She demanded guarantees for the Greek Church and also that the Greek Orthodox subjects of the Sultan should be placed under her protection. This would have affected the independence of Turkey, and could not be entertained by the Porte, in which attitude she had the support of England and France. On 18th May 1853, Diplomatic relations were broken off with Russia by Turkey, and Russia proposed to occupy the Danubian Principalities. The British Fleet of 7 battleships and 8 frigates was ordered to Besika Bay and arrived on 13th June, being joined later by 9 battleships and 4 frigates of the French Fleet. Here many weary months were spent. At the end of October, the Allied Fleets moved up to Therapia in the Bosphorus.

Conferences took place without much result, and on 30th November the Russians attacked and destroyed a Turkish Squadron at Sinope, which was escorting troops to Asia Minor. The Allied Fleets entered the Black Sea on 3rd January 1854 and going to Sinope escorted the Turkish troops to the Eastern end of the Black Sea and then returned to Constantinople. As nothing came of the conferences, war was declared by the Allies on 27th March 1854. On 6th April 1854 the *Furious* was sent to Odessa to bring off the British Consul and subjects, and though carrying a flag of truce, was fired on. Meanwhile British and French troops were arriving and being landed at Gallipoli.

On 20th April HMS *Terrible*, *Tiger*, *Furious* and *Retribution* with three French Ships went to Odessa and on the 22nd commenced a bombardment. HMS *Arethusa* stood in to the Mole, the fort of which was blown up, and the batteries ceased firing. The British ships then stood in and set the enemy shipping on fire and destroyed the batteries and brought off the people. On 29th they made a reconnaissance of Sevastopol but did nothing.

An incursion to the East end of the Black Sea was then made and on 19th May, after a bombardment of Redoubt Kaleh, Turkish troops were placed in occupation of it.

At the end of May it was decided to blockade the mouths of the Danube, and to transport the Armies to Varna, which was done, but no further action was taken till the autumn, when an invasion of the Crimea was determined on.

Meanwhile action was being taken in other quarters, first in the Baltic[237] and also in the Pacific, where an abortive but instructive attack was made on Petropaulovski on 30th August. This place was very strongly fortified, but the Allied Commanders with inadequate forces proceeded to attack it. The British ships *President* (50), *Forte* (40), Pique (40), *Virago* and *Amphitrite*, with three or four French ships, attacked on 30th August. (For some reason the British Admiral shot himself during

---

237 See pages 35 – 37.

the engagement.) It was renewed on the 31st against three batteries of 3, 5 and 11 guns. A party from *Virago* landed and spiked the guns of the three-gun battery, but the Russians also landed men from their ships and they had to retire. The other batteries were also silenced but were repaired during the night.

Three American deserters came off and acting on their information a Council of War decided to attempt to seize the town and take the batteries in reverse. On 4th September, 700 Seamen and Marines were landed under Captains Burridge and La Grandiere, after two batteries of 5 and 7 guns had been silenced by *President*, *Forte*, and *Virago*. There was a wooded hill in rear of the landing place and the Russians were driven back to it and one battery was destroyed. The Hill was then carried with difficulty, the top being covered with brushwood and brambles whilst skirmishers opened fire on the attackers; in a bayonet charge Captain C A Parker RM was killed, and the British had to retreat to the boats. This was effected, but not without loss and confusion, the British losing 107 killed and wounded, and the French 101. Besides Captain Parker, Lieutenants McCallum and A H Clements RM were wounded, and the attempt had to be abandoned. The landing place had been badly chosen, as the wooded hill commanded it and when they occupied the hill they could not be covered by the fire of the ships.

The Campaign in the Crimea[238]

Eupatoria.
When it was finally decided to invade the Crimea and attack the great fortress and arsenal of Sebastopol, the British, French, and Turkish Forces put to sea on 7th September 1854 and were disembarked at Old Fort, near Eupatoria, on the 14th. The disembarkation was completed on 18th, when the Army began its march to the Southward; on the 19th was fought the Battle of the Alma, resulting in a victory for the Allies. The Corps took no part in these operations, except landing parties to cover the seamen working parties employed in removing the wounded after the battle. But in order to protect the flank of the Allied Armies HMS *Vesuvius* and *Retribution* had been sent on 15th September with a detachment of 12 Officers and 418 Royal Marines from the larger ships, the whole under Captain Brock RN, to hold Eupatoria and to act in conjunction with the French afloat and ashore, to secure the town from enemy attacks, and to defend the Bay when transports were anchored there. They established a police and fortified three strong points: (i) the Lazarette at the South-West extremity of the Bay; (ii) a large house in centre of the Bay; and (iii) a strong stone magazine at the Eastern extremity. These were loopholed and strengthened with sandbags and breastworks. On 19th September a strong body of Cossacks attempted an attack but were repulsed without loss. On 23rd September, 300 French Marines reinforced the British, and later the Turks landed 200 Marines. On 26th September, HMS *Leander* landed 100 men.[239] The place was now strong enough to resist attack, but it was never used as a Base owing to the change in the plans. It was left in peace until 12th October. On that day a force of Cossacks, apparently about 800 strong,

---
238 Authorities: History of the British Army (Fortescue); Crimean War (Kinglake); Life of Admiral Sir E Lyons; Life of Admiral Sir W R Mends; Manuscript Records in RMO; Diary of Sir S Fraser; Globe and Laurel, 1904.
239 Life of Sir B. Lyons.

was observed advancing on the town. Captain Brock mounted 30 Royal Marines with a 12 pdr howitzer and some Tartar horsemen sallied out to meet the enemy. When about 600 yards distant the Cossacks opened out and disclosed four Horse Artillery guns which opened fire. Captain Brock retired and took up a defensive position; after a few shots the Cossacks retired.

HMS *Firebrand* arrived the following day with a reinforcement of 400 men of the Egyptian Army, with 24 and 12 pdr guns from the Fleet. These added to the defensive power of the place, which was not attacked again until November.

Balaclava.
After the Battle of the Alma, the Armies marched towards Sebastopol; moving round the East side, they invested the fortress on the South and East Sides, the British on the right and the French on the left. It was therefore necessary to move the main bases of both Armies; the French moved theirs to Kameisch Bay, which was very convenient for them; the British had to be content with the small harbour of Balaclava, which was to their left rear and not covered by their siege lines and was also open to attack from the North-East. The British position was on a plateau with heights looking to their rear over the plain of the River Tchernaya; these were known later as the Marine Heights. In order to protect his rear and flank Lord Raglan, the British Commander, requested Admiral Dundas to land his Royal Marines. On 28th September accordingly, a Battalion of 25 Officers and 988 NCOs and Men were landed from the squadron under Lieutenant Colonel T Hurdle RM, and two days later a further draft of 10 Officers and 212 Men were landed, making a total of 35 Officers and 1200 Men. They were formed into two Battalions. The Brigade was commanded by Lieutenant Colonel Hurdle with Captain Aslett as Brigade Major. The 1st Battalion was commanded by Lieutenant Colonel F A Campbell, Adjutant Lieutenant H G Elliot; and the 2nd Battalion at first by Major McLeux and later by Lieutenant Colonel T Holloway.

They were stationed on the heights 1200 feet above the sea and proceeded to construct a continuous entrenchment about two miles long, extending to Kadikoi - a small village where Colonel C Campbell, commanding at Balaclava, had his Headquarters. At intervals along these entrenchments Batteries were made, armed with an assortment of guns from 6 pdr field pieces to 32 pdr ships' guns. To work the guns a certain number of Marines were allotted from the two Battalions.[240] General Fraser records that the tents were old and dilapidated and that they suffered great hardships from wet and cold and bad food.

The outer line of defence was a chain of smaller redoubts upon a low range of heights, which stretch across the plain at a distance about one and a half miles from the gorge leading into Balaclava; these were manned by the Turks. The 93rd Highlanders with a field battery were in Kadikoi.

The RM Batteries were manned, No 1 by Captain Alexander and 78 RM, No. 2 by Lieutenant Joliffe or Pym and 56 RMLI, No. 3 by Captain S Fraser and a company of Royal Marines from the 1st Battalion, No. 4 by Captain Blyth and a party of RMLI. Lieutenant Bradley Roberts RMA acted as Gunnery Officer to the Batteries helping them cut fuses, etc.

---

240 Life of Sir E. Lyons.

The landing of the RM allowed all available troops to be employed in the actual siege works. The Navy also landed a Brigade with 50 guns, which were employed in the trenches and siege batteries; to this Brigade were attached Lieutenants Douglas and Steele and a party of RMA. Both officers were wounded and specially mentioned in dispatches.

By 17th October the Fleet had landed 1786 Officers and Seamen and 1530 Royal Marines, besides 400 Marines at Eupatoria.[241]

The Royal Marines had their first brush with the enemy on 6th October when the Russians drove in a Marine picket, but the 12 pdrs opened fire and the Russians retired.[242]

On 17th October there was a heavy bombardment by the land batteries assisted by the squadron.

Owing to the position of the Allied investing lines, the isthmus of Perekop was open to the Russians, who were thus able to pour troops and supplies into the Crimea, and they had also a large field army operating outside the invested fortress.

On 18th October the Russians, about 10,000 strong, appeared in the plain below the Marine Heights and with them large bodies of cavalry. They were met by our cavalry and retired across the river. The 2nd RM was moved to the lower part of the Heights to keep up communication with the Cavalry and Artillery; the 93rd Regiment were on the right, with one wing between the 1st and 2nd Battalions RM. It proved however only to be a reconnaissance in force.

On 20th October the Russians advanced again and the whole of the forces at Balaclava were under arms; two companies RM under Captain Timpson were sent to left of the RM lines, about the centre of the position, but it proved to be a false alarm. On 25th October, however, the Russians really advanced in force on the redoubts held by the Turks before described. The Turks were driven out of them, but the guns of Nos 1 and 2 Batteries RM covered them, rendering useful service - "a fire was opened with good effect upon the Russians as they followed up the Turks who were running across the open after having been driven out of the advanced redoubts."

The Russians came on and then took place the magnificent charges of the Heavy and Light Cavalry which are of immortal memory. Before the charge of the Heavy Cavalry, the RM Batteries opened fire on the Cossacks at about 200 yards range but had to cease fire after the first round as the Heavy Cavalry had closed with the enemy.[243] No. 2 Battery however opened on the Russian cavalry reserve and caused them to withdraw. No. 1 Battery fired into the Cossack right as they were reforming to charge again and dispersed them and shelled them as they retired across the plain. No. 4 Battery was also heavily engaged.[244] Colonel Campbell in his reports says, "During

---

241 Life of Sir E. Lyons.
242 Life of Sir W. Mends.
243 Globe and Laurel.
244 Ibid, 1904.

this period our batteries on the hills manned by the RMA and RM made most excellent practice on the enemy cavalry which came up the hilly ground in front." General Fraser gives a graphic account of the firing of No. 3 Battery on the Russian Cavalry after the charge of the Light Brigade*[245] but it is probable that he refers to the Heavy Cavalry charge.

Lord Raglan became doubtful of holding the base at Balaclava, but Admiral Sir E. Lyons was against any change, and it continued to be used as the Main Base until the end.

Inkerman.
On 2nd November two Companies under Captains Hopkins and March[246] were sent to join the Light Division before Sebastopol to replace a wing of the Rifle Brigade sent to Balaclava. These companies took part in the battle of Inkerman on 5th November, when the Russians combined a sortie by the garrison with an attack by the Army outside the fortress. Fought amidst fog and smoke, the British were more or less surprised, and this has become known as 'The Soldiers' Battle', in which the two companies of the Corps bore a distinguished part. The attack fell on the right of the British, the enemy coming up from the valley of the Tchernaya. The Companies were at first told to hold their ground and prevent a junction or communication between the troops and the town. The Inkerman Caves had however been occupied by the enemy's sharpshooters, who were picking off the officers and gunners. A Russian frigate was covering the open space in front of the caves. The RM were then ordered to clear the caves, but as soon as they appeared the frigate opened fire; Captain March was severely wounded in the jaw and several men were killed and wounded. Sergeant Richards and Corporal Prettyjohns then proceeded to clear and hold the caves, which they did quickly, but they were promptly counter-attacked; ammunition was nearly all expended and Prettyjohns led them in collecting stones which they threw down on the advancing enemy. Prettyjohns gripped the leader in a wrestling grip and threw him. Later in the day they were recalled and had to avoid the fire of the frigate.[247] Corporal Prettyjohns was awarded the Victoria Cross and Colour Sergeant Jordan the Distinguished Conduct Medal and annuity. Captain Hopkins received the CB.

These two Companies remained in the trenches for several months, after which they re-joined the Brigade at Balaclava.

The Brigade remained throughout the winter on the Heights and in the defences of Balaclava, suffering with the rest of the Army in the disastrous gale of November 14th, when the Fleet was much damaged, and several transports were wrecked with the winter clothing for the troops and large quantities of ammunition. They shared with the Army the great hardships of that winter.

On 10th December the garrison at Eupatoria was withdrawn and replaced by a Division of the Turkish Army, which was attacked again on 17th February 1855, but assisted by the ships drove off the Russians.

---

245 Globe and Laurel.
246 Life of Sir E. Lyons. Captain Portlock Dadson says four and Sergeant Turner 312 NCOs and Men.
247 Globe and Laurel, 1904.

Light Infantry.
In January 1855, as already stated, the Corps of Royal Marines was granted the title of Royal Marines Light Infantry.

On 1st February, Sir H Keppel RN, records in his diary that making his way up to Army Headquarters in the snow, he passed the Royal Marines, who occupied the lower ground, and above them were the Guards, and on the higher ground the 93rd Highlanders.

In March the Russians made a sortie which was repulsed.

On 9th April there was an ineffective bombardment by the Fleet and land batteries.

Attack on Redan.
In May 1855 a Division of the French Army, having taken up a position on the Tehernaya River, the Royal Marine Brigade was advanced in support of the French to cover their extreme right.[248] This enabled a detachment of the RMA from the Balaclava Lines to be transferred to the Siege Train, to reinforce the Royal Artillery. This detachment, under Brevet Major Alexander, joined the right attack on June 17th, in time to take part in the bombardment preceding the unsuccessful attack on the Redan on 18th June; they continued with this attack until 11th July when they were transferred to the left attack, rendering valuable aid in both positions.[249]

But in the meantime, the detachment with the Naval Brigade had added yet another leaf to the laurels of the Corps. For on 5th June, Bombardier Thomas Wilkinson of the RMA had gained the Victoria Cross; a terrific fire from the Russian guns had knocked to pieces the advanced works of the British. Wilkinson, jumping on to the parapet, replaced the sandbags as they were brought to him, rebuilding the parapet under intense fire and so saving many lives.

On 6th June the Mamelon was taken by the French.

Sea of Azoff.
The Russians had their depots for supplies to the garrison from Middle and South Russia round the Sea of Azoff, to which the entrance was through the Straits of Kertch on the East of the Crimea. The Navy were anxious to destroy these if possible, but it was first necessary to gain possession of the forts defending the Straits. On 1st and 2nd May, an expedition of 8500 French troops with 2500 British and 4 Batteries of Artillery started with a large squadron of ships, but on 3rd May the French squadron was recalled by the French C-in-C and the enterprise had to be abandoned. On 20th May there was another Council of the Commanders, and it was decided to proceed, the French providing 7000 Infantry and 3 Batteries of Artillery; the British 3000 Infantry, which included one RM Battalion and one Battery, the whole under General George Brown.

---

248 Life of Sir E Lyons.
249 Life of Sir E Lyons.

Kertch.
The troops embarked on 22nd May; there were six Battleships and a large number of small vessels and mortar boats. They steered for Kaffa Bay and the landing was effected at the Bay of Kanish Burnu, 5 miles from Kertch, covered by the steam frigates. There was no opposition on 24th May, the enemy retiring and blowing up their Batteries. The troops marched to Kertch and occupied it the same day, the Russians again exploding the magazines and retiring.

Yenikale.
The light draught vessels under Captain Lyons then pushed on to Yenikale to engage the Forts at the entrance to the Sea of Azoff till the Army could come up. On 25th there was a loud explosion and the Russians evacuated Yenikale, where nearly 100 guns were captured, with large quantities of ammunition and grain, which were destroyed. Yenikale was put into a state of defence, with a Turkish garrison. In "The Life of Admiral Mends", who was Flag Captain, he notes that the French and Turkish troops were very lawless, plundering and massacring, and notes "to the honour of the Royal Marines and 93rd Regiment, the only British troops landed, they preserved perfect discipline and the 93rd extinguished a fire that had broken out."

With the flag of Sir E Lyons in the *Miranda*, the squadron of light vessels entered the Sea of Azoff; among them were several mortar boats with RMA crews, the senior RMA Officer being Captain McNamara.

The Admiral then made over the command to his son, Captain Lyons, and returned. The squadron went first to Berdiansk on 26th May, where they destroyed a number of Russian vessels with grain and stores. On 28th they bombarded Arabat Fort, which blew up, but the garrison was too strong for the small Naval force to land.

They then went on to Genitchi, which they fired and destroyed. Passing on then to Taganrog, the principal place at the head of the Sea, on 3rd June the small flotilla anchored 1400 yards from the Mole. As their terms were refused, fire was opened on the Government stores and buildings which were set alight. The garrison of 3000 men were kept in check by the boats' crews. By 3 pm large stores of grain, etc, with the vessels building on the stocks, were set on fire.

On 5th June at Marianpoul, a small force was landed from the squadron[250] and the stores were destroyed. On 6th June, the stores at Gheisk were burnt and thus having swept the Sea of Azoff, they returned to Balaclava. Another raid was made in July under Captain Sherard Osborne with successful results.

The siege continued; the Fleet and mortar boats participating in the bombardments. The RMA in the mortar boats were under Captain Digby RMA, and the following officers were borne on the books of HMS *Royal Albert* for mortar boats; Lieutenants E H Starr, H Hewett, W Festing. When

---
250 There is a picture of this landing, which shows the Marines in the boats.

the weather was too rough for the boats they had to lie in Streletska Bay. They had been fitted on a plan devised by Captain Julius Roberts, RMA, which answered admirably.[251]

The RM Brigade still consisted of two Battalions, the 1st commanded by Lieutenant Colonel F A Campbell, and the 2nd by Lieutenant Colonel T Holloway.

On 28th June Lord Raglan, the C-in-C, died, much regretted. At the funeral the RMLI furnished a Guard of Honour at the pier in the Bay of Kazatch, and also lined the road from the pier inland.[252]

Malakoff and Redan.
In preparation for another attack on the Malakoff and Redan, a bombardment was opened on 5th September, and continued on 6th and 7th; the Russians were expecting an assault and had brought up large numbers of troops and so lost heavily. Bad weather prevented the Fleet taking part, but the mortar boats lying in Streletska Bay were able to bombard the Quarantine Fort. On 8th the French carried the Malakoff, but the British failed against the Redan. With the loss of the Malakoff the fortifications on the South side became untenable, so the Russians blew them up and retired across the harbour to the North side; during the night there were many explosions and the fortifications on the South side were seen to be in flames. The six remaining Russian battleships were sunk at their moorings, and the Southern portion of the Bridge hauled over. The Russian Black Sea Fleet of 18 battleships and numerous frigates was no more.

As the siege operations were finished, the Naval Brigade was withdrawn and re-embarked on 16th September. Sir H Keppel of the *St. Jean d'Acre* records in his diary: "5th October. Busy re-embarking the Royal Marines, the finest body of men in the Crimea."

It is interesting to record that the Royal Marines were the first British troops to re-enter Sebastopol, when in December 1918 the 3rd Royal Marine Battalion after the Great War took over the town from the German occupying troops.

The Admiralty letter to Admiral Sir E Lyons contained the following remarks about the RM and Naval Brigade:

"They command me on the present occasion to desire you to convey their approval of the conduct of the Officers and Men of the Battalion of Royal Marines who have been serving on shore, and more especially the officers and men of the Naval Brigade. That Brigade has shown the most cheerful endurance of the fatigues and hardships of the trenches, as well as the greatest skill and gallantry in working the guns and bearing their part in the danger of the advanced works in the assault on the enemy lines."

---

251 Life of Sir E Lyon.
252 Life of Sir W R Mends.

But the war was not over. Shots were still exchanged with the Russians on the North side of the harbour; the docks were being destroyed and plans were made for its further prosecution.

Kinburn.
The British were anxious to attack Odessa, but the French would not agree; finally, the Emperor Napoleon III by a telegram of 20th September 1855, ordered his generals to attack Kinburn.

Where the Rivers Bug and Dnieper flow into the Black Sea there is a wide estuary, and Nicolaieff, a large arsenal and Naval Station, is on the River Bug. There is a long spit of land on the South shore extending for some miles towards the opposite coast; the Dnieper flows into the eastern extremity of the Gulf. Not far inland from this point is the town of Kherson; through which troops passed to the Crimea via Perekop. Kinburn Spit was fortified; a large stone fort was situated some distance from its extremity. Two other earthwork batteries, offering a very small target, had recently been built with 10 guns each. Fort Kinburn was a solid structure, casemated and with earthworks above the masonry, mounting 55 guns, howitzers and mortars, mostly en barbette. There was a wet ditch on the North front and the garrison consisted of 1500 men. On the opposite side of the channel was Ochakoff Point, on which was Fort Nicolaieff, with 22 guns and also several earthworks.

The plan was to land on the Spit below Fort Kinburn to cut off the retreat of the garrison, and then to bombard the defences with floating batteries and mortars, as the battleships could not approach nearer than 1200 yards.

The occupation of Kinburn would stop communication by sea between Nicolaieff, Kherson and Odessa, and would threaten the rear of the Russian Army and perhaps cause it to evacuate the Crimea.

By 6th October all was ready: the battleships *Royal Albert, Hannibal, Algiers, Princess Royal, St. Jean d'Acre, Sidon,* and Leopard, with two transports carrying 4000 British Infantry, including Colonel Hurdle's Battalions of Royal Marines (950 strong) and a Battery of Artillery, the whole under Brigadier Hon H B Spencer, a similar force of French under General Bazaine,[253] with a French squadron and a large number of steam frigates, sloops, and mortar vessels. The mortar vessels were under Captain Wilcox RN and Captain Digby, RMA; 1st RM under Colonel C Campbell was reinforced by detachments of *Agamemnon, Royal Albert,* St. Jean d'Acre, and *Hannibal* from 15th to 30th October, and carried a colour lent by Captain King RN.[254] The 2nd RM (Lieutenant Colonel Holloway) was reinforced by detachments of *Algiers* and *Princess Royal* for some time. The RMA detachment was under Brevet Major Alexander and Lieutenant Joliffe.

They rendezvoused on 8th October and reached the anchorage on 14th. At night the *Fancy, Boxer, Cracker* and *Climber* (steam gun vessels) with 4 French gunboats forced the entrance into

---
253 Of Metz fame.
254 See Appx. Divisional. Colours.

the estuary, under heavy fire. The following morning the British and French transports landed their troops about 3 miles to the southward of the principal Fort, thus cutting off the retreat of the defenders. In the evening the ships ranged on the forts. The swell prevented operations on 15th, but on 17th with a Northerly breeze the mortar and other vessels took up their position off Fort Kinburn. By noon the buildings of the Fort were in flames and the Eastern face had suffered considerably. At noon 4 British and 4 French battleships approached Fort Kinburn in line abreast. Admiral Houston-Steuart and a small squadron pushed through between the Points to fire from the inside and cover the troops; 4 ships took on the centre battery and 3 the fort at the point of the Spit. The enemy's fire was soon silenced, and a flag of truce was sent ashore with a summons to surrender, which was accepted; the garrison of 1400 marched out with the honours of war. The British loss was only 2 wounded, but the Russians suffered heavily, and 81 guns were captured.

On the 18th the enemy blew up the forts on Ochakoff Point and retired. Kinburn Fort was put into a state of defence, which was finished by the end of October, and garrisoned with 1000 French troops and a small Allied Flotilla.

The expedition returned to Sebastopol on November 2nd. The troops were kept on board till 11th with a view to an expedition against Kaffa and Arabat, but the idea was abandoned. Part of the Squadron was sent to Malta to refit, and Admiral Sir Houston-Stewart was sent with 4 battleships to cruise in the Mediterranean and round the Ionian Islands. Admiral Mende records that the Royal Marines were sent to England on 2nd November, but these must have been supernumeraries as the detachments probably re-joined their own ships on 30th October.

The war dragged on, but there were no great operations. Peace was proclaimed at beginning of May 1856, and in July the evacuation of the Crimea was completed, having begun on 3rd June with the embarkation of the Coldstream Guards. It was completed on 12th July.

Rewards - The following rewards were given for the Crimea:

Colonel T. Hurdle - Brevet Colonel - 29.6.55.	CB	5. 7. 55.
Brevet - Lieutenant Colonels:		
Captain W F Hooking RMLI		13. 6. 55.
Captain G L Alexander RMA		2. 11. 55.
Brevet Majors:		
Captain W F Hopkins, RMLI		12.12. 54.
Captain S Fraser RMLI		12.12. 54.
Captain W E March RMLI		12.12. 54.
Captain G P Payner RMLI		12.12. 54.
Captain H Marriott RMLI		12.12. 54.
Captain W S Aslett RMLI		12.12. 54.
Captain G B Rodney RMLI		2.11.55.
Captain G S Rigby RMA		2.11.55.

The following were awarded the Legion of Honour:

	Col T Hurdle	
	Lt Col T Holloway	
Capt G B Rodney		Sgt C. Horner RMA
Capt G L Alexander		Sgt G Yule RMA
Capt W E Hopkins		Sgt R Richards RMLI
Capt W H Harch		Sgt J Jordan RMLI
Capt G S Digby		Bdr T Wilkinson RMA
Capt D Blyth		Cpl W Chappel RMLI
Lt A A Douglas		Gnr J Bull RMA
Lt H.J.Tull		Gnr F Kerr RMA
Lt F G Pym		Pte J Burton RMLI
Lt A C Steel		Pte J Coborn RMLI

This list is probably not quite complete.

On the 23rd April 1856, a Review of the Fleets that had been employed in the Black Sea and the Baltic was held at Spithead. 240 ships being reviewed by Her Majesty.

The Baltic Campaign 1854-1855[255]

Concurrently with the Crimea, operations were undertaken in the Baltic, with no very great results. It was almost entirely a Naval War on the British side; both the Admiralty and the C-in-C were so fully impressed with the folly of pitting ships against forts without an adequate landing force, lessons that have been so bitterly repeated, that they were almost unduly cautious.

A Fleet was assembled at Spithead under Admiral Sir Charles Napier consisting of 13 screw battleships, 8 screw frigates, 8 paddle frigates and sloops, 6 sailing battleships and a large number of mortar boats, etc. The Press Gang could not be used, so bounties were offered and all sorts of riff-raff, not seamen, were entered; in fact, if it had not been for the Royal Marines and the Coastguard, the Fleet could not have got to sea. Continuous service for seamen had only just been instituted, and the Admiralty acknowledged the value of the Corps in this emergency by the Order-in-Council 11th August 1854, when free rations afloat were granted.[256]

After inspection by HM The Queen, the armament sailed for the Baltic in April 1854, and cruised off the coast of the Gulf of Finland doing nothing; the Admiral was too old and past his

---
255 Authorities: Life of Sir C Napier, Britain's Sea Soldiers, (Field) ; Diary of Lt Durnford-RMA.; Life of Admiral Moresby; MSS Records.
256 See page 27.

work and would take no risks, in which he was backed up by the Admiralty.

Lieutenant Colonel Fortescue-Graham RM had been embarked in the Flagship to take command of any landing party.

Bomarsund.
The Russians had occupied the Aland Islands as an advanced post against Sweden and had erected there a big fort at Bomarsund. It was armed with 92 guns in two tiers. Its rear was protected by two smaller forts on hills in rear, Nottich and Tzee, and by a fort at Presto on a separate island. These were of granite and each had 24 guns in two tiers.

Admiral Napier at last feeling that something must be done, reconnoitred the Channels on 30th June and the Channels were surveyed by HMS *Driver*. Captain Sullivan RN found navigable passages, though they were difficult.

On 2nd July the Fleet returned to Helsingfors. On 30th July the French troops arrived but would do nothing till the arrival of their artillery. The British troops were represented by the Battalion of Royal Marines from the Fleet, and some Royal Engineers under Brigadier-General Jones RE, who was in command of the whole force. It was then decided to attack Bomarsund.

The Royal Marines were under Colonel Fortescue-Graham ADC, with Major Nolloth and Captain W M Heriot; Brigade Major, Captain W Elliot; Adjutant, Lieutenant O F Fraser; Orderly Officer, Lieutenant J M Lennox. The officers of the RMA Company were Lieutenants Mawbey, Poore, Hewett, J R Brookes and E C L Durnford (Acting Engineer). There were 8 RM Infantry Companies (Captains Hamley, Olavell, Naylor, Sayer, H Delacombe, McKillop, Fosbrook, John Elliot), Lieutenants H Evans, Jeffreys, Portlock-Dadson, J Sanders, T Bent, A Tait, W Sanders, Bland Hunt, Murray, with 18 Sergeants, 20 Corporals, 1 Bombardier, 7 Drummers, 70 Gunners, 541 Privates.

On 5th August the bombardment began, assisted by three French steamers. On 7th August HMS *Driver* embarked 700 Marines and 120 RE under Brigadier General Jones, with some naval guns under Captain Sullivan RN, and went round to the Northern landing place near Hulta in rear of the Forts where, covered by the *Edinburgh* under Admiral Chads, they were landed on the 8th and were followed by 2000 French Marines. The Russians were summoned to surrender but refused. French troops in large numbers were also landed at Tranvick Bay, to the South of the Fortress.

The RM advanced guard pushed on to about 1000 yards to the North of Fort Tzee, where it was encamped, and batteries were opened. The French Battery of four 16 pdrs and four mortars was ready and opened fire on morning of 13th; the British battery of ship 32 pdrs took longer to build as the guns had to be dragged up by the Sailors and Marines. The Marines built themselves wigwams, but it took several days to build the battery of three guns; they were further delayed owing to the few real seamen available having to go on board again to help to get off the *Penelope*, which had gone ashore under the big Russian Battery. During the building of the batteries, the fire of the enemy was kept down by the rifle fire directed on the embrasures by the Royal Marines and French chasseurs. A line of skirmishers of Royal Marines connected with the French attack.

The French attack on Tzee on the 13th commenced at 4 am and at 5 pm the Russians hoisted a flag of truce, but nothing resulted from the negotiations and the firing was continued. At 10 pm the other Russian forts opened fire and the French, finding no reply from Fort Tzee, crept up, found it deserted and at once occupied it. The fort caught fire the next morning and about 11 am it blew up. The British were occupied on the 14th in reforming their battery so as to fire on Fort Nottich.

On the 15th the British ships commenced firing on the remaining forts and the British battery opened on Fort Nottich at 8.10. After a considerable time some impression was made by the 32 pdrs on the granite, but it was not until the seamen had been relieved by the RMA, who had up till then been acting as infantry, that Lieutenant Mawby directed all the guns to fire simultaneously at one spot, when the granite fell in masses and a breach was made, and the defenders hung out a white flag. A hundred RM under Major Ord RE, then took possession of the Fort. The Russians had suffered heavy losses.

Presto Island Fort was next attacked; 800 men and 4 guns were landed at the back of the island, and Captain Ramsay opened fire at 1500 yards. This fort had suffered from the fire of the ships directed at the main fort and surrendered on 16th to Lieutenant Colonel de Vascoigne of the French Army and Captain S N Lowder, Royal Marines.

The Main Fort, having suffered badly from the fire of the Fleet and seeing the preparations for the renewal of the bombardment from the rear, surrendered unconditionally and the garrison marched out on the 17th; the Royal Marines and a French regiment of Marines forming a line to the quay, to which the prisoners were played by the Drums and Fifes of the Royal Marines.

As the French were in command they looted Presto Fort, which was blown up on the 30th, and Fort Nottich on the 31st. The Main Fort was blown up on 2nd September, and they were occupied till the 14th blowing up the works. The Russians had themselves burnt the villages on the 9th to prevent their offering cover to the besiegers.

Admiral Moresby records that "none of the shot and shell from the Fleet had penetrated either the sides or the roof of the Fort .... the guns on shore had done the job in two days."

The Allied casualties were very slight. The RMLI had one killed and one wounded but owing to the lack of sanitary precautions the French suffered heavily from cholera; out of 600 landed at Presto, 100 died, and out of 10,000 troops 800 were lost in three weeks.

The British left for Revel on 22nd September and the French went home.

Helsingfors and Sveaborg were reconnoitred and a few small raids were made, but nothing was done, and the 1854 campaign ended, the British ships having to withdraw on account of the ice.

For the 1855 campaign Admiral Napier was replaced by Admiral Dundas, but the cautious policy was still continued.

Many of the battleships and Royal Marines who had served in the Baltic in 1854, had been sent to the Mediterranean, where they served on shore with the RM Battalions. A French Corps d'Armee and floating batteries were to have taken part in the Baltic campaign but had also been diverted to the Black Sea. The Allied Fleet consisted of 21 battleships, 30 frigates and sloops, and 50 gunboats and mortar vessels, in which large numbers of the RMA were embarked. It also included some 'blockships' which were cut down old battleships armed with 60 guns.

The Russian coasts were harried and Cronstadt was reconnoitred; a sketch of the Cronstadt Forts was made by Captain R A K Clavell, RMLI, who afterwards painted it on the wall of the Commandant's Office in the old Forton Barracks.

Viborg.
On 13th July Viborg was attacked by the *Ruby* and boats from other ships under command of Captain Yelverton RN of the *Arrogant*, and another leaf was added to the Corps Laurels by Captain George Dare Dowell, RMA, who earned the VC.

Anchoring close to the South of Stralsund, the boats of the *Ruby*, *Magicienne*, and *Arrogant* with a strong body of Marines under Captain Lowder, RMLI (*Arrogant*) was sent in; when Viborg was sighted the flotilla was stopped by a boom and other obstacles. A masked battery opened on them at 350 yards range with musketry and grape shot; they also came under the fire of the Russian gunboats and had to withdraw to Stralsund, covered by the *Ruby*, which had failed to break the boom. An explosion took place on board one of the *Arrogant*'s cutters, which was swamped and drifted close to the Battery; Lieutenant Haggard RN of *Arrogant* with Lieutenant G D Dowell RMA of the *Magicienne* in the *Ruby's* gig with a volunteer crew, Lieutenant Dowell rowing stroke oar, succeeded in towing out the cutter under a heavy fire and saved the crew. For this Lieutenant Dowell was awarded the VC, as already stated.

On 21st July Captain Yelverton appeared before the batteries recently erected at Frederickshavn on the Finland coast between Viborg and Helsingfors, and opened fire; the enemy abandoned their batteries and the British withdrew without landing.

It was however considered necessary that the fortified island of Kotla should be examined. On 26th the *Arrogant*, with a small squadron including mortar boats and gunboats, anchored off Fort Rotchenholm; the *Magicienne* was detailed to destroy the bridge connecting with the mainland, and vessels were anchored to command the military road to Helsingfors and the channel. All the Royal Marines were landed under Captain Lowder RM, with Lieutenants Dowell, Mudge, and

Holmes, who took possession of the forts without opposition as the garrison had evacuated them. The stores etc were burnt and on 27th the squadron sailed, the Cossack being left in charge of the island.

Sveaborg.
But nothing serious was attempted, as Admiral Moresby says "As a last useless act Sveaborg was bombarded by the Fleet at 3300 yards range" on 9th August 1855. A certain amount of damage was done, but "it had no practical effect on the War". A considerable number of the mortar boats with the RMA were employed, and the mortars had fired so much that they became unserviceable and the boats were sent home. The Fleet returned in September.

The Mortar Boats had however earned the thanks of the Admiral, who said: "My especial thanks are due to the officers and men of the Royal Marine Artillery for the manner in which their important duties have been performed. The cool and steady courage with which they continued to conduct the duties of their station deserves the highest praise; and I have much pleasure in calling Their Lordships' attention to the services of Captain Wemyss as well as to those of Captains Lawrence and Schomberg of that distinguished Corps."

Lieutenant Colonel Fortescue-Graham received the CB in Gazette of 5th July, 1855.

Brevet majorities were awarded in Gazette of 2nd November 1855 to:

Captain S N Lowder RMLI
Captain J M Wemyss RMA
Captain J F Lawrence RMA
Captain G A Schomberg RMA

By the Treaty of Paris signed on 30th March 1856, the War was terminated.

17 – India and China 1857 - 1860

This period, which saw large numbers of the Corps employed on active service ashore, was also one of reorganisation; one of the most important events being the formation of the separate Royal Marine Artillery Division in 1859. It is also notable for the presentation of new Colours in 1858, and a great enlargement of all the Barracks.

In 1857 the numbers were 15,500.

Good Conduct Badges.
By Order-in-Council 6th May, the grant of Good Conduct Badges, which had been given to Seamen and Marines on 15 January 1849, was extended to Sergeants. The Army had granted them on 8th July 1848.

Promotion.
Again the subject of retirement and promotion was dealt with by Order-in-Council 13 November 1858. This did not much alter the 1854 order but laid down that General Officers; Commandants and Staff were not to hold their appointments for more than five years, and that Commandants were to be retired at 60 years of age.

The growth of the RM Artillery had led to the creation of an additional 2nd Commandant to superintend the Artillery duties (Order-in-Council 2nd February 1857) and also an additional QMS.

1858

The numbers were reduced to 15,000 in 104 Divisional and 14 Artillery Companies; the officers of the reduced companies were however retained as supernumeraries.

Barracks.
The RMA moved out of the Gunwharf Barracks into Fort Cumberland at Portsmouth.

In 1857 and 1858 very considerable additions were made to the Barracks at Stonehouse, three passages being added to the main block and a new infirmary. The North Wing was not finished till 1864 and the fine Western Front with vane and clock not till 1867 and the Married Quarters in 1869.

At Chatham the Barracks were enlarged to their present boundaries in 1862; the C, D, E and F Blocks were added in 1864. A and B Blocks and the Paymaster's Offices and Quartermasters' Stores were added in 1865, and in 1867 the single Officers' Quarters and the Field Officers' Houses.

Colours.
In 1858 new Colours were presented to all Divisions.[257] These departed from the 1827 design in many particulars and were evolved by the Heralds College according to recent Army regulations. No ceremony was observed in their presentations, which were mostly made at the DAG's Inspections.

1859

In 1859 the numbers were 16,995, in 112 Divisional and 16 Artillery Companies (Order-in-Council 30 April).

A considerable increase in officers was effected[258] by placing all the Adjutants, Quartermasters, Gunnery and Musketry Instructors on the Staff, instead of being borne on the strength of the Companies as hitherto.

RMA Division. The great event of the year was the creation of the separate Artillery Division, but the formation of the RMA as a separate Corps did not take place for another three years.

By Order-in-Council 22 October 1859, a Commandant, Barrackmaster, Paymaster, Surgeon, Assistant Surgeon, and another Adjutant, Lieutenant and Quartermaster, and one Quartermaster were allowed; the strength of the Artillery Companies being 2,992 as against an Infantry Divisional strength of 3,472 each.

The wording of the Order-in-Council says:

"The Artillery companies have hitherto been attached to the Portsmouth Division; but the present establishment of Artillery Companies being nearly equal to the strength of a Divisional Headquarters, much inconvenience is felt at Portsmouth, in consequence of all arrangements for the accounts of the said Companies having to pass through the Commandant of that Division; and this inconvenience is now greatly increased, as the Artillery Companies are stationed at a considerable distance from the Headquarters of the Division, and on the opposite side of Portsmouth Harbour. It will therefore be desirable, for the benefit of the Corps generally, to place the Artillery Companies on a more efficient footing, by forming them into a separate Division to be called the Artillery Division of the Royal Marines with the same staff and advantages as the other Divisional Headquarters".

The officers however still remained on the general list of the Corps, and the men were drawn from the general recruits and were called 'volunteers for the RMA'.

The Indian Mutiny, 1857[259]
Before dealing with the China War it is necessary to note the terrible doings in India. The Mutiny

---

257 See Appendix.
258 Order-in-Council 12 April 1859.
259 Authorities: With the Shannon's Brigade in India; History of the Indian Mutiny (Malleson); History of the British Army (Fortescue); RMO. Records.

of the Sepoys broke out in May 1857, and though it was far removed from the usual duties of the Royal Marines, yet a small portion of the Corps was able to render some assistance in that terrible struggle.

Calcutta.
The detachment under Colonel Lemon RMLI of two Captains (S Little and T V Cooke), six Subalterns (Cobb, Inglis, A D Smith, Sparshott and two others), 22 Sergeants, 5 Drummers, 273 Corporals and Privates, with Colour-Sergeant Prettyjohns VC as Sergeant-Major, which left England on March 12th for special service in China, were diverted to Calcutta, where they landed on 1st September, but were retained as garrison at Calcutta in Fort William and did not proceed up country. On 16th October they were reinforced by Captain Foote and 66 Royal Marines from HMS *Sans Pareil*, who however re-embarked on 30th October and Colonel Lemon's detachment left Calcutta for China on 4th November in the troopship *Assistance*. Their presence had released troops urgently required for service up country.

HMS *Shannon* and *Pearl* had also been sent from England to reinforce the China Squadron, but on arrival at Hong Kong, after disembarking their supernumerary RMA (1 officer and 25 other ranks) they were sent back to render assistance; they arrived in the Hooghly on 6th August and landed their Brigades, whose names have passed into history.

HMS *Shannon's* Brigade under Captain Sir William Peel included Captain T C Gray and Lieutenant William Stirling RMLI with 17 RMA and about 45 RMLI and was about 450 strong all told, with heavy guns and rocket tubes.

Fathpur.
They left Calcutta for Allahabad in the river steamer *Chunar* on 18th August, with a flat in tow carrying six 88 pdrs, two 24 pdr howitzers and two field pieces. They arrived at Allahabad on 2nd September and were joined on the 20th by a second detachment from HMS *Shannon* under Lieutenant Vaughan, making them all told 570. The troops were concentrating at Cawnpore and were being pushed up in detachments. A detachment of the Naval Brigade, 104 Officers and Men, escorting the siege train, left Allahabad on 25th October, the second detachment under Captain Peel followed on the 28th with a wing of 53rd Regiment, a detachment of RE and various regiments under Colonel Powell CB.

This detachment reached Fathpur - about half way – at midnight on the 31st, where information was received that about 4000 mutineers were occupying a strong position at Kajwa, 24 miles North-West of Fathpur. Colonel Powell decided to attack, and at 5 am on 1st November set out with a detachment of about 530 men, including 103 Officers and Men of the Naval Brigade under Captain Peel, with two 9 pdr guns. At 3 pm on 2nd November the enemy were sighted in position. Colonel Powell attacked at once, the 53rd in front, the Naval Brigade forcing back the enemy's left so that he was forced to face to left. Powell was killed, and the command devolved on Peel. Peel gave them no time to rally and posting a strong force to secure his new position, he carried his troops round the upper end of the embankment and cut them in two, drove them from this position and captured their camp and two guns. Pursuit was impossible as there were no cavalry, and the infantry had marched 72 miles in three days. The British losses were 95 killed and wounded; among the latter was Lieutenant Stirling RM who was severely wounded.

Peel resumed his march to Cawnpore, where Sir Colin Campbell arrived on 3rd November.

Lucknow.
His immediate object was the relief of the beleaguered garrison at Lucknow, where the Residency was being held by Generals Outram and Havelock; the 32nd DCLI (Bor's Marines) forming a principal part of the garrison under their gallant Colonel Inglis.

From 3rd to 9th November the C-in-C was organising his advance and arranging for the defence of his base at Cawnpore, where a garrison of about 500 Europeans were left, including 47 men and the 24 pdrs of the Naval Brigade (including presumably some Marines and wounded), under Brigadier C Windham CB.

A force of 3,400 men, including the Naval Brigade with eight heavy guns drawn by bullocks, and two rocket tubes mounted in light carts, with 250 Seamen and Marines, having been concentrated, the C-in-C advanced - on 12th November - on the Alumbagh, which was held by a force of 950 men left by General Sir Henry Havelock in the first relief. After a short opposition it was relieved, and the force halted next day. On 14th they moved to Dilkusha Park and the enemy after some resistance was driven out over the crest to the Martiniere and retired across the canal to the city.

The GOC was making arrangements to secure the ground won, when the enemy delivered a counterattack, which was soon defeated; but as the troops were settling down into bivouac, the mutineers at 5 pm made a fresh attack, which the British - who were now lining the Canal – repulsed. The Naval Brigade during the fight was posted on some high ground to the left of the bridge between the Martiniere plain and the Hazratgani main street and brought a heavy fire to bear on the enemy who were massed in this angle of the Canal and crushed them out.

On the 15th arrangements were made for the main advance to the Residency. The baggage was stored in Dilkusha Palace under cover of a strong rearguard.

On 16th the advance was continued, the first point of attack being the Sikanderabagh. It is not possible here to describe all the operations, but only to indicate the part taken by the Naval Brigade and the Royal Marines. The Sikanderabagh and the Barracks were carried with great gallantry, but the troops now found themselves held up by the Shah Najif, which was a large mosque situated in a garden, enclosed by a high loopholed wall, nearly square and very strong; also, between it and the plain was a fringe of jungle and enclosures.

The afternoon was going on, and the GOC considered it essential to secure this point. General

Adrian Hope with his Brigade was at hand, "Captain Peel brought up his 24 pdrs, mortars and rocket frames and placed them in battery against the Shah Najif in an oblique line, with their left resting on the village. The musketry fire of the enemy was very severe and interfered seriously with the fire of the guns; Major Barnston's Provisional Battalion tried to clear the fringe of jungle and enclosures but was unsuccessful, and after three hours' battering the Shah Najif was still unsubdued. The narrow lane leading up from the rear was crowded and confusion reigned; some of the houses were alight; reinforcements and ammunition had the greatest difficulty in getting forward. At 4 pm the enemy brought up a heavy gun to bear from the opposite bank of the river, and the first shot blew up one of the Naval ammunition waggons, and their musketry caused Captain Peel to withdraw his men from one gun. The position was critical, retreat was impossible, and it was necessary for the infantry to do with the bayonet what the artillery had failed to do." [260]

The GOC addressed the 93rd in this sense; Middleton's Battery RA passed Peel's guns on the right, got as close as possible, and opened with grape shot; Peel redoubled his fire;[261] the 93rd formed in open column on the plain and rushed on, Sir Colin leading them himself; but there was no breach or scaling ladders, so they halted and commenced a musketry fire. Two of the Naval guns were brought up to within a few yards of the wall and shot as fast as they could but could make no impression. The rocket frames were brought up and threw in a fire which, just skimming the top of the wall, plunged into the interior of the building and searched it out. Under cover of this the guns were drawn off. Meanwhile Sergeant Paton of the 93rd had discovered a hole in the wall and General Adrian Hope with some of the 93rd got through about 50 yards on the right and officers and men were pushed through; the sappers enlarged the hole and supports rushed in and, gaining the gate, threw it open. The enemy appear to have been panic-stricken by the rockets, as they gave up the struggle just as victory seemed certain for them. The troops bivouacked on the ground won. On the next day the attack was made on the Mess House, which was carried under cover of the fire of the Naval guns from early morning till 3 pm. The Mess House was actually carried by Captain Wolseley, who also continued his pursuit and carried the Moti Mahal as well.

Though the intervening space was exposed to fire from the Kaisar Bagh, Generals Sir Colin Campbell and Sir James Outram met, and the relief was effected.

The main point was how to withdraw the garrison with the women, children, sick and wounded, etc. It is impossible here to describe all the movements necessary, but on the 20th the Artillery and Naval guns commenced a heavy fire on the Kaisar Bagh, which they maintained all that day, also on the 21st and 22nd, and by evening of the latter day the breaches in the wall invited assault, but this was not intended, as the bombardment was to cover the withdrawal. The women and children safely reached the Dilkusha Park and during night of 22nd/23rd all the troops were withdrawn to the same place. On the evening of the 24th the convoy had reached the Alumbagh, and Outram - who had been forming the rearguard - rejoined on the 25th.

---

260 Malleson.
261 From reminiscences of an old Marine in the Globe and Laurel, 1904. We know the RM were there.

Cawnpore.
On the 27th a garrison having been left in the Alumbagh, Sir Colin arrived at the Banni Bridge to find that the garrison at Cawnpore were engaged in a desperate fight with the mutineers and the Gwalior Contingent. At Cawnpore there were 9 guns worked by a detachment of the Naval Brigade. On 26th November General Windham fought a very serious action, in which two 24 pdrs and two 24 pdr howitzers of the Naval Brigade were engaged; two of the pieces were for a time in the hands of the enemy but were recovered by the 34th Madras Native Infantry. Windham was only saved from disaster by the arrival of Sir Colin on the evening of the 28th. During the night of the 27th/28th, the convoys and troops were arriving from Lucknow. The Naval Brigade with the heavy guns, after a 30 mile march, only reached the ground an hour before sunrise. The mutineers had brought down their heavy guns to try and break the bridge of boats. The Naval Brigade was only allowed one hour for rest and food and were then sent to a point above the bridge where they could fire on the enemy's guns. The guns from Cawnpore entrenchment were also turned on the same point. For some time the artillery duel seemed equal, but gradually the British guns asserted their superiority and the Cavalry and Horse Artillery with Adrian Hope's Brigade were sent across, and by evening of the 30th the convoy was safely across on the Cawnpore side, though the rebels were still holding the town.

On 3rd December the convoy of women and children with the wounded was dispatched to Allahabad. Allowing time for the convoy to get away, Sir Colin Campbell determined to fight on 6th December. The Naval Brigade took part in this battle, which is outside the scope of this History. It resulted in a great victory and dispersed the enemy's troops and the dangerous Gwalior Contingent. Captain Gray RM appeared to have been wounded in this battle.

On 31st December the mutineers sent down a party to destroy the suspension bridge over the Kali Nuddi at Fathgarh (Futtegurh), but a party of Adrian Hope's Brigade with two 21 pdrs and one 8-inch howitzer of the Naval Brigade under Lieutenant Vaughan was sent on and saved the bridge and repaired it. They were soon after counterattacked by the rebels, but the main body was coming up, and a very severe defeat was inflicted on the rebels.

The next operation in which the *Shannon's* Brigade was engaged was the capture of Lucknow. The two 24 pdrs and two 6-inch howitzers of the Naval Brigade accompanied the force; the operations are outside the scope of this history, but it must be mentioned that in reconnoitring for a position for his guns in order to breach the Martiniere on 9th March 1858, Sir William Peel was severely wounded. Lucknow was in British hands by 19th March and on 1st April the Naval Brigade started for Cawnpore and Calcutta; on 2nd March Captain Peel had been created KCB and ADC to the Queen, but on 27th April at Cawnpore he succumbed to an attack of small-pox and died there.

In the London Gazette of 5th January 1858, Captain Gray and Lieutenant Stirling RM are mentioned in despatches, and Captain Gray is also mentioned in the London Gazette of 16th January 1858 as wounded and in the Gazette of 25 May 1858 he is mentioned as "deemed deserving of honourable mention" for services at Lucknow. A telegram from HMS *Pylades* dated Calcutta 7th September 1858 says; *"NCOs of Shannon's Brigade served during the whole of that Brigade's campaign in Provinces; Commander J W Vaughan RN and Lieutenant Stirling RM bear the highest testimony to their zeal and gallantry in the execution of their duties."*[262]

Chatham Division Sergeant Leo Hinder and Artillery Company Sergeant George Young of HMS *Shannon* were mentioned in dispatches.

Gorakhpur.

We must now turn to the proceedings of the Pearl's Brigade. This Brigade of 125 men under Captain Sotheby, which included Lieutenant F G Pym RMLI with 5 RMA and about 25 RMLI, were attached to a column under Colonel Rowcroft, which had been organised to clear the rebels out of the districts of Benares and the East of Oudh.

The Column also consisted of 50 Bengal Police and 359 Nepalese troops with four 12 pdr howitzers. It was to move to Tirhut along the Gandah towards Gorakhpur. Leaving their camp at Mirwa, they attacked a force of 1,200 sepoys and 4,000 armed irregulars at Sohunpore on 26th December 1857. The enemy were occupying a strong position at a village, covered in front by a tank with high trees and on the right by a tope of trees. Colonel Rowcroft halted at a distance of half a mile and rode forward to reconnoitre; he decided to turn the enemy's left, which was done with great success. Captain Sotheby managed the Artillery. "The Minie Rifles of the Royal Marines directed by Lieutenant Pym produced a striking effect."[263] The attack commenced at 11 am and by 1.30 pm the enemy was beaten back, pursued, and driven across the Gandah. "Rowcroft followed up his victory the next day by crossing the river and destroying the houses of the leading rebels."[264]

The Nepal Army in the meantime had turned the rebels out of Gorakhpur on 6th January 1858.

On 17th February, Captain Sotheby, with a force of 130 Seamen and Marines and with 50 Nepalese and 35 Sikhs, when escorting the boats up the River Gagra assisted by the river steamer *Jamna*, attacked and captured the Fort of Ghandepur.

Phoolpore.

On 19th February the Nepal Army reached Barari and that evening Rowcroft's force arrived within four miles and landed on the right bank. On the morning of the 20th he was joined by a Nepal Brigade and six guns; the boats were brought up, so that the Nepalese could cross at Phoolpore, but as that place was in enemy hands, Rowcroft marched on, capturing it and dispersing the rebels; he also captured three guns. Lieutenant Pym and Sergeant F Butler were mentioned in dispatches for this action.

---

262   RMO Papers.
263   Malleson.
264   Malleson.

General Rowcroft with the Pearl's Brigade, Yeomanry, and two Nepalese regiments garrisoned Gorakhpur, whilst the Nepalese continued the operations.

Amorah.
Soon after Colonel Rowcroft, with Captain Sotheby, advanced on Amorah, 68 miles to the West of Gorakhpur, and on 4th March took up a position close to the enemy's entrenched camp at Belwa, which was occupied by a large force of rebels. On 5th March the rebels to the number of 14,000 advanced to attack the British camp which was distant about 7 miles. They were resolutely met. The Naval Brigade distinguished itself, and the enemy were driven off, followed by Yeomanry, and retired to their entrenched camp at Belwa. This was known as the Battle of Amorah, and besides Lieutenant Pym, Sergeant Argent (Portsmouth), and Sergeant F Butler (Woolwich) were mentioned in dispatches. (London Gazette, 2 May and 4 August 1858). Rowcroft was not strong enough to attack Belwa, but on 17th at the village of Thanrowlee, and on 25th at Puchewas, he again met and defeated them in the plain between the positions.

On 28th April Rowcroft captured the Fort at Nugger; Acting Bombardier W Bates (Portsmouth) was mentioned in dispatches. The Brigade remained in the neighbourhood of Amorat; there was an engagement at Ranee's Cote on 9th June and another at Hurreah on 18th June.

The Pearl's Brigade was engaged again in September 1858 in the relief of Bhansi;[265] after which they were withdrawn.

* * * * * * * * *

But meanwhile large numbers of the Corps were being actively engaged in yet another theatre of war, namely China, where we meet again many of the places made familiar by the war of 1840-3.

China War 1856-60 [266]

In 1856 there was a renewal of the trouble with China; non-observance of the treaty arrangements, interference with merchants, and general difficulties with the Chinese head officials culminated in the seizure of the crew of the British vessel *Arrow*, for which no redress could be obtained. The C-in-C on the China Station therefore determined to take action against Commissioner Yeh at Canton and the following details are taken from Sir M Seymour's despatch of 14 November 1856.[267]

The Admiral moved HMS *Calcutta* (80 guns), his Flagship, above the Bogue Forts.

---

265 A full account of the Relief of Bhansi is given by Sergeant Sutler in Britain's Sea Soldiers, Volume II.
266 Authorities: Life of General Hope Grant; Per Mare Per Terram. (Major Poyntz); Life of Sir H Keppel; War in China. (Times Correspondent); RMO Records.
267 London Gazette, 8 January 1857.

Canton.

On 23rd October 1856, the force employed consisted of HMS *Coromandel, Sampson, Barracouta*, small steamers and gunboats with the RM detachments and the boats' crews of the *Calcutta, Winchester* and *Bittern*, and the boats' crews of the *Sybille* and *Encounter* (the RM detachments of these ships were protecting the English factory at Canton).

The *Sampson* and part of the force were sent up the Macao Passage to capture Blenheim Fort; the Admiral with the *Coromandel* and *Barracouta* went up to the Barrier Forts, below the City, where they anchored, and sent on the boats to capture the Forts; who, having effected their object and having destroyed the guns and ammunition and burnt the buildings, proceeded on to Canton at 2 pm. The *Barracouta* having joined the *Sampson*, they occupied Blenheim and Macao Forts armed with 86 guns; 250 Marines were placed in Macao Fort, which they held till the expedition of the following year.

The reply of the Chinese was unsatisfactory, so on the 24th the Admiral landed a portion of the Royal Marines to aid the *Sybille's* and *Encounter's* Marines in protecting the factory on the West side of the town.

Bird's Nest Fort on Honan Island and the Shameen Forts on the West of Canton were occupied without opposition and the guns destroyed. As still no satisfaction could be obtained from the Chinese the remainder of the Royal Marines and a body of Seamen with field guns were landed near the factory; posts and field guns were established at all available points, and boats kept watch against fire rafts.

The work was in charge of Captain W K Hall CB, the Flag Captain. The Royal Marines were under Captain P Penrose (*Winchester*) "who showed great ability and promptitude".

On 25th the Dutch Folly Fort in the river opposite the centre of the town was occupied by the seamen of the *Calcutta*. At 12.30 pm the Chinese made an attack on the factory; after being warned by the Consul, they were driven back by the Royal Marines under Captain Penrose.

On 27th October, demands for satisfaction were renewed; also for proper treatment of British officials and reception as at other Treaty Ports. As there was no reply, fire was opened by the *Encounter* with her 10-inch gun, which shelled the Yamun; Gough's Fort on the heights behind the town was shelled by the Barracouta. Eighteen Royal Artillerymen under Captain Rotton joined up and were sent to man the Dutch Folly Fort. On the 28th and 29th fire was kept up by the Dutch Folly Fort with some 32 pdrs from the ships and a breach was made in the City Wall.

The landing party landed at 2 pm, the Seamen under Captain Stewart, and the Royal Marines under Captains Penrose and Hoyle. They seized the parapet and diverging left and right, within ten minutes they were in possession of the defences between the two gates. "Captain Penrose on gaining the wall hastened to the gate on the right on which he planted a small flag to show the position to Captain Hall, who then landed the boats' crews of *Calcutta* and *Barracouta*, and having pushed his way through the streets to the City Gate effected an entrance; the gate was blown to pieces and part of the arch destroyed. There was only scattered desultory fire from the Chinese. Three Privates RM were killed, 11 Seamen and Marines were wounded.[268]

The Admiral landed and went over to the quarters of the Chinese Commissioner, and the troops were withdrawn, re-embarking quietly and in good order. At 5 pm a fire broke out in the suburb; the breach was filled up again by the Chinese during the night but was blown down again on 30th and also on 1st November after further repairs.

The Chinese still continued refractory, sending inferior officers to treat and refusing to accede to the British demands. Therefore at 11 am on 3rd November slow fire was opened from the *Encounter*, *Sampson* and Dutch Folly Fort, which was continued on the 4th and 5th.

On the 5th, the Chinese projected an attack on the factory and ships: as there were 26 war junks anchored off French Folly Fort, Commodore Elliot in the *Barracouta*, with the *Coromandel* and a detachment of Royal Marines and ships' boats was sent to disperse them and capture the Fort. At daylight on 6th he proceeded, towing the boats, and engaged the junks, who replied fiercely with 150 guns. After 35 minutes the *Barracouta* and the boats drove the Chinese out of the junks, and turned on the Fort. The guns and ammunition were destroyed; only two junks escaped, one of which was the Admiral's ship. The others were burnt.

On 11th November the Bogue Forts were destroyed. The *Sampson* and *Niger* were sent to protect the factory; the remainder of the Squadron went down river and attacked the two forts on the Wangtong Islands, which were taken possession of by the boats and the Royal Marines after considerable resistance, 201 guns being captured. On 13th the Forts on Anunghoy, on the opposite side, were similarly taken without any casualties, and the command of the river was in British hands. In the London Gazette of 6th January 1857, Captains Penrose and Boyle, with Lieutenants R P Henry, H Smale (wounded), C F Burton, W W Allnutt and Private Lye were mentioned in dispatches. Captains Penrose and Boyle were again mentioned in the London Gazette of 30 January, 1857.

On 14th December 1856, the Chinese burnt the British factories at Canton, but the Admiral put the Church and Clubhouse in a state of defence with two Companies of the 59th Regiment, and the RM detachment of the *Calcutta* (Captain Boyle); the RM detachment of the *Sybille* garrisoned Dutch Folly Fort, and that of the Nankin Macao Fort. Reprisals continued, parts of the city being burnt, but hostilities ceased for a time.

Escape Creek.
On 25th, 26th, and 27th of May 1857, an attack was made on 41 junks lying in Escape Creek by

---

268 Times Correspondent: War in China.

Commodore Elliot with the *Hong Kong* and some gunboats; the junks were armed with 24 or 32 pounder guns in the bows and four to six 9 pdrs. There was a brisk action, after which the Chinese crews fled; five junks were brought off, the remainder being destroyed. The Royal Marines were landed to clear the village and had 9 men wounded.

Fatshan Creek

On 1st June a large expedition under the Admiral himself destroyed 75 war junks in Fatshan Creek. The *Coromandel*, flying the flag of Sir M Seymour, towed up the boats with 300 Marines and arrived at Macao Fort on 30th May. Here she joined the gunboats which had been on watch. In Fatshan Creek two miles from the entrance, is Hyacinth Island; there is a steep hill on the left bank opposite the island, crowned by a fort with 19 guns. Higher up two small creeks go off right and left. Along the creeks and across the Channel above the island were moored 72 junks, their bow guns commanding the two channels. There was also a six-gun battery on the shore opposite to the Fort.

The *Coromandel* went first, towing the Marines under Captain Boyle RM in boats; she was to cover their landing. The gun-boats and boats were to follow her, but to wait till she was well up. At 3 am 1st June they started; the Chinese opened fire at dawn from the junks and the Forts. Going up the left hand channel the *Coromandel* ran aground, on a line of sunken junks, under heavy fire. The boats were cast off and rowed under the land; Captain Keppel coming up in the *Hong Kong* stood-in between the *Coromandel* and the bank; the *Haughty*, towing the boats of the *Fury*, *Inflexible* and *Cruiser*, with other gunboats, came up. Sergeant Christian RMA was killed here.

The *Opossum* went up the right hand channel. Several gun-boats went ashore, but the boat continued up the creek. As the tide was rising the *Coromandel* and gunboats floated off again and the scene was like a regatta.[269]

The Chinese fire now slackened. The Royal Marines and the boats' crews had by this time landed and advanced up the precipitous side of the hill on which the fort was situated, where the Chinese had not expected them; the latter threw down 32 pdr shot as they could not depress the guns sufficiently. Led by Commodore Elliot and Captain Boyle, who ran a race up to the embrasures, the fort was captured; Boyle missed a mandarin, but Elliot shot him. The Admiral also climbed the hill. The Chinese resisted bravely and continued firing their guns until the attacking party were within 50 yards.

The British turned the forts' guns on the junks, who replied. The Seamen then returned to their boats, followed Captain Keppel in the *Haughty* and made their way above the island. The Royal Marines descended on the far side of the hill, and wading into the water up to their waists, joined in the attack on the junks. The gunboats and boats placed themselves alongside the junks, whose crews made off across the paddy fields; the junks were then blown up or set on fire. Commodore

---
269 Cooke.

Keppel in his galley with some boats' crews, charged among the junks and forced his way about 6 miles up the creek, almost to the town of Fatshan, where the Chinese turned out and stopped him; he then returned with his captures. The British loss was 13 killed and 40 wounded, of which the RM had 3 killed and 6 wounded. In the London Gazette of 1st August 1857 the following were mentioned in despatches; Captains R Boyle and T Magin; Lieutenants G L Blake, R P Henry, C W Burton, E Swale, A I Ozzard, A H F Barnes and A H Pascoe; 2nd Lieutenants W Allnutt, F T Cooper and C L Owen.

In the meantime, the Government had decided on making the Chinese observe the treaties; reinforcements were being sent from England; Lord Elgin was sent out as a Plenipotentiary to arrange matters. HMS *Shannon*, *Pearl* and *Sans Pareil* were sent from England.

Royal Marine Battalions.
Lieutenant Colonel Lemon with Captains Little and Cooke, and Lieutenants Inglis, J Cobb, A L Smith and E A Sparshott and 300 NCOs and Men, were sent from Plymouth for special service on 12th March. But the Indian Mutiny had broken out and they were diverted to Calcutta (q.v.) as were the troops under orders for China and did not reach the squadron off Honan Island till 19th December, where they formed the nucleus of the Provisional Battalion Royal Marines, which was completed by the detachments of the Fleet. It is interesting to note that Colour-Sergeant Prettyjohns VC was Sergeant-Major of the detachment. HMS *Shannon*, *Pearl* and *Sans Pareil* were also sent to India, where we have already seen their doings.

A Brigade of Marines was also ordered to be sent from England. The Admiralty Letter to the C-in-C in China, dated 8th August 1857, said: "In consequence of the troops originally destined for China having been unavoidably diverted for service in India, Their Lordships have determined to strengthen the forces employed under your orders by the addition of 1,400 RMLI and 100 RMA as stated in detail in margin. They will leave England in less than 10 days from this date.[270] They are to be borne on the books of the Flagship as Royal Marines serving in the Fleet, but as far as practicable the Battalions are to be kept distinct for special service.

"Captain J. C. Travers, now serving in China, shall act as Brigade Major, and is to be borne specially for that service."

Colonel Holloway was appointed to command and the detail was:

	Lt Col	Capts	Subs	Sgts	Cpls	Drms	Ptes & Gnrs
Artillery Coy	-	1	4	5	8	2	80
1st Bn Chatham & Woolwich	1	8	18	34	32	8	600

---

270 As a matter of fact they left within three days.

| 2nd Bn Portsmouth & Plymouth | 1 | 8 | 18 | 34 | 32 | 8 | 600 |

The Officers were:
    Lieutenant Colonel Holloway
    Brigade Major - Major J O Travers   ADC - Lieutenant C J Ellis

Artillery:
    Brevet Major G A Schomberg
    Lieutenants C Williams, Footing, Crease, and Crawford

1st Battalion:
    Lieutenant Colonel A S S Walsh
    Captains P M Croker, Gritton, Morrison, Masters, E L Pym, S J Tribe, E P Ussher, R Parke
    Lieutenants H L Evans, J F Hawkey, C F Coppin, E Willis, R J H Douglas, W Portlock-Dadson, C F Short, G O Evans
    2nd Lieutenants H Wolrige, H J Barker, J S Straghan, L Rokeby, A Fonblanque, M Heriot, S T Collins, E P Thomson
    Adjutant - Lieutenant J C Travers
    Quartermaster - Lieutenant Carrington
    Sergeant-Major - J B Woon

2nd Battalion:
    Lieutenant Colonel E Hocker
    Captains Kinsman, Ward, Jackson, Driver, Fox, Budd, Spratt, J B Prynne
    Lieutenants J de C Meade, W Connor, W H Wroot, W G Hale, E Bazalgette, C J W Napier,
    J D Broughton, F Parry
    2nd Lieutenants W H Smith, J A Godfrey, W Armstrong, J W O'Grady, J W Scott, W H Poyntz, C E Servante, C E W Oliver
    Adjutant - Lieutenant J H Maskerry
    Quartermaster - Lieutenant Gill

There were three medical officers with each Battalion, the senior being Dr Little.

The Artillery, Staff, and Woolwich Companies embarked in the transport *Adelaide* at Deptford on 15th August 1857, and arrived at Hong Kong on 30th November 1857.

The Chatham and two Portsmouth Companies embarked in the P&O *Imperatrix* which sailed from Portsmouth on 12th August and arrived at Hong Kong on 5th November.

Two Portsmouth Companies and the Plymouth Companies left Plymouth in the P&O *Imperader* on 13th August, and after a record passage arrived in 80 days at Hong Kong on 28th October. They were at once sent on to Canton and landed their Marines at the Wang-tong Islands below the City.

The French contingent was also arriving, as well as the British gunboats.

On 18th November HMS *Calcutta* (flagship) left Hong Kong for Canton, and anchored off Tiger Island where the *Adelaide* arrived on 1st December. On 4th December the *Assistance* arrived with Colonel Lemon's Battalion from Calcutta.

The Admiral, Sir M Seymour, issued an order against looting, and took the opportunity of thanking the officers and men of the Fleet for their services during the past year.

The force now available for the operations against Canton consisted of:

Army: RA and RE, 59th Regiment, Madras Native Infantry	800
Royal Marines	2200
Naval Brigade	1500
French Troops and Sailors	900
	5700

Major General Van Straubenzee was in command, with Majors Clifford and Crealock as his Staff Officers.

Honan Island.
On 15th December 2nd RMLI and 150 French Sailors were landed on the back of Honan Island, an island facing Canton; it is about 11 miles wide and 4 to 5 miles long. They were followed by the 1st RMLI and occupied the big warehouses on the shore. Colonel Holloway was in command. In his Report Colonel Holloway mentions the excellent work of Lieutenant Crease RMA, who, with only the artificers of the Brigade, constructed a fine magazine for the safe storage of their large amount of ammunition.

Lord Elgin's demands were that Canton should be opened as the other Treaty Forts to commerce; compensation for the damage to British merchants to be paid (the factories had been burnt), and the occupation of Honan to be acquiesced in as a guarantee. The Chinese Commissioner Yeh treated all negotiations with contempt, so preparations for the attack went on.

Life on Honan Island was not pleasant, the mosquitoes rejoicing in the men just out from England. The Times Correspondent wrote: "How the Marines do swear".

On 20th December, divine service was held in the Warehouse, 1,200 Marines attending.

Colonel Hocker had formed a choir from his Battalion.

Capture of Canton.
On 23rd December the General and Admiral made a reconnaissance in force with 70 Marines, at Tsing-poo, where Gough had landed in 1841 on the West side of the City, but decided against it. On 24th a reconnaissance was made on the East side, and it was decided to attack the East and North-East Gates and the Lin - or Eastern - Fort.

Yeh was informed that if he did not yield in 48 hours, the City would be bombarded.

The force was very healthy; the 2nd RMLI had only 15 sick out of 700; the weather was cold, rations were good and plentiful, and they had an extra supply of quinine. On 28th December the 59th Regiment arrived.

GENERAL ORDER.

Headquarters,
Honan.
26th December

Troops under command of General Van Straubenzee, CB, will be formed in Brigades as follows:

1st or Colonel Holloway's Brigade.
   Colonel Holloway ADC
   Brigade Major, Captain J O Travers RM
   Orderly Officer, Captain Ellis.
   1st Battalion RMLI
   2nd Battalion RMLI

2nd or Colonel Graham's Brigade.
   Colonel Graham.
   Brigade Major, Major Luard, 77th Regiment
   Orderly Officer, Captain Hacket, 59th Regiment
   RE and Volunteer Sappers
   RA and RMA
   Provisional Battalion RMLI (Colonel Lemon)
   59th Regiment
   38th Madras Native Infantry

Colonel Lemon's Battalion was completed on 19th December by the detachments from HMS *Calcutta, Nankin, Sybille, Sans Pareil, Esk, Highflier*, to a strength of about 800 Officers and Men. Lieutenant C W Burton (*Calcutta*) was appointed Adjutant.

The Artillery were under the orders of Colonel Dunlop RA.

Captain Morrison, 1st RMLI, was appointed Provost Marshal.

GENERAL ORDER

Before Canton.
26th December.

The Naval and Military Commanders-in-Chief of the Allied Forces before Canton have agreed to the following operations against the City.

First bombardment to commence at daylight on Monday 28th December. The ships and vessels named in the note under Letter A (viz. Actaeon, Phlegethon, and Gunboats) on signal being given will open fire on South-West angle of the City walls, with a view to breach them and impede the communication of the Chinese troops along the parapets to the Eastward.

Ships and vessels in note under Letter B (viz. Mitraille, Fusee, Cruiser, Hornet, Niger, Blanche) and the Dutch Folly Fort with a similar object will breach the City walls opposite the Viceroy's residence; the mortar in Dutch Folly Fort shelling the City and Gough Heights.

Ships and vessels in note under Letter C (viz. Nimrod, Surprise, Dragon, Marcia and gunboats), between Dutch Folly Fort and French Folly will open fire on South-East angle of the New and Old City walls and walls forming East side of City.

To commence simultaneously when White Ensign is hoisted at fore of Actaeon, and yellow flag from Phlegethon, Hornet and Avalanche will repeat these signals.

Bombardment to be in very slow time and continued day and night, not to exceed per each gun 60 rounds during the first 24 hours; C ships to fire 100.

Immediately bombardment opens, landing of Allied Troops will take place at the creek in Kupur, where British and French flags will be planted, in following order, commencing at daylight:

1. *Sappers and Miners, 59th Regiment, RA Stores and Ammunition, etc.*
2. *French Naval Brigade, Stores, etc.*
3. *Naval Brigade under orders of Hon. C. Elliot.*
4. *Naval Brigade from Canton.*
5. *Colonel Holloway's Brigade of Royal Marines.*

etc., etc..

Following will be dispositions after landing:

British Naval Brigade on left.
Centre Brigade:
    Lieutenant Colonel Lemon's Provisional Battn RM.
    59th Regiment.
    RA.
    Sappers.

French Naval Brigade on left.

Colonel Holloway's Brigade with RMA in reserve

After getting into position, Allied Force will remain in Line of Contiguous Columns of Brigade until further orders for advance, which will be made to a position for the night preparatory to active service in the morning.

                                              M. Seymour, Rear-Admiral.
                                   E. Regnault de Guouilly, Rear-Admiral.
                                   C. V. Van Straubenzee, Major-General.

In the Dutch Folly Forts platforms had been built for two 13-inch mortars and two 10-inch SS mortars and two 24 pdr rocket tubes. These were under Major Schomberg RMA and played on Magazine Hill, the City Heights and Gough's Fort.

The slow bombardment began at daylight and continued all day; the gunboats embarked the troops and went down to Kupur, and the General made a close reconnaissance of Lin Fort whilst the troops were disembarking. The covering force of the 59th was posted to protect the RE and Volunteer Sappers and working parties, whilst constructing piers etc. to land the guns and making a road across the marshy paddy fields to the hard ground about 400 yards inland. The tide prevented the disembarkation till 9 am on 28th, but all were landed before nightfall. At 10 am the French force, having landed, moved forward to some rising ground where fire was opened on them, and part of the 59th advanced to the right of the French. The French drove the Chinese from the undulating ground, covered with Chinese graves in front, but it was difficult to cross the paddy fields in front. The French howitzers opened on Fort Lin, and the 59th moved to the Joss House within 300 yards, covered by the fire of the British howitzers. The troops pushed on and kept up a heavy fire on the embrasures until the 9 pdr field guns got into action. The Fort was partially surrounded, the storming parties carried the Fort and the Chinese fled up the hill to Gough's Fort, which our heavy guns could not reach. The British and French flags were hoisted on Fort Lin, where the troops bivouacked for the night. Fires broke out in various parts of the town during the night.

On the next morning troops were formed up for the assault, the French Naval Brigade commanding the direct road to the East Gate, the 59th in rear and under cover of Fort Lin; the Provisional Battalion RMLI to the right on a range of hills fronting NNW; and on its right the Naval Brigade as if to advance towards Fort Gough, North of the City on the heights and the feint succeeded. The 3rd Division of the Naval Brigade was placed in rear and to the right of the Joss House, occupied by the Allied Commanders during the night. One Battalion of Colonel Holloway's Brigade was on the left, the other at the landing place protecting stores and keeping open the communications. The Artillery were in position in front of Fort Lin.

The guns opened fire on the East Wall to clear off the Chinese; the assault had been timed for 9 am but the French started at 8.40, followed by the 59th, but fortunately Major Schomberg RMA, in the Dutch Folly Fort was able to stop the guns and the French, 59th Regiment, and the RE escaladed the wall about a mile to the North of the East Gate, and turning northward started clearing the walls.

At daylight on the 29th the large Joss House had been occupied by parties of the Naval Brigade, supported by the RM Battalion under "that deserving old Officer" Lieutenant Colonel Lemon. The artillery bombardment was to continue till 9 am to give time to bring up the ladders, but this was effected with more despatch owing to the great exertions of all concerned, particularly of the "RA and RMA, whose energy and zeal were worthy of high commendation", by whom two guns were brought close up the ditch. Captain Bate RN was killed reconnoitring for a place to put the scaling ladders;

Captains Blake and Cooke RMLI brought up their two Companies of Royal Marines with scaling ladders and kept up a heavy fire on the embrasures, Blake's company losing one man killed and six wounded. When they had quelled the fire, the scaling ladders were placed, and the Naval Brigade and Lemon's Battalion escaladed the walls at a broken embrasure, 200 yards South of the North-East Gate; turning North, they swept along the Wall to Magazine Hill on the North side of the town.

At this time a Chinese Army, now perceiving "we did not intend to attack Fort Gough, descended the hill, and necessitated my sending some companies of Colonel Lemon's RMLI Battalion to protect our right, and afterward to direct Colonel Walsh's Battalion to extend to their right to prevent advance of the enemy which was judiciously executed by all officers concerned, though I regret to say Colonel Holloway and some men were wounded."[271] Colonel Holloway's Brigade had been posted to the North-West of Fort Lin to meet such an eventuality.

The Tartars came on in skirmishing order, but were driven off by the RN and it was difficult to prevent the Marines from charging the enemy; but they drove the Chinese out of a little village and a small wood, and were pressing forward to complete their defeat, when the General recalled the Brigade; there was much discontent among the RM at this order; the men had thrown off their knapsacks in the fight and when recalled Colonel Holloway and a few had to bring them in.

---

271 GOC's Dispatch.

By 9 am the greater part of the force was on the Walls, the enemy making slight resistance except at the Gateways. The Naval Brigade and Royal Marines proceeding past the five-storied Pagoda and the Magazine, the enemy rallied at the North Gate; part of the Naval Brigade charged down the hill and the enemy were driven back. At this point he showed a bold front. Brigadier Graham with the 59th and the 38th NI took the East Gate and proceeded round the walls nearly to the South Gate of the City.

About 2 pm Gough's Fort - above the town - was assaulted and taken. The British remained on the Walls for the next 3 or 4 days; no tents were available and there was heavy rain for 70 hours, during which Colonel Lemon's Battalion was in the open and consequently there was a good deal of sickness.

In the London Gazette of 5th March 1858, the following were mentioned: Colonel Holloway ADC, Lieutenant Colonels Walsh, Hocker, and Lemon, Captain and Brevet Majors Boyle, J A Morrison, Parke, Jackson, and Foote, Major J O Travers, Brigade Major, "whom from personal observation I recommend as a valued officer", and Captain Ellis.

Brevet Major Schomberg, i/c Mortar Battery in Dutch Folly Fort, and that "indefatigable young officer" Lieutenant Festing RMA were also mentioned.

Gough's and Bluejacket's Forts were blown up, but without effect on the Chinese. After a pause to see if the Chinese would surrender, and as no move was made, on 5th January 1858 operations, were resumed and advancing from Magazine Hill, 250 of the French Naval Brigade entered the Yamen and secured the Tartar General where they were joined by the 2nd RMLI and two howitzers; two Companies of the 1st RMLI with two howitzers, under Colonel Holloway, forced their way into the Yamen of the Governor of Kwang Tung and made Pek-wai prisoner. The Provisional Battalion with two guns first marched to the Temple, where the Imperial Commissioner Yeh was supposed to be hiding, but failed to find him, and later joined by 200 of 1st RMLI - the whole under Captain Parke - they secured the Treasury and a large quantity of silver.

Captain Cooper-Key and 100 of the Naval Brigade secured Yeh later in the day. Escorted by Colonel Hocker and two files of Marines, he was brought before the General and the Admiral; as he was still recalcitrant, he was eventually sent to India. In order to control the City, the Governor Pek-wai was reinstated with a council consisting of Colonel Holloway, Captain Martineau (French), and Mr. Parkes the Consul, who governed the City for the next year. Later a Constabulary was raised, to which the RM contributed 3 officers and about 30 men under Captain E L Pym RM.

The casualties had been; RMA, Colonel Holloway, 1 Sergeant and 2 Gunners wounded; Colonel Lemon's Battalion, 10 wounded; 1st RMLI, Lieutenant Portlock-Dadson severely, and 1 Sergeant and 3 Privates wounded.

1858

The Royal Marines remained in garrison with two Sepoy Regiments. The 2nd RMLI were quartered in the monastery of Celestial Bliss, and one day a priest, waiting till the senior officers were out on a reconnaissance, presented an order from the General to recover his property, and carried off vast quantities of treasure that had been hidden in the idols, the guards being unable to prevent him.

As fighting was still going on in India, the Army Staff Officers wished to rejoin their regiments, so Major J O Travers became AQMG of the force vice Colonel the Hon. A Clifford, Captain T V Cooke became DAQMG vice Major Crealock and Captain Carrington DAAG.

Captain Ellis became Brigade Major of the RM Brigade, Lieutenant J C Travers ADC to Colonel Holloway and Lieutenant J F Hawkey Adjutant of 1st RMLI.

White Cloud Mountain.

The garrison duty at Canton was varied by one or two expeditions. On 2nd June 1858 General Van Straubenzee made a reconnaissance of the White Cloud Mountain, where Chinese Forces were reported. He discovered an encampment and sent back for reinforcements; by 7 pm 1,400 men had started. Colonel Holloway with about 600 Marines and 100 of the 59th with 4 guns joined the General; the remainder consisting of the Naval Brigade, RA and Sepoys, embarked in gunboats, and went down the river to land next morning. The advance began at daybreak and it was found that only the two RMA rocket tubes could accompany them. At 11 am the enemy camp was sighted, and the Advanced Guard pushed on, 3 officers and 8 men being wounded. Owing to the great heat the troops had to halt until the evening, the Marines carrying a village in which they were able to shelter. At 5 pm the force again advanced and crossed the mountain, 1200 feet high, but found the enemy camp deserted.

They returned to Canton on 4th, having burnt three villages. Lieutenant Rokeby and 26 men were wounded, but a lot of men were lost from sunstroke. In the London Gazette of 28th July 1858, the following were mentioned:[272] Brevet Major R Boyle, Lieutenants G McCallum, W E Clements, E H Norton RMA, H B Savage RMA, 2nd Lieutenants W W Allnutt and H T Cooper.

Nantow.

In August another expedition was sent to the walled town of Nantow. They proceeded by water in gunboats and landed at 11 am on the 10th, to the South-East of the City, the covering party being provided by the Naval Brigade. This entailed an advance through a populous suburb. The advance was made in two parallel columns; 40 officers and 489 Naval Brigade formed the outer column; 3 officers and 64 men RA, 3 officers and 22 men RE, 5 officers and 104 men the 104th Regiment, 2

---

272 These were all officers serving afloat.

officers and 100 men 12th Madras NI, 5 officers and 140 men RMLI forming the inner column. The RMLI under Captain Foote were in reserve. They moved along the canal in great heat under constant fire from the right flank.

After reconnaissance, at 1 pm the ladders were placed, and the Naval Brigade stormed the walls, covered by the 59th and 12th NI, whilst the RM covered the right flank. During the escalade of the walls the force under Colonel Graham was attacked by several hundred Braves who were most gallantly repulsed by Brevet Major Foote and the Royal Marines[273] though not without loss. The wall was gained, and the enemy fled; the gate was blown in and then after burning the city they returned to Canton the following morning. Unfortunately, three officers were killed by the accidental discharge of the seamen's rifles.

The Royal Marines lost 8 wounded, one mortally. On 23rd August Lieutenant Colonel Walsh was invalided, and on 1st October Colonel Lemon assumed command of the 1st RMLI.

Provisional Battalion.
On 22nd September 1858, a Brigade Order was issued that, as the Provisional Battalion had been so reduced by the re-embarkation of the detachments of which it was composed, the remainder were to be drafted into the 1st and 2nd Battalions, to take effect from 1st October. Its strength was then only about 350. The Companies of the 1st and 2nd Battalions were made up to 75 men each, all above this and the NCOs were borne supernumerary.

British Columbia.
On 24th November 1858, Captains Bazalgette and Magin, 5 Subalterns (C L Owen, Henry, G L Blake, Sparshott and ?) with 80 men from each Battalion were sent to British Columbia, where they occupied the island of San Juan which was garrisoned by the British and American Marines until 1872, when the German Emperor gave the decision in favour of the United States.

Canton.
On 4th January 1859 the Brigade was attacked, whilst on its weekly route march outside Canton. Just after having their dinners they saw a large body of Chinese advancing on them. Colonel Holloway decided that from the point of view of prestige they must return by the same route, so flankers and skirmishers were thrown out and the march began. The Chinese followed to within three miles of the walls, and they had to pass through some villages, but the enemy fire was kept down by the skirmishers; the only chance of the getting to close quarters occurred when Captain Ussher, the Provost Marshal, who had gone out to draw in the skirmishers of the 2nd Battalion (who had become too much extended) charged at the head of a few men and cut down and dispersed a party of Chinese. As the day was closing in, and in view of the General's instructions that they were not to take the offensive, Colonel Holloway did not feel justified in taking any further steps. They arrived at the North Gate at 6 pm in good order. Colonel Lemon was in command

---

273 London Gazette.

of 1st RMLI, and Captain Little 2nd RMLI. Lieutenant O'Grady was slightly wounded. The Quantung Braves had been driven off with loss.

On 8th January a force of 1,700 men was sent to take the town of Shek-Tseng, about 9 miles off. This force marched to a village about 1000 yards from the walls, whilst 400 of the Naval Brigade went by water to the mouth of the river. The only means of approach was across a narrow wooden causeway and the bridge; in the middle of the river was a well armed island. Two hundred French, 150 from 1st Bn Royal Scots, 150 RE formed the fighting line, and 1st RMLI. under Colonel Lemon in support, the remainder in reserve. The French charged forward, but were checked by a volley. General Straubenzee sent forward the 65th Bengal NI to support them, whilst rocket tubes and howitzers covered the Royal Scots and RE, who worked up the river. The Naval Brigade, who had landed on the Shak-Tseng side, came down on the Chinese flank; panic seized the Chinese, so the Royal Scots, followed by the RE and RM Battalion, crossed the bridge. Large quantities of ammunition and stores were captured, and the destruction of the city created a great impression on the Chinese, who had considered the place to be impregnable.

But failing to make any impression on the Chinese Imperial authorities from Canton, the Allies decided to make an attack in the North, nearer Peking, with a view to getting them to observe the Treaties. In May 1858 the Squadron had attacked and occupied the Taku Forts with a naval landing party, but they had only been held temporarily, and the Chinese were now on their guard.

Taku Forts.
In June 1859, Vice Admiral Sir James Hope (who had succeeded Sir M Seymour) determined to attack the forts with a view to forcing the Chinese to admit the two Residents in accordance with the Tientsin Treaties. Colonel Lemon, with 400 of 1st RMLI and a small party of RMA under Lieutenant Williams and Lieutenant Tuson were sent from Hong Kong; about 400 Royal Marines were provided by the Fleet and a half company of RE with 19 gunboats reinforced Sir James Hope, who with other vessels was lying off in the Gulf of Pechili. The Royal Marines were formed into a small Brigade under Colonel Lemon, with Captain Parke in command of 1st RMLI, Captain Masters of a 2nd Battalion formed from the ships' detachments; Captain Croker was Brigade Major, Lieutenant Rokeby ADC, and Lieutenant Evans Adjutant of the 2nd Battalion. The small party of RMA were under Lieutenant Williams.

These operations are worthy of careful study as an example of how not to do it: Colonel Lemon objected strongly to the plans.

On 17th June a single vessel with the Admiral on board went to the anchorage off Taku; the rabble prevented any landing, and it was found that the Pei-Ho River was obstructed. On 20th the Residents arrived and told the Admiral to make his own arrangements to open the river. Against the advice of his military advisers in charge of the troops, the Admiral insisted on making a frontal attack on the Forts; on 25th under cover of the gun-boats the Seamen and Marines were landed on the mud flats, through which they had to struggle to attack; 4 gunboats were sunk, including the Admiral's and he himself severely wounded - he was rescued by the US ship. Out of the landing party of 1,100, 434 were killed or wounded and the Royal Marines lost Lieutenants Inglish and Wolrige, with 21 NCOs and Men killed or died of wounds, 15 officers and 142 NCOs and men wounded.

The Reports of Colonel Lemon and Captains Parke and Masters give an excellent picture of what occurred.

Colonel Lemon's report says that the boats with the Royal Marines assembled round the *Nimrod* on the evening of 25th June, and were joined by the RE and the Royal Naval Battalion under Captain Chadwell, RN. They attacked the fort on the right bank of the Pei-Ho River and landed on the mud in front; the 1st RMLI was the first to arrive and advanced in skirmishing order to cover the parties carrying the bridges and ladders; the RE acted as coverers on the left. The ground was tenacious, and the men sank knee deep in the mud, and could only advance slowly. Colonel Lemon says it was impracticable and injudicious to adopt a regular formation as they were under heavy fire, and that he led the main body forward until cover could be obtained for forming; that on arriving at a wet ditch the covering party waited for the bridges, but as there were none available they crossed by wading; advancing until they arrived at another deeper and more difficult ditch which they also crossed, and advanced until they got cover from the advanced trench, where they waited for the ladders, and here Colonel Lemon was severely wounded in the head and handed over the command to Captain Parke.

Captain Parke's report says that the 1st RMLI embarked in the boats at 5.45 pm and were taken in tow by an American steamer, *Taiwan;* as there was great difficulty in towing, all the boats except one had to cast off and were taken in tow by the *Forrester*. On arriving at the Stakes, the boats went alongside the *Cormorant* (1 Lieutenant and 46 NCOs and Men had been left in the American ship). Here Captain Willis RM ordered them all to follow him and pull ashore. The boats shoved off, the men pulling with all their might to be the first on shore.

The Battalion landed without any order and there was great confusion. All efforts to advance in anything like military formation were futile; the men jumped out anyhow, some up to their waists in water. Parke says he tried to extend them, but they rushed on in masses, all arms intermingled, towards the fort under a tremendous fire of guns and gingalls, which told with great effect. The men and officers pushed on gallantly; the ground was tenacious, clayey mud, into which the men fell down and rendered their arms useless; they arrived at the first ditch; they had no ladders, or bridges, but the seamen brought up some ladders; only one was serviceable and they crossed by wading.

Those who managed to keep their ammunition dry, kept up a heavy fire to cover the crossing of the rest. After a rest they advanced again and encountered another large ditch; there were then only about 100 men but many officers of the 1st RMLI and they succeeded in crossing, but as the ammunition was quite wet their fire slackened. Colonel Lemon being wounded, Captain Parke took command of the Brigade. Night was falling and only one efficient ladder was up; as the British fire lessened the Chinese assembled in large numbers and kept up a heavy enfilade fire. Under these conditions Parke - after consulting with Commanders Commerell and Heath RN, and Major Fisher RE - decided to withdraw; the men were ordered to move off noiselessly in parties of twos and threes; the retreat commenced at 2 am, the enemy firing light balls etc unceasingly. Most strenuous efforts were made to bring off the wounded; all behaved well and although invidious to mention any one, Captain Parke calls attention to acts of gallantry by Lieutenant Wolrige, who was shot dead whilst cheering on his men; by Lieutenant Rokeby who volunteered to advance with only one ladder; by Lieutenants Evans and Straghan in assisting to carry off the wounded under a very severe fire and by Sergeant Major Woon and QMS Halling, whose gallantry was most conspicuous.

From Captain Master's report of 2nd RM we learn that he himself and his party were transferred to the *Forrester* and proceeded inshore to well within range of the forts who were firing; Captain Willis ordered them to land and the Admiral ordered them to take the fort by assault and to lose no time, as the sun was setting. The first boat contained Lieutenant Williams and a party of RMA; Masters himself was in the next. The boats could not get near the land and they jumped into the water up to their middles under a galling fire of guns and musketry and were ordered to make the best of their way and to form up when they reached firmer ground; on arriving at the Stakes they formed up, some of the 1st and some of the 2nd. They were kneeling in the mud, which was over their ankles. Masters tried to get them to advance, but they were exhausted and could not use their muskets, which were unfit from salt water. Here he himself was wounded and taken off, and the Battalion was brought off by other officers. The Chaplain, the Rev W Huleatt, was severely wounded with the 1st RM

After this reverse the 1st RM returned to Canton on 6th August in HMS *Magician* and the Northern operations were abandoned till the properly organised expedition of the next year.

At this date the 1st RMLI numbered 696 and the 2nd RMLI 625. Colonel Lemon was invalided to England on 26th July 1859 and in the London Gazette of 16th September 1859 the following were mentioned in dispatches; Colonel Lemon, Brevet Major Parke, Captains W G Masters, P K C Croker, Lieutenants Rokeby, J F Hawkey, H L Evans, J Straghan, Sergeant Major Woon, and QMS Halling. The following Brevets were given for the operations in 1857-59:

To be Colonel -	Lieutenant Colonel T. Lemon.	
To be Majors -	Captain J C Travers	Captain J C Morrison
	Captain W F Foote	Captain G E O Jackson
	Captain P C Penrose	Captain C J Ellis
	Captain R Boyle	Captain R Parke
	Captain T V Cooke	

RM Brigade - broken up.
On 26th December 1859, the following Brigade order was issued by Colonel Holloway ADC at Canton.

"The Board has directed that the Brigade shall be broken up and formed into one Battalion of 8 Companies, each consisting of 1 Captain, 2 Subalterns, 5 Sergeants, 6 Corporals, 1 Drummer, 76 Privates, with the following staff, 2 Lieutenant Colonels, 1 Adjutant, 1 Acting QM, 1 Acting SM, and one Acting QMS."

Lieutenant Colonel Hocker CB was appointed to command, but he was invalided on 27th January 1860, and Lieutenant Colonel J O Travers vacated his appointment of AQMG and assumed command. Lieutenant Carrington was appointed Adjutant, Lieutenant Meade QM, Lieutenant Cobb Assistant Adjutant, Sergeant Denslow to be Sergeant Major (died at Tientsin), Sergeant Brown to be QMS. The Medical Officers were Drs Little, Shin and Cope. Mr Spark, Paymaster.

The Company Officers were
- 1 and 2 Chatham: Captains Evans and Gritton
- 3 and 4 Woolwich: Captains Prynne and Ussher
- 5 and 6 Portsmouth; Captains Symonds and Jackson
- 7 and 8 Plymouth; Captains Budd and Spratt

NCOs and Men employed in the Military Train and Constabulary were formed into a Supernumerary Company; the Battalions were at once formed into four companies each of medically fit men; the men of the Bengal Artillery were attached to the RMA Company and 34 Privates were selected to complete the RMA Company proceeding to Macao Fort, and 51 Privates were sent to complete the Fleet; remaining Officers and NCOs to be borne supernumerary as well as the volunteers from the Indian Army. Colonel Holloway and the surplus officers and men returned home on 11th January 1860. A draft from England under Captain Slaughter arrived.

General Van Straubenzee published the farewell order on 31st December 1859:

"My sense of the efficiency, good order and high state of discipline of the Brigade, which reflect also much credit upon the Officers of the Battalions; the forbearance of the NCOs and Men of the RM Brigade since the capture of this city and their general very good character during the two years they have been quartered in it are most creditable to them, as soldiers, and to the splendid Corps of which they form part, and merit my highest approbation."

As serious prosecution of the war was now inevitable and as the Indian Mutiny had been crushed, troops were now available and were sent from India and from England. Colonel Gascoigne and Brevet Lieutenant Colonel March with a draft were sent from England to replace Colonels Hocker and Lemon.

General Sir Hope Grant of Indian fame was sent to command. The French Commanding Officer was General de Montaubam, afterwards known as Count de Palikao.

About 14,000 British and 7,000 French troops concentrated at Hong Kong and proceeded North in March 1860.

Shanghai.
The 87th Regiment relieved the Marines at Canton and the RM Battalion was the first to move North; the left wing arrived at Shanghai on 6th April under Lieutenant Colonel March, where the Taeping rebels were threatening trouble. Owing to want of accommodation they remained at first in the *Assistance*; they were accompanied by Lieutenant Williams' Company of RMA.

The right wing under Colonel Travers went to Chusan.

Lieutenant Colonel Gascoigne joined the left wing on 15th May and took up a defensive line from the Stone Bridge, by the grandstand of the racecourse, to Ning Po Joss House on the North-East extremity round the walls to the City gate. On 16th June General Sir Robert Napier approved of these arrangements. The French - about 200 strong - were on the South side. On 15th June there was considerable anxiety about an advance by the rebels, but it did not materialise then.

A state of the Battalion dated 13th June 1860 gives an interesting account of their distribution:

Location	Officers	NCOs & Men
On board Transport Octavio at Shanghai	11	214
In Barracks, Shanghai	6	110
Ning-po Joss House	3	79
Souchon Bridge	3	80
Hospital	-	6
At Chusan	12	228
On board HMS *Encounter*	2	58 (on passage)
Hong Kong on Staff	2	8
Chinese Coolie Corps	4	33
Hospital Ships	-	5
Canton Constabulary*	3	132
Supernumerary	14	218
RMA		
Shanghai	2	87
Macao Fort, Canton	1	9
Coolie Corps	-	2
Barrack Sergeant at Canton	-	1

*Captain E L P Pym

On 21st July, leaving Lieutenant Colonel March as senior officer at Shanghai, with 300 RMA and RMLI and about 600 French, Lieutenant Colonel Gascoigne embarked with Nos 5 and 6 Companies (207 all told) but they did not arrive at the rendezvous till the 29th, too late to be present at the taking of the Taku Forts. Colonel Travers with Nos 1 to 4 Companies were not long at Chusan; leaving there on 11th June they joined the force in the North, where the ultimatum to the Chinese had been sent on 8th March.

The British Force was organised into:

> A Cavalry Brigade – King's Dragoon Guards, Fane's and Probyn's horse, and Stirling's Battery RHA.
> 1st Division - General Sir John Michel - Two Brigades
> 2nd Division – Major General Sir Robert Napier - Two Brigades

Taku Forts.
The 1st Battalion RMLI was attached to the 4th Brigade, consisting of 67th, 99th and 19th Punjab Native Infantry.

About the middle of May the force embarked for the Gulf of Pe-Chi-Li and the British landed at Talienwan and the French at Chefoo, where they formed depots.

On 20th July the troops re-embarked, and on 28th anchored off Pei-Tang-Ho. On 30th Sutton's Brigade (2nd), the Rocket Battery, and a 9 pdr with a party of French were towed ashore, landing through the mud, and next day, found Pei-Tang evacuated.

On 31st a storm prevented disembarkation, but it was continued next day. That night was spent in repairing roads, which occupied the next ten days; the British were kept making roads and building wharfs and so kept out of mischief, but the French went plundering.

On 3rd August a reconnaissance was made of the causeway leading to the Taku Forts; and on 9th August it was discovered that the country was traversable by all arms. The RM Battalion under Travers, with Lieutenant G Mairis as its Adjutant, had now joined the Army.

On 12th August the French and the First Division advanced frontally along the causeway, the 2nd Division and the Cavalry Brigade followed the reconnaissance of the 9th instant; with the British were two batteries of the new 12 pdr Armstrong guns.

The First Division pushed along the causeway and captured the village of Sinho. About two and a half miles South-East of Sinho the Chinese were holding an entrenched position about Tong-Ku to which the causeway led with a wet ditch on either side.

On 13th August, General Grant caused the canals to be bridged, refusing to be hurried by the French. He ascertained that the Chinese forces had retired to the South (right bank) of the Pei-Ho end that there were no troops on his side of the river except in Tong-Ku and the Taku Forts to the South-East of him.

The First Division advancing on the right and the French on the left, crossed the space between the causeway and the Pei-Ho. The 60th Rifles advanced under cover of the field guns, which silenced the Chinese artillery; the 60th entered the works at Tong-Ku and found the Chinese in full retreat; the French further to the left met with some resistance. The Allies then arrived without difficulty within two miles of the Taku Forts. There was a halt of six days whilst ten day's supplies were collected at Sinho, and the heavy guns and ammunition brought up; a bridge of boats was thrown over the Pei-Ho at Tong-Ku and a close reconnaissance made of the forts. On each bank there was a detached fort to westward of the larger and principal fort; on the North bank this detached fort was only two miles from Tong-Ku and could be approached by a detour clear of fire and without cross fire from the Southern bank. If taken it would be possible to enfilade the large fort to the South-Eastward and it also overlooked the detached fort on the Southern bank. General Grant decided to attack this point. General Montauban refused but had to give way. By August 20th all was ready, the road built, and the canals bridged. Batteries were established against the North face of the detached fort; the Admiral had not brought up his gunboats, so the Chinese turned the guns in the cavaliers of the river forts to bear on the attackers.

The obstacles to be surmounted were a deep dry ditch, then an open space with abatis, then a wet ditch and a strip of ground 20 feet wide with pointed bamboo stakes, and then another wet ditch and another staked strip; there was also a thick wall of unburnt brick with loopholes.

At daybreak on 21st August the batteries opened vigorously, and the Chinese replied; at 6 am the magazine in the fort blew up, and at 6.30 am a shell from a gunboat blew up another magazine. At 7 am every gun in the detached fort was disabled and two batteries of field guns and the storming parties of the 44th and 67th Regiments advanced to the gate; the French on the right approached the Western angle. The wing of the RM Battalion had been detailed to carry pontoons for crossing the ditches, but owing to casualties unfortunately blocked the causeway and the stormers had to swim; it was sometime before sufficient troops were assembled; Major Anson - of the Staff - got to the post and hacked down the ropes of the drawbridge and some men got across, whilst Captain Prynne RMLI was the second man over the wall and shot the Head Mandarin with his revolver; Lieutenant Pritchard RE was the first. The garrison resisted bravely, but after three and a half hours the fort was taken.

Captains Barker, Carrington, and Straghan RMLI were among the wounded, and were mentioned in dispatches.

The heavy guns were brought forward to the attack on the main fort, when the Chinese on the South bank hoisted the white flag. They were told that unless the main fort was surrendered within two hours the Allies would re-open fire, and towards the end of that time the troops advanced; the enemy offering no resistance, they walked in and took possession. The Political Officer forced the Chinese commander to sign a capitulation giving up all the country and strong places on the river as far as Tientsin, including that city.

After a day removing obstacles in the river, the Admiral and Mr Parkes steamed up the river to Tientsin. On the 25th the troops followed, and by 5th September all had followed except the 44th Regiment, which had been sent to Shanghai on account of the Taeping Rebels. A party of Marines and a battery of artillery were left to garrison Tong-Ku.

On 7th September the Convention was to have been signed, when it was suddenly realised that the Chinese authorities had not, and could not produce, any authority to treat; on which negotiations were broken off.

Peking.
Meanwhile Lieutenant Colonel Gascoigne and the two Companies from Shanghai had joined the other half battalion, and Colonel Gascoigne assumed command. On 8th September the First Division and the Cavalry Brigade, with the French, began their march on Tung-Chow, sixty miles up the river and twenty miles below Peking. The RM Battalion was now with the 2nd Brigade. The 2nd Division was left at Tientsin; they marched in small detachments, the siege train and part of the supplies going by water. Major Poyntz says that the regiments will remember how the Royal Marines managed to keep up a supply of bitter draught beer throughout the march, which was much appreciated.

Captain C L Barnard with his party of RMA were brought to notice for the manner in which the heavy guns were brought up from Tientsin to Tung-Chow; the labour of pulling the boats over the flats was very great and it was "due to their exertions that the guns were brought up so rapidly and safely."[274]

On the 13th the troops reached Ho-Si-Wu, where the medical officers of the RM Battalion established a general hospital. On the 17th the Cavalry Brigade and 1st Division left Ho-Si-Wu. Mr Parkes and other officers and officials had preceded on the 16th to Tung-Chow to make arrangements; but the force had hardly advanced two miles before hostile forces were observed, and whilst waiting for the return of the advance party, suddenly a commotion was observed and Colonel Walker, AQMG, and other officers were seen galloping towards the column, some of them wounded. As there were no signs of Mr Parkes' party, General Hope Grant advanced in attack formation. Fire was opened by the Chinese, who were holding an entrenchment several miles in length with a battery of 16 guns. After a sharp engagement of two hours (the RM Battalion was in reserve), the enemy gave way and were severely cut up by the cavalry. Captain Ussher RM, the Provost Marshal, was nearly cut down by a Tartar, having been unhorsed.

---

274 Letter from General Hope Grant.

Following up the enemy, the 99th and 15th Punjabis entered Ching-Kia-Wang, which was given over to plunder as a reprisal for the capture of Mr Parkes' party. On 20th September there was a reconnaissance and the enemy were found to be in front of the Yang-Liang Canal, the waterway between the Pei-Ho and Peking, over which were two bridges, one of marble, at Pa-Li-Chao. The other - of wood - was about a mile to the West. The French were directed on Pa-Li–Chao, and the British Infantry on to the wooden bridge, with the cavalry to the left: the cavalry charged and, followed by three batteries of Armstrong guns and two Battalions, inflicted great loss. The pursuit was stopped six miles from Peking. The 2nd Division was hurried forward and by 2nd October the full force had arrived. On 6th October the advance was resumed through a tangle of ruined fortifications, and Tung-Chow was occupied. The Royal Marines and a party of French taking possession of the City, Colonel Travers disarmed and dispersed a lot of Chinese soldiers who were hovering about the suburbs.[275]

The letters of application show that they served in these actions, by which the Tartar covering army was driven off, and the road to Peking opened, together with occupation of Tung-Chow protecting the convoys of stores and supplies upon which the army before Peking depended.

On 7th October the French reached the Summer Palace and started plundering. The prisoners from Mr Parkes' party were restored on the 8th, but only 19 remained out of 39, the remainder having been tortured or murdered.

General Grant threw up breaching batteries to blow down the city, and at noon on the 13th they were ready to open fire, when the Chinese surrendered and agreed to terms. On the 18th and 19th as a punishment for the treatment of our prisoners, the 1st Division burnt the Summer Palace. On the 24th a Convention and ratification of the Treaty of 1858 were at last signed by the Chinese Imperial Authorities.

On 8th November the troops began the march back to the transports; on the 12th Desborough's Battery, Probyn's Horse, the RM Battalion and 99th Regiment, the whole under the command of Colonel Gascoigne, marched for Tientsin, where they arrived on the 14th and embarked in HM Troopship *Adventure*. As the transport was not big enough, 31 officers and 629 men went in *Adventure*, whilst 4 officers and 240 men went in HMS *Sampson, Fury, Inflexible*, and *Minerva*; the RMA went in the *Highflier*.

Memorial.
The RMA Battery and the RMLI Brigade erected a memorial to their comrades at Hong Kong. This shows that from 1857-60 the loss in all ranks was: killed or died, 3 officers, 2 staff-sergeants, 13 corporals, 214 gunners and privates; wounded, 27 officers, 16 sergeants, 20 corporals, 4 buglers, 155 gunners and privates.

---

275 The fact that they were present at these two actions of the 18th and 20th September was the grounds on which they were awarded the clasp for Peking. (WO Letter, 20th February, 1863.)

In a Board Letter it was said that, *"My Lords observe with pleasure that the Marines, as usual, had conducted themselves with the spirit and gallantry which have always been evinced by that Corps."* [276]

Colonel Holloway, Lieutenant Colonels Lemon, Travers, Hocker and Gascoigne were awarded the CB, and there were many mentions in dispatches and brevet promotions.

London Gazette - 6th November 1860: Mentioned-in-Dispatches: Lieutenant Colonel J O Travers, Captains C W Carrington, G Mairis, W J Barker, J Straghan, J C Symonds, J C Morrison, J B Prynne; Lieutenant T H Brenan, Sergeants G Tearle, T Knapp, Privates F Kelly, Brady, R Bowerman, for the capture of the North-West fort at Taku, and Sergeant H Trent for 'deserving all praise for exertions to get the pontoons up although wounded'.

In the London Gazette of 15th February 1861, the following brevet promotions were awarded:

Brevet Colonel	Lieutenant Colonel J H Gascoigne
Brevet Lieutenant Colonel	Captain & Brevet Major J C S Morrison
To be Brevet Majors	Captains J C Symonds and J B Prynne

Taeping Rebellion.
The RM detachment left at Shanghai was engaged on operations against the Taeping Rebellion from 1860 to 1863. In 1860 a fierce attack on Shanghai was driven off, and in the London Gazette of 14 November 1860, Lieutenant Colonel March, Captain Budd, Lieutenants O'Grady and O L Williams (RMA) were brought to notice; also, Lieutenant F R Phillips who volunteered to carry a flag of truce to the rebel camp, "a service of great danger".

In April 1862 troops were sent from Tientsin under General Staveley to keep a radius of 30 miles round the city clear of the rebels. The Shanghai merchants also raised a force under European officers under an American officer named Ward. He was succeeded by an RM officer, Captain Holland, who was however defeated at Taitsan, 22 February 1863. He was replaced by Colonel Charles Gordon RE (Chinese Gordon) who with this force - named the 'Ever-Victorious Army' - eventually stamped out the Rebellion after two years.

The RM detachments were engaged in the capture of the Walled Cities of Kah-Ding and Singpoo, and in numerous engagements in neighbourhood of Shanghai.

---

276 10 November, 1860.

VOLUME THREE 1837 – 1914

18 - Woolwich and Deal; Japan and New Zealand
1861 – 1869

During this period the Corps was subject to some drastic changes, which considerably altered its outlook. First was the final separation of the Officers into two Lists - RM Artillery and RM Light Infantry - and the dropping of the title 'Royal Marines Light Infantry'. Also, it saw the formation of the Depot at Deal for training Recruits for all Divisions, and the abolition of the Woolwich Division.

In 1860 the numbers were 16,000, in 118 Divisional and 17 Artillery Companies.

In 1861 the numbers were 18,000.

Depot Royal Marines.
About the 4th May 1861 there appears to have been a detachment of Royal Marines at Deal; but on 7th May of that year the CO, Lieutenant Colonel W R Maxwell is addressed as Commanding Depot RM Deal, so that it is evident that the decision to form a depot for training recruits had been made, and steps were promptly taken to carry it out. On 8th May detachments from Chatham and Woolwich Divisions were sent for duty, shortly after followed by 100 Recruits from each Division to commence training. They were accommodated in the East Barracks[277] and by August of that year the Depot was in full swing. All recruits for the Corps were sent there, those of the requisite standard being allowed to volunteer for the RMA, until the removal of the RMA Company in 1897 to Eastney. At first the Depot was commanded by a Lieutenant Colonel, but later by a Colonel Second Commandant. As it expanded they took over the South and Cavalry Barracks, and later the North Barracks was built, the smaller blocks being completed in 1900.[278]

RM Artillery.
In 1862 by Order-in-Council 21st March the Officers of the Corps were finally divided into two separate lists (the recruits were however still drawn as before up to 1897) The wording of the Order gives the reason for the change: *"Attention has been called to the position of the Officers of the Artillery Division of the RM Forces, and the present system of promotion, by which the Officers of the Artillery and Officers of the Infantry Divisions are placed on one general list, the consequence of which is, that the proportion of subalterns in the Artillery is much greater than in the Infantry, and the opportunities of promotion less (Artillery, 4 Subalterns to 1 Captain; Infantry, 2 Subalterns to 1 Captain). Artillery Officers are generally promoted to the Infantry companies, and are afterwards brought back to their own Corps as vacancies occur, often while on foreign service; thus not only subjecting the officer to the expense of providing new uniform etc, but causing a great inconvenience to the Service; as the officer, on his return from the other branch of the Corps, necessarily requires a fresh course of instruction to fit him for his duties as a Captain of Artillery; it being impossible for him to keep pace with*

---
277 Formerly the RN Hospital.
278 See 'History of Depot, RM' Globe and Laurel.

the various improvements which are constantly being made in rifle ordnance[279] while not employed in the discharge of Artillery duties."

The Order consequently reduced the Artillery subalterns to two per company, but increased the companies to 24. The General List was divided into two separate and distinct lists for promotion and seniority, one "to be composed of the Officers of the Royal Marine Artillery and the other of the Officers of the Royal Marine Light Infantry." (This was the Order by which the historic title Royal Marines was dropped, the title of the Corps since 1855 having been Royal Marines Light Infantry.) The order went on to say that the division was made on the understanding that "after the lists have been formed no more interchanges by promotion shall be allowed". But the General Officers List remained common till on 10 November 1868 three generals were added to the list and the Generals' List divided into Artillery and Infantry.

1862

In 1862 the numbers were 18,000.

Barracks.
The Barracks for the RMA at Eastney were commenced but were not occupied till 7th November 1864 when the depot from Fort Elson took over, but it was on 1st April 1865 that the Barrackmaster assumed charge, and they were not in complete occupation till 1867.

Inspector General.
A reform was instituted by Order-in-Council 6 January 1862 that is often advocated in recent times, but which after an extended trial was abandoned owing to the friction with the DAG.

An Inspector General was appointed, with a Captain as his Assistant; the first holder was Major General A R Stransham, an officer with a very fine record, and his Assistant was Major J C Travers. The wording of the Order says; *"The strength of the Corps is now 18,000 whereas in 1839-40 it was only 9000"…………..* the Board *"feeling the necessity of maintaining the Corps in a high state of efficiency, we consider it essential that a General Officer RM should be appointed Inspector-General."*

The holders of the appointment were:

Major General A B Stranshan	9th January 1862 to 30th June 1867.
Major General J O Travers CB	9th June 1867 to 18th December 1868

---

279 This was a period when great strides were being made in development of guns and ammunition.

1863

In 1863 the numbers were 18,000.

Colonels.
The Colonelcies of Divisions, which had been held by Naval Officers up to 1837 were revived by Order-in-Council of 20th March 1863 but were in future to be held by General Officers Royal Marines. The Order-in-Council sums up the situation: "Owing to the peculiar nature of the RM Service, General Officers are debarred from all further advantage, having no lucrative commands or appointments to look forward to like their brother officers in the Army; and although various measures have been submitted from time to time to improve the position of officers and men, by placing them as nearly as possible on a footing with the Army, nothing has been done for the General Officers." It was therefore proposed to appoint a General Officer as Colonel to each of the five Divisions (on the principle adopted in the Army of Colonelcies of Regiments) and to raise the pay of those officers from £702.12.6 to £900 a year. "This measure will in our opinion give general satisfaction, as it will not only afford a means of conferring a reward upon a very meritorious class of old officers but will be beneficial in giving the Corps a few honorary appointments."

These appointments were abolished on 31st March 1870.

The holders were;

Chatham:
    Lieutenant General H I Delacombe   28th March 1863.
    Major General H Anderson   23rd August 1866.

Portsmouth:
    Major General Sir S B Ellis KCB   28th March 1863.
    General J Tatton Brown   28th March 1865.

Plymouth:
    Major General Fortescue Graham   1st June 1863.
    Lieutenant General Thomas Lemon   14th February 1867.

Woolwich:
    Lieutenant General J A Philips   28th March 1863.
    General Sir A B Stransham   14th February 1867.

RMA:
    General Sir C H Menzies KH   28th March 1863.
    Lieutenant General Fortescue Graham   23rd August 1866.

The post of Honorary Colonel Commandant of the Divisions was revived again in 1923, one being allowed for each Division. These are purely honorary appointments; no pay or allowances are granted, but they are allowed to visit their Divisions once a year and are a very pleasant method of allowing officers to keep in touch with their old comrades.

1865

In 1865 the numbers were 17,000, in 24 Artillery and 116 Divisional Companies - a reduction of 1000.

Greenwich Hospital Pensions - four of £80 for Field Officers and four of £50 for Captains - were established by Order-in-Council 16th February 1866. Also, a very welcome concession was made to Quartermasters promoted from the ranks by granting them an allowance to pay the mess and band contributions on promotions.[280]

1866

In 1866 the numbers were 16,400.

Naval Savings Banks for RN and RM were established on 10th November 1866, which after fulfilling a very useful purpose for many years were abolished in 1933.

1867

In 1867 the numbers were 16,400, in 18 Artillery and 105 Infantry Companies. (Order-in-Council 3rd August 1867)

Quartermasters.
This Order-in-Council also finally abolished the appointment of Lieutenant and Quartermaster, and all Quartermasters were in future promoted from the ranks.

Second Captains.
It also instituted the rank of Second Captain, 46 being allowed with pay at 10/6 per day; it further laid down that Adjutants should hold their appointments for five years unless previously promoted to Captain.

1868

In 1868 the numbers were 14,700 (Order-in-Council 28 March).

---

280 Order-in-Council 3 February.

It was laid down that a Quartermaster and 4 Staff Clerks were allowed to the RMO and a Schoolmaster to Deal.

Pay. An increase of pay of 2d per day to NCOs and 1d per day to re-engaged men was made.

1869

Examinations for Promotion.
On 19th June 1869 it was laid down that it was compulsory for all Officers under the rank of Captain RM to pass an examination for promotion similar to that in the army, with such modifications as were considered necessary. This was extended to include Captains for Major on 18 March 1880, and in 1903 the examination of Majors in Tactical Fitness for Command prior to promotion to Lieutenant Colonel was instituted. After the War of 1914-18 this last examination was replaced by a course at the Senior Officers' School of the Army.

In 1869 the numbers were 14,000 in 16 Artillery and 84 Infantry Companies.[281] The number of 2nd Captains was reduced to 21.

Woolwich Division.
A heavy blow fell on the Light Infantry by the abolition of the Woolwich Division, which was ordered by Mr Childers, the reduction was carried out with great hardship and callousness. A certain number of officers and men were sent to Deal, being dumped on the beach with their belongings from the coasting cruisers that brought them round; 200 men were summarily dismissed by being marched out of the barrack gates and turned adrift, similar scenes being enacted at the other Divisions. Several hundreds of men in uniform paraded in front of the Admiralty in London with sandwich-boards, stating they had been discharged from the Corps. The scandal resulted in some being reinstated. The Mess property was distributed to the other Divisions and Depot, and the Colours were sent to the Depot where they now hang in the Depot Church. The Order-in-Council dated 17 March 1869 placed surplus officers, except Lieutenants, on half pay; they were placed on a special list with a view to re-absorption in vacancies. The barracks were exchanged with the War Office for the barracks at Deal.

Mexico.
Internal disturbances had prevented payment of the interest on the debts of the Mexican Government and increased taxes had been imposed on foreign goods. By the Convention of London of 1st October 1861, England, France and Spain decided to send armed forces to Mexico for the protection of their nationals. Accordingly, three squadrons with troops were sent to demand satisfaction.

The British contingent included a Battalion of Royal Marines under Lieutenant Colonel S N

---

281 28 Chatham, 26 Portsmouth, 30 Plymouth.

Lowder RMLI, consisting of 4 Officers, 63 RMA, and 28 Officers and 669 RMLI. This Battalion carried the old pair of 1827 Colours now hanging in the Officers' Mess at Plymouth.

On 8th January 1862 the Allies occupied the city of Vera Cruz with the Fort of San Juan de Ulloa. The city was so unhealthy with yellow fever that the troops were moved out to camps inland, the Spaniards at first under General Prim to Orizaba, the French under de la Greviere to Tehuacan, and the British under Sir C Wyke to Cordova. There was no C-in-C and no method of routine. The RM Battalion extemporised a field battery of ships guns drawn by mules under Captain Power RMA. Negotiations were opened, and the President Juarez was very insulting; but eventually the treaty of Soledad, a sort of truce, recognised Juarez as Liberal President. The French, however, who had harboured the leaders of the Mexicans, also showed a tendency to interfere in local politics, and in addition to their contingent of 2000 troops they sent a further reinforcement. The British and Spanish, on the Mexican Government's promising to satisfy their claims, withdrew their troops in March 1862 who returned home. The French occupied Mexico City on 17th January 1863 and offered to crown Maximilian of Austria as Emperor; he accepted it, only to be dethroned and executed a little later.

Japan.
Eastern Waters were not long without a Battalion of Marines. Trouble had arisen with Japan. After several attacks on the Legation in 1861 and 1862, in September 1862 a Mr Richardson encountered one of the daimios or feudal nobles named Satsuma, whose guards cut him down and killed him. As no redress could be obtained a small squadron under Admiral Keefe proceeded to his principal town, Kagosima, on 11th August 1863, bombarded it and burnt it after dismantling the batteries and burning three new steamers. A Legation Guard commanded by Captain Smith RMLI was sent to the Legation from England to relieve the men of the Military Train, but a stronger force was needed. A Battalion was put under orders, formed of two companies from each of the four Infantry Divisions. Colonel W G Suther was Commanding Officer, with Lieutenant Colonels Penrose and C W Adair, Lieutenants H S Poyntz, Adjutant; J A Stewart, Paymaster; Hill, Musketry Instructor; Barker, Quartermaster: one Captain, two Subalterns to each company. It consisted of 700 of all ranks with 1 Surgeon and 2 Assistants. They were inspected at Plymouth on 19th December 1863, by General Stransham, the Inspector General, and embarked from the Victualling Yard in HMS *Conqueror*, a fine line of battleship with her main deck guns taken out. This Battalion carried the same pair of 1827 Colours now hanging in the Officers' Mess at Plymouth.

After calling at Hong Kong they proceeded to Yokohama where they were encamped on the Bluff in charming surroundings. Here they were joined by the 2/20th Regiment (now Lancashire Fusiliers) a detachment of RE and RA. The Royal Marines were on one side of a ravine, the soldiers on the other, the ravine between making a fine ground for sports, drill, etc.

Simonoseki.
At this time the daimios or nobles were at the very height of their power and very troublesome. One of the most powerful was Prince Chesiu, whose territory commanded the Eastern entrance to

the Inland Sea. He had erected batteries on shore and had fired on the vessels of different nations. An Allied force of English, French, Dutch and Americans was ordered to assemble in the Inland Sea to punish him. On 29th August 1864 the RM Battalion re-embarked in the *Conqueror*.

The squadron consisted of nine British ships, three French, four Dutch, and one American together with the Battalion.

On 5th September the bombardment of the batteries commenced, the Fleet being formed in two lines; the *Conqueror* was anchored beyond the squadron and well out of range of the batteries. The Japanese batteries returned the fire and several casualties were caused. The *Conqueror* would not be left out, so the Armstrong pivot gun, manned by Lieutenant Lye and some gunners of the RMA fired over the other ships and made excellent practice at long range. The batteries were much knocked about, and by 6 pm the Japanese fire ceased and parties from the *Perseus* and the Dutch *Medusa* landed and spiked the guns of No 5 Battery. Orders were issued for parties to be landed on the 6th.

The British force was under Colonel Suther with Major Wolrige as Brigade Major. The 1st Battalion commanded by Lieutenant Colonel Penrose, and the 2nd Battalion composed of the ships' detachments by Lieutenant Colonel C W Adair. There was also a Naval Brigade under, Captain Alexander and a Dutch battalion of Seamen and Marines.

The landing was covered by the ships and boats with howitzers in the bows, the latter under Captain Luard RN. They disembarked without opposition, and an advance was made along the line of deserted batteries to the town of Simonoseki, which was found to be evacuated, as Prince Chesiu had declared he would pay a large ransom for the sparing of the town.

Whilst the troops were at dinner some officers examined the town; in the evening on their way back to the beach fire was suddenly opened on the RM Brigade as it was crossing the foot of a ravine, densely wooded on either side and with a marshy valley in the centre.

Skirmishers were thrown out and Colonel Suther ordered an advance towards what proved to be a large well-built stockade with two field pieces at the gate. The RM were on the right and the RN on the left; the Dutch had taken another route. Colonel Adair was winded by a spent ball. They advanced through a dense undergrowth, the men falling down frequently. The stockade was built of strong wooden stakes with barrack buildings inside and a large entrance gate. The troops scrambled over the stockade, but the Japanese escaped through an opening in rear into the woods, leaving a good many dead. Many of the Japanese were clad in armour, samples of which can be seen in the Officers' Mess at Chatham.

The barracks and magazines were burnt or blown up, and the force re-embarked. Two Officers (Captain de Courcy and Lieutenant Inglis) were severely wounded and some NCOs and Men killed and wounded.

On 7th, 8th, and 9th strong working parties with covering forces were landed to destroy the five batteries etc. bringing off 62 guns. Several brass field pieces were brought off, two of which were given to the Battalion and are now in the Officers' Mess at Plymouth. The Battalion returned to Yokohama, but this time to the excellent huts erected by the RE, where they remained with the other troops until they embarked on 24th August 1865 in HMS *Conqueror* for home. On their way to Hong Kong they encountered a typhoon and had it not been that the *Conqueror* was such a fine ship and so well handled by Captain Luard they would probably have been lost.

Officers and men were shoulder to shoulder at the hand pumps, as the steam pumps were useless. Major Poyntz says: "I always look back with pride on the good humour and cheery behaviour of all hands amid such terrible surroundings."

Before leaving the East at this period it is necessary to place on record that there was trouble with Chinese pirates in 1868 and 1869. In November 1868 the Marines of the Fleet under Major Hall were landed for the capture of Yangchow and again in January 1869 for the capture and destruction of three walled villages at Swatoo. Major Hall and Lieutenant Baldwin were mentioned in dispatches, and Lieutenants Crosbie and Ogle, well known officers of the Corps, were in the Battalion.

New Zealand 1800-64.
During these greater events, small detachments of the Corps were again engaged in operations in New Zealand.

Trouble had arisen with the Maories over the taking of their land for the settlers, and the Chiefs had rebelled.

In this instance land on the Waitara River, North of Taranaki, in the North Island had been sold and the question of surveying it had arisen. There was a quarrel between the Chiefs and on 29th January 1860 the Governor declared martial law in Taranaki and ordered the survey to be made. There were about 1,000 British troops in the Island - RA, RE, and 65th Regiment - scattered in four or five stations. That nearest the scene of the trouble had 200 men at Wanganui and New Plymouth. Colonel Gold, the Commander, took the field with about 400 men, with some rockets and howitzers. The Chief Te Rangiki had built a pah on the land which he was ordered to burn within 20 minutes. He obeyed, but on 15th March built another and pulled up all the surveying posts.

On the 17th Colonel Gold opened fire and after a bombardment on the 18th advanced to the assault; the pah was found deserted and there was little loss on either side. The Maoris, then murdered some settlers, on which the local Militia were called out, and the 65th Regiment and a Naval Brigade of Seamen and Marines from HMS *Niger* stormed the pah in which the Maoris had taken refuge, killing 30 of them.

Reinforcements of the 12th and 40th Regiments with some RA arrived at the end of April from Australia - all told about 600 - who landed at New Plymouth and moved into an entrenched camp at the mouth of the Waitara River. Opposite it was another pah - Puketauere - with a ditch, stockade and rifle pits on a ridge with deep gullies on either side full of brambles and bracken.

Major Nelson of 40th Regiment and Captain Seymour RN (afterwards Lord Alcester of Alexandria fame), after a bombardment by two heavy howitzers advanced with two columns, 350 men each, of the 40th Regiment and a Naval Brigade. The ground was slippery clay, soaked with rain, and they were beaten back with a loss of 30 killed and 34 wounded, mostly of the 40th Regiment. The wavering natives now joined the rebels and many settlers were murdered.

On 3rd August Major General Pratt arrived at New Plymouth from Australia and took command. He had nominally a force of 3,500, including 900 volunteers. The Coast was most dangerous, with no good harbour; the country was difficult forest and no information of enemy's movements could be obtained. The Maoris however evacuated the Puketuaere pah. On 8th September information was received about three pahs on the South Bank of Waitara River. Pratt dispatched three columns of 1,000 men over very difficult country; the Maoris evacuated their posts when he arrived and leaving garrisons in them, he moved on to three other pahs on the Kakiki River.

On 11th October he opened trenches within 250 yards of them and then sapped his way forward, whilst a Naval 8-inch gun kept up a steady bombardment. The Maoris resisted steadily for a time and then fled, leaving a lot of provisions.

News was now received that the Waikato tribes were moving South on the Waitara River. General Pratt returned and converted Fuketuaere pah into a fortified signalling post, and then proposed to occupy a place called Ilakoetaki, when in November he learned that the Maoris were already in vision. He advanced on it in two columns, one about 800 strong from New Plymouth, the other about 300 from Waitara. On nearing the pah he was met by fire, so the guns were brought up; the 65th attacked in front and the Militia on the left. They contained the pah with fire until the 2nd Tailara Column (12th and 40th) came up on the right, when after a couple of hours' resistance, the enemy fled and were pursued, eight very important chiefs being killed. Leaving 300 men to garrison the pah, they returned to New Plymouth. In the London Gazette-of 5th February 1861, the gallant behaviour of the Naval Brigade and Marine Artillery (Lieutenant Morris RMA and 22 Rank and File) are mentioned.

This was a heavy blow to the Waikato tribes who considered themselves very fine fellows. General Pratt however had to leave to defend Auckland; therefore after providing for the posts of Taraniki, the remainder were embarked in sloops and taken to the port of Auckland; after a rough and crowded passage they arrived to find that five companies of the 14th had arrived from Australia, so the detachments were sent back to New Plymouth and 1200 men were concentrated on the Waitara River.

The Maoris were reported to have three pahs five miles up the river, and to be building a fourth called Matarorikoriki. Leaving 300 men to hold his base, on 29th December the General advanced to within 800 yards of the pahs, where he entrenched half his force. On 30th the Maoris hoisted the white flag and evacuated the forts.

By 14th January 1861 the remainder of the 14th Regiment had arrived, so that 1,500 men were now available. General Pratt then proceeded to sap towards Matarorikoriki; on 23rd the Maoris counter-attacked but were driven off and lost heavily; on the 24th another redoubt was ready and by 10th February there were eight redoubts and the sap was within 200 yards of the pah; they were working by rolling sap. On 11th March as the Armstrong guns were arriving, the Maoris asked for a truce and on the 19th hostilities, pending conclusion of peace, came to an end. On 31st March General Pratt returned to Australia and was succeeded by General D Cameron. In General Pratt's dispatch, Captain Morris RM was mentioned and received the Brevet of Major.

In 1862 Sir George Grey became Governor. In 1863 hostilities broke out again.

Covered by the fire of the Squadron and a battery of Armstrong guns, General Cameron with men of the 57th, 65th and 70th Regiments attacked the principal Maori stronghold on the Katikaro River, which was carried with the bayonet. On 12th July General Cameron crossed the creek and established a redoubt in the Kokeroa Hills and collected supplies. In October the Maoris retreated up the Waikato to Rangiriri and closed the ground across the isthmus, dividing Lake Waikari from the river with a strong earthwork. On 19th October after a long and heavy bombardment from the gunboats and Armstrong guns, an assault was made; the outer works were carried, but the central redoubt, which had a ditch 12 feet wide and walls 18 feet high, defied all attacks by the seamen and artillery. At dawn on the 29th the Maoris hoisted the white flag, having suffered heavy loss; the British casualties were 40 killed and 90 wounded.

On 8th December General Cameron occupied Nguwakia, at the junction of the Waikato and Waikara Rivers and halted until 24th January 1864. Replenishing supplies etc, he was joined by the 43rd and 50th Regiments from India. The Maoris then retired to the Pateragi pahs which were too strong to be assaulted.

On 21st February a depot of provisions at Rangiaokia was taken with little difficulty, and on 22nd at Taawamuta he drove the Maoris South-East to Manitatori with a loss of 40 killed. On 31st March with a force of about 1,300, General Cameron surrounded Orakau, but three attempts to assault were repelled, and he decided to sap up to it.

Gate Pah.
On 2nd April after bombardment the pah was summoned but refused to surrender; the outer works were carried and then he again summoned the inner works. The defenders formed a column and coolly marched out; another chief came in and surrendered, but by cool cheek most of them got off.

The Maoris were now surrendering, but there remained Tauranga, 40 miles East of Cameron's Headquarters, the seaport of the Waikato tribes. The now celebrated Gate Pah was at Pukekinakina, three miles from Tauranga, situated on a ridge between two swamps. On 21st April, Cameron shifted his HQ to Tauranga and on 27th reconnoitred the pah. It was oblong in shape, 70 yards by 30 yards, with strong palisades and surrounded by a strong fence of timber; the slopes leading to the swamps were honeycombed with rifle pits. The strength of the Naval Brigade from HMS *Niger* and *North Star* was 429; he had also 6 companies of the 43rd and 732 of the 88th Regiments. Besides field guns he had 3 heavy guns.

On the evening of 27th April half the force encamped within 400 yards of the pah and on that day and the next the guns were placed in position. After dusk on the 28th a feint attack was made, under which the 68th - taking advantage of the low tide - passed along the beach outside the swamps on the enemy right and extended themselves across the rear to cut off the retreat.

Soon after dawn on the 29th the guns opened fire and continued till 4 pm, making a practicable breach in the exterior fence and palisades. The assaulting party was composed of 300 men from the Naval Brigade and 300 from the 43rd. It was divided into 150 from each for storming party and 150 each for reserve. They gained the breach with little loss but were met by a heavy hail of bullets from concealed passages and pits; nearly all the officers were shot down and the men were seized with panic, the Naval Brigade losing 4 officers and 40 men, and the 43rd 9 officers and 73 men. Three quarters of an hour afterwards, the Maoris tried to retire, but were driven back by the 68th Regiment. General Cameron took up an entrenched line 1,000 yards from the pah and deferred operations until the next day, but at daylight on the 30th the Maoris retreated and left the pah.

They then threatened the 68th at Tauranga, four miles from the pah, but Colonel Greer with 600 of the 68th and the 43rd marched against them on 21st June and being reinforced by 259 men, charged the rifle pits. The Maoris stood for a while but then gave way, pursued by the British for miles, and suffered heavy loss. The remainder in August surrendered their lands, of which the Governor kept one quarter as a punishment.

A medal was issued for these operations.

19 - Long Service, Army Reform and Africa 1870 - 1880

Fortunately for the Corps the great changes that took place in the Army were not reflected in the Royal Marines, which now became the only long-service unit in the Kingdom, though the compulsory retirement age for officers was introduced. As purchase of Commissions had never been allowed in the Royal Marines, that great army reform did not affect them.

Officers.
The perennial question of the promotion of officers was to the fore: as the result of enquiries and a Committee, a scheme of promotion and retirement was established by Order-in-Council 22 February 1870, which in many ways affected the Corps.

1. The system of compulsory retirement for age was extended to all higher grades, so as to cause a more even flow of promotion. The number of General Officers was fixed at 12.

2. The posts of Colonels of Divisions were abolished.

3. The establishment was fixed at RMA - 2,877, RMLI - 11,103.

4. A Second-Commandant was allowed for command of Depot at Deal.

5. The HQ Staff at the RMO was fixed at 1 Deputy Adjutant General, 1 Assistant Adjutant General, 1 Quartermaster, 1 Chief Clerk and 3 Staff Sergeant Clerks.

6. Any Officer placed on the Retired List in no case to be replaced on the *Active* List.

7. The grant of a step in rank on retirement was approved.

8. The ages of compulsory retirement were laid down, as were the scales of retired pay, varying from £600 for a Colonel to £225 at 42 years of age.

Recruiting.
On 17th August (Order-in-Council) Recruiting Bounties were discontinued and shorter periods for award of GC Badges were introduced. The 1d a day extra pay on re-engagement was abolished.

On 7th September HMS *Captain*, the first turret ship, was lost in the Bay of Biscay. The Admiralty had rigged her with masts and yards as well as the turrets, and she is believed to have turned turtle in the heavy seas. Only 18 men were saved.

Japan.

On 5th November yet another Battalion was sent to Japan, consisting of 4 Companies under Lieutenant Colonel F J Richards; Adjutant, Captain A Hill; Quartermaster, Lieutenant E N H Gray; 4 Captains (E B Snow, C W Burton, A H Walsh, P R Holmes), and 8 Lieutenants. It was quartered on the Bluff at Yokohama and remained in garrison there till 1875. Japan at that period was being opened up and becoming Westernized, whilst the feudal damios were losing their power, and it was necessary to have protection for the Europeans. At the same time our men acted as a model for their new armies, in fact Lieutenant Hawes was employed as an Instructor for many years. Other officers, among them Lieutenant Q S Fagan, were employed as Assistant Engineers in laying their new railways.

Pensioner Reserve.

On 29th November 1870 the Seamen Pensioner Reserve was established, but the Royal Marine Pensioner Reserve not until 25th June 1872, when special rates of pay whilst at drill were laid down.

Schools.

With a view to securing uniformity in the Schools, on 10th May 1872 a Sub-Inspector of RM Schools was appointed to the Staff of the DAQ with pay at 10/- a day, retiring at 60; the holder was a Captain T Smith. This appointment was abolished in 1895. The Schoolmaster's position was established as ranking next to Sergeant-Majors but under no NCO. (Warrant Officers were not yet in existence in the Royal Marines.) Provision was also made for NCOs and Marines to be employed as School Assistants; this of course was the era when compulsory education was introduced into England.

In 1871 the numbers were 14,000.

Second Lieutenants. On 31st October 1871 the rank of 2nd Lieutenant was abolished and was not reintroduced till 1887.

In 1872 the numbers voted were 14,000.

1873

In 1873 the numbers voted were Artillery 2,675, Infantry 10,980, Staff 7: Total 13,660 (Order-in-Council) in 16 Artillery and 48 Infantry Companies.

Officers' Entry.

A very important change was inaugurated by Order-in-Council 16 January 1873. Since 8th June 1838 and 25th February 1841 there had been a Naval College at Portsmouth to train Officers RN and RM; this new Order abolished the College at Portsmouth and established the College at Greenwich, which included in its staff a Professor of Fortification, who was in charge of the Marine Cadets. The RMA Recruit Officers were trained for two years at this College, but the RMLI

Recruit Officers after training at their own Headquarters received six months instruction at Forton or Eastney from the Military Instructor prior to confirmation in their appointments. The post of Military Instructor was instituted by Order-in-Council 4th August 1873; he was to be an Officer qualified at the Staff College and was appointed in lieu of one of the Adjutants of the Artillery Division. At one time Officers, who had failed to qualify for the RMA., were transferred to the RMLI, but this arrangement was soon stopped, though many distinguished officers were saved to the Corps by this means. These arrangements continued until 1889.

In May 1873 it was laid down that Probationary Officers' commissions would in future be signed by the Admiralty, but all first commissions to permanent rank would be made under His Majesty's Sign Manual and notified by the Admiralty; no other commissions would be issued, which was a great change from the old custom and a great relief to officers, as the stamp duty of 30/- on each Commission was a heavy tax.

Second-Captains.
On 4th August 1873 the rank of Second-Captain was abolished. New rates of pay were laid down for Lieutenants which lasted till 1902, and an extra 2/- for Captains of over 8 years' Service when afloat introduced.

In 1874 the numbers were 14,000.

1875

In 1875 the numbers were 14,000.

On 1st September the new ironclads *Vanguard* and *Iron Duke* were in collision off the coast of Ireland and the *Vanguard* was sunk with a loss of many lives.

Musicians.
In May for the first time provision was made for the introduction of the rank of Musician for the Divisional Bands - 25 being allowed to each Division.

On 27th November the Royal Marine Schools were placed under Naval Regulations and rates of pay were laid down for school-mistresses, the maximum being £50 a year.

India.
On 22nd July 1875, HMS *Serapis* (one of the Indian troopships) was commissioned to take HRH The Prince of Wales (afterwards HM King Edward VII) on his visit to India in the winter of 1875-76. The RM Officers were Brevet Major E B Snow RMLI and Lieutenant W M Lambert RMA. The Band of the Portsmouth Division, RMLI was specially embarked for the occasion, and on their return were privileged to wear the Prince of Wales' Feathers on their cap and helmet badges.

In 1876 the numbers were 14,000.

1877

In 1877 the numbers were 14,000.

Naval Gunnery.
In 1877 an important step was taken as regards training in Naval gunnery. The standard for the RMLI was ordered to be the same as that for Seaman Trained Man, and NCOs and men who attained the standard were given 1d a day extra pay (TM), for which they had to requalify every three years. There was some discussion as to the necessity of the RMLI qualifying in the Cutlass Exercise, which was one of the subjects required by Seamen, but My Lords were at last persuaded that, as RM were armed with a bayonet and not a cutlass, this was hardly necessary. The RMA, of course, who were paid as Artillerymen, were required to obtain the standard of Seamen Gunners. It was not till about 1904 that the rating of QMs at 2d a day (i.e. the same as Seaman Gunner) was opened to RMLI, though for many years they had formed separate guns' crews in HM ships.

1878

In 1878 the numbers were 14,000.

This year the system of weekly payments of pay in lieu of daily was introduced by Colonel Lambrick for NCOs and men.

On 24th March HMS *Eurydice* capsized off the Isle of Wight with a loss of 318 lives.

Officers: Majors.
Following a Committee in 1877, the retirement question was again raised by Order-in-Council 15 January 1878. General Officers were to retire at 65 instead of 70 years of age; the Reserve List of Lieutenant Colonels was abolished; but most important of all the substantive rank of Major was restored, 8 being allowed for Artillery and 24 for the RMLI at 16/- a day with forage allowance; there were also to be four Artillery Lieutenant Colonels instead of three.

A reward for Special Merit and Promise was instituted by the power to grant one special promotion per annum to be published in the London Gazette. Also, selection of Colonels and Lieutenant Colonels for promotion was introduced. The Chief Clerk at the RM Office was made a Quartermaster and 5 Staff Clerks were allowed. The compulsory age for retirement of Majors was fixed at 48 years on £300 and for Captains at 42 on £225.

It was also laid down that the number of first entries of officers were to be carefully regulated according to Actuarial advice - a provision which was neglected and led to the great blocks in promotion in later years.

1879

In 1879 the numbers were 13,000.

Army Discipline Act.
This year marks a great departure in the Acts governing the Corps. Hitherto the Army had been governed by a Mutiny Act and Articles of War passed annually by Parliament. The Marines had followed the same rule, though the Marine Act and Articles, after passing through Parliament were signed by the Admiralty and then promulgated. The Army now consolidated their regulations in the Army Discipline And Regulation Act of 1879,[282] which is brought into force by the Army Annual Act. The Royal Marines on shore were now brought into the provisions of this Act by a special provision with certain modifications; but the provisions of the old Marine Mutiny Acts 11 & 12 Vict. C63 and 20 Vict. C1 as regards conditions of service were and are retained in force.

In consequence of the provisions of s. 171 (11x) of this Act, the Admiralty issued an Order-in-Council 26th February 1880 by which Royal Marines when embarked became subject to the provisions of the Naval Discipline Act of 1868, and also made provision for the RM when landed for active service on shore from the Fleet to be subject to the Army Act. These provisions became necessary owing to the cancellation of the Marine Mutiny Act and Articles of War on these points. There were revision Orders-in-Council of 6th February 1882 and 26th February 1888, but the principle that the Marines when embarked became subject to the Naval Discipline Act was not affected.

Flogging.
The Army Discipline Act was replaced by the Army Act of 1881 and with these Acts finally disappeared the punishments of flogging, as by s44 the Rules for Field Punishment were substituted for it on Active Service.

In the Navy in 1830 the number of lashes had been limited to 48. In Order-in-Council 1 July 1840 it had been laid down that no Marine wearing a Good Conduct Badge was liable to corporal punishment except for mutinous conduct. In 1871 there were further restrictions and it was practically abolished in 1879. The last case in the Navy occurred in 1882.

Operations - The Ashanti War 1873-74.[283]
In 1873 renewed trouble arose with King Coffee of Ashanti, partly over the purchase of Elmina from the Dutch by the British. The Ashantis, a fierce and warlike tribe, invaded the British Protectorate and advanced towards Cape Coast Castle and Elmina with an army of 12,000 men. The local troops consisting of the West India Regiment, Volunteers and Native Levies, were not sufficient to cope with them, and the Naval Squadron on the Station was very small. The *Druid* and other small craft landed their Seamen and Marines to garrison Cape Coast Castle, Elmina, and Fort William.

---

282 Now replaced by the Army Act.
283 Authorities: Coomassie (HM Stanley), Officers' Services., Britain's Sea Soldiers (Field); Globe and Laurel.

On the news reaching England, a detachment of 110 RMA and RMLI under Captain and Brevet Lieutenant Colonel F V Festing RMA, Captain Despard RMLI, Lieutenants Cheetham and Allen RMA, Lieutenants J H Price and J J Quill RMLI with two mountain guns and 200 war rockets was sent out in HMS *Barracouta*. She arrived at Elmina on 7th June and Martial Law was proclaimed.

Elmina.
On the night of 12/13th June, Colonel Festing with 300 Royal Marines, Houssa, West India Regiment and Volunteers occupied the land side of the town. Between 2 and 4.30, 300 men from the *Barracouta, Druid, Decoy, Seagull* and *Argus* were towed in boats up the river by the *Argus* and the boats were moored in line with their guns and rockets laid on King's Town, the disaffected quarter. The inhabitants were ordered to hand over their arms and ammunition and as they did not comply at 12 noon, the boats and Castle opened fire; the inhabitants fled into the bush, where they were pursued by Colonel Festing's detachment, supported by the seamen under Captain Fremantle RN.

Just after their return 2,000 Ashantis were reported advancing out of the forest on the loyal part of the town. They were at once engaged by the Royal Marines and Houssas whose fire checked their advance, whilst the seamen of the *Barracouta* who had not yet re-embarked caught them in flank and they were driven off with heavy loss, being pursued by Colonel Festing for two miles. Lieutenant Quill was mentioned in dispatches for having skirmished his men with zeal and alacrity.

There was a pause in the fighting, but punishment was inflicted on several of the coastal villages, and reconnaissances of the route to Prahsu and Coomassie were made. The Royal Marines suffered heavily from fever and had to be nearly all replaced, Captains Crease RMA, Allnutt RMLI, Lieutenant T Moore RMA, Lieutenants Gray, Stephens and P Hearle RMLI being sent out with 50 RMA and 150 RMLI on 17th July in the SS *Simoon*. Captain Crease invented a filter for water which proved most valuable. Lieutenants Stephens and Hearle were sent up country to train native Levies.

The Government had now decided to send an expedition to punish the Ashantis, but as the British troops could not operate until December, General Sir Garnet Wolseley and a number of Special Service Officers were sent out to make the necessary preparations and to raise Native Regiments, organise carriers, etc.

These arrived on 4th October. At this time a large Ashanti army was encamped at Essaman, about 6 miles north of Elmina, and was being supported and helped by the local Fantee Chiefs.

Essaman.
On 14th October General Wolseley attacked Essaman with a force composed of 29 RMA, 129 RMLI, 29 Seamen, 205 2/WI Regiment, 126 Houssas, 40 Native Levies and 270 carriers with one 7 pdr and a rocket tube. They advanced in single file and when near the village fire was opened on

them, to which they replied and then pushed on; the shells from the 7 pdr set the village on fire, the RM attacked in front and soon rushed the village, the Houssas turning the right flank. The village was deserted and after a short rest the column moved on to Amquana, about 4 or 5 miles further on. The RM were leading in extended order, when they were attacked from the bush. The advanced guard composed of Houssas and WI Regiment then moved over a grassy plateau, keeping up a heavy but ill-directed fire, whilst a wood on the left was attacked by the RMA under Captain Crease, supported by the Seamen with the gun and rocket tube. The main body, pushing on, reached the village - which was on the sea beach - without further opposition.

Here Captain Luxmoore of HMS *Decoy* landed with his Seamen and Marines to reinforce the Column. The village was found to be deserted and was burnt; the villages of Akimfoo and Amponee were also burnt after being bombarded by the *Argus* and *Decoy*. The loss in the column was 2 killed and 23 Officers and men wounded. They had marched 22 miles and suffered greatly from the heat.

Fortified posts were established on the road to Prahsu, where the river Prah had to be crossed. Colonel Festing was in command of Dunquah, which he had occupied on 11th October. Scouts kept the General well informed as to the movements of the Ashantis, who were variously estimated at from 10,000 to 40,000 men. The Fantees in the British Protectorate were useless as soldiers; it was therefore necessary to ensure the peace of the Protectorate before advancing into the Ashanti country.

On 27th October, Colonel Festing from Dunquah (15 miles north-west of Cape Coast Castle) surprised Escaibo to the west of his post, where an Ashanti army was encamped; they fled but opened fire from the bush; the village and encampment were however destroyed. Out of 9 officers, 5 were wounded, 4 of the 2/WI Regiment were wounded and 42 of the Native Levies.

Abrakrampa.
On 28th General Wolseley advanced from Abrakrampa with 100 Royal Marines under Captain Allnutt, 158 Seamen, some Houssas and Native Levies. Festing was unable to co-operate, so leaving a garrison at Abrakrampa, Wolseley returned to Cape Coast Castle.

Abrakrampa was a strategic point on the main route to Coomassie and Major Baker Russell, 13th Hussars, was placed in command with 50 Royal Marines and some Native Levies, amounting in all to 1,000 men, with a rocket tube. On 5th November, just as the Marines were falling in to return to Cape Coast Castle, the Ashantis attacked in force, estimated at 10,000 men. The RM Snipers fired volleys and after 1½ hours' severe fighting the enemy retired; but during the night the Ashantis were reinforced to 15,000 and renewed their attacks on three sides. A reinforcement of 502 2/WI Regiment arrived during the night but in response to appeals, General Wolseley arrived at 6 pm with 50 Seamen and Marines, and 196 2/WI Regiment and Native Levies. The Ashantis then retired and returned to Coomassie, taking six weeks to reach their capital. General Wolseley reported "*the successful defence was solely attributable to the admirable conduct of Major Russell and the officers[284] under his orders who with only 50 Marines in addition to Native Levies held the town against numbers at least twenty-fold during two most fatiguing days and nights."*

It was impossible to follow up the retreating Ashantis, but on the 26th Amanquatsia, one of their principal Chiefs, was defeated at Faisoon, the defeat being much due to rockets fired by three RM Artillerymen whose *"cool courageous bearing it was a pleasure to witness."*

On 4th November Festing with his Native Levies had a brush with the Ashantis in which he was himself wounded. The bulk of the Marines had by now been invalided and sent to Ascension to recuperate.

British reinforcements were now arriving, among them a Battalion of Royal Marines commanded by Lieutenant Colonel de Courcy RMLI; Lieutenant A A Allen, Adjutant and Quartermaster; composed of one company of RMA and 3 of RMLI. To their great regret the RM Battalion was not disembarked, nor was the greater part of the Royal Welsh Fusiliers.

Coomassie.
The force detailed for the advance to Coomassie consisted of the 42nd Highlanders, 2nd Rifle Brigade and part of the Royal Welsh Fusiliers, two Battalions West India Regiment, 1 Battalion Houssas, 2 Battalions Native Levies, Houssa Artillery, with a Naval Brigade of 210 men under Captain Hewett VC, divided into two wings under Captains Hunt-Grubbe and Luxmoore RN with whom were 70 RM formed into two companies under Lieutenants A B Crosbie and R N Deane RMLI of HMS *Active*.

On 23rd December General Wolseley went to Chamali, at the mouth of the Prah river in the Flagship and landed with the RM detachment to look for the natives, but met with no opposition. The Prah River runs diagonally across the country from NE to SW. The plan was for Captain Glover, the Administrator, with his levies, to march from the Volta River; Wolseley's column to advance from Prahsu, which was 69 miles by road from Cape Coast Castle. The two columns would thus advance on two sides of a triangle whose apex was Coomassie. The advanced base was at Prahsu, where there was a well laid out camp. From Prahsu to Coomassie the distance was 78.5 miles, to be covered in 9 stages.

From 4th October to 13th December with the Royal Marines, Seamen, West India and two Native Regiments, General Wolseley had driven 20,000 Ashantis across the Prah.

On 20th December the Naval Brigade and Rifles crossed the Prah.

On 26th January 1874 Russell's Native Regiment and Giffard's Scouts with part of the Naval Brigade reconnoitred Addibassee, where they attacked and drove out the enemy without

---
284 Captain Allnutt and Lieutenant Moore.

loss. On the 28th Borborassi was found occupied and was attacked on 29th; the enemy were surprised and fled, though an attack was made on the Naval Brigade, including the Royal Marines, on the left flank which was driven off. The dispatches said, "*Discipline and conduct of the Bluejackets under Captain Grubbe, who formed the advance and rearguard afterwards, merited my special commendation.*"

Amoaful.

On 1st February was fought the battle of Amoaful, which broke the power of the Ashantis. When the force advanced, the Black Watch were in the centre, followed by the Royal Artillery and a portion of the Royal Welsh Fusiliers; the left column was composed of the right wing of the Naval Brigade, Russell's Native Regiment, some RA and RE; the right column of the left wing of the Naval Brigade, Wood's Native Regiment, and some RA and RE; the Rifle Brigade were in reserve.

The action opened at 8 am; by 9.15 am the centre had reached the village of Eggniassie, which had been carried at 8.5 am by Lord Giffard's Scouts. The right column was then seriously engaged, the Ashantis fighting with great gallantry. Colonel Wood was wounded, and the RWF were ordered up to support him to the north-east; two companies of the Rifle Brigade were also ordered up as the Highlanders were meeting with strong resistance. The Naval Brigade of the left column was hotly engaged for 1½ hours but fighting their way forward they lost touch with the main body and then had to move diagonally through the bush and eventually came in on the right of the Black Watch to reinforce them and enable them to carry the big Ashanti camp in their front. The Ashantis retreated at 12, and Wolseley reached Amoaful at 5 pm.

Another attack was made on the rear guard 2.5 miles in rear at Quarman which lasted till midnight but was driven off by the Rifle Brigade and Russell's Natives.

On 1st February the advance was continued to Becquah; the Naval Brigade with one gun and a rocket tube, some RE, Russell's Natives and Gifford's Scouts formed the advanced guard; the main body consisted of RWF and 5 Companies of the Black Watch. They moved to the west of Amoaful by a road from the north end of the town. After going about 1.5 miles, firing commenced and the Ashantis took to the bush; at first, they made some resistance, but were driven off by volleys fired by companies of the advanced guard. The main body was not engaged. Becquah was set on fire and destroyed.

Coomassie.

On 2nd the advance was resumed to Coomassie, Russell's Natives and Gifford's Scouts forming the advanced guard. There was a skirmish at the crossing of a stream, but the main body was not engaged. On 3rd they advanced to the Ordah river; during the morning there was a skirmish, but the RE were able to command the bridge. The Native Levies bivouacked on the north bank, the main body on the south. Very heavy rain fell, but at 7 am on 4th February the advance was continued, the Rifle Brigade leading. They were resisted by heavy fire from the bush, but the enemy was cleared off by volleys fired without aim level with the ground. The town of Ordahsu was only 1.5 miles from the river, but it was 9.30 am before they reached within 600 yards of it, when it was carried by the Rifle Brigade. The baggage was brought up, but the enemy swung round both flanks and attacked the rear; they were driven off by the Naval Brigade supported by Wood's and Russell's Natives.

The Black Watch were then ordered to advance on Coomassie, covered by the Artillery. Advancing in file they were met by fire on both flanks which was countered by volleys fired by companies to right and left without halting; when the way was cleared, the porters with SAA and medical stores went on, the Naval Brigade formed the rear guard. They passed through the deadly swamp which insulates Coomassie and by 6 pm entered the broad avenue of "pretentious looking edifices of porticoes and alcoved houses."

That night fires broke out and burnt part of the town; King Coffee fled to the bush, so the Palace was burnt and destroyed, and a certain amount of loot collected. It was undesirable to retain white troops there, so the return march commenced on 8th February. The troops on return to Cape Coast Castle were re-embarked at once. Glover's Column of 4,600 natives, coming by the other route, arrived in Coomassie on the 12th, having been preceded by Captain Sartorious the day before, who found Coomassie still deserted.

Lieutenant Colonel Festing was promoted to Brevet Colonel and given the CB on 31st March 1874, and KCMG on 8th May 1874. Lieutenant Crosbie RMLI, for this campaign and his services in the Congo in August and September 1879, and the *Niger* in August 1876, was specially promoted to Captain 3rd December 1878. Lieutenant R N Deane was mentioned in dispatches; after retirement from RM he joined the Royal Canadian North-West Mounted Police and became Superintendent.

HMS *Shah*.
On 28th May 1877 there were internal troubles in Peru and a Peruvian Turret-Ship, *Huascar*, was seized by the rebels and carried off. She was engaged by HMS *Shah* and *Amethyst* and forced to surrender; the first occasion of British armoured ships being in action. Captain J Phillips RMLI and Lieutenant W M Lambert RMA were the RM Officers.

South Africa and Zulu War 1879 [285]

During 1876-77-78 there had been considerable trouble with the natives in South Africa, in Cape Colony, Natal, etc.; parties had been landed from the Squadron, including Marines, to assist the local troops - parties from the *Active* were present on 7th February 1878 at the battle of Guintana; but at the end of 1878 a serious quarrel arose with the great military tribe of Zulus, who under their king, Ketchwayo, had been thoroughly trained in warfare and military organisation. He had 40,000 warriors and a good supply of fire-arms; they were a warlike race and the ensuing campaign was chequered with several disasters to the British Forces. The immediate cause of

---

285 Authorities; Official Account, Officers, Services, etc.

hostilities was a dispute over some territory on the Blood River, which was transferred to the British when the Transvaal was annexed in 1877.

It was important to secure Natal and the Transvaal from invasion; it was therefore decided to advance in three columns - the main column composed of two Battalions of the 24th Regiment under General Lord Chelmsford advanced by Rorke's Drift over the Buffalo River; the left column under Colonel Flood VC, with the 90th Regiment and mounted troops; the right column under Colonel Pearson composed of the Buffs, Naval Brigade from HMS *Active* - about 170 Seamen and Marines - under Commander Campbell, with Lieutenant T W Dowding, RMLI in command of the RM (about 60 men); they had two 12 pdr Armstrong guns, a Gatling and two rocket tubes, and details of mounted troops. All columns had Battalions of the Natal Native Contingent, 105 of whom were armed with rifles but who were very unreliable.

The right column moved through the coast district to the Lower Tugela Drift; the ground here was a high open grassy down furrowed by deep watercourses and rocky ridges, and there was low lying alluvial land along the coast. The Tugela and Buffalo Rivers crossed the track of the Right and Centre Columns.

The Naval Brigade landed on 19th November and proceeded by the Coast road to Fort Pearson, which was being built to protect the Lower Tugela Drift. Arriving on the 24th, they relieved two companies of the Buffs who went on to Thring's Post.

From 6th to 10th January 1879 they were occupied in placing a steel hawser to work a punt ferry at the Drift, whilst the stores were being collected at Stanger and Fort Pearson. Stores were also being collected at Greytown, Ladysmith and Holpmakaar for the Centre Column, and at Newcastle and Utrecht for the Left Column.

On 6th January 50 Seamen and Marines from the *Tenedos* joined the Brigade.

On 11th January, Pearson's Column was formed up, consisting of:

8 Companies Buffs
6 Companies 99th
2 guns RFA
2nd Company RE
Naval Brigade, 220.
2 Battalions Natal Native Contingent.
No 2 Company Native Pioneers.

On 12th the Naval Brigade crossed to the left bank of the Tugela without opposition and by the evening of the 18th all were across, the punt working very successfully. Fort Tenedos was constructed on the left bank by evening of the 17th, and stores and transport collected there.

Inyezane.
At 6 am on 18th the advanced parties, including the *Active's* Brigade, 5 Companies of the Buffs, RE, and mounted troops, reached the Inyoni River with 50 waggons and next day crossed that river to Umsundusi, the rear portion with 50 waggons reaching the Inyoni. On the 21st they reached Kwasamabela; on 22nd they came to the Inyezane River where was fought the Battle of Inyezane. The Zulus were seen at 8 am on a hill 400 yards from the left flank and the Native Company of the advanced guard was driven in. Colonel Pearson with two companies of the Buffs, two of the Naval Brigade and two guns, advanced to a knoll on the ridge leading to the Mission Station at Etshowe; the Zulus, advancing on the right, were met by the Buffs and the 99th, who forced them back. They however pushed forward on the British left but were stopped by the rockets of the Naval Brigade; portions of the Native Contingent supported by the Naval Brigade carried the kraal in their front and set it on fire; a company of the Buffs was then sent up in support and they then occupied the Maja's Hill. At 9.30 am the Zulus retreated and the troops advanced and occupied a ridge four miles further on where they bivouacked; next morning they occupied the Mission Station of Etshowe without opposition and placed it in a state of defence as a depot on the line of advance and here they were beleaguered till 3rd April.

Isandhlwana.
On 22nd January disaster befell the Centre Column; the greater part of the 2/24th having gone out with Lord Chelmsford on a reconnaissance, the Zulus attacked the troops in camp - consisting of the 1/24th and details - who were massacred almost to a man when their ammunition was exhausted. The gallant defence of the River crossing at Rorke's Drift by Lieutenant Chard RE and Lieutenant Bromhead 24th, with one company of 1/24th prevented the Zulus bursting into the Colony and enabled some of the fugitives from Isandhlwana to escape. They were relieved the next morning by the reconnoitring column. The left column also met with a reverse at the Inhlobane Mountain and had to withdraw to the White Umvolosi River, so that operations came to a standstill till reinforcements could arrive from England, Mauritius, etc.

Etshowe.
Lord Chelmsford sent instructions to Colonel Pearson's column to fall back to the Tugela, but they decided to hold Etshowe and to send back their empty waggons under escort to Fort Tenedos. On three sides the fort was commanded at short range, dangerous wooded ravines ran up close to it; there was good water, but the stock of provisions was not large; they sent back all mounted men and two battalions of the Native Contingent who reached Fort Tenedos in safety. A convoy of supplies reached them safely on 30th January and the garrison took shelter under the waggons which formed their defence line; 1,000 of the animals were sent away, but the Zulus captured 900 of them and drove the rest back to the fort. They did not hear of the disaster at Isandhlwana till 7th February but ignored Lord Chelmsford's recommendation to fall back. They were not interfered with until the 16th. On 1st March, four companies of the Buffs and one of the 99th, with one company RE and 20 Royal Marines (Lieutenant Dowding) burnt one of Dubulmanzi's kraals about 7 miles from

the Fort, communication being established with GHQ by flashing mirror.[286]

On 7th March they commenced making a road back towards the Tugela. There was a good deal of sickness, but on the morning of 2nd April the relieving force was seen to be engaged at Gingihlovo and on the evening of 3rd April the blockade was raised. Four Officers and 27 NCOs and men died and there were 120 sick.

Ginghilovo.
Reinforcements were now arriving; HMS *Shah*, on her way home from South America embarked one Company of the 88th and a battery of artillery at St. Helena and reached Durban on 6th March, where she also landed her Naval Brigade of 400 including her RM detachment under Captain J Phillips RMLI and Lieutenant Lambert RMA; HMS *Boadicea* also landed her Brigade of 200 including the RM under Lieutenant Robyns RMLI, on the 15th. The total Royal Marines numbered about 100.

Heavy floods in the Buffalo and Tugela Rivers had stopped the Zulus. A column was at once formed for the relief of Etshowe; it was assembled at Fort Pearson and consisted of the 57th, 91st, 2/60th and 99th Regiments, with 2 companies of the Buffs and the Naval Brigade from the *Shah*, *Tenedos*, *Boadicea*, with mounted volunteers; they had two 9 pdr guns, two Gatlings and 4 rocket tubes. The troops were divided into two Brigades.

On 28th March they were on the left bank of the Tugela and on the 29th the advance commenced near the coast and over more open country; heavy rain on the 27th and 28th had made the progress slow; an entrenched camp was formed at the Inyoni River.

On 30th they moved to the Amatikulu River, crossing on the 31st. On 1st April they made an entrenched camp one mile from the Inyezane River close to the Gingihlovo stream, which was free from bush, but the long grass gave cover to the enemy, large numbers of whom were seen. At dawn on the 2nd, mounted men went out to reconnoitre and at 6 am the Zulu army was reported to be advancing; two columns appeared on the further bank of the river. One column attacked the south and west faces and in spite of the heavy fire the Zulus pushed on to within 20 yards of the shelter trench, but at last recoiled; mounted men then attacking their right flank they turned and fled, incurring heavy loss in the ensuing pursuit. The Naval Brigade had 6 wounded; the Zulus - who were about 10,000 strong - lost about 1,200.

The 2nd April was spent in lager, and on the 3rd, a portion being left in camp, Lord Chelmsford moved on with a force including 190 Seamen and 100 Royal Marines who belonged to the 2nd Brigade; they marched 15 miles and did not reach Etshowe till midnight; the other 350 of the RN Brigade were attached to the 1st Brigade. On 4th April a small force including the Royal Marines destroyed Dabulmanzi's kraal about 8 miles away and the whole force then returned to the Tugela.

---
286 Heliographs were not yet in use.

Preparations were now made for the advance into Zululand to attack Ulundi, Ketchwayo's capital.

The force was divided into two Divisions, and the Naval Brigade was attached to the 1st Division under Major General Crealock; 350 Seamen to the 1st Brigade, and 190 Seamen and 100 Royal Marines to the 2nd Brigade.

The 2nd Division under Major General Newdigate, who was accompanied by Lord Chelmsford and his staff, and Colonel Wood's column on the left, advanced direct on Ulundi and fought a battle there on 4th July, which broke the power of the Zulus and decided the campaign. Ketchwayo became a fugitive and was captured by a patrol of the KDGs on 28th August. Meanwhile the 1st Division had marched from the Lower Tugela and Gingihlovo at the end of April; they marched through the low lying coast region which was very unhealthy and there was much sickness.

The Naval Brigade was now armed with three 9 pdrs, 4 Gatlings and 4 rocket tubes. They reached Port Durnford - about 6 miles north of the mouth of the Umlalaz River - on 28th June, where there was an open beach and on the 29th and 30th the Naval Brigade and troops were sent to land stores etc. through the surf. Two hawsers were taken ashore and made fast, the other ends being 400 yards out to sea and the surf boats were warped backwards and forwards along the hawsers; they also commenced to build a fort, called - after the Commodore - Fort Richards. General Wolseley, who had been appointed to relieve Lord Chelmsford - arrived in the *Shah* on 2nd July but was unable to land owing to the surf and returned to Durban. He objected to the plans being followed, but before he could intervene the Battle of Ulundi had been fought and the war was practically ended.

A Battalion of Royal Marines had been asked for by General Wolseley before he left England, so 44 Officers and 1,028 men RMA and RMLI were embarked in the transport *Jumna* and arrived at Capetown. They were however too late and were not required, so returned to England on 19th July.

The Naval Brigade and Royal Marines were inspected by Lord Wolseley on 21st July at Port Durnford and returned to Durban in a transport from which they were sent to their ships. Captain Phillips RMLI was mentioned in dispatches and received the CB. Lieutenant Burrowes RMA was mentioned in dispatches and Lieutenant T W Dowding besides being mentioned in dispatches was specially promoted to Captain on 15th November 1879.

VOLUME THREE 1837 – 1914

20 - Egypt 1881 - 1882

In 1881 the numbers were 12,400

Great changes were made in the Corps and with very far reaching results. Warrant Rank, as in the Army, was for the first time introduced into the Marines.[287] It was granted to Sergeant-Majors, Superintending Clerks, Bandmasters, and Schoolmasters.

Commandants were now only to hold the appointment for 3 years and Staff Officers for 5; Lieutenants to be promoted to Captain after 12 years' service; special rates of pay for QMS and First Sergeants Instructors of Gunnery, Musketry, Infantry, etc. were granted (promotion to QMSI came many years later). The pay of all NCOs was revised and raised, in consequence of which deductions for rations when on shore continued and the 1d a day Beer Money was abolished for them but not for men. Re-engaged pay was discontinued, also Good Conduct pay for Corporals and Bombardiers (restored in 1919) and Lodging Money for Married Men was fixed at 8d a day instead of 4d and 2d.

Naval Savings Banks, which had been authorised for Marine Divisions by Order-in-Council 10th March 1882, were later assimilated to the Naval Regulations.

Chevrons.
It was ordered that NCOs were to wear their chevrons on the right arm only.

Boer War 1881.
The Navy was called on again to assist the troops in Natal, when war broke out with the Boers in 1881; a Naval Brigade, including a detachment of Royal Marines under Lieutenant Robyns RMLI was present at the engagements at Laing's Nek, but fortunately none of the RM were included in the part of the Naval Brigade that accompanied the force under General Colley, which was involved in the disaster of Majuba Hill. Peace was soon patched up with the Boers, but it was not long before large bodies of the Corps were again engaged in active operations.

1882 - The numbers were 12,400.

Ireland.
In 1882 a Battalion was sent to Ireland where the Fenians and others were again causing trouble. It was commanded by Lieutenant Colonel H S Jones and was on duty in the west and south parts of the country. In addition 200 of the Corps were employed on duties far outside the scope of their ordinary duties. Those were specially picked men who, dressed in plain clothes, were used to reinforce the police in Dublin and rendered invaluable service.

---

287 Order-in-Council, 29th November 1881.

HRH Admiral the Duke of Edinburgh was created Honorary Colonel of the Royal Marine Forces.

Egyptian War, 1882[288]

Trouble was brewing in Egypt where the Army, under Arabi Pasha, had rebelled against the authority of the Khedive, and after much hesitation owing to international complications, the British Government supported the Khedive and demanded that Arabi should cease the arming of the batteries at Alexandria and surrender them for the purposes of disarmament by the morning of 11th July 1882.

Arabi returned a confused rambling reply, which the Admiral, Sir Beauchamp Seymour (whom we have already seen in New Zealand), refused to accept, and the bombardment of Alexandria took place on 11th July.

The Mediterranean Fleet was available, and the Channel Fleet had been ordered to reinforce them; it was due to leave Malta on 9th July with two regiments of Infantry and some RE, but did not arrive until after the bombardment.

In addition, HMS *Orontes* was sent from England with the following Royal Marines:

RM Artillery: - Lieutenant Colonel Tuson, 2 Majors, 2 Captains, 5 Lieutenants; Lieutenant Noble, Adjutant; Lieutenant Burrower, Pay and Quartermaster; 342 NCOs and men, formed into 3 Companies.

RM Light Infantry: - Lieutenant Colonels Ley and Le Grand; 3 Majors; 5 Captains; 12 Lieutenants; Lieutenant Sandwith, Adjutant; Lieutenant L. Edye, Quartermaster; Lieutenant Frampton, Paymaster; 568 NCOs and men (298 Chatham, 170 Portsmouth, 117 Plymouth) formed into 5 Companies.

At Gibraltar on 4th July they were transferred to HMS *Tamar* and sailed the same day arriving at Malta on the 9th. After drawing stores, they left on 11th for Cyprus where they arrived on 15th; they left that night for Alexandria, where they arrived on the 17th, nearly a week after the bombardment.

Alexandria.
Returning to the Fleet; for bombardment purposes it had been divided into two Squadrons, the Inshore consisting of the battleships *Invincible* (Flag), *Monarch*, *Penelope*, with the gunboats *Beacon*, *Bittern*, *Condor*, *Cygnet*, and *Decoy*; the Offshore consisting of the Battleships *Sultan* (SNO) *Alexandra* (Flag), *Inflexible* (Turret), *Temeraire*, *Superb*. This squadron was to the eastward

---

288 Authorities; Official Account; Officers' Services; War in Eqypt (Lieut Goodrich USN - Official USA Report); Diaries (Captain Edye, etc.); Britain's Sea Soldiers (Field).

of the Corvette Pass. Foreign men-of-war and merchant vessels were off the mouth of the Central or Borghaz Pass out of the line of fire.

To the east of Alexandria was a small circular harbour called New Port; enclosing the harbour is the breakwater; and covering the town is the reef through which are three passages, the East or Corvette Pass close to the breakwater, the Borghaz or Central Pass which was the main one, and the Marabout or West which was seldom used. The fortifications consisted of a nearly continuous series of open works, with closed works at the principal salients.

The principal Forts were:

East of the City:	1.	Fort Silsileh.
North of the City:	2.	Fort Pharos.
	3.	Fort Ada.
	4.	Fort Ras el Tin.
	5.	Light House Fort.
South of the City:	6.	Fort Aga.
	7.	Unnamed open battery.
	8.	Oom-el-Kabobo.
	9.	Fort Kumania.
South-West of the City:	10.	Mex Lines.
	11.	Fort Mex.
	12.	Namusia or Mex Citadel.
West of the City:	13.	Marsa-el-Khanat.
	14.	Marabout Fort.
	15.	Adjemi Fort (the newest).

Most of them were well sited, armed with modern Armstrong ML rifled guns, mounted in the open or *en barbette*; only Fort Pharos had casemates. They were constructed of sand, with retaining walls of soft limestone bonded with coarse lime mortar. The parapets were of sand at 30 degree slope and the embrasures admitted of 60 degree of training. The guns were 10-in., 9-in., 8-in., and 7-in. MLR, and 40 pdr Armstrong BL with some 15-in., 10-in., and 6.5-in. smooth bores, 10-in. howitzers and the usual 13-in. and 10-in. mortars. The Northern Line had 103 guns and the Inner line 102.

The British guns were much the same; the Off Shore Squadron could fire a broadside of 2 x 16-in. MLR, 1 x 12-in., 21 x 8-in., 2 x 9-in., with the 3 x 12-in and 2 x 10-in. MLR of *Temeraire* and was able to bring 33 guns to-bear on Forts Aga and Pharos. The Inshore Squadron had a broadside of 4 x 12-in., 5 x 9-in., and 4 x 8-in, all MLR.

The bombardment was to commence at 5 am by a ship firing at the Hospital Battery near Fort Ada. List of RM Officers at Bombardment of Alexandria:

Alexandra   Lieutenant Colonel J Phillips RMLI, Lieutenants G D Raitt, RMA, Paris RMA
Invincible

Penelope	Captain E S Innes RMLI
Monarch	Captain E S G Schomberg RMLI, Lieutenant W M Marriott RMA.
Sultan	Captain C J Cleethen RMA, Lieutenants A G Tatham RMA, J Swanton RMLI
Inflexible	Captain W Campbell RMA
Temeraire	Captain A Allen RMA, Lieutenant F White RMLI
Superb	Captain Matthias, Lieutenants G Trotter, H Talbot RMA

Channel Squadron arrived later:

Achilles	Captain de la P Beresford RMA, Lieutenant Ussher RMA., C H Willis RMLI
Minotaur	Captain A French RMA, Lieutenant G Kappey RMA Lieutenant J R Johnston RMLI
Agincourt	Captain F A H Farquharson RMLI, Lieutenant W Gaitskell RMA, Lieutenant J Oldfield RMLI
Northumberland	Captain G A Gore RMLI, Lieutenant Swinburne RMA and Peake RMLI
Ismailia:	
Orion	Captain R B Kirchoffer RMLI
East Indies:	
Euryalus	Captain J Baldwin RMLI

The Ras-el-Tin batteries were to be attacked, especially the Light House Battery; when silenced the *Sultan*, *Superb*, and *Alexandra* were to move to the Eastward and attack Pharos and Silsileh Forts; the *Inflexible* in the afternoon was to deal with the Mex Lines from the Corvette Pass and to support the Inshore Squadron, whilst the *Temeraire*, *Sultan*, and *Alexandra* dealt with the flank works at Ras-el-Tin; the gunboats to remain outside until there was a favourable opportunity to attack Mex. It was to depend on the state of the weather whether they anchored or remained under weigh. The Admiral himself was in command of the Inshore Squadron, and Captain Hunt-Grubbe of the Offshore. Shell was to be used with caution. Should the *Achilles* arrive in time she was to engage Pharos.

Fire commenced at 7 am and was kept up steadily till 10.30 am, when the *Sultan*, *Superb*, and *Alexandra* anchored off the Light House Fort and assisted by the *Inflexible*, which had weighed and joined them at 12.30 pm, silenced most of the guns in Ras-el-Tin; but some heavy guns in Fort Aga remained in action. At 1.30 pm a shell from the *Superb* blew up the magazine of the Fort and the garrison retreated. The ships then turned on Pharos, and one of its guns was dismounted. The Hospital Battery was well fought but was silenced by a shell from the *Inflexible*; it however came again into action later on.

The *Invincible*, *Penelope*, and *Monarch* assisted at intervals by the *Inflexible* and *Temeraire* after some hours silenced and partially destroyed the Batteries and lines at Mex. Marsa el Khanat was apparently destroyed by the explosion of its magazine after half an hour's duel with the *Monarch*; as a matter of fact, the fort itself was undamaged, the explosion having taken place in a guncotton store in rear of the fort.

At 2 pm the gunners in the Lower Mex Battery abandoned their guns, when twelve volunteers under Lieutenant Bradford RN, and some officers, under cover of the gunboats, destroyed two 10-in. MLR guns with guncotton and spiked some others. HMS *Condor*, commanded by Lord Charles Beresford, with only a 7-in. MLR gun attacked the forts most bravely.

The action terminated at 5.30 pm when the Fleet anchored for the night. The Offshore Squadron bore the brunt of the fighting; the upper works of the *Inflexible* and *Invincible* were much knocked about, whilst the *Sultan*, *Superb* and *Alexandra* were hulled, the latter being hit sixty times.

On the morning of 12th the *Temeraire* and *Inflexible* engaged Fort Pharos, but after two or three rounds a flag of truce was hoisted at Ras-el-Tin, and in the evening, it was found that the town was evacuated.

Yet another lesson of the difficulties of attacking forts with ships was learnt. The British fuses had proved very bad and there were a large number of prematures and failures; they had fired vast quantities of ammunition and in fact some ships could not have continued much longer. They found that when anchored the advantage of knowing the range outweighed the risk of being hit; they used their machine guns, but results were unknown. The British casualties amounted to 6 killed, 27 wounded.

"The Forts were bruised but not knocked out and could have been repaired in a night. It was only ships that could attain a steep angle of descent for their shells who did any good." [289] An American observer summed up in his report: "*Ships cannot continue the action beyond a certain time, limited by the capacity of their shell rooms and magazines; the garrisons of the forts may quietly wait under cover until the fire slackens and can then return it with interest and continue it indefinitely and absolutely at their leisure.*"

Policing of Alexandria.

On the 12th under cover of the white flag, Arabi withdrew his troops and took up a position in rear of the town, and the town was left at the mercy of the mob. As an American observer reports: *"This memorable battle was followed by one of the most shocking, wanton and deplorable catastrophes of the century."* The town was set on fire in two places, the main square and many other streets were burnt down, massacres, pillaging and disorder reigned, and it was with the terrible conditions prevailing that the Corps had now to deal.

Admiral Seymour in his report says that on the 12th, Arabi Pasha was reported to be at Pompey's Pillar and that he had to proceed cautiously; that he sent two parties from the *Invincible* and *Monarch* under Captain Fairfax RN, to spike the guns bearing on the harbour and that he sent the gunboats to bring in the Marines of the Offshore Squadron. "Ras-el-Tin Palace was occupied, and the guns spiked and at 4 pm the Khedive surrendered at the gate of the Palace and was guarded by a guard of Marines from the Fleet."

---

289 Goodrich.

He also says; "On the evening of 13th landed all the Marines of the Offshore Squadron and sent a small patrol into the streets, but they were of little service" which was not a fair way of putting it and shows how little he knew of what was going on ashore. Under Lord Charles Beresford the Royal Marines and the few seamen landing parties were doing invaluable work.

The first party - consisting of 150 RM and 250 seamen - who were landed from *Monarch*, *Invincible* and *Penelope*, reached the Ras-el-Tin Palace at 10.30 am on the 13th and seized the western end of the peninsula; they threw out a line of sentries north to south from shore to shore. At 12.30 pm a small party of seamen with a Gatling gun pushed towards the town and guarded the streets in the immediate neighbourhood and occupied the Arsenal, which became a place of refuge for the Europeans. In the afternoon the seamen re-embarked, their places being taken by the Royal Marines of *Superb*, *Inflexible*, and *Temeraire*. A patrol of RMA went through the Arab and European quarters and shot some natives and police who were pillaging. In the evening the RM of the *Achilles* and *Sultan* also landed; the *Inflexible*, *Temeraire*, and *Achilles* anchored off Ramleh to cover the land approaches to the south and east. On the 14th as many men as could be spared were landed and Captain J A Fisher RN was appointed to command the Naval Brigade. The RM were formed into a Battalion, Major J Phillips RMLI in command.

The damage to the town was enormous by this time; the Channel Fleet had arrived and also landed their Marines and the entire City was occupied -

> The Ramleh Gate by the Marines of the *Monarch*
> Rosetta Gate by the Marines of the *Temeraire*
> Moharrem Bay Gate by the Marines of the *Alexandra* and *Inflexible*
> Fort Kam-el-Dih Gate by the Marines of the *Sultan*
> Pompey's Pillar Gate by the Marines of the *Superb*
> Caracol by the Marines of the *Achilles*
> Gabarri Railway Station by the Marines and Seamen of *Alexandra*
> Zaptieh and Arsenal by the Marines of the *Invincible*

Major Phillips was at Ras-el-Tin in charge of the Khedive and the United States Marine Corps and Seamen occupied the European Quarter and Club.

On the 15th there were rumours of an attack by Arabi Pasha, so Seamen and Marines were landed, and each reinforced its own detachment. The *Minotaur's* Marines reinforced the Ramleh Gate, the Seamen between Pompey's Pillar, and the Marines at Barsab; the *Alexandra*'s seamen were sent to the Bridge over the Mahmoudieh Canal; but Arabi had retired to Kafr Dewar, where he proceeded to erect strong fortifications across the isthmus that connects Alexandria with the mainland. Large numbers of Royal Marines were now formed into a police force under Major A French, RMA who, under Lord Charles Beresford, cleared the streets of looters and re-established order in the town.

On 17th July the 1st Bn South Staffords and a company of RE were landed from HMS *Northumberland* and relieved the Marines between Pompey's Pillar and Ramleh, who were nearly worn out, by attacks of insects, fleas and mosquitoes and want of sleep. *"Up to this time a few hundred men had held the City against a force estimated to be ten times as strong and in presence of an inimical and violent population."*[290]

Defence of Alexandria.
On the 17th the RM Battalions arrived and were landed that afternoon and went to the Gabarri Gate and took charge of the Western Lines from Pompey's Pillar Gate to the Mahmoudieh Canal with two Companies of RMLI and one of RMA on Outpost. Lieutenant Colonel Le Grand assumed command of the Battalion from the Fleet.

On 18th July the 3rd Bn 60th Rifles arrived in HMS *Agincourt* and relieved the Staffords at the Moharrem Gate who were then concentrated at the Rosetta Gate and the land defence was assumed by the Army, assisted by the Royal Marines of the *Alexandra, Superb*, and *Temeraire* at the Ramleh Gate under Lieutenant Colonel Le Grand with the seamen and Gatlings. Major General Sir Archibald Alison had now arrived and assumed command.

The remainder of the Royal Marines were employed policing and patrolling the town, being allotted as follows;

Ras-el-Tin	half	*Agincourt's* detachment
Coast Guard Station		*Sultan's* detachment
Zaptieh		*Monarch's* detachment
Tribunal		*Minotaur's* detachment
Caracol	half	*Agincourt's* detachment
Caracol		*Achille's* detachment
Gabarri Railway		*Infexible's* detachment

It was not possible at first to raise: A Native Police, so the RM were acting as Police Constables. It may be of interest to note that the RM from the Fleet were wearing blue serges and their caps had white covers with a "cape or havelock".

On 25th July Lieutenant Colonel Ley was invalided home and Major Strong was temporarily in command of the RMLI Battalion; Captain Sandwith, the Adjutant, was appointed a DAQMG on the Army Staff.

Reinforcements of troops were now arriving in large numbers and on 24th July Ramleh was seized and occupied by Sir Archibald Alison, and fortified, the RMA of the *Inflexible* under Captain Campbell being sent to help the RA in mounting the 40 pdr guns there.

---

290 Cdr Goodrich USN.

On the 28th, 300 of the 35th Regiment were told off to relieve the RM of the police duties in the town, and on the 30th all Royal Marines belonging to the Fleet were withdrawn to their ships, but on 2nd August 200 from the *Alexandra* and *Superb* were sent to the Mex lines under Lieutenant Colonel le Grand to guard that important outpost.

On the 26th July, one Company RMA and three Companies RMLI of the Battalion under Major Strong took part in a reconnaissance in force, but with no result returning to quarters at 4 pm. Again, on the 29th a company of RMA and one of RMLI under Colonel Tuson with a party of RE were sent out to repair the railway line from Gabarri Station towards Cairo which was effectively carried out under a screen of Mounted Infantry without opposition.

The Egyptians had retired to their entrenchments at King Osman and Kafr Dowr. At the eastern extremity of the Alexandria Peninsula were the Aboukir Forts, very powerful and held by 5000 men. The main body was at Kafr Dowr. Lake Mareotis, as it was summer time, was nearly dry and the Egyptians could easily advance. The length of the line to be held by the British was ten or eleven miles; the Fleet could guard the ends, but troops were necessary; the waterworks and tower being the centre of the defence.

Mellaha Junction.
On 5th August Sir Archibald Alison made a reconnaissance in force, known as the action of Mellaha Junction. The left column was composed of a half Battalion each of DCLI and South Staffords with some Mounted Infantry and a 9 pdr gun, and advanced along the east bank of the Mahmoudieh Canal; the 60th Rifles and a 9 pdr gun along the west bank to where the railway from Cairo approaches the Canal.

A strong Battalion of Royal Marines drawn from the RMA and RMLI Battalions under Majors Ogle and Strong, the whole under Colonel Tuson, left Gabarri Station by train and detrained about 800 yards from Mellaha Junction and formed up under cover of the railway embankment, where it acted with the Naval armoured train with a 40 pdr gun and two 9 pdr guns, under Captain J A Fisher and formed the right attack under Sir Archibald Alison himself.

The left attack advanced at 4.45 pm and soon came into action against the enemy who were strongly posted; the positions were carried, and the enemy retired to a new position on the east bank, half a mile in rear, from which they were also driven with loss. The right attack closed the chord of the arc formed by the left attack and moved forward under cover of the railway embankment rapidly and out of sight to within 350 yards of the enemy, but the enemy discovered them and opened artillery fire. They pushed on in file, the 9 pdrs coming into action on the embankment, to the junction of the railway and canal, where Major Donald's Company of RMA doubled across, dislodging the enemy from their entrenchments and which they used in reverse. The RMLI companies lined the embankment and fired volleys; here they were enfiladed by a house on the railway line; Captains Heathcote's and Byrch's RMLI companies were sent to reinforce Donald's towards the canal and then four more companies still more to the left upon the bank and across the canal so that they formed a diagonal line across the canal and railway, and the enemy fell back slowly. The enemy were completely dislodged from their works except on their left, where the entrenchments were very strong. At about 5.30 pm the enemy opened with rockets, on which the 40 pdr came into action with great effect. As there was a chance that the companies might penetrate the lines too far, the GOC sent orders to prevent any further movement to the front. At 6.15 the GOC having obtained all the information he required, ordered the Battalion to retire. This they did by alternate companies, A, B, and C, RMLI forming the rearguard. Sergeant Holdstock distinguished himself in bringing in a wounded man. They withdrew by alternate companies, covered by the Naval guns. General Alison in his dispatch said, "Movement was carried out with the most perfect gallantry and precision by the Marine Battalion under Colonel Tuson" and "fell back by alternate companies with the regularity of a field day." They entrained and returned to Alexandria and the left attack was also withdrawn, the casualties being:

Army	1 Officer,	1 Man killed;	3 wounded.
Navy	1 man killed;		4 wounded.
Royal Marines	1 man killed;		20 wounded.[291]

The reconnaissance was unfortunately barren of results, as the Egyptians who were 12,000 to 10,000 strong, did not develop their strength and they regained the positions from which they had been driven.

On 8th August another Battalion consisting of RMA - 1 Major, 2 Captains, 2 Lieutenants, 108 NCOs and men, and RMLI - 1 Major, 5 Captains, 8 Lieutenants, 432 NCOs and men under command of Major and Brevet Lieutenant Colonel S J Graham RMLI who had left England on 27th July in SS *Dacca* arrived, who were sent on to the *Northumberland* at Port Said. Lieutenant Colonel E S Jones RMLI also arrived and assumed command of the RMLI Battalion.

On 12th August the *Alexandra*'s and *Superb*'s detachments were relieved by a company from the RMA Battalion at Mex and the guns were destroyed by the seamen. A garrison was left in Alexandria under General Sir Evelyn Wood, which included some Marines, and on 19th and 20th September some Marines of the Fleet under Major French RMA occupied the Aboukir Forts.

At Suez, Admiral Hewett, C-in-C East Indies, in *Euryalus* with *Eclipse*, *Ruby*, and *Mosquito*, had landed 450 men to protect the town and docks without opposition.

Seizure of Suez Canal.
Admiral Hoskins was at Port Said with *Penelope*, *Agincourt*, *Monarch*, *Northumberland*, *Tourmaline*, *Ready*, and *Beacon*. The *Orion* and *Carysfort* were at Ismailia, but Arabi's troops were holding these places.

---

291 Several of whom died later.

General Sir Garnet Wolseley, the C-in-C, arrived on 16th August and the Army was formed into two Divisions and a Cavalry Division. There was also an Indian contingent to arrive at Suez. The First Division was composed of the 1st or Guards Brigade under HRH the Duke of Connaught, the 2nd Brigade under General Graham with Divisional Troops. The RM Battalions were attached to the First Division, the RMA (acting as infantry) to the Divisional Troops and the RMLI Battalion to the 2nd Brigade, the other regiments of which were 2nd Bn Royal Irish, 1st Bn Royal West Kents, 2nd Bn York and Lancaster, 1st Bn Royal Irish Fusiliers.

General Wolseley's objects were:

1. Crush Arabi Pasha.
2. Save Cairo from the fate of Alexandria.
3. Re-establish the Khedive's authority.

He therefore determined on a secret change of base to Ismailia, leaving a garrison in Alexandria, and to make his advance along the railway and Sweet Water Canal to Cairo; the distance was only 96 miles and the route was more healthy; there was also a sheltered inland harbour for the transports.

To cover his movements a feint was made on the Aboukir Forts. The *Temeraire*, *Inflexible*, *Minotaur*, and *Superb* anchored in Aboukir Bay at 3.30 pm on 19th August with transports. The transports *Euphrates* with the DCLI and 60th Rifles, the *Rhosina* with the RMLI Battalion and *Nerissa* with the RMA Battalion and RE pushed on to Port Said; the last two broke down but were towed by the *Alexandra* and *Euphrates* and after dark the other transports followed, arriving the following morning.

But meanwhile Admiral Hoskins with the Seamen and Marines of his Squadron and Colonel Graham's Battalion of RM had secured the Canal. The following account is extracted from the reports of Admiral Hoskins and Captains Fairfax and Fitzroy RN.

Commander Edwards was sent down the Canal on the night of 19/20th to seize the telegraph station at Kantara, etc, also all barges and dredgers and to make sure that the Canal was clear.

On 18th two companies of RMLI under Major Scott and Captains Pine-Coffin and Eden from *Northumberland* were placed on board *Monarch* and *Iris*, and on the evening of the 19th the remaining three companies under Colonel Graham were placed on board *Dee* and *Ready*, to proceed to Ismailia with two launches to facilitate landing. At sunset the *Falcon* and, after dark on 10th, the *Northumberland* went off to Fort Ghemil to prevent the exodus of the coal heavers.

At 4 am on the 20th the movement was executed simultaneously at all places and the Canal was in British hands, despite the unfriendly attitude of M de Lesseps and his French employees and the presence of Arabi's troops in all three ports.

Port Said.

At Port Said, Captain Fairfax RN reported that the landing commenced at 3.30 am and that they got ashore without being observed. A Colonel Tulloch and six Marines, landing from an open boat, had seized the sentries on the quay. The Iris Brigade (80 Seamen and 28 Marines) with Captain Pine-Coffin's Company of the RM Battalion landed abreast the ship and seized the beach and the RM went to one side of the Barracks.

From the *Monarch* two companies (100 Seamen and 48 RM) went out and barred the egress from the town and Captain Eden's Company of the RM Battalion went to the other side of the Barracks and the two RM Companies secured the 160 soldiers quartered there. The *Monarch's* guns commanded the main street, and the *Iris* was to seaward where she could command the beach and town. Port Said was held by the Seamen and Marines of the Fleet until relieved on 16th September by 207 RMLI and 78 RMA under Major Colwell, RMLI, who left England in SS *Quetta* on 7th September.

Ismailia.

At Ismailia where Captains Fitzroy and Stephenson RN were in command with Commanders Kane and Napier, 565 Seamen and 74 Marines were landed including:

From *Orion*	40 RM (Captain Kitchoffer), one 9 pdr, one Gatling, and a Torpedo party.
From *Northumberland*	1 Rifle Company and one Gatling seaman.
	21 RMA under Captain Swinburne.
	1 RMLI under Captain Gore and Lieutenant Neils.
From *Coquette*	One 7 pdr
From *Nyanza*	100 Seamen and Marines from *Northumberland*.

Enemy pickets were in the town; there were also 2000 men and six guns at Nefiche Station and there were also an unknown number of Bedouins.

At 3 am the *Orion's* and *Coquette's* landed, followed by the *Carysfort's*, and seized the Canal Lock Guard. The Governor's Guard laid down their arms to Lieutenant Napier and Lieutenant Swinburne RMA

Commander Kane seized the railway and telegraph stations and the *Orion's* men the Canal Lock Bridge and town. Captain Stephenson's party (*Carysfort*) met with no opposition in Arab Town. He advanced his 200 men, including 74 RM under Captain Gore, with a strong advanced guard through the European and Arab quarters, the latter was occupied and loopholed for defence. At 3.40 am the ships had bombarded the Guard House and by 4 am the whole place was occupied.

Nefiche.

Later it was reported that the enemy were advancing on Nefiche Station in force, and it was decided to dislodge him from there before reinforcements could arrive. The *Orion* and *Carysfort* began a slow bombardment at 11 am on the 20th at 4200 yards, and by noon the camp there was destroyed, and the enemy were retreating towards Cairo. One train on the railway to the south was damaged, but at 4 pm another train was observed discharging men, so the bombardment was continued, and that train was wrecked, blocking the line from Nefiche to Suez. The shelling continued till 10 pm and afterwards on Nefiche at intervals of half an hour to prevent the lines being cleared.

At 6 pm 340 of Colonel Graham's Royal Marines were landed; 200 reinforced Commander Kane at Nefiche and 140 were sent to Captain Stephenson, who had entrenched himself in advance of Arab Town and the Royal Marines were posted along the high canal bank. Lieutenant Napier had secured himself in the Governor's Palace.

Arabi Pasha with 3000 men had advanced to within three miles of Nefiche.

At 10.30 pm 20th, General Graham arrived with the advanced guard of the Army and assumed command; he relieved Stephenson's party in Arab Town with 300 of the 1st Royal West Kents. On the evening of the 20th Captain Fitzroy, expecting a night attack, had placed the *Ready* and *Dee* close inshore in a position that would cover the retreat of the parties if necessary through the town. At 4 pm on 21st August Captain Fitzroy with the Seamen and RM guards were relieved by the Army. On the 21st the transports with the RMA and RMLI Battalions arrived at Ismailia; they were landed and went into bivouac there, on the 22nd.

At Suez Admiral Hewett in *Euryalus* with 200 Seaforth Highlanders, and his Seamen and Royal Marines after slight opposition had secured the approaches to the town.

On 21st the *Tourmaline* and *Dee* were sent to Kantara to establish a permanent post. Troops were now arriving at Ismailia in large numbers and were pushed on along the railway and canal.

The RM Battalions were amalgamated into two; the RMA acting as infantry, under Lieutenant Colonel Tuson, 13 Officers and 450 men; the RMLI under Lieutenant Colonel H S Jones, 37 Officers and 1,006 Men.

Transport was the great difficulty, and also the horses of the cavalry had not recovered from the effects of the sea voyage.

The country in front of Ismailia was a desert with loose sand; the railway and Sweet Water Canal ran side by side; there is a ridge to the north and the ground slopes to the south past the canal; there are a lot of hummocks and mounds; the sand increases in firmness towards Tel-el-Kebir where it is fairly compact gravel. From 9 am to 4 pm the heat was intense, but it was cold at night; the flies and mosquitoes were terrible; water could only be obtained from the Canal, where it had to be filtered to get rid of sand etc. and it became very contaminated.

El Magfar.
General Graham started on 21st August with 800 men and a small Naval party under Captain Stephenson, including 104 RM from HMS *Northumberland* under Captain Gore and Lieutenant Peile. They reached El Magfar station at 1.30 pm and captured 30 trucks with provisions and ammunition; here they entrenched to cover the railway from Suez and that from Zagazig. On making a reconnaissance the enemy was located four miles away.

The 22nd and 23rd were occupied in bringing up stores, the RM Battalions being in bivouac near Ismailia.

Tel-el-Mahuta.
On 24th the action of Tel-el-Mahuta took place; this place was 9 miles west of Ismailia. It was necessary to secure the Canal and prevent the water being tampered with; the enemy was building a dam across the canal, so the Cavalry and Artillery were sent forward. Starting at 4 am on the 24th the Household Cavalry, Mounted Infantry with two guns RHA, the York and Lancaster Regiment, and the RMA Battalion reached Nefiche at daybreak; at 7.30 they reached a point on the canal half way between El Magfar and the village of Tel-el-Mahuta, where the enemy had constructed a dam which was captured by the Household Cavalry; the enemy in force were holding a line across the canal about 1½ miles further on and also a ridge curving round the British right flank on north site about 2000 yards off.

The canal and railway were close together and passed through cuttings with mounds which were strongly entrenched. At Mahuta there was a solid wide dam across the canal and an embankment across the railway; reinforcements were reaching the enemy, whose strength was later ascertained to be 7000 men with 12 guns and an unknown number of Bedouins. It was decided to hold the ground and await reinforcements from Nefiche.

At 9 am the British left was on the captured dam and the enemy were trying to work round it and opened artillery fire. The two RHA guns arrived, and the enemy infantry formed a line of shelter trenches about 1000 yards off; they approached close on the left, but were checked by the York and Lancaster Regiment. From 10 to 11 am the attack developed; fortunately, the enemy only used common shell. General Drury Lowe manoeuvred the Cavalry and Mounted Infantry on the right and checked the enemy, but his horses were not fit to charge. The Naval Gatlings arrived and came into action; the "energy shown by them and by the Marine Artillery drew my highest commendation". N Battery RHA worked their guns with great steadiness, exposed to the fire of 12 guns; later in the day "when the men were extremely tired, the men of the RMA requested permission to help them and did so until the close of the action."

At 3.30 pm the Household Cavalry and MI moved forward on the right, and the DCLI arrived at 1 pm.

At 5.15 pm the enemy advanced his left, again bringing four guns into action and moving cavalry and infantry down the slope but did not come under effective infantry fire. At 6 pm the 4th and 7th Dragoon Guards and the Brigade of Guards arrived but the enemy retired across the ridge to Mahuta.

The RMLI Battalion under Colonel Jones left Ismailia at 4 pm on the 24th, reached El Magfar at 1.30 am on the 25th and left at 4 am with the general advance. At 5 pm on the 25th they marched into camp at Mahsameh. "Such a good piece of work deserves record."

Mahsameh.

At daybreak on the 25th General Graham's force advanced and occupied Tel-el-Mahuta, the enemy abandoning their works retired to Mahsameh. At 6.25 am the artillery came into action and the mounted troops pushed forward and occupied Mahsameh, which was an extensive camp where they captured 7 Krupp guns, ammunition, and two large trains of provisions.[292] The enemy fled in confusion, but the British horses were not yet fit to gallop.

The water supply was now secure, and the canal cleared for more than half the distance between Ismailia and the Delta; the railway line also for 20 miles was in the possession of the British. The troops were undergoing considerable privations as food supplies were not yet organised and Colonel Field tells us how useless the RM transport carts were purchased at Malta.

Kassassin.

On the 26th, the 7th Dragoon Guards occupied the Lock at Kassassin and later in the day the DCLI and the York and Lancasters, and the RMA Battalion, with a small Naval Brigade under Captain Fitzroy consisting of two Gatlings and 70 RM from *Orion* and *Carysfort* marched up and established themselves there.

The cavalry were permanently quartered in Mahsameh Camp, and the RMLI Battalion was also there.

The enemy fell back to Tel-el-Kebir and commenced entrenching; on the 27th the advanced British troops were distributed between Kassassin Lock, Mahsameh and Tel-el-Mahuta.

On 28th August the Egyptians made a serious attack on Kassassin astride the canal but were driven back and the cavalry inflicted severe punishment. General Graham had now about 1,875 troops (including 427 RMA) with two guns, fronting north-west and west. At 11 am a large force of the enemy was reported moving round the right flank behind the ridge and two heavy guns opened fire on our left front. At 3 pm the Mounted Infantry reported that the enemy were retiring, and the troops were ordered back to camp.

At 4.30 pm the enemy advanced again in great force, their skirmishers supported by artillery

---

292 The two RM Battalions are mentioned as the only ones who kept up with the mounted troops.

overlapped on the left. The RMA were posted on the south bank of the canal facing north to north-west; in the centre were the DCLI, about 800 yards in rear of the RMA, with 2nd York & Lancasters on their right. The Mounted Infantry and Dragoon Guards were covering the gap between the RMA and the DCLI and prevented all efforts to break through; "the steady fire of the RMA stopped attempts to cross the canal."

At 4.30 pm the Cavalry and the RMLI Battalion at Mahsameh were sent for, and the cavalry fell on the left flank of the skirmishers and rolled up their line. At 5 pm enemy reinforcements arrived by train.

"Near the right of our position an 8 cm Krupp gun, captured at Mahsameh, had been mounted on a railway truck and was worked by a detachment of RMA under Captain Tucker; it was admirably served and did great execution, as our other guns had to cease fire from want of ammunition; it became the target but no one was hit, man or gun, and it expended 93 rounds."

At 6.45 pm the order was given to the infantry to close, as the cavalry charge was expected; the RMLI came up on the right and advanced in order of attack and the advance continued for two or three miles, supported by the DCLI; the 1st York & Lancasters being kept in reserve, "the enemy fell back, only one attempt at a stand being made on our left which broke at the first volley from the Royal Marines." The infantry had been advancing for 1½ hours in the moonlight and as there seemed no further chance of co-operating with the cavalry, the DCLI and RMLI were ordered to return to camp at 8.45 pm. The Household Cavalry had made a most dramatic charge in the moonlight and dispersed the enemy. At daylight the next morning the battlefield was clear. Lieutenant Colonel Tuson was mentioned in dispatches and he had brought to notice Major Ogle, Captain Rawstorne, Lieutenants Pym and Talbot, with Captain and Adjutant E Noble. The RMA lost 7 killed and 23 wounded. "*The RMLI Battalion under Lieutenant Colonel Jones although arriving too late to take any decisive share in this action, showed by the promptitude of their march to the field a steadiness of their advance that they are well capable of sustaining the high character of their Corps.*"[293]

Captain Tucker's gun, by constant shifting of the truck on the rails and protected by sandbags, escaped injury.

Till the locomotives arrived from Suez, the troops underwent great privations: the water in the canal was very polluted and there was always the danger of the railway being cut by raiders.

On 1st September the 3rd Brigade of the 2nd Division (Highlanders) arrived, and on the 2nd the Indian contingent reached Suez.

On 6th September the distribution of the Royal Marines was as follows;

---

293 Official Dispatch.

At Kassassin.
RMA   15 Officers,   424 NCOs and men.   21 Horses.
RMLI   37 Officers,   850 NCOs and men.   61 Horses.

At Ismailia.
RMLI   3 Officers,   101 NCOs and men.

The artillery staff were preoccupied in getting up stores and provisions ready for a further advance and troops were concentrating, when there occurred the second Battle of Kassassin on 9th September. The Egyptians, employing a force of 30 guns, 17 battalions, several squadrons of cavalry, and some thousands of Bedouins, advanced in two columns, one from the north from the Salileh direction, the other direct from Tel-el-Kebir.

At daybreak 50 men under Colonel Pennington, 17th Bengal Lancers, when posting vedettes, discovered the enemy advancing; first dismounting and opening fire, they then counted and charged 5 squadrons of cavalry which gave the alarm. The enemy guns came into action on the North Hill at 2000 yards on the British right front where they made good shooting. The 1st Division moved out to attack; the RMA and DCLI were to the south of the canal; the RMLI and 60th Rifles formed the firing line with other Battalions in support between the canal and the railway. The RMA Krupp gun and the Naval detachment with the 40 pdr gun on a truck were on the railway; the cavalry and artillery to the north of the railway.

Advancing in attack formation they gradually drove back the enemy and the "RMLI Battalion advancing in regular formation for attack came on a battery of four Krupp guns", which were in action. The RM did not return the fire but kept on until within 400 yards when they opened volleys by half companies, still continuing to advance; the steady fire proved too much for the Egyptians who fled; two of the guns were captured by Captain Pine-Coffin's company, Lieutenant B C Money being mentioned in dispatches for gallantry in capturing them.

The ground was held for 1½ hours, till it was clear that the attack from the north had been dealt with, and at 8.30 the advance was resumed, the right being refused. The enemy was again engaged and at 9.30 am they retired, and the British advance was continued to within 5 or 6000 yards of Tel-el-Kebir entrenchments. At 12.30 pm they returned to Kassassin. General Wolseley in his dispatch of this action says, "General Graham has specially brought to my notice the dashing manner in which the Krupp guns were taken by the Battalion RMLI and the excellent manner in which that Battalion was handled by its CO, Lieutenant Colonel H S Jones."

The total loss was 3 men killed, 2 officers and 70 men wounded; one RM diary speaks of 42 casualties but does not specify if they were all RMLI.

Tel-el-Kebir.
Till 12th September the Battalions remained in camp at Kassassin. When General Wolseley was

ready to attack, he determined to make a night march and attack on the entrenchments at Tel-el-Kebir, which one diary speaks of as a second Plevna.

The Tel-el-Kebir entrenchments were about 9 miles distant and were held by about 24,000 infantry, 1000 artillery with 60 guns, 1000 cavalry and about 2500 irregulars.

Near Tel-el-Kebir station the ground rises gradually to the west, culminating in a range of hills that stretch from the railway (about 1½ miles east of the station) northward to Salihieh; to westward of this range and parallel to the Sweet Water Canal, there is a second line of hills intersecting the first at a point about two miles north of the railway; viewed from the railway this east and west rise appears as a moderate hill, really it is a tableland sloping northward with rather a steeper descent to the south. The country is barren and desolate. The Egyptian entrenchments ran along the crests of the two ranges, the north and south line being prolonged over two miles beyond the intersection; the east and west line faced north-west and so could be taken in rear and flank when the front line fell.

The works consisted of a breastwork about four to six feet high, with a banquette: there was an ample ditch in front, 8 to 12 feet wide, and 5 to 9 feet deep; there were occasional salients with well designed redoubts with wide command on either flank. In rear were frequent shelter trenches irregularly placed, and there were passages at intervals for field guns etc. to come through, protected by traverses and breastworks. The sand and gravel was revetted with grass and reeds, but readily gave way, the passage of a few men invariably broke down the side of the trench, making a causeway for those in rear.

The southern portion near the rail and canal was practically completed, but work was still in progress on the north and western lines, in fact at the north end the works were hardly more than traced out. The extent of the works was very large for the numbers of defenders. At the south end of the line were two well built, redoubts, one on each side of the canal with three guns each, and there was a dam across the canal; also, a gun emplacement on each side of the railway. In front of this portion of the line was a formidable redoubt with 8 guns. At the intersection of the two lines above mentioned was a most elaborately finished redoubt with 5 guns, traverses, etc. This was the point struck by the left of the British main attack - the 2/HLI.

Further North was another formidable redoubt mounting five guns, which was also completed; luckily the attack of the 2nd Division passed to the southward of this and turned it. Two other redoubts north of this, opposite the front of the 1st Division, were only just begun.

As Lord Wolseley says in his dispatch, there was no cover between Kassassin and Tel-el-Kebir; a daylight attack would have entailed an advance over a glacis exposed to artillery fire for five miles, whilst to have attempted to turn either flank would have entailed long marches and have been a slow business, so that the enemy could probably have retired to the cultivated ground in rear, cut up by irrigation ditches and canals; no decisive action would have been possible and the enemy would have been able to make a desperate resistance and possibly destroy Cairo, etc. He therefore determined on a night march.

Orders were issued at 2 pm on 12th September. Men carried two days' rations and 100 rounds SAA with 30 rounds on mules in rear. Valises, blankets and baggage were stacked alongside the railway. The battalions left parade at 6.30 pm and formed in brigade where they bivouacked. The 1st and 2nd Divisions advanced in line. Commencing from south and facing the railway station were the Indian contingent and Seaforth Highlanders; then the 2nd Division, its left directed on the point of intersection of the before-mentioned entrenched lines and the redoubt, covering a front of 1000 yards. The Highland Brigade in the front line from left to right, the HLI, Camerons, Gordons, and Black Watch; the 4th Brigade - 3/60th Rifles and DCLI in rear. In rear of the 60th was GHQ with the RMA Battalion and a troop of 19th Hussars as escort. Battalions were in line of half battalions in column of double companies at deploying interval. Then an interval of 1200 yards filled by the seven batteries of Royal Artillery and connecting files at 10 paces distance; the artillery in line with the supporting brigades. Then the 1st Division, with the 2nd Brigade in front line and the Guards Brigade in support. The 2nd Brigade was formed from left to right: RMLI Battalion, Royal Irish, Royal Irish Fusiliers, York and Lancasters; they occupied a front of 1000 yards and were formed in line of half battalions in column of companies at deploying intervals. The Cavalry Division with the Mounted Infantry and RHA were about 2½ miles to the right rear of the 1st Division. When formed they bivouacked till about 1.30 am when they advanced to within two miles of the works. "The night was very dark, and it was difficult to maintain formations."[294] They marched by a line of telegraph posts till they ceased, when Lieutenant Wyatt Rawson RN directed them by compass and stars, connection being maintained by connecting files.

The Indian Brigade and the Naval Brigade did not start till 2.30 am. The works were reached just at daylight; an enemy scout had dashed into the 2nd Brigade just before but had been captured. The official account says, "Leading Brigades reached the enemy works within a couple of minutes of each other." The enemy were completely surprised but were sleeping in their works and when roused by the sentries they quickly opened fire from guns and rifles. The official report says, "Troops advanced steadily without firing, in obedience to orders they had received, and when close to the works went straight for them, charging with a ringing cheer." The HLI on the left hit the enemy picket in front of the redoubt at 4.55 am, and the enemy opened a heavy artillery and musketry fire, which the Brigade did not return, but advanced another 100 yards when the fire became a perfect blaze; at 150 yards bayonets were fixed and the men charged. The centre companies of the HLI hit the redoubt fair, but the flank companies got round, the rest of the Brigade swept over the parapet and took three field batteries, also taking the next big redoubt to the north in flank and the east and west line of entrenchments in rear. The enemy halted at sixty yards and opened fire, but Arabi Pasha fled at once and the Highlanders seized his quarters.

The 2nd Brigade also swept over the line of entrenchments in their front; in the official dispatch

---

294 Official Report.

it is said that the 2nd Brigade supported by the Guards Brigade reached the works a few minutes after the Highlanders. The American observer reports that at dawn the 2nd Brigade was 900 yards from the entrenchments and that partly owing to the difficulty of keeping the proper alignment during the night march, partly to the fact that the line of march was not at right angles to the line of works, and partly to the surprise caused by the Egyptian scout who galloped into the lines, the 1st Division had to change front forward on its left company (the RMLI) before assaulting and deploying, and then deployed into attack formation. This coincides with Colonel Field's account,[295] who says that four companies formed the firing line and four were in support. At 300 yards the British fired a volley and then rushed to 100 yards, fired a second volley, and then reached the ditch (Colonel Field says they advanced by rushes, firing volleys). Here the firing line was joined by the supports; they delivered a last volley, jumped the ditch and the works were cleared at the point of the bayonet. As soon as they reached the parapet the Egyptians broke and ran, some stopping to fire back at their pursuers, who chased them for a mile, only desisting when the artillery got over the entrenchments and started shelling the fugitives; "they were longer exposed to the fire than the Highlanders, who had surprised the enemy.' It was argued for some time as to who was the first over the parapet - the Highlanders or the RMLI but it was never settled. Colonel Field says that Major Strong was killed as he dismounted near the entrenchments, and Captain Wardell as he crossed the parapet, his assailant being decapitated by Lieutenant Luke.

General Graham in the official despatch says, "*The steadiness of the advance of the 2nd Brigade, 2/Royal Irish, RMLI, 2/York & Lancasters, 1/Royal Irish Fusiliers under what appeared to be an overwhelming fire of musketry and artillery will remain a proud remembrance*".

The Seaforth Highlanders and the Indian contingent had also carried the entrenchments on the extreme British left in a most gallant manner. The Cavalry Division now came round the right and sweeping along the rear of the entrenchments cut up the fugitives and continuing the pursuit to the railway station captured locomotives and trains, and then formed up ready to advance to Cairo. General Drury-Lowe, without wasting any time, started on his journey to Cairo with the Cavalry, Mounted Infantry and RHA. He bivouacked for the night at Belbeis, struck across the desert and reached Cairo at 4 pm on the 14th, having covered 65 miles in two days. Here he demanded the surrender of Arabi and the troops, 10,000 of whom laid down their arms, and Cairo was saved from the fate of Alexandria which had been planned by Arabi. The Guards Brigade arrived there on 15th and every-thing was secured.

The total British casualties were:

Killed:	9 Officers, 43 NCOs and men.
Wounded:	27 Officers, 353 NCOs and men.

The RMLI Battalion casualties were:

---

[295] See Britain's Sea Soldiers.

Killed:	Major H Strong, Captain Wardell, 11 NCOs and men.
Wounded:	Lieutenant E McCausland, and 50 NCOs and Men.

Cairo.
The battalions remained at Tel-el-Kebir clearing up the battlefield till the 18th, when they entrained at 6.30 am for Cairo, arriving there at 12.30 pm and occupied the Kasr-el-Nil Barracks.

On the 21st they marched out to the camp at El Gezireh, where they remained for the rest of their time in Egypt. On 25th September they marched into Cairo to line the streets for the formal entry of the Khedive. On the 24th Colonel Graham was invalided home and on the 25th Lieutenant Coke RMLI died at Alexandria.

On 28th the RMA were ordered to occupy the Aboukir Forts, but not for long.

On 30th September the RMLI Battalion was inspected by the Khedive and General Sir Garnet Wolseley, and marched past in white helmets, scarlet tunics, and white trousers: Major Scott was in command.

On 9th October they started for home, leaving Cairo at noon and arriving at Alexandria at 1.15 am on the 10th they embarked in the SS *City of Paris*. After calling at Malta on the 13th, they arrived at Plymouth on 21st October.

The following honours were awarded in the London Gazette of 17 November 1882.

To be CB
  Colonel H S Jones RMLI
  Colonel S J Graham RMLI
  Colonel H B Tuson RMA
To be ADC to The Queen
  Lieutenant Colonel H S Jones RMLI
  Lieutenant Colonel H B Tuson RMA
To be Brevet Lieutenant Colonel
  Major A French RMA
  Major F A Ogle RMA
  Major J O Scott RMLI
To be Brevet Majors.
  Captain E J W Noble RMA
  Captain W G Tucker RMA
  Captain J Craigie RMLI
  Captain J H Sandwich RMLI
  Captain R W Heathcote RMLI
  Captain R Pine-Coffin RMLI

Medjidie
- 2nd Class — Lieutenant Colonel H S Jones RMLI
- 3rd Class — Lieutenant Colonel H B Tuson RMA
- 4th Class — Captain J H Sandwith RMLI
  - Captain R W Heathcote RMLI
  - Captain R H Les Barres RMLI
  - Captain and Adjutant E J W Noble RMA
  - Captain W G Tucker RMA

Oemanieh
4th Class — Lieutenant Colonel S J Graham RMLI
- Major J Scott RMLI
- Major F A Ogle RMA

VOLUME THREE 1837 – 1914

21 - Egypt and Specialisation 1883 - 1886

In 1883 the numbers were 12,400.

An Order-in-Council of 31st December 1883 dealing with various rates of extra pay throws great light on the activities and employment of the Corps in these days:

Officers' Mess.
Officers' Messes were now allowed a grant of £450 a year (Depot £250) which included Regent's Allowance, and from this all charges for fuel and light, furniture, crockery, glass, linen, wages etc, had to be met; as these amounts were obviously insufficient for upkeep, a considerable levy on officers' subscriptions was entailed.

Paymasters.
The pay of Paymasters was fixed as for other officers instead of a salary of £500 per annum and 5% on the amount of imprests.

Allowances were given for the upkeep of the Men's Recreation Rooms.

An allowance of £100 a year for each Divisional Band was granted.

Clothing compensation was very different from what it is today: £3 for Sergeants, £1-10-0 for Rank and File.

As shewing the varied employments open to NCOs and men, provision was made for pay of RM Wardmasters in the RN Hospitals at Bermuda, Yokohama, and Cape of Good Hope. Scales of working pay were laid down for the working party at Bermuda who lived in Commissioner's House; Officer Superintending, Subalterns, Sergeants and Corporals, whilst Artificers were paid as first class 1/6, second class 1/4, and labourers 1/3 a day. These included masons, carpenters, sawyers, painters, plumbers, smiths, and shoemakers. Similar artificers at Ascension received 1/6 a day and boot money, where the men employed included also the various kinds of farm labourers such as cowmen etc.

On 29th November 1884 the pay of the DAG was fixed at £1500 and of the AAG at £800 a year.

Naval Gunnery.
A departure which has led to great developments was made by an Order-in-Council dated 27th January 1885, which authorised the payment of 2d a pay to Captains of Guns (ie Gunlayers) Royal Marines. This payment had hitherto been confined to seamen. It was now extended to the Marines, and from now on the RM have shared in the various gunnery ratings of the Navy.

On 27th June 1885, prizes for good rifle shooting and judging distance were introduced.

405

Separation Allowance.
By the same order, Separation Allowance under Army Regulations and conditions was allowed for wives of NCOs and men, and proved an inestimable boon during the Great War of 1914-18.

Ward Room Servants etc.. An Order of 19h January 1886 authorised a departure that had had very far reaching effects on the Corps. It says, "It would be advisable to employ men of the Royal Marines on board ship in the ratings of Barber, Butcher, and Lamptrimmer, and to grant extra pay at the rate of 2d a day"; and about the same time the provision of attendants for wardroom officers was inaugurated. The provision of these ratings has often strained the resources of the Corps and rendered the revision of drills and the provision of specialist ratings very difficult, but they have undoubtedly solved a very difficult Naval problem. A precedent which also enabled the provision of printers for the Navy to be solved in 1917, instead of instituting another branch of the Navy.

In 1886 the system of Divisional Numbers to distinguish NCOs and men was introduced; and they ceased to be known by the number of their Divisional Company.

The Soudan, 1884-1885 [296]

As early as 1881 a carpenter, Mahomed Ahmed, had proclaimed himself as the expected Mahdi, and the revolt in the Soudan had been spreading, very inadequately coped with by the Egyptian garrisons. After the defeat of Arabi Pasha and the occupation of Egypt by the British, some British officers were lent to the Egyptian Government to endeavour to deal with the situation. In an attempt to relieve El Obeid, Hicks Pasha with his army was annihilated at Kashgil in October 1883, losing 7,000 rifles and 14 guns, and by this time the Mahdi had possessed himself of large numbers of rifles and guns. In January 1884 General Gordon was sent from England and appointed Governor-General of the Soudan with a view to withdrawing the garrisons and dealing with the revolt.

Meanwhile in the neighbourhood of Suakin on the Red Sea, Osman Digna, a slave trader and merchant, who had been ruined by the suppression of the Slave Trade, encouraged by the success of the Mahdi, had raised a revolt of his own on 3rd August 1883. He demanded the surrender of Suakin and Sinkat and attacked the barracks at the latter place, but was driven off with loss; he invested it again in October and it surrendered. A relief force accompanied by the British Consul at Suakin was sent to relieve Tokar, but was annihilated at El Teb on 5th November. Suakin was again attacked and 700 black troops were cut to pieces at Tamai on 2nd December. Colonel Valentine Baker Pasha was sent with 3,000 Egyptian troops to relieve Tokar; after establishing Fort Baker on the inland side of the morass that separates Trinkitat (the port) from the inland country, he advanced and was attacked by Osman Digna in great force. His force was annihilated and massacred, and on 8th February Sinkat was evacuated and the garrison annihilated on its way to the coast. The British Government, as paramount power in Egypt, felt constrained to interfere.

---

296 Authorities; Official History of Soudan Campaign; RM War Diaries and Returns; Officers' Services; Britain's Sea Soldiers (Field).

On 8th February 1884 it was decided to defend Suakin. Admiral Hewett, in command of the East Indian Squadron, was informed that 100 Royal Marines on their way home from China were at his disposal, but he demanded 500. In consequence of which a Battalion was formed at Malta from the Royal Marines of the Fleet under Major G H T Colwell RMLI from HMS *Temeraire*, Captain Allen RMA and Lieutenant F White RMLI; HMS *Superb*, Captain Tucker RMA, Lieutenants Prendergast and C Rogers RMLI; HMS *Alexandra* (Flag), Major Colwell RMLI, Lieutenant G Aston RMA and D Kysh RMLI; *Monarch*, Captain Schomberg RMLI, Lieutenant E Brittan RMA, and 463 NCOs and men. They were embarked in HMS *Hecla* and arrived at Port Said on 12th February, where they picked up the *Monarch's* detachment and the whole were transferred to HMS *Orontes*. They arrived at Suakin on 19th February and left for Trinkitat where they arrived the same evening. Here they landed on Sunday 24th and were placed under the Army Discipline Act and attached to the 2nd Infantry Brigade under Major General Davis. On the 27th Colonel Tuson CB ADC RMA, who had arrived from England, assumed command with Captain W H Poe as his Adjutant.

Captain F Baldwin RMLI of *Euryalus* (Flag) had been landed with detachments of *Euryalus* and *Carysfort* and the East Indian Squadron and the men on their way home from China at Suez, so that the force of RM available on 28th February was:

At Trinkitat:
    RMA   5 Officers   116 NCOs and Men
    RMLI   7 Officers   289 NCOs and Men
At Suakin:
    RMA   36 NCOs and Men
    RMLI   3 Officers   177 NCOs and Men

Orders had been sent to the GOC in Egypt to organise a force at Suakin to be reinforced by troops on their way home from India, and General Sir Gerald Graham was appointed to command.

El Teb.

In consequence on 28th February a force of 2850 infantry, 750 mounted troops, 150 Naval Brigade, 100 RA, 80 RE with 6 mountain guns and 8 x 7-pdrs of the RA was concentrated at Trinkitat and marched to Fort Baker about 4 miles off. Trinkitat and Fort Baker were garrisoned by some companies of 3/60th Rifles; each place also had a Krupp gun and two bronze guns which were manned by the RMA.

On the 29th the troops advanced to El Teb (about 5 miles) where the rebels were found entrenched with the captured Krupp guns. Their strength was estimated at 6000. The other British regiments were the 1/Gordons, 2/Royal Irish Fusiliers, 1/York and Lancasters, and the 3/60th. The enemy were on a low range of hills covered with scrub. The Krupps were in a redoubt on the enemy's left; there were three brick houses and an old sugar mill in the centre and in front shelter trenches and rifle pits. On a higher knoll in rear was a village of reed huts and the wells were below the knoll. The cavalry and mounted infantry were skirmishing in front; the square approached the enemy's right and then moved to the right in order to turn the left of the entrenchments which were then stormed. To quote Colonel Tuson's report: "*the Royal Marines formed part of the 2nd Infantry Brigade under Major General Davis. Formed left side of square with 1/York & Lancaster Regiment in passing the enemy's position at Teb to their left flank; became front face in attacking left position and redoubt mounting two Krupp guns and one mountain gun (carried by both regiments at the point of the bayonet)*. He also reported that Lieutenant White was ordered with his Company to charge the left redoubt, which he carried after a hand to hand encounter with the enemy in which he, Sergeant Major Hurst and Privates Birtwhistle and Yerbury displayed the greatest gallantry. The Diary also says: "*Manned the guns in the redoubt by Major Tucker with RMA and turned them on the enemy's right position (very good practice)*." General Graham in his Dispatch dated 6.5.84 says: "*Brevet Major Tucker RMA showed great readiness and intelligence in at once turning the captured Krupp guns, taken in the first position at El Teb, on the enemy's remaining battery, thereby facilitating the advance of the infantry.*" A rapid advance was made on the enemy; he stood firm in the central position and was bayonetted out of the Mill; he then stood again round the wells whence he was driven by two companies and the Gordons worked round his rear, whilst the cavalry charged round the left flank. After three hours' desperate fighting they fled. The British losses were 34 killed and 155 wounded, of which the RM lost 4 men killed, 3 officers and 13 men wounded. Captain and Adjutant Poe though wounded in the leg continued to perform his duty.

General Graham in his Dispatch of 2nd March 1884 says: "*The York & Lancaster Regiment which had some hand to hand encounters with the enemy, and the Royal Marines behaved with great steadiness and gallantry.*"

On 1st March they advanced to Tokar and relieved the Egyptian garrison; bringing back the inhabitants of Tokar on the 3rd they marched to Fort Baker and then to Trinkitat where they embarked in HMS *Humber*, and returned to Suakin on the 4th; here they disembarked and encamped. On the 5th they were joined by the detachments under Captain Baldwin RMLI and he became Adjutant vice Poe to hospital.

Tamai.
As no answer was received to the proclamation calling on the rebels to submit, General Graham decided to march to Tamai, Osman Digna's camp. The force, including Cavalry, was 116 Officers and 5216 Man, including the RM Battalion now formed into six companies, of 14 Officers and 464 NCOs and men. Lieutenant Brittan RMA, and 100 NCOs and men were left to garrison Suakin.

They left Suakin on 11th March and moved to Baker's zeriba about 8 miles from the town. On the 12th they advanced to within about a mile of Osman Digna's position, where they formed another zeriba for the night; from 1 am the enemy opened a sniping fire. On the 13th they advanced in two squares. The 1st Brigade under General Buller composed of KRR, 1/Gordons, 1/Royal Irish Fusiliers, and the Camel Battery in echelon to the right rear of the 2nd Brigade under General Davis, which was also formed in square and was composed of the Black Watch, 1/York &

Lancasters, and the RM Battalion with the Naval Brigade and 9 pdr Mule Battery.

The Official Report says that: "*On arriving at the edge of the ravine in which the enemy were concealed, the 2nd Brigade was attacked by a great mass of Arabs from the front and right flank, which for a moment made it fall back in some disorder and allowed the enemy to capture the machine-guns which however had been locked by the Naval Brigade.*" [297] The retirement also left the battery of four guns unprotected, but the gunners stood by them and fired inverted shrapnel.

The 1st Brigade was also attacked but stood firm and by its steady fire helped the 2nd Brigade to rally whilst the cavalry protected its left. But Lieutenant Colonel Tuson's diary gives a more detailed picture;

"*Formed outside zeriba about 7.30 am and advanced on wells of Tamai, formed the rear face of the square. Y. & L. formed the front and right faces, Black Watch front and left face with RN machine guns in centre between them. Enemy attacked guns and right front face of square in great numbers, forced back Y. & L. on to the Royal Marines, took the machine guns temporarily, spearing the RN officers and men defending them. Highlanders were then attacked and forced back on our left, causing a temporary check in the advance of the square. Major Colwell and Captain and Adjt Baldwin with great exertion getting two of our companies through the temporary retirement of the square* [298] *which were the last to come back, as we reformed into line; Highlanders on left, Y. & L. in centre, Royal Marines on right of the line, with the 1st Brigade square on our right, charged the enemy's position again, the Royal Marines retaking the guns and although charged in numbers along the 2nd Brigade line, succeeded in forcing back the enemy who were completely routed.*"

Colonel Tuson reported also that

"*Major Colwell, Captain Baldwin, and Surgeon Cross I have brought to notice of the GOC for their gallant conduct, Major Colwell being the means of bringing two of our companies through the temporary retirement of the square; Surgeon Cross attending the wounded till shot in the forehead.*"

The 1st Brigade then carried a ridge 800 yards off and Tamai was seen; by 11.40 am Osman Digna's huts and wells were in our possession.

Besides the above officers Private S Patterson was specially brought to notice for bravery in saving the life of a comrade at the risk of his own and was awarded the Conspicuous Gallantry Medal, as were Gunner Bretwell RMA, and Private D Brady RMLI, who gallantly saved the life of Surgeon Prendergast RN, carrying him to the rear; Private John Davis was also brought to notice for gallantry and Corporal Bale RMLI, who although twice wounded returned to his company till ordered by his company commander to the rear.

---

297 It was here that Admiral Sir Arthur Wilson, then a Captain, earned his VC.
298 Major Colwell, who had a very fine voice, is reputed to have called out "Men of Portsmouth Division Rally:"

On the 14th the wells and huts were burnt and the force returned to Suakin on the 15th. The British loss was 5 officers killed, 8 officers wounded, 104 NCOs and men killed and 104 wounded, of whom the Royal Marines had killed 1 gunner RMA, 2 Privates RMLI, and wounded 2 gunners RMA and 12 Privates RMLI.

It is well to remember that this Battalion, which displayed such gallantry and with such disciplined results was drawn from the ships of the Mediterranean, East Indies, and China Fleets; only brought together 14 days before this action. As the CO says, "*The number of officers was totally inadequate to its strength, the NCOs and men, especially those who had served abroad for many years in different stations were not so well up in their drills as I should have wished; but with all that the work they have done has been admirable and I feel proud of having commanded them in the field.*"

On 17th March, Captain Baldwin with 17 RMA and 58 RMLI rejoined their ships *Euryalus* and *Briton*.

Tamanieb.
On 22nd March a reconnaissance was made to Tambuk, but it was decided that want of water etc rendered it inadvisable to advance to Berber. However on the 25th the RM Battalion, forming part of the 2nd Brigade, advanced to the first zeriba on the road to Tamanieb, 78 men falling out exhausted on the march owing to the heat. The next day they escorted a convoy of provisions to the second zeriba, which was formed at the foot of the mountains; on the 27th they advanced at daybreak on Tamanieb in two squares with cavalry and mounted infantry on the flanks and front; the mounted troops had a brush with the enemy and after burning the village the troops returned to Suakin the next day, where 19 RMA and 109 RMLI re-embarked in *Orontes* for home.

In the London Gazette 6th May 1884, Sir Gerald Graham reported that the Royal Marines under Colonel Tuson CB ADC were in the fighting line at El Teb and by their gallantry and steadiness contributed largely to the success of that day's operations. At Tamai they were in the square of the 2nd Brigade and assisted in forming the rallying line.

The following were mentioned in dispatches;

> Colonel Tuson for the admirable manner in which the RMA and RMLI were handled.
> Major Colwell RMLI
> Surgeon Cross RN
> Sergeant-Major J Hirst RMLI
> Private J Birtwhistle RMLI
> Private Yerbury RMLI
> Gunner Rolfe RMA
> Private S Patterson RMLI
> Private J Davis RMLI
> Gunner A. Bretwell RMA

Private D Brady RMLI

Captain Tucker RMA was specially promoted to Major, Major Colwell to Brevet Lieutenant Colonel, and Captain W N Poe to Brevet Major. Lieutenant Colonel Colwell was later awarded the CB.

Suakin.
It was decided to abandon the attempt to relieve Khartoum from Suakin. On 3rd April Sir Gerald Graham left for Suez and the troops were withdrawn, only the Royal Marines and the 3/60th being left to garrison Suakin. The latter were withdrawn in May, being replaced by two Egyptian battalions, and the Royal Marines were left to hold Suakin throughout the rest of the year through all the hot weather. Colonel Tuson's Battalion rejoined their ships and the work was done by a battalion from England under Lieutenant Colonel Ozzard RMLI, whose doings we must now chronicle.

On 7th February 1884 orders were issued for a force of Royal Marines to embark on 9th February at Portsmouth and the 10th at Plymouth in SS *Poonah*, consisting of

RMLI
  1 Major (Rose)
  4 Captains (Montgomery, Bridge, Robbins, Gordon)
  8 Lieutenants (Roche, Horniblow, Darling, Money, Stamper, Holman, Townshend, David)
  181 NCOs and men from Chatham
  54 NCOs and men from Portsmouth
  204 NCOs and men from Plymouth

RMA
  1 Captain (Connolly)
  2 Lieutenants (Orford and Campbell)
  98 NCOs and men

They disembarked at Ramleh, Alexandria, on 3rd March, were joined on 6th by Lieutenant Colonel Ozzard RMLI to command, with Quartermaster J Murphy.

On 5th April, Captain Montgomery with 2 Lieutenants and 100 NCOs and men - reinforced later to 189 - were detached to form the garrison of Port Said, and Captain Poe became Adjutant of the Battalion and Gritton became Paymaster.

The Battalion left Ramleh by rail on 30th April for Suez, where they embarked in HMS *Orontes* on 1st May and arrived at Suakin on 6th May, transferring to HMS *Tyne* when two detachments of about 4 officers and 100 men took over the garrisoning of Forts Eurylaus and Carysfort. The Battalion remained for the time on board the *Tyne* and the detachments on shore were relieved every week.

On 7th May another draft of four companies RMLI - two Majors (Way, Alston), 4 Captains (McKechnie, Hobart, Burrowes, Pearson), 8 Lieutenants (Onslow, Cotter, Brine, E Evans, Lloyd, N White, Curtoys, Logan-Home) with 283 NCOs and men - embarked in SS *Deccan* and were landed at Port Said on 19th May; these joined the Battalion at Suakin on 17th June. The officers and men left at Port Said under Captain Montgomery had joined the Battalion per HMS *Iris* on 10th June.

The rebels continued to make night attacks on the garrison, but contented themselves with firing at long ranges. The RMA manned all the guns and on 26th May Lieutenant Townshend RMLI with 22 NCOs and men were detached to join the mounted infantry, who were composed of Egyptians. Lieutenant Orford and 36 RMA joined the Battalion as also some regimental transport from Egypt, which was put under charge of Lieutenant Onslow.

The Companies in the forts and in the ship were regularly exchanged owing to the heat and trying conditions on shore. In the first week of June the rebels made several night attacks, but nothing serious resulted.

When the drafts arrived, the New Barracks on the north-east side of the island were taken over and eventually became the HQ, whilst the garrisons of the forts were strengthened, Fort Euryalus to 200 men; also the Police Post, Camel Post, Right Water Fort and Left Water Fort. The health of the Battalion began to give cause for anxiety and it was considered that after six weeks or two months service at Suakin the men should be exchanged with men at Port Said; this was not found to be practicable and it was decided that a depot should be formed at Suez to take men from Suakin; therefore on the day that Colonel Way's draft arrived, Major Rose with 218 NCOs and men embarked for Suez, and from now on it was arranged to send companies in rotation to Suez for recuperation. At Suez they were quartered in the Victoria Hospital and in huts. On 28th June they reported that the weather had been somewhat cooler at Suakin, viz; 95-100 degrees in the buildings, and 105-112 degrees in the tents!

A company of RE arrived to commence the construction of piers, jetties, etc for the proposed railway to Berber. The works were also strengthened and the Mounted Infantry increased to 40 men.

On 18th July the Mounted Infantry under Lieutenant Townshend had a skirmish with the enemy and narrowly escaped being ambushed; but were well handled and firing from the saddle galloped round the enemy's flank and returned to Suakin.

On 20th July, Major General Lyon-Fremantle arrived to command at Suakin and relieved the Commodore of all responsibility for defence.

On 28th July owing to a threatening advance of Osman Digna the Battalion, with all the Marines from the Squadron with some seamen, manned the defences; no attack was made, but owing to the men having to man the defences in the midday heat there was a great increase in the number of sunstroke cases and general sickness.

Captain Crooke with 58 NCOs and Men, relieved a similar number under Captain Swinburne, who went to Suez to recuperate.

On 4th August it is reported that the heat in the tents ranged from 110 degrees to 125 degrees. The Headquarters of the Battalion were transferred from HMS *Tyne* to the New Barracks. All through August the diaries are full of the arrangements to exchange the companies with those at Suez, and complaints of the rising sick list; the night attacks also continued.

By 20th September the sick had risen to 142.

On 27th September, Captain A St L Burrowes assumed command of the mounted infantry in place of Lieutenant Townshend, but on 11th October in view of Army arrangements they were broken up.

As separate returns were now being rendered of the RMA, we learn that they were manning the following guns:

Fort Euryalus	2 Krupps, 1 Howitzer, 2 Gardners, 1 Gatling, with 2 Officers and 41 NCOs and men.
Right Water Fort	1 Krupp, 1 Howitzer, 1 Gardner, with 1 Officer and 15 men.
Sphinx Redoubt	1 Krupp, 1 Gatling, with 7 NCOs and men.
Island Redoubt	1 Gardner with 3 NCOs and Men.

There were of course infantry garrisons in these places as well.

Lieutenant Stamper RMLI died at Suez on 17th October, and on the 24th the SS *Bulimba* which had brought out drafts and reliefs was retained for use as a hospital ship; the sick had hitherto been retained on board the *Tyne* until they could be sent to Malta, Suez or Ramleh. The sick list from fever seemed to be increasing.

At home the Government were occupied with the question of the relief of General Gordon at Khartoum, and though the War Office had raised the subject as early as April and were pressing for a decision, Mr Gladstone's Government could not make up their minds, and it was not till August that it was definitely decided that the advance was to be made up the Nile and the wonderful expedition under Lord Wolseley, when the troops rowed themselves up the river in 800 whalers was undertaken. Lord Wolseley arrived in Cairo on 9th September 1884.

As well as the troops moving up in boats it was decided to form four Camel Regiments of detachments; one from the Mounted Infantry, one from the Guards, one from the Heavy Cavalry, and one from the Light Cavalry regiments.

The Guards Camel Regiment was formed of 40 men from each of the Battalions of Guards at home making three companies; the fourth company was provided by the RMLI from Suakin. The officers were Captain and Brevet Major W H Poe, Captain A C Pearson, Lieutenants C V F Townshend, and H S N White, Colour Sergeant Drew (Ply), 4 Sergeants, 6 Corporals, 2 Buglers, 80 Privates, who left Suakin for Egypt on 10th October 1884.

Lieutenant Townshend transferred to the Indian Army and afterwards became famous for his defence of Chitral 1896, and later as commander of the British forces in the early part of the Mesopotamian Campaign at the Battles of Ctesiplean and the siege of Kut-el-Amara. Lieutenant White afterwards became Commandant, Depot RM, 1913-1917. Lieutenant David transferred to the Egyptian Army and was commanding a Brigade in Lord Kitchener's reconquest of the Soudan when he died.

By 15th October a new post at Suakin - called the Sandbag Redoubt, about 2000 yards outside the lines - had been erected to protect the head of the railway, and a post of 25 RMLI under Lieutenant E F David was sent to garrison it; on the 22nd two companies RMLI were sent to the same place from Fort Eurylus, who formed an entrenched camp.

By the end of November the night attacks by the rebels had recommenced.

The sick list had assumed the alarming proportions of 250; on 20th November it was ordered that the Royal Marines at Suez should be formed into a separate Battalion under Major and Brevet Lieutenant Colonel Way to include all the sick in Egypt and those recuperating there; in fact what nowadays would be called a Base Depot. The Battalion at Suakin was reduced to a strength of 500.

On 7th and 8th December there were attacks by the rebels, which were dispersed by artillery fire from the forts and ships; they again attacked the advanced posts on the night of 12th, but without result. The diaries state that sickness was now going down.

The state at the end of the year 1884 was

	RMA	RMLI
At Suakin	3 Offrs. 46 NCOs & men	27 Offrs. 534 NCOs & men
At Suez	2 Offrs. 31 NCOs & men	11 Offrs. 88 NCOs & men
Sick Hospital Suez etc.	20 NCOs & men	2 Offrs. 74 NCOs & men
Camel Corps (Nile)	4 Offrs. 95 NCOs & men	

Camel Corps (Nile).

We must now turn to the detachment of RMLI under Major Poe which was on its way to join the Guards Camel Regiment. As it was such an unusual duty for the Corps it may be of interest to describe how they were equipped. Each man had:

1 Serge Frock (Scarlet)	1 Spine Protector
1 Serge Frock (Grey)	Clasp knife and Lanyard
1 Greatcoat or Cloak	Tin of Grease
1 White Helmet	Housewife
Veil	Canvas Bag
1 Pair Goggles	Waterbottle
Puggaree	Haversack
2 Pairs Ankle Boots	Surgical Bandage
1 Pair Puttees	Pocket Filter
1 Blue Jersey	Grey Flannel Shirts and socks
1 Pair Tartan Trousers	Rifle and Sling
1 Pair Pantaloons (Bedford Cord)	Sword Bayonet
1 Pair Jack Spurs	Bandolier
2 Flannel Belts	Infantry Waistbelt and Pouc

They had a Namaqua Bucket for the Rifle and Sword Bayonet (as used by RMA) instead of the triangular bayonet. They had a Sulleetah which was passed over the saddle tree and covered by a red saddle cover which carried on the near side - shirt, towel and soap, cleaning gear, knife, fork and spoon, holdall, cavalry canteen, and 50 rounds of SAA; on off side - days' rations and 50 rounds SAA. A water skin to hold 6 gallons was attached to the back of the saddle, an Egyptian waterbottle to hold 2 quarts on cantle of saddle. Picketing gear, tente d'abri between two men, whip, knee lashing, headstall and rope, nose ring. Forage - 3 days' grain. The blanket was generally carried in lieu of great coat, also a tripod to keep the water skin off the ground. A camp kettle and fuel was distributed between 8 men.

On 19th October it was decided to concentrate at Debbeh, south of Dongola, in advance of the infantry and mounted force, so that if it became necessary to send urgent help to Gordon they might be able to cross the Bayuda Desert to Metemneh where they could meet Gordon's steamers from Khartoum. The Commandant of the base was therefore ordered to send on the Camel Battery, the 19th Hussars and the RMLI Company by the first opportunity, and on 26th October a general order was issued constituting the four Camel Regiments. They had to march from Wady Halfa to Debbeh, a distance of 337 miles, and by 13th November the Guards Camel Regiment was between Dongola and Dal, with the RM Company at Sarras. On 16th December Lord Wolseley made his Headquarters at Korti, which became GHQ during the campaign. The Guards Camel Regiment with the Mounted Infantry had arrived there on the 15th, where also the Royal Sussex Regiment and the South Staffordshire Regiment had arrived by whalers.

At the end of Decemher Lord Wolseley had decided that the column must he sent across the desert under Brigadier General Stewart. Owing to want of sufficient camel transport it was necessary to establish a depot at the Jakdul Wells, about 98 miles from Korti.

Accordingly on 30th December 1884 a column consisting of the 19th Hussars, the Guards Camel Regiment (19 Officers and 365 Rank and File), and the Mounted Infantry Regiment - in all about 1100 men, with the camels of the Heavy and Light Cavalry Regiments acting as transport

- left Korti, and after halting at Tambuk and El Howeiya Wells arrived at Jakdul at 8 am on 2nd January. Here the Guards Regiment and RE were left to improve the water supply and make fortifications, in which work they were occupied for the next nine days. General Stewart returned to Korti with the remainder and reported. In his Dispatch he said that during his absence the Guards had built two strong forts of stone, "*made roads and footpaths over stony ground and the water supply for men and camel had been improved. Nothing but extreme hard work on the part of officers and men could have effected so complete a metamorphosis in this post.*" And we may be sure our old soldiers, with their varied experience, had a large share in this work.

General Stewart started again on 8th January with half Battery RFA, one Squadron 19th Hussars, the Heavy Camel Regiment, the Mounted Infantry Camel Regiment, HQ and 400 men of the Royal Sussex, one Company the Essex Regiment, Naval Brigade and details; they arrived at Jakdul on the 12th. The Essex were left at El Howeiya and 150 of the Royal Sussex at Jakdul, and the remainder with the Guards Camel Regiment left Jakdul on the 14th - a total of about 1800 combatants.

On 16th January the Hussars gained touch with the enemy, and at 11.30 am the enemy was reported to be in force between the column and the Abu Klea Wells. The column therefore halted about 3½ miles from the Wells and constructed a zeriba for the night. It was decided to attack next day - 17th January leaving the sick and baggage etc. in the zeriba with a guard of the Royal Sussex.

On the 17th the square was formed on foot - front and right faces the Guards Camel Regiment, front and left face the Mounted Infantry Camel Regiment, the RA in front face between them; the rear and left face the Heavy Camel Regiment; the remainder of the right face the Royal Sussex Regiment, the Naval Brigade and machine guns in the centre of the rear face. Camels for SAA and water in the centre. The enemy were reported in force on the left on high ground. When the square advanced with skirmishers out, it came under a heavy fire. The guns were brought into action against the enemy on the right and right rear, and the cavalry checked the enemy trying to work round to the zeriba. The square at first moved down the centre of the valley to the Wells, which was covered with clumps of long grass and bushes, but then it took ground to the right, parallel to the Khor. Here there was a little command, though the ground was more difficult and undulating. The advance was slow and they were obliged to halt constantly. A line of flags on the left front was observed and when shells were fired at them at a range of 1500 yards, large bodies of the enemy sprang up and retreated, and their fire was silenced. When 500 yards from the flags, the right front corner of the square (Guards Camel Regiment) was on a slight rise, and halted to allow the rear face to close up. Five thousand of the enemy from behind the line of flags charged the left front corner of the square; unfortunately the skirmishers, running in, masked the fire of the square; the 7 pdrs were run out from front and left faces, and these with the fire of the front and left faces forced the enemy to swerve to their right, so that the weight of the charge fell on the Heavy Camel Regiment and the Naval Brigade on the left and rear faces, where they were a little disordered by lagging of the camels etc. In spite of their fire they were pressed back by sheer weight of numbers, the Gardner gun jammed and nearly half the Naval Brigade was killed. Many rifles also jammed. There was a desperate conflict in the centre of the square; the Guards and Mounted Infantry on slightly higher ground brought a heavy fire to bear over the heads of the combatants and stopped the rearward Arabs, causing them to fall back. In five minutes "*by sheer pluck and muscle*" the Heavy Camel Regiment had killed the last of the fanatics. The dispatch said: "*Steadiness of the troops enabled the hand to hand conflict to be maintained, whilst severe punishment was still being meted out to the enemy continuing to advance, with the result that a general retreat of enemy under heavy artillery and rifle fire took place.*" At the same time the fire of the Royal Sussex checked a charge of Arab cavalry on the right rear face of the square and the enemy fled.

The square moved to the wells where they bivouacked at 5 pm, but 9 officers and 65 NCOs and Men had been killed, 9 Officers and 85 rank and file wounded. The RM Company lost 2 killed, 2 wounded.

The camels and party in the zeriba were brought in to the wells during the night and next morning. A fort was constructed and garrisoned by the Royal Sussex Regiment; at 3.50 pm on the 18th the Column moved off for Metemneh, aiming to strike the Nile two or three miles above that town. At nightfall two companies of the Guards and two companies of the MI were dismounted to form the advanced guard as they had to pass through the Shebakat Bush. There was no moon, the camels were tired and they had to move through most difficult country; the men were sleepy and tired, and great difficulty was experienced with the civilian camel drivers; the result was a good deal of confusion, but they got through the bush and they halted at dawn, having taken 14 hours to cover 18 miles.

At 7 am on the 19th the Nile was sighted, and the enemy were seen in force, prepared to contest the road. Consequently a laager of camel saddles and biscuit boxes was made and the men were sent to breakfast; a detachment was sent to occupy a knoll that commanded the zeriba. The enemy kept up a hot fire from the long grass and General Stewart was severely wounded, with many others. The command then devolved on Colonel Sir C Wilson. The baggage was placed in the zeriba and at 2.30 pm the square was formed to fight; Colonel Boscawen of the Guards Camel Regiment being placed in executive command. The Guards and Mounted Infantry were in front, Royal Sussex and Heavy Cavalry in rear. There was a gravel ridge between the zeriba and Abu Kru on the river, and the long grass was full of the enemy. No skirmishers were sent out and they felt their way by halting and firing volleys, the guns and Gardners doing good service.

At 600 yards from the ridge the enemy fire ceased and they charged in good numbers, but as there were no skirmishers the full force of the fire could be developed and only one got within 100 yards, whilst a large force on the left front of the square was held in check by the artillery and machine gun fire from the zeriba.

The square continued the march to the Nile, which was reached half an hour after dusk; the casualties were 1 officer and 22 men killed, 8 officers and 90 men wounded, of which the RMLI had 5 killed and 13 wounded; in the reports Plymouth Sergeant Chislett and Bugler W Shire, who were wounded, were specially mentioned. The latter died of his wounds.

On the 20th-the greater part of the force moved back to the village of Gubat, on the gravel ridge, which was placed in a state of defence, and the wounded were brought in and placed under a guard of the Royal Sussex; the Guards occupied the side facing the desert. Gubat was about 700 yards from the river and 3500 yards from Metemneh. On 21st January the British made an attack from the south on Metemneh, a long village with loop-holed walls and two or three guns, but they met with a strong resistance. During the attack Gordon's steamers arrived and their troops were landed to join in the attack. As however they brought reports of heavy enemy reinforcements moving down from Khartoum, the attack was broken off and the force returned to Gubat after destroying the intervening villages. Major Poe and 1 Private RMLI were severely wounded; the former suffering amputation of the leg.

In view of the reported advance of the troops from Khartoum, the camp was moved down to the banks of the Nile, and Gubat was only held as an outpost.

On 22nd, Colonel Wilson and Lord Charles Beresford with two companies of Mounted Infantry went down the river to Shandi in the steamers to ascertain what was between them and the column coming up the river. After shelling Shandi, they returned, and the next day was spent in repairing the machinery of the steamers and changing their crews. At 8 am on 24th January, Colonel Wilson left with the two steamers for Khartoum, which he reached on the 28th, only to find that Khartoum had fallen and Gordon had been killed on the 26th. Having come under heavy fire the steamers had to return, but on the way down both were wrecked; Colonel Wilson and his party were rescued after desperate adventures by Lord Charles Beresford in the *Saf'iyeh*, which after a severe fight, in which the boiler was pierced by a shot and repaired under fire by Chief Engineer Benbow RN, succeeded in reaching them and bringing them back to Gubat on 4th February.

On 23rd January a column was sent to bring up supplies from Jakdul so that the garrison at Abu Kru was reduced to 73 officers and 912 rank and file; on the 27th a party of the Guards and Mounted Infantry Camel Regiments turned the enemy, who were firing on the outposts, out of a village close by. Convoys were now being sent to and fro to Jakdul bringing up supplies and taking back wounded and sick. General Sir Redvers Buller, the Chief of Staff, arrived on 11th February with the Royal Irish Regiment to take command vice General Stewart.

The news of the fall of Khartoum altered all the plans and necessitated communication with the Home Government for fresh instructions. Lord Wolseley felt that he had not sufficient troops and the season was too late for an advance to retake Khartoum; at first the troops, of both the river and desert columns, were ordered to stand fast; the Royal Irish and Royal West Kent Regiments were sent to reinforce the Desert Column; but General Buller had already decided that as the position at Gubat was impossible, he would fall back to Abu Klea. The River Column fought the action of Kirbekan on 10th February, where General Earle was killed, and though the Dervishes were heavily defeated it was not considered advisable to advance further at present.

On 13th February a convoy left Gubat under Colonel Talbot, taking with it General Stewart and all the remainder of the sick and wounded, those unable to walk being carried on stretchers by the Egyptian soldiers.

The escort was provided by the RM Company and one other of the Guards Camel Regiment, a wing of the Heavy Camel Regiment and a company of the Mounted Infantry Regiment. After going about 8 or 9 miles through the bushy district of Shekabat, a large convoy of camels was sighted. The Royal Marines were sent out in skirmishing order to take the convoy. Captain Pearson found the enemy too strong for him and was reinforced by a company of the Guards and some men of the Heavy Cavalry.[299] The MI were in rear and the sick and wounded were placed among the camels, with the Egyptians on the flanks. The enemy came round the convoy on three sides and kept up a well directed fire for 1½ hours, when a body of troops were observed advancing on the left flank and were received with a volley which fortunately did no damage, as they proved to be the Light Cavalry Regiment. At 1.15 pm the enemy withdrew and the convoy proceeded to Abu Klea with a loss of two killed and six wounded, where they arrived on the 14th. Marching again on the 16th, General Stewart died of his wounds and was buried at Jakdul.

General Buller evacuated Gubat on the 14th. On 20th February, General Sir Evelyn Wood, now in command at Jakdul, reported that the Heavy Cavalry and Guards would require all new camels, and as on this day Lord Wolseley had decided that no further advance was possible, orders were issued to both columns to return to Korti.

On 23rd February Abu Klea was evacuated. On 21st the Guards had left Jakdul for Abu Halfa, where they remained strengthening the post till they marched to Korti, arriving on 4th March; the rest of the Colunn did not get in till the 14th.

With a view to an autumn campaign, the Guards were to have spent the summer at Dongola, but on 12th April the Government decided that the expedition must be abandoned (no doubt owing to the threatening state of affairs on the Afghan frontier) and on 11th May the withdrawal of the troops from the Soudan was ordered. The Guards Regiment left Assouan on 21st June and had left Egypt by the beginning of July; they arrived at Cowes on 15th July, where the RM Company with the remainder of the Guards regiment were disembarked and inspected by HM Queen Victoria.

On arrival at Portsmouth they were invited to an entertainment in London by the Brigade of Guards, which took place at Chelsea on 20th July, and from here they rejoined their Divisions.

Major Poe was awarded the CB; Captain Pearson was promoted to Brevet Major: Colour Sergeant Drew, the Company Sergeant, who had acted for some time as Sergeant Major of the Regiment, was noted for advancement, as were Sergeants Chislett and Walton (the QMS). Privates Mees, Slade, McEntee, and Golding, with Bugler Brown were specially promoted to Corporals.

---

299 Official Report.

Suakin.

Returning to affairs at Suakin. On 8th February in anticipation of the summer occupation of the Soudan and the renewal of the campaign in the autumn, Lord Wolseley had requested that Osman Digna should be dealt with at once and the Government decided that the railway from Suakin to Berber should be constructed. On 20th February, Sir Gerald Graham was appointed to command the Suakin Field Force, and orders were issued by the RM Office that the Royal Marines at Suakin were to be organised into an RMA Gardner Gun Battery and a Battalion RMLI of 8 Companies with a detachment of Mounted Infantry.

The force at Suakin which had been increased by the addition of a battery of RHA, a Company of RE, the 2/East Surrey and 1/Berkshire Regiments etc, was further increased by the 5th Lancers, 20th Hussars, a four Company Battalion of Mounted Infantry, the Guards Brigade of three Battalions and two Batteries of RFA. The 2nd Brigade was formed of the RMLI, the above two regiments, and the King's Shropshire Light Infantry, who had relieved the 2nd RM Battalion at Suez. A Brigade of Native Infantry and a Regiment of Cavalry came from India; also a Battery of Artillery and an Infantry Battalion from New South Wales; with the latter was Lieutenant Colonel S Spalding, late RMLI.

On 12th March, General Graham arrived and assumed command, with General Greaves as Chief of Staff. General Sir John McNeill VC was in command of the 2nd Brigade.

On 13th the contractors commenced laying the railway. General Graham had been instructed that his first objective was the destruction of Osman Digna's power, and then to push on and secure the road for the construction of the railway and to pacify the tribes. The water supply was however one of the main difficulties.

Before dealing with the operation, we must go back a little and record the doings of the RM Battalion since the beginning of the year. The 1st Battalion, in garrison at Suakin, was subjected to the nightly sniping and attacks by the rebels, but the sickness decreased and the health of the Battalion improved; the Musketry Instructor from Malta (Captain Byron Woods) with his staff was sent to them and they commenced a musketry course.

On one day - 17th January - the rebels appeared in force, but were driven off by the guns of HMS *Dolphin*, *Sandbag*, Right and Left Water Forts, but soon all was in preparation for the expedition to Berber.

On 19th February, a detachment of 50 RMA under Captain Swinburne arrived from Suez.

Mounted Infantry.

On 6th February Captain A St L Burrowes RMLI with 2 Sergeants, Corporals, 1 Bugler, and 21 Privates were detailed for Mounted Infantry and joined E Company of 2nd Battalion Mounted Infantry; Captain F D Bridge became Adjutant of the Battalion, as Lieutenant Congdon who had been appointed was sick. By 28th February the RMLI Battalion was organised into eight Companies under Lieutenant Colonel Ozzard, and on the 2nd Battalion joining on 11th march, Major Way became 2nd-in-Command and the 162 officers and men were incorporated in the 1st Battalion. Soon after the remainder of the 2nd Battalion under Captain Edye also joined from Suez. The officers now were Majors Way and Alston, Captains Allen, McKechnie, Woods, Pine-Coffin, C G Gordon, Pyne, Hawkins, Kirching; Lieutenants Horniblow, Darling, Cotter, Brine, Holman, David, Marchant, Maclurcan, Evans, Curtoys, Trotman, Lalor, Harries, Hubbard, Onslow (Transport Officer), Kysh (Signal Officer); Captain Edye (Signals); Captain Hungerford (Paymaster).

Gardner Battery.
By 16th March Major Crooke had organised the RMA Battery of four 5-barrelled Gardner guns on the lines of a Field Battery drawn by mules, which were led by men on foot, with Captain Swinburne and Lieutenants Orford and Slessor. They were encamped with the RE; Lieutenant Bonnon RA was attached and they came under the orders of the CRA of the force. The RMLI was encamped with the 2nd Brigade to which it was attached on 9th March.

The enemy was very bold and active, penetrating the camps, stabbing sentries, sniping etc, and the force had a taste of what had been the lot of the Marines for so many months.

Before starting the construction of the railway it was necessary to destroy Osman Digna's forces, and the first point of attack was Hasheen where there was an enemy gathering.

Hasheen.
From the seacoast a sandy plain rises quickly in a westerly direction for a distance of 10 or 12 miles to a height of about 200 or 300 feet above sea level till it meets the foot of a volcanic range of mountains. In the immediate vicinity of Suakin, one or two miles of the country to the north and west is fairly open; beyond the radius and to the south-west (ie towards Tamai) there is thick scrub of prickly mimosa six to eight feet high, and belts of lower bushes lining the numerous khors or watercourses which run generally in a north and north-east direction. The railway was roughly to follow the caravan route to Berber in a north-west direction from Suakin.

The enemy were on a line Tamai-Hasheen-Handoub. It would be necessary to make two advances, first to Tamai to crush Osman Digna, and secondly to clear the railway route.

Hasheen threatened the right of the advance on Tamai, besides being the place from which the nightly raids on Suakin were organised.

On the 19th the mounted troops made a reconnaissance, supported by infantry. Hasheen lay 7 miles due west. At this point a group of rocky hills rises up; the highest was called Zeriba Hill; here is the beginning of the thicker undergrowth spreading west to the base of the Waratab range. Dihilbat or Hasheen Hill is an isolated ridge, 1½ miles further on, running East and West,

421

culminating in the centre with steep and rugged sides destitute of vegetation and almost precipitous, with bushy thorny thickets, six to eight feet high, at the base; it is separated from Zeriba Hill and Beehive Hill by a ravine with gullies and slopes.

On 20th March a force composed of the Guards Brigade, 2nd Brigade less the Shropshire Light Infantry, the Indian Brigade, Cavalry Brigade and G/RHA with the RMA Gardner Battery, Ammunition Column etc., left Suakin at 6.20 am. The 2nd Brigade in line of company columns in fours, the Guards and Indian Brigades in column of companies, with the cavalry on the flanks.

Zeriba Hill was occupied at once and the East Surrey Regiment was left to build redoubts and strengthen it. The enemy fell back on Dihilbat and Beehive Hills, between which were the huts of the village. The Berkshire Regiment and RMLI were ordered to occupy Dihilbat Hill, supported by the Indian Brigade and RHA. The Guards Brigade, with which was the RMA Gardner Battery, was in reserve.

The Berkshire Regiment advanced up the hill in attack formation; four companies RMLI under Colonel Way in support. The other four companies under Major Alston with Colonel Ozzard were on their right rear to turn the enemy's flank. Reaching the crest of the first spur, heavy fire was opened by the enemy, but volleys drove them off the summit, which was occupied by Berkshires and RM. Colonel Ozzard's half battalion "pushed up the gorge on the right; the gorge was covered with thick scrub and in it were a quantity of native huts and wells; turning movement was successful as enemy fell back."[300] The RMLI crowned the heights on the right of the Berkshires and the Mounted Infantry moved through the village and passed the wells and engaged a large force beyond. The Guards and Indian Brigades with the RHA and RMA Gardners moved forward and occupied the gorge between Dihilbat and Beehive Hills; the Cavalry charged the enemy with great effect.

The huts, wells, etc. having been destroyed, the force fell back to Zeriba Hill, formed in two squares. The Gardner Battery with the Guards Brigade came into action outside the square (mules inside) to cover the retirement, sweeping the bush with volley firing. The retirement was also covered by the MI; Captain Burrowes reported that he dismounted his men and held the enemy off by cool and accurate fire and then retired into the square.

When the force was reassembled South of Zeriba Hill, the East Surrey Regiment and the RMA Gardner guns were left to hold the fort and zeriba and the remainder returned to Suakin. The mules of the RMA Battery accompanied them. During the action some of the RMA had manned two Krupp guns (9 cm). The RM only had one wounded. The arabs had lost heavily and the destruction of the village stopped the harrassing night attacks on Suakin.

---

[300] Colonel Ozzard's Report.

Tofrek.

The next objective was to crush Osman Digna at Tamai; but it was first necessary to establish an intermediate post for supplies, water etc, so a force under General Sir John McNeill, commanding the 2nd Brigade, composed of one Squadron 5th Lancers, the Berkshires, a Field Company RE, the Naval Brigade with Gardner guns, the Indian Brigade etc [301] was detailed. They moved off in two squares on 22nd March, marching south-west towards Tamai, the British square in advance. Their orders were to advance 8 miles and then form three zeribas, two to hold a battalion each and one to hold 2000 camels. The march was very difficult owing to the scrub in the watercourses crossing the route, and the camels were overloaded and badly packed. The enemy were reported retiring, but on reaching a place with a horse-shoe clearing - known later as Tofrek - only 6 miles out, the General decided to halt and form the zeribas, otherwise the Indian Brigade could not get back that night. The British Brigade formed up on the east, clear of the ground intended for the zeriba.

The RMLI formed their zeriba at the north-east corner on the side nearest Suakin, half the Berkshires at the south-west corner, the large zeriba for the camels between them. The 28th Bombay NI and two companies of the 17th Bengal NI were placed in line to cover the north front during the building, the 15th Sikhs, similarly formed, faced west, and six companies of the 17th Bengal NI faced south. The other half Battalion Berkshire Regiment were in square on the east guarding the camels etc as they were unloaded. Two Naval Gardner guns each were with the Berkshires and RM zeribas. The zeriba building went on rapidly and men were out on all sides building and getting in material. By 1.30 pm the RMLI zeriba was nearly complete and guns mounted, as was also the Berkshire zeriba. Of the main zeriba, only about half was completed; the other half-Battalion of the Berkshires were having their dinners, the camels were unloading and filing out of the central place, when at 2.30 pm the cavalry reported the enemy to be advancing and the working parties were recalled; the cavalry however suddenly came gallopping in, and in their retirement rather unsteadied the 17th NI. The weight of the attack came from the west and south, and fell on the Berkshires, the 15th Sikhs, and the 17th Bengal NI. The enemy came swarming over the zeriba; the Berkshire Regiment put up a magnificent defence, as did the Sikhs on their right, but the 17th Bengalis after firing one volley broke, some into the Berlshires square but the rest to Suakin. The enemy came swarming round, charging the fence in every direction and came in masses into the large zeriba, stampeding the camels and transport animals who streamed back to Suakin; the half-Battalion of the Berkshires to the east formed rallying squares and repelled two successive attacks and held their ground; they then marched to their own zeriba. The RMLI held their own zeriba with volleys and then with the Berkshires cleared the Arabs out of the central zeriba where they were killing followers and the animals. The attack took place at 2.50 and fire ceased at 3.10 pm

In that short time 1500 Arabs were killed and more than that number wounded. Colonel Ozzard reported that "*the conduct of the officers and men merited the highest praise; the enemy penetrating into the zeriba were instantly killed.*"

---

301 The RMA mules under Lieutenant Slessor were lent to the Naval Brigade.

Parties of the RMLI and the Sikhs were then sent out to examine the field and by 4 pm all was quiet. The RM had 9 killed and 17 wounded, but the total losses were 100 killed, 148 missing (mostly followers), and 174 wounded. The RMA lost 13 out of their 27 mules.

Two cavalry squadrons on the road to Suakin were able to charge the enemy and by dismounted fire to stop the pursuit and save many followers and transport animals.

This affair was known as McNeill's Zeriba, but the medal clasp is inscribed 'Tofrek'.

On 23rd March, General Graham with the Guards Brigade and a convoy of camels arrived at the zeriba, which was completed and strengthened. The Indian Brigade with wounded and sick and two battalions of Guards then returned to Suakin.

On 24th March another convoy with 8000 gallons of water, escorted by the Indian Brigade, left Suakin and three miles from Tofrek was met by the RMLI and Coldstream Guards, who had advanced in square to meet them. *"Large numbers of the enemy were discovered on our right flank and we occasionally halted and returned their fire. Lieutenant Marchant and one Private were wounded....... On returning with the convoy to Tofrek both battalions were formed in one square, the RMLI forming rear and half right and left faces, the enemy attacked persistently but failed to penetrate though making several attempts."* [302] Lieutenant Maclurcan, and 5 Privates were wounded.

On 25th March the East Surrey Regiment and the RMA Gardner Battery were withdrawn from Hasheen and the zeribas there dismantled. On the way back the enemy annoyed them with long range fire so Captain Swinburne brought one of the Krupp guns into action and dispersed them after a few rounds at long range.

Tamai.
Convoys were sent out daily to the zeriba to accumulate supplies of water, stores etc, prior to the advance to Tamai. On 27th March, Colonel Ozzard was taken ill and later invalided, but died shortly afterwards. Major and Brevet Lieutenant Colonel N F Way assumed command of the Battalion and on the 28th the RMLI Battalion was brought back to Suakin for a rest.

On 1st April the Mounted Infantry and Cavalry reported that Tamai was still held, and at 4.30 am on the 2nd, the three Brigades and Artillery left Suakin formed in one long oblong Square 70 yards front and 750 yards deep, with the convoy inside. On reaching Tofrek, the 28th Bombay NI and two of the RMA Gardners were left as garrison (the mules being used for the Naval Brigade) and the Grenadiers and Berkshire Regiment joined the column. At 4.30 pm they reached Teselah Hill and formed a zeriba 300 yards in rear where they bivouacked.

At 8.30 am on 3rd they advanced in two squares, the 2nd Brigade leading with the Berkshires

---

302 Colonel Ozzard's Report.

in line, the RMLI on the right the 15th Sikhs on the left each in column of companies, the rear being open and the guns being in rear of the Berkshires. The Guards Brigade in line of columns with the NSW Infantry in rear. The East Surreys, Shropshire LI and the two RMA Gardners were left to guard the zeriba and transport at Teselah. The Cavalry and Mounted Infantry were out in front and flanks.

The ground between Teselah and the khor where Tamai was situated, was broken by three low ridges between which lay the village. This was occupied without serious opposition and by 9.30 am the squares had reached the edge of the khor. The 2nd Brigade crossed to the far side, supported by artillery fire; the Berkshires occupied the high point in the centre and the 15th Sikhs crossed the detached hills on the left and in front. The RMLI Battalion came under long range fire from the enemy who shot well; *"after surrounding the hills at Tamai the square was halted, and my face being annoyed by enemy fire I sent out Captain Woods and some marksmen and they soon drove the enemy away. This duty was well performed."* [303]

G/RHA and the mountain guns came into action on the far side of the khor; the Guards and NSW Infantry crowned the ridges on the north side of the khor and the arabs withdrew to the mountains to the south-west. Wells were found closed and only a thin brackish stream in the khor. It was useless to pursue and as Osman Digna's power was broken, the village was burnt and a quantity of ammunition was destroyed; they marched back at 10.30 am and reached Teselah at noon. Lieutenant Lalor and one Private were wounded. After dinner they marched back to Tofrek, the Cavalry and Artillery to Suakin; and on the 4th April the force returned to Suakin. During the next few days stores etc were withdrawn from Tofrek and attention turned to clearing the line of the railway.

The tribes were becoming willing to submit, but unfortunately in view of the absence of any settled Government policy the General was unable to guarantee them protection, so that it was necessary to guard the route of the railway. On 6th April a small force of the Guards established No 1 Post half way between Suakin and Handoub, where they formed a zeriba, and on the 8th occupied Handoub. On 9th April the RMA Battery received four of the new 2 Barrelled Gardner guns (out of six) in lieu of the 5-barrelled guns.

On the 11th the RMLI Battalion proceeded to a zeriba four miles out towards Handoub with the Berkshire Regiment and on the 16th proceeded to Handoub, on which day the advanced troops occupied Otao 4½ miles beyond Handoub without opposition; and on the 19th advanced troops occupied Tambuk, 5 miles beyond Otao. The railway had reached within one mile of Handoub.

Camel Corps.
On 18th April, 500 riding camels having arrived from India, the Camel Corps of five Companies was formed; the RMLI contributing Captain G T Onslow, 1 Sergeant, 1 Corporal and 30 Privates,

---
303 Colonel Wray's Report.

who formed No 2 Company, with detachments from 2/East Surrey and RE. Each camel was ridden by two men, as three camels were ridden by 5 soldiers and one native driver. Lieutenant Cotter became Transport Officer of the Battalion, vice Onslow. The Camel Corps consisted of 400 British soldiers and 100 native Indian drivers.

The railway was pushed on and by 30th April was completed to Otao. On 24th April the RMLI Battalion with the Berkshire Regiment marched four miles towards Otao, and there formed a zeriba and the diary records that the health of the Battalion was very good.

But the Government, as before stated, had now made up its mind to discontinue the railway and to evacuate the Soudan as quickly as possible. On 28th April at 5.30 am the RMLI Battalion left their zeriba and marched into Handoub, where they entrained for Suakin and embarked that afternoon in SS *Australia*. The baggage and gear was carried in on camels (16 miles) and also arrived during the afternoon.

That day a telegram was received from England directing that Captain C G Gordon, Lieutenants Horniblow and Holman, 1 Colour Sergeant, 4 Corporals, 2 Drummers and 65 Privates were to embark in SS *Arab* for passage to China, which was done; this detachment formed the garrison for Fort Hamilton. [304]

The *Australia* left Suakin at 6 am on 29th April with the RMA and RMLI and arrived at Alexandria on 5th May.

Captain Onslow and the Camel Corps, and Captain Burrowes with the Mounted Infantry were left at Suakin

The Battalion state on 5th May was RMLI:
In SS *Australia*	32 Officers	1 WO	528 NCOs and Men
At Suakin	4 Officers		85 NCOs and Men
At Suez	1 Officer		3 NCOs and Men
Total	37 Officers	1 WO	816 NCOs and Men

There was of course also the Camel Corps still up the Nile, and the RMA numbers.

On arrival at Portsmouth on 16th May the Battalion was inspected by the DAGRM before dispersal to their Headquarters.

General Graham sent the following message to the Commander-in-Chief Mediterranean, who forwarded it to the Admiralty and it was promulgated in Divisional Orders at all Divisions.

---
304 See Page 428.

"As the RMLI are under orders to embark, the Lieutenant General Commanding takes this opportunity of recording his high appreciation of the services rendered by them since he has assumed command and he wishes to thank them for the spirit with which they have carried out their duties under him after their long exposure to this trying climate."

T'Hakool

The Mounted Infantry and Camel Corps had still to undertake some operations. A Mohammed Adam Sarden had assembled a force at T'Hakool, 18 miles west of Suakin and 10 from Otao; it was the only organised Arab force remaining, so a combined attack was made from Suakin and Otao. The Camel Corps with two companies of MI and the Bengal Cavalry left Suakin at midnight on 6th May and at daylight reached the head of the T'Hakool Valley; the Bengal Cavalry closed the south-west entrance of the valley and the main body the south entrance. The Otao column of 1 Company MI and the 15th Sikhs reached the north end of the valley, drawing the enemy to attack them; the enemy were driven back in confusion by the fire of the MI and were pursued by the friendly native tribes to the south-west. Two companies of the Suakin MI crowned the lower heights to the westward, gained the higher ridges and drove them from spur to spur; the enemy fled and large flocks of sheep and goats were captured and the village destroyed. On the way home they met parties of the enemy, coming up to take part in the fight, who were driven off.

This finally broke all resistance and the tribes were ready to submit, but evacuation had been finally ordered and on 17th May General Graham and the Guards Brigade left Suakin, quickly followed by the other troops.

On the breaking up of the Mounted Infantry the Commanding Officer published the following Order: *"I am anxious to record my sense of the very excellent service rendered by Captain Burrowes and every NCO and man of his detachment. Crime has been absolutely unknown. Men rode well; cheerful and willing as they have always been, no officer could have desired to command a finer body of men whether in camp or the field."*

In Lord Wolseley's final Despatch, 15 June 1885, the following were mentioned:

Brevet Major J H Sandwith	RMLI	(Army Staff)
Brevet Major W H Poe	RMLI	(Nile Camel Corps)
Captain A C Pearson	RMLI	(Nile Camel Corps)
Lieutenant D Kysh	RMLI	(Battalion & Staff)
Sergeant Major Scudamore	RMLI	(Bn Signal Officer Suakin)

London Gazette, 25th August, 1885.

Lieutenant Colonel Way and Major Poe were awarded the CB, and Captain Pearson a Brevet Majority. Lieutenant Kysh was specially promoted to Captain dated 15th June 1885. Later Captain Crooke RMA was awarded a Brevet Majority and Sergeant Major Scudamore a DCM.

The following extracts from General Graham's final despatch are of interest.

"19. Looking upon all these operations as trying the qualities of the troops, it cannot be denied that they were severe tests and that no troops could have stood them better. The harassing night alarms with enemies, having all the stealthy cunning and ferocity of wild beasts, prowling about in their midst, only served to increase the vigilance of the men in outpost duties, and while teaching them caution made them more eager to meet their enemy in open fight. The long march and toilsome convoy duties under a tropical sun; the repulse of the enemy's sudden charges in the bush; the toilsome ten nights' watch in the zeriba amid the carnage of a battlefield, are achievements of which any troops may be proud.

"20. By their effort the power of Osman Digna was so broken that for all practical purposes the country was completely cleared; the railway was being pushed on as fast as the plant could be landed; the tribes were submitting to us............I am convinced the enterprise could have been successfully carried out."

With reference to the harassing night attacks etc., it is well for us Marines to remember that General Graham is speaking of the three months when the Expeditionary Force was engaged; but further that the Royal Marines had been exposed to these harassing tactics in addition to the great sickness for over 12 months.

Port Hamilton 1885-1887

In the early part of 1885 a dispute known as the Penjdeh incident took place with Russia over a violation of the Afghan frontier near Herat, and war appeared imminent.

In these circumstances it was desirable to have an advanced base for the Fleet nearer to Vladivostock than Hong-Kong; for this purpose the China Squadron occupied Port Hamilton on 14th April. This place comprised a group of islands - Sodo, Sunhode, and Observatory Islands - enclosing an anchorage in the Nan-How group off the South Coast of Corea [sic] about 120 miles to the westward of Nagasaki. The Fleet protected the anchorage with booms and mines, and a telegraph cable was laid to Shanghai. Corea, China, and Russia protested, but the British Government ignored their protests; however unless it had been heavily fortified it would not have been much use to the Fleet. As related, the draft under Captain Gordon was taken from the RMLI Battalion as it was leaving Suakin[305] and proceeded to Suez. Here they met a detachment from England of Lieutenant Trotter and 25 NCOs and men RMA, and Lieutenant Macdonnel RMLI in relief of Lieutenant Horniblow invalided. They proceeded on 18th May to China.

On arrival at Hong-Kong on 1st July the war scare was over, but a considerable part of the China Squadron was still at Port Hamilton. Tents and stores were drawn and the men re-equipped

---

305 See Page 426.

as the majority had been on active service at Suakin since February 1884, and had little more than the clothes they stood up in. They reached Port Hamilton about 23rd July, and were quartered on Observatory Island; at first in tents which were blown down once or twice by typhoons, and later in huts. Here a telegraph station and camp was established and they settled down in garrison. They asked for the same pay and allowances as the Japanese Battalion 1870-75, ie double pay and Field Allowance, but this was not granted; they however received Field Allowance and 1/6d a day ration money. They established a canteen and Lieutenant Trotter started a poultry farm and imported sheep and goats for milk; and as usual with Marines in such circumstances, they made themselves very comfortable. Captain Gordon went home in 1886 and Lieutenant Trotter, having been promoted, relieved him in command. They were withdrawn in January 1887, and arrived home in April 1887.[306]

Burmah 1885-87

The Third Burmese War was caused by King Theebaw, as a culmination of pinpricks, trying to extort an impossible fine from the Burmah and Bombay Corporation, which led to an ultimatum on 22nd October 1883. On 9th November the Burmese refused the terms and an expedition was dispatched with a view to the occupation of Mandalay and the dethronement of Theebaw.

It was decided to advance by the River Irrawaddy to the capital and a Naval Brigade was landed from HMS *Bacchante, Turquoise, Woodlark, Osprey, Ranger, Mariner,* and *Sphinx*. The total force was 9,000 troops, 67 guns and 24 machine guns. The Naval Brigade under Captain Woodward of *Turquoise* included the Royal Marines under Major Lambert RMA. They manned the light draught steamers armed with machine guns, whilst heavy guns from the *Turquoise* were mounted in barges which were secured alongside the steamers and protected by iron plates etc. The troops were embarked in the steamers.

The force assembled at Thayetmyo on 14th November, the Burmese being taken by surprise at the rapidity of the advance. The armed steamers *Irrawaddy* and *Kathleen* engaged the Burmese batteries and brought out the Burmese armed steamer from under their guns and also the barges which had been prepared for sinking to block the passage of the river. The Burmese were in force with a strongly fortified redoubt commanding the river.

On 17th November at Minhala on the right bank of the river, the enemy held a barricade strongly fortified, and a pagoda. A brigade of Native Infantry was landed, which, covered by the ships' bombardment, advanced and defeated the enemy and captured the place with a loss of 4 killed and 27 wounded. The advance was continued on the following days, the Naval Brigade and the heavy artillery leading, and silencing in succession the enemy's river defences at Nyangu, Patukhu, Myingan (24th November). On 26th November the flotilla approached Ava, the ancient capital,

---

306   See Random Records, pp 55-57 for fuller details.

which had been strongly fortified. There the Burmese envoys came out to meet the General, and on the 27th they acceded to his demands when the ships were off Mandalay ready to commence firing, and King Theebaw surrendered.

Three strong forts full of men were occupied, many Burmese laid down their arms, but considerable numbers escaped into the jungle to give trouble as Dacoits for the next two years.

By 28th Mandalay had fallen and the king was a prisoner; 186 pieces of artillery had been taken. On 28th December, Bhamo was occupied, but the real work of the campaign etc only just beginning, as owing to the chaos in the country and the activity of the Dacoits, it was not until 1887 that the country was finally subdued and during this period Naval Brigades were patrolling the rivers. Large numbers of troops were employed and eventually Lord Roberts assumed command and finally settled the operations.

Major Lambert was awarded the DSO.

22 - Jubilee, South Africa and China 1887 - 1898

1887 - 1888

The numbers voted for this year were 12,709.

Jubilee.
In this year were celebrated the ceremonies in connection with the Jubilee of HM Queen Victoria on completion of fifty years of her reign. A Brigade of Royal Marines took part in the Review at Aldershot, and during the procession for the Thanksgiving Service at St Pauls, a Battalion of RMA lined the streets and a Battalion of RMLI lined Cockspur Street. A Review of the Fleet was also held at Spithead.

From this event a new spirit arose, and the feelings that bound the Dominions and Colonies to the Empire were freshly aroused by the thronging of all the sons of the Empire to render homage to the Great White Queen.

Among other matters a new impulse was given to the Royal Navy, which at that time was still in transition from sail to steam; all the cruisers and many of the battleships still having masts and yards, whilst the squadrons consisted of a heterogeneous mass of samples of Naval architecture, mostly useless for either fighting or keeping the seas. The personnel, including the Royal Marines, were few in number, and training was at a low ebb, the greater part of the energies of officers being devoted to 'spit and polish'.

The ranks of Probationary Second Lieutenant and Second-Lieutenant were reintroduced, but officers were promoted to Lieutenant on qualifying for their commissions, though they did not draw the increased pay till they had completed 3 years' service.

Training.
In 1888 there were a few efforts to improve the Royal Marine training; the importance of signalling was being recognised and a paid NCO instructor was allowed to each Division by Order-in-Council 3rd May 1888. It was also laid down by Order-in-Council 17th March 1888 that vacancies for General or Lieutenant General in RMA or RMLI should be filled by the promotion of a Lieutenant General or Major General of RMA or RMLI, unless there was good cause otherwise; and when a vacancy occurred for Major General any qualified Colonel might be recommended by the DAG for promotion; in absence of such recommendation promotion was to be given to the senior Colonel on the serving strength of that branch, so that even as late as this the separation of the RMA and RMLI was not complete.

On 3rd May prizes and rewards were offered for the study of foreign languages, and many officers became Interpreters.

Quartermasters.
On 17th December the honorary rank of Major for Quartermasters when holding positions of trust and responsibility was instituted; for many years these were only considered to be the Quartermasters at the RM Office.

1889

In 1889 the numbers voted were 12,700.

Naval Defence Act.
In consequence of the growing uneasiness of the country at the state of the Navy, and the general dissatisfaction with its condition, the Naval Defence Act was passed by which a homogeneous squadron of eight battleships of the *Royal Sovereign* class was built and also classes of cruisers of greater speed, armament, and protection; destroyers also came into being; great increases were made to the Naval personnel, whilst the dockyards were also enlarged.

Arrangements were made for improving the mobilisation plans, and large working parties of the Marines, as many as 100 rank and file under a Captain and Subaltern, proceeded to the dockyards daily to arrange the stores etc. for the Reserve Ships; for this a very welcome addition to the meagre pay of those days was given in the shape of extra pay.

Steam Reserve.
This was followed by the embarkation of a small proportion of a detachment (about one-fifth) in the ships of the Steam Reserve, who lived in the depot ships - *Pembroke* at Chatham, *Duke of Wellington* or *Asia* at Portsmouth, and the *Indus* at Plymouth. Several hundreds of men were employed in this way, doing purely working party and dockyard work, which had most disastrous results on the training and even the discipline of the Corps, as the Major and two Subalterns borne in the depot ship could not exercise adequate supervision, and the men though nominally drilling once a week rarely did so more than once a month. This system was followed in 1904 by the nucleus crews, in which a proportion of the detachments with their officers were embarked, and the ships were treated as practically fully commissioned. This had good results as to discipline, but It rendered the training of specialists very difficult, and resulted in large numbers of men practically never revising their drills at Headquarters.

Officers.
In October 1889 a great departure in the entry and training of Officers was made. The RMA had for many years attended the RN College, Greenwich, for two years prior to joining their Division. The RMLI Probationary 2nd Lieutenants, who had hitherto joined their Division direct and later undergone a six months' course under the Military Instructor at Forton or Eastney, were now also sent to Greenwich for a year's training (actually nine months) in Military Subjects, Riding, and Gymnastics with the RMA before joining their Divisions to complete their training.

Field Training.
The first attempts were also made to send detachments at Headquarters through what is now known as Tactical Training. It was then known as Military Training and was based on a book of Questions and Answers. Both officers and men were much at a loss and doubtless much time was wasted, and it is difficult now - watching a detachment at training - to realise what elementary difficulties, even in such matters as pitching a tent, building a fire, or digging a trench, were then experienced, when Officers and NCOs knew very little, if anything, more than the recruits they were instructing.

In the gun-batteries the drill was mostly concentrated on the muzzle loading guns; only a few breech loaders were available and these varying very much in type, whilst the variety of machine-guns rendered it very difficult to give a general training.

1890

1890 - The numbers were 13,882.

Depot Band.
There were no outstanding events in this year, but by Order-in-Council 21st March 1890, the band at the Depot Royal Marines was established with a Sergeant as Bandmaster and 17 Musicians, in lieu of 17 Privates RMLI; no doubt some Buglers were attached. They were given an annual grant of £100; as the Order-in-Council said, it would *"tend to discipline and good health among recruits passed through Depot"*.

Slave Trade.
For many years past the Navy had been endeavouring to put down the slave trade, and for this purpose the cruisers on the East Indian and African stations were not only occupied in chasing slave vessels, but their boats were frequently away cruising and looking for dhows etc., in which officers and men of the Corps took their part. It was now beginning to be realised that the matter would have to be dealt with by attacking the centres of the trade on the mainland. For this purpose, a Naval Brigade landed from the East Indies Squadron under Admiral Sir Edmund R Freemantle to attack the Sultan of Witu.

Witu.
This potentate had massacred some German Colonists and refused to give up the assassins; as it was in the British sphere of influence, a force was landed, consisting of a field battery of four 7 pdrs ML, and 4 Gardner guns, 2 Battalions of Seamen (450), RM Battalion (200) under Major E Poole RMLI, and Lieutenants J R Lalor and J E Hoskyns-Abrahall RMLI, and an Indian Contingent of 150 Askaris from Mombasa. A landing was effected under fire at Lamu, covered by the armed boats, on 24th October, and the natives driven off and villages burnt. HMS *Conquest* had landed men and occupied Kipini, and the fleet assembled there on 25th October where the landing party was disembarked. A zeriba was made about 3 miles inland by the advanced guard where the night was spent; during the night the natives made a most determined attack on the

advanced party but were driven off by fire. The main body spent the night on the beach.

Marching at 8 am the next day, on reaching the zeriba the force was formed in square with flanking parties; one company of RMLI forming the rearguard who had also to keep up the carriers. They encountered occasional sniping and reached the Kall wells at 5 pm, which proved to be only a swampy marsh. Three zeribas were built in echelon, one being built by the RM. Sniping drove in the Indian skirmishers, so the RM were ordered out to engage the enemy and advanced up the hill, two companies of seamen coming up on their left; the enemy were thus repulsed with heavy loss. On the morning of 27th October, they advanced on the town at first in square; then, with the RM in the centre and the RN Battalions on the right and left, the gate was blown in under heavy fire from the enemy and the town was carried with few casualties. The stockade was well built and in a good position. The town having been burnt and the remainder of the enemy driven off, they returned to the wells that night, and re-embarked the next day, having suffered a great deal from the heat.

Malta Clothing Depot.
By Order-in-Council 29th November owing to the large increase in the Mediterranean Squadron, a Clothing Depot was established in the Dockyard at Malta, with a Warrant Officer in charge, who combined the duties of Sergeant Major of the ship battalion when landed; he was given 5/4d a day pay and allowed one tailor or storekeeper to assist him. The Depot was under the supervision of the Captain of Marines of HMS Hibernia, who acted as Examiner of Accounts.

Royal Military Tournament.
In 1833 the Royal Military Tournament for the encouragement of skill at arms and to help the military charities was inaugurated at the Agricultural Hall at Islington. In 1886 competitions in regiments or districts were started, but it was not till 1890 that 10 prizes of 10/- each were offered to each of the Light Infantry Divisions and Depot for Fencing and Bayonet, but up to 1894 not all these prizes were claimed, which in these days seems astonishing.

In 1894 however, the RMA entered a team for the tug-of-war, as did the Depot, Royal Marines, and also a squad for the new competition in Physical Drill which had not long been introduced.

1891

In 1891 the numbers were 13,882.

Again, there is nothing of interest to chronicle, but the expansion of the Fleet was steadily progressing, and in May the Naval Ordnance Department was constituted so that the Navy henceforth became responsible for the provision of its own guns and ammunition, and the scandal of new ships lying idle for months in the dockyards waiting for their guns was put an end to.

Staff Officers.
The system in existence since 1763 by which the Senior Adjutant became the Office Adjutant for the conduct of the correspondence etc. of the Division was abolished, and he was replaced by a more senior officer, generally a Major, who became Staff Officer to the Commandant. In 1913 their title was changed to that of Brigade Major.

Printers.
The printing of Orders, which had hitherto been duplicated by copying press; which in its turn had replaced the system of dictating to the Orderly Sergeants daily, was recognised, and commencing from 1st October 1891, extra pay of 6d a day was approved[307] for the printers employed; the type and machines were however purchased locally and were the property of Divisional Funds.

RMA Recruits.
But by Order-in-Council a very important change was made in the training of the RM Artillery recruits; hitherto on completion of their infantry drill they had been sent to Eastney to undergo a course in Field Battery drill, if they failed to qualify they reverted to the infantry; by this Order-in-Council 25th June 1891 this test was abolished and a short elementary course in Naval Gun Drill was substituted to qualify for Gunner 2nd Class; if they failed they reverted to the infantry.

1892

In 1892 the numbers were 14,505.

Naval Gunnery.
Training was more to the fore, and the gun-batteries at the Divisions were being re-armed with breech-loading guns; though the instruction was still principally given at the muzzle-loaders.

Training.
A battalion of RMLI was sent to Aldershot for a month's training with the Army, from which all ranks gained great benefit, and from this time annually up to 1899 one or more battalions took part in the annual army Manoeuvres at Aldershot or Salisbury Plain, which included always a march from Portsmouth to Farnborough, Pirbright or later Salisbury, the bands of the Divisions taking it in turns to accompany the battalion.

For several years also at Plymouth a battalion marched with the regiments in garrison to Okehampton, and in co-operation with the artillery, took part in the field firing exercises at Okehampton.

A new drill book was published this year which simplified some of the drill and introduced physical drill with arms for the old backboard and pole drill.

---

307 Order-in-Council, 6 February 1892.

Military Instructor and DAAG.

The Military Instructor, who had hitherto instructed the young RMLI officers at Eastney, was not now required and was abolished; instead, by Order-in-Council 28th October 1892, an officer with the title DAAG was appointed to the Staff of the DAG RM to combine his remaining duties with those of the Acting Deputy Judge Advocate who had been formerly attached to the Staff and paid by fees. The new DAAG was paid a salary of £600 a year from 28th September 1892. He was available for all duties in the office, which included many of those of a DA & QMG.

Globe and Laurel. In May 1892 the first number of the Globe and Laurel was published at Chatham through the public spirited efforts of a small group of officers, among whom Captains C G Brittan, G T Onslow, and G E Matthews were prominent.

1893

The numbers voted were Staff 13, RMA 2868, RMLI 11,930.

Esquimalt Defences.

An experiment was made of sending a detachment of RMA to take over the defences of Esquimalt in Canada; a party proceeded in August 1893 to British Columbia and took over the defences under Lieutenant Barnes, and the remainder followed at intervals. Brevet Lieutenant Colonel G A Rawstorne was in command with Lieutenants Barnes, Templer and Poole.

A proportion had been trained as Submarine Miners and took over these duties from the Royal Engineers. Extra pay was granted of 15/- a day to the Commanding Officer, other officers 10/-, NCOs and men 1/6, whilst NCOs and men employed as Submarine Miners were paid at army rates. This party remained at Esquimalt until 1899 when they were relieved by the Royal Garrison Artillery.

Equipment.

The old 1882 pattern valise equipment was exchanged for the Slade-Wallace. The former with its heavy buff straps and large black waterproof canvas valise (much the same pattern as the present web valise) fitted badly; besides being heavy it was very painful to wear and contained a lot of useless articles e.g. tartan trousers etc. The Slade-Wallace, though better balanced, had the coat rolled on the waist belt and therefore unprotected from the weather, with the canteen on top; whilst the valise was small but rode awkwardly on the shoulders, it could however be detached and left behind. The old wooden water bottles were superseded by enamelled iron, covered with felt. The haversack was of white duck canvas.

HMS Victoria.

On 22nd June, during manoeuvres off the Coast of Syria, the flagship, HMS *Victoria*, was rammed by HMS *Camperdown* and lost with nearly all hands; after doing what was possible to close watertight doors etc. the detachment under Major A C Smythe and Lieutenant H G Farquharson

RMLI fell in on the quarterdeck where they remained until the ship heeled over and sank; 68 out of 98 NCOs and men were drowned, those saved clambering over the side and bottom as she heeled over. Lieutenant Farquharson was awarded the Royal Humane Society's silver medal for saving the Fleet Paymaster. As Kipling says of this incident in his poem on the Marines:

> *"To stand and be still to the Birkenhead drill*
> *Is a damn tough bullet to chew."*

Swimming.

After this disaster great attention was paid to swimming instruction; baths were built at the Depot and all recruits had to qualify, and on 2nd July a paid staff was allowed of a Superintendent at 2/6d a day, 1 Swimming Instructor 1st Class at 3/7d, Sergeant Instructors etc.

Works Department.

Considerable numbers of artificers were employed in the Works Department and in the Dockyards at Bermuda and at Ascension, whilst the men under training at Headquarters were also employed on the maintenance of the Barracks, so that there might always be trained men for these places and later Wei-Hai-Wei. Rates of pay were fixed from 1st Grade 1/6d a day for skilled men to the 5th Grade at -/10d a day.

Pumwani.

There was again trouble in East Africa; a Naval Brigade from the *Blanche, Swallow* and *Sparrow* assisted by Soudanese and Zanzibar troops landed from 7th-13th August 1893 to punish a robber chief, Fumo Omari. His fortified strongholds of Pumwani and Jongeni were stormed and captured with great gallantry. A clasp to the African General Medal was awarded for this service.

The Royal Marines were commanded by Sergeant J Battin RMLI (afterwards Major and Quartermaster) and the SNO in his report said, "I should have mentioned also the coolness and gallantry of all under my command, particularly the Marines under Sergeant J Battin RMLI."

With a view to improving the rifle shooting this year was formed the Royal Marine Rifle Association and this competition for the selection of those to shoot in the United Service Cup at Bisley, and the institution of the Eight Badge the next year, 1894.

Ascension.

The island of Ascension which was run on the lines of one of HM Ships, had been garrisoned in 1815 when the Emperor Napoleon I was imprisoned at St. Helena. The garrison was principally composed of Royal Marines, a number of Seamen and Kroomen, but there was a Captain RN in command. [308] The Royal Marines, in addition to their military duties, had gradually assumed all the Works Department services, besides providing men to run the farm, turtle ponds etc,

---

308 During the period 1828-1843 a Royal Marine officer appears to have been often in command.

established to provide fresh food for the garrison. later the island became a cable station and employees of the Eastern Telegraph Company were stationed there. When some guns were mounted a Subaltern of the RMA was added to the garrison as OC Artillery and Ordnance Officer. About 1893 the RMLI Officer Commanding the detachment before proceeding to the island underwent a course of instruction at the School of Military Engineering and became Officer-in-Charge of Works with a Sergeant as Foreman of Works under him. In 1905 the Naval Officers and Men were withdrawn, and the Officer Commanding Royal Marines became Officer in Charge of the island, the Royal Marines being borne on the books of the flagship of the Cape Station. This arrangement continued until 1922, when in consequence of cable stations becoming neutral under International Agreement, they ceased to be fortified and the Royal Marines were withdrawn. The hundred years' connection with the island left many pleasant and interesting memories to members of the Corps.

1894

In 1894 the numbers voted were Staff 13, RMA 2686, RMLI 12,085.

Gambia.
The penetration and civilisation of West Africa had begun, but some of the local chiefs were troublesome and interfered with the settlements. Such a case occurred in February 1894, when Fodi Sillah made himself a nuisance to the settlements on the Gambia. An expedition consisting of two columns, one under Captain Gamble RN, and the other under Major Corbet RMLI, were dispatched: Captain Gamble's column, after effecting its object, was ambushed on its return to the boats and badly cut up; Lieutenant F W Hervey RMLI commanding the rearguard with his Marines charged the enemy with great gallantry, which enabled the force to make good their retreat to the boats. Lieutenant Hervey, 2 Naval Officers and 10 Men were killed, and 40 men wounded. Major Corbet's column with 50 Marines and 50 men of the West India Regiment with one 7 pdr ML gun dragged by the Marines left Bathurst on 22nd February and, accompanied by the Administrator and Admiral Bedford, proceeded to Sukotta, where the headman was made to hand over his guns and powder which were destroyed; his stockade was pulled down and burnt. The Column then returned to Bakotti and bivouacked; next day they marched to Busamballa, fording two rivers and dragging the gun through the jungle. As soon as the head of the column emerged from the bush, fire was opened on them from the stockade and men in the grass; a couple of shells cleared the village and set it on fire; the defenders joined the enemy in the grass and kept up a heavy fire, retiring slowly; the Marines and WI Regiment followed them up in skirmishing order for 5 miles. The pursuit was then discontinued and the stockade, which was very strong with two rows of palisades, was burnt; the force then marched to Aboka in British territory, having marched 20-24 miles dragging the field gun. On the 24th the column marched to Cape St Mary, but on the next day, hearing of the disaster to Captain Gamble's Column, they marched to Sabajee to take up an entrenched position to protect the frontier of the Colony; the tools had not arrived, so they could only clear away the bush. On 26th February they were attacked by 1500 Mandingoes who were repulsed and driven back over the border. On 1st March, being reinforced with 50

more Royal Marines and 10 WI Regiment, Major Corbet took up another position at Isawary, and on the 5th having received further reinforcements of seamen etc, bringing his force to 500 men, he marched to relieve 200 West India Regiment under Major Madden RA, entrenched at Busumbula. He then returned to Sabajee. The Royal Marines, having been re-embarked, Major Corbet went round with the *Alecto, Satellite, Magpie,* and *Widgeon* to Gunjar and after two days bombardment landed with the Royal Marines, 270 seamen, and a portion of the WI Regiment and destroyed the place. The General South African Medal with clasp for 'Gambia 1894' was awarded for this service. Major Corbet was awarded the CB.

Colours.
On 22nd August at Osborne, Isle of Wight, HM the Queen presented new Colours to the Portsmouth Division RMLI, the battalion being conveyed to Osborne in gunboats. The opportunity was taken to revert to the design of the Colours as established by HM King George IV in 1827 with modifications signed and approved by Her Majesty in her own hand.[309]

Cycle Corps.
In 1894 Major L Edye RMLI, with Lieutenant H D Farquharson as his assistant, formed a Cycle Corps, which was semi-officially recognised by the DAGRM. The head-quarters and one section were at the Depot, and a section of one officer and varying numbers of members at each Division. The members were volunteers and mostly came from the Sergeants' Mess. They provided their own cycle and a uniform which was very smart. When available, they were employed at field days and at manoeuvres. As organised units they remained in existence for a few years.

1895

In 1895 the numbers voted were 15,005.

Brass River and M'Weli.
There was more fighting on the West Coast of Africa in which the Royal Marines were concerned. In February a punitive expedition had to be undertaken against King Koko of Nimby in the Brass River; a Naval Brigade from the *St George*, *Thrush* and *Widgeon* under Admiral Sir Frederick Bedford was landed and destroyed the chief town of Brass on the River Niger. Major R Denny RMLI was the senior RM Officer. In August a Brigade was landed from HMS *St George*, *Phoebe*, *Barrosa*, *Racoon*, and *Blonde* under Admiral Rawson to punish a Chief called M'Baruk on the East Coast of Africa. The force landed at Mombasa and accompanied by 60 Soudanese and 50 Zanzibar Askaris advanced and captured the stronghold of M'Weli on 17th August. Instead of a clasp M'Weli was engraved on the rim of the General African Medal. Major Denny was made a Brevet Lieutenant Colonel for this and his services on the West African Coast.

---

[309] See Random Records for full account.

Arms.
The Corps was re-armed with the Lee-Metford Magazine Rifle Mark II, the long rifle with smokeless powder and a short sword bayonet in lieu of the Martini Henry and the old triangular bayonet which with the sergeants' swords, a link with the past, disappeared. It was a curious experience to fire a rifle with very little recoil in lieu of one whose recoil was like the kick of a horse; and in the light of later experience to hear the old shots complaining that it was not so accurate:

Recruiting Staff Officers.
A great innovation was made as regards recruiting. All active service officers except the officer in London were withdrawn, and replaced by 10 retired officers (3 Class I at £350 per annum, and 7 Clase II at £300) who were allotted certain districts; it was further ordered that the London Recruiting Officer should be replaced by an Inspector of Marine Recruiting at £800 a year who was to be in charge of all recruiting for the Royal Marines.[310]

Schools.
At the same time the Sub-Inspector of. Schools was abolished, and the Director of Naval Education arranged for the Inspection of the RM schools.

Quartermasters.
Owing to the growth of the Divisions and the great increase in instructional stores another Quartermaster was added to each Division who took over charge of all instructional stores, the shoemaking fund and similar duties from the other two.[311]

By Order-in-Council 22nd April the white clothing required on foreign stations was issued gratuitously instead of on repayment as hitherto.

1896

In 1896 the numbers were 16,000.

In consequence of the threatening state of affairs in Europe, a Particular Service Squadron was commissioned from 14th January to 21st October and cruised in the Channel and the Atlantic.

Soudan.
In the Soudan the Anglo-Egyptian forces commenced the first advance against the Mahdi, which led to the reconquest of the Soudan; several Royal Marine Officers were employed as Special Service Officers with the troops, and a small body of RM ANCOs serving in gunboats in charge of the guns at the capture of Dongola etc.

---

310 Order-in-Council 22 June 1895.
311 Order-in-Council 22 June 1895.

Zanzibar.
On 27th August owing to the recalcitrant behaviour of the Sultan of Zanzibar, his palace was bombarded by the Squadron; the Royal Marines under Major T de M Roche RMLI being landed to protect the British Agency during the action.

Colours.
On 22nd June HRH the Duke of Edinburgh, the Honorary Colonel of the Corps, presented new Colours to the Chatham Division, and on 3rd July he presented another pair to the Plymouth Division.

Uniform.
There were several changes in uniform; the most important being the introduction of the new pattern straight thrusting sword for RMLI officers with a steel hilt instead of the brass-hilted cut and thrust sword hitherto in use. This was designed to meet the new Italian exercise recently introduced with a straight arm guard.

The RMLI following the Guards, adopted the present pattern Mess Jacket in lieu of the gold laced shell jacket and laced waistcoat.

The Austrian pattern Field Service Cap replaced the Glengarry in the RMLI and for drill in the RMA, who however retained their pill-box for walking out.

1897

In 1897 there was an increase in numbers; Staff 12, RMA 3591, RMLI 12,828 - a total of 16,431.

West Africa: Benin.
In the early part of the year the Corps was again involved in hostilities in West Africa. A mission sent to the capital city of Benin was massacred and it was decided that the Cape Squadron should undertake the punitive expedition in conjunction with the Houssas of the West African Regiment (five companies under Colonel Bruce-Hamilton). Admiral Rawson was in command and he landed a Naval Brigade from HMS *St George* and smaller ships; the RM of the Naval Brigade were under Major T de M Roche of the *St George*, with Lieutenant N F J French RMA and F D Bridges RMLI; to reinforce them HMS *Theseus* and *Forte* were detached from the Mediterranean Station, Captain G L Beaumont being the RM Officer. A detachment of 100 RMLI under Captain G T Byrne and 20 RMA with a machine-gun under Lieutenant Dibblee were sent from England and were known as the Royal Marine Battalion.

On 10th February a base was formed at Warrigi and the force landed and advanced on Benin. On 13th there was a skirmish at Oglobo and the enemy driven off. On 16th the force consisting of the Marine Battalion, the RMLI of the *St George* and *Theseus*, two companies of seamen with a demolition and rocket party advanced on Benin City; after covering only 5 miles owing to the heat and thick bush they halted at Ogaji.

On 17th, starting at 4.30 am, the troops bivouacked at Awoke where they were attacked by the natives who were driven off. On the 18th they started to attack Benin City, under constant fire from the bush, but fortunately with few casualties. On reaching a wide open road leading directly to the city, considerable opposition was encountered including the fire from several guns loaded with scrap iron; two gunners RMA were killed, Captain Byrne was mortally wounded; 312 four Privates were wounded as well as five Naval ratings. The Maxim guns and rockets replied and drove off the gunners. Admiral Rawson then ordered a charge, which being sounded by Bugler Allen RMLI, Houssas, Marines and seamen charged the guns and into the town where they opened fire on the fleeing enemy. The king escaped but was captured a few weeks later; a good many trophies were secured. Major Roche was awarded the DSO and Captain Beaumont a Brevet Majority.

Crete.
In February an insurrection against the rule of the Turks broke out on the island of Crete, and the Royal Marines were landed from the squadron on 15th February at Canea to protect British interests. From January to March Major Bor RMA had been in charge of an International Gendarmerie but in March he resigned. The island was blockaded by the squadron to prevent the Greeks interfering, and Marines were also in garrison at Candia where they were relieved in March by the Highland Light Infantry. In April HMS *Camperdown* was obliged to open fire on the insurgents outside Port Tzeddin, and Major Bor was landed with the detachment and took possession of the Fort till relieved by the Army. Major Bor was awarded the CMG.

Diamond Jubilee.
In June, HM Queen Victoria, celebrated the Diamond Jubilee of her reign by a procession and thanksgiving service at St Paul's Cathedral. A Battalion of RMA lined the street at St George's Square in South London, and a Battalion of RMLI with Colours in Trafalgar Square opposite the National Gallery. A Guard of Honour with Colour and Band was mounted near St Paul's Cathedral.

A Review of the Fleet was held at Spithead, when there were 165 ships and 38,577 men, and 12 foreign men-of-war.

On the occasion of the Jubilee, the first Grand Cross of the Bath was awarded to the Corps in the person of General Sir Anthony Stransham RMLI, who had been Inspector General in 1862. He entered the Corps on 22nd December 1805 and retired in August 1875. He died 6th October 1900, aged 94.

KCBs were awarded to Lieutenant General H S Jones CB and Major General J Phillips CB and a civil CB to a retired officer, Colonel Somers Lewis.

---

312 He reached England but died in St Thomas's Hospital on 14th March.

Edinburgh Cup.
HRH the Duke of Edinburgh presented a handsome cup for competition between the Divisions, half of each team to be composed of young soldiers.

The RMRA had now collected a considerable number of prizes in the Annual Competition.

1898

The numbers were 18,000.

Soudan.
Although there were great operations up the Nile, resulting in the capture of Khartoum, the Corps was only concerned with a few Special Service Officers and NCOs, RMA and RMLI, lent to the Army. But when the advancing British met the French troops under Major Marchand at Fashoda, who had come across from West Africa, the tension between the two nations became acute, and in the autumn the British Fleet was partially mobilised and the Coastguard Battleships and Cruisers, filled up to full crews, assembled at Portland.

Wei-Hai-Wei.
On 24th May 1898 Wei-Hai-Wei, having been leased by the British Government from the Chinese, was taken over from the Japanese who had captured it in the late war; as usual in the Corps, Captain Mercer RMLI, and 25 RMLI were sent to take over from the 4000 Japanese who had been holding it and had great difficulty in preventing the camps etc from being looted; they were relieved later by a garrison of RMLI under Major Maclurcan with 2 Captains and 4 Subalterns, and the Army authorities raised a regiment of Chinese to assist in the garrison duties. The place became a Naval Base and RM artificers were sent out for the Works Department as at Ascension; the Marine guard remained at varying strength till the end of the Great War in 1919.

Rations.
Efforts were made to improve the rations and in consequence of more compulsory physical training, the issues to recruits at the Depot and Eastney was raised to 1 lb of meat and 2 lbs of bread from 1st January 1898 – (Order-in-Council 2nd February 1898) without any increase of the charge of 4½d to the men.

Games and Sports.
During this decade the importance of games for NCOs and men became more recognised. Hitherto cricket had been the only game for which any efforts were made to maintain Divisional and Corps Teams. Both rugby and association football had depended on spasmodic efforts of officers who had been sufficiently keen to play themselves and who formed the majority of the teams. Though the Army Association Football Cup had been won once or twice, a regular team at each Division was unknown. It now became a recognised sport and teams were regularly played, and in time became almost entirely formed of NCOs and men. Hockey also began to be played.

Crete.
On 6th September an unexpected attack was made on the troops stationed in Crete at Candia, cutting them off from the shore and causing casualties; HMS *Hazard*, a gunboat, at once landed her Sergeant (Bunn) and 8 Marines, who behaved magnificently and rescued the Colonel of the Highlanders; the Captain of the *Hazard*, landing just after, had two of his boat's crew killed and others wounded, but covered by his Marines they held the landing place for four hours. Private Priestner was promoted to Corporal. HMS *Camperdown* came round as soon as possible from Canea and landed Major Drury and 60 Royal Marines. They had to land on the beach in the surf as the harbour was held by the insurgent Turks and brought welcome aid to the hard-pressed Highlanders; later in the day the remainder of the *Camperdown's* Marines and those of the *Astraea* were also put ashore and reinforced the Highlanders until the French, Italian and Russian troops arrived; later also a British Battalion from Malta arrived, when the Royal Marines returned to their ships.

23 – South Africa and China 1899 - 1901

1899

The numbers voted were 18,005.

RMA Recruits.
In 1897 the Artillery recruits had been withdrawn from Deal to be trained at Eastney, when an additional Sergeant Major, Sergeant Instructor of Infantry and Instructor of Gymnastics were added to the staff and by Order-in-Council 2nd February 1899 an Assistant Adjutant was allowed at Eastney. This had important results, as the Artillery ceased to pick and choose their recruits at Deal, and soon afterwards, owing to the rising standard of Naval Gunnery in the Infantry, the transfer of RMA recruits who failed to qualify for Gunner 1st Class to the Infantry was stopped.

QMSI.
On 11th July 1899[313] the 1st Sergeants Instructors of Infantry, Gunnery, Musketry, Swimming, and Gymnastics, were raised to the rank of Quartermaster Sergeant with the title of QMSI with Class II rates of pension.

Rations.
Further efforts were made to improve the rationing of the men, and on 8th August increased pay was granted to the Sergeant Cooks and on the same day was published an Order-in-Council which had the effect of raising the men's pay by about 2d a day, but its wording is so involved that it is a monument to the mentality of the Treasury and the Finance Branches of the Admiralty, and must be quoted:

> "From 1st July 1899, the emoluments of NCOs and men to be increased by 2d a day. To be arrived at by abolishing 1d a day Beer Money for Privates [314] and making the following alterations in deductions for Bread and Meat Rations. (a) As regards NCOs a deduction of 2½d a day instead of 4½d. (b) As regards men a deduction of 1½d a day instead of 4½d. When rations in kind were not issued 2d to NCOs and 3d to men, except when on furlough, when allowance to all ranks was 2d a day." [315]

Training.
Men were also allowed a free issue of canvas shoes per annum to relieve the feet after marching. At this time, in consequence of some rather disastrous experiences on manoeuvres in the Army,

---

313 Order-in-Council.
314 Abolished for NCOs in 1881.
315 This left the stoppage for food 5d. a day instead of 7d.

great attention was being paid to route-marching and training in march discipline; a training which was carefully followed by the Royal Marines and which was to bear fruit in the next few years.

Bandmasters.

By Order-in-Council 27th December; provision was made for two Bandmasters, Royal Marines, to become 2nd Lieutenants.

But we now approach a period when the energies of the country were concentrated on the South African War and the Boxer Rising in China; though comparatively small bodies of the Corps were employed in each theatre, they had great results on its training and organisation.

South African War 1899-1902

The quarrel between the Boers in the Transvaal and the British had been growing for some time, and in October 1899 came to a head. The first British reinforcements for the South African Garrison from India were sent to Natal, so that there was a great shortage of troops in Cape Colony. HMS *Terrible*, which was relieving the *Powerful* on the China Station was also sent out via the Cape, as was the *Powerful* on her homeward journey, so that these two large cruisers were available. To reinforce the troops a small Naval Brigade of two 12 pdr guns, some seamen and 260 RM under Major Plumbe RMLI from HMS *Doris* (Flag), *Powerful, Terrible*, and *Monarch* were landed at Simonstown under Commander Ethelston of the *Powerful* and sent to Stormberg to protect the railway junction there. They arrived on 21st October and reinforced the 2nd Battalion of the Royal Berkshire Regiment. Remaining here for about a fortnight, they were recalled to Queenstown, further from the border. Remaining here for 10 days, they were ordered to return to their ships, as the troops were now coming up to relieve them. On arrival at East London, the detachment of the *Terrible* (under Captain Mullins RMLI) was sent on to Durban to rejoin their ship, where they were employed in guard duties in Durban and the Umlass Waterworks, and also in the armoured train guarding the Zululand Border and the railway. A 12 pdr gun's crew under Sergeant Roper RMLI, accompanied the Naval Brigade, manning the heavy guns, which was attached to General Buller's Army and took part in all the engagements that were undertaken for the relief of Ladysmith.

The others on returning to Simonstown were at once re-organised, the command being assumed by Captain Protheroe RN, and with more seamen to two more 12 pdr guns under Commander Ethelston at once proceeded up country to join Lord Methuen's column advancing to the relief of Kimberley.

Graspan.
They left De Aar Junction on 22nd November; during the night 22nd/23rd November the Guards and 9th Brigades advanced to the attack of the enemy in position at Belmont, but at daylight the position had not been taken, so the field artillery and the Naval 12 pdrs were pushed across the

railway in support, the Marines acting as escort to the guns and helping to drag them into position as well as bringing up the ammunition. The enemy was driven off, and the next day the column advanced; the guns going with the armoured train, 50 seamen and 190 Royal Marines marching with the main column. Bivouacking for night 24th/25th, the Naval Brigade was detailed with the KOYLI in support to carry a strong hill about two miles off. The Guards and 9th Brigades were in support. At 5.45 am the cavalry located the enemy in a position about 3 miles long on some broken kopjes, known as Enslin or Graspan, with an ideal field of fire and the flanks drawn back; there were no positions for the attacking artillery, but one battery RFA on the right and the Naval guns on the left managed to shell the position.

The Naval Brigade and 1 Company KOYLI extending to single rank advanced on the enemy's right centre with the remainder of the 9th Brigade in support; inclining to the right, the Naval Brigade attacked the enemy's left, making a diagonal march of about 2 miles. At 7.45 am, when they were 700 yards from the base of the principal kopje, the enemy opened fire and the Brigade turned instinctively to meet it. Advancing by rushes, they carried the ridge, the men moving as if on parade; whilst the ridge was being secured, Major Marchant taking some men cleared out the remainder of the enemy who were hanging on to the kopje in front.

The ridge had been carried, but at great cost. Major Plumbe RMLI and Captain Senior RMA were killed, and Lieutenant N Q C Jones RMLI wounded; 6 NCOs and men were killed and 82 wounded, out of 180. Commander Ethelston was killed and Captain Protheroe wounded, so Major Marchant brought the Naval Brigade out of action. Lieutenant Jones who, though wounded, had continued to lead the advance, was awarded the DSO, as was Lieutenant Saunders RMLI later on. So, ended the action of Graspan, one of the brightest episodes in the long history of the Corps.

Modder River.
On 27th November the Boers destroyed the bridge across the Modder River and occupied the low lying ground on the river banks, where they collected a considerable force to defend the crossing. Lord Methuen continued his advance on the 27th and on the forenoon of the 28th attacked with the Guards Brigade, but it was not till the afternoon that the British reached the south bank of the river and not till 7 pm that the left flank detachment got across and cleared the way.

The Boers retreated during the night, unmolested. A bridge was thrown over the river and the Division occupied Modder River station; a bridge for the railway was commenced and completed by 7th December. Reinforcements now came up, for the Naval Brigade - 2 Officers (Captain Morgan and Lieutenant Wilson RMLI) and 50 Marines with 40 seamen under Commander de Horsey, who assumed command until relieved by Captain Bearcroft RN, on 3rd December; the latter brought up further reinforcements, with Lieutenants Raikes and Poe RMA, and Lieutenant French RMLI, whilst a 4.7 in gun on Captain Scott's mounting joined the Brigade. Major Urmston RMLI of the *Powerful*, who had been sent home sick from China, rejoined his detachment and took command of the Royal Marines till March, when he was appointed Provost Marshal of the 9th Division on the arrival of Major Peile appointed to the *Doris* vice Plumbe killed. More 4.7 in guns came up later.

Magersfontein.

On 4th December the Boers took up a position at Magersfontein, barring the way to Kimberley. Here they were attacked by Lord Methuen on 11th December in a severe action which proved disastrous to the Highland Brigade. The Naval guns, escorted by the Marines, took part; the British were repulsed with considerable loss and matters came to a stand-still; especially as General Buller had also suffered a repulse at Colenso on 15th December in Natal.

1900

The Naval Brigade remained opposite Magersfontein until 16th February 1900, when in consequence of Lord Roberts' great flanking march with the Cavalry, 6th and 7th Infantry Divisions to relieve Kimberley, the Boer Commander, Cronje, broke up his laager and retreated to the eastward.

Paardeberg.

On 17th February, the Naval Brigade moved on Jacobsdaal; Captain Bearcroft with Major Urmston and Lieutenant Saunders RMLI, with the 12 pdr guns and escort of Royal Marines moving into the Free State; Commander de Horsey with the remainder moved direct on Jacobsdaal. The whole Brigade of three 4.7 in. guns and four 12 pdrs with the Royal Marines, followed the 6th Division to Paardeberg, making a splendid march covering the distance from Jacobsdaal to Paardeberg, nearly 31 miles, in 23 hours.

Arriving in the evening of 19th February, they came into action from Gun Hill with the artillery of the 7th Division. On the 20th Major Peile RMLI, joined the Brigade and took command of the Marines. Two of the 4.7 in guns were sent to the north bank over the river and came into action on Signal Hill; the bombardment was not very successful, and the Boer riflemen, creeping out, made it uncomfortable for the gunners on Gun Hill.

The Boers finally surrendered on 27th February and the advance was resumed on Bloemfontein. The 4.7 in guns were in action at Osfontein on 1st March and again on the 8th at Poplar Grove. On the 15th the Brigade moved into Bloemfontein, the capital of the Free State, where it remained for nearly two months, costng heavily from enteric fever, the result of the conditions at Paardeberg, so that when the advance was resumed only Majors Peile and Marchant, Lieutenants Wilson and French were still on duty. On 3rd May Lord Roberts' centre column with which was the Naval Brigade, advanced from Bloemfentein along the railway, the guns were dragged by teams of oxen. Halting for 10 days at Kroonstadt to regulate the advance of General Buller's and other columns to right and left, the advance was resumed on 22nd May, crossing the Vaal River at Viljoen's Drift on the 27th. Here the Free State troops went back into their own state to raise trouble in the British rear, and the Transvaalers retired on Johannesburg. On 28th May Lord Roberts attacked the Boers east of Johannesburg, the guns coming into action. The Boers were outflanked by the cavalry and evacuated their positions on 30th/31st, retiring on Pretoria, and on the 31st Johannesburg surrendered.

Pretoria.
Resuming the advance on 3rd June, the two 4.7 in guns (one of which was now manned by the Royal Marines) came into action against the Boers near Pretoria on 4th June. Commander de Horsey was wounded. On the 5th Pretoria surrendered to Lord Roberts, the Naval Brigade marching past him at 1 pm in the Grand Square. Out of 300 Royal Marine Officers and men who had joined the RM detachment since it started, only 3 Officers (Major Peile, Lieutenants Wilson and French, RMLI), 22 RMA and 41 RMLI were still on parade, Major Marchant RMLI with 25 men was however coming up from Bloemfontein.

Diamond Hill.
On 11th-13th June was fought the Battle of Diamond Hill to the east of Pretoria, in which the 4.7 in guns participated, and the Boers retired to Middleburg.

Belfast.
The two 4.7 in. guns accompanied General Pole-Carew's Division to Belfast. On 24th August Belfast was occupied and the Boers were found in a strong position beyond; the Cavalry Division was sent round the north, whilst Buller's force, which had come up from Natal, was pressing in on the south. The guns were present at the Battle of Belfast on the 26th; about 4.30 pm the RM gun came into action on the north-east corner of Monument Hill; Lieutenant Wilson was wounded, and the gun was now commanded by Major Marchant. The next day the Naval gun was sent to the right flank and the 12 pdrs prepared to follow the advance of the Army. On the 27th the RM gun had a duel with a Boer gun and put it out of action at 10,500 yards, having sunk the trail into the ground. This was their last action, as the country was now too hilly for their further employment. On 5th September the Naval Brigade was split up and soon after the remnants returned home. Majors Peile and Marchant RMLI were awarded the CB, Lieutenants Wilson and Saunders the DSO.

There were a considerable number of RM Officers lent as Special Service Officers, who filled various positions on the Staff, with the transport, and lent to various units, whilst Colonel Paris RMA was in command of one of the flying columns. Lieutenants Clark and Nelson RMLI served as Company Officers with the Royal Dublin Fusiliers. Major F White RMLI gained the DSO for a very gallant defence of Ladybrand. Detachments of several ships were landed to protect various outlying places, such as Walfisch Bay, Mossel Bay, Saldanah Bay etc.

1900

Before dealing with the operations in China there are a few administrative details that should be noted.

The numbers voted for the year were 18,000.

On 20th January the Greenwich Hospital Pensions for retired officers were reorganised and fixed at:

>   10 of £65 per annum for Field Officers and Captains
>   2 of £50 per annum for Quartermasters
>   1 of £25 per annum for Warrant Officers

Band at Depot.

The numbers of the Band at the Depot were also raised to the same as at a Headquarters, viz: Bandmaster (WO), 2 Sergeants, 2 Corporals, 25 Musicians, and 10 Supernumeraries.[316] The Order said that the number of recruits at Deal had risen to 1300; as a matter of fact, they often touched 1800 during this year.

Clothing Depot.

Owing to the great increase in the numbers of the Fleet in China, a Clothing Depot with a Warrant Officer in charge, on the same lines as at Malta, was established by Order-in-Council 15 May 1900, with the RM Officer of the *Tamar* as auditor. Native tailors were employed as necessary.

Naval Gunnery.

On 27th September 1900 a new rating of Second Captain of Gun RMLI was introduced, as the order said certain guns were manned by complete crews of RMLI and with the exception of the Captain of Gun the only gunnery rating was TM. An extra 1d a day whilst afloat was allowed for this rating.

China - The Boxer Rising 1900 [317]

Peking.

At the end of May anxiety as to the safety of the Legations in Peking was felt owing to the growth of an anti-foreign movement, semi-religious in its character, but encouraged by the Imperial authorities against the foreigners, for they were smarting under the encroachments of the foreign nations made in the form of leases of territory and spheres of influence after the Chino-Japanese War of 1894. Captain Strouts RMLI had been detached from Wei-Hai-Wei with 25 RMLI as a winter guard in the British Concession at Tientsin.

It was decided that Allied guards should proceed to Peking, so on the 30th Captain Wray with 25 more RMLI from Wei-Hai-Wei arrived in Tientsin and joined Captain Strouts; these two guards and 50 RMLI from HMS *Orlando* under Captain L S T Halliday were ordered to proceed to Peking; as this would have made the British guard too strong in proportion to the other Allies,

---

316 Order-in-Council, 3rd March 1900.
317 Authorities: World's Navies in Boxer Rebellion (Lieutenant C. Dix, RN); Britain's Sea Soldiers (Field); Lives of Sir P. Scott and Admiral Sir D Beatty, letters of Officers, etc. Commission of HMS *Terrible* (Crowe); History of US Marine Corps (Collum); Diaries Lieutenant Armstrong and Captain Mullins RMLI.

25 of the *Orlando's* Marines were left in Tientsin where detachments of seamen had arrived to guard the Settlement. The total force for the Legations was 3 Officers, 79 RMLI with 3 Naval ratings as armourer, signalmen, and sick birth attendant. They also had a five-barrel Nordenfeldt gun, but were very short of ammunition, but fortunately just as the train started the First Lieutenant of the *Orlando* gave them two more boxes.

Reaching Peking at 7 pm they marched to the Legations, a distance of five miles, leaving Captain Halliday and 18 NCOs and men at the station as baggage guard until the following morning, when the German and Austrian guards also arrived.

It was found that the Austrian Naval Captain was the Senior Officer of the Allies. This proved unsatisfactory after the siege had begun, and the British Minister, Sir Claude Macdonald, an old officer of the 74th HLI, took over command with Captain Strouts RMLI as his Chief Staff Officer.

The total force available was 543, which included 125 volunteer civilians, student interpreters etc, many of whom were English. The regular British troops consisted of the 79 RMLI and 3 Naval Ratings with Captain Poole, East Yorkshire Regiment, Captain Percy Smith, South Staffords, and N Oliphant, Scots Guards. The guns consisted of one Italian 1 pdr, the British 5-barrel Nordenfeldt, and an American Colt gun. The American Marines under Captains Myers and Hall, and Surgeon Lippett who worked with the British, numbered 53. It was decided that the British and American Legations should be the final point of defence; the former was surrounded by a wall 10 feet high and contained 5 wells of good sweet water; a small bastion called Fort Halliday was pushed out covering the main gate of the Legation and flanking the canal and road on the north side. The area to be defended was about half a mile long by half a mile broad, bounded by the Austrian and Italian Legations on the east side; on the north by the street running over the North Bridge of the Canal; on the west by the Russian Legation; on the south by the street running at the foot of the Great Wall of the Tartar City on which the barricades were erected, to the Austrian Legation. On the west was the Mongol Market; at the north west corner adjoining the British Legation (between it and the Imperial City) were the buildings of the Hanlin University; the area to be defended also included the Fu (i.e. the palace and grounds of Prince Su) where the Christian refugees were accommodated.

Working parties were organised from these under the missionaries.

The guards were occupied in preparing defences and bringing in native Christians.

By the 9th June the situation became so threatening that a telegram for further assistance was sent to Admiral Sir Edward Seymour lying with the Fleet off Taku. In response he and the allies at once landed a column at Tong-Ku (although the Chinese still held the Taku Forts) which left Tientsin on 10th June and whose proceedings will be dealt with later. The Admiral took command himself.

At Peking on 13th June, the Boxers attacked the French Legation and the Methodist Chapel, but were driven off. Vigilance was redoubled and the excitement in the City grew, because the Boxers commenced massacring the native Christians and fires in the City were innumerable.

At 10.30 pm on the 14th, Captain Halliday's picquet on the North Bridge was attacked, but a volley stopped the Boxers whose bodies were left lying there as a warning that they were not invulnerable, which was one of their tenets.

From the 16th to the 19th the guards were occupied in patrols, completing the defences, and bringing in what native Christians they could, and incidentally in killing a number of Boxers; there were also some attacks on the North Bridge.

News now arrived that the Allied Fleets had bombarded and taken the Taku Forts on the 17th and this materially altered the situation, as the Imperial Troops which had hitherto been neutral now joined the Boxers.

At 4 pm on the 19th the Chinese Government sent an ultimatum that the ambassadors and all with them should leave the City within 24 hours. Although several were in favour of obeying this order Baron von Kettler, the German Ambassador, objected and volunteered to go and interview the Chinese authorities; on his way there on the morning of the 20th he was murdered, which prevented any further idea of evacuation. Preparations for defence were pushed on; more native Christians with a guard of American Marines came in and at 4 pm firing opened. On 22nd June an alarm of an attack caused all the guards, except the Japanese in the Fu, to fall back on the British Legation, but it was a false alarm and fortunately all the posts were recovered except the Austrian Legation, which necessitated a rectification of the defences in the Fu and the Austrian Captain was replaced in command by Sir Claude Macdonald as before explained.

The Chinese now attempted by setting fire to buildings contiguous to the Legations to drive out the defenders; on the 23rd they set fire to the Hanlin University which adjoined the north-west corner of the British Legation, thereby burning priceless manuscripts, etc. The flames came over the Legations, so a small party of Royal Marines under Captain Poole, East Yorkshire Regiment, drove out the Chinese and extinguished the fire, many of the buildings having to be pulled down. A timely change of wind turned away the flames. The Russians, Japanese and Americans were dealing with similar difficulties.

The Chinese also brought a Krupp gun into action from the Chien Men Gate, which caused the defenders to construct dugouts. The missionaries and refugees were used as working parties. The Germans and Americans advanced along the City Wall to try and capture the gun, but the opposition was too strong for them.

On 24th June the Boxers and Imperial troops made a fierce attack on the West Wall of the British Legation, setting fire to the West Gate of the South Stable quarters; the fire was with difficulty extinguished owing to the firing of the Imperial troops; the presence of these troops in the buildings was a grave danger to the Legation, so Captain Strouts organised a sortie by Captain Halliday and 20 Royal Marines -"a hole was made in the wall and Captain Halliday leading, was at once engaged with the enemy." Before he could use his revolver he was shot through the left shoulder at point blank range, the bullet fracturing the shoulder and carrying away part of the lung; notwithstanding the severe nature of his wound, Captain Halliday killed four of his assailants and telling the men to 'carry on and not mind him' walked back unaided to the hospital, refusing aid so as not to diminish the number of the men in the sortie. It was feared that the wound was mortal, but happily he recovered and was awarded the Victoria Cross.[318] Captain Strouts then took charge and led the men forward and the enemy were cleared out with heavy loss, Captain Strouts being slightly wounded and one Marine severely.

Sniping continued, the Royal Marines using Martini-Henrys to save the Lee-Metford ammunition. On the 28th the Chinese brought up a Krupp gun to bear from the Mongol Market about 300 yards away and did considerable damage to the south end of the British Legation. A sortie was organised, but the Allies lost their way and it proved a fiasco; however the gun was withdrawn and more buildings were burnt, which improved the field of fire for the garrison.

On 29th there was a fierce attack on the French at the south-east corner and on the 30th the Germans and Russians were hard pressed on the City Wall; Corporal Gregory and 7 Royal Marines were sent to reinforce the Germans, and eventually relieved them. Private Tickner was wounded in the legs but refused help to take him to the first-aid post. At daylight on 1st July the Germans and Royal Marines found the Chinese had brought up three field guns at about 100 yards distance; as there were only 8 Germans and 3 British, the German NCO ordered a retirement; the Americans on the wall seeing their rear thus uncovered also retired; fortunately this was not observed by the Chinese and 12 Royal Marines under Captain Wray were able to reoccupy the position; Captain Wray was wounded whilst trying to build a barricade to replace the German one in order to cover the Americans; owing to the heavy fire this proved impracticable and the Americans had to build another for themselves.

Seymour's Column.
Turning to the movements of the relieving column, on receipt of the telegram from Peking an International Force was at once landed, by means of a flotilla of destroyers, tugs, and boats, which slipped past the Forts at Taku in the dark and landed their men at Tong-Ku, the terminus of the railway, on 10th June. This force was about 2,000 men, commanded by the Admiral himself and his Flag-Captain Jellicoe; it included 915 British Seamen and Marines; the Royal Marines were under Major Johnstone RMLI and Lieutenant Beyts RMA (*Centurion*), Captains Doig (*Endymion*) and Lloyd (*Aurora*). They entrained in four trains and took with them railroad repairing material. They left Tientsin on 11th June.

---

318 became General Sir Lewis Halliday, VC KCB, AGRM 1927-30.

Beyond Yangtsun where the railway crosses the Pei-ho River, the track was found pulled up and it was necessary to bivouac and wait whilst repairs were made. Starting at 11.30 am on the 11th near Lofa, the line was found to be torn up in several places, and an advanced guard under Major Johnstone was sent ahead; they were attacked in the afternoon by a strong force of Boxers, but reinforcements coming up, the enemy were driven across the front and sought shelter in the villages, which were then stormed and the Boxers driven out.

By 6 pm the trains were able to advance and arrived within 3 miles of Langfan, which was their furthest point. On the 12th a party of Seamen tried to push on to Antung, the next station, but failed and had to return. The trains now closed up and on the 13th Major Johnstone and 60 Royal Marines went to Antung. On the 14th the line was out behind the column at Yangtsun, and a determined attack was made on the trains which was repulsed with heavy loss. Lo-Fa was attacked, and the Admiral went down with reinforcements and in the evening of the 14th Major Johnstone was withdrawn from Antung.

On the evening of the 15th two trains were left at Lo-Fa and two at Lang-fan and by the good work of the working parties a train got through to Yangtsun; here it was found that not only was the station wrecked, but also the bridge over the River Pei-Ho, so that return by train was impossible: on the afternoon of the 17th the force at Lang-Fan was attacked by 7,000 Imperials, who had evidently received news of the taking of the Taku Forts. Only one course was now open to the Admiral, viz to retire on Tientsin by the road along the left bank of the Pei-Ho. Crossing by junks, the column started the retreat at 4 am on the 18th, carrying half rations for two days in their haversacks. The wounded and stores were towed in junks by captured Boxers.

They marched over very difficult country, numerous villages and irrigation ditches lying in the way; these had to be cleared of Boxers and the exposed left flank was threatened by masses of cavalry and horse artillery. The Royal Marines formed the left flank guard; marching at 4 am they reached camp at 7 pm, having made good little more than six miles. The bivouac the first night was on damp ground and they were tormented by mosquitoes. Marching at 1 am on the 19th, as the ammunition for their field guns was short they were placed in the junks. At 3 am the Royal Marine companies routed a Chinese outpost and found the town they were moving on to be deserted. They were then suddenly challenged, and a heavy fire opened: fortunately the darkness saved them and they replied.

The junk with the guns foundered and others broke adrift, but two gallant seamen swam over and towed them back; only one field gun and 4 machine guns were saved, five of each being lost. The foreign contingents were by now mostly out of ammunition; on the 20th after a severe fight - in which the Flag-Captain Jellicoe was wounded - they captured the town of Pei-Tsang, but they were still ten miles from Tientsin.

Hsi-Ku.
On the 21st they had to pass the fortified Hsi-Ku Arsenal on the opposite bank; it was determined

to try and pass it in the darkness. During the advance the Royal Marines took one village in column of fours, but it caught fire and lit up the country round. The Americans and Germans were leading the column, the British and Russians bringing up the rear. When opposite the arsenal they were challenged and as soon as they replied fire broke out all along the parapet; but luckily the Chinese fired too high. Major Johnstone with the Royal Marines and half a company of Seamen hastened back up the bank and by means of a bridge of junks got across to the arsenal side; cover was available up to 200 yards and the Chinese surprised at seeing this party, deserted the North Wall and the Marines charging over with the bayonet, the Boxers and troops fled; the Germans who were opposite the gate of the arsenal kept down the fire of the Chinese artillery. There was fierce fighting inside the enclosure, made more difficult by the local knowledge of the Chinese of the buildings and enclosures. But after an hour the place was cleared and the Chinese guns, manned by the Allies, were turned on the village nearby. It was 3 pm before all the force had crossed.

The arsenal was about 40 acres in extent with a mud wall 15 feet high and 12 feet broad at the top. The store houses were at the south end, surrounded by a brick wall, which was made the inner line of defence. Guns were mounted, and preparations made to hold the arsenal. At 3 pm General Nieh sent 8,000 regular Chinese troops and 3 field batteries to try and recapture it, but they were driven off after hard fighting. In making arrangements for the defence it was unfortunately considered that the perimeter was too large to be held by their strength and it was decided to hold only the inner line.

The 22nd passed quietly, but on the 23rd the Chinese made a determined attack and charged up to the south-west corner and a party, getting into some long rushes inside the embankment, were discovered by a RM patrol under Lieutenant Beyts RMA, who at once counterattacked them with the bayonet and drove them out. Unfortunately, Lieutenant Beyts and 2 Sergeants were killed. The main attack by 25 Chinese Battalions was beaten off, but ammunition and medical supplies were getting very short; the puggarees of the Marines' helmets being used for bandages.

In the Arsenal were found large quantities of modern field and machine guns, ammunition, medical supplies, and a large quantity of rice.

On the night of the 23rd an attempt was made by 100 Royal Marines under Captains Doig and Lloyd RMLI, to make a way through to Tientsin with a view to obtaining help. They left the arsenal at 9 pm and crossed the river by boat, the idea being that some might at least get through with the information of the plight of the column. They were guided by a railway official; who at first led them in the wrong direction and they had to return to the river. Starting afresh, they had marched three miles when they were fired on, and after returning the fire they captured the position with the bayonet; reaching the railway embankment they were engaged on all sides and bugles sounded the 'Cease Fire'; they found they were in the centre of General Nieh's forces. Tientsin railway station could be seen about 11 miles away and they tried to advance towards it, but fire was opened all round so Captain Doig ordered a retirement which was carried out in square, leaving 5 casualties. They reached the arsenal at 2.30 am, being taken across the river in junks.

Admiral Seymour reported that "the attempt was made with skill and credit", but the strength of the enemy was overpowering. Captain Doig died of enteric fever at Wei-Hai-Wei about a month after the column was relieved.

On the 24th there was a bad sand storm, a well was dug, and the good water was most desirable as they had been drinking the water from the river. This day the defences were rearranged, the British and Germans taking the three most dangerous walls, the Russians the fourth wall. The French and Japanese manned the Inner Line.

They were subjected to long range fire till 10 am when the American and Russians were attacked on the North Wall and had to be reinforced by the British, when the attack fizzled out and the Chinese contented themselves with sniping. Up to this time the British losses were 27 killed and 97 wounded.

Tientsin.
Leaving Admiral Seymour's column temporarily in safety in the arsenal, it is necessary to trace the events that had been taking place at Tientsin. By the 11th June trade had ceased in the settlements and on that day a reinforcement of Seamen and Marines from HMS *Barfleur* under Commander Beatty, viz 2 companies of Seamen with Major V Luke and Sergeant H Armstrong RMLI and 26 RM and two Maxims had reached the place. The RM joined with the remainder of the *Orlando's* RMLI detachment under Lieutenant Carpenter to form one company under Lieutenant Armstrong and were quartered in a 'go down' where the seamen of the *Aurora* already were. Preparations were made to put the place into a state of defence, under Captain E H Bayley RN. German and Russian reinforcements were also arriving and were stationed on the left bank of the river. Communication with the Fleets was very precarious, as the Taku Forts were still in Chinese hands and the river was mined.

The foreign settlements on the right bank of the Pei-Ho were surrounded on three sides by a mud wall which also enclosed the native city. It was 12 feet high and broad enough at the top to allow four men to walk abreast. It was continued on the left bank. It enclosed a total area about 6 miles long from north to south and 5 miles from east to west. Four miles north-east of the British settlement was the Pei-Yang Arsenal on the left bank of the river, whilst 12 miles south-west was the Hai-Yuan-Su Arsenal. Six and a half miles to the north was the Hsi-Ku Arsenal where Admiral Seymour had taken refuge. The foreign settlements were two miles south of the Native City, but the railway station from which the railway ran to Peking and Tong-Ku was on the opposite or left bank of the river; here the Russians were quartered. The Native City was surrounded by high walls, it was about 2 000 yards long by 1,400 yards wide and situated at the junction of the Grand Canal with the Pei-Ho River. The ground between the city and settlements is covered with houses and gardens and there is some marshy land to the south of the city.

Large numbers of Chinese troops were seen on 15th June and fires broke out all round the city of Tientsin. On the night of 15t/16th June a great part of the French Settlement was destroyed. Two trains - one manned by the RM under Major Luke and the other with Lieutenant Armstrong and a 3 pdr gun - were sent to patrol the line to Tong-Ku; they went and returned without opposition. Two hundred Russians were sent to garrison a station half way between Tientsin and Taku. On the night of the 16th/17th an attack in force was made by the Boxers who burnt the native suburbs between the Concessions and the city; they were driven off by the Russians and drifted across the front of the British also and they retired at 5 am. On the 17th an armoured train under Lieutenant Field RN, with the Russians drove the Chinese off the line. Heavy shell fire opened on the Concessions as the Chinese were well supplied with artillery, in which the Allies were very deficient. The Chinese had two 4 in. guns south-west of the city, and the Black Fort at the angle of the canal and the river; the Tree Battery with two 15 pdrs; two 3 pdrs. were at the intersection of the canal with the Mud Wall about 200 yards north-east of the railway station. There were also guns in the villages to the south of the city. The Chinese had about 15,000 troops, the Allies about 2,400 with some old 9 pdr ML field guns and a few machine guns. The perimeter to be defended was about five miles long, one-third protected by the Mud Wall, one-third by the river, but one-third had the Chinese houses close up; the Allies' Ammunition supply was also very limited.

Outside the east end of the British positions on the Bund, on the opposite side of the river, stood a number of buildings forming the Military College, where a battery of Krupp guns was established which was causing casualties. The College was held by the Military Cadets. On the 17th, before they could open fire, they were attacked by a party of Royal Marines under Major Luke, supported by some British and German seamen; they stormed the buildings and after some desperate fighting hand to hand in which numbers of Chinese were killed, they were driven out; the guns and buildings were destroyed. The RM had 1 killed and 3 wounded.

The Chinese guns continued the bombardment and on the 10th they attacked the defences thrown up all along the Bund. The 200 Russians at Chin-Liang-Ching station were cut off and the armoured train was sent to relieve them but failed to get through owing to the breaking of the line. As the Russians at the terminal railway station were being hard pressed, two companies of seamen under Commander Beatty were sent to reinforce them and deployed on the Russian left; there were four hours of heavy fighting and the Russian Field Battery was forced to retire; the 9 pdr ML of the *Orlando* however, in spite of losses, turned the scale and at 4 pm when the Russians advanced, the Chinese broke and fled. The RM Company was sent to reinforce the Germans at the Taku Gate who were also being hard pressed.

On the 19th there were attacks and counterattacks, an attempt by 180 seamen under Commander Beatty and 400 Russians to capture two guns on the Mud Wall failed, Beatty and 4 other officers and 13 men being wounded, and the shelling of the Concessions continued. A civilian named Watts rode through to Tong-Ku on the 22nd and informed the Allied Commanders there of the serious state of affairs and asked for reinforcements. On the 20th the bombardment continued, and on the 21st the Hospital at the Club was hit, and the French Settlement shelled, but at last on the 23rd relief arrived.

Taku.

Great events had been taking place at Taku. Alarmed at the stoppage of communication with the forces up the river, the Commanders of the Allied Fleets (in the absence of Sir Frederick Seymour, Admiral Bruce in the *Barfleur* was the senior officer) decided to attack the Taku Forts and summoned the Chinese to evacuate them by midnight on the 16th. As we have seen in 1860 there were four forts, two on each side, and the stretches of mud covered by sea in front of them prevented a landing in front. The severe lesson of 1859 was not forgotten. The large ships had to lie 11½ miles out owing to the bar, and their guns were therefore useless. The forts were armed with modern guns and the river was mined. On the landward side it will be remembered there is a large plain intersected by small canals and irrigation ditches, having in rear the villages of Tong-Ku (the railway terminus) and Taku on the other bank.

There was a small Naval Yard at Taku where four new Chinese destroyers were lying. The ships available for bombardment were HMS *Algerine* (six 4 in QF guns), *Fame*, and *Whiting* TBDs with one 12 pdr and five 6 pdrs each. The *Iltis* (German) with four 1 in guns, *Gilyak*, *Bobre*, and *Korsetz* (Russian), *Lion* (French), *Atago* (Japanese), with a miscellaneous collection of BL guns and the *Monocacy* (American), a wooden sloop with ML guns.

On the 16th June a tug left HMS *Barfleur* with the British portion of the landing party (320 Officers and men; there seem to have been some Marines from Wei-Hai-Wei under Captain Dustan in this party - doubtful) who were told off into companies on the way ashore. The tug went alongside the *Algerine* and transferred her men, and the ship then moved up to her appointed station after dusk; she was the van ship of the line. The *Fame* and *Whiting* went up the river (Lieutenant Keyes RN[319] in command) and seized the four Chinese destroyers at 1.30 am. The bombardment was to have commenced at 1.30 am but at 12.45 am the Chinese opened fire on the *Algerine*, fortunately firing too high, for her decks were crowded. The landing party at once got into the boats and the bombarding ships opened fire.

The bombardment lasted 6 hours, for the first hour of which the landing parties remained alongside, then landed at 2.30 am.

The force consisted of:

British	23 Officers	298 men
Japanese	4 Officers	240 men
Russian	2 Officers	157 men
Italian	1 Officer	24 men
German	3 Officers	130 men
Austrian	2 Officers	20 men

---

319 Now Honorary Colonel, Portsmouth Division RM.

The *Gilyak* used her searchlight and was badly hit. After capturing the Chinese destroyers and taking them to Tong-Ku, the *Fame* and *Whiting*, joined the line.

The landing party commanded by Commander Craddock RN (Alacrity) attacked the north-west fort (the one attacked in 1860). The British, Japanese and Italians in the front line, the Germans, Austrians, and Russians in support and reserve. They advanced 1,300 yards to within 30 yards of the moats on the north front, then swung to the right and charged along the military road. The fort had suffered very slightly from the bombardment and they waited till daylight at 4 am. The fire of the ships, especially the *Algerine*, was very accurate and the magazine of the south fort exploded. In the north-west fort the Chinese fought their guns very pluckily. By 4.30 its guns were silenced and the stormers advanced and carried the north-west corner of the fort: after advancing over a hard mud flat with no cover. There had been crowding to get on the road where they suffered casualties. After rushing the west gate, they gained the outer fort and the enemy fled to Peh-Tang; it was some minutes before the Inner Fort (i.e. the old Cavaliers) was gained and the flags hoisted.

The North and South Forts opened fire on the Inner Fort, but the attackers brought the captured guns into action and as the fire from the North Fort diminished, they made their way along the covered way between the forts. A shell from the *Algerine* exploded the 6 in magazine of the North Fort, but the Chinese maintained their fire, the *Iltis* suffering heavily, until the Chinese lost heart and the Germans entered by one gate and the British by the landside embrasures.

A 6in QF gun in the South Fort continued its resistance but was eventually silenced by the gunboats and guns of the North Fort after a hard fight. Boats were procured, and parties crossed to the right bank and secured the South and New Forts; the guns in the latter would not bear it and surrendered. By 7 am the parties, after garrisoning the Forts, returned to their ships. The Allies lost about 172, mostly wounded. The British garrisoned the North-West Fort and made new magazines.

This action had serious repercussions on the campaign, as it brought in the Chinese Imperial Regular troops who had not up to this time supported the Boxers. Unfortunately, a small fort up the river still remained in the enemy hands and obstructed communication with Tientsin. Tong-Ku became the shore base (Captain Warrender RN was Base Commandant) but matters appear to have been rather chaotic.

On the 21st, HMS *Terrible* arrived, bringing 300 Royal Welsh Fusiliers and 40 RE with Brigadier-General Dorward from Hong Kong; she also had four 12 pdr guns mounted on extemporised field carriages ready for landing.

A Relief Column was at once organised at Tong-Ku, consisting of:

1,200 Russians (General Stoessel)
30 Italian Seamen

150 American Marines
300 Royal Welsh Fusiliers
British Naval Brigade under Commander Craddock, RN
50 Seamen (*Terrible*) with one 12 pdr gun
100 Seamen: various ships.
50 RMLI Captain Mullins (*Terrible*)
50 Royal Marines (*Barfleur*) under Lieutenant Lawrie (*Terrible*)

For some unexplained reason in spite of the urgent need of artillery, Admiral Bruce only allowed one 12 pdr to accompany the force; the others had to be sent up later.

When eighteen miles from Tientsin the engine and some carriages were derailed. The night was spent at Chin-Liang-Ching held by the Russians; an attempt by a small force of Russians and Americans to reach Tientsin was repulsed. On the 22nd they cleared the neighbouring villages and the train advanced six miles; they were reinforced by two 6 pdr QF guns and on the night of the 22th/23rd, part of the 1st Chinese Regiment from Wei-Hai-Wei, and the *Terrible's* 12 pdr joined them. Starting at 3 am leaving the gun and their heavy gear with 50 men to guard the camp, the British and Italians with the Americans advanced on the left of the railway embankment with their left flank on the river, the Russians and Germans with a six gun battery advancing on the other side of the railway. They were checked opposite the Pei-Yang Arsenal. The Germans and Russians tried to take it but failed and were driven over the railway, but this covered the flank of the other contingents whilst clearing the villages; the Red Ensign was seen on Tientsin Town Hall, so the villages were burnt, and the pursuit continued up to the Military College, where they crossed the river on a raft of logs and the Settlements were relieved. The Russians remained on the left bank. The 12 pdr gun with some of the Hong-Kong Regiment (Pathans) arrived shortly after.

On the night of the 23rd/24th a signal was got through from the top of the Gordon Hall to Admiral Seymour at Hsi-Ku and again on the night of 24th/25th.

The first duty was to send out a relief column to bring in Admiral Seymour's column. It consisted of 1,000 Russians with 2 Maxims, 600 British (including the Royal Marines under Major Luke, who had been formed into 3 Companies under Captain Mullins and Lieutenants Dustan and Armstrong; and the Royal Welsh Fusiliers) and 300 other Allies under the command of Colonel Shirinsky (Russian). On the evening of the 24th the Naval 12 pdr set Hai-Kuan-Su Arsenal on fire; the column started at 11.30 pm on the 24th, rendezvousing at 1 am on the 25th. At first, they missed the bridge over the Lutai Canal, but crossed by means of sampans and planks placed on the ruined bridge under fire from the forts; advancing up the left bank of the Pei-Ho, they arrived opposite the arsenal. As they approached, Admiral Seymour shelled the city and forts with the guns of Hsi-Ku Arsenal and the relief was effected. The Marines of the relieving column drew up in line and sounded the Admiral's Salute. The wounded were transferred across the river under continuous shell fire and a small attack of the Chinese was driven off. At 2.30 pm on the 26th the whole force retired. The arsenal was set on fire, but they failed to destroy the heavy gun ammunition and the field guns. They reached Tientsin railway station at 11 am on the 26th.

Before any attempt could be made to relieve the Legations at Peking, it was necessary to clear the ground round Tientsin.

The first objective selected was the Pei Yang Arsenal on the left bank of the river about 2½ miles North-East of the Concessions. The Russians commenced the attack at 10 am on the 27th, but very soon needed reinforcement. Six companies of seamen under Commander Craddock and six companies of Marines under Major Johnstone with two companies of the Wei-Hai-Wei Regiment with 50 American Marines crossed the bridge; the RM were in their shirt sleeves, but only the *Terrible's* were in khaki. The *Barfleur's* were actually in white uniform. They prolonged the Russian left, the advance was resumed under heavy fire covered by the fire of the *Terrible's* 12 pdr. At 11 am the main magazine was hit and exploded. As the attack advanced the seamen and Marines wheeled to the right so as to be nearly at right angles to the attacking line; the Chinese after letting off a lot of crackers dispersed in a disorganised mob, suffering great loss from the fire of the Marines. Four thousand Boxers however attacked the left of the British in rear, but were met by the Chinese Regiment in support, who drove them back. The RM casualties were 2 Marines killed, 1 Sergeant and 1 Marine wounded. The seamen had 5 killed and 19 wounded.

On the 30th there was desperate fighting at the railway station held at that time by the Russians.

Reinforcements continued to arrive for both sides, including RM from Wei-Hai-Wei. On 1st July the British and Russians made a reconnaissance in force and discovered that the Chinese artillery had been greatly reinforced. On 2nd July the British HQ Barracks caught fire and on the 3rd the attack was renewed, so the women and children were evacuated to Taku.

The Chinese attacked the railway station but were driven off by the *Terrible's* 12 pdr and the French and Japanese artillery. The Russians declined to hold the station any longer, and it was occupied on the 4th by Captain Mullins and 50 RMLI from HMS *Terrible*, with 50 men of the Hong Kong Regiment and some details of French and Japanese. About 3 pm the Chinese launched a fierce attack on them, in which they got to within 100 yards of the buildings; strong reinforcements were sent up, when the enemy were driven off with severe loss. The *Terrible's* detachment had 4 men wounded. The little force had fired not less than 100 rounds per man.

On 5th July two 4 in guns from the *Algerine* and *Phoenix* were mounted and manned by *Terrible's* seamen at Pei-Yang; on the 6th the Allies bombarded the Native City with 25 guns; the Royal Marines manning two 15 pdr Krupp guns that had been captured, when the breech of one blew out, wounding Captain Mullins and two men. The Native City was much damaged. The bombardment was repeated on the 7th.

On 9th July a sortie was made to capture the Hai-Kuan-Su Arsenal by 2,200 British, Japanese, and Russians; the RM were under Major Luke. Issuing from the Taku Gate in the Mud Wall at

2.30 pm, they made for the race-course; the Japanese guns shelled the enemy out of their trenches, and they were driven across the plain pursued by Japanese cavalry; some guns were found in the village. The Allies changed front to the right and covered by shell fire from the Japanese and an Indian mountain battery, the British and Japanese made a frontal attack and the American Marines under Major Waller made a flank attack which carried the arsenal at 10 am, the Chinese offering but slight resistance.

On the 10th a fierce attack was made on the railway station held by the *Terrible's* Marines, who made a most gallant defence; the seamen of *Barfleur* and a company of the Hong-Kong Regiment were sent to support them; when they arrived, the Chinese were within 30 yards of the Royal Marines. The Chinese then retired, losing heavily when they got into the open, but they replied with such heavy artillery fire that at dawn on the 11th the Allies had to leave the locomotive shed and take shelter in the engine pits and content themselves with holding the trenches etc round the platforms. When a company of Sikhs arrived in relief, they drove the Chinese from the railway trenches round which the enemy had taken cover.

On 12th July Admiral Seymour returned to his ship, taking with him the seamen and Major Johnstone with the Marines of the *Centurion*.

It was now necessary to attack the Native City, which was held by 12,000 regular Chinese troops and about 10,000 Boxers.

Hsi-Ku Arsenal had been re-occupied by General Ma's troops.

The Allies had about 6,000 men (710 British, 900 American, 1,500 Japanese, 45 Austrians, 900 French, the remainder Russians and Germans). The Royal Marines, commanded by Major Luke RMLI, consisted of 4 companies - *Barfleur* and *Orlando* (Lieutenant Armstrong), *Terrible* (Captain Mullins, Lieutenant Lawrie), Wei-Hai-Wei (Captain Harris, Lieutenant Dustan), *Aurora* and *Endymion* (Captain Lloyd).

Leaving the Taku Gate, with the British leading, they circled round by the racecourse where the position was untenanted, and then formed into 5 columns, the RM with the Naval Brigade and Royal Welsh Fusiliers forming the left column, and advanced on the arsenal. After an artillery bombardment, the Japanese occupied the Arsenal, meeting with only slight resistance. On issuing from the arsenal, they were met by heavy fire which checked the advance; the RM and RN who were in support, whilst lying down in the open, had some casualties and Captain Lloyd RMLI was killed. After a time, the advance was resumed to attack the South Gate of the city, the Japanese on the left, the Americans on right of the line, the British in support. The road from the arsenal was held by the French and Japanese. As they advanced a terrific explosion of dynamite occurred on the other side of the City.

On a report that the Japanese were in the city, the Royal Marines and one company of seamen went up the road, which was a causeway about 1,200 yards long and 15 feet wide, with a canal on both sides; one company of seamen was sent to reinforce the Americans opposite the south-east corner of the city. The *Terrible's* RM Company who were in khaki and so escaped casualties which fell on the others, led in single file followed by the others. About half way there were some huts in which they halted under enfilade fire, and then gained some houses which were put into a state of defence, when some more Allied troops came up. The night was spent there, the *Terrible's* 12 pdrs covering them by their fire. The Royal Welsh Fusiliers were protecting the left flank; after dark the Americans and the Seamen Company fell back to the Arsenal.

The Japanese recommenced the attack on the suburbs and the South Gate was blown in at 2.30 am. The British rushed in and occupied the South Wall, the *Terrible's* RM were sent along the wall to the westward to fight their way round to the gate on the other side of the City, which they accomplished and were relieved at 5 pm by a company of the Wei-Hai-Wei Regiment. After the Japanese had captured the city, the French cleared the villages on the north side of Boxers and the Japanese helped the Russians to take the city forts and batteries on the east of the city. There were about 775 Allied casualties.

Indian troops were now arriving for the British - cavalry, artillery, and infantry - whilst reinforcements for all nations also arrived. Field Marshal von Waldersee (Germany) was appointed to the Chief Command but did not arrive till long afterwards. General Sir Alfred Gaselee was in command of the British. In consequence of the arrival of the troops the British Naval Brigades were withdrawn to their ships on 21st July for rest and refreshment, and preparations were made for the relief of the Legations. A Naval Battery was formed and on 31st July a small Battalion of Royal Marines was formed to accompany the relief column, commanded by Major Luke, Lieutenant C L Mayhew Adjutant. The Company Commanders were Captains Harris, Mullins, Lieutenants Dustan and H Armstrong, and Lieutenant Harmar.

Our sister Corps, the US Marines, who were clothed in khaki, solved the difficulty of our men being clothed in white by providing them with the necessary khaki garments.

Peking.
In the Legations at Peking the month of July was productive of some fierce fighting and heavy casualties.

A strong attack was made on the Japanese in the Fu and a Krupp gun was brought into action; a combined sortie under the Italian Officer was made. Unfortunately, the party lost their way and lost 3 men killed, and the officer and 1 man wounded. The next day in spite of a desperate resistance the Japanese under Colonel Shiba were driven further back. The Chinese had been making approaches to the City Wall and created a tower to command the American barricade which it was necessary to clear away; a sortie commanded by Captain Myers USMC with Sergeant Murphy, Corporal Gregory and 26 Royal Marines and 15 US Marines and 15 Russians was made, the British and Americans attacking on the left, the Russians on the right. The Chinese were surprised and driven from their barricade with loss; this barricade was strengthened and held.

On 5th July the British Legation was subjected to a bombardment from smooth bore 14 and 7 pdrs to the northward, fortunately receiving little damage. The Japanese were however being severely pressed in the Fu, whilst the Austrian and Italian men, shaken by the loss of their officers, were proving rather unreliable. An old British gun was found in the Legation Street and proved capable of firing Russian ammunition; it was mounted on an Italian carriage and proved very useful.

On 10th July, Captain Wray was sent over to command the British and Italians who were holding the left portion of the entrenchments in the Fu. On the 13th the Chinese sprang a mine under the French Legation, and the French and Austrians were driven back to an inner line which they held tenaciously. The Chinese who had effected an entrance into the Club near the German Legation were thrown out by the Germans. A mine also was dug under the British Legation, but they were evidently diverted by the British countermining.

On 14th July, Corporal Preston RMLI gained the Conspicuous Gallantry Medal for the following gallant act: After the enemy had been driven from their barricade on the Imperial Carriage Park Wall, near the West Hanlin by shell fire, this NCO climbed on the wall some 12 feet high, with the intention of capturing a banner left on the barricade by the enemy. Finding that he could not reach it, he called for his rifle to be given to him and pushing down part of the barricade kept the enemy - some fifty in number at bay, while an American gunner named Mitchell was enabled to lay hold of the flag. Corporal Preston, then jumped down and assisted Mitchell in drawing the flag over with difficulty, as the enemy had laid hold of the other end. He was struck on the head at the same time by a brick which partially stunned him.

On 15th May the enemy succeeded in making a strong attack on the north-west corner of the Fu and had battered down the barricade, which however was rebuilt during the night. At 7 am on the 16th Captain Strouts RMLI with Colonel Shiba and Doctor Morrison was making his rounds when crossing a dangerous place Captain Strouts was mortally wounded in the thigh and died soon after, a victim to shock and fatigue; an irreparable loss to the besieged.

From this date to the date of the departure of the relieving column from Tientsin, with the exception of sniping the guards had to meet no real attacks, but on 19th July the Chinese began a barricade and sniping near Fort Halliday (an improvised caponier in front of the main gate). Firing recommenced vigorously on 5th August and again on the 8th and 9th, and attacks defeated by the Allied machine guns were made.

At 8 am on the 14th the shells of the relieving force were seen to be bursting over the eastern gate of the Tartar City, and that afternoon General Gaselee and his staff appeared, having come via the Chinese City through the Water Gate in the Tartar City Wall to the south of the Legations. The besieged at once assumed the offensive, the Russians and Americans advanced to the Chien Men Gate and let in the 1st Sikhs and Hong-Kong Artillery. The British Marines and Volunteers under

Captain Poole occupied the Carriage Park, the Japanese and Italians cleared the Chinese out of the Fu, whilst the Germans drove back the enemy to the Hata Men Gate.

The relief was thus effected after two months' siege.

It remains to tell of the movements of the relieving column. The Allied Forces, now comprising all arms, the British contingent consisting mostly of Indian troops but including the Naval Brigade with heavy guns, and the small RM Battalion, left Tientsin on 3rd August.

On 7th August was fought the battle of Yangtsun, which cleared the way. On the 8th they marched to Tsi-Tsun; there was no fighting, but it was very hot and the RM suffered terribly, two men dying of sunstroke. The enemy had retired to Ho-Si-Woo (which evokes memories of 1860). On the 9th the Naval guns and Royal Marines marched 5 miles to take up a position, but the Chinese had departed and Ho-Si-Woo was occupied at 4.30 pm Captain Mullins with 50 RM, a troop of Indian Cavalry, G Company 9th US Infantry, 300 Russians, 140 Japanese and 30 Germans, were left to hold this post, which was very important. The banks of the river had been tampered with by the Chinese, which fortunately was discovered in time.

On the 10th the Japanese reached Matao; the Naval guns going by river had to travel 30 miles, the land distance being 8 miles. At 4 pm the force pushed on to Shai-Matao. At 3.30 am on the 11th they started for Tung-Chow; before which occurred a short engagement.

On the 12th the Allies formed for attack; at 1 am the Japanese blew in the South Gate and marched into the town; this day was a rest day. On the 13th was made the final march and they halted 3 miles from the walls of Peking. On the 14th the Russians entered by the Tung-Pin Gate and were reinforced by the Americans at daylight. A sortie in the centre was beaten back by the Japanese, and after a heavy engagement the Japanese entered the City, blowing up two forts. The British as related had entered by the Shan-Huo Gate unopposed. A small party of officers and men, with whom was Lieutenant Harmer and 4 Marines, who had come up by river, followed the Japanese and entered with them, reaching the Legations at 7 am. The RM Battalion entered not long after.

On the 15th there was hard fighting, falling chiefly on the Americans who occupied the approaches of the palace. The RM Battalion with some Indian troops and 500 Russians were detailed to relieve the French and native Christians who had been bravely defending the Peitang Cathedral. The Royal Marines were ordered to assault one of the large gates on the inner wall, Captain Harris' Company advancing along the top of the wall and one company on either side. They advanced covered by a French battery; when they reached the gate, the Chinese fled. Captain Harris' Company was detailed to hold the gate, the other two with the Russians went on and encamped outside the Palace grounds. On the 18th the Royal Marines and the Russians entered the Palace grounds and encamped at Coal Hill. From now on they supplied Officers' Guards for the Palace and parties for organised looting; the loot was to be taken to a central loot committee for division, but never was.

On 21st August the RM Battalion assisted the French to clear their quarter of Boxers, a very terrible business.

On 28th contingents from all nations marched through the Palace and on that day the RM Battalion started to return to Tientsin by river, arriving at 10 pm on 4th September. They returned to their ships on 7th September. Just after they returned 400 RM under Major Kappey RMA, arrived from England in SS *Jelunga* and were sent to garrison the north-west forts at Taku where they remained until July 1901. During the campaign detachments of Royal Marines had been landed at various places in China such as Shan-Hai-Kwan etc, to protect British subjects and interests.

Besides the VC awarded to Captain Halliday and the CGM to Corporal Preston, Captain F Wray received a Brevet Majority; Sergeant Murphy, Corporals Gowney, Preston, and Gregory received the DCM and all members of the Legation Guard were granted six months' service towards pension or retirement.

Majors Johnstone and Luke RMLI were promoted to Lieutenant Colonel in the Gazette of 9 November 1901, Lieutenant Armstrong RMLI was specially promoted to Captain, and Captain Dustan mentioned in dispatches. Majors Luke and Johnstone were subsequently awarded the CB

The casualties at Peking were Captain Strouts killed, Captains Halliday and Wray wounded; 2 NCOs and Men killed, 20 wounded. The casualties at Tientsin and in the relieving columns were Captain Lloyd, RMLI killed; Captain Doig, RMLI, died of fever.

In conclusion we may quote Sir Claude Macdonald's Report on the Legation Guard and also Queen Victoria's telegram to Major Wray.

"They were exposed day and night for two months to the most arduous, irksome and responsible duties, which they fulfilled with a cheerful alacrity and with a courage and endurance which excited the admiration of everybody. Their bearing under fire was quite excellent and could not have been surpassed by the best veteran soldiers. During the entire siege I did not observe the slightest signs of liquor in any of the men, neither was a case reported to me and this though the facility for obtaining drink was great. To sum up, the general good conduct, soldierly bearing, and steadiness under fire of the men of the detachment was worthy of the highest traditions of the British Army and the Corps to which they belong. This high state of excellence was undoubtedly in a great measure due to the Officers and Non-Commissioned Officers. Captain Strouts was an excellent soldier and a gallant gentleman. He was killed in the defence of the Legation on 16th July and his loss to me and to the defence generally was irreparable. Had Captain Strouts lived I should certainly have recommended him to the Lords of the Admiralty through Your Excellency for promotion or for the Distinguished Service Order."

Telegram from HM The Queen.

"I thank God that you and those under your command are rescued from your perilous situation. With my people I have waited with the deepest anxiety for the good news of your safety and a happy termination of your heroic and prolonged defence. I grieve for the losses and sufferings experienced by the besieged.
VRI"

1901

The numbers voted wave 19,800.

On 2nd January, HRH the Duke of York, now His Majesty King George V, was made Colonel-in-Chief of the Royal Marine Forces, an office which he graciously continued to hold on his accession to the throne in 1910.

On the 26th February he sailed in the *Ophir* for a tour of the Dominions and Colonies, returning in November. A special RM detachment under the command of Major C Clarke was embarked; also the Band of the Chatham Division RMLI, which in commemoration of their services was granted the 'White Rose of York' to be worn on their helmets and caps.

At the end of the year a change was made that affected the NCOs of the Corps a great deal; all Active Service Recruiters who had performed the duty since 1755 were withdrawn and replaced by pensioners, who received 2/- a day pay and levy money with their pension, free uniform clothing: this followed on the abolition of the Active Service Officers.[320]

On the evening of 22nd January HM Queen Victoria died at Osborne, Isle of Wight, and for a time the world seemed to stand still; it was impossible to realise that that great personality had passed away.

The ceremonies connected with her funeral have been described, but we must put on record the part played by the Corps.

The Band of the Portsmouth Division RMLI, under Lieutenant Miller, played the procession from Osborne to the pier at East Cowes; being relieved at intervals by the Massed Drums of the RMA and RMLI (no bugles or fifes) who played a special funeral march for drums only which had been originally selected by Her Majesty to be played at the funeral of HRH Prince Henry of Battenberg which tore the heartstrings of all who heard it. Those who saw the Royal Yacht bearing the coffin passing through the lines of the Fleet at Spithead and heard the minute guns, will not forget the wonderful gleam of sunlight that bathed the Yacht as she turned and made for the harbour at Portsmouth. The Yacht was berthed in the Victualling Yard at Gosport and

---

320 Order-in-Council 4 November 1901.

immediately a Guard of RMLI under Captain C J Thoroton from Forton was mounted with a sentry with reversed arms at the head of the coffin and one at the foot, and a similar line of sentries on the quayside above the Yacht. They were relieved every half hour as it was a cold and foggy night, and the Guard was inspected at 10 pm by HM King Edward and the German Emperor. The next morning the coffin was placed in the train for London and the Guard dismounted. As the train passed the Drill Field at Forton, the Division was drawn up with the Colours which she had presented to them, draped in crepe, and paid their last salute.

A guard of honour from Chatham Division RMLI was mounted at Paddington Station under Captain E H Morres and paid the last salute as the funeral party left on its last stage to Windsor.

24 - Reorganisation and the Rising Threat 1902 – 1914

The twelve years that followed the close of the South African War were a period of reorganisation of all the British Forces, the raising of new units, the perfecting of mobilisation and other arrangements. In the Royal Navy it was a period of feverish building of new classes of ships. The possibility of war with our old enemy France had passed away, being finally sealed by the Entente Cordiale in 1904, but a new competitor - the German Empire - was rising to the east, threatening our existence in all spheres and evidently bent on world conquest.

Royal Fleet Reserve.
In 1901 the question of reserves for the Fleet on mobilisation and to replace casualties in war was dealt with. Though arrangements had been made in 1863 to make Seamen and Marine pensioners available, this was not considered sufficient and a more trained reserve was now necessary. For this purpose the Royal Fleet Reserve was instituted in 1901 consisting of three classes: Class A of pensioners up to the age of 50; Class B of men who had completed 12 years or less with the colours and who voluntarily joined this Class; Class C Immediate Reserve to consist of men of Class B who voluntarily undertook to come up within 48 hours without waiting for the proclamation calling out the reserves. Classes A and B were required to perform one week's drill a year, Class C one month if required. During drill they received pay and allowances of their rank. Classes B and C received also retainers and on completion of 20 years' service; or attaining the age of 45, a gratuity. Class A were to receive the 5d a day additional Greenwich Pension on attaining the age of 55. All were required to keep a minimum kit, and supplies of arms, equipment and clothing were maintained at Headquarters to fit them up on mobilisation. When war came in 1914 these reserves were invaluable.

Cadet Corps.
In 1900-01 Major Harkness RMA started the RMA Cadet Corps at Eastney for the sons of Non-Commissioned Officers and men of the Corps, an example quickly followed by the Depot Royal Marines, Gosport, Chatham and Plymouth. By November 1903 the Corps at all Divisions were in working order, and have provided many fine soldiers to the Corps.

1902

The number voted were 19,600.

Selborne Scheme.
The year 1902 saw the inauguration of Lord Fisher's reforms of the Navy when as Second Sea Lord he began to deal with the personnel. He was inspired with no friendly feelings for the Corps and in fact is reported to have tried to abolish it.

The first to see the light was that known as the Selborne Scheme, by which boys were entered for training as officers at Osborne at the age of 13 for all the three branches of the Navy - Executive, Engineering, and Marine - and after a common training at Osborne, Dartmouth, and at sea, they were to become specialists in one of the three branches Elaborate scales of pay, relative rank, and training courses were drawn up, but like most of Lord Fisher's schemes the War of 1914-19 dissolved it into thin air. As far as the Corps was concerned, only three officers were obtained from this source and it gave two to the Navy. It is therefore unnecessary to go into the details.

Unfortunately, it had very disastrous repercussions, because entry under the old system ceased after 1907, and with the exception of three Corps Commissions from the Sandhurst and Woolwich lists entry of officers ceased for five years. Alteration of training of the officers entered between 1902 and 1907 was also made; both RMA and RMLI remained at Greenwich for two years and passed all their examinations there, and in the Gunnery Schools together, those passing out at the top of the list being allotted to RMA. At last when matters were becoming desperate it was decided to recommence Direct Entry into the Corps, and the Order-in-Council 9th August 1911 was published, which provided that officers for the Corps should pass in by direct examination; they were granted the same relative rank and rates of pay as in the 1902 scheme and a most rigorous course of Naval and Military training lasting 4½ years, of which six months was spent in a training cruiser, was laid down. Only one batch completed a full course as owing to the War of 1914-18 all training had to be suspended or modified. But as a result of all these experiments the war found the Corps short of over 40 officers. As long as the two branches RMA and RMLI existed officers were allowed to select their branch according to their places on the passing-out list. This last scheme with modifications exists today.

Reviews.
The year 1902 was principally notable for the ceremonies concerned with the coronation of HM King Edward VII. A review was held on Laffans Plain on 13th June which was attended by a Marine Brigade of one Battalion from the RMA and three from the RMLI. Colonel Commandant Pine-Coffin was Brigadier. The Battalions were encamped at Rushmoor Hill, Aldershot, for four days. The weather was very bad, and the infantry had to march past before the cavalry owing to the state of the ground. The RM Brigade which was led past by the Colonel-in-Chief, HRH the Prince of Wales (now HM King George V), followed after the Royal Navy and preceded all the Army troops. Owing to the illness of the King, the salute was taken by Queen Alexandra.

During his convalescence on board the Royal Yacht, the Band of the Portsmouth Division, RMLI was embarked and His Majesty conveyed to them his thanks for their services. He also paid a visit to the Portsmouth Division RMLI at Forton and inspected the Battalion on parade.

The actual coronation took place on 9th August, when a Battalion RMA was stationed in St George's Square, Southwark; they exercised the right of marching through the City with fixed bayonets, Colours flying and bands playing. A composite Battalion RMLI under Lieutenant Colonel H C Money with the Portsmouth Colours lined the streets in Cockspur Street and had considerable difficulty in keeping back the weight of the crowd in the Haymarket. A guard of honour with Colour under Captain A W Wylde RMLI, with band from Chatham was mounted in Trafalgar Square. The RMA Band played at the Admiralty, the Portsmouth RMLI in the grounds of Marlborough House, the Plymouth Band at the War Office in Whitehall, and the Depot Band with the Battalion.

Uniform.
HM King Edward directed many alterations in the uniform of the services and this year the old slashed cuff worn prior to 1870 was restored to the RMLI. The frock coat (double-breasted) with waist sash and a forage cap very similar to 1840 were reintroduced, whilst white belts for officers, sabretaches and some of the horse furniture were abolished. For the men the Brodrick cap replaced the field service cap.

Physical Training.
In consequence of the abolition of masts and yards and the increasing numbers of machines to replace manual labour on board ship, it was realised that it was necessary to introduce some form of physical exercise to be undertaken afloat. A form of Swedish drill was adopted by the Navy and a School of Physical Training started at Portsmouth on 24th March 1902 under a Captain RN. Two Lieutenants RM were attached to the School as well as several NCO instructors; pay was allowed for instructors afloat, so that the extension of the gymnastic training at Deal, which had hitherto followed Army lines, was made general and the new exercises were used at all Headquarters and in ships.

Naval Gunnery.
On 2nd August 1902 there was a revision of the pay granted to Captains of Guns (the present Gunlayers) RMA and also the ratings of Captain and 2nd Captain of Gun were thrown open to the RMLI.

On 11th June an Order-in-Council authorised an increase of pension of £50 a year for each year of service to the DAGRM, the total not to exceed £950.

1903

In 1903 the numbers voted were 19,800.

For some years Intelligence Officers, in connection with the Intelligence Department of the Admiralty, had been allowed in various Coaling Stations overseas; their services had been found so useful that an increased number of appointments were made and an Order-in-Council of 16th February 1903 authorised pay to Naval and Marine Officers holding these appointments.

Reserves and Drafting Officers.
The question of mobilisation and drafting had been engaging attention, and the matter was now placed on sound lines. At each RM Headquarters a senior Major was appointed to superintend

the drafting, to be called the Drafting Officer. He took over the duties of keeping the rosters, drafting and mobilisation arrangements etc which had hitherto been performed by the Staff Officer and Adjutant.

By Order-in-Council 12th March 1903 it was ordered that all officers under the rank of Lieutenant Colonel who retired from the service at their own request on retired pay or gratuity should automatically become liable to recall for service up to the age of 50; also officers who had resigned might apply to join if medically fit and under age. They were placed on a list of Reserve Officers. These provided a most valuable reinforcement to the officer cadre in 1914-18.

Officers' Employment.
With the increasing activities of the Fleet the transfer of officers to the Indian Army, Army Service Corps etc practically ceased, but new openings were being provided. The Intelligence Officers have been mentioned above, but now one of the factors that was to revolutionise the world was making its appearance, to wit, wireless telegraphy. Many RM officers became expert in this new science; at first by Order-in-Council 11th August 1903 RM officers were employed as instructors at the Torpedo Schools and were granted 2/6d a day extra pay and in 1907 they were also employed at sea; by Order-in-Council 21st December 1907 instructors at 2/6 and assistants at 1/- being allowed. Many officers also qualified at the Royal Artillery College for the Army Ordnance Corps.

Naval Gunnery.
By Order-in-Council 10th August 1903 the higher gunnery ratings of Turret Gunlayers and Turret Sight-setters were opened to both RMA and RMLI NCOs. By the Order-in-Council of 16th November the old titles of Captain and 2nd Captain of Gun were dropped and that of Gunlayers and Sightsetters instituted. A new rating of QM for RMLI at 2d a day was created, the qualification being the same as for Seaman Gunner RN and the whole trend of the training both of RMLI and RMA became more and more concentrated on naval gunnery.

RN School of Music.
The question of bands in the Navy was now dealt with. Hitherto they had grown up in a haphazard way, the oldest practice being to engage musicians from the shore for the ship's commission and to discharge them on paying off. This practice served very well in the Mediterranean, where foreign bandsmen were easy to obtain, but it was most unsatisfactory in every respect on other stations, besides being very expensive for the officers who had to pay the whole cost. The Admiralty then entered bandsmen for non-continuous service and later for continuous service and some sort of training was given in the Naval training ships to boys, but men still entered from the shore. The whole cost of instruments and music were borne by the officers of the ships. Lord Fisher took the matter in hand in 1902 and the result was the Order-in-Council 20th May 1903. *"We are of opinion that it is desirable to improve the efficiency of Naval Bands and to reduce the expense which at present falls upon officers of Your Majesty's Naval Service."*

1.) Band Ratings to be enlisted as Royal Marines and form part of HM RM Forces; the total number of the Force being correspondingly increased, existing ratings to be transferred as far as possible.
2.) Pay to be at rates except Boys at 8d a day. Sergeants were called Bandmasters I and II and Chief Bandmasters.

They were granted an Instrument Allowance for care of instruments which became public property.

Training.
A School of Music was established at which all Bandsmen and Band Boys were to undergo a course of training with the following staff: Commandant, a Major RM at 5/- a day; a Musical Director (a Warrant Officer) at £250 a year; an Adjutant and a Quartermaster RM with extra pay. Two Bandmaster Instructors and a Sergeant RM as Schoolmaster.

Major F M B Hobbs RMLI was the First Commandant and the first Musical Director was Mr C Franklin from the Egyptian Army.

It was found at once that the Central School at Eastney was insufficient. The Band Boys and other ranks were therefore distributed to all Divisions, where they were placed under the supervision of the Adjutant and Divisional Bandmaster for instruction; civilians and musicians from the Divisional Bands being employed as instructors and the boys were brought up with the Drummers under the care of the Drum Major.

By Order-in-Council 24th October 1904, the Central School at Eastney was re-organised and rates of extra pay were laid down for the Staff for the Divisional Schools.

Boys were enlisted from 14 to 17 years of age but could not be rated Musicians until they were 18 or if embarked before that age.

The School was not concentrated at Eastney until 1910 when the quarters that had been used originally for married families and later for the RMA Recruit Depot, were handed over to them.

All boys were trained in two instruments, one for military band and the other for string orchestra, whilst the NCOs have to pass a very high examination in music. At first, they were also trained in First Aid so as to act as stretcher bearers, but later it was considered that they would be more useful if trained in the Fire Control Instruments on board ship, which is now the case universally.

This School has now become an integral part of the Corps, imbued with all its traditions.

1904

The numbers voted were 19,000.

This year witnessed the coming into the Fleet of the new type of Dreadnought ship which, heralded with a loud flourish of trumpets, was said to revolutionise the whole of Naval warfare and the Navy proceeded to give itself up to a period of technical and material development to the exclusion of all thought of its strategical use.

Early in the year the old Steam Reserve was abolished.[321] The officers and men returned to barracks and as at the same time a large number of obsolescent ships on foreign stations were paid off the barracks for a short time were full of men. This year's Orders in Council give the numbers as 19,845 and was the last published prior to the War, the Admiralty having decided that the annual issue of this Order-in-Council which had existed ever since 1664 was unnecessary; about this opinions are divided. The numbers within this limit are now fixed in the Annual Parliamentary Estimates; for many years the numbers did not approach this establishment.

Nucleus Crews.
Lord Fisher now produced his scheme of Nucleus Crews, by which with a certain proportion of the battleships and cruisers were kept manned with three-fifths complements of active service men and on mobilisation were to be completed with active service officers and men from the RN and RM Barracks who were undergoing courses; whilst the remainder known as the Third and Fourth Fleets only had one-fifth crews on board to be completed by reservists etc. The Second Fleet carried out all drills and exercises as if fully commissioned and was always completed each year for manoeuvres; the rest of their time was spent at their Home Ports where the RM carried out as much musketry and field training as possible.

Revue.
On 17th March Their Royal Highnesses the Prince and Princess of Wales visited the RMA and Portsmouth Division RMLI and made a short inspection.

In 1904 war broke out between Russia and Japan which kept the China Squadron on the qui vive and the number of ships was increased. The Russian Fleet from Europe on its way from the Baltic, when crossing the Dogger Bank on 22nd October opened fire on the British trawlers fishing there, which caused serious diplomatic disturbance and a Special Service Squadron was commissioned, but nothing came of the incident.

Somaliland.
The Colonial Forces had been contending with the Mullah in Somaliland for some time, and in order to prevent his obtaining supplies of arms etc it was decided to attack Illig, his chief seaport. Illig was situated about 3½ miles south of the Gullule River and consisted of an upper and lower

---
321 See page 432.

village situated on hilly ground with caves: the lower village was strongly fortified, zerebas and embrasures had been constructed and covered the entrance to the caves over the whole face of the cliff. HMS *Hyacinth*, *Fox*, and *Mohawk* bringing 125 of 1st Bn Hampshire Regiment arrived off the mouth of the Gullule River on 20th April.

The landing place was a strip of beach where the cliffs on either side were precipitous and 300 feet high. The advanced party of 162 seamen under Captain Hood and 43 RMLI under Major Kennedy landed to find a road; the right bank was found impracticable but on the left bank after a steep climb they reached the top of the height and extended to wait for the main body. This consisted of 327 seamen with 4 Maxims and 51 RMLI (under Lieutenant Colley) and 125 1st Bn Hampshire Regiment. Owing to the surf the landing was very dangerous and they were all wet through. As soon as they had formed they advanced, 3 companies of seamen on the right and the RMLI in the centre, the Hampshires on the left with 3 companies of seamen in reserve. After sighting the enemy, who opened a heavy fire, they advanced by rushes and when at 75 yards charged and soon took the upper village, losing 3 seamen killed and 6 wounded. After a short rest they were ordered to clear the lower village which, owing to the desperate men taking refuge in the caves and sniping from them, proved to be a very dangerous business. It was some time before fire ceased. One Private was wounded, Corporal Flowers was specially mentioned for gallantry as he dashed through a burning hut to the cave behind and succeeded with Captain Hood RN and Midshipman Onslow in dispatching the four occupants who refused to surrender. He was awarded the Conspicuous Gallantry Medal.

After the capture Lieutenant Colley and 50 RM were left to assist the Hampshire Regiment to build a zereba to prevent the Mullah reoccupying the place. Next day the *Fox* shelled parties of the enemy who were approaching and dispersed them. The parties remained on shore till 26th April, blowing up the towers and walls etc. The re-embarkation owing to the surf was very difficult but was carried out without loss.

Pay and Rations.
The Order-in-Council 7th March 1904 made some long overdue concessions. Dealing first with the rations. The stoppage of 7d a day for bread, meat, and groceries modified in 1899 for men ashore was abolished; issues of bread and meat were in future to be free, but the stoppage of 2½d a day for vegetables and groceries remained in a way, as an allowance of 2½d a day per man was allowed for purchase of these articles, the money being drawn and expended by Captains of Companies; there was a proviso also that a man must have completed training or attained the age of nineteen. These concessions were a very great boon and enabled the food of NCOs and men to be much improved.

There was also a very substantial increase of pay, but this was given in a very wise manner and not in the haphazard methods of 1919.

1. NCOs as well as men were allowed to receive 1d per day for each badge.

2. 2d a day was granted to all WOs and NCOs and men who attained certain standards in field training, gunnery, and musketry provided they had 18 months service or embarked before that time. This allowance was forfeited if they failed to requalify after three years. It was known as EA (Efficiency Allowance).
3. 1d a day to all who qualified as First-Class Shots or above, which was known as GSA (Good Shooting Allowance).

For Bandsmen and Buglers EA and MPA were allowed for special qualifications.

These allowances led to the introduction of the well-known Drill History Sheets and also to a great improvement in the standard of training.

A further concession was made to WOs and NCOs that they were allowed to count 'lance' time towards pension if subsequently promoted to substantive rank.

One result of these reforms was that the curious ¼d a day hitherto included in the pay of Gunners and Buglers RMA disappeared.

Clothing.
A Clothing Committee was also held this year under the presidency of Lieutenant Colonel Bor RMA which made considerable alterations in the patterns, scales of issue etc for NCOs and men.[322] The main effect on the appearance of the Corps was the abolition of the red kersey of the RMLI which had hitherto been used for all drills, duties and walking out, and the substitution of a plain blue frock. White cap covers were introduced for all ranks, the RMA lost their pill box cap; and brown canvas leggings, the curse of the Corps for the next generation, were introduced in place of the black leather which had superseded the old spatterdashes.

Tattoos.
For some years Torchlight Tattoos had been held at practically all Divisions in aid of the various Divisional charities, the initiative having been taken by Captain and Adjutant Luard and Lieutenant Colonel Johnstone RMLI at Portsmouth; in this year a departure was made by the RMLI at Portsmouth to celebrate the 100th Anniversary of the taking of Gibraltar, when a display of Trooping the Colour in the uniforms and with the drill of that date was given, this being the first of those displays that have since become so popular.

1905

In 1905 the numbers were 18,266.

In 1904 the Entente Cordiale with France had been ratified and to further cement the bonds of

---

322 Vide Order-in-Council 14 November 1904.

friendship in the summer of 1905 the French Fleet visited Portsmouth where it was received and entertained by the British Fleet. Among the other events the Royal Marines at Eastney and Forton gave sports and entertainments for the amusement of the visitors.

Review.
In the summer of this year a Brigade of one Battalion RMA and one of RMLI (from Portsmouth) attended a Review held in honour of the King of Spain on Laffan's Plain at Aldershot.

In November HMS *Renown* was specially commissioned to convey Their Royal Highnesses the Prince and Princess of Wales to India to hold a Durbar on behalf of HM the King. Major H S N White with a specially picked detachment were embarked, returning to England early in 1906.

1906

1906 - The numbers voted were 17,000.

Recruiting.
An anomaly which had long intrigued the Royal Navy was swept away by Order-in-Council 8th January 1906. The fee fixed on 3rd December 1883 for raising a Royal Marine recruit was £1, whilst for a Naval recruit it was only 5/-. In future it was ordered that the fee for both services should be 10/-.

HMS *Indefatigable*.
In 1906 in consequence of the concentration of the squadron in Home Waters and also the withdrawal of the regiments from the West Indies, it was felt that a mobile landing force was necessary in the event of local disturbances. For this purpose, the 2nd Class Cruiser *Indefatigable* was especially commissioned on 9th January and the experiment was made of giving her only sufficient seamen to work helm and lead and a few other similar duties, and also a full engine-room complement, all the rest of the crew being RMLI under Major Chown, Captain Dalton and two subalterns. The Royal Marines provided all duties, boats' crews etc, whilst the officers did Officer of the Watch both at sea and in harbour, cable duties etc. The experiment proved most successful and was continued till the outbreak of War in 1914.

Physical Training.
In view of the increasing importance of physical training, RM instructors were granted pay at 6d a day for seven days a week instead of only being paid for days on which employed.

1907

1907 - The numbers voted were 17,426.

The Fleet which had been increasing in size was now principally concentrated in Home Waters and the Mediterranean. After the spring manoeuvres off the coast of Portugal in which both Fleets were engaged, the Home Fleet was re-organised into six Battle Squadrons of 8 ships each, and six Cruiser Squadrons of 6 ships each.

In this year occurred the tercentenary of the founding of the colony of Virginia USA. Celebrations were held in Hampton Roads which were attended by the 1st Cruiser Squadron from England.

Non-Commissioned Officers. A reorganisation of the Petty Officers of the Navy in August 1907, which abolished the rating of Petty Officer 2nd Class, caused a certain amount of difficulty for the Royal Marines as their relative rank was Corporal, a substantive NCO, whilst the leading seaman who took their places was only an acting rank.

1908

In 1908 the numbers voted were 17,426.

In the spring of the years up to the war of 1914, the Fleet usually carried out cruises and exercises with the Mediterranean Fleet off the coasts of Spain and Portugal; whilst a larger mobilisation of nucleus crew ships and sometimes of the Third and Fourth Fleets took place in the summer, when various strategical problems were worked out.

Training.
Training at Headquarters continued on intensive lines, the greater part of the time being taken up by naval gunnery. In this year the now well-known terms GL I, GL II, and GL III, took the place of the various Gunlaying and Sightsetting ratings.

On 1st August an increase of pay was granted to Captains RM, the amounts being:

After 11 years to receive	RMA	15/1
	RMLI	14/7
After 14 years to receive	RMA	15/7
	RMLI	15/1

Gunlayers Tests.
During those years the Corps was earning a great reputation in the Gunlayers Tests, carrying off the prizes in all classes of ships. About this time owing to the expansion of the Fleet it was laid down that the RM Artillery were only to be embarked in ships carrying more than 4 power worked guns and in flagships on foreign stations, which resulted in the RMLI being placed in charge of turrets in some of the older classes of ships.

1909

1909 - The numbers were 16,000.

By Order-in-Council 11th August the old list of Reserve Colonels,[323] was re-established, by which Colonels Commandant on completion of their term of command could be placed on a special list and be eligible for selection for DAGRM

Brevet Rank. Another Order-in-Council on 22nd November regularised a matter about Brevets providing that officers of the Corps whether RMA or RMLI when employed on the duties of the Corps when holding brevet rank for length of service took precedence according to their substantive rank in the Corps. It is curious that this matter had arisen in 1766 and been similarly settled.

1910

In 1910 the numbers were 15,800.

On 6th May this year occurred the lamented death of HM King Edward VII, and our Colonel-in-Chief HM King George V ascended the Throne and was graciously pleased to continue as our Colonel-in-Chief.

The Corps took the following part in the funeral arrangement. On 17th May the coffin was taken to Westminster Hall; a Guard of Honour with Colour under Captain W T C Jones DSO from Chatham Division being mounted at Westminster Hall and a composite battalion of RMA and RMLI under Lieutenant Colonel A Orford RMA lining the streets in Whitehall. On 20th May, the day of the funeral, a Guard of Honour RMA under Captain Troup was mounted at Paddington Station; in the actual procession were 100 RMA under Captain J Brough, and 100 RMLI under Major Lywood from Portsmouth. Lining Whitehall under Brigadier General L T Pease was No 1 Battalion, Lieutenant Colonel H L Talbot, 300 RMA and 300 RMLI Chatham and No 2 Battalion, Lieutenant Colonel Roe, 400 RMLI Portsmouth and 200 RMLI Plymouth. The Chatham RMLI Band was among the massed bands in the procession.

Arms and Equipment.
The Corps was re-armed with the short Lee-Enfield rifle and long bayonet. Also, with a new pattern of web equipment. For reasons of economy these were at first issued only to detachments embarked in certain ships, so that considerable time elapsed before all the Corps was so equipped, and in fact when war broke out in 1914 there was only the Slade-Wallace equipment available for the reserves.

Musicians.
A great concession was made to the Musicians in the Divisional Bands by Order-in-Council 10th January 1910, whereby they were allowed to count all service above five years on the establishment as Corporal's time for the purposes of pension, and this privilege was extended to Privates and Buglers of the Bands on 4th June 1914.

---

323 Established in 1870 but abolished in 1878.

RM Gunners.
In consequence of the increasing employment of Royal Marines in the turrets of battleships, it was decided that a rank of Warrant Officer, called Gunnery Sergeant Major and later RM Gunner, who would be responsible for the working of the ammunition supply etc under the Officer of the Turret, should be introduced. These were specially selected from the younger sergeants with gunnery qualifications who were put through a special course in HMS *Excellent*, and on passing were given the rank of Warrant Officer with the same status as Naval Warrant Officers, i.e. above the usual Marine Warrant Officer and with the same pay as Gunners WO RN with gunnery allowance of 1/6 and 1/- a day. They were however pensioned on the RM scales plus 6d a day. Between embarkations they were borne in the local Gunnery Schools. The rank caused a great deal of heart burning and was never very satisfactory, though most excellent men came forward and received promotion in due course.[324] The title was changed by Order-in-Council 29th February 1912 and after 1918 (when the status of all RM Warrant Officers was assimilated to that of Naval Warrant Officers) when not afloat they were borne at Headquarters and utilised for ordinary duty and in the gun batteries; they then became eligible for and received promotion to Lieutenant and Captain RM. The rank was abolished in 1931.

Dubai Persian Gulf.
On 24th December occurred one of the few cases of active service. The East Indian Squadron was constantly on the watch to prevent gun-running in the Persian Gulf into Baluchistan etc. A Naval Brigade from HMS *Hyacinth* under Captain Dick RN, with Major Heriot and Lieutenant Brewer RMLI and 33 NCOs and men were landed at Dubai to search for arms. While so occupied fire was opened from the houses on the search parties and men on the beach; Major Heriot entrenched himself on the beach and the guns of the ship quickly silenced the enemy. One Sergeant and 1 Private were killed, and 4 Privates wounded. Major Heriot was awarded the DSO.

1911

In 1911 the numbers voted were 15,820.

The year was principally occupied in the ceremonies connected with the Coronation of Their Majesties King George and Queen Mary, in which the Corps took part.

Captain Scott's 'Director' which had such an important influence on the gunfire of British ships, was first experimentally fitted to HMS *Neptune* and tried out in the Mediterranean and elsewhere.

Coronation.
For the Coronation ceremonies a very large Fleet was assembled at Spithead and practically denuded Headquarters of officers and men. The result was that on the day of the Coronation, 22nd June, the RMA provided a Guard of Honour at Westminster, whilst a composite Battalion of RMA

---
324 Order-in-Council 7th November 1910.

and RMLI which lined the streets in Whitehall was drawn from the Fleet, under the command of Major Harkness RMA SO RM at Portsmouth. On 23rd June for the procession through the City, the RMLI Portsmouth provided a Guard of Honour with Colour under Captain Filmer-Bennett at St. Paul's, and Headquarters provided a representative detachment under Major St G B Armstrong who took part in the procession. The composite battalion RMA and RMLI was drawn from the Fleet, and which lined Constitution Hill was commanded by Major H E Blumberg RMLI (the Fleet RM Officer). Colonel Commandant Daniell with staff from Chatham was in command of the Marine details on both days.

The following day, the Royal Marines having re-joined their ships during the night and morning, Their Majesties reviewed the Fleet at Spithead and were received with the usual salutes and guards.

The Home Fleet then proceeded to Kingstown, Ireland, for Their Majesties' visit. On 8th July a Naval Brigade lined the roads from Kingstown to Monkstown, the RMA Battalion (Major S Gaitskell) and the RMLI Battalion (Major H E Blumberg) being posted near Monkstown.

On 11th July a Review of the troops was held in Phoenix Park in which a Royal Naval Division took part and furnished a very magnificent sight, there being two Brigades of seamen and a Brigade of two Battalions RM. The RM Bands of the Fleet were massed. (The RM Brigade was commanded by Major S Gaitskell, the Battalions RMA and RMLI by Majors Patterson and Blumberg respectively.) The weather was very hot, the dress being tunics and white trousers. The Battalions marched past in Column of Double Companies; which, as they were formed of the detachments of nearly 100 ships, was a sufficient test of training and discipline.

Agadir.
On 26th July there was a war scare owing to movements in Germany which passed over but was revived in October when occurred what is known as the Agadir crisis between France and Germany which very nearly plunged the world into war and caused the Navy and Marines to take stock of their arrangements. The next two years consequently witnessed many improvements in mobilisation and training arrangements.

India.
In the autumn the SS *Medina* was commissioned to convey the King and Queen to hold the Coronation Durbar at Delhi. A special Guard of Honour of RMA under Captain P Phillips with Lieutenants Tuke and Hutton were embarked with the RMA Band. They accompanied Their Majesties to Delhi. On their return the RMA Band was granted the privilege of wearing a special badge in their helmets and caps.

1912

In 1912 the numbers voted were 16,500.

Recruiting.
On 19th June the title of Inspector of Marine Recruiting was changed to Inspector of Recruiting, as he was now responsible to a certain extent for Naval Recruiting also.

Relative Rank.
By Order-in-Council October 1912 the question of relative rank of Naval and Marine Officers afloat was altered. It had originally been laid down by Order-in-Council 10th February 1747, but in course of time the age of officers had altered, and the position was very anomalous. For officers entered under the 1900 and 1911 schemes the matter had been adjusted, but nothing had been done for those entered prior to that date. As the order said, "Owing to the extended periods served as Lieutenant and Captain and the later ages at which promotion is obtained in Royal Marines, compared with officers of other branches, as well as by the nature of the duties allotted to then while afloat." Therefore, it was ruled that Lieutenants RM over two years' seniority and also Captains should rank with Lieutenants; Majors with Commanders, according to dates of seniority; though very soon modifications were introduced. It only applied afloat.

Pay.
On 16th December 1912 a very welcome increase of pay to the Rank and File was made in the shape of an increase of 3d and 4d to all ranks when afloat only, but the officers' allowance did not come in till the following year.

1913

In 1913 the numbers borne were 16,500.

Promotion from Ranks
With a great flourish provision was made for promotion of Warrant and Non-Commissioned Officers and men to commissioned rank, by Order-in-Council 11th February, though as we have seen this was already by no means unknown in the Marines.

This however provided a chance for younger men who might have a reasonable chance of reaching the higher ranks.

Two commissions were to be awarded each year to men specially selected with the necessary educational and other qualifications and under the age of 23. They were to be appointed to Acting RM Gunners and after undergoing courses in HMS *Excellent* and *Vernon* and a modified musketry course, if qualified, they were granted the rank of 2nd Lieutenant. After further courses at Greenwich and in military subjects and passing for Lieutenant RM, they were embarked as Probationary Lieutenants for six months and if satisfactorily reported on were confirmed as Lieutenants. In 1922 this was modified so that on selection the chosen candidates were promoted to Probationary 2nd Lieutenant and underwent all their courses with officers entered by direct entry.

Provision was also made for promotion to Lieutenant RM of any Warrant Officer, NCO or Private who might perform some specially meritorious service or for distinguished war service. These commissions were in addition to the numerous commissions for Quartermaster and later for those promoted to RM Gunners so that the Corps may be said to have made ample provision for commissions from the ranks even under peace conditions.

Brigadier Generals.
By Order-in-Council 14th October, Colonels Commandant were given the temporary rank of Brigadier General without any increase of pay or emoluments; and the old Office Adjutants who had been entitled Staff Officers in 1891 or 1892 became known as Brigade Majors.

Signalling and Naval Examination Service.
The School of Signalling was also expanded, and a Superintendent appointed at 3/6 a day[325] because the Royal Marines had assumed the responsibility for the Naval Examination Service at the majority of the defended ports at home and abroad, so that it was necessary to train considerable numbers of men for this duty.

Cromarty.
As it became necessary at this time to create Naval Bases on the North Sea, it was decided to fortify Cromarty as an advanced Naval Base, and to garrison it with Royal Marines. As the War Office methods were considered too slow and elaborate, the Admiralty decided to erect the fortifications themselves, making use of some older ships' guns and mountings. A nucleus garrison under a Lieutenant Colonel with a Staff Officer was to be provided in peace time, expanded as necessary in war. The necessary work was begun and on 29th December 1913, Cromarty was declared a Dockyard Port and in June 1914 the nucleus Marine garrison under Lieutenant Colonel Conway-Gordon, RMA, took over the guns and mountings. By Order-in-Council 16th July 1914, the Lieutenant Colonel received £100 per annum and the Adjutant 3/6 a day extra pay.

1914

The numbers voted were 16,900 and 1450 RN School of Music, but the Corps was considerably under establishment, officers being 40 short and the RMA as many as 300.

Adjutant General.
By Order-in-Council 21st January, the title of DAG Royal Marines, was changed to that of Adjutant General Royal Marines, and an order of 16th July altered the arrangements of the emoluments of the ADCs to the King who lost the £150 a year allowance, but the number of GSPs for Commandants was raised to four of £150 a year. The net result to the Royal Marines was the loss of two appointments of £150 a year which apparently went to the Accountant Officers RN.

---

325 Order-in-Council 13th October 1913.

Bandmasters.
By Order-in-Council 14th May two Musical Directors with the rank of Honorary Lieutenant were allowed to the Divisional Bands in lieu of Bandmasters, to be promoted to Honorary Captains after 10 years, and Honorary Majors after 15 years.

But the Great War of 1914-18 was at hand, which changed the world and with it the Corps was subjected to upheavals which it met in its usual manner and survived with an enhanced reputation but a considerably changed outlook.

Appendix I – Part 1

The Divisional Colours[326]

The Duke of York and Albany's Maritime Regiment 1664-1689

Before 1633 armies and the retainers of feudal nobles, etc, carried banners and insignia, which displayed all manner of arms, devices, etc., usually those of the King or Baron whom they followed; but in the Civil Wars we get definite records of the first real regimental flags, and Regimental Colours came into general use. These usually consisted of (1) a Colonel's Flag; (2) a Lieutenant Colonel's Flag; (3) the flags of each Company Commander, to distinguish each company.

On 13th February 1661, was published the first Royal Warrant to control the Regimental Colours, and it gives us some idea of the Colours of that time. This Warrant refers principally to the Colours of the Regiments of Foot Guards, but a very interesting point is contained in the last four lines: *"Of the usual largeness, with stands, heads and tassels"*…….. *"some of our Royal Badges painted in oil, as our trusty servant Sir Edward Walker, Knight, Garter Principal King of Arms, shall direct."*

So, we learn that early standards were painted, not embroidered, and the designs were to be regulated by the Garter King of Arms, as they still are. By 1684 the King's Colour was embroidered, but the other Colours were frequently painted until the post Waterloo period; however, by that time a regiment that had its colours painted was rather looked down on.

The first Marine Regiment, the Duke of York and Albany's, following the custom of that time, carried several colours. Thanks to the researches of Major Edye in his *History of the Royal Marine Forces* (of which only the first volume was printed) we know that these colours were - described heraldically:

The Colonel's - a Field Or (i.e. a plain sheet of yellow).

The Lieutenant Colonel's - on a Field Or, a cross gules fimbriated argent (ie on a plain yellow sheet, a red cross with white edges).

The Major's - on a Field argent, a sunburst proper, over all a cross gules, fimbriated of the first (i.e. on a White sheet, a red cross with white edges, and a yellow sunburst issuing from the four angles of the cross).

---

[326] Official records have been consulted and assistance obtained from the standard work on the subject by the late Mr. Milne, Standards and Colours of the British Army, and a book by Mr. S. C. Johnson, Flags of our Fighting Army. I am grateful to all those who have helped in the laborious researches through old records, Divisional Letter Books and orders, which have resulted in new facts being brought to light.

The Company Colours - as for the Major's, but with either a cypher or number in the centre; probably the latter, as in the Coldstream Guards.

The original drawings of these Colours are in the Royal Library at Windsor Castle, and Her Majesty Queen Victoria gave permission for their reproduction by Major Edye; they have also been reproduced in Britain's Sea Soldiers. The staves had pike heads with gold tassels.[327]

In 1676 Captain Charles Middleton's Company was detached to form part of a composite regiment to quell troubles in Virginia (North America); this company carried a colour: "The field white, waved with lemon, equally mixt with ye red cross quite through, with J D Y in cypher in gold".[328] This colour has a spear head on the staff (perhaps the forerunner of the later skeleton spear head used until 1894.[329]) The cost of painting on both sides *"in oyle"* was £18.2s.0d.

In 1680 a reinforcement was required for Tangier (North Africa), which was besieged by the Moors, and a composite regiment of 600 men in five companies was drawn from the 1st Guards, Coldstream, The Duke's (ie Marines) and the Holland Regiment (ie The Buffs). A Colour was sanctioned for each of these companies. The design is not specified, but the "Duke's" company was to have crimson, white and yellow (i.e. the same as the Virginian Company), but *"18 large cypres."* Edye suggests that these were the ciphers of the Duke of York and those of the Captains of Companies from which the men were drawn. The cost is interesting:

4 ells Crimson Taffeta at 13 shillings	£2	12	0
4 ells White Taffeta at 11 shillings	£2	4	0
4 ells Yellow Taffeta at 11 shillings	£2	4	0
	£7	0	0
For making one Ensigne	£1	10	0
For painting in oyle with fine gold			
18 large cypres at 7/6 apiece	£6	15	0
For one Ensigne staff		8	0
For one Tassel of yellow, white and red		2	6
	£8	15	6

Milne gives the account of an observer, Nathan Brooks, at a great review held on Putney Heath on 1st October, 1684, in which he describes the Colours carried by the various regiments. There were present (to give them their present designations): 1st and 2nd Life Guards, the Blues, 1st Royal Dragoons, the 1st (Grenadier) Guards, Coldstream Guards, Royal Scots, The Queen's, The Duke's (Marines), The Buffs and The King's Own. Of the 'Duke's' he says; *"The Admiral's flyes the Red Cross, with rays of the sun issuing from each angle of the Crosse - Or."*

---

327 Vol. I. page 16.
328 Edye.
329 See Britain's Sea Soldiers Vol. I. page 16.

APPENDIX 1

There is no record of the disposal of these Colours when the regiment was disbanded on 28th February 1689, nor whether there was any change when they became the Prince George of Denmark's Regiment in 1685 (i.e. when the Duke of York ascended the throne as James II), although the uniform was changed from yellow to red.

Torrington and Pembroke's Marines 1690 - 1699.

In 1690 two Marine Regiments were raised, named after their Colonels - the Earls of Torrington and Pembroke - both of whom were naval officers. Luttrell says *"these two regiments were to be clothed in blew (blue), lined with white, and to have grenadier caps"*.[330] There is no record as to the colours carried, but Luttrell says *"they had no ensigns."* It is not clear whether he is referring to colours or to officers of that rank; Edye thinks the latter; anyway, since that date Marines have always had 2nd Lieutenants and not Ensigns.

In 1698, owing to the casualties they had sustained, they were combined into one regiment, known as Brudenell's, whilst three line regiments - Colt's, Mordaunt's and Seymour's - were turned into Marine Regiments and placed on the naval establishment

There is no record of the Colours carried by these regiments, but it is probable that they carried the three Colours - the Colonel's, i.e. one plain colour; the Lieutenant Colonel's, i.e. one with same ground with a red St George's Cross on a white field, and the Major's, i.e. probably with some device. Milne says, *"During the reign of William III standards and colours were reduced gradually from one per troop or company to three for a regiment."*

Speaking of the four regiments in 1698, Edye says[331] *"There is no record of their carrying Colours, and the inference undoubtedly is that none were borne"*. However, it is difficult to believe that the three line regiments at least did not have their Colours. Of course, the two Marine regiments were commanded by naval officers, and further, they seem to have been almost wholly embarked as detachments in quite the modern way, and to have been regarded as a nursery for seamen, so that Major Edye's deduction is probably correct as regards them.

The Marine Regiments 1702 - 1713.

According to the Warrant of Queen Anne (now in the Officers' Mess at Chatham) 6 Regiments of Marines were raised in 1702 and 6 Line Regiments were allocated for Sea Service. Three of the six Marine Regiments were transferred to the Line in 1713 and wear the Battle Honour, "Gibraltar 1704-5," viz 30th (1/East Lancs), 31st (1/East Surrey) and 32nd (1/DCLI), the others were disbanded. The six Line Regiments are now the Royal Warwicks (6th), Green Howards (19th), Lancashire Fusiliers (20th), 1/Border (34th), 1/Royal Sussex (35th), 2/Worcesters (36th). The King's Own (4th) also served as Marines from 1703 to 1711.

It is undoubted that all these regiments carried Colours, because the Prince of Hesse (commanding

---
330 Edye.
331 Page 555.

the Marines at the taking of Gibraltar in 1704), arranged to signal to Admiral Sir George Rooke, by *"raising all the Colours of the Regiments."* The design of these Colours is unknown and the Librarian of the War Office tells me that no help can be obtained from the regimental histories.

Milne says, *"As regards the devices borne upon the Colours of the Army during the reigns of William III and Queen Anne, nothing appears to be known. It may be certain, however, that it was the Colours of the Senior Officers that survived, and that the Colonel's and Lieutenant Colonels' flags headed our regiments in Marlborough's campaigns."*

In Johnson's book are shown some examples of slightly later date, where the Colonel's crest is embroidered in the Colours. (See also the Royal Warrant of 1743 below.)

Milne also says, *"The Union with Scotland, 1707, had a marked effect upon the appearance of the Colours of the Army; The Red Cross of St George, used generally with a white edging or border to separate it from the varied ground of the Lieutenant Colonel's, Major's or Captain's flags (and also no doubt to satisfy heraldic requirements the Red Cross on a white field) was simply placed with the white edging intact upon the Scottish ensign, - The White Saltire Cross of St Andrew on a blue field; this forming the combination known as the Great Union or Union Flag."*

The Regiments of Marines 1739 - 1748.

In December 1739, an Order-in-Council authorised the raising of six Marine Regiments and in 1740 four more were added.

Before giving a description of the Colours carried, it is interesting to note that the Adjutant General's Department of the War Office commenced about 1743 to regularise the many different devices then appearing on Regimental Colours. A Royal Warrant was issued in 1743 which laid down inter alia:

"No Colonel is to put his arms, crest, device or livery on any part of the appointments of his regiment."

"The first Colour of every Marching Regiment of Foot is to be the Great Union; the second colour is to be of the facing of the regiment, with the Union in the Upper Canton; except those regiments faced with white or red, whose second colour is to be the Red Cross of St George in a White field, and a Union in the Upper Canton.

In the centre of each colour is to be painted in Gold Roman figures the number of the rank of the regiment within a wreath of Roses and Thistles . . ."

"All the Royal Regiments, the Fusiliers and the Marine Regiments (and several others) are distinguished by particular devices and therefore are not subject to the preceding articles for Colours."

I have put the order about the Red Cross in italics as it may have a bearing on the Marine

Colours from 1755-1802, when the facings of the Corps were white - we have no exact particulars of these colours except those of the battalion at Belleisle, described below, when the Regimental Colour appears to have been plain white.

This Warrant was followed by a series of orders from which we learn that the size of the flags was six feet six inches horizontally, and six feet two inches vertically; the width of the St George's Cross one foot one inch, the width of the white edging, five inches, the width of the St Andrew's Cross, nine inches. The length of the pikes was nine feet ten inches and of the spear head four inches; the length of the cords and tassels three feet, each tassel was four inches.

By the courtesy of the Librarian of the Royal Library at Windsor Castle, I am enabled to give a copy of the MS of the Royal Warrant of 1751 (now in the Royal Library) in which the Colours of the 1st Marine Regiment (44th of the Line), disbanded in 1748, are given in colour.

This Warrant says:

"All the Marine regiments to wear in the centre of their colours a ship with the sails furled, the rank of the regiment underneath, but their Caps, Drums and Bells of Arms to be according to the general direction of the Marching Regiments." This Warrant also repeats the above quoted provisions of the Royal Warrant of 1743 as regards the King's Colour and the Second Colour.

Description.
King's Colour. The Union Flag; In centre a full rigged ship with sails furled, with the rank of the regiment underneath.

Regimental Colour. Square flag of the colour of the facing of the Regiment, with small Union in upper canton; in centre a full rigged ship with sails furled, with rank of regiment beneath.

Skeleton spear heads with gold cords.

Colonel Field[332] has given us the facings as follows: -

1st Regiment	44th of the line	Yellow
2nd "	45th " "	Green
3rd "	46th " "	Yellow
4th "	47th " "	White
5th "	48th " "	Primrose
6th "	49th " "	Green
7th "	50th " "	White
8th "	51st " "	Yellow
9th "	52nd " "	Dark Buff
10th "	53rd " "	Light Buff

---

332 Britain's Sea Soldiers Vol. 1, Chap VI.

There were also three regiments, raised in North America, afterwards formed into one known as Gooch's Marines and taking precedence as 43rd of the Line.

It would be interesting to know if the 4th and 7th Regiments had a white Regimental Colour, or white with red St George's Cross.

In 1747 all these regiments were transferred to Admiralty control, and by Admiralty orders of May 1747 all the facings were ordered to be yellow, and it was further ordered that the Foul Anchor was to be embroidered on the caps, which has therefore become one of the oldest badges of the Corps.

As the Warrant of 1751 was published after the ten regiments had been disbanded, the drawings in the Royal Library probably followed the latest Admiralty order as to facings, viz that of 1747.

1755 To Present Day.
In April 1755 the Ministry authorised the Admiralty to raise a force of 5,000 Marines, in fifty independent companies, so that the Corps on its present footing came into existence.

Probably owing to this method of raising, and possibly, as Colonel Field suggests, because they were clothed as Fusiliers or Grenadiers, Colours do not appear to have been issued at first.

1760 The Belleisle Battalion.
When a battalion was put under orders for the expedition to Belleisle a single pair of Colours was ordered to be handed to them. On 24th October 1760, the Admiralty letter ordered Colonel Burleigh, the Commandant at Plymouth, to send a pair of Colours to the battalion.[333] The bill for this pair is as follows:[334]

Messrs. William Nicholson
24th October, 1760.

To Silk, making Union Sheet of Colours	£5 15 6
To Embroidering the Arms of the Lord High Admiral within a largo Ornament of Roses and Thistles	£5 5 0
To Silk and making a plain sheet with a small union.	£4 14 6
To painting the sheet as above	£3 0 0
To two Colour Staves and Cases	£2 6 0
To two pair of Rich Crimson and Gold Tassels and Cord.	£2 12 0
	£23 13 6

Colonel C Field found this Bill in the Admiralty "Out Letters" in the Record Office. It was approved for payment on 9th March 1761 and signed by *"Anson"* (Lord Anson) *"G Hay"* and *"J Forbes,"* and was ordered to be paid by the Paymaster of the Marines.

---
333 Plymouth Letter Books.
334 Britain's Sea Soldiers, Vol. III, p 113.

Description.
From this we may deduce that they were as follows:

King's Colour.
The Union (as in 1751) on which were embroidered the Arms of the Lord High Admiral (i.e. the Foul Anchor) with a large Wreath of Roses and Thistles.

Regimental Colour.
Silk; plain white sheet with small union in upper canton, the Anchor and Wreath as on King's Colour, but painted on the sheet.

The dimensions must have been those laid down in 1751.

It seems clear that the sheet of the Regimental Colour must have been plain white, but there is some uncertainty as to whether there was a Crown above the Anchor or not. The probability is that the Crown was not over the Foul Anchor (which was the same as that now on the Navy List), as *"the Crown only forms part of the Badge when the King himself is Lord High Admiral, as Charles II and James II were."* (Admiralty Librarian)

Milne, speaking of the Army Colours of the period, beginning with 1751, says:

"........extremely plain at first, only the number within its flowery surroundings, the flowers will be observed to become more ornate; tokens of honour (the remembrance of some gallant action or campaign) added from time to time, and alternately the name of various victories duly and discreetly authorised to be emblazoned; and all surrounding and centring upon the old regimental number (for Marines the Foul Anchor) ever enhancing its value in the eyes of those who had the honour of serving under it."

The 1765 Colours.
A note in the papers of the late Colonel W Gage Armstrong RMLI[335] that a pair of Colours had been given to the Chatham Division about this date, led to a search being made in the records of the Chatham Division, with the following interesting result:

Admiralty Office
26th July 1765

Sir,

The Storekeeper of His Majesty's Yard at Deptford having been directed to send by the first convenient opportunity to Chatham a Pair of Colours directed to you, I am commanded by My Lords Commissioners of the Admiralty to acquaint you therewith, that you may receive the same for the use of the Marine

---
335 Who made such a complete extract of the Plymouth Order and Letter Books.

Officers and Private men of your Division.

I am, Sir,
Your most obedient servant,
(Sgd) Philip Stephens.

Commanding Marine
Officer at Chatham.

The receipt of these Colours was acknowledged on 2nd August 1765.[336]

A careful search in the Portsmouth Division records resulted in the finding of the following letter:

Admiralty Office
16th July, 1785

Sir,

With respect to that part of your said letter wherein you represent that it will be a very great advantage to the discipline of the Corps to give the men better accoutrements than those they have at present, that the want of pouches makes it impossible to put them through all the firings of a battalion, as the largest cartouche boxes hold but eighteen rounds of powder, and many which hold but nine; I am also to acquaint you their Lordships have under consideration the alteration of the accoutrements, and that you will soon receive their determination, and with regard to that paragraph of your before mentioned letter setting forth, that it would also be advantage that your officers and men should be acquainted with the use to be made of Colours in a Battalion and desiring those in store at Portsmouth may be delivered to you. I am likewise to inform you that the storekeeper at Portsmouth is directed to cause those Colours to be delivered, upon application being made by you for that purpose.

Sir,
Your most humble servant,
Philip Stephens

Colonel Boisrond, at Portsmouth.

The words printed in italics would seem to show that the old Marine regiments (1739-1748) must have returned their Colours to the local yard, and that these were re-issued to the Divisions in 1765; because even if Chatham or Portsmouth had received the Belleisle Colours, how are we to account for the other pair.

So far, no record has been found of Colours having been issued to Plymouth at this time, unless we may assume that the Belleisle Colours having been issued by that Division were returned there.[337]

---
336 From Chatham Letter Books.
337 See also under 'Botany Bay.'

APPENDIX 1

Various interesting problems are raised by these two letters; (1) May we assume that the badge of the Full-rigged Ship was worn on the Colours until they were worn out? (2) At what date were they replaced? (3) Presumably as the Belleisle Colours were new they followed the Admiralty Order of 1747 re *The Foul Anchor*.[338] (4) The Laurel Wreath gained at Belleisle first appears on the Colours of 1827.

As the Keeper of the Great Wardrobe supplied Army Colours up to 1789 the designs may yet be found among his accounts in the Public Record Office, or possibly from the storekeeping records of the Admiralty, as the Marine Colours seem to have been issued by the Navy Board.

1766 - 1810

The records of this period are very scrappy.

The first definite record is a letter from the Admiralty to the Commandant at Plymouth:

2nd February 1775.
Commanding Officer, Plymouth.

I am commanded by the Lords Commissioners of the Admiralty to signify their directions to you to send the Colours of your Division to Boston with the Marines, and to acquaint you that they will be replaced by new ones.

(Sgd.) Philip Stephens[339]

There is a similar letter addressed to the Commandant Portsmouth.[340]

These two pairs of Colours were taken out by the draft of 41 Officers and 673 NCOs and men that reached Boston in May 1775 when the two battalions were formed. One set was carried at Bunkers Hill by the 1st Marines but only the Grenadier and Light Infantry Companies of the 2nd were present in the battle. It would be interesting to know whether these were the Colours issued in 1765, and if so, were they the old Colours of 1740-48. The battalions were amalgamated in 1777 into one which returned to England in 1778, but there is no record of the disposal of the Colours, unless they were deposited at Plymouth.[341]

The late Captain Portlock-Dadson told me that when he visited Greenwich in 1864 he saw hanging in the Painted Hall eight or twelve Marine Colours[342] and that the Curator, an old man who had

---
338 See also under 1810. Unfortunately, the Badge is missing.
339 Plymouth Letter Book.
340 Letter Books Vol III.
341 See later.137.
342 These were the 1810 Colours, see later.

lost both his legs, told him that among them was a Colour which had been carried at Bunker's Hill.

In 1913 I was shown at Messrs Spinks in Piccadilly, the medals and orders of Major General Sir James Lyon, which had been bought at Christie's in December 1912; with them was an embroidered letter-case containing a piece of red silk, with some white, as if it was part of a St George's Cross on a white field, which was said to be a piece of the Marine Colour carried at Bunker's Hill. With it was a letter from Lieutenant Colonel Timmins [343] as follows:

"Lieutenant Colonel Timmins has the honour of enclosing to Sir James Lyon [344] a portion of the Colour borne by the Marines at the battle of Bunker's Hill.
Wednesday Morning."

On back of letter:

"Remnant of the Colours borne by the Battalion of Marines engaged at Bunker's Hill.
Toylord (?), 18th May 1818."

This precious relic is now in the Officers' Mess at Plymouth. (Ed: Subsequently moved to the *Royal Marines Museum*.)

Botany Bay.
When the detachment under Major Ross was being prepared for the expedition to Botany Bay in 1786, he appears to have requested that the four companies might be supplied with a *"Sett of Colours"*. On 2nd January 1787 the Admiralty reply to the Commandant at Plymouth is as follows:

"Major Ross having requested that the Detachment of Marines for Botany Bay may be supplied with one of the Setts of Colours at Plymouth Headquarters, I am directed to signify their directions to you to supply the same accordingly – if they can be spared.

(Sgd.) Philip Stephens."

That letter is in the Plymouth Letter Books[345] and shows two points: that these companies carried Colours, and secondly that the Colours from America had been returned there and possibly one of them may have been the Belleisle Colours.

At the defence of Acre, General Berthier, the French GOC, says that the Marine sortie parties carried Colours[346]. Colonel Field has verified this from the journal of Midshipman Budd RN:

---

343 SORM at Trafalgar in 1805.
344 139 Sir James Lyon was GOC of the Portsmouth Garrison and was in command of the parade when Colours were presented to Portsmouth Division, by HRH The Duke of Clarence, 27th October, 1827. He himself had served in the fleet in 1794, and was the son of an officer killed at Bunker's Hill.
345 Colonel Armstrong's extracts.
346 Britain's Sea Soldiers Vol. II, p. 217.

Appendix 1

"Monday, 7th January, 1799 - Moored in the harbour of Constantinople. Fired a salute of twenty-one guns and manned ship on occasion of Marine Corps being presented with a stand of Colours from HBM Ambassador's lady."

Chatham and Portsmouth orders make several mentions of Colours, e.g. "Divisional Colours will be carried by the Guard of Honour ordered to attend H.M. George III at the Thanksgiving Service at St Paul's in 1797."[347] (The guards marched there and back.)

Someday, probably, the design of these Colours will come to light, but they probably very much resembled the Belleisle Colours.

In 1800 we come on further records:

Union with Ireland.
On 13th December there is a Plymouth Division Order giving directions that in consequence of an Order-in-Council 5th November 1800 certain alterations are to be made in the Royal Ensigns, Armorial Flags and Banners following on the Union of Great Britain and Ireland.

On 22nd December 1800 the Commanding Officer at Plymouth wrote to the Lords of the Admiralty:

"You will be pleased to inform my Lords Commissioners of the Admiralty that the Colours of this Division are become totally unfit for further use, being old and worn out, and to request their Lordships will be pleased to order another sett to be forwarded here, and agreeably to the plan proposed relative to the Union.

(Sgd.) J. Bowater."

The last sentence seems to refer to the Union with Ireland, which was finally signed in 1801, when the general plan adopted (according to Milne) was to sew red strips along the white limbs of St Andrew's Cross, to provide for the St Patrick's Cross, and to add the Shamrock to the wreath of Roses and Thistles.

There is also a letter of May 1801, asking that the Navy Board may supply new Colours in lieu.[348] There is an answer from the Admiralty dated 28th December 1800, *"that the Division will be supplied with new Colours agreeable to the Union, and that the Navy Board has been directed to supply the same."*

That new Colours were supplied early in 1801 to all Divisions is corroborated by the Portsmouth

---

347 Gillespie in his History, says that bodies of Marines drawn from Chatham and Portsmouth attended the Thanksgiving Service at St Paul's on 19th December 1797, and that they were drawn from men who had served in the recent campaigns, and together with the seamen were allotted for the protection of the trophies which their valour had conquered.
348 Colonel W G Armstrong.

Letter Books dated 1st January 1801. The Commandant had represented that there were no Divisional Silk Colours in store conformably to the new regulation and requesting to be supplied therewith, the Lords Commissioners of the Admiralty replied that they *"have given directions to the Navy Board accordingly."*

This is further confirmed by the report of their condition by the Commandant at Plymouth under date 1st November 1802:

"In reply to your letter of 30th October, [349] *I beg leave to inform you that though the Colours of this Division are in a good state, yet as the Corps has been made Royal since they were issued, it will be necessary that the Divisional Colours should be altered accordingly, nor until this is done can we strictly be called Royal.*

(Sgd.) J. Bowater."

But the reply of the Commandant at Portsmouth of the same date gives the astonishing information that the Regimental Colour to be replaced was red, as follows:

"Our present colours were received about eighteen months since, and are perfectly good; but in consequence of the late alteration in our uniforms and appointments [350] *the Regimental Colour is of no use whatever, for I need not remark it would be preposterous to take out a red colour with blue facings........I feel it incumbent upon me to remind you that the Egyptian regiments have been honoured with a mark of Royal approbation in their Colours, and I trust it will be admitted that our services have upon every occasion been as zealous and exemplary as any other of His Majesty's troops; and as we had a battalion of more than 500 men serving in that country I hope you will use every endeavour that a distinction as honourable to the discipline and bravery of that army is not withheld from the Corps of Marines."*

(Sgd.) T Avarne. Major General.

Lieutenant General Souter-Johnstone, RM

Note that the second paragraph refers of course to the grant of the 'Sphinx' for the Campaign of 1801; it was before the grant of the Globe to the Corps. There would appear to have been little uniformity about the Colours.

In 1806 a Battalion of Royal Marines was landed from the fleet and took part in the ill-fated attack on Buenos Ayres. They carried a Union Jack and a small Red Ensign, evidently made on board with the letters 'RMB' in white. When the garrison surrendered, these flags, together with the Colours of the other regiments, were given up to the enemy, and they are now hanging in the Convent of San Domingo.

---

349 Note the speed of transmission of letters between London and Plymouth.
350 See Orders of 8th May 1802.

Although the Woolwich Division was formed in 1805 the Brigade Major at Chatham tells me that a careful search of the Woolwich records reveals nothing as to whether Colours were issued on its formation.

The 1810 Colours.
From this time onwards, the records are more definite. In 1810 General Barclay [351] was ordered by the Admiralty to provide Colours of proper pattern for the several Divisions of Marines and these were apparently supplied in 1810 and 1811. Presumably they were in accordance with the latest regulations, e.g. the new Union Flag and the Blue Silk for the Regimental Colour; they appear to have been embroidered.

20th February 1811.
Major-General Bright (Commandant, Plymouth)

"*I have also to acquaint you a sett of Colours for the Division under your command will be sent from London this day directed to you.*"

(Sgd) John Barclay [352]

A pair of this set can now be seen in the Royal Naval Museum at Greenwich.

King's Colour.
The Union Flag, but no badges are discernible.

Regimental Colour.
Dark Blue Silk, with remnants of a Union Wreath of Roses, Thistles and Shamrocks. The poles are of ash with spear heads.

No further information is forthcoming, but presumably, as in 1780, the Foul Anchor must have been in the centre. What we should like to know is what scrolls and mottoes were borne and where the Laurel wreath was placed.

On 17th December 1810 the British Envoy at Lisbon presented a pair of Colours to the 1st Battalion, commanded by Major R. Williams.[353]

On 5th August 1812, approval was given for a pair of Colours to be given to the 2nd Battalion, commanded by Major J Malcolm, under orders for the Peninsula. On 6th August 1812, in acknowledging the order the Commandant of the Portsmouth Division says: "He does not know

---
351   The Commandant in Town.
352   CO's Letter Book, Plymouth.
353   Afterwards Major Commandant of the Artillery Companies, and later Commandant of the Portsmouth Division.

where the different sets lately provided to the Divisions were ordered, as they were sent down by the Naval Board."[354]

As this Battalion sailed on 14th August for the Peninsular War in Spain, it is believed that they took the Portsmouth Division Colours.[355]

After service on the north coast of Spain, this battalion went to North America for the latter part of the war 1812-14. It would seem that the piece of a Colour said to be that of the 2nd Battalion at Bunker's Hill, now in the Officers' Mess at Eastney, really belongs to this Battalion, because in the first place only the Grenadier and Light Infantry Companies of 2/Marines were engaged at Bunker's Hill. Also, the donor of this fragment, General Whylock, only joined the Corps in 1804, became full Colonel 1851, retired on full pay as a Major General 20th June 1855; served in Spain and the Mediterranean 1808-9 and 1812-13; was OC detachments at the storming of Sidon 1840. It would therefore seem as if the Colours of Malcolm's Battalion were torn up, as was often the case at that time.

Disposal.
Correspondence in the Royal Marine Office, dated 6th August 1828, shows that these 1810 Divisional Colours, when replaced in 1827, were ordered to be sent to the Chapel of Greenwich Hospital by the Lord High Admiral, the Duke of Clarence (afterwards HM King William IV); Divisions were ordered to attach to the staves any details of presentation, service, etc.

A letter from Greenwich to the late Major Edye dated 1st December 1892, says:

"We have the Colours of the RM sent to Greenwich by William IV; you shall have full information by Saturday.

Yours sincerely,
(Sgd.) G F Lambert"

This is endorsed in pencil - *"In the School."*

Enquiries made on 21st January 1930 elicited that the only pair is now in the museum.

Among Major Edye's papers is a letter from a member of the Royal Household, signature illegible, dated 23rd August 1892, from which the following is extracted:

"I cannot imagine what can have become of the old Colours which were sent on board the Royal Sovereign, unless they are stored carefully away in Portsmouth Dockyard. I think I may say they are not in any of the Royal Palaces, for I have ransacked them completely. I found some Colours of great

---
354 From this and previous letters it would appear that the Navy Board supplied Marine Colours.
355 A note in the index of the Letter Book lends colour to this idea.

historic interest, but not any belonging to the Marines........I think that the Royal Sovereign yacht was a Portsmouth ship and always had her moorings in that harbour."

These Colours belonged to the Plymouth Division, having been sent there after the presentation of the 1827 Colours.[356]

The 1827 Colours.

The design of these Colours materially differs from those hitherto in use. It had become customary to place Battle Honours on the Regimental Colour, and a list of actions, about 106 in number, was submitted to HM King George IV, in order that he might select those to be placed on the Colour[357] but *"The greatness of their number and the difficulty of selecting amidst so many glorious deeds, such a portion as could be inserted in the space, determined His Majesty, in lieu of the usual badges and mottoes on the Colours of the troops of the line, to direct that the 'Globe encircled with Laurel' should be the distinguishing badge as the most appropriate emblem of a Corps, whose duties carried them to all parts of the globe, in every quarter of which they had earned laurels by their valour and good conduct"*[358] and in his speech at Chatham, HRH referred to this and other badges, and at Woolwich he pointedly said that Gibraltar was for the capture and defence of the Rock in 1704-5. He also said *"His Majesty had given them the most peculiar and honourably distinctive badge of his own cypher; further that it might be known to posterity that King George IV had bestowed on them such an honourable mark of his appreciation, HM directed that whatever King or Queen they might serve under hereafter, though the cypher of the reigning sovereign must of course appear on their standard, still on those of the Royal Marines the cypher GVIR was for ever to remain".*

These Colours are rather inaccurately illustrated in Cannon's Historical Record of the Royal Marines[359] but the design can be seen in the pair now hanging in the Officers' Mess at Plymouth.

King's Colour.

The Union. In the centre the Globe, silver, encircled with the Laurel Wreath, gold with red berries; above the globe, the Foul Anchor, gold entwined with the Royal Cypher GVIR, ensigned with the Crown; above "Gibraltar" in black letters on yellow scroll; under the Globe a yellow scroll, bearing the motto "Per Mare Per Terram" which lies across the stems of the laurel wreath.

Divisional Colour.

Dark Blue Silk, with union in upper canton; the same badges as on the King's Colour. The poles had the usual spear heads, gold and silver tassels and cords. The cost of the four pairs of Colours was £207. 8s. 0d.

---

356 Colonel Armstrong.
357 For full list see a contemporary pamphlet reprinted in The Globe and Laurel, Vol I. p 210.
358 From speech of HRH The Duke of Clarence, Lord High Admiral, at Portsmouth.
359 Published in 1845.

Presentations.
The Colours were presented by HRH The Duke of Clarence; the Lord High Admiral as follows:[360]

> To Chatham on 26th September 1827.
> To Portsmouth on 27th October 1827.
> To Plymouth on 21st December 1827.
> To Woolwich on 10th October 1827.

It is an interesting note of Corps history to recall that two of the Drummers who witnessed this presentation at Plymouth also saw the new Colours presented in 1858, and finally yet another new set, when pensioners in 1896, viz Major and QM Uriah King and QMS Jew.

On 4th December 1829 the RM Office directed the Commandant at Woolwich to send his two Colours to Mr Morton, of 52 Upper Charlotte Street, Fitzroy Square, London, and *"to permit them to remain there for such short time as may be required to enable him to introduce them into a painting of HRH the late Lord High Admiral, on which Mr. Morton is now occupied, for the officers' mess rooms of the several Divisions,"* - where they can now be seen to-day.

Disposal.
An order was sent from the RM Office, dated 6th August 1858, that on the receipt of the new Colours the 1827 Colours were to be returned to the Royal Marine Office.

As regards the Portsmouth set, the late Major and Quartermaster Murphy RMLI told me that he remembered that the old Colours were torn up on parade when the new Colours were presented in 1858.[361] No record exists of the disposal of the Chatham or Woolwich sets.

On 6th November 1861, a pair of the 1827 Colours were sent from the RM Office to the Commandant at Plymouth, to be handed over to Lieutenant Colonel Lowder for the use of the Marine Battalion under orders for Mexico. Lieutenant Colonel H S Bourchier RMLI, wrote in 1912 *"I carried these Colours myself when we landed at Vera Cruz."*

On 5th December 1863, a letter was sent from the DAGRM directing that the Colours lately carried by the Mexican Battalion were to be prepared for issue to the battalion under orders for Japan. The late Lieutenant Colonel H J Norcock RMLI, wrote to me in 1912, *"I carried these Colours myself when we marched out of barracks to embark."* They must therefore have been at the storming of the batteries at Simonoseki in 1864 and must have been the last RM Colours carried in action.[362] This pair of Colours now hangs in the mess room at Plymouth. From Colonel Armstrong's papers we learn that he found these Colours in the Commandant's office, and obtained the permission of the Commandant, Colonel McArthur, to fix them on the picture

---
360 RMO Records.
361 Major Murphy was then a boy of eleven or twelve years old and joined the Corps shortly after as a drummer.
362 See also Britain's Sea Soldiers Vol. II, p 146.

of the Duke of Clarence, who had originally presented them.

Another Battalion of Royal Marines served as a garrison in Japan from 1870 to 1875, and a photograph in the officers' mess at Chatham shows that they had colours. There is no record of these, but they may possibly have been another pair of the 1827 Colours sent from the RM office.

The 1858 Colours.
In 1858 it was decided that the Royal Marine Colours were to be replaced, and the design was entrusted to the Inspector of Colours at the College of Heralds. This officer appears to have departed from the instructions given by King George IV and to have followed the principles approved for the army about 1855. The laurel wreath was removed from around the globe and put back into its old place round the foul anchor, and the cypher of George IV was entirely omitted. HM Queen Victoria herself approved the design and the Board letter notifying her approval was dated 17th February 1858.[363]

It is interesting to note that the bugle was never incorporated in the Colours, though on 30th January 1855, the following minute had been promulgated by the Admiralty:

"Most humbly submitted your Majesty by the Lords Commissioners of the Admiralty:

"That the Corps of Royal Marines may be designated a Light Corps, and equipped and instructed as such, agreeably to your Majesty's Regulations for Light Infantry Regiments of the Line, this training being considered best adapted to the nature of the service which the Corps is generally required to perform on shore."

Appd (signed) Victoria R.

Description.
Poles with spear head; the size of the Colours was 6ft 2ins by 5ft 6ins.

Queen's Colour.
The Union; in centre a gold Crown on upper limb of St George's Cross; Royal Marines in black on a gold scroll beneath on transverse arms of cross.

Divisional Colour.
Dark Blue Silk, with Union in upper canton; the Royal Cypher VR in each of the other corners in gold. In the centre the Globe (silver) encircled with a circular red scroll inscribed. "The Royal Marines" in gold, surrounded by a wreath of roses, shamrocks, thistles and oak leaves, with red and white bow. Below (or in base) the foul anchor, gold, encircled by a laurel wreath, green with red berries; beneath this a yellow scroll inscribed "Per Mare Per Terram" in black; below this a yellow scroll inscribed "Gibraltar" in black.

---

363 RMO records.

These Colours were supplied by Messrs Hamburger and Rogers, who also supplied those in 1894 and 1896.

Presentation.
It was decided that the Naval Commanders-in-Chief at the several ports were to make the presentations, and as far as can be ascertained, there was very little ceremony. Plymouth orders merely state *"Division will parade in Review order tomorrow for presentation of Colours."*

The dates and the several Commanders-in-Chief were:

At Chatham	28th June 1858	by Vice-Admiral E. Harvey.
At Portsmouth	8th July 1858	by Admiral Sir G F Seymour.
At Plymouth	17th June 1858	by Rear-Admiral Sir Thomas Palley.
At Woolwich	15th July 1858	by Commodore Charles Shepherd.

Disposal.
On presentation of the new (i.e. the present) Colours in 1894-96, the 1858 Colours were disposed of as follows:

Chatham Division were presented to HRH the Duke of Edinburgh; a silver circlet was put on them to record the fact, and they were taken to Clarence House. These Colours are now hanging in the North West corner of St George's Hall, Windsor Castle, having been placed there in September 1901.

Portsmouth Division. This pair were hung in the Officers' Mess at Forton; on the amalgamation of the RMA and the RMLI in 1923 they were laid up in St Andrew's Church at Eastney.

Plymouth Division are now hanging in the Officers' messroom at Plymouth.

Woolwich Division. On the break-up of the Division in 1869 they were sent to the Royal Marine Office, where they remained until 1895. On 3rd October 1895, they were sent to Deal and hung in the Officers' messroom until 22nd March 1909, when the Commandant (Colonel E A Wylde) obtained permission to lay them up in the Depot Church, where they now are.[364]

The 1894-96 Colours.
In 1891 it was reported that the Portsmouth Division Colours were in such a bad state that it was necessary to replace them.

---

364 When the Royal Marine Battalion was landed for the Capture of Kinbourn (Crimean War) in October 1855, Lieutenant Hugh Rose carried a Colour which had been lent by Captain King RN. It was a silk Union Jack, properly mounted and was returned to Captain King on the return of the battalion to the ships. (Captain Portlock-Dadson).

In 1892 the Garter King of Arms, or rather the Inspector of Regimental Colours in his office, was asked to prepare designs. In the first place the army Colours had recently been reduced in size to 3ft 9ins by 3ft with a bullion fringe round them; the lion and crown had superseded the spear heads on the poles, which had been reduced in length to 8ft 7½ins. Following the 1858 pattern, and embodying these modifications, a design was prepared and submitted, but the historians and senior officers of the Corps, remembering the speeches of the Duke of Clarence represented that the cypher GVIR should appear.

After a good deal of correspondence and preparation of drawings of the 1827 Colours from the pair in the Plymouth mess, the design of the Garter King of Arms was dropped and one following the 1827 design, but of small size and without the bullion fringe, was submitted to HM Queen Victoria, who personally made several alterations, including inserting her cypher VRI in the three corners of the Divisional Colour, and finally approved the Colours as they now appear in her own handwriting.[365]

Description.

Queen's (now King's) Colour.
The Union: in the centre the Foul Anchor with the Royal cypher interlaced, ensigned with the Imperial Crown, "Gibraltar" on a scroll above; in base the Globe surrounded by a Laurel Wreath, motto "Per Mare Per Terram" on a yellow scroll beneath.

Divisional Colour.
Dark Blue Silk. In the centre the Foul Anchor interlaced with the cypher GVIR, ensigned with the Imperial Crown; "Gibraltar" on a scroll above; in base the Globe surrounded by a Laurel Wreath; motto "Per Mare Per Terram" on a yellow scroll beneath. In the upper dexter canton the small Union, in the remaining three corners the Royal and Imperial cypher.

It will be noticed that contrary to the army practice the Queen's Colour bears the distinctive badges of the Corps, as the Marine Colours always have since the beginning.

Presentation. HM Queen Victoria conferred a signal honour on the Portsmouth Division by presenting the Colours personally at Osborne on 28th August 1894. The presentations to the Chatham and Plymouth Divisions were made by HRH The Duke of Edinburgh, the Honorary Colonel of the Corps, who presented them to Chatham on 22nd June 1898 and to Plymouth on 3rd July 1896.

---

365 The original drawing with the alterations and signature are in the RMO. Records.

Notes.

1. In an old book *"Drum and Flute Duty for HM Army"* that was in the possession of the Drum Major of the Portsmouth Division, I ascertained that the Royal Marines had a special salute on the drum for receiving the Colour.

2. Following on the loss of life incurred in saving the Colours in the Afghan War, and again in the Zulu War, it was henceforth forbidden to carry Colours into action; so that we may say that the Colours of the battalion for Japan in 1864 were the last RM Colours to be carried in action.

3. In the War 1914-18 no battalion actually carried Colours, but in some cases platoon flags were carried. At the Battle of Passchendaele (in Flanders) on 28th October 1917, A Company, 2/RMLI, gallantly led by Lieutenant P Ligertwood, who had connected his men with spunyarn to prevent their leaving the narrow tracks through the mud, crossed the Paddebeeke and made good their position there. He had provided each of his platoons with a small red flag, which had been blessed by the battalion Chaplain, and these were carried forward, and served as rallying points for the platoons; three of these now rest at Chatham, Portsmouth and Plymouth; the bearer of the fourth was killed and the flag lost in the Flanders mud. Lieutenant Ligertwood, who had gained his commission from the ranks during the war, unfortunately died of his wounds *("Britain's Sea Soldiers" Vol III, p 335)*. The casualties in this battle were: 1/RMLI - four officers killed, six wounded; 270 NCOs and men killed and wounded. 2/RMLI - four officers killed, four wounded; 391 NCOs and men killed and wounded.

4. Owing to the large number of battles in the war of 1914-18, HM George V ordered that those selected which had hitherto been confined to the Regimental Colour, were to be inscribed on the King's Colour, and each regiment was allowed to select ten from a list prepared by the War Office to be so inscribed.

If it had been customary for the Royal Marines to inscribe such honours, it is interesting to note that they would have had to select from the following, in addition to the naval actions, such as Jutland and more particularly Zeebrugge:

Chatham Bn. RMLI	Portsmouth Bn. RMLI
Antwerp	Antwerp
France and Flanders 1914	France and Flanders 1914
Anzac	Anzac
Helles	Helles
Krithia	Krithia
Egypt 1915	Egypt 1915

Plymouth Bn. RMLI	Deal Bn. RMLI
Antwerp	Antwerp
France and Flanders 1914	France and Flanders 1914
Landing at Helles	Anzac
Helles	Helles
Krithia	Krithia
Egypt 1915	Egypt 1915

After 13th July, 1915, the Battalions were so reduced owing to casualties (the Portsmouth Battalion had not one officer left), that they were amalgamated into 1st and 2nd Battalions RMLI in August 1915.

1st RMLI formed from	2nd RMLI formed from
Chatham and Deal Bns.	Portsmouth and Plymouth Bns
Helles	Helles
Krithia	Krithia
Gallipoli 1915-16	Gallipoli 1915-16
Macedonia 1916	Macedonia 1915
Somme 1916-18	Somme 1918-18
Ancre 1916-18	Ancre 1916-18
Arras 1917-18	Arras 1917-18
1st RMLI formed from	2nd RMLI formed from
Chatham and Deal Bns	Portsmouth and Plymouth Bns
Vimy	-
Scarpe 1917	Scarpe 1917
Arleux	Arleux
Ypres 1917	Ypres 1917
Passchendaele	Passchendaele
St Quentin	St Quentin
Albert 1918	Albert 1918
Bapaume 1918	Bapaume 1918

Owing to the casualties in the Retreat of March 1918, culminating in the final counter-attack on 6th April in Aveluy Wood, in which both battalions charged in line, it was found impossible to reinforce both up to strength, and they were amalgamated into one, 1st RMLI.

1st RMLI	
Drocourt-Queant Line	Cambrai
Hindenburg Line	Pursuit to Mons
Canal du Nord	France and Flanders 1916-18

5. After the Armistice, 11th November 1918, the 1/RMLI (the sole remnant of the RMLI Brigade) settled down in the neighbourhood of Mons. The Colours of the Chatham Division were sent to them, which they carried until the cadre returned to England on the final break-up of the R.N. (63rd) Division, 6th June 1919, when they were returned to Chatham.[366]

---

366 Britain's Sea Soldiers Vol III p 381.

Appendix 1 - Part 2

Summary of the Presentations of Colours to the Royal Marines at various dates - No accounts prior to 1827 exist

1827

The following account of the ceremony at Portsmouth is taken from a contemporary pamphlet (which is printed in full in The Globe and Laurel Vol I pp 197-210).

Portsmouth .
The troops in garrison paraded in line on Southsea Common, under command of Major General Sir James Lyon KCB on 27th October 1827, in the following order: Royal Marine Artillery, 58th Foot, Provisional Battalion (Depots 27th, 28th, and 95th Regiments), Royal Marines, a Light Infantry Battalion (Depots of 51st, and 60th Regiments). In front a Guard of Honour of Royal Artillery.

The new Colours, in charge of Colonel Phillott, RA and Lieutenant Colonel Darley, 58th Regiment.

On arrival of HRH The Lord High Admiral (later William IV) with the Naval Commander-in-Chief, the Commissioner, the DAGRM (Major General Campbell) and staff, he was received with a general salute and then passed down the lines and returned to the saluting point. The Royal Marines then advanced in line and on the march formed open column of companies right in front. Upon the centre arriving opposite HRH they halted and formed three sides of a square. The RMA formed in close column in rear of the right face, the 56th and Provisional Battalion in rear of the rear face, and the Light Infantry Battalion in rear of the left face.

The Royal Marines saluted the old Colours, which, being dropped, were not again raised.

HRH then directed all Officers and Sergeants of every Corps to be formed in the centre of the square - as well as the young gentlemen of the RN College - who were formed into two lines by the Lieutenant Governor and his staff.

HRH with Lady Stopford on his right arm and Lady Lyon on his left, accompanied by a large party of officers and ladies and gentlemen, entered the square, together with the Guard of Honour.

He commenced his speech: *"Colonel Moncrieffe (the Commandant), Lieutenant Colonel Sir*

Richard Williams, Officers, NCOs and Privates of the Royal Marines and Royal Marine Artillery, as Lord High Admiral and General of Marines............ "[367]

HRH then delivered the King's Colour to 2/Lieutenant Johnson-How and the Divisional Colour to 2/Lieutenant George Griffin. Colonel Moncreiffe replied, after which the Brigade saluted and cheered, and HRH returned to the saluting point. The troops then formed contiguous column and deployed into line; they then fired a feu-de-joie, broke into open column of companies and marched past in review order in slow and quick time and in quarter distance columns; wheeled into contiguous columns, deployed into line, and saluted when HRH left the ground.

Divisional Orders, Portsmouth Division, 27th October 1827, contain a letter from the DAG (Major General Campbell) to the Commandant, enclosing the following memorandum from HRH and also conveying his own congratulations on their good discipline and fine appearance.

Memorandum, Portsmouth, 27th October 1827

HRH The Lord High Admiral congratulates Colonel Moncreiffe, the officers and men of the Portsmouth Division of Royal Marines on the distinguished marks of His Majesty's favourable consideration, which they have this morning received, and which HRH, both as Lord High Admiral and General of Marines, has felt much gratification in personally obtaining for and presenting to the Corps.

HRH derives additional satisfaction from the confident assurance that these honourable badges will stimulate their future conduct, and that wherever their King and Country may require their services, they will be marked by the same undaunted courage, discipline and loyalty as they have hitherto displayed. HRH cannot conclude this order without calling to the minds of Lieutenant Colonel Sir Richard Williams KCB, the Officers, NCOs and Privates of the Royal Marine Artillery, that as being an integral part of the Corps of Royal Marines, they must participate in the honour and distinction thus conferred by their Most Gracious Sovereign; and as HRH, both as Lord High Admiral and General of Marines, trusts and believes that this highly distinguished and drilled Corps will equally continue to merit the approbation of their King and the gratitude of their Country.

By Order,
(Signed) William Davis, Adjutant,

Woolwich.

The presentation at Woolwich was marred by rain.[368] The following extracts may be of interest: After receiving HRH and marching past in slow and quick time, the rain became so heavy that the battalion was ordered to quarters; crowds kept pouring into the barrack field, until it seemed to be a forest of umbrellas. As there was no hope of the weather clearing, HRH ordered the parade to be

---

367 The whole speech can be read in the Globe and Laurel.
368 The full account is given in The Globe and Laurel 1905 p 71.

held in the riding school[369] with as many of the Artillery Brigade as could be accommodated. In the centre was a platform for the Duchess of Clarence, the Princess Augusta and other ladies with the principal officers. HRH then addressed Colonel McCleverty (the Commandant) and the Royal Marines, pointing out the badges, etc. It is interesting to note that in this speech HRH says "for the Capture and Defence of Gibraltar, 1704-5" HM had selected "Gibraltar" as one of the badges.

After the general salute and three cheers the Commandant addressed HRH, and then the Duchess, Princess Augusta with the Generals and effective Field Officers of the Artillery, Engineers and Marines, repaired to the *"Green Man"* at Blackheath, when HRH entertained the company to a *déjeûner* of great profusion and splendour.

From Blackheath many of the principal officers, and especially the Field Officers and staff of the Brigade of Engineers and Artillery, returned to Woolwich, being engaged to dine with Colonel McCleverty and the Royal Marines in their barracks; about ninety sat down and well kept up the *joyous feeling of the day*. The NCOs, Royal Marines, invited the Staff Sergeants of the RA and RE, with their families, to a dinner and dance in a temporary building, which would have been illuminated, but that the rain defeated all efforts in this respect.

Plymouth.
The following account of the presentation at Plymouth is taken from Mr Whitfield's *"Plymouth in Times of Peace and War,"*

HRH the Duke of Clarence presented the Colours, and made a speech lasting one and a half hours. Rain fell all the time with remarkable violence, but the Duke *"in a firm and manly voice"* persisted to the end.

In the evening the barracks were illuminated, each entrance gate displayed the emblem of the Lord High Admiral, the crossed Double Anchors and Cables, with the letters 'W' and 'A' (later Queen Adelaide) surmounted by a coronet. Another transparency (whatever that may have been) depicted *Fame* drawing aside a curtain and displaying to *Britannia* the new flag, surrounded with trophies of war.[370]

The 1858 Colours.
It has been impossible to trace any account of these presentations, though doubtless there must be a record in some of the local papers. In any case there seems to have been very little ceremony e.g., the Plymouth orders merely state that *"The Division will parade in Review Order tomorrow for presentation of Colours."* In some cases the presentation seems to have coincided with the DAG's inspection.

The 1894-96 Colours.
Her Majesty Queen Victoria conferred on the Portsmouth Division the signal honour of

---
369 Presumably the RA School.
370 The full local newspaper account may be seen framed in the Commandant's Office at Plymouth.

presenting the Colours personally at Osborne on 22nd August 1894. The presentations to the Chatham and Plymouth Divisions were not made until 1896, when HRH The Duke of Edinburgh, the Honorary Colonel of the Corps, presented them at Chatham on 22nd June 1896 and at Plymouth on 3rd July 1896.

These ceremonies were the first occasions which I have been able to trace where the old Colours were "trooped" before the presentation of the new Colours. The religious service appears also to have become standardised, because none was held in 1827.

Portsmouth.
A Battalion of six companies, under Lieutenant Colonel F Baldwin, was convoyed in gunboats from Gosport to Cowes and marched up to Osborne House. They were then formed in line on the lawn facing the NW front of the house; a battalion of RMA, under Lieutenant Colonel Pengelley, was formed up on either flank at right angles to the RMLI.

About 5 pm Her Majesty drove on to the ground, and was received with a general salute by the troops under Lieutenant General Davis CB, Commanding Southern District. With Her Majesty were the Princess Louise and the Duchess of Connaught, and in a second carriage Princess Beatrice and the ex-Empress Eugene, HRH The Duke of York (now HM King George V) accompanied Her Majesty on foot with the Naval Commander-in-Chief, Sir John Commerrell VC.

Her Majesty drove down the line and then returned to the saluting point. Colonel Commandant J Philips CB, then assumed command. The old Colours were trooped (Major H C Money with Lieutenants F Phillips and Whitmarsh being the officers of the escort), and were then marched to the rear of the Battalion to the tune of *"Auld Lang Syne"* and cased. The line then advanced to fifty yards from Her Majesty's carriage and formed hollow square, with the drums piled, on which the new Colours were laid; the band was also in the centre. After the singing of the hymn *"Brightly gleams our Banner"* - the first and last verses being sung by the whole battalion, the second and third verses by the right and left half battalion respectively; the prayers of consecration were read by the Chaplain, the Reverend C E Yorke RN.

Majors Quill and Money then handed the new Colours to Her Majesty, who delivered them to Lieutenants J B Pym and J E Crowther. Queen Victoria then said: *"I have much pleasure in presenting you with these Colours. They carry on them the badge of my uncle, George IV, and the motto defining your services by land and sea. I am confident that they will always be safe and honoured in your keeping."* Colonel Philips replied, and the battalion reformed line and saluted the Colours, which were then marched to their places in line whilst the National Anthem was played.

The troops then marched past in column, reformed line advanced in Review Order and gave a Royal Salute by command of Colonel Philips. Her Majesty expressed her satisfaction at the appearance of the troops and the manner in which the ceremony had been performed.

Her Majesty provided the troops with refreshments in the meadow near the Royal Stables (lately the RN College) and the officers were entertained at Barton House Farm.

As an instance of Her Majesty's solicitude for the troops (she was a soldier's daughter and prided herself on it), having heard that they could not return to Gosport until a late hour, she telegraphed the next day her hopes that they had reached their destination all right. It is sad to recall that these Colours were carried at Gosport at the funeral in January of 1901 of this most gracious sovereign.

HRH The Duke of Connaught also telegraphed his congratulations on the honour conferred on them.

The WOs, Staff Sergeants and Sergeants celebrated the presentation by a dinner and entertainment at Forton, and the Junior NCOs held a smoking concert.[371]

Chatham.
The details of presentation were much the same in this case.[372] A battalion of eight companies, under Lieutenant Colonel A B Crosbie ADC paraded on the Great Lines. HRH The Duke of Edinburgh was received by a Guard of Honour of the Royal Scots and escorted to the ground by a troop of the Royal West Kent Yeomanry. Colonel Commandant G H T Colwell CB received HRH with a Royal Salute. Colonel F H Poore RMA attended HRH as equerry.

The Consecration Service was read by Reverend Dr Dickson LLD RN, the Chaplain, and the Colours were handed to the Duke by Majors Horniblow and Matson, who delivered them to Lieutenant W L G Connolly and Lieutenant J H Lambert. The Duke than made a speech:[373]

"Colonel Colwell, Officers, Non-Commissioned Officers, Buglers and Privates of the Chatham Division, Royal Marines. It is peculiarly gratifying to me as your Honorary Colonel, as having been so intimately connected in my capacity as a Naval Officer with your Corps and serving with its members in all parts of the world, that the duty of presenting you with new Colours should have fallen upon me. It is not necessary for me to speak of the way in which the Royal Marines have at all times done their duty, and will, I doubt not, at all times do it in future, not to mention the various occasions upon which the reigning Sovereign has shown marked appreciation of their faithfulness by bestowing some special distinction on the Corps. These facts are well known to all present here today, but in presenting the new Colours I would draw attention to the fact that in addition to the monogram of Her Majesty, they bear that of King George IV, who in 1827, when the Duke of Clarence was fulfilling the same duty which it is my privilege to perform today, directed that the Colours of the Royal Marines should for ever after bear his monogram, in addition to that of the reigning Sovereign, and this is a distinction which I know is highly prized in the Corps.

---

371 For fuller details see The Globe and Laurel 1894 p 97.
372 See The Globe and Laurel 1895-96 p 102.
373 As it has not hitherto been published, it is reproduced here in full.

"In delivering these Colours into your custody, I feel satisfied that they will be in safe hands, and that it will be the pride of the Corps to show in the future, as in the past, their loyalty and devotion in the service of their Queen and Country."

Colonel Colwell replied, and mentioned the fact that the Colours which were being replaced were presented to the Division in the same year in which HRH had entered the Royal Navy, viz 1858.

HRH then returned to the barracks and after being photographed with the officers lunched with them in the mess. The officers' friends were entertained in the theatre. As the Duke left the barracks all ranks were on the pavement and cheered him as he drove away.

In the evening the Sergeants' Mess gave a dinner and smoking concert, and on 17th July the Officers gave a ball, a special dancing floor being laid in the drill shed.

On 30th June Colonel Colwell, with Lieutenants Connelly and Lambert, took the old Colours to Clarence House, where they were handed to HRH, a silver plate with an inscription having been placed on them to record the fact.

The Dean of Rochester (Dean Hole) had offered them a resting place in Rochester Cathedral, but as HRH had accepted them, the offer had to be declined.

Plymouth.
On 3rd July 1896, HRH The Duke of Edinburgh, attended by the DAG, General Sir Henry Tuson KCB, the DAAG, Colonel C H Scafe, and his Equerry, Colonel P H Poore RMA, arrived at Millbay station at 7am. He was received by a Guard of Honour and Band and escorted to barracks by the Mounted Company of the 2nd Volunteer Battalion Devon Regiment. He breakfasted with the Commandant (Colonel E L Rose).

In the forenoon the Battalion paraded on the Brickfields under Colonel R B Kirchoffer. HRH, who wore the full dress of a Colonel Royal Marines, with the Star and Ribbon of the Garter, was received by the Colonel Commandant with a general salute.

The Service of Consecration was read by the Reverend S S Browne RN, Majors Cotter and Barrett then handed the Colours to the Duke, who delivered them to Lieutenants R Prynne and B C Howard. He then addressed the battalion, to which Colonel Commandant E L Rose replied. The Duke then returned to barracks and lunched with the officers and afterwards was photographed with the Officers and Colours; he then left Millbay for Windsor, a Guard of Honour being mounted at the station.[374]

On 31st July the Officers gave a ball, a special floor being laid in the drill shed, and supper

---
374 See The Globe and Laurel 1895-96 p 110.

in the mess room, the new Colours being marched from the drill shed with ceremony to their permanent home in the Officers' Messroom, where they hang in company with their forerunners of 1858 and 1827.

Appendix II - Commanding Officers

Chatham

Date	Appointment	Name	Remarks
25 March	1755 Lieutenant Colonel	Charles Gordon	To retired full pay.
22 April	1758	James Burleigh	To Plymouth by exchange.
1 July	1758	Richard Bendyshe	To retired pay.
16 April	1771 Colonel Commandant	John Mackenzie	To Commandant in Town.
1 August	1783	Walter Carruthers	Died at Chatham
24 December	1791	John Tupper	To Commandant in Town.
6 November	1794	Harrie Innes	
24 December	1803	John Barclay	To Commandant in Town.
24 September	1806	Henry Anderson	
25 July	1809	Henry Bell	To Commandant in Town.
29 April	1814	Robert Winter	
1 October	1819	Lawrence Desborough	
28 July	1821	James Campbell	
20 June	1825	J. Boscawen Savage	
13 March	1831	Walter Tremenheore KH	
16 July	1837	Elias Lawrence CB	
13 July	1844	John Wright, KH	
30 April	1849	Walter Powell KCB	
1 November	1851	John Montreeor Pilcher	
17 June	1854	Thomas Wearing	
23 June	1855	John A Philips	
7 February	1857	Edward A Parker	
13 August	1859	Edward Rea	
28 February	1862	Thomas Lemon CB	
18 March	1865	J O Travers CB	
30 November	1886	George Lambrick ADC	
31 March	1870	Charles Louis	
30 September	1873	G B Rodney CB	Promoted.
18 September	1875	P H Fellowes	
1 October	1877	G Wentworth Forbes	
28 December	1877	E L Pym	
28 June	1879	E J R Connolly	
3 June	1882	R W Bland-Hunt ADC	To retired pay
3 June	1885	Geoffry Mairis	Promoted
22 May	1886	Samuel J Graham CB	"
25 June	1887	Gustavus F Morro	"

8 April	1889		Ponsonby R Holmes	
25 March	1892		James W Scott CB ADC	To retired pay
26 March	1895		George H T Colwell CB	Promoted.
9 May	1897		Frederic V G Bird	Died at Chatham
30 December	1899		Herbert S G Schomberg	Promoted
12 December	1901		Roger Pine-Coffin	"
11 April	1903		Cosmo G Gordon	To retired pay
11 April	1906		George T Onslow	"
11 April	1909		Edwin L McCauslan	Promoted
19 May	1910		John F Daniell	"
11 April	1912		C H Kennedy CB	To retired pay
11 April	1916	Brigadier General	A E Marchant CB ADC	To retired pay
11 April	1918		H M C W Graham CMG	"
11 April	1921	Colonel Commandant	A R Hutchison CB CMG DSO ADC	Promoted
1 January	1924		F C Edwards	To Plymouth by exchange
21 June	1924		R H Morgan CBE	Promoted
3 December	1926		P Molloy	"
1 October	1928	Brigadier	F H Griffiths	"
10 July	1930		R F C Foster CB CMG DSO	"

Portsmouth

23 March	1755	Lieutenant Colonel	James Paterson	To Commandant in Town
19 Decembe	1755		Richard Bendyshe	To Plymouth
17 February	1756		T Dury	To Acting Commandant in Town
23 February	1761		Hector Boisrond	Colonel Commandant
16 April	1772	Colonel Commandant	H Smith	To Commandant in Town
24 December	1791		W Souter (later Souter-Johnstone)	To Plymouth by exchange
1 February	1793		Harrie Innes	To Chatham by exchange
5 November	1794		Maurice Wemyse	Placed half-pay sentence GCM 10.12.1797
9 February	1798		Thomas Avarne	To retired full pay
24 December	1803		George Elliot	"
28 April	1814	Major General	R Williams	
19 July	1821	Colonel Commandant	Robert Moncrieffe	
20 December	1827		Sir Richard Williams KCB	
17 July	1835		Harry P Lewis	
10 July	1837		E C Hornby	
27 December	1837		George Jones	
9 November	1846		Thomas Aelett	

Appendix II

17 August	1848		Charles Menzies	
21 June	1854		George B Bury	
1 August	1854		James J Willes	
22 June	1855		Fortescue Graham CB	
20 February	1857		Thomas Hurdle CB	
21 November	1859		Alexander Anderson	
16 May	1862		John J G Ayles	
3 November	1864		William H March	
21 November	1865		Hayes Marriott	
13 February	1867		William S Aslett	
13 February	1872		Richard Clavell	Died
29 July	1878		Charles W Adair	
2 September	1878		Hamond W Gwyn	
1 July	1880		William E Worthy Bennett	To retired full pay
1 July	1883		John M de C Meade	
7 November	1885		Howard Sutton Jones CB	
18 July	1886		Ardley F H Barnes	
29 August	1888		John Cairncross	
20 November	1889		John M Moody	To retired full pay
20 November	1892		Joseph Phillips CB	"
20 November	1895		Edward W G Byam	"
20 November	1898		Christopher F Fagan	Promoted
1 March	1900		Robert B Hirchoffer"	
23 April	1902		Arthur E Chapman	To retired full pay
23 April	1905		Thomas J P Evans	"
23 April	1908		Albert F Gatliff	"
22 February	1910		Francis J Cotter	Promoted
21 November	1910		John R H Oldfield	To retired full pay
21 November	1913		Edward C B Roe	"
21 November	1916	Brigadier General	Charles N Trotman CB	Promoted
21 November	1919	"	Herbert E Blumberg CB"	
30 November	1920	"	St George Bowes Armstrong CB CMG	"

Division Amalgamated with RMA

23 June	1923	Brigadier General	Picton Phillipp CMG MVO ADC	Promoted
		"	John Bruce Finlaison CMG	
		"	Arthur G Little CMG	
		"	H A Hathway Jones	
		"	G R S Hickson CBE	

Plymouth

24 March	1755	Lieutenant Colonel	T Dury	Transferred to Portsmouth

14 April	1756	"	R Bendyshe	To Chatham by exchange
1 July	1758	"	James Burleigh	To retired full pay
15 April	1771	Colonel Commandant	James Bell	" "
15 September	1784	"	A Tooker Collins	Died
4 January	1793	"	Harrie Innes	To Portsmouth by exchange
1 February	1793	"	William Souter (Souter-Johnstone)	To Commandant in Town
19 February	1795	"	John Bowater	To retired full pay
27 December	1803	"	R Bright	" "
26 May	1814	"	T Strickland	Promoted Lieutenant General
1 October	1819	"	Watkin Tench	To retired pay
19 July	1821	"	George Elliot Vinicombe	
22 July	1830	"	T Abernethie KH	
10 July	1837	"	George Lewis CB	
26 August	1839	"	Thomas B Adair	
12 February	1842	"	George Beatty	
9 November	1848	"	Edward Smith Mercer	
27 December	1847	"	John McCallum	
25 April	1849	"	William Fergusson	
26 February	1851	"	Abraham Henry Gordon	
23 December	1851	"	John Rawlins Coryton	
14 July	1855	"	Joseph Childs	
1 April	1857	"	Thomas Peard Dwyer	
21 November	1859	"	Thomas Holloway CB ADC	
29 May	1863	"	John Hawkins Gascolgne CB ADC	
23 August	1886	"	Samuel Netteville Lowder ADC	To Deputy Adjutant General
1 July	1867	"	William Francis Foote	
31 March	1869	"	William Grigor Suther CB	
29 November	1872	"	Penrose Charles Penrose CB	
7 May	1877	"	John Henry Stewart	
2 December	1877	"	Charles McArthur	
13 April	1879	"	George Bayles Heaety	To retired full pay
13 April	1882	"	Horatio Charles Nelson Blanckley	
13 April	1886	"	Francis W Thomas	Promoted
1 February	1888	"	Frederic Gasper le Grand	
16 April	1887	"	G F Monro	To Chatham by exchange
22 June	1887	"	Arthur Huntly Hill Walsh	
8 September	1889	"	Mackay A J Heriot	To retired pay
8 September	1892	"	Nowell Fitzupton Way CB	" "

APPENDIX II

8 September	1895	"	Edward Lee Rose	Promoted.
31 January	1898	"	C H Scafe	"
10 February	1900	"	F Baldwin	"
30 January	1902	"	A D Corbet CB	To retired full pay
30 January	1905	"	William T Adair	Promoted
29 September	1906	"	H C Engler	"
14 July	1909	"	H C Money CB ADC	"
12 October	1910	"	Charles George Britten	To retired full pay
12 October	1913	Brigadier General	Charles L Gordon	Promoted
21 June	1915	"	Charles E Curtoys CB	To retired full pay
21 June	1918	"	Edward J Stroud CB CMG	Promoted
21 June	1921	Colonel Commandant	G J H Mullins CB	"
21 June	1924	"	F C Edwards	"
16 June	1926	"	R C Paterson OBE	"
1 April	1928	Brigadier	G L Raikes DSC CB	"
3 December	1929	"	George Carpenter OBE CB	"

Woolwich

15 August	1806	Colonel Commandant	John Fletcher	Dismissed Service by GCM
10 December	1808	"	Andrew Burn	
29 April	1814	"	Theophilus Lewis	
19 July	1821	"	Lewis Charles Meares	
12 November	1826	"	Robert M'Cleverty CB	
10 January	1837	"	George Prescott Wingrove	
26 August	1839	"	William Connolly	
12 February	1842	"	T A Parke CB	
19 November	1851	"	D J Ballinghall	
10 January	1852	"	Robert Mercer	
18 October	1852	"	Samuel Burdon Ellis CB	Promoted
22 June	1855	"	John Ashmore	
30 October	1855	"	John Tatton Brown	Promoted
8 September	1858	"	Anthony Blaxland Stransham	To Inspector General
22 December	1860	"	F A Campbell	
1 March	1862	"	John Mitchell	
28 March	1863	"	John Alexander Philips	
13 June	1865	"	William Robert Mitchell	
10 November	1866	"	Richard George Connolly	
29 November	1867	"	William Grigor Suther CB	To Plymouth 31 March 1869

519

Blumberg's History of the Royal Marines 1755-1914

Royal Marine Artillery

Major Commandant

1 January	1816	Maj & Bt Lt Col	Sir Richard Williams KCB	Lt Col 12 Jul 1821 to Portsmouth Div.
22 July	1830	Bt Maj	T A Parke	Act Lt Col 31 Dec 1832 To Woolwich Div.
10 July	1837	Lt Col	C H Menzies KH	To Command Portsmouth Div.
10 July	1844	"	D A Gibsone	
4 September	1851	"	J A Philips	To Command Chatham

Abolished as separate Unit, 7 February 1832 and placed under Commandant, Portsmouth
Re-established 1859
Separate List 1862

21 November	1859	Colonel Commandant	J Fraser	
20 June	1862	"	H C Tate	
28 November	1865	"	G G Alexander	
10 April	1867	"	G A Schomberg	
1 April	1870	"	C L Barnard	
10 July	1872	"	J W C Williams	Promoted
3 May	1876	"	G S Digby	
20 March	1877	"	H Adair	
3 July	1880	"	H W Mawbey	To retired pay
3 July	1883	"	E H Cox	Promoted
3 September	1883	"	G Brydges	To retired pay
3 September	1886	"	Sir F W Festing KCMG CB	
5 October	1886	"	F E Halliday	
22 November	1886	"	H B Tuson CB	
21 May	1888	"	John F Crease	To retired pay
21 May	1891	"	G C Suther	Promoted
29 August	1892	"	F A Ogle	To retired full pay
29 August	1896	"	F H Poore	To retired pay
29 August	1899	"	W G Tucker	Promoted
28 September	1902	Colonel Commandant	William Campbell	Promoted
1 August	1904	"	John B Leefe	"
10 August	1906	"	W C Nicholls	
1 July	1908	"	J H Bor CMG	To retired pay
26 June	1911	"	W I Eastman	Promoted
7 February	1912	"	L T Pease	"
6 June	1914	"	H L Talbot	"

Appendix II

24 September	1914	Brigadier-General	Sir George Aston KCB	To retired pay
24 September	1917	"	George M Campbell	Promoted
2 July	1920	"	L Conway-Gordon CB	
3 October	1921	Colonel Commandant	G R Poole CMG DSO	
11 December	1922	"	Picton Phillipps CMG MVO	

Amalgamated with Portsmouth Division 23 June 1923

Depot Royal Marines

	1861	Lieutenant Colonel	W R Maxwell	To Woolwich
21 September	1864	"	P H Fellows	
29 November	1869	Col 2nd Commandant	G B Rodney	From Woolwich
18 September	1873	"	J H Stewart	To Plymouth
7 May	1877	"	G W Forbes	To Chatham
25 December	1877	"	G B Heasty	To Plymouth
13 April	1879	"	H Worthy Bennett	To Portsmouth
4 July	1850	"	H C N Blanckley	To Plymouth
13 April	1882	"	J H Mashery	
14 April	1883	"	G Mairis	To Chatham
4 June	1885	"	H S Jones CB ADC	To Portsmouth
7 November	1885	"	S J Graham CB	To Chatham
9 May	1886	"	F G Munro	To Chatham
15 April	1887	"	J Cairncross	To Portsmouth
29 August	1888	"	M A H G Heriot	To Plymouth
8 September	1889	"	N F Sampson-Way CB	To Plymouth
8 September	1892	"	G H T Colwell CB	To Chatham
23 March	1895	"	J I Morris	Deputy Adjutant General
23 May	1899	"	A B Crosbie	
19 October	1900	"	T W Dowding	
2 October	1902	"	T F D Bridge ADC	
2 October	1905	"	T H de M Roche DSO	
2 October	1908	"	E A Wylde	
1 May	1910	"	J R Johnstone CB	
22 January	1911	Brigadier General	J H Swanton	
22 January	1914	"	H S Neville White MVO	
22 April	1918	Col Comdt Brig Gen	C McN Parsons CB ADC	
1 October	1920	Colonel Commandant	H D Farquharson CMG	
1 January	1923	"	L S T Halliday VC CB	Adjutant General
11 December	1925	"	R C Temple OBE CB.	
16 June	1927	Brigadier	C L Mayhew	

521

13 July	1928	"	R V T Ford CB OBE ADC	Adjutant General
16 June	1930	"	L C Lampen	

Commandants in Town

19 December	1755	Colonel	James Paterson	Commandant in Town
23 February	1761	Major General	T Dury	Acting Commandant in Town
1 August	1783	Col.Comdt & Lt Gen	John Mackenzie	Commandant in Town
24 December	1791	" " "	Henry Smith	" "
29 October	1794	" " & Maj Gen	John Tupper	" "
15 February	1795	" " & Lt Gen	William Souter (Souter Johnstone)	" "
21 December	1803	Col 2nd Comdt & Lt Gen	John Campbell	" "
24 December	1806	Col Comdt. & Lt Gen	John Barclay	" "
29 April	1814	" " & Maj Gen	Sir Henry Bell	" "

Deputy Adjutant Generals

1 August	1825	Col Comdt & Maj Gen	James Campbell	From Chatham
17 March	1831	" "	Sir J. Boscawen Savage KCB	From Chatham
1 January	1838	Lieutenant Colonel	Sir John Owen KCB KH	
14 December	1854	"	S R Wesley	
1 January	1862	"	G C Langley	
1 July	1867	Colonel Commandant	S N Lowder CB	From Plymouth
10 July	1872	Major General	G A Schomberg CB	From RMA
1 October	1875	Colonel Commandant	G B Rodney CB	From Chatham. Resigned
3 September	1878	Major General	C W Adair	From Portsmouth
3 September	1883	"	J W C Williams	From RMA
29 August	1888	"	Howard S Jones CB	From Portsmouth
29 August	1893	Lieutenant General	Sir H B Tuson KCB	From RMA
1 March	1900	Major General	J I Morris	From Depot RM. Died
19 June	1902	"	W P Wright	From RMO
19 June	1907	"	W T Adair CB	From Plymouth
28 June	1911	"	W C Nicholls	From RMA

Adjutant Generals (from 1914)

21 January	1914	Major General	W C Nicholls	
28 June	1916	Colonel 2nd Comdt	D Mercer CB	From RN Division. Died
2 July	1920	Major General	G M Campbell CB	From RMA. Died
30 November	1920	Colonel Commandant	H Blumberg CB	From Portsmouth
31 March	1924	Major General	A R H Hutchison CB CMG DSO	From Chatham

Appendix II

| 1 October | 1927 | Lieutenant General | Lewis S T Halliday VC | From Depot RM |
| 1 October | 1930 | Major General | R V T Ford CBE | From Depot RM |

Inspector Generals

| 2 March | 1831 | Major General | Sir James Cockburn KCB | ? From Army Office |

(Under Secretary for War & Colonies, 1806) Abolished 10 May 1836

| 9 January | 1862 | " | A B Stransham | R.M.L.I. |
| 9 January | 1887 | " | J O Travers CB | R.M.L.I. |

(Office abolished 18 December 1888)

Appendix III - The Earl St Vincent

The following letters with reference to the portrait of Earl St Vincent in the Portsmouth Mess are abstracted from the Portsmouth Letter Books to the Admiralty 1802 to 1806.

Royal Marine Barracks Portsmouth
May 17th 1804

My Lord,

The Officers of the Division which I have the honour to command, impressed with lasting gratitude for the many benefits conferred by your Lordship on their Corps; beg leave, as a small testimony of their sense of obligation, to solicit through me that you will be pleased to allow some artist of eminence (whoever your Lordship may approve of) to take your portrait that it may be placed in the Mess Room at this Headquarters. Permit me to express particular pleasure in communicating this wish to your Lordship and also to assure you, that I am with the most profound respect, My Lord

Your Lordship's Most obedient servant
George Elliot,
Major General, Royal Marines.

To:
Lieutenant General Campbell,
Commandant in Town.

Royal Marine Barracks Portsmouth
20th May 1804

Sir,

By particular desire of the officers of the Division a letter of which the enclosed is a copy, was forwarded to Earl St Vincent, a copy of whose letter in return is likewise transmitted for your information, you will perceive that Sir William Beechey is the artist alluded to, and I am to request you will wait on that gentleman and give him directions to take a painting of His Lordship, near the size of that of Earl Spencer at Plymouth; our Mess Room not being capable of containing a picture of larger dimensions; and also to wait on his Lordship and express the high sense of the satisfaction we feel at his indulgence and request he will be pleased to inform you of the time it will be most convenient for Sir W Beechey to wait on him.

I am Sir
Your most humble servant

George Elliot,
Major General.

The following letters are taken from the letters of Earl St Vincent.[375]
Earl St Vincent agrees to sit to Sir W Beechey for his portrait for the officers of the Portsmouth Division Royal Marines.

Major General Elliot.
29th May 1804

Colonel Burn,
"I am much gratified by the sentiments which the officers of the Chatham Division of Royal Marines have been pleased to express of the attention I have paid to honour and interest of the Corps, and although I feel the sitting for my portrait very irksome I shall comply with their request and hope they will approve of Sir William Beechey."

It is probable that there is a similar letter to account for the portrait of Lord St Vincent in the Plymouth Mess.

---

375 Navy Records Society.

Index

Accoutrements, 6, 8, 42, 47, 51, 53, 54, 59, 102, 257, 492
Adair W, Mr, Paymaster and Agent, 4 , 250
Adjutant Generals, x, xi, 4, 98, 152, 159, 249, 255, 369, 483, 488, 518, 521, 522
Adjutants, x, 4, 7, 8, 27, 41, 42, 43, 50, 51, 50, 71, 99, 100, 127, 150, 172, 102, 200, 242, 254, 255, 256, 260, 285, 298, 326, 360, 435, 473, 483
Alfonso, King of Spain, 266
Arabi Pasha, Egyptian Commander, 384, 387, 388, 391, 392, 394, 400, 401, 406
Arms
    Enfield Rifle, 309
    Gardner Guns, 433 413, 417, 420, 421, 422, 423, 424, 425
    Krupp Guns, 396, 397, 398, 407, 408, 424, 413, 423, 424, 452, 453, 457, 461, 463
    Lee-Enfield, 479
    Lee-Metford Magazine Rifle, 440, 453
    Martini-Henry Rifle, 309, 440, 453
    Minie Rifle, 309, 331
    Snider Rifle, 309
Armstrong Guns, 351, 354, 363, 366, 379, 385
Army Discipline Act, 373, 407
Anstruther's Regiment, 7
Army Officers
    Abercrombie Sir R, Gen, 128, 130 ,148, 153, 154, 203, 204
    Adams, Col, 282
    Auchmuty Sir S, Col later Gen, 178, 179, 212, 213, 214, 215
    Albemarle Lord, Gen, 32
    Alison Sir A, Maj Gen , 389, 390, 391, 16
    Amherst, Gen, 16, 17
    Anson, Maj, 352
    Apthorp, Col, 304
    Arnold, Maj Gen, 66
    Backhouse, Col, 178
    Baird, Sir D, Gen, 153, 175, 176, 178
    Baillie, Col, 89
    Baker Russell, Maj, 375
    Barker, Lt, 4th Kings Own Regiment , 57, 60
    Barrington, Gen, 20, 22
    Beckwith Sir R, Gen
    Beresford Gen, 175, 176, 177, 178, 179,
    Beresford Lord C, 387, 388, 418
    Blakeney, Gen, Governor of Minorca, 13
    Bligh, Gen, 19
    Boneywood, Col, 4
    Bookland, Maj Gen, 4
    Boscawen, Col , 417
    Braddock, Gen
    Braithwaite, 89, 90
    Bromhead, Lt , 380
    Brook, Lt Col,, 237, 239
    Brooke, Col, 237, 239
    Brown G, Gen, 315
    Bruce, Maj Gen, 120
    Bruce-Hamilton, Col, 441
    Buller Sr R, Gen, 408, 418, 419, 446, 448, 449
    Burgoyne, Maj Gen later Gen, 63, 72, 73
    Burrell, Gen, 282, 284

Cameron D, Gen, 366, 367
Campbell Sir C, Col later Gen, 160, 249, 313, 328, 329, 330
Carleton, Sir Guy, 66
Cathcart, Lord
Chard, Lt, 380
Chelmsford, Lord, Gen, 378, 380, 381, 382
Church R, Capt, 199205
Clarke A, Gen, 125, 126
Clarke, Maj, 199, 205
Clifford The Hon A, Maj later Col , 344
Clinton, Sir H, 73, 74, 81, 84
Clinton Sir W, Gen, 256
Clinton C, Maj Gen later Gen , 63, 65, 69, 71, 72
Cockburn Sir J, Maj Gen, 34, 249, 523
Colley, Gen, 383
Coote, Sir E, Col later Gen, 35, 89, 90, 154
Cotton, Maj, 304
Cornwallis, Lord, Gen, 71, 72, 81, 84, 85
Craig, Maj Gen, 125, 126
Craigie, Lt Col, 289
Crealock, Maj Gen, 382
Crosby, 89
Crauford, Col later Maj Gen, 28, 29, 179
Cuyler, Maj Gen, 119
Cunningham, Maj, Engineers, 13
Davis, Maj Gen, 407, 408, 409
Davis, Lt Gen, 510
de Rottenburg, Gen, 230
Dorward, Brig Gen, 459
Douglas Sir H, Gen , 218
Draper, Gen, 34, 36
Drummond G, Col later Gen, 202, 231, 232, 233, 234
Duff, Capt, 285, 286
Dundas, Gen, 119, 120, 122
Dury-Lowe, Gen, 395, 401
Earle, Gen, 419
Elliot, Gen, 32, 304
Errington, Maj, 304
Evans, Gen, 119, Lt Gen, 266, 267, 269
Fischer, Col , 232, 233, 234
Fisher, Maj RE, 348
Flood, Col, 379
Fratt, Maj, 279
Gage, Gen, 57, 58, 60, 62, 68
Gaselee Sir A, Gen, 463, 464
Gibbs, Col, 214
Giffard, 376, 377
Gillespie, Lord, Col, 212
Godwin H, Maj Gen, 303, 304
Gordon, Gen, 406, 413, 415, 418
Gordon C, Col (Chinese Gordon) , 355
Gough Sir H, Gen, 276, 277, 281, 282, 283, 284, 286, 290, 291, 292, 293, 294, 339
Graham, Gen, 207
Greaves, Gen, 420
Grant Sir H, Gen, 63, 76, 332, 349, 353
Green Sir C, Gen, 167
Grant, Brig Gen, 63
Greer, Col, 367

Grey Sir C, Gen , 121
Hacket, Capt , 339
Hadfield Lt , 285
Handcock, Maj, 230, 231
Havelock Sir H, Gen, 328
Haviland, Gen, 31
Hedgson, Gen, 28, 29, 30
Hope A, Gen , 329, 330, 332
Howe, Col later Maj Gen , 25, 32, 33, 63, 64, 65, 68, 69, 72, 73
Hudson Lowe, Col , 199, 205
Inglis, Col, 328
Jones, Brig Gen , 63, 321
Keating, Col , 202, 203
Knight, Pte, 278
Knyphausen, Gen , 72
Lambert, Brig Gen , 28, 29
Lawrence, Col, 34
Loudon, Lord , 14
Luard, Maj, 339
Ludlow, Gen, 184
Lumley, Col, 178
Lyon-Fremantle, Maj Gen, 412
Madden, Maj, 439
Massy, Gen, 71
Maitland,, Gen, 196, 197
McLeod, Col, 204
McNeill, Sir J, Gen, 420, 423, 424
Mee, Capt, 277
Methuen, Lord, 446, 447, 448
Michel Sir J, Gen , 351
Middleton, 329
Monckton, Gen, 23, 25, 30, 31, 32
Monson, Maj, 35
Montgomerie, Lt Col, 294
Montgomery, Maj Gen, 66
Mordaunt Sir J, Gen, 15
Morris, Lt Col, 283, 289
Morrison, Lt Col, 230
Mulgrave, Lord, Brig Gen, 118
Munro, Sir H, 88, 89, 90
Murray, Gen, 23, 24, 25
Napier Sir C, Col later Gen, 227, 228
Napier, Sir R, Gen, 350, 351
Nelson, Maj (40th Regt), 365
Newdigate, Maj Gen, 382
Nicoll, 38
Nugent, Lt Col, 119
O'Hara, Gen, 119
Outram Sir J, Gen , 328, 329
Ord, Maj RE, 322
Oswald, Brig Gen later Gen, 198, 205, 206, 206
Pakenham, Gen, 242
Paterson, Capt later Lt Col , 29, 237
Paton, Sgt, 329
Pearson, Col, 60, 130, 379, 380
Pearson Lt (69th Regt), 139
Pennington, Col, 398
Percy, Lord, Brig Gen, 58, 60, 63, 69
Phillips, Maj Gen, 84
Pigot, Brig Gen, 63, 64, 65, 75
Pole-Carew, Gen , 449
Poole, Capt , (East Yorkshire Regt) 451, 452, 465

527

Blumberg's History of the Royal Marines 1755-1914

Powell, Col, 327
Pratt, Maj later Maj Gen, 278, 292, 365, 366
Prevost, Col later Gen , 78, 229, 234
Pritchard, Lt RE, 352
Raglan, Lord, 312, 314, 317
Roberts, Lord, 430, 448, 449
Robertson, Brig Gen, 63
Ross, Gen, 236, 237, 238, 239
Rosslyn, Lord , 185
Rotton, Capt RA, 333
Russell, Col, 331, 332
Schoedder, Gen, 294
Scott, Lt Col, 233, 447
Smith,, Lt Col, (10th Regt), 60, 61
Smith Sir C, Col, 272, 275
Smith P, Capt, (30th Regt), 29, 451
Spencer, Lord, Gen, 132, 193
Spencer The Hon H B, Brig Gen, 318
Staveley, Gen, 355
Stewart, Brig Gen, 415, 416, 417, 418, 419
Stuart, Col, 22nd Regiment, 126, 129,
Stuart Hon C, Gen , 143, 144
Stuart, Sir J, Gen, 181
Talbot, Col, 419
Thornton, Lt Col, 237, 242
Townshend, 23
Turnbull, Lt, 211
Van Straubenzee, Maj Gen, 338, 339, 341, 344, 346, 349
Vaughan, Gen, 83
Vilettes, Lt Col , 120
Vincent, Gen, 229, 231
Walker, Capt, Artillery, 18
Walsh, Brig Gen, 31, 342
Webster, Gen, 81
Wellesley, Sir A, Gen later Lord Wellington, 184, 185, 193, 197, 208, 217, 219, 220, 221, 225, 236, 432
Wetherall, Col, 212, 213, 214
Whitelook, Lt Gen, 179
Whyte, Maj Gen, 128
Wilson Sir C, Col, 417, 418
Wolfe, Lt Gen, 4,, 17, 23, 24, 25
Wolfe, Col , 15, 16, 17
Wolseley, Sir G later Lord, 374, 375,, 376, 377, 382, 391, 392, 398, 399, 402, 413, 415, 418, 419, 420, 427
Wood Sir E, Gen, 391, 419
Wood, Col. 212, 213, 214, 377. 378, 382
Worge, Col then Governor of Goree, 18
Wyke Sir C, Gen, 362

Army Regiments
Life Guards, 395, 486
Blues (Blues and Royals), 395,486
Light l Dragoons , 28, 175, 178, 198, 212, 215, 230
Kings Dragoon Guards, 382
Royal Dragoons, 486
6th Dragoon Guards, 179, 396, 397
4th Dragoon Guards, 396, 397
7th Dragoon Guards, 396
19th Hussars, 23, 375, 400, 415, 416, 420
5th Lancers, 179, 420, 423
Coldstream Guards , 319, 486
Grenadier Guards, 424, 486
1st Royal Scots, 119, 233, 234, 348, 486, 511
2nd Regiment, Queens, 121
3rd The Buffs, 155, 379, 380, 381, 486

4th Kings Own, 63, 236 , 236, 237, 238, 239, 237, 487
5th Regiment, 62, 63, 64, 80
6th Royal Warwicks, 204, 487
7th Royal Fusiliiers, 13
9th Regiment, 119, 303
10th Regiment, 60, 62, 63, 230, 490
12th Regiment, 303, 365
13th Regiment, 230, 231
14th Regiment, 212, 214, 366
15th East Yorkshire Regiment, 151, 152
16th Regiment, 78
18th Royal Irish, 63, 278, 282, 282, 284, 285, 287, 289, 293, 290, 401, 407
19th Green Howards , 29, 487
20th Lancashire Fusiliers, 20, 362, 487
21st Regiment, 28, 236, 237, 239
22nd Regiment, 63, 128
23rd Royal Welsh Fusiliers , 13, 62, 63, 85, 87, 376, 377, 459, 460, 462, 463
24th Regiment, 13, 176, 379, 380
25th Regiment, 88
26th Regiment, 277, 278, 279, 282, 284, 285, 288
27tth Regiment, 28, 507
28th Regiment, 277, 293
29th Worcesters, 66, 121, 497
30th East Lancs, 29, 487
31st East Surreys, 43, 256, 420, 424, 487
32nd DCLI, 397, 398, 487
34th Border Regiment, 13, 487
35th Royal Sussex, 63, 205, 303, 369, 415, 417, 487
36th Worcesters, 178, 487
37th North Hampshires later Royal Hampshire Regiment, 474, 475
38th Staffordshire Regiment later South Staffs, 62, 63. 64, 175, 389, 507, 343, 415
40th Regiment, 63, 178, 270, 365
41st Regiment, 233
42nd Royal Highland later Black Watch, 376, 377, 378, 400
43rd Regiment (Gooch's Marines), 63, 64, 367
44th Regiment, 63, 198, 236, 237, 238, 352, 353
45th Regiment later Sherwood Foresters, 63, 120, 489
47th Regiment, 63, 65, 489
48th Regiment, 70, 489
49th Royal Berkshire Regiment, 63, 120, 230, 254, 277, 278 , 283, 284, 285, 286, 287, 288, 289, 290, 292, 293, 423, 425
50th Royal West Kent Regiment, 75, 153, 254, 366, 489
51st Regiment, Yorkshire West Riding, later Kings Own Yorkshire Light Infantry, 303, 304, 447, 490, 507
52nd Regiment, 63, 64, 128, 490
53rd Shropshire Regiment later KSLI, 327, 420, 422, 425, 490
55th Regiment, 288, 289, 290, 291, 293
57th Regiment, 361, 366
58th Regiment, 302, 507
59th Nottinghamshire Regiment, 63, 88, 176, 213, 214, 334, 338, 339, 340, 341, 342, 343, 344, 345
60th Rifles, 23, 352, 389, 390, 392, 398, 400, 407

60th Regiment, 78, 381, 407, 411, 507
61st Regiments, 28
63rd Regiment, 62, 63, 197, 304
65th York and Lancaster, 63, 228, 364, 365, 366, 392, 395, 396, 397, 400, 401, 407, 408, 409
67th South Hampshires later Royal Hampshire Regiment, 28, 351, 352,
68th Regiment, 367
69th Regiment, 29, 86, 130, 203, 204, 212, 213, 214
70th Regiment, 256, 366
71st Regiment later Highland Light Infantry, 176, 177
72nd Regiment, 176
74th Regiment later Highland Light Infantry, 18, 399, 400, 451
75th Gordon Highlanders, 154, 400, 407, 408
77th Regiment, 339
78th Regiment later Seaforths, 214, 401
79th Camerons, 34,, 35, 36, 153, 400
80th Staffordshire Volunteers, 119, 303
82nd Regiment, 84
83rd Regiment, 65, 176
85th Kings Light Infantry later KSLI, 228, 236, 242
86th Regiment, 123, 203, 237
87th Royal Irish Fusiliers, 80, 81, 400, 401
88th Regiment, 80, 367, 381
89th Regiment later Royal Irish Fusiliers, 212, 214, 230, 233, 255
90th Regiment, 123, 153, 379
91st Regiment, 123, 381
92nd Regiment later Gordons, 153, 154, 400
93rd Highlanders, 176, 312, 313, 315,, 316, 329
94th Regiment, 207
95th Regiment later Sherwood Foresters, 507
96th Regiment, 302
97th Regiment later Royal West Kent, 123
98th Regiment, 92
99th Regiment, 351, 354, 361, 379, 380, 381
100th Regiment, 233
101st Regiment, 37, 38
102nd (Royal Madras Fusiliers) later Royal Dublin Fusiliers, 226, 227, 228, 229
103rd (Royal Bombay Fusiliers) later Royal Dublin Fusiliers, 37, 38, 227, 233
104th Regiment, 233, 344
105th Madras Light Infantry, later KOYLI, 447
118th Regiment, 123
2nd Royal Highlanders, 20, 22, 78, 397,401, 409, 444
African Corps, 199
Askaris, 433
Bengal Light Infantry, 203
Bengal Native Infantry, 212, 346, 423
Bengal Lancers, 398, 427
Bengal Volunteers, 277, 278, 283, 384
Bengal Artillery, 349
Bombay Native Light Infnatry, 212, 277, 424
Brudenell's Regiment, 487

528

INDEX

Camel Corps, 416, 417, 419, 426, 427, 428
Chinese Regiment, 460, 461
Colonial Marines, 236, 237, 238, 239
Colt's Regiment, 487
Corsican Rangers, 198, 199, 205
De Roll's Corps, 205
De Watteville's Regiment, 232, 233
Fraser's Highlanders, 78
Giffard's Scouts, 377
Glengarry Light Infantry, 232
Greek Light Infantry, 205
Guards Camel Regiment, 414, 415, 416, 417, 419
Hong Kong Regiment, 460
Madras Native Infantry, 204 255, 277, 278, 283, 284, 285, 303, 330, 338, 339, 345
Madras Artillery, 277, 282 , 283, 289, 294
Madras Sappers, 283, 289
Madras Volunteers, 290
Moghul Cavalry, 37, 38
Mordaunt's Regiment, 487
Mounted Infantry Regiment, 395, 397, 415, 416, 420, 421, 424, 427
Native Infantry, 285, 286, 303, 345, 423
Natal Native Contingent, 379
Nepalese Regiments, 331, 332
New South Wales Battalion, 420, 425
Punjab Native Infantry, 351, 354
Rohilla Horse, 37, 38
Rufane's Regiment
Russell's Native Regiment, 376, 377, 378
Sepoy Regiments, 36, 37, 38, 39, 90, 91, 204, 215, 327, 331, 344
Seymour's Regiment, 487
15th Sikhs, 331, 423, 424, 425, 427, 462, 464
St Helena Infantry, 176, 177
US Infantry, 465
Webb's Regiment, 23
Wei-Hai-Wei Regiment, 461, 463
West African Regiment , 441
West India Regiment, 195, 373, 374, 376, 438, 439
York Rangers, 196

Badges of Rank, 200, 201
Badges, 154, 295, 300, 490, 509
Bands, 48, 297, 371, 435, 472, 473, 479
 Bandmasters, 383, 446, 473, 484
 Depot Band, 433
 Musicians, 484
Barracks, 5, 46, 47, 51, 103, 107, 111, 157, 161, 179, 216, 325
Barrack Locations
 Berry Head, 220, 225, 235
 Cambridge (Woolwich) , 299, 361
 Chatham, 81, 95, 161, 255, 265, 325
 Clarence, 95, 161, 258, 265, 299
 Deal, 357, 361
 Eastney, 358
 Fort Cumberland, 157. 161, 260, 265, 97, 325
 Forton, 299, 323
 Gunwharf, 297, 325
 Hilsea , 96, 137
 Stonehouse, 95, 99, 100, 161, 325
Batavian Republic, 117
Battles/Operations/Engagements/

Commitments
Agadir , 481
Ascension, 376, 437
Afghan War, 419, 428, 504
Algiers, 251
American War of Independence, 57, 58
 Lexington , 60
 Bunker's Hill, 61, 62, 63, 64, 65, 66
 Charlestown, 57, 58, 60, 61, 62, 64, 66
 Gloucester and Yorktown, 84
 Philadelphia, 72, 73, 74
 Savannah, 68, 78
 Dorchester Heights, 57, 62, 66, 68
American War 1812-1815 , 225-241
 Chesapeake, 73, 75, 84, 225-239
 New York, 14, 30, 32, 34, 66, 69, 70
 Washington, George, 70, 72, 84
 Washington, Burning of, 236, 237, 238
 Yorktown and Hampton Roads, 68, 84, 228
Ashanti War, 373, 374, 375
 Abrakrampa, 375
 Amoaful, 377
 Coomassie , 376, 377
 Elmina, 373, 374
 Essaman, 374
Baltic Campaign 320
 Anholt, 210
 Bomarsund, 321
 Viborg, 323
 Sveaborg, 324
Belle Isle or Belleisle, 16 , 17, 26, 28, 29, 30, 32, 47, 490
Boer War 1881 , 383
Botany Bay, 47, 103, 104, 105, 106, 111
Boxer Rising 1900, 450, 452
 Hsi-Ku, 454
 Hsi-Kuan-Su, 460, 461
 Taku, 458
 Tientsin, 456
 Peking, 463
 Capt Hallliday 's VC, 453
British Columbia, 345, 436
Burmah 1824, 255
Burmah 1852 , 303
 Rangoon , 303
 Bassein, 304
 Pegu , 304
 Prome, 304
Burmah 1885-87 , 429
Buxar, 37
 Cadiz, 131
 Calder's Action, 170
Canada, 11, 20, 22, 27, 36, 66, 69, 229, 230, 436
 Esquimalt Defences, 436
 Fort Erie, 233
 Niagara, 229, 230, 231
 Plains of Abraham, 25
 Plattsburg, 231
 Quebec, 12, 16, 17, 22, 23, 24, 66, 229
 Rivers and lakes , 229
 St Lawrence River, 20, 22, 23, 229, 230
 St Johns, Newfoundland , 34
 York now Toronto, 231
Cape of Good Hope, 89, 125, 155, 175, 176, 203, 405
Cape St Vincent, 26, 80, 130
China 1840-1843, 271, 276

Amoy, 277, 287, 288, 292, 295
Anunghoy , 279, 280, 334
Bogue Forts , 277
Canton, 276, 277, 278, 281, 286, 295, 332, 333
Chapoo, 292
Chusan, 276
Hong Kong, 276, 279, 295, 327
Macao, 276, 277, 280, 281
Ningpo and Chinghai, 290
Tsekee, 291, 292
Woosung, 293
Yang-tse-Kiang, 292
China 1856- 1860, 332
 Canton, 333, 334, 339, 345
 Escape Creek, 334
 Fatshan Creek, 335
 Honan Island , 336
 Nantow, 344
 Taku Forts, 346, 351
 Shanghai, 350
 Peking, 353
 Taeping Rebellion, 355
 White Cloud Mountain, 344
 RM Memorial in Hong Kong China, 354
Chinese Pirates , 364
Crimea, 307, 309, 311
 Eupatoria, 311
 Balaclava, 314, 315
 Inkerman, 314
 Charge of the Heavy and Light Brigades, 314
 Redan, 315
 Azoff, 315
 Kertch, 316
 Yenikale, 316
 Kinburn, 318
 Malakoff and Redan, 317
 Sebastopol, 311,312, 314, 317
Dardanelles, 185, 186, 210, 243
Constantinople, 186, 187, 310
Gallipoli, 15, 17, 21, 24, 28, 29, 32, 187, 310
Dubai/Persian Gulf, 480
East Africa, 437
 Pumwani, 437
 M'Weli, 439
 Zanzibar, 440
East Indies, 34, 77, 88, 91, 93, 155, 175
 Karachi, 270
 Madras Roads, 34
 Cuddalore, 34, 35, 89, 91, 92
 Negapatam, 92
 Pondicherry, 34, 35, 37
 Trincomali, 90, 92, 126
Egypt 1799, 145, 153, 188, 272
 Aboukir, 153
 Alexandria, 154
 Battle of the Nile, 142
 Cairo, 142, 145
 Mandora, 153
Egypt 1881-1882, 383, 384
 Alexandria, 384, 387
 Cairo, 390
 Ismalia, 393
 Mellaha Junction, 390 ,
 Port Said, 393
 Seizure of Suez Canal, 391
 El Magfar, 395
 Tel-el-Mahuta, 395

529

Kassassin, 396
Mahsameh, 396
Nefiche, 393
Tel-el-Kebir, 398
Tel-el-Mahuta, 395
Encounter with the Dutch Fleet, 136
  Dogger Bank, 83
  St Marcou, 127, 136, 140, 144
  Surinam, 168
French Revolutionary Wars, 117
  La Vendee, 117
  Toulon, 110
Copenhagen, 151, 184
Corsica, 120, 122
Gaeta, 181
Glorious First of June, 121
Gulf of Mexico, 241
  Mexico, 361, ,
  New Orleans, 11, 241, 242
  Havana, 32, 36
Heligoland, 185
Herqui, 129
Indian Mutiny, 326, 336
  Amorah,, 332
  Calcutta, 327
  Cawnpore, 330
  Fathpur, 327
  Gorakhpur, 331
  Lucknow, 328
  Phoolpore, 331
Indian Ocean, 202
  Mauritius and Reunion, 202
  Point du Diable, 203
Ireland,, 132, 142, 183, 245, 260, 302, 383, 481, 495
Japan, 292
  Chapoo, 292
  Simonoseki, 362, 363, 501
  Woosung, 293
  Yang-tse-Kiang, 2292
Java, 212
Kempenfeldt's Action, 65
Louisburg, 12, 14, 17, 20
Manila, 32, 36, 186
Mediterranean, 204
  Carthagena, 16
  Crete, 442, 444
  Gibraaltar, 13, 16, 26, 77, 80, 83, 86, 88, 487. 499, 509
  Grao, 206
  Languelia, 217
  Lissa , 206
  L'Orient, 127
  Matagorda, 207
  Minorca, 12, 13, 14, 20, 36, 80, 85, 93, 143
  Navarino, 257
  Palamos, 206
  Point du Che, 207
  Porto Ferrajo, 122
  Santa Maura, 205
  Tangier, 486
  Toulon, 13, 14, 16, 25, 26, 117, 118, 120, 122, 142, 163, 169, 181, 194, 198, 206
New Zealand, 302, 357, 364
North America, 11, 14, 16, 22, 30, 58, 74, 77, 84,, 87, 155, 196, 222, 486, 498
  Amoa, 79
  Savannah, 78

Passchendaele, 504
Peninsular War, 193
  Figueiro, 193
  Hague, 221
  Lisbon, 188, 193, 208, 209, 256
  Rosas, 194
  Vimiero, 193
  Vittoria, 221
Persian Gulf, and Aden, 270
Peru, 378
Port Hamilton, 428
Porto Cavallo, 79
Porto Praya, 89
Porto Novo, 89, 92
Porto Ferrajo, 122, 152, 153, 155
Portuagal, 155, 185, 188, 193, 197, 256, 260, 301, 477, 478
Rochefort and Aix, 9, 14, 15, 16, 30, 169, 174, 194
Russian War 1854-1856, 310
  Constantinople, 310
  Petropauloyski, 310
Santa Cruz, 138, 154
Senegal,18
Goree, 18
Seven Yearss' War 1756-1763, 11
  St Malo, 19, 77
  Ushant, 12,
Slave Trade, 433
Witu, 433
Soudan 1884-1885, 406, 419
  Dongola, 415
  El Teb, 407
  Hasheen, 421
  Khartoum, 411413, 415, 418, 443
  Suakin, 411
  T'Hakool, 427
  Tamai, 408
  Tamanieb, 410
  Tofrek, 423, 268
Soudan 1896, 440
  Zanzibar, 440
Soudan, 1898, 443
South Africa and Zulu War1879, 378
  Etshowe, 380
  Ginghilovo, 381
  Inyezane, 380
  Isandhlwana, and Rorke's Drift, 380
South African War 1899-1902, 446
  Belfast, 449
  Bloemfontein, 448
  Diamond Hill, 449
  Graspan, 446
  Johannesburg, 448
  Magersfontein, 448
  Modder River, 447
  Paardeberg, 448
  Pretoria, 449
  Transvaal, 446
South America, 300
  Buenos Aires, 176, 179
  Buenos Ayres, 301497
  Dutch Guiana, 128
  Surinam, 166
Strachan's Action , 174
Syria 1840, 272
  Acre, 275
  Caiffa, 274
  Tyre, 274

Sidon, 274
Trafalgar, 163, 171
  After Trafalgar, 191
War in Spain 1836-1839, 266
  Hernani, 268, 269
  San Sebastian, 266, 267, 268, 269
Waterloo, 223, 241, 245
Wei-Hai-Wei, 437, 443, 450, 458, 460
West Coast of Africa, 104, 302
  Benin, 441,
  Brass River and M'Weli, 439
  Gambla, 430, 439
  Lagos, 26, 302
  Senegal, 18
West Indies, 164, 169
  St Kitts, 86
  Battle of the Saintes , 87
  Cayenne, 197
  Curacao, 165, 166, 182, 183, 210
  Diamond Rock, 165
  Dominica, 169
  Dutch Guiana, 128
  Grenada, 77, 93
  Guadeloupe, 122, 195, 201
  Jamaica, 87, 127, 239
  Martinique, 20, 21, 22, 30, 37, 80, 84, 87, 120, 121
  San Domingo, 130, 165, 166, 175
  St Lucia , 32, 76, 80, 84, 87, 93, 121, 125, 128, 155, 164
  St Vincent , 26, 36, 77, 93, 128
  Tobago, 36, 84, 93, 119, 164

Barney, American Commodore, 236, 237, 238
Bayonet Exercise, 182, 192, 209
Beatson, xiii
Beer Money, 121
Bermuda, 191, 226, 236, 255, 405, 437
Berthier, French General, 495
Birkenhead Drill, 302
Blue Colonels, 250
Boys, 168, 169, 180, 209, 215, 469, 472, 473
Brevet Rank, 44, 45, 48, 479
Brigadier Generals, 483
Bute, Lord, 33
Cadet Corps, 469
Caffarelli, French General, 218
Camel Corps (Nile), 414
Canteens and Taxation, 179
Captain-Lieutenant, 168
Captain Scott's 'Director', 447, 480
Casteau, French General, 118
Chauvelin, French Ambassador , 117
Chelsea Hospital, 4
Children, 100, 112, 129, 177, 179, 255, 303, 329, 330, 461
Clarence, Duchess of, 509
Clothing, 6, 7, 41, 53, 54, 74, 102, 105, 109, 141, 182, 307, 406, 467, 476
Clothing Depots
  China, 450
  Maltas, 434
Colonelcies of Divisions, 359
Colonels Commandant-en-second , 102
Colour Sergeants, 222
Colours, 4, 47, 150, 160, 257, 325, 326, 361, 439, 441, 468, 485, 490, 504, 507
Botany Bay, 47

Index

Laurel Wreath, 30
1827 Colours, (The Globe and Laurel), 499
1765 Colours, 491
1810 Colours, 497
1858 Colours, 501
1894-96 Colours, 503
Summary of Presentations of Colours, 507
Disposal, 498, 500
Potential WW1 Battle Honours, 504
Presentations,
  at Douglass 507
  by Queen Victoria, Aug 1894, 503
  at Chatham, 500, 502, 503
  at Plymouth, Dec, 500, 502, 503
  at Portsmouth, 500, 502
  at Woolwich, 500, 502
Commandants in Town, 523
Comte D'Orvillers, French Admiral, 74, 77
Conflans, French Admiral, 25, 26
Connaught, Duchess of, 510
Corbet's History of the Seven Years War, xiii, 33, 34
Correspondence, 201
Courts Marshal, 42, 46, 74, 137, 204
GCMs, 43, 49, 246
Court Martial of |Maj Gen Wemyss, 137
Cromarty, 483
Cronje, Boer Commander, 448
Cumberland, Duke of, 3, 14, 15, 16
Cycle Corps, 439
D'Ache, French Admiral, 34, 35
Daendels, French General, 212
Death of Captain Cook, 82
Declaration of American Independence, 70
D'Estaing, French General, 35,
D'Estaing, French Admiral, 74, 75, 76, 77, 78
De Bruis, French Admiral, 142
De Caen, French General, 204
De Guichen, French Admiral, 80, 85
De Grasse, French Admiral, 84, 85, 86, 86
De Lesseps, M, 392
De Montaubam, French Gen, later Count de Palikao, 349
De La Clue, French Admiral, 16
De La Greviere, French Commander, 362
De La Mothe, French Admiral, 14
De Vascoigne, French Lt Col, 322
De Winter, Dutch Admiral, 136
Demobilisation, 41, 42, 95, 158, 222, 245
Depot Deal, 357, 361, 369, 445, 450, 471, 502
Diamond Rock, 165
Diezzar Pasha, Turkish Commander, 145,
de Langara, Spanish Admiral, 80
D'Hervilly, Count, French Commander, 124 Discharge by Purchase, 42, 144
Discontent in the Fleet, 140, 342
Discipline, 42, 44, 81, 96, 432, 481
Dockyard Guards, 46, 100, 106, 110, 161
Drill for Reviews, 110
Drill and training, 9, 44, 88, 249
Drummers, 7, 192, 260
Duelling, 216, 297
Dumanoir, French Admiral, 174
Du Quesne, French Admiral, 16
Edinburgh Cup, 442
Elections, 48
Elgin, Lord, 336, 338
Elliot, Capt, British Envoy to China, 278

Embarkation Muster Roll, 99
Equipment, 436, 479
E. Regnault de Guoully, French Rear Admiral, 341
Expressions of Loyalty 1798, 141
Eylon, American General, 236
Falkland Islands, 49
Ferdinand, King of Spain, 16, 30, 266
Field, Col, ix, x, xiii, 6, 53, 218, 251, 272, 320, 373, 384, 396, 401, 406, 450, 489, 490, 491, 495
Fifers, 100, 103, 260
Flogging, 100, 373
Florida, 37, 83, 93, 226, 240, 242
Fodi Sillah, Gambian Chief, 438
Formation of the Corps 1755, 3
Fortescue, Sir John, History of the British Army, xiii, 3, 8, 13, 29, 37, 62, 63, 76, 90, 91, 117, 134, 169, 195, 196, 212, 218, 222, 227, 239, 242, 303, 311, 326
Franklin C Mr, Musical Director, 473
French Revolution, 109, 110, 112, 117
Fu, Palace of Prince Su, 451
Peking, 277, 279, 346, 353, 450, 451, 452, 463, 466
Fumo Omari, African Robber Chief, 437
Funds, 50, 200, 255, 435
Gambier, Dockyard Commisioner, 66
Games and Sports, 443
Ganteaume, French Admiral, 169, 194
Gardner Battery, 421, 422, 424
Gibraltar, 13, 16, 26, 77, 80, 83, 85, 88, 120, 122, 127, 130, 143, 476, 487, 488, 499, 503, 509
Gillespie A (Historian), ix, xiii, 19, 20, 28, 63, 65, 66, 81, 91, 96, 119, 151, 495
Gladstone, Mr, Prime Minister, 413
Globe and Laurel Magazine, ix, x, xiii, 107, 146, 147, 311, 313, 314, 329, 357, 373, 436, 507, 508, 511, 512
Glover, Administrator of the Ashanti Protectorate, 376, 378
Good Conduct Badges, 299, 300, 325
Greenwich Hospital, 6, 129, 133, 259, 498
Greenwich Hospital Pensions, 360, 449
Grey Sir G, Governor of New Zealand, 302, 366
Half Pay, officers, 4, 41, 42, 45, 49, 51, 95, 98, 99, 104, 107, 110, 141, 151, 246, 247, 250, 255, 256, 361
Hall, Capt USMC, 451
Hamilton, Lady, 141
Hampton, American General, 230
Hanover, 11, 12, 14, 15, 16, 20
Hassan Bey, Turkish Commander, 146, 275
Hastings, W, Governor General of India, 88
Hessian Troops, 11, 69, 73, 78
Hessian, 59
Hicks Pasha, Egyptian Mercenary. 406,
HMS *Victoria*, 436
Hospital Sergeant, 102
HRH Prince Henry of Battenburg
HRH The Duke of Clarence, 250, 257, 494, 498, 499, 500, 503, 501, 509, 511
HRH The Duke of Connaught, 392, 511
HRH The Duke of Edinburgh, 384, 441, 443, 502, 503, 510, 511, 512
HRH The Duke of Gloucester, 47
HRH The Duke of York, later George V,

123, 467, 510
HRH The Prince of Wales, 108, 371, 470
Hungerford, American General, 236
Hyder Ali, Sultan of Mysore, 88, 89, 90, 92
Ibrahim Pasha, Turkish Viceroy of Egypt, 145, 257
Income Tax, 144
Inspector of Colours, 501
Inspector of Recruiting, 481
Inspector General, 249
Intelligence Officers, 171, 172
Ireland, xi, 79, 95, 132, 140, 142, 150, 169, 183, 245, 260, 302, 383, 495
Jackson, American General, 241
Janssens, Dutch General, 212, 215
Jockmus J, Turkish General, 273
Juarez, President of Mexico, 362
Jubilee 1887, 431
Jubilee 1897, 442
Junot, French General, 188, 193
Ketchwayo, Zulu King, 378, 382
Kettler, Baron von, German Ambassador to Peking, 452
King Coffee of Ashanti, 373, 378
King Edward V11, 371, 468, 470, 471, 479
  Coronation, 470, 480
  Coronation Durbar, 481
King William 1V, 250, 259, 269, 498
King George 11, 3, 27
King George 1V, 257, 439, 499, 501, 511
King George V, 467, 470, 479, 480, 510
King Louis XV1, 111, 117
King of Naples, 148, 181
King of the Netherlands, 253
King of the Sicilies, 122
King of Spain, 477
King's Pardon, 67, 191
Kings Regulations, 174, 182
Khedive of Egypt, 272, 384, 387, 388, 392, 402
Kwan, Chinese Admiral, 280
La Perouse, French Admiral, 106
Lafayette, French General, 84
La Grandiere, French Commander, 311
Lally, French General, 34, 35
Le Poypeau, Italian General, 118
Lenox, Lord G, 96, 134
Lessegues, French Admiral, 175
Libraries, 271
Lind, Dr and Surgeon, 219
Liniers, Spanish General, 177, 178
Lippett, Surgeon, 451
Lloyds Patriotic Fund, 179
Ma, Chinese General, 462
Macdonald Sir C, British Minister, Peking, 451, 452, 466
Mahomed Ahmed (Mahdi), 406
Marmont, French General, 217
Marine Mutiny Acts and Articles of War, 3, 42, 44, 298, 373
M'Baruk, African Chief, 439
Medals
  Army Distinguished Conduct Medal
  Conspicuous Gallantry Medal, 309, 409, 464, 475
  Good Conduct Medal, 259, 299
  Long Service and Good Conduct Medal
  Meritorious Service Medal, 299

531

Naval War Service Medal, 298
Victoria Cross, 314, 315, 453
Mess Funds, 255,
Military Instructor, 371, 432, 436
Milne Mr, 485, 486, 487, 488, 491, 495
Miller, Capt USMC, 237
Minto, Lord,, Govenor General of India, 212
Misserssy, French Admiral, 169
Mitchell, American Gunner, 464
Montcalm, French Admiral, 12, 14, 24
Morrison, Dr, 164
Mullah of Somaliland, 474, 475
Musketry Instructors, 326, 362, 420
Mutiny at the Nore, 136
Mutiny at Spithead, 132, 134
Mutiny at Stonehouse, 134, 135,, 136
Myers, Capt USMC, 451, 463
Napier, Historian, 208, 220
Napoleon Buonaparte, 118, 142, 143, 145, 147, 151, 168, 169, 170, 171, 174, 181, 183, 185, 188, 193, 194, 198, 212, 221, 222, 241, 245, 246, 437
Napoleon III, 318
Naval Defence Act, 432
Naval Discipline Act, 44, 373
Naval Gunnery, 76, 258, 300, 372, 405, 435, 445, 450, 471, 472, 478
Gunlayers Tests, 478
Naval Sixpence, 6, 259
NCOs, 4, 200
Newcastle, Duke of, 3, 13
Ney, Marshal, French General, 198
Nieh, Chinese General, 455
Nucleus Crews, 97, 432, 474
Officers,
Educational Requirements, 266
Employment, 472
Entry, 370
Entry and Training, 432
Examinations for Promotion, 361
Employment, 472
Promotion, 250
Promotion and Retirement 251, 369, 870
Retirements, 107, 158, 245, 247, 251, 265, 325, 369, 372
Officers' Messes, 405
Osman Digna, Soudan Slave Trader, 406, 408, 409, 413, 420, 421, 423, 425, 428
Parkes, Mr, British Consul in China, 343, 353, 354
Parliamentary Elections, 48, 179
Pay, 5, 50, 52, 137, 160, 180, 199, 245, 250, 253, 359, 482
Lodging Money, 111
Pay and Rations, 475
Sea Pay, 6, 50, 200
Separation Allowance, 67, 406
Paymasters, 405
Pensioner Reserve, 370
Pedro 1 of Brazil and as Pedro 1V of Portugal, 258
Philipeaux, Col, French Engineer, 145, 146
Pikes, 137, 151, 257
Pitt W, (the elder) later 1st Earl Chatham, 14, 20, 30, 169
Portier, Spanish General, 219
Pottinger Sir H, Political Officer, 287
Precedence in the Line, 254
Prim, Spanish General, 362

Prince Chesiu, Japanese noble, 362
Prince Frederick, Austrian Commander, 275
Prince George of Denmark's Regiment, 487
Prince of Hesse, 181, 488
Princess Augusta, 509
Printers, 406, 435
Prisoners of War, 73, 83, 123, 127, 166, 203, 210, 245, 299
Promotion, 49, 250, 265, 300, 308, 325, 358, 369, 431
Promotion Examinations, 361
Promotion from the Ranks, 141, 482
QMSIs, 383, 445
Quartermasters, 256, 297, 326, 360, 432, 440
Queen Alexandra, 470
Queen Anne, 487, 488
Queen Caroline, 254
Queen Maria 11 of Portugal, 260, 301
Queen of Naples, 143
Queen Victoria, 54, 265, 269, 419, 466, 467, 488, 501, 503, 509, 510
Jubilee 1887, 431
Diamond Jubilee, 442
Ramrods, 49
Rates of pay,
(1689), 5
(1806), 180
(1812), 215
1902 Selborne Scheme, 469
Rations, 6, 111, 123, 132, 150, 168, 297, 307, 308, 320, 383, 443, 445, 475
Recruiting, , 5, 44, 79, 81, 83, 108, 109, 123, 140, 142, 149, 155, 162, 163, 169, 179, 191, 201, 369, 440, 477, 481
Regent's Allowance, 210, 235, 405
Relative Rank, 470, 478, 482, 471
Reserves and Drafting Officers
Reviews, 110, 470
Rewards, 192, 309, 319, 431
Rickman Mr, Surgeon, 4
RM Gunners, 479, 482, 483
RN School of Music, 472, 483
Rollo, Lord, 30
Fleet Reserve, 469
Royal Marine Artillery, 167, 191, 253, 255, 259, 325, 358, 520
Officers' Maths examination, 191
RMA Recruits, 435, 445
Royal Marine Light Infantry, ix, 309, 315, 357, 358
Royal Marine Rifle Association, 437
Royal Military Tournament, 434
Royal Review, Aldershot, 431, 470, 477
Royal Review, Chatham, 86
Royal Review, Phoenix Park, 481
Royal Review, Plymouth, 108
Royal Review, Portsmouth 1773, 52

Royal Marines and Royal Marine Artillery Officers and Other Ranks,
Abernethie, Capt, 161, 208, 218, 518
Adair C, Paymaster, 171
Adair C W, Lt, later Lt Col, 273, 362, 363, 517, 522
Adair H, Colonel Commandant, 520
Adair T B, Maj later Col, 242, 256, 260, 517
Adair W, Mr, 4, 250
Adair W T, Colonel Commandant, 519, 522

Adlam, Capt, 92
Alexander G L, Capt RMA, 312, 315, 318, 319, 320, 407
Allen A, Capt RMA, 61, 386, 421
Allen, Lt RMA, 374
Allen, Bug, 442
Allnutt W W. Lt, 334, 336, 344, 374, 375, 376
Alston, Maj, 412, 421, 422
Anderson A, Lt, 275, 276, 517
Andrews H, Maj Gen, 359, 515
Apthorpe, Capt, 85
Archbold T, 50
Argent, Sgt, 332
Armstrong W G, Col, 491
Armstrong W, 2nd Lt later Capt, 337, 456, 457, 460, 462
Armstrong H, Lt, 463, 466
Armstrong H, Sgt, 456
Armstrong St G B, Maj, 461
Aslett T, Capt later Lt Col, 254, 269, 276, 312
Aslett, W S, Capt, 319, 517
Aston G, Lt RMA, later Brig Gen, 407, 521
Atcherly L, Capt, 171, 295
Atkinson, R G, Lt, 210
Averne T, Capt later Maj Gen, 62, 65, 69, 72
Bagg, Lt, 87
Bagnell, Lt, 216
Baillie, Col, 89
Baillie, Capt, 147
Baillie, Lt, 164
Baldwin, Lt, 364
Baldwin F, Capt later Lt Col, 407, 408, 409, 410, 510, 519
Baldwin J, Capt, 386
Bale, Cpl. 409
Ball, Lt, 171
Ballchild, Lt RMA, 194
Ballingall O H, Lt, 149, 150, 177
Barclay, Capt later Lt Gen, 73, 160, 182, 245, 497, 515, 522
Barker H J, 2nd Lt, 57, 60, 337
Barker W J, Capt, 352, 355
Barnard C J, Lt RMA later Col Comdt, 301, 353, 520
Barnes A H F, Lt, 336, 436, 517
Barnston, Maj, 329
Barrel, Lt, 92
Barrett, Maj, 512
Barry, Maj,, 226
Bartleman, Maj, 221
Barton, Lt, 231
Bate W, Lt, 203
Bates W, Bdr, 332
Battin J, Sgt later Maj, 437
Baxter G, Lt, 253
Bazalgette E, Lt, 337, 345
Beaumont G L, Capt later Maj, 441
Beatty G, Lt, 146, 165, 246, 247 (Note 213)
Bell Sir H, Maj Gen, 241, 245, 249, 515, 522
Bell, Capt, 87, 258
Bell, J, Col, 50, 518
Bendyshe R, Maj, 3, 50, 515, 516, 518
Bennett, Lt, 171
Benson J, Lt, 172

INDEX

Bent T, Lt, 321
Beresford de La P, Capt RMA, 386
Beyts, Lt RMA, 453, 455
Birtwhistle, Pte, 408, 410
Bissett J P B, Lt RM,A, 253
Blackaller, Sgt, 134
Blake G L, Lt, 336, 345
Blake, Capt, 342
Bland-Hunt, R W, Lt, 321, 515
Blumberg H E, ix-xiii, 481, 517, 522
Blyth D, Capt, 312, 320
Boileau, Lt, 187
Boisrend, Maj, 23
Bor, Maj RMA, 442, 476, 520
Bourne, Lt, 140
Boyd W S, Lt, 165
Boyle R, Capt, 334, 335, 336, 343, 344, 348
Bourchier, H S, Lt Col, 500
Bowater Sir J, Maj Gen, 134, 135, 158, 164, 495, 496, 518
Brewer Lt, 480
Bretwell, Gnr, 409, 411
Bridges F D, Lt, 441
Brittan E, Lt RMA, 407, 408
Broom H, 2nd Lt, 198
Brough J, Capt, 479
Broughton J D, Lt, 337
Brown J, Pte, 231
Budd, Capt, 337, 349, 355
Bull J, Gnr RMA, 320
Bullman, Sgt, 134
Bulkeley R, Lt, 138
Bunce, Capt, 181, 213
Bunn, Sgt, 444
Burleigh J, Maj later Col, 3, 50, 490, 515
Burdwood, Lt, 119
Burn, A Capt, 136, 137, 519
Burns, Sgt, 222
Burrower, Lt Pay and QM, 384
Burrowes A St L, Lt RMA, 382
Burrowes, A St I, Capt,, 412, 413, 421, 422, 426, 427
Burns, Sgt, 222
Burton C F, Lt, 145, 253
Burton J, Pte, 320
Burton W M, Lt and Adjt, 219
Busigny S, Capt, 172
Butler F, Sgt, 331, 332
Brace, Capt, 138
Brady D, Pte, 355, 409, 411
Brannan J, Pte, 135
Brereton, Capt, 36
Bretwell, Gnr RMA, 409, 411
Brewer, Lt, 480
Bridge F D, Capt, 411, 421, 441, 521
Bright R, Col later Maj Gen, 164, 245, 497, 518
Bright Maj, 119, 128
Brine, Lt, 412, 421
Brisbane A, Lt, 65
Brittan C G, Capt, 436
Brittan E, Lt RMA, 407, 408
Brookes J R, Lt, 321
Brough J, Capt RMA, 479
Broughton J D, Lt, 337
Brown J, 2nd Lt 198
Brown, Maj, 126
Brown, Capt RMA, 276
Brown, Sgt, 349

Brown, Bug, 420
Brown J, Pte, 231
Brown G, 45
Burton C F, Capt, 253, 334
Burton C W, Lt, 336, 339, 370
Burton W M. Lt and Adjt, 145, 219
Burton J, Pte, 320
Byrch, Capt, 390
Byrne, G T, Capt, 441, 442
Byron Woods, Capt, 420
Caldwell, Lt, 231
Cahusac, D Lt, 166
Clark, Lt 106, 449
Clarke C, Maj, 199, 205, 206, 267
Clavell R A K, Capt, 323, 517
Campbell A, Capt, 62, 65, 83, 106
Campbell of Glenlyon, J, Maj, 22, 31, 33
Campbell G M, Maj Gen, DAGRM, 135, 160, 202, 247, 249, 507, 508, 522
Campbell, Sir C, Col, 312, 313, 318, 328, 329, 330
Campbell W, Capt RMA, 386, 389, 520
Campbell, Lt RMA, 411
Cambell F A, Lt Col, 73, 152, 221, 312, 317. 519
Campbell, Maj 163
Campbell G M, Brig Gen, 521
Carden P H, Lt, 217
Carey, Capt, 80
Carleton, Col, AQMG, 22, 25
Carrington, Lt, 337, 349
Carrington C W, Capt, 344, 252, 355
Carrol G P, Lt, 181
Carruthers, Capt later Col, 29, 102, 110, 515
Carter, Lt, 118, 226, 227
Cassel J, Capt, 136
Cathcart, Lt, 7
Chambers Lt, 136
Chance, Sgt, 282
Chaundy, Lt, 21
Chapman J, Sgt and Temp Lt and Adjt, 242
Chappel W, Cpl, 320
Cheetham, Lt RMA, 374
Chislett, Sgt, 418, 420
Chown, Maj, 477
Christian Sgt Maj, later Lt and Adjt, 8, 42, 51
Christian Sgt RMA, 335
Chudleigh, Capt, 65
Clapperton, Lt RMA, 267
Clark, 2nd Lt, 106, 449
Clarke C, Maj, 199, 205, 206, 467
Cleethen C J, Capt RMA, 386
Clements A, Capt, 174, 239, 311
Clements W E, Lt, 344
Clogstone R, Capt, 92
Cobb J, Lt, 327, 336, 349
Coborn J, Pte, 320
Cock W B, Lt, 217
Coffee D, Pte, 135
Coke, Lt, 402
Collins A T (Tooker), Maj later Col, 17, 29, 33, 66, 69, 70, 71, 107, 167, 518
Collins D, Capt later Lt Col and Governor of Tasmania, 107, 161, 162, 172
Collins S T Lt, 337
Collet S J, Lt, 203
Colley, Lt, 475
Colwell G H T, Maj later Col, 393, 407, 409, 410, 411, 511, 512, 516, 521

Conche J, Lt, 208
Congdon, Lt, 421
Cooke T V, Capt, 327, 335, 336, 342, 344, 348
Conner, Sgt, 134
Connor W, Lt, 337
Connolly W L, Lt RMA, 411, 511
Connolly E J R, Col, 515
Cooper E T, 2nd Lt, 336
Cope, Dr, 349
Coppin C F, Lt, 337
Corbet A D, Maj, 438, 439, 519
Cotter F J, Maj, 512, 517
Cotter, Lt, 412, 421, 426
Coulter J, Lt, 208
Conway-Gordon, Lt Col RMA, 483, 521
Craig W A, Lt, 166, 402
Crawford, Lt RMA, 337
Crease, Lt later Capt RMA, 337, 338, 374, 375
Crease J F, Col, 520
Creswell, Capt, 143, 147
Croker P M, Capt, 337, 346
Croker P K C, Capt, 348
Conway-Gordon, Lt Col, 483
Crooke, Capt RMA, 413, 421, 427
Crosbie A B, Lt later Lt Col, 364, 376, 378, 511, 521
Crowther J E, Lt, 510
Curtoys Lt later Brig Gen, 412, 421, 519
Cuthbert, Capt, 136
Curls, Lt, 21
Curtoys C E Lt later Brig gen, , 412, 421
Dair, Sgt, 144
Dalton, Capt, 7, 477
Daniell, Col Comdt, 481, 516
Darling, Lt, 411, 421
David, Lt, transferred to Egyptian Army, 411, 414
David E F, Lt, 414, 421
Davey, Lt, 106
Davis, Lt, 86
Davis W, Capt and Adjt, 508
Davis J, Pte, 409, 411
Dawes, 2nd Lt, 105, 111
Deane R N, Lt, 376, 378
Debrissay J H, Lt, 198
de Courcy, Capt later Lt Col, 363, 376
Dehan J, 2nd Lt, 198
Delacombe H, Capt later Lt Gen, 321, 359
Denny R, Maj later Lt Col, 439
Denslow, Sgt, 349
Desborough L, Lt, 74, 354, 515
Despard, Capt, 374
Dexter, Capt, 118
Dibblee, Lt RMA, 441
Digby, G S, Capt RMA later Col, 316, 318, 320, 520
Doan, Sgt, 134
Doig, Capt, 453, 455, 456, 466
Donald, Maj RMA, 390, 147, 147
Douglas Maj later Sir J Col, 134, 145, 146
Douglas C, Lt, 152
Douglas R H J, Lt, 337
Douglas A A, Lt RMA, 313, 320
Dowding T W, Lt later Col 2nd Comdt, 379, 380, 382, 521
Dowell G D, Capt RMA, 323
Drew, Lt, 86
Drew, Clr Sgt, 414, 420

533

BLUMBERG'S HISTORY OF THE ROYAL MARINES 1755-1914

Driver, Capt, 337
Drury T, Maj later Lt Col, 444
Duncan, Col, 142
Durnford E C L, Lt RMA, 320, 321
Dustan, Capt, 458, 460, 462, 463, 466
Dyer J, Lt, 65
Eden, Capt, 392, 393
Edwards, Lt, 92, 276
Edwards F C, Col Comdt, 516, 519
Edye L, Lt and QM later Maj, 384, 421, 439
Edye, Maj, (Historian), ix, 485, 486, 487, 498, 499
Elliott, Lt Gen, 161, 164, 192, 220, 245
Elliott G, Capt, later Col Comdt, 242, 292, 516, 525, 526
Elliott H, Lt, 242
Elliott H G, Lt and Adjt, 312
Elliot, Col, 160
Elliot J, Lt, 304, 305, 321
Elliot W, Capt and Adjt, 321
Ellis C J, Lt, 337, 339, 343, 344, 348
Ellis S, 65
Ellis E B, Capt later Maj Gen, 270, 276
Ellis Sir S B, (Note 221), 276, 278, 281, 282, 285, 286, 287 and note 228, 288, 290, 291, 292, 359, 519
Ensor, Lt, 140
Entwistle, J, L/Cpl, 134
Ewer, Capt, 16
Evans E, Lt, 412
Evans H, Lt, 321, 337, 348, 349
Evans G O, Lt, 337, 346
Evans T J P, later Col Comdt, 517
Ewer, Capt, 16
Faddy, Capt, 143
Faden, Lt and Adjt, 192, 209
Fagan Q S, Lt later Col Comdt, 370, 517
Fairbrother W, Pte, 182
Fairweather F, Clr Sgt, 285, 289 (note 230)
Farber, Lt, 191
Farmer J, Lt, 150, 285
Farmer, Maj Gen, 245
Farquharson F A H, Capt, 386
Farquharson H Lt, later Col Comdt, 436, 437, 439, 521
Fegan C, Capt, 272, 273
Fernyhough, Lt, 177
Festing F V, Lt Col later Sir F, Col RMA, 374, 375, 376, 378, 520,
Festing W, Lt RMA, 316, 343
Fielding J, Lt and Adjt, 58, 62
Filmer-Bennett, Capt, 481
Finch, Brig Gen, 154
Finnie W, Lt, 65
Fischer J N, Capt, 211
Flight, Lt Col, 131
Flowers, Cpl, 475
Fonblanque A, 2nd Lt, 337
Foote, Capt, later Col Comdt, 327, 343, 345, 348, 518
Footing, Lt RMA, 337
Forbes J, Lt, 177, 191, 491
Fortescue-Graham, Lt Col later Lt Gen RMA, 321, 324, 359, 517
Fosbrook, Capt, 321
Fox, Capt, 337
Frampton, Lt, 384
Frazer, Lt, 130
French A, Capt later Maj RMA, 386, 388,

391, 402
French N F J, Lt RMA, 441
French, Lt, 447, 448, 449
Fynemore, Lt, 187
Gaitskell S, Maj, 481
Gaitskell W, Lt later Maj RMA, 386
Gard, Lt, 65
Gardiner F, Lt, 65
Gardiner, Capt, 20
Garmston, Capt, 267
Gascoigne, Col, 349, 350, 351, 353, 354, 355
Gauntlett, Lt Col, 66
Gibson, Lt, 100
Gibsone D A, Lt Col (Maj Comdt), 520
Gilborne A, Sgt
Gillespie, Col, 177, 194, 212, 213, 214
Gillespie, Capt, 278, 280
Glazier, Lt Col, 78
Godfrey J A, 2nd Lt, 337
Golding, Pte, 420
Gordon A H, Col Comdt, 518
Gordon C G, Lt, 100, 421, 426, 429, 515
Gordon O, Lt Col, 3
Gore G A, Capt, 35, 386, 393, 395
Graham, H M C W, Brig Gen, 516
Graham S J, Maj later Lt Col, 75, 209, 218, 339, 343, 345, 391, 392, 394, 402, 403, 515
Grant, Maj, 68
Gray E N H, Lt, 370, 374
Gray T C, Capt, 327, 330
Green R, Lt, 172
Gregory, Cpl, 453, 463, 466
Griffin G, 2nd Lt, 508
Griffiths F H, Brig Gen, 516
Griffith C, Lt, 198
Griffiths, Lt 84, 246
Gritton, Capt, 337, 349, 411
Haggart, Lt, 72
Hale W G, Lt, 337
Hall, Capt, 288
Hall, Maj, 364
Halliday L S T, 2nd Lt later Col Comdt and Adjt Gen, 266, 267, 450, 451, 452, 453, 466, 521, 523
Halling, QMS, 348
Hambly A J, Lt, 292
Hamley, Capt, 321
Harch W H, Capt, 320
Harkness, Maj RMA, 469, 480
Harman, Capt, 86
Harmar, Lt, 463
Harris, Capt, 462, 463, 465
Harries, Lt, 421
Harrison, Capt RMA, 238, 274
Harrison R, Lt, 274
Harwood E, Lt, 166
Hawes, Lt, 370
Hawkey J F, Lt, 337, 344, 348
Hawkins, Capt, 421
Hearle P, Lt, 374
Heathcote R W, Capt, 390, 402, 403
Henfry, 2nd Lt, 253
Henry C C, Lt, 210
Henry R P, 2nd Lt, 242, 334, 336, 345
Hepburn, Capt, 29
Herald W, Lt, 295
Heriot M, 2nd Lt, 337
Heriot W M, Lt later Maj, 80, 321, 480
Heriot M A H G, Col 2nd Comdt, 521

Hervey F W, Lt, 438
Hewitt C C, Lt, 294, 316
Hewett H, Lt RMA, 232, 233, 287, 288, 291, 321
Hewitt, Sgt, 209
Hill, Maj, 125
Hill A, Capt, 370
Hill J G, Lt, 217
Hill, Paymaster, 362
Hinder L, Sgt, 331
Hobbs F M D, Maj, 470
Hocker E, Lt Col, 337, 339, 343, 349, 355
Hobart, Capt, 412
Hodges, Lt, 86
Holdstock, Sgt, 391
Holland, Capt, 355
Holloway T, Lt Col later Col, Comdt, 312, 317, 318, 320, 336, 337, 338, 339, 340, 341, 342, 343, 344, 345, 348, 349, 355, 518
Holman, Lt, 411, 421, 426
Holmes P R, Lt later Col Comdt, 370, 516
Holt D, Lt, 187
Holtaway, Capt, 211, 233
Hopkins T, 45, 46
Hopkins W F, Capt, 143, 314, 319, 320
Horner C, Sgt RMA, 320
Horniblow, Lt later Maj, 411, 421, 426, 428, 511
Hore, Lt, 195
Hornby, Capt, 218
Hornby E C, Col Comdt, 516
Hoskin C F, Lt, 275
Hoskyns-Abrahall J E, Lt, 433
Howard B C, Lt, 512
Howard S J, Maj Gen, 517, 522
Howe, Lt, 194, 195
Howell J, Lt, 148
Hubbard, Lt, 421
Hudson, Capt, 81
Hull, Capt, 246
Hungerford, Capt, 421
Hunter, Capt, 106
Hurdle T, Capt later Lt Col, 301, 312, 318, 319, 320, 517
Hurst, Sgt Maj, 408
Hutton, Lt RMA, 481
Inglis, Lt, 327, 336, 347, 363
Innes E S, Capt, 386
Innes H, Col Comdt, 515, 516
Innes, Lt Gen, 160, 161
Instone J, 134
Jackson G E O, Capt, 337, 343, 348, 349
Jeffreys, Lt, 321
Jew, QMS, 500
Jewell, Lt, 143
Jewell, Sgt, 100
Johns, Lt, 222
Johnson-How, 2nd Lt, 508
Johnston J R, Lt later Col 2nd Comdt, 386, 521
Johnstone, Maj later Lt Col, 453, 454, 455, 461, 462, 466, 476
Johnstone, D, Lt, 50, 62, 65
Johnstone G, Lt, 92, 106
Johnstone J, Lt, 106
Johnstone, Lt Col, 61, 85
Johnstone, Capt, 107
Joliffe, Lt, 312, 318
Jones H S, Lt Col later Lt Gen, 383, 394,

534

Index

517, 521, 522
Jones E S, Lt Col, 391, 396, 398, 402, 403, 442
Jones W T C, Capt, 479
Jones N Q C, Lt, 447
Jones H A H, Brig Gen, 517
Jordan J, Clr Sgt, 314, 320
Kappey G, Lt later Maj RMA, 386, 466
Kay, 2nd Lt, 106
Kellow, Lt , 106
Kempenfeldt, Capt, 26
Kempster, Lt and Adjt, 218
Kempster F J, Capt, 249
Kendall, 2nd Lt , 192
Kennedy, Maj, 475
Kennedy C H, Col Comdt, 516
Kent, Capt, 187
Kerr F, Gnr RMA, 320
King U, Maj and QM
Kingston, Lt, 172
Kinsman, Capt, 337
Kitching, Capt, 421
Kitchoffer, Capt, 393
Kirchoffer R B, Capt later Col, 386, 512
Knight Sir M A G, Capt, 192
Kysh D, Lt, 407, 421, 427
Laban, Lt , 87
Lalor J R, Lt, 421, 425, 433
Lambert J H, Lt, 511, 512
Lambert W M, Lt later Maj RMA, 371, 378, 381, 429, 430
Lambrick G, Col laterr Col Comdt, 372, 515
Langley G C, Lt later Lt Col, 266, 267
Laurie J, Lt , 198
Laurie W, Lt , 187
Law, Lt, 222
Lawrence J F, Lt RMA, 140, 152, 194, 237, 301, 324
Lawrence E, Col Comdt, 515
Lawrie J, Lt, 232, 233, 460, 462
Le Grand, Lt Col later Col Comdt, 384, 389, 390, 518
Le Vesconte J, Lt , 172
Lee R, Pte, 135
Lees J, 45
Leighton F, Maj, 3
Lely P, Capt, 172
Lemon, Col later Lt Gen, 327, 336, 338, 339, 341, 342, 343, 345, 346, 347, 348, 349, 355, 359, 515
Lennox J M, Lt
Leonard, Capt, 272, 276, 301
Lewis G, Capt 136, 193, 221, 235, 236, 230, 238, 239
Lewis H P, Maj Gen, 137, 516
Lewis S, 442
Lewis G, Col Comdt, 518
Lewis T, Col Comdt, 519
Ley, Lt Col, 384, 389
Liardet I, Capt later Maj, 197, 204, 212, 213
Ligertwood P, Lt, 504
Little A G, Brig Gen, 517
Little, Dr, 337, 349
Little R J, Lt , 208
Little S, Capt, 327, 336, 348
Livingston, Lt , 131
Logan G, Capt, 62, 65, 69
Logan-Home, Lt , 412
Long, Lt, 91

Lowder S N, Capt later Col Comdt, 322, 323, 324, 362, 500, 518, 522
Lloyd, Lt, 412, 453, 455, 462, 466
Luke V, Lt later Lt Col, 401, 456, 457, 460, 461, 462, 463, 466
Luscombe, Lt, 130
Lye, Lt, 363
Lye, Pte, 334
Lyon-Freemantle Sir J, Maj Gen, 412, 494(note 346), 507
Lynwood, Maj, 170
Macdonnel, Lt, 428
Mackay, Sgt Maj, 282
Mackay A J H, Col Comdt, 518
Mackenzie J, Lt Col later Gen, 28, 29, 50, 67, 99, 107, 515, 522
MacLachlan A, Capt, 208
Maclurcan, Lt later Maj
Magin T, Capt, 336, 345
Mairis G, Lt and Adjt later Col 2nd Comdt, 351, 355, 515, 521
Maitland, Hon J, Capt, later Col, 59, 69, 78, 283
Malcolm J, Maj later Lt Col, 219, 220, 229, 232, 233, 236, 239, 240, 241, 498
Maltby, Lt, 7
Mant, Lt, 181
March W E, Capt later Lt Col, 314, 319, 349, 350, 351, 355, 517
Marchant A E, Lt later Brig Gen, 421, 424, 447, 448, 449, 516
Marriott, Maj, 45
Marriott H, Lt, 277, 287, 319, 517
Marriott W M, Lt RMA, 386
Masters, Capt, 337, 346, 347, 348
Masters W G, Capt
Maskerry J H, Lt and Adjt, 337
Mason J T, Maj, 18
Matthews G E, Capt, 436
Matthias, Capt 386
Matson, Maj, 511
Maxwell, Maj, 199
Maxwell H, Lt, 277, 278, 282, 285
Maxwell W R, Lt Col, 357, 521
Maxwell, Lt and Adjt, 288
Mawby, Lt, 322
Mayhew C I, Lt later Brig Gen, 463, 521
McArthur, Capt later Lt Col, 276, 501, 518
McArthur E, Lt, 302,
MsCallum J, Lt Col, 276
McCallum G, Lt later Col Comdt, 311, 344, 518
McCausland E, Lt, 402
McCleverty, Col, 509
McDonald, Lt, 74
McEntee, Pte, 420
McGinnis J, Pte , 135
McGuire P, Act Cpl, 134
McIntyre, Lt , 6, 7, 8, 9, 54
McKechnie, Capt , 412, 421
McKenzie A, Maj, 176, 177
McKillop, Capt, 321
McLeux, Maj, 312
McWilliams J, 2nd Lt, 242
Mead J de C, Lt, later Lt Col, 337, 349, 517
Mercer, Capt, 443
Mercer E S, Col Comdt, 518
Mercer R, Col Comdt, 519

Mercer D, Col 2nd Comdt, 522
Mees, Pte, 420
Menzies Sir C H, Gen RMA, 162, 359, 517, 520
Meredith, Lt, 106
Middleton C, Capt, 486
Miller D, Lt, 198, 238, 276
Miller, Lt DOM, 467
Minto T, Capt/Lt, 134, 144, 154, 167
Money B C, Lt, 398, 411
Money H O, Maj later Col Comdt, 470, 510, 519
Morgan, 2nd Lt, 242
Morgan W, Lt, 253, 447
Morgan R H, Col Comdt, 516
Moncreiffe, Col, 508
Montgomery, Capt, 411, 412
Mooney J, Sgt, 141
Moore T, Lt RMA, 206, 258, 374
Morres E H, Capt, 468
Morris, Lt later Maj RMA, 365
Morris J I, Col Comdt, and Maj Gen, 521, 522
Morrison J A, Lt, 106, 174, 205, 206, 274, 275
Morrison, Lt and Adjt, 301, 337, 340
Morrison J A, Capt, 343, 348, 355
Morrison Dr, 464
Mortimer, Maj, 226
Mould T, Capt, 218
Mournier, Lt, 87
Mudge, Lt , 323
Mullins G J H, Capt later Col Comdt, 446, 450(Note 319), 460, 461, 462, 463, 465, 519
Murphy J, Maj and QM, 411, 500 and note 363
Murphy, Sgt, 463, 466
Murray, Capt, 29
Murray, Lt, 321
Napier C J W, Lt , 337, 393, 394
Naylor T, Lt, 119, 321
Neame J, Lt , 217
Neils, Lt, 393
Nelson, Lt, 449
Nicholas P, Lt and Adjt, 198
Nicholls E Lt (Fighting Nicholls), 140, 141, 241, 242
Nicholls W C, Col Comdt and Maj Gen, 520, 522
Nicholls, Clr Sgt, 285
Nicholson J, Capt, 194
Nightingale, Lt, 304, 305
Noble C, Capt, 219
Noble E J W, Lt and Adjt, RMA, 384, 397, 402, 403
Nolloth, Maj, 321
Norcock, Lt Col, 500
Norman T, Capt, 172
Norris, Maj, 131
Norton E H, Lt RMA, 344
Nugent, Lt, 69
Oates M, Lt, 187
O'Grady J W, 2nd Lt RMA, 337, 346, 355
Ogle F A, Lt later Col Comdt, 364, 390, 397, 402, 403, 520
Olavell, Capt, 321
Oldfield, Maj, 131, 146, 247 (Note 213)
Oldfield T, Capt, 138, 143
Oldfield J, Lt, 386, 517
Olive C, Sgt Maj later 2ndLt, 51, 337
Oliver C E W, 2nd Lt, 337

535

O'Neale, Sgt later 2ndLt, 141
Onslow, Lt, 412, 421
Onslow G T, Capt, 426, 436, 516
Orford A, Lt later Lt Col RMA, 411, 412, 421, 479
Orr, Lt, 90, 91, 92
Owen C L, 2nd Lt, 336, 345
Owen J, Lt later Sir J and DAG, 172, 217, 222, 249, 266, 268, 269, 522
Ozzard A I, Lt later Lt Col, 336, 411, 421, 422, 424
Packwood, Sgt, 192
Paden, Lt and Adjt, 182
Paine S J, Lt, 172
Paris, Lt later Col RMA, 385, 449
Parke R, Capt RMA later Col, 228, 229, 337, 343
Parke T A, Maj later Col Comdt, 260, 269, 519, 520
Parke, Lt later Maj, 276, 346, 347, 348
Parker, Capt, 36
Parker C A, Capt, 311
Parker E A, Col Comdt, 515
Parker J, 45
Parry R, Lt, 154
Parry F, Lt, 337
Pascoe A H, Lt, 336
Patten, Lt, 194
Patterson J, Maj, 481
Patterson S, Pte , 409, 410
Payne Lt, 192
Payne G P, Capt, 319
Peake J G, Lt , 172
Peake, Capt, 386
Pearson A C, Capt, 412, 414, 419, 420, 427
Pease L T Brig Gen, 395, 479, 520
Peile, Lt later Maj, 395, 447, 448, 449
Pengelley, Lt Col RMA, 510
Penrose P C, Capt later Lt Col, 333, 334, 348, 362, 363, 518
Perrot, S Lt, 166
Perry, Lt, 130
Peters R, Pte, 134
Philips J A, Lt Gen, 350, 442, 510, 515, 519, 520
Phillipp P, Brig Gen, 517, 521
Phillips F R, Lt, 355, 378, 381, 382, 510
Phillips J, Capt later Maj Gen, 385, 388, 517
Phillips M, Lt later Col, 62, 82, 83, 151
Phillips P, Capt RMA, 481
Pickard, Lt, 277, 288
Pilcher J M, Lt, 177, 515
Pine-Coffin, Capt, 392, 393, 398, 402, 421, 470, 516
Pitcairn, Maj, 57, 58, 60, 61, 65
Pitcairn J, Lt, 62
Plumbe, Maj, 446, 447
Poe W H, Capt and Adjt later Maj, 407, 408, 411, 414, 418, 420, 427
Poe, Lt RMA, 411, 447
Pollard, Lt, 177
Polkinghorne, 2nd Lt, 282, 285, 288
Poole E, Maj, 433
Poole G R, Col Comdt, 521
Poore, Lt, 321, 436
Poore F H, Col RMA, 511, 512, 520
Portlock-Dadson, Capt, 314 (Note 248), 321, 337, 494, 503(Note 366)
Portlock-Dadson, Lt, 343

Poulden, Lt, 106
Power, Capt RMA, 362
Poyntz, Maj, 332(Note 268), 353, 364
Poyntz H S, Lt, 362
Poyntz W H, 2nd Lt , 337
Prendergast, Lt. 407
Preston, Cpl, 464, 466
Prettyjohns, Cpl, 314, 327, 336
Price J H, Lt, 374
Priest, Lt, 277
Pritchard, Pte, 111
Prynne J B, Caspt, 337, 349, 352, 355, 512
Puddicombe, Lt and QM, 246
Pym E L, Capt later Lt Col, 337, 343, 350, 515
Pym F G, Lt , 312, 320, 331, 332
Pym J B, Lt , 397, 510
Pyne, Capt, 421
Quill J J, Lt later Maj, 374, 510
Quill, Maj
Ragg R, Lt, 65, 69
Raikes, Lt RMA, 447
Raikes G L, Brig Gen, 519
Raitt G D, Lt RMA, 385
Rawstorne, Capt, 397
Rawstorne G A, Lt Col, 436
Rea C, Lt, 136
Read, Lt, 197
Reeves L B, Lt, 172, 199
Renshaw, Lt, 35
Richards E, Sgt, 314, 320
Richards F J, Lt Col, 370
Richardson G, Lt, 150, 152
Rigby G S, Capt RMA, 319
Robbins, Capt, 411
Roberts, Lt, 21
Roberts B, Lt RMA, 312
Roberts J, Capt RMA, 317
Robertson, Lt RMA, 226, 227
Robinson, Maj, 120
Robinson, Lt, 139, 144(Note 138)
Robyns J, Capt, 237, 238, 239, 241
Robyns, Lt, 381, 383
Roche, Lt, 411
Roche T de M, Maj, 441, 442, 520
Rodney G B, Capt later Col Comdt, 319, 320, 515, 521, 522
Roe E C B, Lt Col, 479, 517
Rogers C, Lt , 407
Rokeby L, 2nd Lt, 337, 344, 346, 348
Rolfe, Gnr, 410
Roper, Sgt , 448
Rose, Maj, 412
Rose E L, Col, 512, 519
Ross, Maj, 104, 105, 106, 107, 494
Rotheram, Maj, 86
Rudd H Sgt later 2nd Lt, 51
Ruddle, Sgt, 140
Rycaut, Maj (Local Lt Col), 20, 86
Sabine, W, 42
Sandell, Lt, 177
Sanders J, Lt , 321
Sanders W, Lt , 321
Sandys, Lt, 136
Sandwich J H, Lt later Maj, 384, 389, 403, 427
Saunders, Lt, 121, 447, 448, 449
Savage H B, Lt RMA later Sir J Maj Gen, 268, 344, 515, 522

Sayer, Capt, 321
Scafe C H, Col, 512, 519
Schomberg E S G, Capt RMA later Maj Gen, 324, 337, 341, 342, 343, 386, 407, 516, 520, 522
Scott J W, 2nd Lt later Maj , 337, 392, 402, 403, 447, 516
Scudamore, Sgt Maj, 427
Secker, Sgt, 171
Senior, Capt RMA, 447
Servante C E, 2nd Lt, 337
Seddon W, Lt, 172
Shairp A, Lt, 105
Shea R, Lt , 65, 106
Sherman, Capt, 208
Shillabeer, Lt , 201
Shin, Dr, 349
Shire W, Bug, 418
Short, Maj, 62, 65
Short C F, Lt, 337
Shute, Capt RMA
Slade, Pte , 420
Slaughter, Capt, 349
Slessor, Lt RMA, 421, 423 (Note 303)
Smale H, Lt , 334
Smith A D, Lt , 327
Smith A L, Lt , 336
Smith F T, Capt, 39
Smith H, Lt Col, 51, 110 , 516, 522
Smith J M. Lt, 198
Smith T, Lt, 62
Smith T, Capt, Inspector of Schools, 370
Smith W, Capt, 121, 153, 154, 362
Smith W H, 2nd Lt, 337
Smythe A C, Maj, 436
Snow E B, Capt, 205, 206, 370, 371
Somers Lewis, Col, 442
Souter-W, Capt later Col, 57, 62, 71
Souter-Johnstone, Lt Gen, 137, 496, 516, 518, 522
Spalding S, Lt Col, 420
Spark, Mr, Paymaster, 349
Sparshott E A, Lt, 327, 336, 345
Spratt, Capt, 337, 349
Stamper, Lt, 411, 413
Stannus J, Capt, 181
Starr E H, Lt RMA, 316
Stavel, Capt, 65
Steel A C, Lt, 320
Steele R, Capt RMA, 266
Steele, Lt, 313
Stephens, Lt , 232374
Stewart Lt, 83
Stewart J A, Paymaster, 362
Stewart J H, Col Comdt, 518, 521
Stevens J B, Lt RMA, 230, 252
Stevens, Capt, 258
Stevenson C J, 2nd Lt, 174
Stirling W, Lt, 327, 328, 330, 331
Straghan , Lt, 80
Straghan J S, 2nd Lt, 337, 348, 352, 355
Stransham, Lt later Sir A Gen, 378, 280, 282, 285 , 358, 359, 362, 442, 519, 523
Strickland T, Maj later Gen, 147, 245, 518
Strong H, Maj, 389, 390, 401, 402
Strouts, Capt , 450, 451, 453, 464, 466
Sturgeon, Lt, 258
Suther, Lt, 276
Suther W G, Col later Col Comdt, 362,

536

INDEX

363, 518, 519, 520
Swale E, Lt , 177, 336
Swanton J, Lt later Brig Gen, 386, 521
Sweet J, Sgt later 2nd Lt, 136
Swinburne S, Lt RMA, 386, 393, 413, 420, 421, 424
Symonds J C, Capt , 349, 355
Symons J, Cpl, 275
Tait A, Lt, 321
Talbot H L,, 520 Lt RMA later Col Comdt, 307, 397, 419, 479
Tantum, Lt, 71
Tatham A G, Lt RMA, 386
Tatton Brown J, Gen, 359, 519
Tench W, Capt/Lt later Maj Gen , 106, 107, 255, 518
Thomson E P, 2nd Lt, 337
Thoroton C J, Capt, 468
Tickner, Pte, 453
Timmins, Lt later Lt Col, 106, 172, 494
Timpson, Capt, 313
Tooker Collins, Capt later Col Comdt, 17, 29
Torrens, Maj RMA, 210, 211, 235 (Note 199)
Townshend C V F, Lt , 411, 412, 413, 414
Travers J O, Maj, 337, 339, 343, 344, 349, 350, 351, 354, 355, 515, 523
Travers J C, Lt and Adjt later Maj Gen, 276, 336, 337, 344, 348, 358
Tremenheere, Lt, 121
Tribe S J, Capt, 337
Troup, Capt RMA, 479
Trotman C N, Lt later Brig Gen, 421, 517
Trotter G, Lt RMA, 386, 428, 429
Tucker W G, Capt later Col Comdt, 397, 402, 403, 407, 408, 411, 520
Tucker Mr, Paymaster, 4, 250
Tuke, Lt RMA, 481
Tull H J, Lt, 320
Tulloch, Col, 393
Tupper, Maj later Col comdt and Maj Gen, 58, 62, 65, 69, 71, 86, 110, 515, 522
Tuson Sir H, Lt later Gen, 346, 384, 390, 391, 394, 397, 402, 403, 407, 408, 409, 410, 411, 512, 520, 522
Uniacke, Capt later Maj, 292, 294, 295
Urmston, Maj, 447, 448
Urquhart J, Lt , 277, 287
Ussher, Lt RMA, 386
Ussher E, Lt, 277, 282 (Note 226), 285, 288, 289 (Note 230), 291, 337, 345, 349, 353
Vallack T, Maj later Lt Col, 253
Walker G, Lt, 136
Walker, Lt Col, 272, 276
Walker, Col, AQMG, 353
Wallen R H, 2nd Lt RMA, 242
Waller, J, Lt and Adjt, 50, 62, 65
Walsh A S S, Lt Col, 337, 342, 343, 345
Walsh A H, Capt later Col Comdt, 370, 518
Walton, Sgt, 420
Ward, Capt, 337
Wardell, Capt, 401, 402
Way N F, 427, Maj later Col Comdt, 412, 414, 421, 422, 518, 521
Weaver, Capt, 219
Webb, Capt, 7
Webb W, Sgt Maj, 241

Weir, Maj, 143, 149, 152
Welchman, Capt, 215
Wemyss J M, Capt later Maj Gen , 37, 137, 147 172, 324
Westroop P, Capt, 172
Whitcomb J, Capt later Maj, 276, 280, 282 (Note 226), 283, 285, 287, 288, 289 (Note 230), 291, 292
White F J, Lt, 277, 386
White F S, Lt later Maj, 278 , 285, 407, 408
White J, Capt, 140
White H S N, Lt later Brig Gen, 414, 477, 521
White N, Lt, 412,
White R, Lt, 212, 269
Whiting, Lt, 282 (Note 226), 285, 286, (Note 230)
Whitmarsh, Lt, 510
Whylock, Capt, later Gen, 272, 275, 276, 498
Williams D J, 154
Williams J C, Lt RMA later Maj Gen, 302, 337, 346, 348, 350, 520, 522
Willliams O L, Lt RMA, 355
Williams Sir R, Lt Col RMA, 92, 142, 167, 208, 218, 220, 226, 227, 228, 229, 231, 234, 238, 240, 241, 245, 247, 253, 260, 498, 507, 508, 516, 520
Willis E, Lt, 337, 347, 348
Willis C H, Lt , 386
Wilkinson T, Bdr RMA, 315, 320
Wilson J K, Sgt Maj later 2nd Lt, 253
Wilson J, Capt, 253
Wilson, Lt, 447, 448, 449
Windham C, Brig Gen, 326, 330
Wingrove, Gen, 126, 129(Note 127), 519
Winter R, Col, 245, 515
Wolrige Lt RMA, 222
Wolrige A R, Lt, 252 , 347, 348, 363
Wolrige H, 2nd Lt, 337
Wolseley, Capt, 329
Wood, Capt, 77, 167
Woods B, Capt, 420, 421, 425
Woon J B, Sgt Maj, 337, 348
Wray, Capt, 425(Note 305), 450, 453, 464, 466
Wright G, 45, 46
Wright J, Capt, 253, 515
Wright W P, Maj Gen, 522
Wroot W H, Lt, 337
Wybourn M, Lt, 148, 226, 227
Wylde A W, Capt, 471
Wylde E A, Col, 502, 521
Yerbury, Pte, 408, 410
Young G, Sgt, 331
Yule G, Sgt RMA, 320
Commanding Officers (Appendix 11) , Chatham, 515
 Portsmouth, 516
 Plymouth, 517
 Woolwich, 519
 RMA, 520
 Depot RM, 521
Colonel Commandants , 520
Commandants in Town, 522
Adjutant Generals ,522
Deputy Adjutant Generals, 522
Inspector Generals, 523
RM Administration , 160, 249
 Continuous Service, 307, 320, 472

Promotion from the ranks, 482
RM Gunners, 180, 210, 271, 479, 482, 483

Royal Naval Officers and Ratings
Alexander, Capt, 363
Anson, Adm, 3, 11, 19, 25, 491
Arbuthnot , Adm, 81, 84
Ball, Capt, 90, 143
Baker, Capt, 221
Barham, Lord Adm, 172, 174, (Note 163)
Barrington, Adm, 76
Barclay, Capt, 73, 229
Barlow, Cdr, 283
Barrie, Capt, 236, 239
Bartle, Adm, 203
Bate, Capt, 342
Beatty, Cdr, 456, 457
Beatty Sir D, Adm, 450 (Note 319)
Bearcroft, Capt, 447, 448
Bedford Sir F, Adm, 438, 439
Benbow, Engineer RN, 418
Beresford, Lord C, 387, 388, 418
Bickerton Sir T, Adm, 92, 163, 171, 235
Bligh, Capt, 166
Boscawen, Adm, 12, 16, 17, 25, 26, 27
Bouchier, Capt, 283
Bradford, Lt, 387
Bremer J G, Cdre, 276, 281
Brett, Sir Piercy, Capt and Col, 27
Bridport Lord, 124, 127, 132, 133, 134
Brisbane, Capt, 183
Brock, Capt, 311, 312
Brown S, Reverend RN, 512
Bruce, Adm, 458, 460
Burridge, Capt, 311
Byng, Adm, 13
Byng, Capt, 227
Byron, Adm, 74, 77
Calder Sir R, Adm, 170, 171, 208
Campbell, Capt , 217
Chads, Adm, 321
Chadwell, Capt, 347
Chatham, Earl of, 14, 107, 197
Christian, Adm, 128
Cochrane Sir A later Lord, Adm, 175, 195, 196, 197, 236, 239, 241, 242
Cockburn, Adm, 226, 227, 234, 236, 238, 239, 240
Codrington, Sir E, Adm, 257
Cole, Lt, 165
Collingwood, Lord, Adm, 170, 172, 174, 186, 194, 198
Colpoys, Vice Adm, 133
Colville, Adm, 34
Commerell, Cdr, 348
Cook, Capt, 82, 104, 151
Cornish, Adm, 35, 36
Cotton Sir C, Adm, 193
Craddock, Cdr, 459, 460, 461
Cross, Surgeon, 409, 410
Curtis, Capt. 85
Darby, Adm, 83, 84, 89
Davis, Lt , 164
Davis Vice Adm, 183
de Horsey, Cdr, 447, 448, 449
Dick, Capt, 480
Dickson, Reverend RN, 511
Douglas, Adm, 30
Downie, Capt, 234

537

Drummond, Capt, 166, 202
Duncan, Adm, 136
Dundas, Adm, 312, 323
Duckworth, Cdre later Sir J, Adm, 143, 144, 154, 175, 186, 187, 188
Durell, Adm, 22, 23, 26
Edwards, Cdr, 392
Elliot, Adm, 277
Elliot C, Cdre, 334, 335, 340
Elphinstone, Capt later Adm, 118, 125, 126, 129
Essington, Rear Adm, 184
Ethelston, Cdr, 446, 447
Fairfax, Capt, 387, 392, 393
Ferris, Capt, 165
Field, Lt, 457
Fisher, Lord, 469, 470, 472, 474
Fisher J A, Capt , 388, 390
Fitzroy, Capt, 392, 393, 394, 396
Ford, Cdre, 120
Freemantle Sir E R, Adm, 433
Furber, Lt, 165
Gambier J, Adm, 183, 184
Gamble, Capt, 438
Gardiner, Adm, 133
Gardner, Rear later Vice Adm, 120, 136
Gifford, Lt, 273
Graves, Capt later Vice Adm 34, 58, 61, 84, 85
Haggard, Lt, 323
Hall W K, Capt, 288, 333, 334
Hallowell, Capt, 164
Hamilton, Lt, 208
Hardy T M, Lt , 138
Hardy, Capt , 125, 126
Hardy, Adm, 16
Hardy, Sir C, Adm, 77, 78
Hawke, Adm, 12, 13, 14, 16, 19, 25, 26, 27
Harvey E , Capt later Adm, 78, 121, 130, 502
Hay, Lord J, Adm, 266, 267, 269
Heath, Cdr, 348
Herbert, Capt, 280, 281, 290, 291
Hervey, Capt , 31, 32, 33
Hewett, Capt later Adm, 376, 391, 394, 407
Holleburne, Adm, 12, 14
Holmes, Adm, 23, 24, 26
Hood later Lord, , 120Adm, 83, 84, 85, 86, 87, 118 165
Hood, Capt later Cdre, 139, 143, 164, 167
Hood, Capt, 475
Hope, Lt, 201
Hope Sir J, Adm, 346
Hoskins, Adm, 391, 392
Hoste, Capt, 181, 206
Hotham, Cdre later Adm, 76, 122
Houston-Stewart Sir, Adm, 319
Howe, R, Capt, later Adm, 12, 19, 27, 69, 70, 73, 74, 75, 76, 88, 96, 101, 120, 121, 132, 133
Hughes Sir E, Cdre later Adm, 20, 77, 89, 90, 91, 92, 92, 93
Huleatt W, The Reverend, 348
Hunter, Capt, 106
Hunt-Grubbe, Capt, 376, 386
Inglefield, Adm, 301
Jellicoe, Flag Capt, 160 (Note 153), 453, 454
Jervis, Adm later Earl St Vincent, 119, 121, 122, 127, 130, 131, 143, 157, 159, 161, 162 (Note 155), 163, 164, 525, 526

Johnstone, Cdre, 89
Keates, Capt, 124
Keefe, Adm, 362
Kempenfeldt, Adm, 35, 36, 75, 85
Keppel, Adm, 11, 27, 28, 74, 75, 99, 315
Keppel, Cdre, 18, 30, 32 , 336
Keppel Sir H, 315, 317, 332 (Note 268), 335
Keyes, Lt, 458
King, Capt, 177, 318, 502 and 503 (Note 366)
King Sir R, 135
Knowles, Adm, 15
Lake, Lt , 165 and Note 159
Lake, Capt, 219
Lambert,Cdre, 304
Lock, Capt, 134
Louis, Adm, 171, 186, 188
Luard, Capt, 363, 364
Luttrell, Cdre, 79, 487
Luxmoore, Capt, 375, 376
Lydiard, Capt, 183
Lyons Sir E, Adm, 311 (Notes 240, 241), 312 (Notes 242, 243), 314 and Notes 248, 250, 251), 316, 317
Lyons, Capt (son of Adm), 316
Mackinnon, Lt, 301
Maurice, Capt, Governor of Anholt, 210
Mende, Adm, 319
Moresby, Adm, 320 (Note 257), 322, 324
Mudge Z, Capt, 165
Mulcaster, Capt, 230
Muller, Capt
Moore, Cdre, 20, 21, 22
Napier Sir C, Cdre later Adm, 272, 273, 320, 321, 323
Napier, Cdr, 393
Nelson Sir H later Lord, 120, 122, 130, 138, 142, 143, 147, 151, 152, 154, 163, 167, 170, 171, 172
Newcombe, Capt, 126
Nisbet W, Capt, 202, 203
Norman, Lt , 203
Onslow, Mid, 475
Osborne, Adm, 16
Osborne S, Capt, 316
Palley Sir T, Rear Adm, 502
Palliser, 74
Pane, Capt, 206
Parker Sir H, Adm, 76, 77, 83, 151, 152
Parker Sir P, Adm, 16, 71
Parker Sir W, Adm, 260, 287, 288, 290, 291, 301
Parker, Capt, 36
Peebles G, Lt, 183
Peel Sir W, Capt, 327, 328, 329, 330
Pellew Sir F, Adm, 251
Pigot, Capt, 241
Pocock, Adm, 32, 34, 35, 35
Popham Sir H, Cdre later Adm, 175, 176, 178, 181, 185, 216, 218, 220
Popham, Cdr, 233
Prendergast, Surgeon, 409
Price, Lt, 137, 140, 144
Protheroe, Capt, 446, 447
Rainier, Adm, 126, 129
Rawson W, Lt later Adm, 400, 439, 441, 442
Reynolds, Capt, 183
Rice, Lt, 304
Robinson, Capt, 273
Rodney Sir G later, Lord, Adm, 25, 30, 31,
32, 71, 75, 77, 80, 83, 84, 86, 87
Rowley, Cdre, 202, 203
Rowley, Capt, 217
Saunders, Adm, 22, 23, 24, 25, 26, 27
Seymour Sir B, Adm, 384, 387
Senhouse Sir F, Adm, 279, 281, 287, 456, 460, 462
Seymour, Sir E, Adm, 451, 456
Seymour Sir G F, Adm, 502
Seymour Sir M, Adm, 335, 338, 341, 346
Seymour, Capt later Lord Alceater, 192, 365
Shepherd C, Cdre, 502
Slaughter, Lt, 206
Spencer, Lord, 132, 153 and Note 146, 525
Stanhope, Sir T, Capt, 28, 29, 30
Stewart, Lt later Capt, 83, 333
Stopford Sir R, Adm, 213, 215, 272, 275
Stirling, Adm, 176
Smith Sir S, Capt later Adm, 186, 188, 145, 146, 153, 181
Stephenson, Capt, 393, 394, 395
Stevens, Adm, 34, 35
Stot, Capt, 49
Strachan, Sir R, Capt later Adm, 174, 175, 197
Sullivan, Capt, 321
Swanton, Cdre, 30, 31
Tarleton, Cdr, 304
Trollope, Capt, 129, 136
Troubridge, Capt, 138, 139, 147, 148
Vaughan J W, Cdr, 327, 330, 331
Vernon Sir E, Cdre, 88
Warren Sir J, Cdre later Adm, 124, 125, 142, 149, 150, 152, 226, 227
Warrender, Capt, 459
Watson, Adm, 34
Watson, Capt, 294
Wilkinson, 144
Wolseley, Lt, 91
Woodward, Capt, 429
Wright, Lt, 146
Yelverton, Capt, 323
Yeo, Capt, 229, 231, 232, 233
Young, Rear Adm, 132

Retirements 1787, 107
Rosas, Dictator of Buenos Ayres , 301
Russian War, 310
Saluting, 8
Sandwich, Earl of , 59, 68, 157
Sashes, 47, 53, 131
Satsuma, Japanese Noble , 362
Schools, 100255, 370, 371, 440
School of Physical Training, 471, 473, 474, 476, 477
Scott, J, Mr, Surgeon, 4
Sea Rosters, 8, 42, 48, 67, 191
Sebastiani, French Ambassador to Turkey,185
Second Captains, 191, 360, 371
Second Lieutenants, 41, 68, 101, 112, 127, 158, 163, 173, 191, 221, 265, 370
Selborne Scheme, 469
Sergeant Majors, 8, 108, 298, 383
Shiba, Japanese Colonel, 463, 464
Spanish (British) Legion, 266, 267, 268

Ships: Royal Navy:
Abercrombie, 202, 204, 208

Index

Acasta, 196
Achillle, 172
Achilles, 386, 388, 389
Actaeon, 77, 340
Active, 206, 376, 378, 379
Africa, 172
Africaine, 203
Agamemnon, 318
Agincourt, 199, 386, 389, 391
Ajax, 171, 186
Albion, 21 (Note 19), 239, 252
Alecto, 439
Alexandra, 384, 385, 386, 387, 388, 389, 390, 391, 392, 407
Algerine, 252, 270, 281, 282, 287, 288, 293, 458, 459, 461
Algiers, 318
Alliaance, 145
Alligator, 276, 279, 282, 287
America, 126, 217
Amethyst, 192, 378
Amoy, 276
Amphion, 129, 163, 181, 206
Amphitrite, 310
Anholt, 211
Anson, 183
Apollo, 188
Arethusa, 128, 183, 310
Argus, 374, 375
Armide, 207
Arrogant, 323
Arrow, 332
Asia, 57, 239, 240, 257, 258, 432
Assistance, 111, 327, 338, 350
Astraea, 444
Augusta, 73
Aurora, 164, 453, 456, 462
Australia, x
Bacchante, 429
Badger, 1337, 144
Barfleur, 130, 456, 458, 460, 461, 462
Barrcouta, 333, 334, 374, 333
Barrosa, 439
Beacon, 384, 391
Bedford, 107, 136
Bellerophon, 127, 172
Belliqueux, 136
Bellona, 174
Bellepoule, 205
Benbow, 274, 299
Bentick, 293
Berwick, 21, 83
Birkenhead, 302, 437
Bittern, 333, 384
Blanche, 165, 166, 166, 340, 437
Blenheim, 130, 165, 191, 235 (Note 199), 279, 280, 282, 285, 286, 287, 288, 289 (Note 230), 290, 291, 292
Blonde, 84, 282, 285, 287, 288, 290, 291, 293, 294, 295, 439
Bloodhound, 302
Boadicea, 202, 203, 381
Boyne, 57, 122
Britannia, 62, 130, 509
Briton, 410
Bristol, 20, 21
Broke, 234
Bruno, 235
Brunswick, 127, 182

Burford, 91
Caesar, 87, 141, 174
Calcutta, 162, 332, 333, 334, 338, 339
Caledonia, 207, 260
Calliope, 278, 279, 280, 281, 282, 285, 287
Cambrian, 206, 258
Cambridge, 33, 280
Camperdown, 436, 442, 444
Canopus, 21 (Note 19), 186, 187
Captain, 122, 130, 369
Carysfort, 173, 274, 391, 393, 394, 396, 407, 411
Castor, 266, 267, 272, 274
Centaur, 84, 143, 144, 164, 165
Centurion, 24, 68, 126, 453, 462
Cerebrus, 62, 66, 206
Ceylon, 203. 234
Charlotte, 106
Charwell, 232
Chatham, 68
Charon, 79, 242
Clio, 294
Colossus, 130, 143, 172
Columbine, 282, 285, 288, 289 (Note 230), 290, 291, 293, 294
Condor, 178, 384, 387
Confiance, 197, 234
Conqueror, 174, 362, 363, 364
Conquest, 433
Constance, 270
Conway, 282, 287
Coquette, 393
Cormorant, 347
Cornwall, 221
Cornwallis, 292, 293, 294, 295
Coromandel, 333, 334, 335
Courageux, 164
Cruiser, 270, 282, 285, 288, 289 (Note 230), 290, 335, 340
Culloden, 130, 131, 138, 142, 143, 147, 148
Cumberland, 34, 221, 240
Curacao, 217
Cygnet, 384
Decoy, 374, 375, 384
Dee, 392, 394
Defence, 184
Delft, 84
Derwent, 199
Diadem, 87, 130, 175, 177, 218, 226
Diamond, 127
Diana, 62
Dido, 272, 273
Diomede, 126, 177, 222, 226
Dolphin, 196, 420
Doris, 446, 447
Dragon, 28, 31, 32, 33, 239, 340
Drake, 82, 165, 215
Dreadnought, 474
Driver, 321
Druid, 277, 278, 279, 280, 282 (Note 226), 285, 287, 288, 373, 374
Eagle, 70, 77, 181
Eclair, 217
Eclipse, 391
Egmont, 122, 130
Elephant, 70, 151
Elizabeth, 36, 80
Encounter, 176, 177, 333, 334, 350
Endymion, 186, 187, 453, 462

Esk, 339
Essex, 28
Europa, 120
Eurydice, 372
Euryalus, 386, 391, 394, 407, 410
Excellent, 130, 194, 195, 258, 259, 480, 482
Exeter, 77
Falcon, 392
Falmouth, 36
Fame, 195, 195, 195, 458, 459, 509
Fantome, 337
Fero, 304
Firebrand, 312
Fisgard, 149, 183
Formidable, 127, 174
Forte, 310, 441
Forrester, 347, 348
Fox, 138, 219, 226, 303, 304, 305, 474, 475
Friendship, 106
Furious, 310
Freya, 201
Fury, 335, 354
Games, 183
Genoa, 257
Gipsy, 166, 166
Glasgow, 64, 65, 70, 252, 254
Glatton, 129
Glendower, 210
Glory, 136
Goliath, xi, 130
Hampton Court, 16, 28
Hannibal, 154, 318
Haughty, 335
Hazard, 302, 444
Hecla, 407
Herald, 279, 282, 287
Hercule, 166
Hermes, 242, 303
Hero, 89, 174
Hesper, 215
Hibernia, x, 434
Highflier, 339, 354
Hong Kong, 335
Hound, 280
Humber, 408
Hyacinth, 276, 277, 282, 285, 474, 480
Hydra, 275
Imperieuse, 195, 217
Impregnable, 252
Implacable, 17 (Note 15), 175
Indefatigable, 477
Inflexible, 184, 335, 354, 384, 386, 387, 388, 389, 392
Inspector, 134
Invincible, 384, 385, 386, 387, 388
Iphigenia, 202, 203, 242
Iris, 89, 392, 393, 412
Irresistible, 130
Iron Duke, 371
Juno, 49, 181
Juste, 127
Kent, 70, 206
Lancaster, 136, 175
Larne, 277
Latona, 183, 219
Leander, 138, 139, 144, 252, 253, 311
Leda, 175
Leonidas, 205, 242
Leviathan, 143, 144, 217

539

Linnet, 231, 234
Lion, 215
Lively, 62, 138
London, 133
Lowestoft, 79
Lucifer, 187, 188, 194
Lynn, 28
Lyon, 21
Madagascar, 278, 279, 280, 281
Magician, 348
Maynamme, 15, 91, 92
Magnificent, 87, 106, 205, 219
Magpie, 439
Majestic, 185
Malabar, 127
Marcia, 340
Mariner, 429
Marlborough, 33, 133, 229
Mars, 140, 171, 172
Mediator, 183
Medusa, 219, 294, 304, 305
Melpomene, 235
Melville, 279, 280
Meteor, 188, 194
Merlin, 73
Minden, 212, 252
Minerva, 130, 354
Minotaur, 133, 143, 148, 184, 386, 388, 389, 392
Minstrel, 206, 207
Miranda, 316
Modeste, 279, 280, 281, 282, 285, 288, 290, 291, 293, 294
Mohawk, 227, 474
Monarca, 92
Monarch, 384, 386, 387, 388, 389, 391, 392, 393, 407, 446
Monmouth, 16, 89, 91
Montagu, 80, 205
Montreal, 232
Mosquito, 391
Namur, 127, 130, 174
Nankin, 339
Narcissus, 175, 177
Nassau, 183
Neptune, xi, 480
Nereids, 202, 203
Niagara, 232
Niger, 334, 340, 364, 367, 378
Nimrod, 282, 283, 285, 340, 347
Nisus, 203, 215
Norfolk, 21
Northumberland, 121, 246, 386, 389, 391, 392, 393, 395
North Star, 269, 294, 302, 367
Nyanza, 393
Nymph, 77
Ophir, 467
Opossum, 335
Orion, 130, 172, 183, 386, 391, 393, 394, 396
Orlando, 450, 451, 456, 457, 462
Orontes, 384, 407, 410, 411
Orpheus, 126, 129
Osprey, 429
Otter, 84
Panther, 21
Pearl, 152, 267, 327, 331, 332, 336
Penelope, 322, 384, 386, 388, 391
Perseus, 363

Phaeton, 215
Phlegethon, 290, 294, 294, 303, 304, 340
Phoebe, 215, 439
Phoenix, 70, 134, 174, 261, , 281, 266
Pique, 166, 272, 274, 310
Pluto, 294, 304
Pomona, 79
Pompee, 136, 181, 186, 187, 196
Porcupine, 23
Powerful, 136, 272, 446, 447
President, 215, 310, 311
Prince George, 74, 130, 487
Prince of Orange, 28
Princessa, 87
Princess Caroline, 221
Princess Charlotte, 272
Princess Royal, 318
Prometheus, 251, 252
Prosperine, 304, 305
Protector, 176
Pylades, 281, 282, 285, 288, 331
Queen, 278, 279, 290,
Queenborough, 34
Queen Charlotte, 132, 252
Racoon, 439
Raisonnable, 175, 177
Ramillies, 7, 12, 25, 239
Ranger, 429
Rattler, 303
Ready, 391, 392, 394
Regulus, 130, 235, 240
Renown, 21, 68, 149, 152, 477
Repulse, 87, 186, 187
Retribution, 310, 311
Reyna, 267
Rippon, 20, 21
Roebuck, 21, 70
Rodney, 80, 272
Royalist, 267
Royal Albert, 318, 316
Royal George, 25, , 75, 80, 132, 133, 186, 187
Royal Oak, 87, 239
Royal Sovereign, 171, 172, 432, 499
Ruby, 293, 391
Salamander, 267, 303
Sampson, 333, 334, 354
Sandbag, 420
Sandfly, 144
San Domingo, 226
Sans Pareil, 327, 336, 339
Sandwich, 28
Satellite, 439
Scarborough, 68, 106
Sceptre, 202, 226
Seagull, 374
Seahorse, 36
Semarang, 279
Serapis, 371
Serpent, 303
Sesostris, 290, 294 303, 304
Severn, 252
Shah, 378, 381, 382
Shannon, 222, 225, 234, 327, 330, 331, 336
Sheldrake, 211
Sidon, 318
Sirius, 104, 106, 202, 203
Somerset, 57, 61, 64, 70
Solebay, 199
Sparrowhawk, 206, 207

Sphinx, 429
Standard, 186, 187, 188, 210
Stanley, 281
St George, 130, 439, 441, 442, 470
St Jean d'Acre, 317, 318
Star, 232
Starling, 293
Staunch, 203
Stromboli, 275
Success, 70, 144
Suffolk, 126
Sulphur, 279, 280, 282, 283
Sultan, 91, 92, 384, 386, 387, 388, 389
Superb, 43, 91, 92, 170, 184, 252, 253, 384, 386, 387, 388, 389, 390, 391, 392, 407
Supply, 104, 106
Surprise, 239, 340
Surveillante, 219
Sutherland, 23, 24
Swallow, 18, 437
Swiftsure, 16, 28
Sybille, 333, 334, 339
Tamar, 384, 450
Tartar, 70, 211, 284, 302
Temeraire, 30, 172, 384, 385, 386, 387, 388, 389, 392, 407
Tenedos, 379, 381
Tennasserim, 294, 304
Terrible, 302, 310, 446, 450 (Note 319), 459, 460, 461, 462, 463
Theseus, 138, 143, 145, 146, 166, 441
Thrush, 439
Tiger, 310
Tigre, 145, 146, 188, 199
Thunderer, 171, 186, 274
Tonnant, 171, 235, 236, 239, 240
Torbay, 87
Tourmaline, 391, 394
Tremendous, 127
Triumph, 127
Turquoise, 429
Tweed, 267
Tyne, 411, 412, 413
Valiant, 184, 207
Vanguard, 7, 12, 142, 143, 183, 371
Venerable, 136
Vengeance, 77
Vesuvius, 311
Victory, 109, 118, 130, 163, 170, 171, 172
Ville de Paris, 131, 163
Virago, 310, 311
Volage, 206, 270, 276
Wasp, 272, 274
Wellesley, 270, 276, 278, 279, 280, 282, 283, 285, 287, 288, 289 (Note 230), 290, 291, 292
Whiting, 282 (Note 226), 458, 459
Widgeon, 439
Winchester, 21, 333
Winchelsea, 122
Windsor Castle, 186, 187
Wizard, 188
Woodlark, 429
Woolwich, 21
Worcester, 77, 92
Zebra, 274

RN Steamers
Atalanta, 282
Boxer, 318

INDEX

Chunar, 327
Climber, 318
Cracker, 318
Cyclops, 273, 274
Fancy, 316
Gorgon, 272
Irrawaddy, 304, 429
Jamna, 331
Kathleen, 429
Nemesis, 219, 276 (Note 221), 278, 279, 280, 281, 282, 283, 288, 289, 294
Pluto, 294, 304
Saf'iyeh, 418

British Merchant Marine/transports
Australia, 426
Adelaide, 337, 338
Adventure, 354
Assistance, 111, 327, 338, 350
Bulimba, 413
City of Paris, 402
Dacca, 391
Deccan, 412
Dromedary, 123
Euphrates, 392
Grand Duchess of Russia, 68
Imperader, 338
Imperatrix, 337
Increase, 70
Jelunga, 466
Jumna, 382
Kars, 184
Kent, 256
Mary, 222
Medina, 481
Nerissa, 392
Ocean, 162
Poonah, 411
Quetta, 393
Rhosina, 392
Romney, 260
Simoon, 374

Austrian Ships
Guerriera, 274

French Ships:
Albion, 165
Achille, 121, 172
America, 121
Ardent, 87
Bienfast, 17
Bucentaure, 171
Caesar, 87
Caton, 87
Ca Ira, 122
Censeur, 122
Diademe, 87
Duguay-Trouin, 174
Formidable, 174
Foudroyante, 16
Fusee, 340
Genereux, 144
Glorieux, 87
Harmonie, 165
Hector, 87
Hercule, 140
Impetueux, 121
Jasen, 87

Juste, 121
La Hoche, 142
Lion, 458
L'Orient, 142
Morne Rouge, 21
Mitraille, 340
Modeste, 26
Mont Blanc, 174
Northumberland, 121
Ocean, 26
Oriflamme, 16
Orphee, 16
Prudente, 17
Redoubtable, 26
San Nicholas, 131
Sanspareil, 121
Scipion, 174
Temeraire, 26
Tonnant, 143
Vengeur, 121
Ville de Paris, 87

Dutch Ships
Granicus, 252, 253
Hebrus, 252
Medusa, 363
Vryheid, 136

Peruvian Ship
Huascar, 378

Portugese Ships
Infanta, 197
Voada, 197

United States Ships
Chesapeake, 225
Delaware, 72
Monocacy, 458

United States Steamer
Taiwan, 347

Spanish Ships
Algeciras, 171

Turkish Ships
Gulsefulde, 274

Indian Ships
Ferooz, 303
Mahannuddy, 304
Mozaffur, 303, 304
Sesostris, 303
Zenobia

German Ship
Iltis, 458, 459

Russian Ships
Bobre, 458
Gilyak, 458, 459
Korsetz, 458

Japanese ships
Atago, 458

Separation Allowance, 406
Shirinsky, Russian Colonel, 460

Sidearms, 259, 266
Signalling and Naval Examination Service, 431, 483
Slave Trade, 406, 433
Soult, French General, 198
Squads 1758 and 1783, 7, 41, 53
Squad Officers, 7, 45, 53, 98, 102, 141, 256
Staff Officers Stagnant Promotion, 256
Straw Bedding, 168
Steele, Sir R, 211
Stoessel, Russian General, 459
Stoppages for Rations, 6, 307
Suarez, Acting President of Uruguay, 301
Suffren, French Admiral, 84, 89, 91, 92
Sultan of Witu, 433
Sumroo, Indian General, 37, 39
Sujah Dowlah, 14, 37, 39
Swimming, 231, 437, 445
Sydney, Lord, 104, 106
Tartars, 293, 342
Tasmania, 162, 172
Tattoos, 476
Ternay, French Captain, 34
Thanksgiving Service St Paul's 1797, 139
The Marine Regiments 1702-1713 , 487, 488
The Regiments of Marines 1739-1748, 488
The Formation of Corps 1755 , 3
Theebaw, King of Burmah, 429, 430
Thuret, French Privateer, 27
Tippoo Sahib, 92
Torrington and Pembroke's Marines 1690-1699, 487
Training, 9, 44, 67, 88, 192, 200, 249, 251, 307, 357, 371, 431, 432, 433, 435, 445, 470, 475, 478
  Bands, 472, 473
  Gunnery, 300, 372, 435, 472
  Physical Training, 471, 477
  Tactical or Field, 433
  RMA recruits, 435
  Swimming, 437, 445
Training of 2/lts 1776, 67
Treatment of wounded man, 182
Treaty of Tilsit, 189, 194
Tucker Mr, Second Paymaster and Agent, 4
Uniforms/Equipment, 53,, 55, 109, 160, 496
United Irishmen, 141
United States Marine Corps, 388
Victor, French Marshal, 207
Villaret-Joyeuse, French Admiral Villeneuve, French Admiral, 121
Villiers Hon G, 160, 250
Virginia, 477
Walcheren, 197
Waldersee von, German Field Marshal, 463
Walker Sir E, Garter, Knight Principal King of Arms, 485
Walker Bey, Turkish Admiral, 275
Waller, Maj USMC, 462
Ward, American Officer in Shanghai, 355
Warrant Officers, 370, 450, 480
Wilkinson, American General, 231
Willaumez, French Admiral, 175
Winder, American General, 237
Wolfe Tone, 42
Woolwich Division, 172, 173, 174
Works Department, 437, 443
Yeh, Chinese Commissioner, 332, 338, 339, 343

541